Intermediate Level

Organisational Management

Textbook

3245/J00

British Library Cataloguing-in-Publication Data

A catalogue record for this book is available from the British Library.

Published by Foulks Lynch Ltd
Number 4
The Griffin Centre
Staines Road
Feltham
Middlesex
TW14 0HS

ISBN 0 7483 4324 5
Printed in Great Britain by Ashford Colour Press Ltd, Gosport, Hants.
© Foulks Lynch Ltd, 2000

Acknowledgements

We are grateful to the Chartered Institute of Management Accountants, the Association of Chartered Certified Accountants and the Institute of Chartered Accountants in England and Wales for permission to reproduce past examination questions. The answers have been prepared by Foulks Lynch Ltd.

CONTENTS

PREFACE

This is the first edition of the Textbook for this paper of the new CIMA Syllabus, which is examinable from May 2001. It has been written specifically to cover the syllabus and learning outcomes published by CIMA and care has been taken to ensure that all syllabus areas are covered.

The new syllabus textbooks continue to bear the hallmarks of our other ranges of acclaimed publications. Particular attention has been paid to producing an interactive text that will maintain your interest with a series of carefully designed features.

- **Introduction with learning objectives**. We put the chapter into context and set out clearly the learning objectives that will be achieved by the reader.

- **Definitions**. The text clearly defines key words or concepts and where relevant we do of course use CIMA's official terminology. The purpose of including these definitions is **not** that you should learn them - rote learning is not required and is positively harmful. The definitions are included to focus your attention on the point being covered.

- **Brick-building style**. We build up techniques slowly, with simpler ideas leading to exam standard questions. This is a key feature and is the natural way to learn.

- **Activities**. The text involves you in the learning process with a series of activities designed to arrest your attention and make you concentrate and respond.

- **Conclusions**. Where helpful, the text includes conclusions that summarise important points as you read through the chapter rather than leaving the conclusion to the chapter end. The purpose of this is to summarise concisely the key material that has just been covered so that you can constantly monitor your understanding of the material as you read it.

- **Self test questions**. At the end of each chapter there is a series of self test questions. The purpose of these is to help you revise some of the key elements of the chapter. The answer to each is a paragraph reference, encouraging you to go back and re-read and revise that point.

- **End of chapter questions**. At the end of each chapter we include examination style questions. These will give you a very good idea of the sort of thing the examiner will ask and will test your understanding of what has been covered.

Complementary Examination Kits and Lynchpins

Examination Kits - contain a comprehensive bank of questions, mainly from past examinations.

Lynchpins - pocket-sized revision aids which can be used throughout your course, contain revision notes of all main syllabus topics, all fully indexed, plus numerous examples and diagrams. They provide invaluable focus and assistance in keeping key topics in the front of your mind.

EXAMINATION PROCEDURES

UK legislation

The examination will be set in accordance with the provisions of relevant UK legislation passed and case law established up to and including 1 December preceding the examination concerned. This date is especially relevant to the following papers:

- Business Law (Foundation level)
- Financial Accounting, Financial Reporting & Business Taxation (Intermediate level)

This means that the Business Taxation paper will be set in accordance with the Finance Act 2000 for the May and November 2001 examinations.

Financial Accounting and Financial Reporting

Examination papers covering Financial Accounting and Financial Reporting will be available in both an International and UK Accounting Standards format. Students can elect to answer in accordance with either of these accounting standards.

Separate syllabuses based on each format are available in these two subjects.

Statements of Standard Accounting Practice and Financial Reporting Standards

The examination will also be set in accordance with relevant Statements of Standard Accounting Practice and Financial Reporting Standards issued up to and including 1 December preceding the examination concerned. The date is especially relevant to Financial Accounting and Financial Reporting (UK Accounting Standards variant).

International Accounting Standards

The examination will be set in accordance with relevant International Accounting Standards issued up to and including 1 December preceding the examination concerned. The date is especially relevant to Financial Accounting and Financial Reporting (International Accounting Standards variant).

Exposure Drafts

The date of 'up to and including 1 December preceding the examination' also applies to material contained in Financial Reporting Exposure Drafts, which are especially relevant to the Financial Reporting paper.

Students are advised to refer to the notice of examinable legislation published regularly in the monthly CIMA Student to ensure they are up to date.

Local law and tax

Where examination are not based on UK legislation and practice, overseas students may take appropriate opportunities to cite examples of local practice in their answers. Such examples should be supported with references that will validate their answers.

New syllabus

THE SYLLABUS AND LEARNING OUTCOMES
Intermediate level

11 – Organisational Management

Syllabus overview

This syllabus introduces students to the concepts, tools and issues of management in organisations of all types. The emphasis is on the role of the Chartered Management Accountant as supervisor and manager of staff in an open social system and the relationships necessary with other specialists within the organisation. As well as their specialist role, Chartered Management Accountants are participants in the management process at the supervisory and managerial levels. This syllabus aims to provide students with an awareness of the skills required to operate effectively as a manager in the finance department of an organisation.

Aims

This syllabus aims to test the student's ability to:

• Evaluate and recommend improvements to the management of organisations in an international context

• Evaluate and recommend alternative structures for organisations

• Apply Human Resource Management techniques in the management of a finance department

• Advise on the management of working relationships

• Advise on the management of change

Assessment

There will be a written paper of 3 hours. The paper will comprise two sections.

Section A will contain a series of compulsory questions each with its own scenario. Section B will offer a choice of questions, with or without short scenarios.

All learning outcomes and knowledge domains apply to both sections of the paper, but the optional questions are more likely to cover topical issues or specific areas.

Questions will not be phrased in such a way that they require knowledge of the work of specific writers. Examples of suitable alternatives are given for guidance, and students should use the theories or approaches with which they feel most comfortable, or which appear most appropriate to the circumstances described in the question. This is essentially a practical examination, and the theoretical models mentioned in the syllabus provide a framework for analysis and problem solving.

Learning outcomes and syllabus content

11(i) Organisational management - 25%

Learning outcomes

On completion of their studies, students should be able to:

• Explain the concept of strategy and its possible effect on the structure and management of business organisations	3
• Identify the stakeholders of an organisation and explain their influence on its management and structure	2
• Recommend appropriate organisational goals	2
• Analyse and categorise the culture of an organisation, and recommend changes to improve organisational effectiveness	4
• Explain the importance of organisational and professional ethics	4
• Recommend ways in which ethical behaviour can be encouraged in organisations	4
• Discuss ways in which the conflict between centralised control and individual creativity can be managed	5
• Explain the usefulness of both classical and contemporary theories of management in practical situations	1
• Explain trends in the general management and structure of organisations	5
• Evaluate the management of an organisation and recommend improvements	5

Syllabus content

• The determinants and components of strategy	3
• Organisational objectives (i.e. stakeholder analysis and organisational mission, goals and targets)	2
• The reasons for conflict between the objectives of an organisation, or between the objectives of the organisation and its stakeholders, and the ways in which this conflict might be managed (eg compromise or identification of a dominant coalition)	2
• The process of strategy formulation (i.e. the steps required and the order in which those steps might be undertaken)	3
• The various approaches that might be adopted to determine an appropriate strategy for the organisation (i.e. rational, adaptive and interpretative approaches)	3
• The determinants of culture, the different models available for categorising cultures (eg Deal and Kennedy, Harrison, McKinsey 7-S, Peters and Waterman, Peters)	4
• The importance of culture in organisations (eg the 'organisational iceberg')	4

11 (ii) The functional areas of organisations - 15%

Learning outcomes

On completion of their studies, students should be able to:

Syllabus content

- The organisation and activities of the marketing function (i.e. marketing research, market segmentation, marketing strategy formulation) 8

- 'The concept of the marketing mix and the major tools therein (i.e. branding, product mix, pricing, advertising, sales promotion, public relations, packaging, distribution) 8

- The information required by managers in the various functional areas of a business organisation and the role of the Chartered Management Accountant in identifying and satisfying those information needs 7

11 (iii) Human resource management 30%

Learning outcomes

On completion of their studies students should be able to:

- Explain the process of human resource planning and its relationship to other types of business plan 9

- Produce and explain a human resource plan for an organisation 9

- Produce a plan for the recruitment, selection and induction of finance department staff 10

- Produce a plan for the induction of new staff into the finance department of an organisation 10

- Explain the importance of human resource development planning 12

- Evaluate the tools, which can be used to influence the behaviour of staff within a business, particularly within the finance department 11

- Explain the process of succession and career planning 12

- Produce a training and development plan for the staff of a finance department and analyse the major problems associated with the design and implementation of such a plan 12

- Produce and explain a plan for the delivery of a training course on a finance-related topic 12

- Evaluate a typical appraisal process 13

- Analyse the issues involved in managing the dismissal, retirement and redundancy of individual staff 9

Syllabus content

- The relationship of the human resource plan to other types of business plan 9

- The determinants and content of a human resource plan (i.e. organisational growth rate, skills, training, development, strategy, technologies, natural wastage) 9

- The problems, which may be encountered in the implementation of a human resource plan and the ways in which such problems can be avoided or solved 9

11 (iv) Management of relationships 15%

Learning outcomes

On completion of their studies, students should be able to:

	Chapter location
• Explain the problems of maintaining discipline and evaluate the tools available to help a manager achieve it	17
• Explain how the legal environment influences the relationships between the organisation and its employees, and between the employees of an organisation	18
• Explain the responsibilities of the organisation, its managers and staff in relation to health and safety and advise how a manager can promote the health and safety of subordinates	18
• Explain the various ways in which fair treatment of employees can be achieved, and the role of government in ensuring this	18
• Analyse the causes of inter-group and interpersonal conflict in an organisation and recommend ways in which such conflict might be managed	19

Syllabus content

• The concepts of power, authority, responsibility and delegation and their application to organisational relationships	14
• The characteristics of leaders and managers	15
• Management style theories (eg Likert, Tannenbaum and Schmidt, Blake and Mouton)	15
• The advantages and disadvantages of different styles of management	15
• Contingency approaches to management style (eg Adair, Fiedler)	15
• Theories of group development, behaviour and roles (eg Tuckman, Belbin)	16
• Disciplinary procedures and their operation, including the form and process of formal disciplinary action and dismissal	17
• The nature and effect of legal issues affecting work and employment, including the application of appropriate employment law (i.e. law relating to health, safety, discrimination, fair treatment, childcare, contracts of employment and working time)	18
• The sources of conflict in organisations and the ways in which conflict can be managed to ensure working relationships are productive and effective	19

Note.

Only the application of general legal principles will be required in this examination, and the English legal system will be used in suggested answers purely as an example. Students will be free to use relevant law from their own country.

11(v) Management of change 15%

Learning outcomes

On completion of their studies, students should be able to:

• Evaluate the determinants of change in organisations and the different levels at which change must be managed	20

Syllabus content

EXAMINATION TERMINOLOGY

Learning objective	Verbs used	Definition
1 Knowledge		
What you are expected to know	List	Make a list of
	State	Express, fully or clearly, the details of/facts of
	Define	Give the exact meaning of
2 Comprehension		
What you are expected to understand	Describe	Communicate the key features of
	Distinguish	Highlight the differences between
	Explain	Make clear or intelligible/state the meaning of
	Identify	Recognise, establish or select after consideration
	Illustrate	Use an example to describe or explain something
3 Application		
Can you apply your knowledge?	Apply	To put to practical use
	Calculate/compute	To ascertain or reckon mathematically
	Demonstrate	To prove with certainty or to exhibit by practical means
	Prepare	To make or get ready to use
	Reconcile	To make or prove consistent/compatible
	Solve	Find an answer to
	Tabulate	Arrange in a table
4 Analysis		
Can you analyse the detail of what you have learned?	Analyse	Examine in detail the structure of
	Categorise	Place into a defined class or division
	Compare and contrast	Show the similarities and/or differences between
	Construct	To build up or compile
	Discuss	To examine in detail by argument
	Interpret	To translate into intelligible or familiar terms
	Produce	To create or bring into existence
5 Evaluation		
Can you use your learning to evaluate, make decisions or recommendations?	Advise	To counsel, inform or notify
	Evaluate	To appraise or assess the value of
	Recommend	To advise on a course of action

PILOT PAPER

Foundation Level

ORGANISATIONAL MANAGEMENT

PILOT QUESTIONS

RATIONALE

PILOT ANSWERS

Instructions to candidates

Section A contains **three** questions: candidates should answer **all** of these.
Section B contains **four** questions: candidates should answer **two** of these.

Time allowed: 3 hours

Note

This is a **Pilot Paper** and is intended to be indicative of the style of questions that will appear in the future. It does not purport to cover the range of the syllabus learning outcomes.

The mark allocations for particular topics within the paper are subject to change in the future, as is the range of topics covered.

The layout of the printed paper may be subject to slight variation in the future.

PILOT QUESTIONS

Section A: 60 marks
Answer all three questions

Question 1

Like many other companies, X has to respond to a variety of pressures for change. Increasing competition has forced company X to reduce costs by downsizing its personnel numbers and reducing the size of the head office. Further measures have included a greater concentration on its core business and processes. To date, these pressures have had a limited effect on the finance department, but the finance director is now under pressure to reduce the number of personnel employed in her department by 30 per cent over the next two years, and by a total of 50 per cent within a five-year period.

In the initial review of the task facing her, the finance director appreciates that she has to take into account a number of changes that are affecting the finance function. These include the ever-increasing application of IT, the increasing financial pressure to outsource transactions and other routine operations to large service centres, and the expectation by the chief executive that finance personnel will play a fuller part in the management of the business.

The department currently employs 24 people divided almost equally between three areas: financial accounting, management accounting and the treasury function.

The age/experience profile is a mix of older, experienced specialist staff, a young to middle-aged group of qualified accountants (many of whom also possess MBA degrees), and a group of trainees with limited experience who have yet to qualify.

Three of the older staff are within five years of the statutory retirement age; two more will move into this category within the time period set by senior management. One or two of the younger qualified staff have been looking for other jobs and one of the trainees has applied for maternity leave.

The finance director has arranged a meeting with the human resources director to discuss the development of a human-resource plan for future staffing, training and development of personnel in the finance department.

Requirements

(a)   Describe the main stages of the human resource planning process and briefly explain how manpower planning fits into this process.   **(8 marks)**

(b)   Taking the role of the finance director, prepare a paper by way of preparation for your forthcoming meeting. Explain the key considerations that you will need to take into account in the development of a human resource plan for your department.   **(12 marks)**
                                                                                      (Total: 20 marks)

Question 2

The B Company is in many respects a dinosaur, with a culture and structure from a time that has now passed. The company enjoyed much of its growth during the 1950s and 1960s under the leadership of its founder manager, Ben Tough. The company originally provided fittings for ships built in the local shipyards but, as the shipyards declined, the company moved into manufacturing a range of fixtures and fittings for the new homes being built for an ever-more prosperous population. As the company grew, it developed the characteristics typical of an organisation that enjoys a relatively secure market. In the interest of economies of scale it developed mass-production techniques and these, combined with good control systems, enabled the company to keep costs low.

Though Ben Tough retired long ago, B has maintained the hierarchical, centralised command and control structure that had been his hallmark from the early days. Over time, B also developed rules and procedures for almost every aspect of the business. In times of stable markets and steady growth, these set routines and procedures served the company well, but as the company moved into the latter end of the twentieth century, the market for B's products became saturated and senior management realised that, if they were to survive into the future, they would have to diversify into new products. Building on what they considered to be a core competence - B's manufacturing capability - the company moved into the growing and fast-moving world of consumer electronics.

At first, things went well. The company was able to transfer the skills it developed in the assembly of household fixtures and fittings to the production of a range of electronic consumer goods. However, as time went on, the market became increasingly competitive and less stable. This was partly to do with the increasing number of imports from developing countries, and partly to do with the increasing pace of change brought on by developments in microelectronic technology and by consumer demand for state-of-the-art gadgetry.

Despite its best efforts, senior management has found it difficult to cope. It is not that the management lacks an active approach to problems: the company has invested heavily in the latest production technology and recruited designers and electronic engineers to help it to respond rapidly to the developments in the market. Just why the company is not doing better is difficult to identify, but a chance remark by one of the designers leaving to work for a competitor provides a clue. Asked why he was leaving after such a short time, he replied, 'It's the way you do things around here. I just don't seem to be able to fit in. People at higher levels seem remote, and even those lower down don't appear to want to listen. Everybody seems cosy in continuing to do things in the same old way.'

Requirements

As a consultant hired by the company, you have been asked to conduct an investigation into the degree of fit between the culture of the company and the demands it now faces in the market place, and to come up with a set of recommendations.

You are asked to structure your report into three main sections as follows:

(a)   describe the existing organisational culture of the company in terms of any well-known classification; **(6 marks)**

(b)   explain the lack of fit between the existing culture and the demands of the market place; **(6 marks)**

(c)   make recommendations for the type of organisational culture that you consider will best fit B's new situation, and justify your choice. **(8 marks)**

(Total: 20 marks)

Question 3

TR is a transportation company involved in all aspects of the movement of people and goods around the country. Recently it has experienced considerable conflict between the Research and Development (R&D) department and the Operations department.

Research managers are responsible for developing operational innovations to improve efficiency, while operations managers are responsible for the scheduling and running of planes, trains, lorries and coaches. The conflict is manifested in constant complaints about 'the other department', and by a general sense of ill feeling and lack of co-operation between the staff of the two departments.

The operations managers are frustrated by the way in which the R&D department operates. They claim that research personnel take too long to carry out projects because, instead of seeking practical, cost-effective solutions to problems, they go in for 'the perfect solution' - which is often very costly and often late.

R&D managers are equally scathing about what they consider to be the unhelpful attitude of the operations personnel. They feel that Operations has been so uncooperative and resistant to adopting some of their innovations, such as the automated loading platform and the training simulator, that the point has now come for senior management intervention.

The personalities and attitudes of the heads of the two departments do not help the situation. Both are strong characters with authoritarian attitudes, and both are earnestly committed to achieving the aims of their respective departments. Communication, except for some routine interchanges and the usual abuse, has almost ceased between the departments.

Things have now come to a head and the chief executive has appointed a manager from within the organisation to investigate the problems affecting the relationship between R&D and Operations and to report back with findings and recommendations.

Requirement

You are the manager from TR appointed to investigate and to write a report. Divide your report into two parts.

(a)   Describe how conflict is manifested in the TR case and explain the causes of this conflict.

(10 marks)

(b)   Explain how the conflict might best be resolved.   **(10 marks)**

(Total: 20 marks)

Section B: 40 marks
Answer two questions only

Question 4

You have been invited to give a talk to members at your local CIMA branch.

The chairperson of the branch is keen to encourage the involvement of students in branch meetings and has invited you to give a talk that will be of particular interest to students, but which will also be of some interest to the qualified, experienced membership.

In order to meet the different needs of both of these groups the chairperson has decided on two topics. The first of these - *the relationship of management accounting with other management activities* - will be aimed primarily at the student audience, while the second - *the changing role of the management accountant* - will be aimed at the membership as a whole.

Requirement

Prepare a paper for a talk on the following two topics, including a series of headings supported by brief explanatory notes, that could be used as a basis for your overhead projector slides or whiteboard/blackboard headings.

(a)   Describe the general relationship between management accounting and the key activities of management.   **(12 marks)**

(b)   Describe how the role of the management accountant is changing and explain briefly the key forces driving the changes.   **(8 marks)**

(Total: 20 marks)

Question 5

(a)   Explain why the actual strategy pursued by a company over a three - to five-year period may diverge from the deliberate strategy that the company initiated at the outset of that period.   **(8 marks)**

(b)   A D Chandler and others have argued that a multi-product organisation is best served by a divisional structure. Discuss the arguments for and against this claim.   **(12 marks)**

(Total: 20 marks)

Question 6

The problem of keeping staff motivated is one with which managers in all departments have to cope.

Requirements

Assume that you are the senior manager in the finance department of an organisation and that you have been asked to respond in writing to the following two requirements posed by a less-experienced colleague who has just taken up a similar post elsewhere in the same organisation.

(a)   Describe the use of financial incentive schemes as a means of improving employee motivation.   **(10 marks)**

(b)   Explain how non-monetary methods can be used to motivate employees.   **(10 marks)**

(Total: 20 marks)

Question 7

Y is one of the five main high street banks in the country. Since banking deregulation in the late 1980s, Y, like other banks, has been facing increasing competition, first from other existing financial institutions but more recently from new entrants who have started to offer deposit accounts and a number of other financial services.

In seeking to respond to these competitive threats, the bank's senior management has started to implement a number of changes. These involve a significant restructuring of the organisation with the removal of a number of layers of management, and a consequent reduction in staffing levels in most divisions. The closure of a number of high-street branches is also planned. The telephone-banking arm is being substantially enlarged, and a major investment in IT is being undertaken. The effect on staff will be considerable. A programme of voluntary redundancy and redeployment is planned and, given the demand for new skills, a considerable amount of training will need to be carried out. Despite clear evidence of the threat to the future of the bank, the plans set forth by management are meeting resistance from the workforce. The banking unions in particular seem determined to obstruct the changes wherever possible.

Requirements

With reference to the above scenario:

(a)   Explain why the implementation of organisational change often proves to be so difficult.

(8 marks)

(b)   Advise Y's management about the ways in which change can be facilitated.   **(12 marks)**

(Total: 20 marks)

RATIONALE

General

All the questions seek to test candidates' ability to apply theoretical concepts, frameworks and models to the problems and issues involved in the management of organisations. Management accountants, like all other professionals, can be regarded as part of the management team and the questions asked in this specimen paper are based on that assumption. This is a three hour, unseen examination.

Section A - three compulsory questions

Question 1 seeks to test (a) candidates' knowledge of the human resource planning process and (b) their ability to construct a human resource plan for the finance department of a large corporation. It also tests the skills required to communicate the plan to management colleagues. The scenario, involving the finance department, was selected for its relevance to management accountants and the references to changes in the corporation under consideration reflect current real world developments. Syllabus section (iii)

Question 2 is based on a scenario that reflects the kinds of changes that many large traditional companies have had to face in recent years. It is designed to test candidates' ability to describe the organisational culture of a particular organisation using any well-known classification of their choice, and to devise recommendations for change so as to improve organisational performance. Syllabus section (i)

Question 3 takes a common problem, that of the conflict that sometimes occurs between departments or divisions of a large organisation, and seeks to test candidates' knowledge of the manifestations and causes of such conflicts in part (a). Part (b) is intended to test how candidates might use their knowledge to overcome this conflict. Syllabus section (ii)

Section B - two questions from four

Question 4 uses a situation that candidates may face after qualification (or even before) - to produce notes for a talk to members of their local CIMA branch. The topic has been selected for its particular relevance to management accountants. Part (a) tests the ability to formulate the key points necessary for a discussion of the relationship between management accounting and the main activities of business, while part (b) seeks to test knowledge of the changing role of management accountants and the reasons for these changes. Syllabus section (iv)

Question 5. Part (a) seeks to test candidates' knowledge of the differences between deliberate and emergent strategy and, in so doing, brings out the nature of strategy as applied to business organisations. Part (b) is concerned to test the ability of candidates to explain the links between strategy and structure and to evaluate the claim - often taken for granted - that strategy determines the kind of structure required for optimum organisational performance. Syllabus section (i)

Question 6 has been selected for its relevance to management accountants. It is a practical question concerned with actual methods of motivation in the work place, rather than the usual test of the theories of motivation. Syllabus section (iii)

Question 7 makes use of a contemporary situation of organisational change to test (a) candidates' ability to explain why 'the implementation of' organisational change is difficult and (b) to suggest ways in which change can be facilitated. Again, this particular scenario has been selected because it is one likely to be familiar in general terms to candidates, and allows a discussion of the problems of organisational change to be related to a specific organisation and to a realistic set of circumstances. Syllabus section (v)

PILOT PAPER ANSWERS

Answer 1

(a)   Human resource planning (HR planning) was previously described as manpower planning, and has been defined as 'a strategy for the acquisition, utilisation, improvement and retention of an enterprise's human resources'. Manpower planning still provides a good starting point for the development of a human resource plan, but in recent years it has been recognised that there is more to people planning than quantitative estimates of the demand and supply of personnel.

Four main phases are involved in manpower planning:

(i)   an analysis of existing staffing resources - its strengths and weaknesses, age spreads, experience and training levels etc;

(ii)   an estimation of likely changes in resources - flows into, within, and out of, the organisation - and the ability of relevant labour markets to supply existing or future demands;

(iii) an estimation of the organisation's future manpower needs in terms of numbers, type, quality and skill composition; and

(iv)   the identification of gaps between supply and demand and the development of policies and plans to close these.

The HR planning process goes beyond this simple quantitative exercise by taking into account the broader environmental factors eg, patterns of employment and developments in automation and uses qualitative techniques, such as scenario planning, for estimating future manpower requirements. The process is also linked to the development of the organisation as a whole, and should be related to corporate objectives and to an organisation structure capable of achieving those objectives. It is also concerned with developing people so that they have the skills to meet the future needs of the business and with improving the performance of all employees in the organisation by the use of appropriate motivation techniques.

(b)   Briefing paper: Development of a human resource plan for the finance department

The key considerations for developing the human resource plan for the department will focus on three main areas:

(i)   making the required reductions, in line with the downsizing strategy;

(ii)   addressing the changes that are affecting the department; and

(iii) identifying the future role, in playing a fuller part in the management of the business.

Reducing staff numbers from 24 to 17 over the next two years and to 12 by the target date (in five years time) will be by using natural wastage and early retirement wherever possible. Hopefully, this will avoid (or at least reduce) the need for compulsory redundancies, and will avoid or reduce the adverse effects on staff morale and motivation.

There is a good chance of achieving the reductions over the time period set, provided that the necessary steps are taken. Three of the older members are within five years of retiring; two more will move into this category within the five years set by senior management. If those employees nearest retirement could be encouraged to leave by offering them a generous retirement package and an enhancement of their pension, it would be the least painful option.

One or two of the younger qualified members of staff are already looking for posts elsewhere, so they may be encouraged to leave earlier when the news that the organisation is looking to slim down the department has been communicated to the department. One of the trainees has applied for maternity leave. She will have the right to return to work, provided that she comes back within the period set out in legislation, so we have no room for manoeuvre there. Some of the trainees will qualify within the time period under consideration, and the reduction in costs will not allow me to increase salaries substantially, so I think that they will look elsewhere for work.

The age/experience of the existing people, spread over financial accounting, management accounting and the treasury function, is a mix of older, experienced specialist staff, a young to middle-aged group of qualified accountants (many of whom also possess MBA degrees), and a group of trainees with limited experience who have yet to qualify. I would like to keep a similar spread and one of the problems will be retaining the most able of my staff. This will mean planning a package of financial inducements and a clear career structure.

Reducing staff will be possible, but coping with the current workload with the reduced resources will be more difficult. There are several solutions to help me to deal with this problem:

- The department's existing operations will be thoroughly reviewed to make sure that it matches the corporate objectives, and its structure is capable of achieving those objectives. It may be that, following the general downsizing, there may be a reduced need for some of its services.

- There are many changes in technology and the department can make more use of IT and the latest developments in computer software. This could allow an increase in productivity and result in better quality output from the department. It will mean developing some of the staff, so that they have the skills to meet the future needs of the business. Although staff training is expensive, it will provide some motivation and reassurance to staff that the organisation is still prepared to invest in them and is ready to equip them with the latest IT skills.

- The department has been under increasing pressure to outsource transactions, and some of its other routine work, to one of the new service centres. Although I am not keen to do this, it may be the only way of coping with the existing volume of work.

For the future plans, the department will have to monitor its expenditure to keep in line with the budget. Early retirement and additional staff training will add considerably to costs, but perhaps outsourcing some of the routine work will allow us to offset some of these costs.

It is inevitable that some of the department members will have to become more flexible and be ready to take on a wider range of responsibilities. The younger staff will welcome this, as their education and training has already prepared them for wider management responsibilities, and those with MBA degrees are in a good position to accept more responsibilities. However, additional training and development to handle future demands will need to be planned for some members of the department.

Answer 2

Report
To: The Board of Directors, B Company
From: Consultant
Date: 15 May 20X0
Subject: Recommendations on the changing cultural environment for the B Company

(a)   The existing organisational culture could be described as a 'role culture', as identified by R. Harrison and others. In this type of organisational culture there is a formality of organisational structure, procedures and rules, which determine what is to be done. It is a role culture in that people act in terms of the roles specified by the job description. It is typical of large organisations, which operate in a relatively stable environment, such as that occupied by the B Company until recently. The Civil Service is probably the best example of a bureaucratic organisation, but large hospitals, large educational establishments and big corporations all exhibit aspects of this cultural type to some degree.

(b)   The increasing competition faced by B, together with the decreasing length of the product life cycle for consumer electronic products, has made for greater uncertainty and the need on the part of the organisation to be more flexible. The 'role culture' as outlined above is best suited to an environment, which is relatively stable and large sized organisations, as was the case with the B Company until relatively recently. Although it can adapt, this ability is restricted and the company will have problems in surviving a dramatic change, because the detailed rules and procedures, and the hierarchical centralised control structure will inhibit any kind of innovation. The chance remark by one of the designers leaving to work for a competitor seems to support this idea. His comments suggest that the only communication is downward in the organisation and that there is a reluctance to listen to employees. Individuals who work for this kind of company tend to learn an expertise without experiencing risk; many do their job adequately, but are not encouraged to be over-ambitious. This attitude is not conducive to changing market demands requiring flexibility.

(c)   The organisational type that would fit the B Company's new situation is the task culture, where management is seen as completing a succession of projects or solving problems. It is called a task culture because of its task, job or project orientation. This type of culture is reflected in a matrix organisation that is characterised by a lack of rules and a 'can-do' attitude to getting jobs done. Teams are established to achieve specific tasks, with team members having the requisite drive, skills and expertise to achieve the organisation's objectives. In such organisations, there is no dominant or clear leader. The principal concern in a task culture is to get the job done. Therefore, the individuals that are important are the experts with the ability to accomplish a particular aspect of the task. Individuals in the team have more influence than they would have if the work was organised on a formal 'role culture' basis. Information is likely to flow freely up, down and horizontally, so that the conditions of organisational learning are more easily met in this climate of co-operation. This type of culture is particularly suited to cope with rapidly changing product markets and production processes, such as the B Company is experiencing.

A change in the corporate culture of the B Company is a vital ingredient of the long-term success of its programme of change. The recommendation of this report is for the company to make a start on changing from its present role culture to a task culture. Because the culture of an organisation is very difficult to change, due to its deeply ingrained sets of values, beliefs and behaviour patterns of which participants may not even be conscious, the company may require some outside assistance to facilitate the change.

Answer 3

Report
To: Chief Executive
From: Manager
Date: 18 June 20X0
Subject: Conflict between the R&D and Operations departments

(a)   Within TR, there are many examples of how conflict is manifested. They include the following:

- constant complaints about 'the other department';

- a general sense of ill feeling and lack of co-operation between the staff of the two departments.

- communication between personnel in the R&D and Operations departments, except for some routine interchanges, has almost ceased;

- verbal disagreement between the departments, resulting in abuse that is considered usual;

- expressions of frustration about the behaviour of managers and members of the other department;

- unfair criticism of the achievements of the R&D department by Operations staff;

- the Operations department are perceived to be uncooperative and resistant to adopting some innovations developed by R&D.

The conflict between the Operations and R&D departments stems from a misunderstanding by each about what the other is trying to do. Operations claim that research personnel take too long to carry out projects because, instead of seeking practical, cost-effective solutions to problems, they go in for 'the perfect solution' - which is often very costly and often late. They do not appreciate that innovation depends partly on a mix of science and chance and is not something that can be scheduled and produced, like a train timetable. The misunderstanding on the part of the people in the R&D department is that they are unaware of the pressures that Operations managers and staff are under to implement an efficient service.

The heads of both departments are earnestly committed to achieving the aims of their respective departments and to achieving the goals of the organisation. They both want to produce a more efficient service for customers and ultimately to earn higher profits for the organisation. Traditionally, both departments have developed their own specialisation, which has produced barriers with other departments. Operations and R&D have become preoccupied with trying to achieve their own goals, even though it has sometimes been at the expense of the goals of the other department and of the overall goals of the organisation. Where, as in this case, the achievement of the goals of the two departments are interdependent, then the situation is aggravated by the frustration caused when the goal of one department is blocked by that of the other. Unfortunately, there is a structural problem within the organisation, because of the separation of the task of the development of new methods and techniques from the task of implementing the resulting innovations. This arises wherever a division of labour occurs in an organisation.

Another cause of the conflict is the clashing of personality types at the head of each of the respective departments. They are both strong characters with authoritarian personalities and a deep commitment to their own departmental goals, which is likely to exacerbate the conflict. Authoritarian people tend to be rigid in their beliefs and conform to rules and regulations, and are not inclined to change unless compelled to do so. Their commitment to their own departmental goals is a good thing in itself, but blind commitment without regard to the super-ordinate organisational goal of increased efficiency and effectiveness is not acceptable to the organisation.

(b)   Resolving the conflict between these two departments will depend on each department head having an increased understanding of what the other is trying to achieve and of the pressures and difficulties that each faces in trying to meet its objectives.

This can be achieved using a programme of re-education for the staff of both departments. Members of each department need to understand each other's problems and perspectives. This process needs to start with the heads of the respective departments, who will require a degree of retraining and a reminder that co-operation between their departments is essential to the well-being of the whole organisation. Authoritarian people prefer to work in organisational situations that are highly structured and unambiguous, each needs to know what is expected of them. They are likely to respond to relatively autocratic and directive leadership styles.

There are a number of methods that are available to carry out this programme, ranging from briefing meetings, through to workshops in which members from the two departments come together to work on simulated, or even real, problems. However, real understanding will not come about unless there is an exchange of staff between departments. If members of the R&D department are actually confronted with the problems of meeting timetable schedules on a daily basis, they will come to appreciate the pressures facing operations staff. Similarly, if and when members of the Operations department experience the frustrations of trying to devise new methods and techniques for increasing efficiency, they will really come to appreciate the difficulties experienced by staff in R&D.

Alternatively, to encourage co-ordination and communication, TR management could change the structural arrangements and form temporary project teams to work on small projects, with members of both departments working together to solve the problems. A project leader with the relevant skills and a non-authoritarian personality could be chosen to lead the group.

Answer 4

(a)   **Management role**

Management is not an activity that exists in its own right. It is really a description of a variety of activities carried out by those members of organisations whose role is that of a manager - having formal responsibility for the work of at least one other person in the organisation.

Management as a description of its activities

The activities of managers have generally been grouped in terms of:

*   planning;
*   organising;

- motivating;
- communicating; and
- controlling.

They do not depict the full account of what constitutes management but they are a convenient way of describing the key aspects of the work of managers in practice.

Activities of management accountants

We can discuss the relationship between management accounting and these key activities of managers by comparing the activities performed in general by management accountants. A recent survey suggests that these activities include the following:

- Interpretation and management of accounts and cash flows - this involves the analysis and allocation of costs.

- Managing and organising others in the finance function.

- Operations planning, budgeting and budgetary control.

- Investment appraisal - involving analysis of funds before they are committed to projects and advising on operational decisions, programmes and projects;

- The design, development and operation of financial and management information systems.

Type, size, level and structure of organisation

As with any other role in an organisation, there will be variations due to the type of industry and size of business that the management accountant is employed in, the level at which he or she operates and the structure of the company (divisional, functional or a matrix combination). The amount of time and effort devoted to each of these activities by a particular management accountant will vary according to these factors.

Relationship between management accounting and the key activities of management

- **Planning in the longer term** - the management accountant helps to formulate plans for the future by providing information that will help managers in the various functional areas to decide what products to sell, what markets to enter and at what prices and to evaluate proposals for capital expenditure.

- **Planning in the short term** - the management accountant makes a contribution in the budgeting process by providing data on past performance as a guide to future performance. By establishing budget procedures and timetables, the management accountant also co-ordinates the short-term plans from all the various functions or sections of the business, so that they are in harmony with each other. This is achieved by assembling all the various plans into an overall plan (master budget) for the business as a whole.

- **Organising** - the management accountant will often be included in the management team to advise on the kind of organisational structure that will be most useful for the development of an internal reporting system.

- **Motivating** - management accountants play an important role in the motivation process using budget and performance reports. Because budgets represent targets, they can be used to motivate people to improve their performance, if they are used carefully. They are designed to do this by communicating performance information in relation to targets set. The management accountant may also advise on incentive schemes and their likely impact on labour costs

- **Communicating** - by advising on how to install an effective communication and reporting system, the management accountant assists in the organisation's communication process. When communicating budgetary information, an effective reporting system enables budget plans to be conveyed to functional managers, as well as providing feedback at various times to show whether or not the departments concerned are within budget. As a communicator, the management accountant has a role to play in educating functional managers in the ways that financial information can help them in the fulfilment of their duties as managers of the various functions, whether in marketing, R&D, production, distribution or after-sales service.

- **Controlling** - management accountants assist in the control process by providing performance reports that compare actual outcomes with planned outcomes for each of the business area functions or responsibility centres. Using the management-by-exception process, a manager's attention is drawn to particular activities that do not conform to agreed budget limits or to planning targets. This type of control activity frees managers from unnecessary concern with those operations that are sticking to agreed limits and plans.

(b) Many of the roles in an enterprise are changing because of changes in the business environment, associated changes in organisations and developments in information technology. The role of the management accountant is at the forefront of these changes.

Key forces driving the changes

The key drivers of change in management accounting include:

- globalisation and internationalisation;
- changes in the business environment;
- organisational restructuring;
- communications; and
- information technology.

There are other trends, which must be considered eg,

- quality and continuous-improvement initiatives - including the spread of accounting knowledge amongst an increasing number of managers;

- outsourcing - of routine accounting transactions,

- new management accounting techniques eg, activity-based costing, benchmarking, business process re-engineering and the 'balanced scorecard';

- developments in the education and training of accountants. and the spread of accounting knowledge amongst an increasing number of managers.

How the role of the management accountant is changing

The major changes to the management accounting role arising from these drivers include:

Globalisation and internationalisation - where management accountants are employed in global organisations they need to be more involved with the provision of information on the activities on a world basis, reporting on matters that affect the organisation in other countries. Details of the basis of trading with foreign countries, such as fluctuations in exchange rates, political payments at home and abroad, labour policies on pay and pension schemes as well as policies on safety, health and green issues, must be accounted for.

Changes in the business environment - it is crucial that the organisation interacts effectively and efficiently with its external environment. To achieve this, chief executives need better advice in an increasingly turbulent and uncertain environment and they are encouraging management accountants to take a more proactive strategic role in business decision-making. Crafting strategy involves:

- managing stability
- detecting discontinuity
- knowing the business
- managing patterns
- reconciling change

The organisation's management information system must be flexible enough to enable the management accountant to use the financial models to describe the effect of emergent strategies. Developments in both the education and training of management accountants and the number of new management accounting techniques are providing the means to enable accountants to meet these demands.

Environmental concerns and the demands of corporate governance are also increasing the requirements for management accountants to provide new types of information for a wider range of stakeholders. There are always pressure groups representing the public's concern about something eg, GM products, the treatment of waste and the safety procedures and safety records of companies.

Information technology - the development of accounting software packages, allowing easier collection, storing, manipulation and accessing of financial data, has led to a reduction in the importance of some of the traditional contributions of management accountants eg, measuring and reporting costs and performance. This data is more accessible to managers, who are themselves now much better educated, both in accounting matters and in the use of IT, than they were in the past. However, the widespread use of management information systems allows accountants to conduct sensitivity analysis, improving their ability to carry out their analytical tasks more efficiently and to present relevant and timely information to managers.

Communications - developments in IT have also made location of the management accounting function less important than in the past. The use of electronic data transmission means that accounting transactions can be carried out at more remote and cheaper locations than major cities. Some large companies have taken advantage of these developments and outsourced their routine transactions, either in-house or to service centres.

Answer 5

(a)   Strategy formulation is a continuous process of refinement based on past trends, current conditions and estimates of the future, resulting in a clear expression of strategic direction, the implementation of which is also planned in terms of resource allocation and structure.

The strategy then comes about or is realised in actuality. This process is shown in the diagram below as the planned intended strategy (also known as the deliberate strategy). However, the actual strategy pursued by a company over a three - to five-year period may diverge from the deliberate strategy for many reasons, as outlined below.

The obvious reason is that an intended strategy is not implemented because its underlying assumptions turn out to be invalid or because the pace of developments overtakes it. Factors affecting the strategy realisation will include changes in the organisation's external environment eg, changes in the market for the goods and services that the firm produces and in the nature of the competition facing the company, and also its internal environment.

Mintzberg argues that strategies can emerge, perhaps as a result of the processes of negotiation, bargaining and compromise, rather than being due to a deliberate planning process. This emergent strategy would be one that arises from an external stimulus not envisaged in the planned strategy. For example, a supplier pursuing modern ideas on supplier/customer relationships, might encourage a partnership approach to sourcing. It is easy to imagine that buyers in the customer organisation might see benefits in this, and could pursue the idea to the point where sourcing strategy took on an aspect not at all contemplated when planned strategic developments were laid down.

Sometimes changes from the intended strategy come about in opportunistic or entrepreneurial ways eg, an enterprise can find a new process or resource that enables dramatic cost reductions

Finally, strategy may be imposed. For example, recession and threat of a takeover may force a strategy of cost cutting and retrenchment. Technological developments may cause an organisation to develop new products to replace the ones that have become obsolescent.

(b)   Chandler traced the growth and development of a sample of large US corporations from 1909 to 1959. His research showed that:

- diversification led to the need for a new administrative system that would ensure the efficient use of resources;

- the multi-divisional structure had evolved as an adaptive response to this need; and

- this created a type of managerial environment that placed a premium on economic performance and the skills of generalists.

The diversified corporations that Chandler was charting were about to become multinational corporations. As markets opened up, the evolution of a product-market strategy would impose changes on the organisation, leading to a transition from a functional to a multi-divisional structure, based on product-market relationships. This is how Chandler's idea that 'structure follows strategy' came about. He also argued that managers who are close to the operational base and its markets, deal with the day-to-day operations of a large organisation's various divisions more efficiently. Long-term strategy, on the other hand, he saw as best undertaken by those who can stand back and take an overview of the whole organisation.

Scott, following Chandler, developed a model of growth and development that viewed the corporation as moving through several stages as its product-market complexity increased. He saw firms as developing from one-person enterprises to functionally organised (sales, production and research) single business organisations. As the firm began to diversify and to develop multiple product lines, it would then adopt a multidivisional structure.

Subsequent studies by Channon, Galbraith and Nathanson confirm the general claim by Chandler that it is impossible for senior managers at the corporate centre to be sufficiently familiar with the different products and markets served by the different divisions of the corporation, and to make informed decisions. Divisionalisation enables each division to concentrate on the problems and opportunities of its particular business environment. The products/markets in which the organisation operates may be so different that it would be impractical to bring the tasks together in a single body. It is more sensible to split the organisation according to the different products/markets or operations and then to ensure the needs of each division are met by tailoring the operations within the division to the particular business needs.

Most writers seem to agree that organisation structure logically follows after strategy has been decided. However, there are some, including Mintzberg, who cast some doubt on this claim. They argue that, whilst the strategic activities need co-ordinating, the existing structure of the organisation is likely to provide a major barrier to change, as the vested interests of existing personnel are tied up in it. Their view is that the structure limits the strategic options and information flow and shapes strategic thinking. To the extent that such a situation prevailed it could then be argued that 'strategy follows structure'.

The view of modern contingency theorists is that there is a range of factors involved in the relationship between strategy and structure, and the structure that is actually selected is likely to be a compromise between pressures which pull in opposite directions. The assumption of any simple relationship is likely to be mistaken.

As with other areas of organisational management, it is not clear if there are any universal generalisations that can be made about the relationship between strategy and structure.

Answer 6

Examiner's note - Candidates who describe the use of incentive schemes largely in theoretical terms can gain substantial marks, provided the application of the theory is appropriate.

(a)   Motivation is a perennial organisational problem. The context in which it is faced, however, changes from generation to generation as economic and social values change. Motivation can be either positive or negative. Positive motivation, sometimes called anxiety-reducing motivation or the carrot approach, offers something valuable to the individual such as pay, praise or permanent employment for acceptable performance. Negative motivation, often called the stick approach, uses or threatens punishment by dismissal, suspension or the imposition of a fine if performance is unacceptable.

Money can never be overlooked as a motivator. Whether in the form of a salary, piecework, bonus, stock option, company-paid insurance or any other financial incentive that may be given to people for performance, money is important. Most managers and economists place money high on the scale of motivators. This stems from the work of Taylor and the school of scientific management. Taylor believed that there was a right (meaning best) way to perform any task and that it was management's job to determine the right way. Workers gain from this approach because the right way is easier and pay is enhanced as a result of increased productivity.

On the other hand, behavioural scientists such as Maslow and Herzberg tend to place money low on the scale as a motivator. Their content theories offer ways to profile or analyse individuals to identify their needs and they stress the limitations of monetary reward as the main, or even as a major, means of motivating people at work. Their work emphasises the need for employees to feel valued, to attain a sense of achievement in their work and to have an opportunity to exercise responsibility. Another approach, and one that many believe goes far in explaining how people are motivated, is expectancy theory. Victor Vroom's theoretical perspective stresses the role played by subjective factors, such as the employees' estimation of the chance of promotion, for striving hard to fulfil organisational objectives. Pay is only one of many work rewards that may be valued by individuals at work. When instrumentality and expectancy are high, pay can be a source of motivation.

When discussing money as a motivator it is necessary to recognise its effects at two levels. Money in absolute terms, as an exact amount, is important because of its purchasing power. Because money can be exchanged for satisfaction of needs, money can symbolise almost any need an individual wants it to represent. The next increase in salary could mean affording a better car, or an extra holiday. Money is also important as an indication of status. Increasing differentials between jobs creates feelings of a senior status in the person enjoying the higher salary.

Financial incentive schemes have been used to motivate people to perform well for a long time. All such schemes are dependent upon the belief that people will work harder to obtain more money. The most direct use of money as a motivator, is a 'payment by results' scheme, whereby an employee's pay is directly linked to his or her results. The system can be applied to individuals, groups or the whole of a plant. Traditionally these systems are common in the factory of a manufacturing business and have been less commonly applied to non-manual work such as administrative, managerial or professional.

Performance related pay (PRP) is a method used to motivate non-manual workers. However, research has shown that money will only motivate if the prospective payment is significantly large in relation to the normal income of that person. Small increases can prevent feelings of dissatisfaction but to create motivation in a person, who will be motivated by money, it is necessary for the amounts to be large. PRP comes in a number of different forms. The NHS introduced the system, starting with senior managers, in which up to 20% of the salary was dependent upon achieving short-term and long-term objectives. Performance was evaluated according to results achieved against these objectives and classified in five grades. The amount of bonus, which could be nothing, was dependent upon the grade allocated and had to be re-earned each year. An alternative approach is to pay one-off bonuses to reward individual or team performance. Under this alternative system the bonuses are not consolidated into base rates.

Other methods of seeking to motivate employees by monetary means include various kinds of profit-sharing schemes and profit-related payment schemes. The most common profit-sharing scheme is simply to pay employees a cash bonus, calculated as a proportion of annual profits.

(b)   **Examiner's note** - Again, candidates who make good use of theoretical models of motivation to explain the viability of non-monetary methods of motivation can gain substantial marks, provided the theory is applied appropriately.

There are many other ways that managers can increase the motivation of their employees apart from pay and incentive schemes. Several non-financial motivators that have been suggested by various writers include participation in decision-making and quality of work life. The content theories of Maslow and Herzberg point to the job itself as a source of motivation. The job content can be interesting and challenging and can meet needs for advancement, social standing, professional recognition and self-esteem. The methods used include job enrichment, job enlargement and job rotation. The human relations' approach expressed the importance of the work group and leadership style in determining levels of job satisfaction.

The work of Maslow and Herzberg emphasises the need for employees to feel valued, to attain a sense of achievement in their work and to have an opportunity to exercise responsibility. There is no doubt that people are motivated by being involved in the actions and decisions that affect them This view leads to an approach towards employees that encourages contribution and self-direction, advocating full participation on matters of significance to improve the quality of decision-making and the nature of supervision. Participation also recognises the value of staff, since it provides a sense of accomplishment and 'being needed'. A manager seeking to raise performance by increasing motivation could involve staff in the planning and inspection aspects of the work encouraging staff to participate in the design of the work planning schedules. Staff would be motivated to achieve the targets that they had helped establish.

An interesting approach to motivation is the recent development of 'quality of work life programmes'. Basically the approach is a very wide-ranging application of the principles of job enrichment. The intention is to improve all aspects of work life, especially job design, work environment, leadership attitudes, work planning and industrial relations. It is an all-embracing systems approach, which usually starts with a joint management and staff group looking at the dignity, interest and productivity of jobs.

The team approach shares a similar philosophy to the new approach to job design. It seeks to harness the influence of the group, which provides its members with the opportunity for social interaction, and has been shown to be a source of job satisfaction. Associated with working in groups, two major aspects of leadership have been identified as sources of job satisfaction. Firstly the leader who has a supportive relationship with their subordinates and takes a personal interest in them is seen to contribute positively to job satisfaction. Secondly the leader who encourages involvement and participation in the group similarly enhances job satisfaction. Management/leadership style is of particular relevance in this respect. A democratic style has been found to assist in the motivation process because it provides a degree of worker participation and involvement. The achievement of employee involvement in turn is considered to be a useful contributory factor in the motivation process.

Goals are also important motivators. They not only provide a basis for the measurement of performance necessary for administration of payment systems, but they can also serve to assist motivation in themselves. A goal provides a target to aim at, something to aspire to. This means the existence of a goal generates motivation in a person to work towards the achievement of the goal. Goals provide a standard of performance; a person is doing well if they have achieved a goal or are on the way to achieving it. Feedback on an excellent level of performance can be rewarding in itself and can spur individuals to greater efforts. On the other hand failure to achieve a goal or at least to make some progress toward it is evidence of unsatisfactory performance.

Research has investigated the importance of goals in motivation and concludes that for goals to be significant motivators they must be specific, sufficiently difficult to be challenging and they must be accepted by the person as their own particular goals and not as something imposed from outside.

Answer 7

(a)   Change in organisations has positive and negative attributes. On the positive side, it means experiment and the creation of something new. On the negative side, change means discontinuity and destruction of familiar social structures and relationships. Despite the positive aspects, change may be resisted because it involves both confrontations with the unknown and loss of the familiar. Change presents those caught up in it with new situations, new problems, ambiguity and uncertainty. Many individuals, groups and organisations find change, or the thought of change, painful and frustrating.

Individuals - seek to protect a status quo because they have a fear of the unknown. They develop a vested interest in the perpetuation of particular organisation structures and accompanying technologies. Changes may mean the loss of jobs, power, prestige, respect, approval, status and security. In the case of 'Y', it may also be personally inconvenient for a variety of reasons. It may disturb relationships and arrangements that have taken much time and effort to establish. It may force an unwanted location or geographical move or alter social opportunities. There could be problems with learning new skills. Some employees will fear that they will fail and will be reluctant to take on retraining. Perceived as well as actual threats to interests and values are thus likely to generate resistance to change.

Groups - there will be groups of people who see their position threatened and who will combine to resist any threats to their position. In particular, the middle management groups, fearing de-layering, will feel threatened and will be looking to their trade union to protect their interests. There may well be calls for industrial action or action to obtain the highest possible severance pay or redeployment terms. Even without the help of a trade union, groups may collude informally to resist change. They may do this by withholding information or by not being wholly co-operative with those seeking to implement change.

Organisational - at this level there will be a number of factors that will make the change process difficult. These include the existing investment in resources and past contracts and agreements with various organisational stakeholders. It is especially difficult to renegotiate the terms of the contracts with stakeholders, such as the trade unions. However, the main factor is the existing structure and culture of the organisation. Firms that change from a role culture, in a relatively stable and a large-sized organisation, to a different culture that requires a flatter, more organic, organisational structure to cope with competition in the open market, will have problems in surviving such a dramatic change

(b)   There are a number of ways that change can be facilitated. Kurt Lewin developed a general-purpose diagnostic and problem-solving technique to bring about change and improve performance. His force field model suggests that in any situation there are forces that push for change (driving) as well as forces that hinder change (restraining). If the forces offset each other completely, it results in equilibrium and status quo. Change can be brought about by increasing the driving forces or by reducing the restraining forces. Lewin's force-field theory of organisational change is illustrated below:

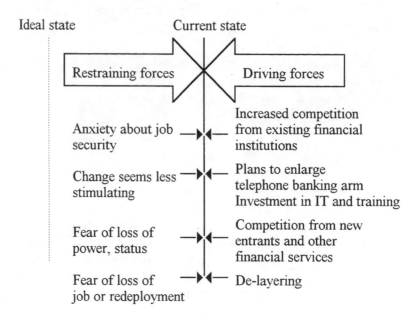

Using this model, we can show that the major driving force for change is the increasing competition brought about by changes in the industry environment. There are few options for 'Y' except to respond to it by becoming leaner and more effective. Reducing management levels and its consequent reduction in staffing levels should help to cut costs. The strengthening of the telephone banking division should help the bank's competitiveness, as should the investment in IT and training.

Despite clear evidence of the threat to the future of the bank, the plans that management have produced do not seem to have convinced the employees. The management should attempt to communicate the message to managers and other employees more effectively. It is not clear from the scenario what methods have been used to communicate to the workforce either the seriousness of the bank's situation, or the rationale behind senior management's plans to combat this situation, but this must be an early priority for the senior management team.

J Kotter and L Schlesinger suggest education and communication, along with other means, such as participation, manipulation and coercion as specific methods for overcoming resistance to change.

Resistance may be based on misunderstanding and inaccurate information. When this happens, it is important to get the facts straight and to discuss and reconcile opposing points of view. Managers should share their knowledge, perceptions and objectives with those who will be affected by the change. This may involve education eg, a training programme, face-to-face counselling, reports, memos and group meetings and discussions. However, the managers should tread carefully because bank employees generally have a high level of education and it would not help the case for change if management underestimated this.

A method associated with communication and education is that of facilitation and support. The management at 'Y' may be able to alleviate the fears of some individuals by the use of counselling and group discussion.

Participation is another way of reducing resistance to change, involving all employees from the start of the change process. Collaboration can have the effect of reducing opposition and encouraging commitment. It helps to reduce the fears that individuals may have about the impact of changes on them and makes use of their skills and knowledge. By putting the problem the bank is facing to employees in a series of face to face meetings, and offering the possibility of participation in the decision-making and planning process, it may be possible to get more employees to buy into the planned changes.

Given that the decisions have been made at 'Y' and that resistance has already been encountered it may well be that the best way forward is now through a process of negotiation and agreement with representatives of the workforce. Trade union officials will probably represent the employees' side. A process of negotiation and bargaining may result in concessions from management, in terms of built-in safeguards and appropriate compensation for the union members. The bank could then be allowed to continue without further interference.

Management could always try the manipulation or co-optation approach. They can put forward proposals that deliberately appeal to the specific interest, sensitivities and emotions of key groups involved in the change. Alternatively, they can use information that is selective and distorted to only emphasise the benefits of the change. Co-optation involves giving key people access to the decision-making process eg, 'buying people off' with the promise of some kind of reward for going along with the proposed changes. These techniques may work in the short run but create other problems. Manipulation will eventually be discovered and will discredit the reputations of those involved. Trouble-makers who are co-opted tend to stay co-opted and may continue to create difficulties from their new position of power.

The last approach - the use of explicit and implicit coercion - is where the management abandons any attempt at consensus and may involve mass redundancies without right of appeal. This would have to be the approach of last resort since the image of the bank would suffer and the morale of the remaining workforce would be badly affected.

1 CLASSICAL AND CONTEMPORARY THEORIES OF MANAGEMENT

INTRODUCTION & LEARNING OUTCOMES

Syllabus area 11(i)   The views expressed by both classical and contemporary writers on business management and the practical value and limitations of the approaches they propose. For example, scientific management, administrative, human relations, systems and contingency approaches when compared with contemporary writers such as Peters or Handy.

As its title suggests, this syllabus is largely concerned with the study of 'organisations'. The title embodies certain assumptions that are not explicitly stated. For example, it is assumed that:

- entities called 'organisations' exist;
- these entities can somehow be distinguished from other entities which do not rank as organisations;
- despite any differences between individual organisations, there is enough common ground to make general statements possible and meaningful;
- to derive general conclusions about organisations is in some way valuable, and specifically is valuable to a management accountant working in some particular organisation.

A major aim of this introductory chapter is to justify these assumptions. It explains what is meant by the term 'organisation', what common features can be observed in many different organisations and how the study of such features can help you perform your work role more effectively.

The chapter begins with a general introduction to the nature of organisations and their classification. To help identify the main trends in the development of organisational behaviour and management theory, it is usual to categorise the work of writers into various 'approaches', based on their views of organisations, their structure and management. This provides a framework in which to direct study and focus attention on the progression of ideas concerned with improving organisational performance. The framework is based on four main approaches: classical, human relations, systems and contingency.

When you have studied this chapter you should be able to:

- Explain the usefulness of both classical and contemporary theories of management in practical situations

---

1 THE NATURE AND CLASSIFICATIONS OF ORGANISATIONS

1.1 Distinguishing features of organisations

We come across 'organisations' many times every day, and the word is very commonly used in conversation and in printed text. But how can the term be defined? What features must be present before we can say 'Yes - that is an organisation'?

In some cases the absence of a clear definition might pose no problem. For example, few people would disagree with the following examples of organisations:

- A multinational company such as General Motors
- A government department such as the Department of Social Security in Britain
- A charity such as Oxfam
- A university
- A professional body such as the Chartered Institute of Management Accountants.

However, the need for a definition, or for a defining list of characteristics, becomes apparent in less clear-cut cases. Consider the following examples:

- A village cricket team
- A professional football club
- A school chess club
- A self-employed plumber selling his services as a 'one-man-band'
- A family unit - say, a mother and father plus two young children
- A market stall run by a family - a mother and father plus their two teenage children.

The difficulties posed by these examples underline the difficulty of arriving at a general definition of 'organisation', and indeed no single definition is likely to command unanimous agreement.

One standard text - **Organizational behaviour** by Andrzej Huczynski and David Buchanan - attempts to confront the problem by offering the following:

[Definition]   'Organisations are social arrangements for the controlled performance of collective goals.'

Before we go on to look more closely at the elements of this definition you might care to refer back to the list of examples above to see whether the definition helps to clarify your thinking about each one. Returning to the definition, we can pick out the following main elements:

- **Social arrangements**. This suggests that organisations involve the interaction of different people. The case of the one-man-band plumber probably fails to qualify as an organisation on this criterion.

- **Controlled performance**. This is really the nub of the definition and above any other criterion helps to distinguish an organisation from any other entity. It can itself be broken down into two further elements: it suggests that performance levels are important and that some kind of control mechanism exists to achieve the required levels. Both of these factors are absent from some of our earlier examples; for instance, it would not make much sense to talk of controlled performance in the day-to-day functioning of a family unit. Even the school chess club, which seems a slightly more formal arrangement, will hardly cease to function if, for example, a few members fail to turn up at most meetings.

- **Collective goals**. Very often, an organisation owes its very existence to the fact that a particular individual is unable on his or her own to achieve a certain objective. For example, an engineer might see a need, and a demand, for a certain kind of machine tool, but he will not himself have sufficient resources of time, money, materials and machinery to create it. However, if he is sufficiently enthusiastic about his idea he may form a company, raise finance, buy materials and machines, rent factory premises and employ skilled personnel to achieve the objective of making and selling his machine tool.

1.2   Classifications of organisations

One thing that should be very apparent is the diversity of the different entities embraced under the heading 'organisations'. One way of trying to grasp the essential meaning of the term is to look at the common features uniting these entities, and this is what we have been doing so far. Another approach is to break down the mass of different entities into appropriate categories.

What criteria should we use to distinguish between the different categories? There are many possibilities that overlap. We could divide the whole mass of organisations into type A and type B on the basis of some particular criterion (such as size). Alternatively, we may choose a division into type C and type D based on a different criterion (such as ownership).

Some of the possible categorisations are discussed in what follows. You may well be able to add to the list. Remember that in each case the objective of defining categories is so that we can make useful general remarks about each category as a whole.

- **Classification by size of organisations.** Clearly, this is a useful method of distinguishing organisations. The organisational principles that apply to a small confectioner's shop may have much in common with those in a small family-owned printing business. However, you would expect to see such principles modified, extended, or even abandoned if the scene of operations is a multinational manufacturing conglomerate.

- **Classification by profit motive.** Most - possibly all - business organisations aim above all to make a profit. Other organisations - such as a charity, a school or an environmental pressure group such as Greenpeace - do not have a profit motive. This may well have an impact on the way the organisation is structured and managed.

- **Classification by ownership.** Here the main distinction is between private ownership and public ownership. Most businesses are privately-owned - from the corner shop owned by a sole proprietor or a husband and wife team, to a major business such as British Telecom owned by millions of private investors. On the other hand, many organisations - usually large ones - are in public ownership: examples in the UK include the National Health Service, the armed forces, the BBC.

We can also use the classifications to begin the process of identifying policies and principles, which apply to different organisations in different circumstances. (This is a point you should try to keep in mind as you work your way through the text.) For example, we might expect to find some or all of the following differences when contrasting large organisations with small ones.

	Large organisations	**Small organisations**
Structure	Well defined, hierarchical, embodied in written documents	Fluid, few or no steps in the hierarchy
Communication systems	Formal, based on written documents; perhaps supplemented by informal 'grapevine'	Informal, oral
Management systems and procedures	Formal, based on procedures manual, consensus	Informal, ad hoc, possibly autocratic

A similar exercise contrasting public and private ownership is illustrated by the case of the regional water authorities in Britain.

Case study

The supply of water to homes and industry in Britain was managed by publicly owned utilities before it was sold to a number of privatised regional water authorities. The aim was to reduce the role of central government, and introduce improved management and greater efficiency by market disciplines, such as accountability to shareholders.

During the dry summer of 1995, a number of the water authorities found difficulty in meeting the demand for water. Reservoirs were depleted and leakages from the system were reported to be at an all-time high. One Northern authority had to resort to desperate measures, threatening to introduce standpipes and undertaking a gigantic programme of bringing in water from outside the area in tankers. Press comment during and after the crisis focused on the organisational and cultural changes brought about by privatisation. The following criticisms were made (amongst many others!):

- The privatisation utilities no longer preserved the 'service' ethos of their publicly owned counterparts.
- The main corporate objective was now to satisfy shareholders by improving profitability, rather than to satisfy customers by improving service levels.
- These objectives often conflicted. For example, reducing staff numbers and neglecting to repair leakages both save money and improve profits; but both led to lower levels of service.
- Managers of the utilities, when quizzed by press and television reporters, often gave an impression of arrogance, and of disregard for customers. The effect was that customers came to see the managers as 'the opposition', rather than as part of a team working on their behalf. This impression was exacerbated by the much-increased levels of pay and benefits awarded to managers since privatisation.

As this case illustrates, the ownership of an organisation can be of vital importance in determining organisational priorities, management styles and relationships with customers.

The efforts of researchers to analyse such effects as these have had a relatively short history. Although occasional remarks on the subject are found in earlier authors, it is only really in the twentieth century that systematic efforts have been made to develop a 'science' of organisational theory. It is to some of these efforts that we now turn our attention.

1.3   The nature of organisations

Despite the differences between various organisations, there are some common factors:

(i)   people;
(ii)   objectives;
(iii)   structure; and
(iv)   management.

Most organisations are based on the interaction of people striving to achieve objectives. Some form of management and structure is required by which the activities of the organisation and the efforts of the members are directed and controlled towards the pursuit of the objectives.

The effectiveness of the organisation is dependent on the inter-relationship of people, objectives and structure, together with the efficient use of available resources. There are two broad categories of resources:

(i)   human - the members' abilities and influence, as well as their management;
(ii)   non human - the physical assets, materials and facilities.

2   CLASSICAL APPROACHES

2.1   Introduction

Classical approaches to organisation include scientific management, administrative theory and the bureaucratic model. The essence of the classical approach is that there exists a single, best approach to management and research was aimed at identifying this. They study the activities that need to be undertaken to achieve objectives and classify human beings into two groups described much later by McGregor as:

[Definition]   'The untrustworthy, money-motivated, calculative mass, and the trustworthy, more broadly motivated, moral elite who organise and manage the mass.'

Schein considered the mass to consist of those he defined as **rational-economic man:**

(a)   'Man is primarily motivated by economic incentives and will do that which gets him the greatest economic gain.

(b)   Since economic incentives are under the control of the organisation, man is essentially a passive agent waiting to be manipulated, motivated, and controlled by the organisation.

(c)   Man's feelings are essentially irrational and must be prevented from interfering with his rational calculation of self-interest.

(d)   Organisations can and must be designed in such a way as to neutralise and control man's feelings and therefore his unpredictable ways.'

2.2   Scientific management (1880 - 1930)

This period saw the rise of the business baron and the industrial revolution. Complex business organisations built by such people as John D Rockefeller began.

The emphasis in this period was on production. Organisations were continually looking for ways to become more efficient and prevent waste. The industrial revolution resulted in standardisation of production and the introduction of the assembly line. Emphasis was on work efficiency, and the foremost exponent of this approach was Fredrick W Taylor 'the father of scientific management' (whose principles were later developed by Henry Gantt and the Gilbreths).

Frederick Winslow Taylor (1856 - 1917) worked his way up through the American steel industry starting as an apprentice machinist and becoming in 1898 the General Manager of the Bethlehem Steel Company. Based on firsthand studies of manufacturing practices at the shop floor, he promulgated a series of principles in his work 'Scientific Management'. He criticised managers for their arbitrary approach to their responsibilities and workers for their apparent lackadaisical attitude. Taylor recommended making management a science, resting on 'well organised, clearly defined and fixed principles, instead of depending on more or less hazy ideas'.

He believed that:

- 'The principal object of management should be to secure the maximum prosperity for the employer, coupled with the maximum prosperity for each employee.'

- If productivity was increased then both could enjoy a larger piece of a larger cake - his differential piece rate system was designed with this in mind. He considered welfare to be of secondary importance - he firmly believed in **high-priced man.**

- 'Scientific Management has, for its very foundation, the firm conviction that the true interests of the two (ie, owners and workers) are one and the same.'

According to Taylor, the duties of management were to:

- Develop a science for each element of a man's work to replace the old rule of thumb method - the **best way** of doing a job.

- Scientifically select and then train, teach and develop the workmen (whereas in the past he chose his own work and trained himself as best he could).

- Heartily co-operate with the man so as to ensure all of the work being done is in accordance with the principles of scientific management.

- Bring about an almost equal division of the work and responsibility between the management and the workmen. The management should take over all the work to which they are better fitted than the workmen.

Taylor's methods led to spectacular results, particularly in the case of Schmidt, a pig iron handler who was trained to move 47.5 tons of iron per day as compared with the average 12.5 tons. However, it was essential for all four principles to be used together. Productivity could be increased without proper training or financial inducement and this, together with inherent defects in the methodology itself, led to many criticisms which are discussed at the end of this section.

Henry Gantt (1861 - 1919), a one time co-worker of Taylor, introduced:

- **Task setting** - goals for the worker to achieve.
- **Gantt charts** - to plan and control production.

Frank Gilbreth (1868 - 1924) was a bricklayer by trade who later ran his own business. His wife, Lillian, was an industrial psychologist, whose interest in attitudes to work linked in with her husband's contributions to scientific management which were to introduce **micro-motion** analysis based on defined elements of work. This formed the basis of time study.

Scientific management principles have encountered a number of criticisms.

- Initiative was removed and workers lost control over their activities. They were no longer required to think and were scheduled as a passive, almost mechanical, resource.

- The emphasis on quick and accurate performance of minutely planned repetitive tasks led to boredom, frustration and negative motivation.

- Unions feared unemployment and exploitation although Taylor claimed the cheaper price should increase demand.

- Employers and academics also opposed Taylor's ideas on **humanitarian** grounds (eg, demoralising for workers) and **economic** and **academic** grounds (eg, oversimplifies people and their behaviour).

2.3   Administrative theorists

As organisations grew and became more complex, a need for systematic understanding of the overall management and organisation process arose. The administrative theorists were concerned with the efficiency of administrative processes through system co-ordination and endeavoured to establish certain **principles of good management practice**.

Henri Fayol (1841 - 1925) qualified as a mining engineer. In 1888 he was appointed General Manager of the Commentary Fourchambault collieries and successfully turned the company round before retiring in 1918 to popularise his ideas. Like Taylor, Fayol undertook research of a technical nature. He recognised he was working on similar lines to Taylor, but he was looking at problems from the top and not from the bottom.

His basic belief was that 'to manage is to forecast and plan, to organise, to command, to co-ordinate and to control.'

In addition to identifying managerial functions, Fayol also developed several principles of management as guides to managerial action.

- **Division of work** leading to specialisation.

- **Authority** - the right to give orders and the power to exact obedience - linked to responsibility.

- **Discipline** - the military tag 'discipline constitutes the chief strength of armies' should be followed by 'discipline is what leaders make of it'.

- **Unity of command** - one man one superior.

- **Unity of direction** - one plan for a group of activities having same objectives.

- **Subordination of individual interest** to the general interest.

- **Remuneration** should be fair.

- **Centralisation** should be at the optimum for the particular purpose.

- **Scalar chain** through which formal lines of authority should pass - permission must be sought for lateral communication but such 'gangplanks' were very important.

- **Order** - a place for everything and everything in its place.

- **Equity** - a combination of kindliness and justice.

- **Stability of tenure of personnel** - high labour turnover is both a cause and an effect of poor management.

- **Initiative** - a manager must be able to sacrifice some personal vanity in order that subordinates can exercise initiatives and gain satisfaction from so doing.

- *Esprit de corps* - Unity is strength - do not divide and conquer.

Fayol accepted that his list had no precise limits and that his **principles** allowed for flexibility in their application. It was his followers who stressed the **universality** of his principles in that they could be applied in any company, both large and small.

He advocated **management education,** in that he felt it was useful and possible for managers to learn from each other that experience in running an organisation could be reflected upon, analysed and described in a systematic way. It would also be profitable to generalise from that experience.

One of the most important contributions of administration theory was to depersonalise the giving of orders.   However, like the scientific theorists, the administrative theorists concentrated on the processes rather than the employee, who was assumed to be more or less a standard production unit.

Woodward established that the principles were not universal.   Others argue that the principles are prescriptive and concentrate on the formal activity with little attention paid to commercial, interactional or motivational aspects.

2.4   Bureaucratic model

Max Weber (1864 - 1920), a German sociologist, is credited with the concept of bureaucracy. Weber classed the bureaucratic (or **rational legal**) form of authority as one of three types. The others being **charismatic**, which is supposed to be wielded by virtue of some innate personal quality, and **traditional**, which has the sanctity of tradition and status associated with it.

Weber stated that bureaucracies should have:

(a)   Clearly defined duties and responsibilities for all organisational members.

(b)   Hierarchically arranged staff with each member reporting to a superior and responsible for subordinates (except for those at the top or bottom of the structural pyramid).

(c)   An elaborate system of rules governing the manner in which each official carries out his duties.   Decisions are recorded and preserved so as to constitute precedents to guide future decisions.

(d)   Officials holding office on the basis of merit formally attested and subject to systematic selection and training (seniority and merit being considered to be the same).   This includes promotion by testing.

(e)   Each official carrying out his duties without regard to any personal or family commitment, impartially and unemotionally. His authority is confined to his official duties and he is motivated by a sense of duty and career prospects.

Weber claims that a bureaucratic organisation is technically the most efficient form of organisation possible:

'Precision, speed, freedom from ambiguity, knowledge of files, continuity, discretion, unity, strict subordination, reduction of friction and of material and personal cost - these are raised to the optimum point in the strictly bureaucratic administration'.

It must be remembered that Weber was referring to an ideal model, which would not exist in reality. However, many organisations are described as bureaucratic, even today, and all organisations will have a degree of bureaucracy. In a bureaucracy, highly complex tasks of administration are broken down into manageable areas such as sales, finance etc. It is the same in the public sector. For example in the Department of the Environment there are separate sections dealing with such matters as inner cities, planning, water, pollution etc.

Conclusion   The Classical approach is based on the identification of a single best approach to management, creating a set of rules whereby managers could operate. Such ideas are now seen as simplistic and unreal by the current contingency authors. Nonetheless, the Classical approach represents a major school of management thought and frequently occurs in examination questions.

3   THE HUMAN RELATIONS APPROACH TO ORGANISATION (1930 - 1950)

3.1   Introduction

This approach developed as a reaction to the dehumanising aspects of the approaches to the organisation of workforce previously described.

In the early 1920s, managers and academics were becoming increasingly aware of signs of worker rebellion against excessive impersonalisation and standardisation. Elton Mayo's work on the famous Hawthorne experiments gave birth to the human relations movement which dominated the field of organisational behaviour during the 1940s and 1950s.

3.2   Social man

As mentioned by one group of American academics, 'human relations dethroned economic man and installed social man in his place.'

Definition   Social man was defined by Schein as follows:

(a)   'Man is basically motivated by social needs and obtains his basic sense of identity through relationships with others.

(b)   As a result of the industrial revolution and the rationalisation of work, meaning has gone out of work itself and must, therefore, be sought in the social relationship on the job.

(c)   Man is more responsive to the social forces of the peer group than to the incentives and controls of management.

(d)   Man is responsive to management to the extent that a supervisor can meet a subordinate's social needs and needs for acceptance.'

3.3   The Hawthorne investigations

Experiments were carried out at the Hawthorne plant of the Western Electric Company. These experiments have become known as the 'Hawthorne experiments'.

Roethlisberger and Dickson, under the general direction of Elton Mayo (1880 - 1949), carried out the main research during the period 1927 - 1937. It has become the most widely quoted investigation in the history of social research. Six female operatives were put into a distinct group so that observers could record the effect on output and morale due to various changes in working conditions. Initially, an incentive payment scheme was introduced; then rest pauses in different forms. Almost without exception, output increased regardless of the changes introduced; the experimenters reverted to the original working conditions with no incentive payments, no pauses for rest or for refreshment and yet output was the highest ever recorded.

It was apparent that the changes in working conditions could not account for the increase in output. It was due to the enhanced work satisfaction that the girls enjoyed, the development of personal friendships and a new social atmosphere which brought a marked change in their attitude to work. Further experiments proved the importance of employees' attitudes to work, to supervision and to working in a group. Previously the individual had been treated as an isolated unit but the emphasis on work groups and supervisory behaviour was to change this view.

The experiments revealed that an organisation was more than a formal structure or arrangement of functions. Mayo wrote: 'An organisation is a social system, a system of cliques, grapevines, informal status systems, rituals and a mixture of logical, non-logical and illogical behaviour.'

As Pugh points out:

'... the significance of the Hawthorne investigations was in discovering the informal organisation which it is now realised exists in all organisations. It demonstrated the importance to individuals of stable social relationships in the work situation.'

3.4   Managerial implications

The result of the Hawthorne experiments and subsequent research into small group behaviour indicate that management should:

(a)   Pay more attention to the needs of the workers and not confine their attention to the tasks that have to be carried out.

(b)   Realise that the satisfaction that individuals gain from group membership may be far greater than can be achieved from what management has to offer.

(c)   Accept groups as a reality and consider group rather than individual incentives.

(d)   Act as an intermediary between the group and higher management and become a facilitator and sympathetic supporter rather than an allocator and controller of work.

Another finding of the studies which is of importance to social researchers has become known as the **Hawthorne effect** - the presence of researchers has an influence on the behaviour of the people being observed.

3.5   Criticisms of the human relations approach

By the late 1950s the human relations approach had fallen into disrepute mainly due to the naive, simplistic concepts that accompanied its implementation. Its solutions to organisational problems included strong cohesive work groups and the training of supervisors who would treat workers with greater fairness and consideration. It was accompanied by typical managerial practices of the time such as:

(a)   Suggestion schemes.
(b)   Fringe benefits to reward company loyalty.
(c)   Canteen committees.
(d)   Programmes for effective leadership.

In the words of one sociologist it humanised the work context but left the nature of the work unchanged. Leavitt called this approach 'people without organisation'.

4   MODERN APPROACHES (1950 - PRESENT)

4.1   Introduction

The modern approaches are characterised by processes of refinement, extension, and synthesis. This has resulted in the extension of the human relations' approach by the use of knowledge gained from the behavioural scientists. The result is a more objective and value-free approach to understanding persons in organisations. A major impact upon current organisational theory is the introduction of systems and contingency theories.

4.2   Behaviouralist approach - self-actualising man

By the early 1960s, the term organisational behaviour began to emerge and management started to use the new behaviouralist approach pioneered by Maslow, McGregor, Argyris and Herzberg. Although not universally accepted, since some prefer to regard it as one of the psycho-sociological approaches, it differed from the human relations approach in two important respects:

(a)   It is concerned both with organisations (structure, tasks, reporting relationships) **and** people;
(b)   There is the belief that people wanted more from their work than financial rewards, job security, humane treatment and a full social life.

Sometimes termed human resource theorists, behaviouralists believe in Schein's **self-actualising** concept of man:

(a)   'Man's motives fall into classes which are arranged in a hierarchy:

       (i)   simple needs for survival, safety and security;
       (ii)   social and affiliation needs;
       (iii)   ego - satisfaction and self esteem needs;
       (iv)   needs for autonomy and independence;
       (v)   self-actualisation needs in the sense of maximum use of his resources.

As the lower-level needs are satisfied, they release some of the higher-level motives. Even the lowliest untalented man seeks self-actualisation, a sense of meaning and accomplishment in his work, if his other needs are more or less fulfilled.

(b)   Man seeks to be mature on the job and is capable of being so. This means the exercise of a certain amount of autonomy and independence, the adoption of a long range time perspective, the development of special capacities and skills, and greater flexibility in adapting to circumstances.

(c)   Man is primarily self-motivated and self-controlled; externally imposed incentives and controls are likely to threaten the person and reduce him to less mature adjustment.

(d)   There is no inherent conflict between self-actualisation and more effective organisational performance. If given a chance, man will voluntarily integrate his own goals with those of the organisation.'

4.3   Managerial implications

Although there are some similarities with the Human Relations approach managers should worry less about being considerate to employees and more about how to make their work more challenging and meaningful.

Moreover, they will no longer be solely concerned with extrinsic rewards, be they economic or social, but also will be providing opportunities for employees to obtain intrinsic rewards for original and well executed work. Indeed, these opportunities may be more important than external factors.

Each manager will have to determine what work his subordinates will find satisfying and will delegate as much responsibility as he feels his staff can handle.

As with the Human Relations approach, participation is an important aspect of this approach. Here, however, it is employed to make better use of human resources untapped by previous approaches.

Participative practices include job enrichment, management by objectives, quality circles and autonomous working groups, all of which will be discussed later.

4.4   Limitations of the behaviouralist approach

As will be seen later, although there have been some notable successes with this approach it does have its limitations because:

(a)   Economic and social man still 'exist'.

(b)   Unions have been very distrustful - Winpisinger pointed out that 'it is difficult to picture enriching jobs at the expense of profit'. Many argue that behavioural techniques are as manipulative as those employed in scientific management

(c)   There are certain behavioural misconceptions:

- Hulin and Blood claim that blue collar workers are '... not alienated from work but from middle class concepts of work.'
- Klein and others found that many did not find routine work boring.
- According to Fein 80-85% of workers obtain their satisfactions outside of work.

(d)   Levitan and Johnston consider that change brings no lasting effects - workers soon forget the old system and the novel becomes the routine.

(e)   There is tremendous resistance to change even if it is intended to bring benefits.

5   SYSTEMS THEORY

5.1   Introduction

The advantage of the 'systems' approach to organisation theory is that it embraces a variety of disciplines to explain how an organisation operates, grows and declines.

Barnard is the main author associated with systems theory. Ackoff defines a system as:

> '... a whole that cannot be taken apart without loss of its essential characteristics and hence it must be studied as a **whole**.'

Closed system thinking stems primarily from the physical sciences and is applicable to mechanistic systems, which are self-contained and deterministic. Classical approaches consider an organisation as sufficiently independent so that its problems could be analysed in terms of its internal structure, tasks and formal relationships - without reference to its external environment. For example, a chemical reaction is a closed system.   The results that a closed system can achieve are wholly determined by the initial configuration of the system.

Open systems have a dynamic relationship with their environment and receive various inputs; these they transfer into outputs, which they then export.   Such systems are also open 'internally' in that interactions between components affect the system as a whole.

Feedback control is an important concept in systems thinking.   For closed systems to preserve their status quo, feedback must be negative and continuous.   However, in order that an open system can survive in a changing environment, it must utilise positive feedback to eventually change its goals and direction and reduce its entropy.

5.2   Organisations as open systems

Organisations can be viewed as social, informational, financial or economic systems and any one firm is in effect a subsystem of a larger suprasystem.   The firm itself is composed of many subsystems with their own goals and objectives.

Suprasystems, and environmental components for such subsystems, are not necessarily the same - a sales department would deal with the firm's customers' purchasing departments whilst industrial relations would be concerned with various union organisations.

Handy recognises four main classes of organisational subsystems.   **Adaptive** systems are concerned with fitting the organisation into its environment, shaping its future, dealing with divergencies and deciding its policies.   **Operative** systems assemble resources/inputs, convert inputs into outputs and finally dispose of outputs.   **Maintenance** systems work to keep the organisation healthy and **information** systems form the decision base of the organisation.

An organisation does not exist in a vacuum. It is dependent on its environment and is a part of larger systems, such as society, the economic system and the industry to which it belongs. The model below shows how the organisation, as an open system, receives inputs, transforms them and exports the outputs to the environment.

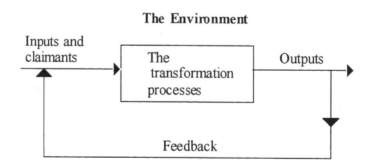

Inputs and claimants - may include capital, raw materials, people, information, managerial and technical skills and knowledge. In addition, various groups of people - stakeholders - will make demands on the organisation. For example, employees push for higher wages, better working conditions and job security. Consumers want safe and reliable products or services at reasonable prices. Shareholders want high returns on their investment and security for their money. Governments expect taxes and compliance of the law and the local community wants the maximum number of jobs with a minimum of pollution. We will be looking at stakeholders in more detail in a later chapter.

The transformation process - Charles Handy considers these processes as sub-systems:

- *Production* - in a manufacturing organisation, the transformation of inputs into outputs would be the production department, in an Insurance company it would be the underwriting department.

The production sub-system is the heart of the organisation and all sub-systems are usually oriented towards it.

- *Maintenance* - keeps the organisation functioning. It may repair and service the building. Alternatively, the human resource department can be seen as a maintenance sub-system, recruiting, retiring, counselling etc employees.

- *Boundary spanning* - organisations must acquire inputs, raw materials data etc, and distribute output - the finished product or service. This sub-system can cover a variety of activities, such as purchasing and marketing.

- *Adaptation* - an organisation needs to adapt in order to survive. This sub-system can cover such activities as research, engineering, planning and development.

- *Management* - is the sub-system which co-ordinates all of the other sub-systems, by means of policies, plans, resolving conflict etc. It is the task of managers to transform the inputs, in an efficient and effective way, into outputs using the managerial functions of planning, organising, staffing, leading and controlling.

Outputs - the type of outputs will vary with the organisation. They generally include products, services, profits and rewards (the satisfaction of the goals of various claimants). For example, employees need not only their basic needs (money for food and shelter) satisfying but also their needs for affiliation, acceptance, esteem and self-actualisation.

Feedback - it is important to note that, in the systems model shown above, some of the outputs become inputs again. For example, the satisfaction of employees becomes an important human input and part of the profits are reinvested in machinery, equipment, buildings and stock.

The systems approach expresses a manager's role as being a co-ordinator of the elements of a system, of which people are only one part. A manager is encouraged to spend greater time and effort in improving, planning, controlling and operating systems than motivating staff, since this will lead to greater efficiency.

5.3   The communication system

Communication is essential to the managerial process - it makes managing possible. Firstly, the communication system integrates the managerial functions of planning, organising, staffing, leading and controlling. It is a means of communicating the objectives of the organisation so that the appropriate structure can be organised. Effective leadership and the creation of an environment conducive to motivation depend on the communication system. Lastly, it is through communication that a manager determines whether events and performance conform to plans.

Another purpose of the communication system is to link the organisation with its environment. For example, it is used to identify the needs of customers. This knowledge enables the company to provide its goods or services at a profit. Similarly, it is through an effective communications system that the organisation becomes aware of competition and other potential threats and constraining factors.

6   CONTINGENCY APPROACHES

6.1   Introduction

The word 'contingency' means 'it depends'. The contingency theory of management contends that whether we are discussing leadership styles, motivation or organisation structure, there is no approach appropriate to all situations. The basis of contingency theories is that the approach depends upon the circumstances, there is no 'one best way' to organise and manage. In the light of prevailing (or forecast) conditions, issues of design and style depend on choosing the best combination of three variables:

(i)   the external environment;
(ii)   technological factors;
(iii)   human skills and motivation.

Prescriptive guidelines depend on these interrelated external and internal variables.

The term 'contingency approach' was suggested by Lawrence and Lorsch in 1967. Their research looked at the environmental determinants that affected the management of an organisation. Other contributors to this approach include:

- Burns and Stalker - who introduced the concept of mechanistic and organic types of structure and discussed them in relation to the environment;
- Joan Woodward - noted for her study on the effects of technological determinants on structure and performance;
- Edgar Schein - who recognises the complexity of man; and
- The Aston Group - who completed some interesting studies into several of the technology-structure variables in organisations.

6.2   Environmental determinants

Between 1965 and 1967 **Lawrence and Lorsch** were concerned with the various economic and market conditions that affected organisations. They investigated the internal functioning of six companies making plastics, which operated in a dynamic environment. The results of these six companies were then compared with two companies in the packaged foods industry, where the rate of change was moderate, and two firms in the container industry, operating in a very stable environment.

The major emphasis of their study was on the states of differentiation and integration in organisations. **Differentiation** was seen as more than the division of labour or specialisation. It also referred to the differences in attitude and behaviour of the managers concerned. Their findings showed that, in their orientation towards particular goals, issues of cost reduction were more important to production managers than sales managers. Production managers tended to be less relationship-orientated than sales managers. In their time orientation, sales and production managers had short-term orientations while research managers had long-term orientations. **Integration** was defined as the level to which units are linked together and their degrees of interdependence - the inter-relationships.   .

Lawrence and Lorsch were hoping to provide a systematic understanding of what states of differentiation and integration are related to effective performance under different environmental conditions. They measured effective performance in terms of:

- the change in profits over the past five years;
- the change in sales volume over the same period;
- the new products introduced over the period as a percentage of current sales.

They concluded that:

- In a dynamic and diverse environment, a high degree of differentiation is required in order to succeed.
- Regardless of the amount of environmental uncertainty, a high degree of integration is required to succeed.
- Conflict increases with differentiation, and the more successful a company, the better it handles conflict.
- Within companies operating in uncertain environments, middle or junior managers resolve conflict, whereas senior managers are involved where the environment is stable.

6.3   Burns and Stalker

Burns and Stalker investigated some twenty firms in the electronics industry in Scotland and Northern England. The research took place in the late 1950s and was primarily concerned with the way management systems might change in response to the demands of a rapidly changing external environment. They found two distinctive 'ideal types' of management system - mechanistic systems and organic systems.

- **Mechanistic systems** are appropriate for conditions of stability. They are typified by formal organisation, vertical communication and set rules with precise job descriptions.

- **Organic systems** are appropriate for conditions of change. They rely heavily on expert power, team work and lateral, informed communication and, as there is great commitment to the organisation, formal and informal systems become indistinguishable.

Burns and Stalker did not see the two systems as complete opposites, but rather as positions between which intermediate forms could exist. They proposed that organisations could move from one system to the other when there were changes in the external environment, and some organisations could operate with both systems at once. Critics of the mechanistic/organic systems approach argue that large organisations, when confronted with periods of change, have to maintain a high degree of structure and formality, even though they are committed to delegation, involvement and communication between groups.

6.4   Technological determinants

Professor Joan Woodward's research was based on the study of one hundred firms in the area of South East Essex. Its pioneering aspect was that it was to reveal a link between technology, organisational structure and management behaviour. The aim of the research was to determine just how far particular forms of industrial organisation could be associated with commercial success. Professor Woodward was able to establish that variations in structure and success did exist. The relationship between these variations could only be understood when the organisations surveyed were placed into three technological areas:

- **Small batch and unit production** - includes custom made products, the production of prototypes and large fabrications undertaken in stages.

- **Large batch and mass production** - includes assembly line production.

- **Process production** - includes the intermittent production of chemicals as well as the continuous-flow production of gases, liquids and crystalline substances.

Once grouped into one of these areas, Woodward identified several trends directly relevant to the link between technology and organisational structure. Her findings can be divided into four areas:

(i)   The more complex the process, the greater the chain of command ie, there were more levels of management in the process production industries than in the other two.

(ii)   Relationships were less formal, as was the type of communication methods used in unit and small batch production and process production. There was far more formality practised within large batch and mass production.

(iii)   Variations in technology seemed to affect industrial relations with disputes tending to be more frequent within mass production than the other two categories.

(iv)   It was discovered that companies enjoyed more financial success when they conformed to the medium organisational characteristics of their technology groups. When companies chose to diverge they were less successful.

In conclusion, Woodward's research showed there was no one best method of organisation and management. Optimum management and organisation structure is dependent upon the type of technology and thus the form of production system used.

6.5   Complex man

Edgar Schein recognised that, because organisations can have different structures and relate in a variety of ways with the environment, they will have an effect on the way managers manage. He made the following assumptions:

- Man is not only complex, but also highly variable. He has many motives, which are arranged in some sort of hierarchy of importance to him. However, this hierarchy is subject to change from time to time and situation to situation. A man's motives in different organisations, or different subparts of the same organisation, may be different.

- The nature of the task to be performed, the abilities and experience of the person on the job, and the nature of the other people in the organisation all interact to produce a certain pattern of work and feelings. For example, a highly skilled but poorly motivated worker may be as effective and satisfied as a very unskilled but highly motivated worker.

- Man can respond to many different kinds of managerial strategies, depending on his own motives and abilities and the nature of the task. In other words, there is no one correct managerial strategy that will work for all men at all times.

Research proves that organisations that adopt forms of structure, consistent with the expectations and perceived needs of their personnel will tend to attract a greater contribution from them towards high performance.

6.6   The size of the organisation

The **Aston Group** - Pugh, Hickson *et al* carried out extensive research in the late 1960s into the effect size, technology, ownership and history, location and market had on an organisation and its management. The Aston group's contribution to organisation theory was based on their multi-dimensional approach to organisations and the context they operated in. The aim was to identify an ideal structure for an organisation, which was determined by the particular set of circumstances (context) that faced it at a specified stage of its life in order to be successful.

The Aston research findings identified five structural variables:

(a)   Specialisation - both role and functional
(b)   Standardisation of procedures
(c)   Formalisation of documentation
(d)   Centralisation of decisions
(e)   First-line span of control

which were considered against a number of contextual variables:

(a)   size of organisation;
(b)   technological features;
(c)   ownership history;
(d)   location;
(e)   market.

They concluded that **size** was the most important contextual variable and that larger size led to more specialisation, standardisation and formalisation but less centralisation.

The researchers believed that it was possible to predict fairly closely the structural profile of an organisation on the basis of information obtained about the contextual variables.

Conclusion | There are task-centred approaches (the classical schools), people-centred approaches (human relations schools) and interactive approaches (behavioural and Contingency approaches). Classical, human relations and behavioural models are generally prescriptive and universalistic ('one best way'), whereas contingency approaches are situational ('it all depends'). Systems thinking pervades all approaches to management. To reach a balanced understanding of organisations a consideration of all of the above perspectives is essential.

7   OTHER PERSPECTIVES

7.1   Learning from the Japanese

During the 80's and 90's management guru's have emerged from the US and Japan who have developed a range of approaches. Japan's economic and industrial successes have been generally attributed to a combination of their culture and their management system, and these two factors are interrelated. The Japanese management system has many distinctive features.

(a)   Job rotation and slow promotion, with experience across functions before promotion.

(b)   Complex appraisal systems, primarily based on loyalty and long service.

(c)   Emphasis on work groups (eg, quality circles).

(d)   Open communication.

(e)   Consultative decision making.

(f)   Concern for the employee.

Whether such techniques will find wide recognition in the UK is debatable. At Nissan's plant in Sunderland, there has not been universal acceptance of Japanese management practices by the workforce. This workforce is largely male, formerly employed in highly unionised traditional industries (eg, shipbuilding, coal and engineering). On the other hand, the largely female workforce of Japanese companies in South Wales and Plymouth, who have limited previous industrial experience, have successfully adopted Japanese practices.

7.2   Theory Z

Ouchi studied 24 large multinational companies, half of them American owned and the other half Japanese owned, and developed what he refers to as the ideal Theory Z type of company which encompasses the best of both worlds.

This theory was based on the belief that it is the spirit of co-operation and consensus decision-making that provides Japanese companies with the advantages of a highly motivated workforce, high productivity and good quality. This theory, therefore, argues that organisations become more efficient by:

(a)   maintaining formal and explicit control mechanisms;

(b)   developing
- formal planning systems
- management by objectives
- sophisticated information and accounting systems;

(c)   ensuring longer-term employment;

(d)   encouraging employees and managers to think and function over longer time frames;

(e)   carrying out frequent cross training and job rotation together with participative decision making and an emphasis on mutual trust.

7.3   The excellence school

Peters and Waterman in their management best-seller 'In Search of Excellence' identified the concept of 'culture', and identified eight cultural values, which they claim are held by 'excellent' companies.   These 'excellent' companies are 'continuously innovative', and the whole company is willing and prepared to adapt to the needs of customers, actions of competitors etc.   Excellent companies tend to 'experiment more, encourage more tries, and permit small failures.' Charles Handy is impressed with their findings, which fit his own contingency ideas.

> **Conclusion**   The contingency approach is the most practical since it adapts management behaviour to suit the particular circumstances.   This could result in an approach being formed, which features several different schools of organisation thought.

8   SELF TEST QUESTIONS

8.1   Give a definition of 'organisation'. (1.1)

8.2   What criteria could you use to classify organisations? (1.2)

8.3   What was Frederick Taylor's contribution to organisational theory? (2.2)

8.4   How did Henri Fayol's approach differ from Taylor's? (2.3)

8.5   What type of organisation could be defined as bureaucratic? (2.4)

8.6   What are the managerial implications of the Hawthorne investigations? (3.4)

8.7   What are the limitations of the behaviouralist approach? (4.4)

8.8   What types of systems exist within organisations? (5.2)

8.9   How have contingency approaches developed the understanding of how organisations operate? (6.1)

8.10   What can be learnt from the Japanese perspective of organisations? (7.1)

9   EXAMINATION TYPE QUESTION

9.1   Systems theory

Management writers have found it useful to conceptualise organisations as open systems.

CA is a company engaged in the assembly and sale of computers. Components are purchased from around the world, briefly sorted using a just-in-time (JIT) system and assembled in a factory employing the latest technology. The assembly of a computer begins after receipt of a customer order. Post, fax or telephone is normally used to place a customer's order because the company sells directly from the factory. Payment is normally in advance by cheque or credit card and the computer is delivered to the customer by a courier service. CA advertises in national newspapers and targets the home and small business market. CA is organised on functional lines and includes departments dealing with customer services, technical support, research and development, storage, assembly, packaging, marketing and sales, accounting, personnel and administration.

Requirements

(a)   Describe the CA organisation using concepts from open systems theory.   **(10 marks)**

(a)   In what ways can open systems theory assist in our understanding of the operation of organisations like CA?   **(10 marks)**

(Total: 20 marks)

(CIMA May 99)

10   ANSWER TO EXAMINATION TYPE QUESTION

10.1   Systems theory

(a)   In the general systems approach, organisations are systems of inter-related activities.   The organisation interacting with its environment is viewed as an open system made up of two aspects - the inputs and the outputs. The inputs or factors of production (people, finance etc) are drawn from the environment and the outputs (the products or services) are offered to the environment. Closed systems, on the other hand, are systems, which are self-supporting and do not interact with the environment outside the system. The interdependence of open systems is particularly important for a company because, if it is to flourish, it must respond to the changes, threats and opportunities in its environment.

Using concepts from open systems theory, we can describe CA as buying components, assembling them into computers, and marketing the completed product, raising money to continue buying inputs and generate outputs. CA makes computers using its own separate resources and identifiable management entity, whilst interacting with others outside itself.   For example, suppliers who are developing new components, customers who want new features, and competitors who want to grab a larger share of the market.

A model could be drawn to show this activity:

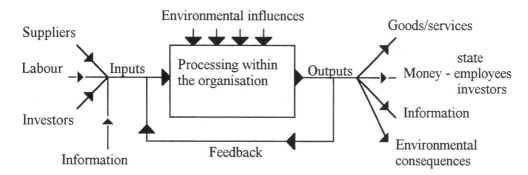

Open systems are composed of several subsystems. CA is not just one entity, but a combination of different departments and different sites. Management is the sub-system that co-ordinates all of the other sub-systems, by means of policies, plans and resolving conflicts etc. The production sub-system is the heart of the organisation but the quality control operation may be distinct from the rest of the production process. Each subsystem will have its own sense of identity, its own physical space and personnel, its own cost centre management, its own leader and its own ways of handling interaction with other parts of CA.

Each part of CA takes in its different inputs, adds value in its own way and generates its own different output. The maintenance sub-system keeps the organisation functioning. It may repair and service the building. Alternatively, the human resource department can be seen as a maintenance sub-system that recruits, retires and counsels employees. Yet, for the world outside CA, the cumulative effect of all their separate (but linked) efforts is the output generated by CA as a whole.

Open systems have a dynamic relationship with their environment and receive various inputs. They transfer these inputs into outputs, which they then export. Such systems are also open internally in that interactions between components affect the system as a whole. Feedback control enables a system to change itself, including its goals, so that it can survive in a changing environment.

(b)   Whilst the classical approach to organisations is impersonal and the human relations and behavioural approaches stress the importance of individuals and informal groups, the systems approach emphasises the need for correct decision making through the interaction of man and machines. Followers of the approach are interested in studying whole situations and relationships rather than segments of an organisation. They recognise the interactive effect of activities and functions upon each other and make efforts to harness the controlling influences.

We can use open systems theory to assist our understanding of the operation of organisations like CA because:

It focuses on the activities, including aspects of the technology employed, the people in the company, their relationships and roles, as well as the interaction with the environment.

It draws attention to the dynamic aspects of organisation and the factors influencing the growth and development of all its sub-systems.

It creates an awareness of sub-systems, each with potentially conflicting goals that must be integrated. When sub-systems pursue their own goals to the detriment of the system as a whole, it is called sub-optimisation.

It focuses attention on inter-relationships between: aspects of the organisation; the organisation and its environment; and the needs of the system as a whole. Managers should not get so involved in detail and small political problems that they lose sight of the overall objectives and processes.

It can highlight 'linear causality' - showing managers that decisions intended to achieve result 'X' may inadvertently create unwanted side-effect 'Y' somewhere else in the system because of the unpredictability and uncontrollability of many inputs.

It underlines the importance of sensitive but firm central co-ordination if the overall outcome of an organisation is to be greater than the sum of the outcomes of it constituent parts.

The systems approach expresses a manager's role as being co-ordinator of the elements of a system, of which people are only one part. A manager is encouraged to spend greater time and effort in improving, planning, controlling and operating systems than motivating staff, since this will lead to greater efficiency. Like any other approach, managers should take what they find useful in practice, without taking it to extremes.

2 ORGANISATIONAL OBJECTIVES

INTRODUCTION & LEARNING OUTCOMES

Syllabus area 11(i)

- Organisational objectives (ie stakeholder analysis and organisational mission, goals and targets)

- The reasons for conflict between the objectives of an organisation, or between the objectives of the organisation and its stakeholders, and the ways in which this conflict might be managed (eg compromise or identification of a dominant coalition).

Every organisation needs to be clear about its goals and objectives. As the environment changes and presents new challenges, organisations need to review and reassess their goals. Some organisations will discover that they are drifting, because their goals are no longer relevant. Others will find that their goals are clear, relevant, and effective. Still others will discover that their goals are no longer even clear and that they have no firm direction. The purpose of developing a clear set of goals for an organisation is to prevent it from drifting into an uncertain future. The issue of setting an organisation's goals breaks into two distinct steps, first determining what the current goals are, and second deciding what the goals should be.

Objectives are normally formulated within a hierarchical structure, with each level in the hierarchy deriving its objectives from the next level above, all therefore emanating from the organisation's overall mission or vision. Objectives therefore cascade downwards in the sequence: mission, goals, objectives, strategies, tactics and operational plans. The hierarchy of objectives suggests, for example, that strategy is planned to achieve objectives, but that in turn it provides targets for the planning of tactics.

In striving to satisfy its goals and achieve its objectives, an organisation cannot ignore the political, social, technical and cultural environmental variables. Organisational survival is dependent on a series of exchanges between the organisation and the environment. These give rise to a number of broader responsibilities to society in general. Objectives in general are likely to be shaped by the needs of different coalitions of interest, sometimes referred to as stakeholders. These needs include those of the strategic decision-makers themselves, and how they, the decision-makers, see the power structure in the organisation.

When you have studied this chapter, you should be able to:

- Recommend appropriate organisational goals.
- Identify the stakeholders of an organisation and explain their influence on its management and structure.

1 MISSIONS, GOALS AND OBJECTIVES

1.1 A systems view of goals and objectives

The goals of an organisation are related to the input-conversion-output cycle. In order to achieve its objectives, and therefore satisfy its goals, the organisation takes inputs from the environment, through a series of activities transforms or converts these inputs into outputs and returns them to the environment as inputs to other systems. A systems view of organisational goals and objectives is shown overleaf:

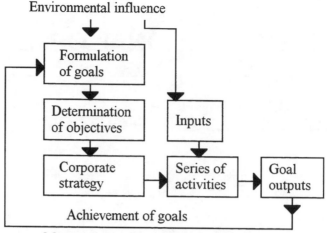

Environmental influence

Measurement of organisational success

Whatever the type of organisation, there is a need for lines of direction through the establishment of objectives and determination of policy. These form the basis of management.

1.2   Hierarchy of objectives

Most writers agree with the idea that there is a hierarchy of objectives, just as there is a hierarchy of managers.   At each higher level in the hierarchy, the objectives are more relevant to a greater proportion of the organisation's activities so that the objectives at the top of the hierarchy are relevant to every aspect of the organisation.   The following diagram illustrates the hierarchical relationship of mission, goals, objectives, strategy, tactics and operational plans.

Within large and complex organisations, it is obvious that objectives at different levels and between different units will be in conflict. However, the existence of a hierarchy of objectives, with lower-level objectives forming the means whereby higher-level objectives are achieved, is a useful concept and has been referred to as a means-end chain.

The topmost statement of organisational objectives is usually termed 'the mission'.   This is where we start.

1.3   The concept of 'mission statement'

[Definition]   A statement in writing that describes the basic purpose of an organisation ie, what it is trying to accomplish.

Characteristics

A mission statement can be viewed as a statement primarily directed towards the employees of an organisation, which should assist in the attainment of the objectives of the organisation. In short, a 'mission statement' will have some or all of the following characteristics:

- It is usually a brief statement of no more than a page in length. (Some companies have produced very effective mission statements consisting of a single sentence, although there are also successful company credos that extend into several pages.)

- It is a very general statement of entity culture.

- It states the aims (or purposes) of the organisation.

- It states the business areas in which the organisation intends to operate.

- It is open-ended (not stated in quantifiable terms).

- It does not include commercial terms, such as profit.

- It is not time-assigned.

- It forms a basis of communication to the people inside the organisation and to people outside the organisation.

- It is used to formulate goal statements, objectives and short-term targets.

- It therefore guides the direction of the entity's strategy and as such is part of management information.

Example

ICI PLC - GROUP PURPOSE

The chemical industry is a major force for the improvement of the quality of life across the world. ICI aims to be the world's leading chemical company, serving customers internationally through the innovative and responsible application of chemistry and related sciences. 'Through achievement of our aim, we will enhance the wealth and well-being of our shareholders, our employees, our customers and the communities which we serve and in which we operate'

1.4   Mission statements with an external orientation

A mission's goals do not have to be 'internal'. Some of the most effective are directed outside the company, on customers, or competitors. Federal Express Corporation's US operation has a short but powerful mission statement: *'Absolutely, Positively Overnight!'* Everyone in the company knows what that statement means. Almost nothing more has to be said to ensure that every action of every person is aimed at total customer satisfaction.   Another short credo that says it all belongs to PepsiCo. PepsiCo's mission has long been simply to *'Beat Coke'*, a mission it has yet to achieve. A longer mission statement on a plaque at Lever House places the emphasis on serving the customer:

The mission of our company, as William Hesketh Lever saw it, is to make cleanliness commonplace, to lessen work for women, to foster health and to contribute to personal attractiveness so that life may be more enjoyable for the people who use our products.

Mission statements like these will prompt people to think first about the customer, and will provide a gauge against which employees can judge their efforts to satisfy customers. It will equip employees with a strong inner compass for navigating their actions. It will stamp the culture of the organisation. Mission statements are like visions or dreams. We should not forget that in a memorable speech, Dr. Martin Luther King, Junior said, *'I Have a Dream'* - he did not say *'I have a strategic plan'*.

In isolation, however, missions can be self-destructive. Concentrating single-mindedly on their mission, many entities lose their way once they have achieved their goal. Having landed a man on the moon, NASA drifted. It has yet to find a new mission as compelling as its first one.

1.5   The search for a mission

According to Peter Drucker there are a number of fundamental questions that an organisation will need to address in its search for purpose. These are:

- What is our business?
- What is value to the customer?
- What will our business be?
- What should our business be?

Part of the process of defining an organisation's mission is to decide what role it is to play. There are at least two ways of looking at the role of a mission statement.

- It is a **description** of the pervading culture of an organisation. It defines the assumptions, values and beliefs regarded as important by those managing the organisation.

- It is **strategic tool**, a discipline that forces managers to think carefully about the goals they should be pursuing. It helps them to formulate plans for achieving them.

2   GOALS

2.1   Introduction

[Definition]   Goals are long-run, open-ended attributes or ends a person or organisation seeks and are sufficient for the satisfaction of the organisation's mission.

Characteristics

In short, goals will have all or some of the following characteristics:

- They are mainly narrative statements derived from the mission.
- More than one goal statement is required to satisfy the organisation's mission.
- Goal statements are set in advance of the objectives. (They separate the organisation's mission from the detailed, time-assigned objectives.)
- They are open-ended (not stated in quantifiable terms).
- In the main, they have no time-assigned basis.

2.2   Clarifying the meaning of 'goal'

The distinction between goals, objectives and targets is a common cause of confusion. Some writers assign different meanings to the same terms, others use them interchangeably and almost all disagree with their relative values and significance. Some examples will serve to exemplify the distinction.

(a)   Lorange, P., 'Corporate Planning, An Executive Viewpoint'

'Objectives, as referred to in this book, are more general statements about a direction in which the firm intends to go, without stating specific targets to be reached at particular points in time. A goal, on the other hand, is much more specific, indicating where one intends to be at a given point in time. A goal thus is an operational transformation of an objective; typically a general objective often gets transformed into one or more specific goals.'

(b)   Vancil, R., 'Strategy Formulation in Complex Organisations'

'One of John F. Kennedy's **objectives** in 1960 was to re-establish and maintain this (USA) country's position as a leader in the fields of science and technology. One of his **goals** was to land a man on the moon and return him safely before the end of the decade.'

However as mentioned previously, in this text we adhere to the view that goals will be a narrative transformation of the mission statement (or mission), and typically a goal will be transformed into one or more specific objectives. Thus, we categorise objectives into five components:

- **Mission**, the primary *raison d'être* set in advance of strategy.

- **Goals**, the secondary and mainly narrative objectives derived from the mission and also set in advance of strategy.

- **Corporate objectives** which are time-assigned aims derived from the goals and also set in advance of strategy.

- **Strategic targets** which are time-assigned and derived from the strategy.

- **Standards of performance** (often identical with targets) assigned to particular individuals.

In this respect we are close to the opinions of writers such as:

(a)   Mintzberg, H., 'Power in and Around Organisations':

- **Mission**: An organisation's mission is its basic function in society.

- **Goals**: An organisation's goals are the intentions behind its decisions or actions.

- **Objectives**: Objectives are goals expressed in a form in which they can be measured.

(c)   Hofer, C., and Schendel, D., 'Strategy Formulation: Analytical Concepts':

'We consider goals to be the ultimate, long-run, open-ended attributes or ends a person or organisation seeks, while we consider objectives to be the intermediate-term targets that are necessary but not sufficient for the satisfaction of goal.'

There is no reason for you to be worried about the confusion of terms. Your examiner will also be aware that they are used interchangeably by writers and practitioners. It is important however, for you to clarify the ways in which you are using them.

3   OBJECTIVES

3.1   Introduction

Definition   Objectives are time-assigned targets derived from the goals, and are set in advance of strategy.

Characteristics - objectives have all or some of the following characteristics:

- They are mainly statements expressed in quantitative terms ('closed') derived from the goals.
- More than one objective may be required to satisfy a goal.
- Objectives are set in advance of strategy.
- They are time-assigned.

Objectives must be capable of being quantified, otherwise progress towards them cannot be measured. For a local authority, for instance, to state a goal as 'to improve the welfare of old age pensioners in the Borough' is not precise enough. The goal needs to be translated into objectives, which state how it is going to measure the achievement. For example:

- the number of places made available in old people's homes by a certain date;
- the number of meals-on-wheels served in certain period;
- the number of patients treated in geriatric wards.

As shown in this example, several targets may make up its overall objective. For objectives to be of use in practice, they must have three components:

- Attribute chosen to be measured, eg, profit, return on capital, output.
- Scale by which it is to be measured, eg, £, %, tonnes.
- Target, ie, the level on the scale which it is hoped to achieve, eg, £1m, 12%, 350,000 tonnes.

As well as being explicit, objectives need to be realistic and attainable. Ideally, existing performance statistics should be used to measure objectives. If a new system of data collection or processing has to be instituted in order to measure progress towards objectives, extra cost will be incurred.

3.2   Objective setting

Ackoff considers objectives to be desired states or outcomes, which may be unattainable within the planning period, but must be approachable: for example, increased market share. A goal is an objective whose attainment is desired by a specified time; for example to obtain a 10 per cent market share by 20XX.

Hofer and Schendel have written that they consider goals to be the ultimate, long-run, open-ended attributes, or ends a person or organisation seeks, objectives are intermediate-term targets that are necessary, but not sufficient for the satisfaction of goals.

Mintzberg defines goals as the intention behind an organisation's decisions or actions. He argues that frequently goals will never be achieved, and may be incapable of being measured. Thus, for example 'the highest possible standard of living to our employees' is a goal, which will be difficult to measure and realise. Although goals are more specific than mission statements and tend to have a shorter number of years in their time scale, they are not precise measures of performance.

Mintzberg goes on to define objectives as goals expressed in a form in which they can be measured. Thus, an objective of 'profit before interest and tax to be not less than 20 per cent of capital employed' is capable of being measured.

Objectives state end results, and overall objectives need to be supported by sub-objectives. Thus, a hierarchy of objectives is formed as well as an interlinking network of objectives between the different functions. Furthermore, organisations and managers have multiple goals, which may be incompatible and create conflict. A manager may have to choose between short-term and long-term achievement and personal interests may have to yield to corporate objectives.

Drucker maintains that there are several factors that should be considered when formulating objectives:

- Objectives are commitments to action through which the mission of the business is to be carried out, and provide the standards against which performance is to be measured.

- Objectives must be operational, that is capable of being converted into specific targets and implying certain courses of action.

- Objectives should be of a fundamental nature to ensure the concentration of resources; that is, objectives must be selective.

- A number of objectives are required to manage a business adequately.

- Objectives are needed in all areas upon which the survival of the organisation depends.

Drucker is an advocate of the hierarchy approach to corporate objective setting whereby the primary objectives are defined before the lower level objectives. In this way, the overall objective specifies the lower or sub-objectives.

The categories that could be involved as overall objectives have been listed by Drucker as:

- profitability;
- innovation;
- market standing;
- productivity;
- financial and physical resources;
- managerial performance and development;
- worker performance and attitude;
- public responsibility.

Not all of these will apply to all organisations, and emphasis could change in response to environmental changes.

Each aspect is seen as a key area of corporate performance and should therefore figure in the overall corporate objectives.

Conclusion Understanding the mission, goals and objectives is a step to grasping why an organisation is following particular strategies. The goals should reveal what it is likely to do in the future. Goals are essentially of the future, and not of the present or the past. They are targets at which the organisation is aiming and could be described as the driving forces, which cause the organisation to go in a certain direction.

3.3   Activity

Consider how goals and objectives could be important in the following situations:

- where the parent company has completed the takeover of a smaller competitor;
- where a company is considering whether to buy-in partly finished goods from countries in Eastern Europe and complete the manufacture in UK

3.4   Activity solution

Where a parent company has taken over a smaller competitor, the setting of specific goals and objectives could achieve the following benefits:

- a means of checking the operating data and results that the parent company believed existed at the time of the takeover;
- identifying areas of performance that are inferior to group standards;
- identifying effective managers;
- evaluating the contribution of particular processes or products;
- checking customer reactions to the takeover.

Where a company is considering whether to buy in partly finished goods from Eastern Europe, then goals and objectives would be important in:

- defining the standards required in areas of quality, delivery promise, design, etc;
- setting improvement targets;
- providing a basis of comparison with other suppliers.

4   EVALUATING EFFICIENCY AND EFFECTIVENESS

4.1   The meaning of efficiency and effectiveness

Establishing organisational goals and objectives is just a start. We also need to measure success in achieving those goals. In this context, it is important to be clear what is meant by two concepts that are often confused - efficiency and effectiveness.

- **Effectiveness** is a measure of the match or mismatch between what an organisation produces (its actual outputs) and what it should be producing (defined in terms of its organisational goals, which in turn will be related to the needs of its 'customers').

- **Efficiency** is a measure of the resources used in producing the organisation's actual outputs.

To illustrate that these concepts are different, note that:

- an organisation may be effective without being efficient - it produces exactly what it intends (or what its 'customers' need), but squanders resources in doing so;

- an organisation may be efficient without being effective - it achieves excellent value from the resources it uses, with no wastage, but its actual outputs do not match customer expectations (perhaps because organisational goals are badly defined).

4.2   The relationship between efficiency and effectiveness

Organisational efficiency measures performance and takes into account how the organisation operates taking account of the way resources and technology are utilised. Improvement of standardisation in terms of procedures and working practices, reducing waste and raising quality are all examples of how organisational efficiency can be improved. Efficiency is an important consideration when determining an organisation's capability in the long, medium or short term.

Organisational effectiveness can be defined as a measure of the quality of the relationship between an organisation and the goals it is aiming to achieve. A viable organisation could be described as recognising the key internal and external variables that will affect its performance and has developed, implemented and achieved its strategic plan that will maximise its position in the environment.

In order for an organisation to enjoy long-term success, there needs to be a balance between efficiency and effectiveness. Handy identifies that the study of organisational effectiveness is complex, and details over sixty different variables that can have an impact on the organisation's effectiveness. Most theorists and managers tend to place these variables in groups and concentrate on one group of variables at any one time, for example:

- Technological environment - condition of plant, type of technology and raw materials used.

- Work groups - size, cohesion, goals, task, age and leader.

Handy believes that it is 'seldom possible to optimise on all the variables'. For example focusing on introducing new technology may result in de-skilling the workforce, which may result in problems. The issue organisations are faced with is how effectiveness is defined. The goals and objectives set will obviously be linked to how the organisation defines both effectiveness and efficiency. This in itself can be a difficult exercise, especially if there are conflicting values and therefore views.

5   ENVIRONMENTAL ANALYSIS

5.1   The effect of the environment on the organisation

Today's organisations must respond to a variety of internal and external pressures. When an organisation operates in a stable total environment, managers need to pay only moderate attention to internal and external conditions.   When the external environment continuously undergoes rapid changes, far-reaching effects on organisations and their management strategies are experienced.

The external environment consists of elements outside an organisation that are relevant to its operations.   The external environment has both *direct-action* and *indirect-action* elements. Stakeholders directly influence an organisation and so are elements of direct-action. Indirect-action elements include technology, economy and market conditions.   Indirect-action elements have the potential to become direct-action elements.   For example, changes in consumer expectations concerning organisational behaviour may lead to the creation of new government legislation.

Koontz, O'Donnell and Weihrich listed three ways in which an organisation is affected by its environment:

- The organisation imports goods and services from the environment.   Labour, public services, materials, finished goods, professional services etc are bought in by the company.

- Outside groups can make demands upon the organisation and can impose constraints.   Such groups are customers, government, employees, shareholders, general public etc.   These constraints can be mandatory (eg safety requirements imposed by law) or self-imposed (eg maintaining clean factory areas, restricting noise levels).

- The environment contains opportunities and threats for the organisation.   A change in market may create an opportunity for a new product or it may hasten the demise of an existing product.   An oil crisis in the Gulf will affect all companies' transport costs but will have more serious repercussions in a company which uses petroleum products in its manufacturing processes.

5.2   Stakeholder theory

Stakeholders can be defined as groups or individuals that have an interest in the well-being of the company and/or are affected by the goals, operations or activities of the organisation or the behaviour of its members. They have a 'stake' in what the organisation does. Stakeholders can be broadly categorised into:

(a)   internal stakeholders - employees, management, etc;
(b)   connected stakeholders - customers, suppliers, competitors, etc;
(c)   external stakeholders - government, pressure groups, etc.

F Abrams speaks of a firm's responsibility to 'maintain an equitable and working balance among the claims of the various directly interested groups'. Management normally undertakes this responsibility but usually the most powerful group of stakeholders, termed the dominant coalition, will determine the organisation's prime objectives.

Bowen (1953) proposed the idea of a social audit, which would establish what needs and expectations of the various stakeholders groups had been satisfied. Similar ideas were expressed by Humble with his social responsibility audit and, since the publication of The Corporate Report, many company annual reports carry sections devoted to this idea.

Johnson and Scholes stress that 'objectives are not permanent or pre-ordained, rather they are the result of a bargaining process and change over time.'

There are obviously close links between stakeholder theory and social responsibility, which is discussed later in this text.

5.3   Internal stakeholders

These include:

- **Entrepreneurs** - who wish to 'do their own thing' - become financial magnates, develop their own technical or commercial ideas, be independent.

- **Managers** - are likely to have a particular interest, and concern for, the size and growth of the organisation and its profitability, job security, status, power and prestige (office size, type of company car, number of staff working for them).

- **Non-managerial employees** - normally concerned with improving pay and conditions and, particularly in the current economic situation, job security. Safety, freedom from discrimination, and industrial democracy are also of concern.

  Employees are more productive when they have a sense of participation in the decisions affecting them. Human resource development has become a major organisational objective for many companies. West German companies have labour representation on management boards, and the Swedish company Volvo has pioneered the concept of job enrichment for assembly-line workers.

5.4   Connected stakeholders

These include:

- **Customers** and final consumers - are interested in value for money, ethical advertising and consumer protection. A customer may be an institution, such as a hospital or government agency; it may be another firm, such as a distributor or manufacturer; or it may be an individual consumer.

The customer market may be highly competitive, with large numbers of potential buyers and sellers seeking the most congenial arrangements. In such markets, managers must be especially concerned about price, quality, service, and product availability if they want to keep old customers and attract new ones.

In recent years, as foreign firms have challenged UK firms, new standards of quality have begun to change customer relationships. For example, when Japanese car manufacturers found it difficult to set up service networks for their products in the UK, they responded by making cars that were more reliable. Now some Japanese car manufacturers work in association with UK manufacturers.

New technology has also led to some homogenisation of markets throughout the world, by making communications and transportation inexpensive and accessible. People around the globe are now exposed to the latest and best products, allowing customers in different countries to become potential customers for the same goods. Manufacturers can now think in terms of a world car, for example, or a worldwide computer networking system.

- **Suppliers** - want a fair price, regular business and payment on time. Every organisation purchases raw materials, services, equipment and labour from the environment and uses them to produce its output. What the organisation brings in from the environment will determine both the quality and the price of its final product.

  Advances in inventory control and information processing have changed organisational relationships with suppliers. Some companies keep zero inventory, relying on several 'just in time' (JIT) deliveries each day. If JIT methods are in operation, this obviously results in a much closer relationship between organisations and suppliers, not only in terms of lead-time deliveries, but also in terms of quality control.

- **Competitors** - competition in an industry is rooted in its underlying economics, and competitive forces exist that go well beyond the established combatants in a particular industry.

  Competitors will therefore be concerned with the degree of rivalry between themselves in their own industry and the degree of potential rivalry or threat of entry from others.

- **Shareholders** - are the owners of companies and are the suppliers of any additional risk capital, which may be required.

  Consideration must be given to the interests of these suppliers of capital by any firm that may require to raise further equity, as well as having regard to their potential control over the company. Ascertaining exactly who owns the firm's shares, and what their particular preferences and objectives are, is important if managers want to act in the shareholder's interests. The information may also provide insights into circumstances where different types of shareholder may have conflicting interests. This information may not necessarily resolve the conflict but will help alert management to it. It may also alert them to potential conflicts between themselves and their shareholders.

  The type of shareholder or shareholders that a company has, will largely determine the sort of information that can be gained from them. There are basically two main types of shareholder:

  (i)   institutions, usually of a large size; and
  (ii)   private shareholders, either individuals or small groups of investors.

An *institutional investor* is the general name given to those institutions, or firms, which make investments in stocks and other securities as principals but raise funds for investments from individuals and other firms. There are four main types of institutional investors.

(a)   *Pension funds* - These invest on behalf of the pension fund members in order to provide members with a retirement pension.

(b)   *Insurance companies* - These operate on behalf of holders of life and endowment policies.

(c)   *Investment trust companies* - These are limited liability companies, who invest in shares, property, etc, on behalf of their own shareholders.

(d)   *Unit trusts* - These are trusts, which invest on behalf of its unit holders.

Due to the increase in the shareholdings of institutional investors, it is no longer meaningful to think of shareholders as being uninformed, uninterested people. They have developed substantial professional expertise and are generally much more aware than the private shareholders, although there has been a growing trend for the private investor to use professional advisers.

The income requirements of each type of investor will differ according to circumstances, tax position, preferences, etc, but generally the institutions will require a stable dividend for pensions, lump sums, their own dividend requirements, etc. The private investor may also require a regular income but again this may alter due to tax positions or personal preferences. For example, an individual who pays a higher marginal income tax rate, may prefer investment for capital growth, and therefore choose low-yielding shares.

5.5   External stakeholders

The external stakeholders include:

- **Governments** - seeking finance through taxation and other means and political support for its legislated activities.

  When industry fails to respond to the pressure exerted by society, the public will turn to the government.   For example, after numerous deaths caused by fires in the homes, investigations revealed that the materials used in manufacturing armchairs and settees were contributing to the seriousness of the fires. Due to a lack of self-regulation by this industry the government had to legislate in respect of the materials that could be used in soft furniture.

  Recent governments have also promoted deregulation, which aims at removing those rules that serve only to restrict competition and do little to enhance the safety of customers. Deregulation increases competition between existing suppliers, and between them and new suppliers who can now enter the market, in order to reduce costs and stimulate the provision of new services for which there is a demand.

- **Pressure groups** - society at large desires an improvement in the 'quality of life' through:

  - the reduction of pollution;
  - the maintenance of an ecological balance by ceasing to rely on non-renewable resources;
  - the minimisation of poverty, assistance with local community projects and help with the young and elderly.

Environmental advocates are examples of a more general trend towards the use of the political process to further a position on some particular issue such as effluent control. Managers can never be sure that a pressure group will not form to oppose the company on any particular issue.

Not surprisingly, environmental regulations have imposed extra burdens on business. For example, the development of the catalytic converter as part of a car's exhaust system reduces engine performance and adds to the overall purchase price of a car. Managers, however, have no choice but to take into account today's current climate of broad and genuine concern for the environment.

5.6 Activity

Rank the stakeholder list given above, according to the criterion of 'depending on the continuing existence of the organisation'.

Draw up three examples each of:

(a) precise, quantified objectives; and

(b) non-precise, subjective objectives.

5.7 Activity solution

The stakeholder list should be ranked in the following order:

workers; managers; directors; investors; suppliers; customers; locality; government.

(a) Examples of precise, quantified objectives:

   (i) increase market share of 2-stroke oil market to 7% by end 20XX;
   (ii) achieve one order for every three sales demonstrations;
   (iii) reduce debtor balance from 34 to 32 days within three months.

(b) Examples of non-precise, subjective objectives:

   (i) to improve the image of the manufacturing unit in its immediate locality;
   (ii) to be recognised as market leader for quality;
   (iii) to improve the flow of information from sales depots to accounts department.

6 CONFLICT BETWEEN OBJECTIVES

6.1 Developing and changing objectives

Nowadays it is axiomatic that in order to survive and prosper, a company must be continually adapting and improving its products, services and technologies. A company ought to change its objectives if they do not reflect its current aspirations: even where they are sanctified in an apparently specific list, new ones should be developed and out of date ones dropped. Corporate objectives are not akin to commandments written on tablets of stone on Mount Sinai and handed down to succeeding generations for them to accept with unquestioning obedience. Humans devise them, and it is a fact that gives corporate objectives both their strength and weakness.

Individual companies have their own unique permutation of corporate objectives, but there are certain common strands and themes. The basic motivators include survival, customer satisfaction and shareholder's wealth.

6.2   Survival

Survival is an implicit, overriding objective in every organisation, although it rarely rates a mention in the Chairman's Annual Report. The first six months of the life of a company are usually the most crucial. However, survival through infancy is no guarantee of a subsequent happy life. Economic recessions and the activities of competitors will threaten an established company, and may cause it to re-examine its capacity for long-term survival.

6.3   Customer satisfaction

Drucker suggests that a company exists to 'create a customer', or, as others have put it, 'to satisfy a customer need'. The view is that unless companies achieve a satisfactory level of customer satisfaction they would soon close down.

Taken to its logical conclusion, customer satisfaction will increase as the quality of the product improves and its price falls. It could be argued, therefore, that customer satisfaction and profit are incompatible corporate objectives. The optimisation of one is a virtual guarantee of low performance by the other because they pull in different directions, eg *'Good Food Costs Less at Sainsburys'* and *'We are never knowingly undersold'* (John Lewis Partnership).

6.4   Pursuit of profit

Despite some disagreement among writers as to a company's main objective, a clear 'winner' emerges.

Although there have been suggestions that the main objective of a company is simply survival, we can surely agree with Argenti that this is inadequate. Survival is not an end in itself; most organisations would want to reach a certain minimum performance level better than just 'hanging on', and if this was not attainable the shareholders might not wish for the survival of the company. Shareholders are obviously a major group to be taken into account when setting objectives. If we ask *'why does the company want to survive?'* the answer must be to make a profit or to maximise the wealth of investors in the company, ie, the shareholders.

What about the objective of customer satisfaction? Again, why does the company wish for satisfied customers - unless to make a profit?

6.5   Factors that pull against profit maximisation

In a practical context, other factors are important because they pull against profit maximisation. These are:

(b)   **Separation of management and ownership** - In large companies there are a large number of shareholders each with a relatively small share of the company and the company is managed by directors who may not have a large shareholding. Provided that they can earn enough to satisfy the shareholders, such directors might be more interested in factors such as geographical market spread, prestigious buildings, the company's public image, and so on, rather than obtaining the maximum return. This ties in with Cyert and March's Behavioural Theory of the Firm. They assert that organisations do not have objectives, only people have objectives, and therefore the objectives that are pursued by an organisation represent a compromise between objectives of various groups within the organisation, shareholders and directors among them.

(b)   **Responsibilities and constraints** - companies have obligations to groups other than shareholders, employees, customers and the public at large. Although the economic objective may remain the primary one, because it is fundamental to the company's survival, the company may set itself other objectives. These could be concerned with improving the welfare of, (or its relations with) other groups; objectives which may well reduce the amount of profit which could otherwise have been earned. These are internal constraints.

There may also be external constraints, for instance in the form of legislation. In formal terms, constraints are decision rules that preclude certain courses of action.

Responsibilities are obligations which the company undertakes to discharge, but which use up a share of profit which has been made, rather than affecting the way in which that profit is obtained. An example would be a donation to a charitable trust. The words constraints and responsibilities are also interchangeable - it could be argued, for example, that constraints are in fact responsibilities. If an examination question is posed, which concerns social responsibilities, you should include a discussion of both internal and external constraints (including the *stakeholder theory*) within your answer.

It seems likely that there will be increasing pressure on firms to have regard to objectives other than profit, and so responsibilities and constraints will assume increasing importance. Indeed, some writers suggest that it is already inadequate to think of profit as being the main objective, or that even if it does retain the primary role, the objective will have to be expressed in more socially acceptable terms.

(c)   **Risk reduction** - seeking large profits inevitably involves taking risks. A firm may therefore decide that it will settle for a slightly lower but surer return. It may be influenced in its attitude to risk by the type of shareholders it has. There are many large institutionalised shareholders, such as pension funds that want some stability of return. If a risky project fails and their return falls, they may withdraw their support, which, because of the size of their shareholding could have a significant, even knock-on, effect on the share price.

(d)   **The flexibility objective** - because companies have only an incomplete knowledge of the future it is important that they retain flexibility, enabling them to react to any given situation. They should be in a position to benefit from any new breakthroughs and must insure against catastrophes. **Internal flexibility** is achieved by having sufficient liquid funds and reserve borrowing power in order to be able to react quickly in a new situation. It is measured by ratios such as the current ratio, acid test ratio, and debt to equity ratio (gearing). However, there is a conflict between high flexibility and return to the shareholders. The high flexibility requires liquidity and reserve borrowing power (low gearing), and high gearing, which implies making use of all available funds (not having surplus liquid funds), boosting the return to the shareholders. Circumstances will dictate which is the most important consideration. The flexibility 'cushion' obviously has a cost in ROI terms. Internal flexibility is also achieved by having an appropriate management structure, a culture that is conducive to change, plus marketing and R & D strengths.

(e)   **Technological competitiveness** - an organisation that is associated with one particular technology tends to have the life-cycle pattern of that technology. Such an organisation will progress through the sequence of birth, growth, maturity and decline (as will its products or services). However, an organisation can avoid stagnation and ultimate demise if it continually renews itself. If developing technologies are brought in to replace declining ones, the organisation can probably survive indefinitely. If the rate of introduction of new technology is the same as the rate of decline of old technology, then the company will not grow. An organisation does not necessarily have to grow to survive but it must renew itself or die.

(f)   **Conflict between long and short-term** - a company might be able to improve its profit in the long-run by sacrificing some profit in the short-term, for instance by spending money on product development. Conversely, if the company concentrated on short-term profitability it would be likely to find itself in an unhealthy position in the long-term.

For all the above reasons, a company should think of profit **optimisation**, ie, maximisation subject to constraints, rather than of profit **maximisation**. Putting together all the points, an acceptable statement of the primary objective of the private-sector company is:

'the achievement over a defined period of time of the maximum profitability consistent with keeping risk to an acceptable level and with any social responsibilities and constraints, internal or external, within which the company has to operate'

Profitability is used as the measure rather than profit. It can be measured by return on capital, or perhaps more appropriately return on shareholders funds, since it is more realistic and practical to think in terms of increasing the return on available resources, rather than of infinitely expandable resources.

7   STAKEHOLDERS AND OBJECTIVES

7.1   Stakeholder and political risk

The 'stakeholder' approach suggests that the objectives of an organisation should be derived by balancing the often conflicting claims of the various stakeholders (or coalitions) in the organisation. These stakeholders consist of coalitions of people within the organisation, and external groups. The organisation has responsibilities to all these groups, and it should formulate its strategic goals to give each a measure of satisfaction.   The difficulty is balancing the conflicting interests and differing degrees of power. For example, there might be conflicts of interest between a company's shareholders and its employees.   If the strategy of the organisation is to reflect the interests of its stakeholders, the strategic planner will need to consider, and be influenced by, factors relating to them.   These are:

- Composition and significance of each group.

- Power that each group can exert.

- Legitimate claims that each group may have on the organisation.

- Degree to which these claims conflict and significant areas of concern.

- Extent to which the organisation is satisfying claims.

- Overall mission of the organisation.

In practice, the assessment of the *political risk* inherent in various strategies can be an important deciding factor between strategies.   For example, a strategy of market development might require the cutting out of wholesalers, hence running the risk of backlash, which could jeopardise the success of the strategy.

Other political risk factors would include a substantial issue of new shares, which might be unacceptable to unions, government or other customers. The understanding of these softer measures of risk is invariably important during strategy evaluation.   It would be unwise to proceed with options that are likely to be undermined by the political activity of either consumers or other organised groups.

Management normally undertakes the responsibility of maintaining an equitable and working balance among the claims of the various directly interested groups, but usually the most powerful group of stakeholders, termed the *dominant coalition*, will determine the organisation's *prime* objectives.

Bowen proposed the idea of a *social audit,* to establish the needs and expectations of the various stakeholder groups that had been satisfied. Similar ideas were expressed by Humble with his *social responsibility audit* and since the publication of the 'Corporate Report', many company annual reports carry sections devoted to this idea.   However, in normal circumstances **all** stakeholders would support Peter Drucker's view that **survival** is the central purpose. Such an activity entails maintaining or increasing the net worth of the organisation.

7.2   Competing values

An organisation's ideology is determined partially by its goals and values, and the direction the organisation is taking. These influences govern relationships in the organisation, people's attitudes, the decisions that are made and the way the organisation reacts to its environment.

However, different departments, functions and support activities will have their objectives, views and opinions that may not be complementary. For example, the sales department may want the company to hold high levels of stock in order to provide a fast delivery time for customers. However, this will most probably add to the cost of operations, overtime may have to be worked or an extra shift put on. There is also the consideration of the cost of storage space. An assessment has to be made whether the added value of keeping stocks high is greater than the additional cost.

A key task of management is to identify where values are in conflict, and attempting to overcome this conflict. The aim is to develop and sustain common attitudes and values amongst all elements of the organisation in order that employees see the organisation's purpose in the same way. For example, engineers always want production machinery adequately maintained, while production operatives see this as an interruption to their work, which may mean targets are not met. The engineers would argue that if the machinery is not adequately maintained it will break down and stop production. By working together to identify common values and objectives, solutions to this problem can be found, whether it be maintenance programmes running at week-ends or during low production periods. Alternatives can be identified by discussion.

Misunderstandings and competing values can also exist between suppliers, buyers and the organisation. The classic example is that buyers always want both low cost and high quality, which may be in direct conflict as far as the manufacturer is concerned.

7.3   Conflicting objectives in a not-for-profit organisation

We know that in the last resort shareholders have the power over the private sector business organisation, but which group of stakeholders prevails if there are conflicting objectives in a not-for profit organisation, such as a comprehensive school? Is it the teachers, the parents, the local authority, the Department of Education or the pupils? The absence of a 'bottom line' like profits means that the management cannot act with clarity and certainty in making decisions.

Education must be its objective, with performance being measured in terms of pass rates at GCSE examinations. However, this straightforward interpretation of the purpose of the school may not suit some people associated with the school. They may see different aims as being important, for example, developing all the different talents of children. There can be a strong lobby for religious education, while others complain about political indoctrination. Most people would acknowledge the part the school plays in preparing children to take a useful role in society. This can extend to having a strong vocational orientation in the way that subjects are selected and taught. Others see this preparation for life to be more to do with developing the children's personality and social skills.

Good strategic managers in these circumstances tend to be able to combine acute political and interpersonal skills with a clear set of values, or a 'vision'. Armed with this clarity of purpose, they are able to set directions and make judgements between conflicting requirements.

8   SELF TEST QUESTIONS

8.1   Sketch the hierarchy of objectives. (1.2)

8.2   What is a mission statement? (1.3)

8.3   What is an organisational goal? (2.1)

8.4   Outline two characteristics of an organisational goal. (2.1)

8.5   For objectives to be useful, they must have three components. What are they? (3.1)

8.6   What are the differences between efficiency and effectiveness? (4.1)

8.7   What is a stakeholder? (5.4)

8.8   Describe two connected stakeholders. (5.4)

8.9   What are the three main corporate objectives? (6.1)

9   EXAMINATION TYPE QUESTION

9.1   Development of a mission statement

(a)   In recent years, many organisations have developed mission statements. It has become increasingly common for such statements to be published within the organisation and also externally.

You are required to contrast the viewpoints that a mission statement is either an embodiment of the prevailing organisational culture or an attempt to change it. Explain other motives for publishing these statements.   **(14 marks)**

(b)   In discussing not-for-profit organisations, Bowman and Asch state ' ... even if the goals are clear but achievement of them is not measurable, then assessing the performance of the organisation becomes extremely difficult'.

Strategic Management, Bowman & Asch
(MacMillan)

You are required to explain how the performance of a not-for-profit organisation could be assessed.   **(11 marks)**
(Total: 25 marks)
(CIMA Nov 93)

10   ANSWER TO EXAMINATION TYPE QUESTION

10.1   Development of a mission statement

(a)   Most writers on the subject of strategic planning agree with the idea that there is a hierarchy of objectives, just as there is a hierarchy of managers. At each higher level in the hierarchy, the objectives are more relevant to a greater proportion of the organisation's activities so that the objectives at the top of the hierarchy are relevant to every aspect of the organisation. The hierarchy forms a relationship between mission, goals, objectives, strategy, tactics and operational plans. The topmost statement of organisational objectives is usually termed 'the mission'. A 'mission statement' is therefore a statement in writing that describes the basic purpose of an organisation, that is, what it is trying to accomplish.

A mission statement can be viewed as a statement primarily directed towards the employees of an organisation, which should assist in the attainment of the objectives of the organisation. In short, a 'mission statement' will have some or all of the following characteristics:

(i)   It is usually a brief statement of no more than a page in length. (Some companies have produced very effective mission statements comprising of a single sentence, although there are also successful company credos that extend into several pages.)

(ii)   It is a very general statement of entity culture.

(iii)   It states the aims (or purposes) of the organisation.

(iv)   It states the business areas in which the organisation intends to operate.

(v)   It is open-ended (not stated in quantifiable terms), and is not time-assigned.

(vi)   It forms a basis of communication to the people inside the organisation and to people outside the organisation.

(vii)   It is used to formulate goal statements, objectives and short-term targets.

(viii)   It therefore guides the direction of the entity's strategy and as such is part of management information.

A statement of corporate mission is inextricably linked with that organisation's goals and objectives, although it is important to draw a distinction between these three aspects of the strategic planning process. Whilst the organisational objectives comprise the specific targets of the company and the goals comprise its broad aims, the mission encapsulates the reason why the entity exists, in terms of the service and utility provided to meet specific needs of society. Johnson and Scholes suggested that 'the mission of an organisation is the most generalised type of objective and can be thought of as an expression of its *raison d'être*'. On the other hand, some commentators believe that the mission statement is the end product of the process of strategic planning, and this illustrates the confusion, which often exists between the organisation's mission and its goals and objectives.

A statement of corporate mission will provide all managers involved in the decision making process within the organisation with a clear indication as to what constitutes the *raison d'être* of the organisation. The existence of a 'mission statement' should assist those responsible for the formulation of strategic plans, since it will focus upon critical issues. This will help to ensure that strategic plans are prepared in accordance with desired norms within the organisation.

Mission statements can provide motivation to the employees of the organisation in the sense that they tell people what is important from the standpoint of executive management. A 'mission statement' will clearly specify the business domain in which the company is to operate thereby facilitating planning activities. Decision making processes within an organisation should be improved as a result of the clarification of the overall direction of the company which is contained within a corporate mission statement. A 'mission statement' will also aid staff, both existing and newly appointed, in their appreciation of the company's philosophies as well as providing a clear indication as to the expectations and attitudes which exist within the company.

A mission's goals do not have to be 'internal'. Some of the most effective are directed outside the company, on customers, or competitors. Mission statements like these will prompt people to think *first* about the customer, and will provide a gauge against which employees can judge their efforts to satisfy customers. It will equip employees with a strong inner compass for navigating their actions. It will stamp the culture of the organisation. Mission statements are like visions or dreams. We should not forget that in a memorable speech, Dr. Martin Luther King, Jr., said, *'I have a dream'* - he did not say 'I have a strategic plan.'

All these points support the view that the 'mission statement' is an embodiment of the prevailing organisational culture.

Although an entity's mission is usually clear in the beginning, it may become less so over time as its environment changes. When defining the current mission of the entity it would be necessary to de-emphasise certain things and assumptions and emphasise others. According to Peter Drucker, the organisation will need to address a number of fundamental questions in its search for purpose. These are:

(i)   What is our business?
(ii)   What is value to the customer?
(iii)   What will our business be?
(iv)   What should our business be?

Although seemingly simple, these questions are among the most difficult the strategist will need to solve. Successful planners will raise these questions and seek to answer them correctly and thoroughly. The mission of an organisation is generally influenced by five key elements:

(i)   The history of the organisation.
(ii)   The current preferences of the organisation's management and owners.
(iii)   The environmental factors influencing the organisation.
(iv)   The organisation's resources.
(v)   The organisation's distinctive competence.

Environmental change and its affect on society and its values, needs and expectations, inevitably place a pressure on management to review and if necessary adapt or change the entity's culture. Because it is the responsibility of the top-level management to prepare the statement of entity mission, it should incorporate the broad aims of executive management. The mission might well be changed to reflect the different views of incoming chairmen, should there be a change. In these ways, the 'mission statement' becomes the basis by which the prevailing organisational culture can be changed. Also, the 'mission statement' is often influenced by 'bottom-up' pressure in situations where the prevailing culture is unacceptable to lower level managers.

(b)   Whereas the objectives and thus outputs of a profit-making entity are quantifiable in monetary terms in relation to monetary inputs, thus providing a ready measure of performance, ie, profit, the same is not true of not-for-profit organisations. Although the inputs to this type of organisation are usually measurable in monetary terms, its outputs are not. Indeed, it may be difficult or impracticable to quantify in any meaningful way the outputs of the entity, let alone measure the qualitative aspects of the service provided. This point is emphasised by Bowman and Asch.

In establishing measures of a non-profit-making organisation's performance, a distinction needs to be drawn between those that measure effectiveness and those that measure efficiency and economy. Effectiveness measures the outputs of an activity against its desired results and thus assesses its ability to accomplish the goals it has set or been set. Effectiveness measurement is not necessarily a straightforward procedure; some goals may not be apparent. For example, effectiveness may, involve the fulfilment of political goals for an organisation operating in the public sector domain. Economy and efficiency are the measures of the costs of inputs and the uses made of these concerning the level of outputs achieved.

What will be important is to establish the desired balance between effectiveness and efficiency, ie, between the service level provided and the norm efficiency levels actually required. The pressures for effectiveness and efficiency may pull in different directions. For example, a police force may be effective at responding to emergencies and reducing road accidents by employing large numbers of police staff, even if from time to time they are under-employed. A *'Rolls Royce'* service may be effective, but surely unlikely to be efficient. For that, the force may need to reduce staff to a *'sensible'* minimum, so that all are fully stretched and occupied, though at the expense of some effectiveness, in terms of service provided to the public.

It is generally recognised that the effectiveness and efficiency of a non-profit-making organisation should be compared, where possible, to predetermined standards or performances. These should be compared over time between geographical areas and with similar non-profit-making (or even similar profit making) activities. Predetermined standards are only possible when outputs can be separately identified, and measured. There are instances when effectiveness and efficiency measures are either impracticable or not possible. With these points in mind, establishing appropriate measures for assessing the effectiveness and efficiency of the non-profit-making organisation is going to be difficult, but nonetheless might be accomplished by using both quantitative and qualitative measures.

3 THE DETERMINANTS AND COMPONENTS OF STRATEGY

INTRODUCTION & LEARNING OUTCOMES

Syllabus area 11(i)
- The determinants and components of strategy.

- The process of strategy formulation (i.e. the steps required and the order in which those steps might be undertaken).

- The various approaches that might be adopted to determine an appropriate strategy for the organisation (i.e. rational, adaptive and interpretative approaches).

The formulation of strategy is a complex process, and in the nature of things it is undertaken by senior management. Most students have no practical experience to guide them, and this can make it hard to appreciate either the value of the exercise or the methods by which it is carried out. In this chapter, we try to overcome these initial difficulties by tackling the subject in the following order.

- What is strategy? Or rather, what alternative views of strategy can reasonably be advocated?

- What are the main approaches to formulating a strategy? How in practice are strategic options arrived at and evaluated?

- What are the various approaches that might be adopted to determine an appropriate strategy for the organisation?

When you have studied this chapter you should be able to:

- Explain the concept of strategy and its possible effect on the structure and management of business organisations.

1 WHAT IS STRATEGY?

1.1 Introduction

There is no one specific definition of a strategy and writers have discussed the lack of consensus over what a strategy actually is. However, it is generally agreed that a strategy is some sort of future plan of action.

> **Definition** Strategy: a course of action, including the specification of resources required, to achieve a specific objective.

This definition, although stated in a single sentence, provides a framework that can be expanded, shaped, applied and developed further. Because of the rapid technological and social changes affecting an organisation's environment, there is a need for strategies to achieve agreed goals and objectives, giving a sense of purpose and direction to the organisation.

In military terms, 'strategy' refers to the important plan. Where the objective is to defeat the enemy, the strategy will be to deploy the resources available in a manner that is likely to achieve the aim.

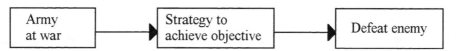

Army at war → Strategy to achieve objective → Defeat enemy

1.2   A wider view

We view strategy as the organised development of resources to achieve specific objectives against competition from rival organisations.   It is the use of all the entity's resources, financial, manufacturing, marketing, technological, manpower etc, in the pursuit of its objectives.

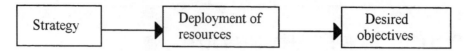

It is a set of policies adopted by senior management, which guides the scope and direction of the entity. It takes into account the environment in which the company operates.

1.3   Adaptation to its environment - Hofer and Schendel

> **Definition**   A strategy is the mediating force or 'match' between the organisation and the environment. (Hofer and Schendel)

Harrison also supports the proposition that strategy is the achieving of the match between the organisation and its environment. It is viewing the internal capabilities of the organisation and, in the light of these, identifying the opportunities or threats that exist externally.

By using the organisation as a strategy for the fulfilment of needs, it must continue to grow and devolve thereby creating more wealth from its environment. The organisation will only be efficient, however, if it controls its wealth and its interaction with the environment providing that wealth.

1.4   Strategy as part of the planning framework

Planning activity will seek to direct the efforts of all towards the common goals of the organisation. A sequence of developing plans that move from general to specific and intent to action would create several levels of planning, which could be illustrated in the triangle below.

Mission - Every organisation will have a purpose for its continued existence. A mission statement expresses their purpose and can therefore be a brief statement eg, Du Pont Company's mission is expressed as 'better things through chemistry'.

Objectives - do not only represent the end point of planning but are the ends towards which management activities and resource usage is directed. They therefore provide a sense of direction and a measure of success achievement.

Strategies - relate to broad areas of an enterprise's operations. Their purpose is to furnish a framework for more detailed tactical planning and action.

Tactics - are actions carried out to put into effect the details of a strategic decision – tactics can therefore be seen as the detailed implementation of a strategy. In addition, some tactical decisions will be made in response to changing circumstances.

Actions, programmes and rules - are the operational practices that will translate the intention of the tactics into action by individuals and are therefore detailed, short term and subject to immediate control.

1.5   Classification of strategies

All organisations should carry out some form of corporate strategy activity. The need for involvement increases with the complexity of the organisation and the uncertainty and turbulence of its environment.

Johnson and Scholes classify strategies into three levels:

(i)   *Corporate strategy* - what business or businesses the firm is in or should be in and how integrated these businesses should be with one another. It relates to the future formula and structure of the company, and affects the rationale of the company and the business in which it intends to compete. For example Racal Electronics' decision to float off Vodaphone as a separate company or TSB's decision to sell Swan national car rentals and concentrate on retail banking and insurance.

(ii)   *Competitive or business strategy* - how each business attempts to achieve its mission within its chosen area of activity. It identifies how individual business units will compete in a particular market or new product launches, eg. Ford's launch of Mondeo model, aimed at fleet car buyers who had not favoured the Sierra, its predecessor and Next Clothing adding mail order to their existing retail business.

Here strategy is about which products or services should be developed and offered to which markets and the extent to which the customer needs are met whilst achieving the objectives of the organisation. It includes corporate planning at the tactical level and consists of the allocation of resources for complete operations. It is means-oriented and is mainly administrative and persuasive in its endeavours.

A term that is often used in relation to business strategy is SBU, or strategic business unit. SBU means a unit within the overall corporate entity for which there is an external market for its goods and services, which is distinct from that of another SBU.

(iii)   *Operational or functional strategies* - how the different functions of the business support the corporate and business strategies. They are concerned with how the various functions of the organisation contribute to the achievement of strategy eg, revising delivery schedules and drivers' hours to improve customer service or recruiting a German-speaking sales person to assist a UK company's sales drive in Europe.

Functional strategy examines how the different functions of the business (marketing, production, finance etc) support the corporate and business strategies. Such corporate planning at the operational level is means oriented and most activities are concerned only with the ability to undertake directions.

However, despite the points evaluated above, the boundaries between the three categories are very indistinct and much depends upon the circumstances prevailing and the kind of organisation. Overall, corporate planning is concerned with the scope of an organisation's activities and the matching of these to the organisation's environment, its resource capabilities and the values and expectations of its various stakeholders.

A number of students complain that the formulation of corporate strategy is too far removed from their likely level of activity, but an understanding is essential for all management in that:

(a)   Through the means-end chain, lower-level objectives are inexorably linked to higher-level strategies. An appreciation of these strategies and how they are formulated can be an effective guide to action.

(b)   The principles of corporate strategy are equally appropriate for the smaller organisation.

(c)   Whatever the level on which a manager operates within an organisation, he or she can have some influence over that organisation's corporate strategy.

2   APPROACHES TO FORMULATING A STRATEGY

2.1   Introduction

Strategy formulation is a continuous process of refinement based on past trends, current conditions and estimates of the future. A visible strategy helps the organisation to focus its efforts, to facilitate commitment on the part of the participants.

Strategies are not static: they evolve over time. However, how they evolve can differ. Certain organisations' strategies tend to merge due to their relationship with their environment. For example, managers working in a fast changing, dynamic environment may not have had time to think about how the organisation's strategies have developed, all they know is that they have reacted to the environmental demands placed on the company. For example, PC based IT industry is research led. The development of new technology eg, the mouse, resulted in strategic developments and company strategies evolving into a new direction.

2.2   Strategic planning process

Top managers get paid for making tough decisions, and although nobody can predict the long-term future with any accuracy, strategic planning forces managers to think critically and analytically about the future. The planning process by which an organisation can move from mission to strategies and actions can be expressed in the diagram below.

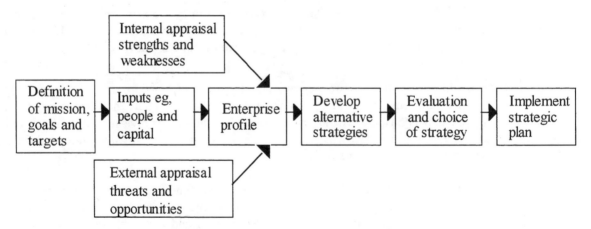

This diagram represents an approach where objectives are defined ahead of, and independent of, the strategies to be pursued. There is a logical sequence of activities. However, it is important to stress that the model is only a device for thinking through complex strategic problems. It is not an attempt to describe how the process actually takes place in the political and cultural arenas of an organisation.

Although the steps taken in the formulation of strategy vary, the process can be identified by the key elements shown in the diagram above. We have already discussed the mission, goals and targets, and also the inputs. In the following sections, we will briefly cover the other steps.

2.3   The enterprise profile

The enterprise profile is usually the starting point where the organisation determines where it is and where it should go. This analysis would cover the following areas:

- The external environmental variables as well as the competitive factors to analyse how they will affect the organisation and its activities.

- The external environmental variables - the resource availability and its relative strengths and weaknesses.

- The aspirations and expectations of the groups that have an interest in the organisation ie, the stakeholders.

- The beliefs and assumptions that make up the culture of the organisation because they are the means of interpreting the environment and resource influences.

Top managers set the organisational climate, clarify the basic purpose of the organisation and determine the direction to go eg, whether it should operate in selected regions or even in different countries. In addition, managers assess the competitive situation of their organisation. Because of their orientation, and the subsequent impact on the strategy, manager's values, preferences and attitude towards risks, have to be carefully examined.

2.4   The external environment

The external environment, both present and future, must be appraised in terms of threats and opportunities. The appraisal focuses on economic, social, political, legal, demographic and geographic factors. In addition, the environment is scanned for technological developments, for products and services available in the market, and for other factors necessary in determining the competitive situation of the enterprise.

Because there is uncertainty associated with any future event, forecasting becomes increasingly hazardous and more subjective as the time element is extended. However, it still remains an essential ingredient in the planning process. Forecasting is an attempt to make the future environment less uncertain. Conscious effort towards anticipating the social, economic, technological and political climate helps the manager avoid pitfalls that might be disastrous.

2.5   The internal environment

The organisation's internal environment ie, its present and future resources, should be scanned, and strengths and weaknesses in production, operations, purchasing, marketing, products, services and research and development identified.

The internal organisation involving a company's structure, systems, people, and culture can be an important source of both strengths and weaknesses. The flexible, entrepreneurial organisational structure of organisations such as 3M, where new project teams and divisions are continually created, is a key to its growth. The systems at fast food outlets, such as McDonalds, are important strengths.

Internal organisation can affect the cost and even the feasibility of some strategies. There must be a 'fit' between a strategy and the elements of an organisation. If the strategy does not fit well, it might be expensive, or even impossible, to make it work. For example, an established centralised organisation with a background oriented to one industry may have difficulty implementing a diversification strategy requiring a decentralised organisation and an entrepreneurial thrust.

2.6   Develop alternative strategies

After analysing the internal and external environment, strategic alternatives are developed. An organisation may pursue many different types of strategy. For example, it may:

- Specialise or concentrate - on a niche in the market eg, Hyundai specialise in lower-priced cars rather than having a complete product range.

- Diversify - extending the operation into new and profitable markets.

- Go international - expand the operations into another country or countries.

- Grow by acquisition.

- Form a joint venture - to pool resources.

- Liquidate - by terminating an unprofitable product line or even dissolving the company.

- Retrench - by curtailing operations temporarily.

These are just a few examples of possible strategies. In reality, organisations pursue a combination of strategies.

2.7   Strategic evaluation and choice

There are two parts to this element. Firstly, managers evaluate the options to assess their relative merits and feasibility. Drucker, in his book *Managing for Results,* discusses business strategies and states that whatever a company's programme, it must decide:

- what opportunities it wants to pursue and what risks it is willing and able to accept;

- its scope and structure, and especially the right balance between specialisation, diversification and integration;

- between time and money, between building its own or buying, ie using sale of a business, merger, acquisition and joint venture to attain its goals;

- on an organisation structure appropriate to its economic realities, its opportunities and its programme for performance.

There are three kinds of opportunities:

(i)   **Additive** - exploitation of existing resources.
(ii)   **Complementary** - involving structural changes in the company.
(iii)   **Breakthrough** - changing the fundamental economic characteristics of the business.

Risks can be placed in four categories:

(a)   those that must be accepted;
(b)   those that can be afforded;
(c)   those that cannot be afforded; and
(d)   those the company cannot afford to miss.

The right opportunities will not be selected unless the company attempts to maximise opportunities rather than to minimise risk. Quantitative techniques can be used to evaluate the likely outcomes of different decisions but the selection is often subjective and likely to be influenced by the values of managers and other groups with an interest in the organisation.

The second part is the selection of the strategy or option that the organisation will pursue. Strategic choices have to be made in the light of the risks involved in a particular decision. Some organisations may not pursue profitable opportunities because a failure in a risky venture could result in bankruptcy. Another critical element in choosing the strategy is timing. Even the best product, introduced to the market at an inappropriate time, may fail. Competitors reactions must also be considered; when IBM reduced the prices of its PCs, companies producing IBM compatible computers had little choice but to reduce their prices as well. There could be more than one strategy chosen but there is a chance of an inherent danger or disadvantage to any choice made.

2.8   Strategy implementation

The implementation process can also be thought of as having several parts.

(i)   Resource planning and the logistics of implementation. The process will address the problems of the tasks that need to be carried out and also the timing of them. There may need to be changes in the mix of resources required to implement the strategy and decisions will need to be taken about who is to be responsible for the changes.

(ii)   The organisational structure may need to be changed, eg, from hierarchical to matrix or from centralised to decentralised.

(iii)   The systems employed to manage the organisation may be improved. These systems provide the information and operational procedures needed in the organisation. It may be that a new information management system is required to monitor the progress of the strategy. Staff may need to be retrained or new staff recruited.

2.9   Contingency view

An alternative approach reflects systems concepts and a contingency view because it recognises that there is an inter-relationship between four major components.

(i)   **Environmental opportunity** (what the organisation might do).

(ii)   **Abilities and resources** (what the organisation realistically can do) - an organisation might not be able to capitalise on a particular opportunity eg, market demand, if it does not have the necessary competencies or resources.

(iii)   **Responsibility to society** - what the organisation should do.

(iv)   **Managerial interests and desires** (what the organisation wants to do). An organisation is unlikely to succeed if its strategic plan is based on managerial interests without reference to opportunity, competence or societal responsibilities.

Integrating these four components of strategy formulation is a delicate and complex task. Being aware of them is an important first step; reconciling their implications and combining them into a viable strategy is more difficult. An organisation may not be able to capitalise on an environmental opportunity, such as market demand, if it does not have the necessary competence or resources. Similarly, an organisation is unlikely to succeed if its strategic plan is based on managerial interests, without reference to competence, opportunity or societal obligations.

3   VARIOUS APPROACHES TO DETERMINING A STRATEGY

3.1   Crafting

Mintzberg likens strategy development to a potter crafting clay.

'The crafting image captures the process by which effective strategies come to be. The planning image, long popular in the literature, distorts those processes and thereby misguides organisations that embrace it unreservedly.'

It must be realised at the outset that there is no one best way of managing the strategy of an organisation. A flexible, reactive style may suit a small firm in a rapidly changing environment, whereas a large company may need to take a long term view and plan accordingly.

Strategies may come about in different ways and Mintzberg has recognised that there are different modes of strategy formulation, which are described below. His views on planned strategies dovetail with what we have already described as the rational model, but his other two modes of strategy formulation lead on to a wider discussion.

3.2   Entrepreneurial model

Strategies may come about in **opportunistic** or **entrepreneurial** ways. An organisation may take advantage of changes in the environment or recognise new skills in an opportunistic manner. Alternatively, a firm may be set up by an entrepreneur because of an opportunity in the market place.

In the **entrepreneurial mode**, strategy-making is dominated by the active search for new opportunities, and is characterised by dramatic leaps forward in the face of uncertainty. Strategy is developed by significant bold decisions being made. Growth is the dominant goal of the organisations, and in uncertain conditions, this type of mode can result in the organisation making significant gains.

The organisation operating in this mode suggests by its actions that the environment is not flexible, it is a force to be confronted and controlled. Power is centralised in the chief executive, with an unwillingness to 'submit' to authority.

3.3   Adaptive mode

It is called the adaptive mode because it fits the description that managers give of how strategies come about in their organisations. They see their role as strategists as being involved in a continual proactive pursuit of a strategic goal, countering competitive moves and adapting to their environment whilst not rocking the boat too much.

This mode is commonly found in the public sector, non-profit making organisations and in organisations that face relatively stable environments. Strategies are developed as a result of the interaction and bargaining among various power/interest groups. As there is no one source of power or influence, strategies are not always automatically clear.

Four major characteristics distinguish the adaptive mode of strategy-making:

(i)   Clear goals do not exist in the adaptive organisation; strategy-making reflects a division of power among members of a complex coalition. The adaptive organisation is caught in a web of political forces - unions, managers, owners, lobby groups, government agencies, and so on.

There is no one central source of power, no one simple goal. The organisation cannot make decisions to 'maximise' any one goal such as profit or growth; rather it must seek solutions to its problems that satisfy the constraints.

(ii)   In this mode, the strategy-making process is characterised by the 'reactive' solution; its the existing problems rather than the 'proactive' search for new opportunities. Adaptive organisations seek conditions of certainty wherever possible, otherwise it seeks to reduce existing uncertainties by, for example, negotiating long-term purchasing arrangements to stabilise sources of supply etc.

(iii)   In this mode, organisations make decisions in incremental, serial steps. Because its environment is complex, the adaptive organisation finds that feedback is a crucial ingredient in strategy-making. Strategy-making focuses on what is familiar, considering the convenient alternatives and the ones that differ only slightly from the status quo.

(v)   Disjointed decisions are characteristic of the adaptive organisation. The demands on the organisation are diverse, and cannot be reconciled easily, therefore decisions are made in a piece-meal manner.

3.4   Planning mode - the rational approach

The implication of the planned approach to strategy formulation - sometimes referred to as the Rational model - is that the organisation takes a systematic and structured approach to its development. Internal and external information is collected, and decisions are integrated into a comprehensive strategy. Managers ascertain, review and evaluate every option available, and they are then able to choose what appears to be the best option in the light of rational criteria.

Planned or **deliberate** strategies come about where there are precise intentions, which are written down and imposed by a central leadership. There are a large number of controls to ensure surprise-free implementation in an environment, which is controllable.

There are three essential features of the planning mode:

(i)   The analyst plays a major role in strategy-making.

(ii)   This mode focuses on systematic analysis, particularly in the assessment of the costs and benefits of competing proposals. Formal planning involves both the active search for new opportunities and the solution of existing problems.

(iii)   This mode integrates decisions and strategies. For example, planning can ensure that the decision to acquire a new company complements (or at least does not conflict with) the decision to expand the product line of an existing division.

In recent times, more and more organisations have used the planning mode to create strategy. The reason for this popularity is that the environments that organisations have to deal with are becoming increasingly complex. Technological, economic and social change is occurring faster than ever before. Strategic planning is seen as a way of preparing for these changes and providing direction for the organisation. It also allows the organisation to co-ordinate its activities internally. However, the assumption that everything an organisation does reflects a carefully planned strategy would clearly be false. Later in this chapter, we look at alternatives to this assumption - the ideas that strategies in some cases just 'emerge' or reflect managers 'muddling through'.

3.5   Imposed strategy

Finally, a strategy may be imposed on the organisation. Government policies may have an impact on the strategy; this has been the case for those public utilities recently privatised. Recession and threat of a takeover may force a strategy of cost cutting and retrenchment. Technological developments may cause an organisation to develop new products to replace the ones that have become obsolete.

3.6   Choice of mode

The conditions that drive an organisation to favour one mode of strategy-making over the others are outlined below.

•   **Entrepreneurial mode** - requires the strategy-making authority to rest with one powerful individual. The environment must be flexible, and the organisation oriented toward growth. These conditions are most typical of organisations that are small and/or young.

•   **Adaptive mode** - suggests the organisation faces a complex, rapidly-changing environment and a divided interest group. Unusually, large established organisations who have invested significant resources in controlling the diverse interest groups fall into this mode. For example, hospitals and amenities.

- **Planning mode** - organisations must be large enough to afford the costs of formal analysis, must have goals that are operational, and must face an environment that is reasonably predictable and stable.

4   EMERGENT STRATEGY AND 'MUDDLING THROUGH'

4.1   Emergent strategies

Even in an environment where a planned approach is pursued, eventual outcomes may not always match what was intended. What can go wrong with a planned approach to strategy formulation?

- The obvious possibility is that an intended strategy is not implemented, perhaps because its underlying assumptions turn out to be invalid or because the pace of developments overtakes it.

- A more subtle point is that defined patterns of behaviour will already exist in an organisation, and superimposing a new strategy is not a straightforward task. Existing patterns of behaviour may themselves help to shape a planned strategy; alternatively, if the planned strategy runs counter to existing patterns of behaviour, this may lead to unintended modifications. The effect described here is that of **emergent strategies** - elements of strategy not laid down in a formal planning process but arising from existing patterns of behaviour.

A simple example of an emergent strategy would be one that arises from an external stimulus not envisaged in the planned strategy. This could happen if a supplier, pursuing modern ideas on supplier/customer relationships, encouraged a partnership approach to sourcing. It is easy to imagine that buyers in the customer organisation might see benefits in this, and could pursue the idea to the point where sourcing strategy took on an aspect, not at all contemplated when planned strategic developments were laid down.

Mintzberg also states that strategies can emerge rather than be due to a deliberate planning process.

'One idea leads to another, until a new pattern forms. Action has driven thinking and a new strategy, has emerged... Out in the field, a salesman visits a customer. The product isn't right, and together they work out some modifications. The salesman returns to the company and puts the changes through; after two or three more rounds, they finally get it right. A new product emerges, which eventually opens up a new market. The company has changed strategic course'

The figure below shows that the actual outcome, the organisation's realised strategy, can come about through a planned, deliberate formulation and implementation. The realised strategy can also come about from a pattern in a stream of decisions (emergent strategy).

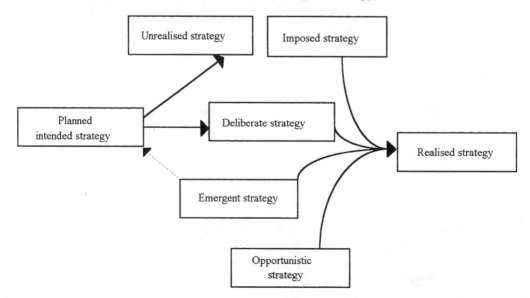

4.2   'Muddling through'

Some researchers have been sceptical about the very idea of the rational model in strategy formulation. Charles Lindblom, in particular, has argued that this model simply does not reflect reality. His criticisms of the rational model can be summarised as follows.

*   It is unrealistic to distinguish between goals and the possible strategies to achieve them. In practice, managers confuse the two.

*   It is unrealistic to imagine a strategic planner carefully sifting through every possible option to achieve predetermined goals. In practice, the range of options that will even present themselves as possibilities will be limited, and of those many will be filtered out without full evaluation.

*   At best, formulation of strategy is a process of evaluating a few slight extensions to existing policies.

Because of the complexity of organisations and the environments in which they operate, it would be difficult for managers to consider all the strategic options and measure them against pre-set, unambiguous objectives.

Lindblom therefore argued that strategic choice takes place by comparing possible options against each other and considering which would give the best outcome. Lindblom called this strategy building through 'successive limited comparisons'.

The aim of this approach is to identify the organisation's current strategy and estimate the threats and opportunities that exist in the environment. Also, the organisation's own strengths and weaknesses are identified together with the key decision makers' values and aspirations. By analysing this information, decisions can be made as to whether the current strategy is appropriate and if not how it needs to be changed. Once the strategy has been agree, the necessary plans can be developed to allow the strategy to be implemented. This process is shown below.

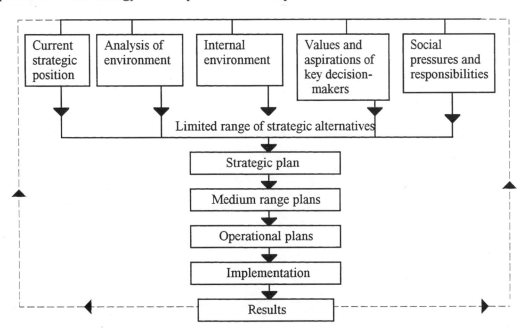

The incremental planning approach

This approach does not try to identify and review all the potential strategies available to the organisation. Rather it provides a way of monitoring the progress and the direction the organisation is moving in, and allows a change in 'course' if required.

Lindblom's conclusions, because of this analysis, are somewhat surprising. He does not argue that this scenario is regrettable and should be improved; on the contrary, he believes that the avoidance of major departures from current strategy is a safeguard against serious mistakes.

Critics of this view point to the difficulties it presents in an environment of turbulence and rapid change, where minor adjustments to current policies will not allow organisations to adapt sufficiently. The same could be said in circumstances where organisations face threats to their survival; moving the deck chairs on the Titanic is not good enough.

4.3   Logical incrementalism

On the spectrum bounded at one end by the rational model and at the other by Lindblom's ideas, the concept of logical incrementalism occupies a middle position. This view has been championed in particular by James Quinn, who argues that:

- Logical incrementalism incorporates both the behavioural realism of 'muddling through' and the advantages of a planned, analytical approach.

- Managers act from a broad awareness of the strategic direction they wish to pursue, without having detailed foreknowledge of the consequences of complex decisions.

- Strategy is determined both by this broad awareness of general direction, and by the need to test changes of strategic direction by means of small steps.

The outcome of this approach is a deliberate policy of small strategic changes within the framework provided by a general sense of strategic direction.

Managers have a view of where they want the organisation to be in the years to come, but they try to move towards that objective in an evolutionary way. They do this by attempting to develop a strong, secure but flexible core business whilst also continually experimenting with 'side issues'. Quinn argues that the decisions taken by management as part of this process should not be reviewed in isolation.

While managers are continually learning from each other, this results in continual testing and gradual strategy implementation, which provide improved quality of information to help decision-making. Because of this continual readjustment, the organisation should be in line with the environmental demands being placed on it.

Quinn's studies recognised that such experiments could not be the sole responsibility of the top managers but they should be encouraged to come from the lower levels of the organisation.

5   SELF TEST QUESTIONS

7.1   What is strategy? (1.1)

7.2   Define three modes of formulating strategy. (2.1)

7.3   What does Drucker's analysis contribute to the understanding of strategic decisions? (2.4)

7.4   What according to Johnson and Scholes are the characteristics of strategic decisions? (2.5)

7.5   Describe three different levels of strategy. (3.3)

7.6   What justifications are there for developing strategic plans? (4.3)

6   EXAMINATION TYPE QUESTION

6.1   Strategic planning versus freewheeling opportunism

McNamee states that 'strategic management .... is considered to be that type of management through which an organisation tries to obtain a good fit with its environment'.

Management Accounting - Strategic Planning and Marketing, McNamee
(CIMA/Butterworth Heinemann)

This approach has been characterised as 'proactive'.

There are many successful organisations that do not undertake strategic planning. This approach has been characterised as 'reactive' or sometimes 'freewheeling opportunism'.

You are required

(a)   to explain, with the help of a diagram, the activities included in the process of preparing a strategic plan;   **(9 marks)**

(b)   to explain the essential characteristics of the two approaches (strategic planning and freewheeling opportunism) mentioned above. What are the advantages and disadvantages of the two approaches?   **(10 marks)**

(c)   to explain in what circumstances you would recommend an organisation to adopt

    (i)   strategic planning,
    (ii)   freewheeling opportunism

(6 marks)
(Total: 25 marks)
(CIMA Nov 93)

7   ANSWER TO EXAMINATION TYPE QUESTION

7.1   Strategic planning versus freewheeling opportunism

(a)   With the understanding that they have limitations for individual companies and situations, the elements briefly outlined below and illustrated in the following diagram typify what is involved in the planning and implementation of strategy.

- A study of the *environment* within which the organisation operates - if the strategic planner does not understand the environment in which the organisation is operating, any plans implemented may have little chance of success.

- Agreeing objectives - setting long-, medium- and short-term *objectives* and *targets*, which will be based on the needs and aspirations of the planning entity. A rational strategic plan involves the building of a path towards explicit goals.

- Analysis of the *current position* - this appraisal exercise involves looking at the current products and markets of the company, its resources, organisation structure, systems and results.

- Carrying out the *corporate appraisal* - the appraisal uses the data provided by the other studies to conduct a critical assessment of the strengths and weaknesses, opportunities and threats (*SWOT analysis*) in relation to the internal and environmental factors affecting the entity in order to establish its condition prior to the preparation of the long-term plan.

- Planning *fundamental strategies* - the corporate appraisal provides a base upon which new strategies are developed. There is considerable distinction between the five strategic models involved.

- Planning *internal* strategies - organisations often find that performance is improved by the strengthening of internal efficiencies.

- Planning external *product-market* strategies - growth in performance can often be achieved by altering the product-market scope of the organisation. This aim can be achieved by different means, although the two main directions are expansion and product-market diversification.

- Planning *resources* required for the strategy - strategists have the task of allocating limited resources among the competing needs. An important aspect of planning strategy is to establish which resources are required and then to assess their availability, taking into account the potential contributions that each give to the plan.

- The *evaluation* of strategic proposals - the merit of each strategic option or proposal needs to be examined in the context of the corporate appraisal and the resources it requires. There is a need not only to consider the *acceptability* of the plan in terms of stated objectives, but also to ensure that the plan is *feasible* to implement, and *suitable* in terms of the *SWOTs* that stimulated its formulation.

- Deciding on the appropriate *strategic plan* - a number of *individual strategies* will be brought together to form the strategic plan.

- The *implementation* of plans the strategic plan has to be implemented within an *organisation structure*. Some consideration thus needs to be given to the decision making processes, organisational structures and management information systems.

- The *control* of the plan - the successful implementation of the strategic plan will require *information* to effect control over both short and long term aspects.

The diagram shown below illustrates the basic framework.

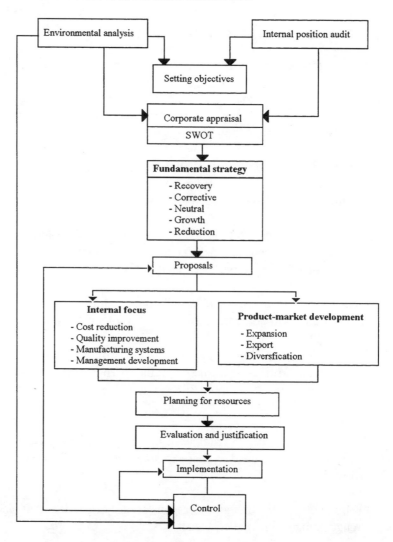

(b)   Strategic planning is the pattern of decisions in an entity that determines and reveals its objectives, purposes or goals. These decisions produce the principal policies and plans for achieving the goals, and help to define:

- the range of business the company is to pursue;
- the kind of economic and human organisation it intends to be; and
- the nature of the economic and non-economic contribution it intends to make to its shareholders, employees, customers and communities.

In other words, to paraphrase Hoffer and Schendel, strategy 'involves matching organisational competence (internal resources and skills) with the opportunities and risks created by environmental change in ways that will be effective and efficient'. Put plainly, the 'rational' strategic planning model is one in which objectives determine strategy rather than the other way round. The planning process involves a structured approach which entails systematic appraisals, the use of techniques and the interpretation and assimilation of business information.

The practice of *free-wheeling opportunism* essentially concentrates on finding, evaluating and exploiting short-term product-market opportunities instead of adhering to the rigidity of a predetermined strategy. It encourages a non-corporate philosophy, and managers who have vested interests will try to exert pressure for the acceptance of their own ideas even if they are incompatible with existing corporate aims. It is perceived by some managers to be dynamic, exciting and innovative. Furthermore because of its unstructured approach, strategy arising from it is seen to bear the stamp of individual managers.

Opponents of structured long-term strategic planning argue that, in instigating explicit long-term strategy, managers are putting their organisations into what is effectively a strait-jacket, resulting in a serious loss of flexibility, rendering difficult the exploitation of opportunities on a more free-wheeling basis. The arguments imply certain weaknesses in the disciplined approach, such as its inflexibility, forecasting inaccuracy, complexity and bureaucratic nature.

Not withstanding these criticisms, planning long-term corporate strategy can be justified. Certain action, which is fundamental to the corporate operations, is irreversible in the short-term at least. It is difficult to imagine managers making decisions, which have a degree of permanency, without first going through some form of formalised strategic planning. Also, the bigger an organisation grows the bigger are the risks involved in top management decisions. Strategic planning helps to identify these risks and either prevent or mitigate their effects. Large entities face dynamic and complex environments and an integral part of the strategic planning process is environmental appraisal which often uses sophisticated forecasting techniques requiring expert interpretation and evaluation of strategic options. The systematic survey of the corporate environment and of the company's internal strengths and weaknesses, acts as 'an early warning system'. The process will, hopefully, identify product/market threats and resource weaknesses in time for the company to bring in preventative or remedial measures.

Some companies have undoubtedly managed quite successfully without strategic planning. However it is probable that they could have performed much better. Even an upward sloping profit line can be criticised if it prevents the occurrence of an even steeper profit line. Strategic planning ensures that performance is targeted, rather than merely assessed against loose expectations. In these terms, strategic planning is concerned with the long-term which is an essential dimension in the overall survival pattern of an entity. The planning disciplines concentrate management's attention on long- term matters, but not at the exclusion of short-term considerations. Free-wheel planning is apt to focus only on the short-term and there is evidence to suggest that this is a dangerous policy.

Also, strategic planning requires the clarification of corporate objectives. The process aids in the formulation of organisational goals and objectives, and the strategy formulation process can be used to evaluate whether or not the tentative objectives established are achievable, given the organisation's resources and the nature of the changes occurring in its environment, and, if not, what other objectives could be achieved. In this way, strategic planning helps to integrate long, medium and short plans and to harmonise the activities of different departments and functions. The planning process results in people from different functions working together in teams, and the plan itself clarifies the contribution made by the different functions to the achievement of overall objectives. The emergent plan should reflect the 'corporate' nature of the entity, instead of merely being an aggregation of the plans of individual departments. The strategy spells out the responsibility and authority of each executive and management activity. This tends to boost morale, and produces improved results since most groups and individuals perform better if they know what is expected of them and how they contribute to the overall progress of the company.

Strategic planning demands a logical deliberation and analytical approach to decision making. It requires the generation of alternative strategies, and the evaluation of the probable results of their execution. The plans formulated can be used as yardsticks against which actual performance can be judged and remedial needs identified. The planning process is continuous and not conducted as a *'one-off'* ad hoc exercise. The systematic approach requires the maintenance of an information system, which will continuously provide up-to-date data for on-going decision making and control purposes. Strategic planning, when carried out imaginatively and conducted in the right atmosphere of communication, participation and incentive, helps to develop a climate conducive to creative thinking, initiative and innovation.

(c)   The system of planning in any entity will depend on a mixture of factors.

- The size and nature of the company.
- The attitudes of the Board particularly the chief executive.
- The information systems in use in the company.
- The structure of the organisation.
- The general trading circumstances of the company.
- The ability of the individuals who occupy planning positions.

(i)   Many organisations are large, complex, diversified and geographically decentralised, and are based on formal organisation structures and bureaucracies. It is hard to imagine how these organisations could be managed effectively without imposing the discipline of long-term corporate strategic planning. A failure to impose this discipline would probably result in the fragmentation of the organisation into separate, uncoordinated management autonomies. (A distinction must be made here between a loose set of uncoordinated autonomies and a deliberate corporate policy to fragment the planning structure into strategic business units (SBUs), of the type used in a conglomerate group.)

(ii)   'Freewheeling opportunism' is more likely to occur at the entrepreneurial stage of an enterprise's development, usually when one person, (or at most a handful of people), dominates strategic-thinking and where strategy is seldom explicit. Senior management of the entity know the business environment and are in direct touch with it by visiting customers, dealing with bank managers, negotiating directly with suppliers and are knowledgeable about competitors and their activities. There is no need for information systems, sophisticated management techniques nor structured planning and evaluation. Consequently, the planning system has to be seen in relatively simple ways. All companies, big or small, with simple or complex environments, diversified or concentrated product-market positions have to cope with environmental uncertainty. Uncertainty can best be managed if a disciplined approach is taken to cope with the future by using skills to identify and analyse trends, and forecast possible future events.

Managers at all levels possess attributes of creativity and innovation. However such attributes need to the encouraged, channelled and developed. The strategic planning system focuses attention, and creates a working environment suitable for creative management.

On balance, it would seem that the arguments for formal strategic planning are strong. The distinctive and identifiable pressures of rapid growth, the rising cost of resources, accelerating technology, government fiscal policies, inflation, ethical, social and political considerations, matched with the development of techniques such as gap analysis, product-portfolio appraisal, sensitivity analysis, capital investment appraisal, computer database processing, forecasting and cost analysis, have provided the impetus and stimulus for the spread of strategic planning converts, even for those managers in small entrepreneurial organisations.

4 ORGANISATIONAL CULTURE AND ETHICS

INTRODUCTION & LEARNING OUTCOMES

Syllabus area 11(i)

- The importance of culture in organisations (eg, the 'organisational iceberg').

- The determinants of culture, the different models available for categorising cultures (eg, Deal and Kennedy, Harrison, McKinsey 7-S, Peters and Waterman, Peters).

- The expectations of stakeholders with regard to ethical behaviour and the role of government (eg, Cadbury Report, ombudsman appointment) and professional bodies (eg, CIMA) in determining ethical standards.

Organisational culture is a concept easier to recognise than to describe. If you have had close contact with a number of different organisations - a college where you have studied, a club to which you have belonged, a company you have worked for - you may well be conscious of differences in the cultures of each. In this chapter, we try to be more specific about what these differences consist of.

We begin by distinguishing between the major types of culture that are found in practice, and the influences which determine the existence of one culture rather than another in any particular organisation. This leads on to a discussion of 'excellence': the concept that excellent companies share certain cultural features. This section refers in particular to the work of Peters and Waterman.

An organisation is a legal entity with no personal existence. Consequently, the problem of ethical behaviour depends on the personal ethics or values of its members, which shape its culture. This may result in the organisation drawing up policies that govern, to some extent, the conduct of its members. The culture of an organisation will also influence its approach to social responsibility. Management must decide, either unilaterally or as a member of an industry, to subscribe to a voluntary code of conduct of behaviour, or to simply comply with government regulations.

Although a person's own values have a considerable influence on their ethical standards, these are often reinforced and supported by the actions of superiors and peers. Professionals are also considerably influenced by the ethical standards maintained within the various institutions of which they are members and this can result in serious dilemmas for such managers.

When you have studied this chapter, you should be able to:

- Analyse and categorise the culture of an organisation, and recommend changes to improve organisational effectiveness.

- Explain the importance of organisational and professional ethics.

- Recommend ways in which ethical behaviour can be encouraged in organisations.

---

1 CULTURE

1.1 Introduction

The term culture has its origins in the work of social anthropologists. They used the term to refer to 'the complex whole which includes knowledge, belief, art, law, morals, custom and the many other capabilities and habits acquired by a person as a member of a society'. Culture was used to refer to total societies and the external environment of the organisation. However, since the mid-1970s the concept of culture has been increasingly applied to organisations. Each organisation is seen as possessing its own distinctive culture, which not only provides a basis for understanding organisational behaviour but also is a key determinant of organisational success.

1.2   The definition of organisational culture

Business strategies rest on two pillars. There is the tangible business situation - the environment of competitive pressures, the firm's reputation, its technology, level of capital employed and so on. The other is the people in the firm - how they think and feel, organise and are led and how they use their intellect and imagination. This human aspect is often referred to as corporate culture.

There is no shortage of definitions of organisational culture. It has been described, for example, as 'the dominant values espoused by an organisation', 'the philosophy that guides an organisation's policy toward employees and customers', 'the basic assumptions and beliefs that are shared by members of an organisation'. More simply, culture has been referred to as the 'way things are done around here'.

> **Definition**   Culture is the commonly held and relatively stable beliefs, attitudes and values that exist within the organisation.

2   DETERMINANTS OF CULTURE

2.1   Introduction

Despite the variety of definitions for culture, it is possible to distil the common characteristics and recognise the common features.

In every organisation there has evolved, over time, a system of beliefs, values, norms of behaviour, symbols, myths and practices that are shared by members of the organisation. The key elements can be shown in a diagram:

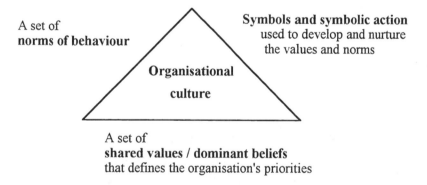

Culture refers to the shared understandings and meanings that members have concerning an organisation. Rather as individuals have distinctive personalities, organisations have their own particular culture. Some will be friendly, relaxed and informal whilst others will be highly formal, aloof and hostile. This raises the important issue of whether there is a 'right' culture for an organisation, and we shall address this question later.

2.2   Shared values or dominant beliefs

These underlie the culture by specifying what is important and they need to be shared by everyone in the organisation so that they are reinforced and widely accepted. Examples of shared values include:

- A belief in the importance of people as individuals.
- A general objective eg, being the most innovative in their field.
- Management style - eg, fostering communication and encouraging creative input.
- A key asset or skill which is the essence of competition - eg, product quality level, customer support or service system.

- An operational focus - eg, guaranteeing delivery on time.
- A focus on output eg, zero defects.
- An emphasis on a functional area - market-driven approach as opposed to a manufacturing or sales focus.

2.3   Norms

Norms guide people's behaviour, suggesting what is or is not appropriate. The commitment to shared values must be strong enough to develop norms of behaviour or informal rules, which influence the decisions and actions throughout the organisation. For example, in a 'quality service' culture, sloppy work affecting the product or service would be informally policed by fellow workers, without reliance on formal systems.

2.4   Symbols or symbolic actions

There are many examples of persistent, consistent and visible symbols and symbolic actions that make up an organisation's culture. These include:

- The organisation's unique roots established by the personal style and experience of the founder and the original mission eg, the concept of entertainment developed by Walt Disney.

- The organisation's logos and slogans eg, 'I think therefore IBM'.

- The activities of an executive can send a strong signal throughout the organisation eg, regularly visiting the factory floor to establish problem areas and speak to employees.

- Rituals such as recruitment techniques, eating lunches and giving impromptu awards help to define a culture.

- Organisational structure can be an attention-focussing process. For example, replacing tables that seat four with ones that seat six in the canteen, increases the chances of employees from different departments meeting and interacting with each other.

3   MAJOR INFLUENCES ON CULTURE

3.1   Cultural characteristics

A problem stemming from the definitions of culture we have looked at is that they do not provide a structured approach to analysing the culture of an organisation. However, Robbins suggests that we can identify ten key characteristics, which influence an organisation's culture:

(a)   Individual initiative - the degree of responsibility, freedom and independence that individuals have.

(b)   Risk tolerance - the degree to which employees are encouraged to be aggressive, innovative and risk-taking.

(c)   Direction - the degree to which the organisation creates clear objectives and performance expectations.

(d)   Integration - the degree to which units in the organisation are encouraged to operate in a co-ordinated manner.

(e)   Management contact - the degree to which managers provide clear communication, assistance and support to their subordinates.

(f)   Control - the degree of rules and regulations, and the amount of direct supervision, that are used to oversee and control employee behaviour.

(g)   Identity - the degree to which members identify with the organisation as a whole rather than with their particular work group or field of professional expertise.

(h)   Reward system - the degree to which reward allocations (ie, salary increases, promotions) are based on employee performance criteria.

(i)   Conflict tolerance - the degree to which employees are encouraged to air conflicts and grievances openly.

(j)   Communication patterns - the degree to which organisational communications are restricted to the formal hierarchy of command.

These ten characteristics provide a framework for analysing the culture of any organisation.

3.2   Cultural elements

Morse and Lorsch identify seven elements that affect an organisation's culture:

(a)   structural orientation (eg, centralised, or satellite branches?);

(b)   distribution of influence (eg size of the business);

(c)   character of superior/subordinate relationships (eg, how is management carried out?);

(d)   relations between staff (eg, good in small, skilled teams);

(e)   time orientation (eg, do we take a short or long term view?);

(f)   goal orientation (eg, people working only for money); and

(g)   management style (eg, 'X' or 'Y').

4   CATEGORISING CULTURES

4.1   Introduction

Deal and Kennedy *(Corporate Cultures: The Rites and Rituals of Corporate Life)* went beyond outlining the cultural elements within an organisation. They believe that the culture of a company affects its policies, decisions, activities and hence its success. Successful companies have strong and cohesive cultures where employees identify with the company goals and band together to achieve them. Alternatively, less well-performing companies have weak and disconnected cultures with minimal employee loyalty. Money is the prime motivator at work.

They suggest that an organisation is capable of being managed from a weak one to a strong one by the process of creating and implementing supporting rites, rituals and ceremonials. These act to communicate and reinforce the beliefs and values that senior management wants all employees to share.

4.2   Risk and Feedback

Deal and Kennedy argue that two crucial factors shape an organisation's culture. The first is the degree of risk associated with the organisation's activities and the second is the speed of feedback provided to employees concerning the success of their decision strategy. They placed these factors on different axis to produce four distinctive types of organisational culture as shown below:

	Fast	Slow
High	Tough guy culture	Bet-your-company culture
Low	Work hard, play hard culture	Process culture

RISK (left axis), FEEDBACK (bottom axis)

FEEDBACK

- **Tough guy culture** - is made up of individualists who thrive on high risks and fast feedback on their performance. Unfortunately, the short term need for feedback may divert attention from longer term efforts. This type of culture is often found in construction, advertising and entertainment organisations.

- **Bet-your-company culture** - is characterised by high stake decisions with a delayed feedback. It is prevalent in oil and aircraft companies where the decisions that risk the company's future are made by technically competent people and necessitate attention to detail.

- **Work hard, play hard culture** - is characterised by low risk taking combined with quick feedback. High activity is the key to survival. This type of culture suits organisations with high volume sales of mass produced goods.

- **Process culture** - has little risk and little feedback. Typical process cultures include government agencies, banks and heavily regulated industries.

4.3   Analysing and comparing cultures

Developing the ideas of Roger Harrison *(Understanding Your Organisation's Character)* Charles Handy *(Gods of Management)* has created a typology, which provides a useful basis for discussing and investigating variations in organisational culture. He has identified four theoretical cultural types and devised a questionnaire for their measurement.

According to Harrison, the four basic classifications of the types of culture one might expect to find in an organisation are:

- power;
- role;
- task; and
- people cultures.

Handy gave each of these types a Greek God's name:

- Zeus is the God that represents the power culture;
- Apollo is the God that represents the role culture (or bureaucracy);
- Athena is the Goddess of the task culture; and
- Dionysus is the God of the existential (people) culture.

(a)   Power orientation

Power-orientated organisations attempt to dominate their environment and those who are powerful within the organisation strive to maintain absolute control over subordinates. They are competitive and have voracious appetites for growth. They buy and sell organisations and people as commodities, in apparent disregard of human values and general welfare. The major source of power and influence is most likely to be the owners (in a small firm the original founders, in a large firm the major shareholding individuals). In this type of culture, there are few procedures and rules of a formal kind. The major decisions are taken by key individuals; others use broad guidelines or knowledge of what has happened previously to decide what should be done. This suggests that this kind of organisation can be very adaptive to changing conditions though this is, of course, dependent on the abilities of the key decision makers. The power culture tends to be found in small organisations where the pattern of communication is simpler than in large ones. Example: entrepreneur heading small company.

(b)   **Role orientation**

This type of orientation emphasises legality, legitimacy and responsibility. Rules and procedures regulate conflict. Rights and privileges are defined and there is a strong emphasis on hierarchy and status. Predictability of behaviour is high and stability and respectability are often valued as much as competence. In other words, it is a bureaucratic organisation. It is a 'role culture' in that people act in terms of the roles specified by the job descriptions.

The structure determines the authority and responsibility of individuals and these boundaries are not to be crossed by any individual. Individual personalities are unimportant; it is the job that counts. This is a feature of many large bureaucracies. People describe their job by its duties, **not** by its purpose.

This kind of culture is best suited to an environment that is relatively stable and a large-sized organisation. Although it can adapt, this ability is restricted and a 'role culture' will have problems in surviving a dramatic change. Examples: civil service, ICI.

(c)   **Task orientation**

This type of orientation evaluates structures, functions and activities in terms of their contribution to the organisational goals. Nothing is allowed to get in the way of task accomplishment. Authority is based on appropriate knowledge and competence. If individuals do not have the skills or knowledge to perform the task, they are either retrained or replaced. Emphasis is placed on flexibility. Collaboration is sought if this promotes goal achievement.

Task culture is best seen in teams established to achieve specific tasks ie, project teams where the emphasis is on the execution of a particular task. People describe their positions in terms of the results they are achieving.

Note: the life of the team lasts for the duration of the task and it ceases to exist after completion. This type of culture is often found in rapidly changing organisations where groups are established on a short-term basis to deal with a particular change. Structurally this culture is often associated with the matrix structure. Examples: market research organisations, entertainment industry, computer software design.

(d)   **People orientation**

Less common than any of the other cultures, the person culture is characterised by the fact that it exists to satisfy the requirements of the particular individual(s) involved in the organisation. Authority may be assigned on the basis of task competence, but this practice is kept to a minimum. Instead, members are expected to influence each other through example and helpfulness. Consensus methods of decision making are preferred and roles are assigned on the basis of personal preferences and the need for learning and growth.

If there is a small, highly participatory organisation where individuals undertake all the duties themselves, one will find the person culture. More commonly, a key individual heads a support team of different skills. Example: barrister in chambers.

4.4   The concept of excellence

Following the impact of Peters and Waterman's much acclaimed book there has been an increasing emphasis placed on the importance of cultural factors in developing standards of quality and excellence. This culture needs to exist at all levels within the company, not just at senior management level. Peters and Waterman show that employees tend to welcome the norms associated with this definite culture or else they leave.

Peters and Waterman suggest from their analysis of 'excellent' organisations that there is a common set of shared values which are to be found in all of them. The study looked at organisations in the United States, which had performed consistently well, in terms of innovation and return on investment, over a period of twenty years. These are listed below:

Amdahl	Delta Airlines	Intel	3M
Amoco	Digital Equipment	IBM	Nat. Semiconductor
Avon	Disney Productions	Johnson & Johnson	Procter & Gamble
Boeing	Dow Chemical	K-mart	Raychem
Bristol-Myers	DuPont	Levi Strauss	Revlon
Caterpillar	Eastman Kodak	Marriott	Schlumberger
Chesebrough-Pond's	Emerson Electric	McDonald's	Texas Instruments
Dana Corp.	Fluor	Maytag	Wal-Mart
Data General	Hewlett Packard	Merck	Wang Labs

However, some five years after the above list was produced, Fortune magazine carried an article suggesting that several of the companies no longer qualified for the term 'excellent companies'.

4.5   Shared values

Peters and Waterman (*In Search of Excellence, 1982*) recognised that a clear, coherent culture was evident in excellent companies. This culture varies between organisations and is expressed distinctly in different companies:

(a)   IBM bases its culture on service;
(b)   McDonald's is based on consistent quality.

The main aspects of culture in 'excellent' companies are:

(a)   **A bias for action** - an urgency to produce and complete results rather than analyse obstacles to action. A positive attitude of 'what can we do now' rather than a negative attitude of 'what is preventing us'.

(b)   **Hands-on, value driven** - showing a commitment to the organisational values.

(c)   **Close to the customer** - a continuous pursuit to understand the customer's needs and improve the quality offered. Peters and Waterman see improving quality as a motivating force for workers as well as affording opportunities for employees to be innovative. Their concern for quality and customer needs must exist in all functions at all levels.

(d)   **Stick to the knitting** - no evidence of conglomerate diversification.

(e)   **Autonomy and entrepreneurship** - teams and individuals are encouraged to establish their own targets for improvement. An element of competition is regarded as invigorating. This self-improvement drive encourages innovation and a customer satisfaction based culture.

(f)   **Simple form, lean staff** - uncomplicated structures without large numbers of employees at head office.

(g)   **Productivity through people** - staff must be treated as intelligent contributors, who are individually valuable and capable of 'extraordinary effort'. Harvey-Jones in his experience at ICI states that he never ceased to be surprised at the exceptional results that motivated people were capable of achieving.

(h)   **Simultaneous tight-loose properties** - tight controls and detailed rules were replaced by common understanding and acceptance of the main guiding values of the organisation. Clearly this philosophy affects a company's recruitment, training and promotion standards and is not attainable overnight. Rather there is a steady change in the balance between control and trust.

4.6   Activity

Peters and Waterman state that staff are capable of exceptional loyalty and effort if the organisation culture is attuned to this. How could this occur?

4.7   Activity solution

Peters and Waterman list three basic requirements:

(a)   The tasks must be obviously worthwhile eg, creating satisfied customers, so engendering pride in staff.

(b)   Staff individuals are treated as winners. Positive attitudes and contributions are highlighted.

(c)   The organisation of work allows staff to satisfy the two desires of being highly regarded in their own right and also as a welcomed member of a successful group.

4.8   McKinsey's 7-S approach

The McKinsey 7-S approach, which was widely interpreted in Peters and Waterman's book *In Search of Excellence,* provides the key aspects of a management system and a practical framework for its analysis. The seven Ss are:

(i)   **strategy** (objectives and resource allocation) - in this context it refers to the organisation's business and competitive strategies;

(ii)   **structure** - this refers to the formal organisation structure (eg the division of tasks, responsibility and authority);

(iii)   **systems** (processes and procedures) - an important example of a system is an accounting system, which processes financial data and produces information. The whole gamut of information and processing systems is referred to here;

(iv)   **style** (image, management behaviour) - this refers to what might be called culture, 'the way we do things around here', or even the informal organisation;

(v)   **staff** (motivation, groups, abilities);

(vi)   **shared values** (super-ordinate goals, common purpose) - these are the guiding beliefs as to why the organisation exists;

(vii)   **skills** (capabilities of organisation as a whole) - this is what the organisation does well. This is more than just the aggregate of individual skills, because it results from the ways in which these are deployed in pursuit of organisational objective.

Peters and Waterman believed that any intelligent approach to organising had to encompass, and treat as interdependent, at least these seven variables. The diagram below outlines the relationship between different organisational aspects.

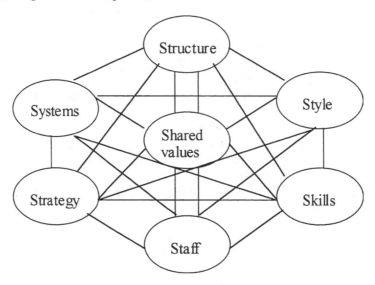

The importance of this model is that it emphasises the importance of issues that are not quantifiable other than strategies, systems and structure, which are more easily measured.

5   THE IMPORTANCE OF CULTURAL FACTORS

5.1   Culture and organisational effectiveness

An initial point that should be made here is that until the late 1970s organisations were, for the most part, seen as rational means of co-ordinating and controlling a group of people. Effectiveness was to be achieved by a purely rational approach. Just as decisions needed to be taken on the most rational basis, so organisational problems of size and structure had to have rational solutions. The idea that factors such as myths and symbols, values and beliefs can affect organisational effectiveness is relatively new and increasingly influential.

A simple distinction can be drawn between strong and weak cultures. A strong culture is marked by the organisation's core values being both intensely held and widely shared. On the other hand, weak cultures show a lack of uniformity and limited commitment. Some writers, noticeably Peters and Waterman in their book *In Search of Excellence*, have suggested that a strong organisational culture is a key factor in determining organisational effectiveness.

Although a number of the original 'excellent' organisations have since fallen from grace, there is definitely a relationship between an organisation's culture and its effective performance.

5.2   Are cultures uniform?

We are perhaps mistaken to speak of **an** organisational culture. Though it may well be that an organisation possesses a dominant culture, all members do not always share it. Groups form in organisations eg, departments and informal work groups who create distinctive shared understandings of their own. This leads to the existence of **sub-cultures** which, though they may share the core features of the whole organisation, are nonetheless distinct. For example a research and development department may well have its unique culture as a result of its specialist role, its qualified staff and its geographical separation from other employees.

At the extreme, organisations may be faced with the existence of **counter-cultures** where the aim is to undermine the dominant culture. Examples of this might be in groups, which seek to undermine management control, groups who practise vandalism and sabotage, or groups who are simply alienated and apathetic.

In the light of these observations, it is important to remember that most writers on organisational culture are referring to the **dominant culture** and tend to ignore or underplay the existence of sub- or-counter cultures.

5.3   The organisational iceberg

In their book *Organisational Behaviour*, Hellriegel, Slocum and Woodman suggest that one way to recognise why people behave as they do, is to view an organisation as an iceberg. 'What sinks ships is not always what sailors can see, but what they can't see'.

They portray an organisation as having overt, formal aspects on the tip of the iceberg and covert, behavioural aspects hidden underneath.

The formal aspects (the visible bits) include:

- Physical facilities
- Financial resources
- Customers
- Technology
- Organisational design
- Surface competencies and skills
- Formal goals
- Rules and regulations

The covert, behavioural aspects (the hidden bits) include:

- Underlying competencies and skills
- Communication patterns
- Informal team processes
- Attitudes
- Personalities
- Conflict
- Political behaviour

There are four types of icebergs:

(i)   the ones you can see and basically know what they are doing;
(ii)   the ones that are half above the water, which means there is still a little bit of mystery, but you have a good idea of what is coming;
(iii)   the one that is just below the water level and you only have a general idea of the effect it will have; and
(iv)   the one that is well below the surface, which you cannot anticipate and you have no idea what it will do.

The managers who can understand the potential effect of the iceberg well below the surface will go a fair way down the journey to success.

The pervasive nature of culture, in terms of 'how things are done around here' and common values, beliefs and attitudes, will have a significant effect on organisational processes such as decision-making, design of structure, group behaviour, work organisation, motivation and job satisfaction, and management control.

6   CULTURE AND THE INDIVIDUAL

6.1   Culture and job satisfaction

There does appear to be a strong relationship between culture and job satisfaction, though it is not straightforward. In general terms, job satisfaction will be high when the organisational culture is complementary to the needs of the individual. If an employee has a high need for autonomy and achievement, a culture which is marked by being low in structure, having loose supervision and a high level of recognition for achievement will produce more job satisfaction than a culture marked by a tight structure, close supervision and low recognition for achievement.

6.2   Culture and individual performance

Socialisation into a culture has important effects on employee performance. Clearly, an individual's performance will depend on knowing the right and wrong ways to perform the job. Understanding the right way to do the job is evidence of successful socialisation. There is also the broader issue of fitting in and working well with colleagues, which enables the person to perform well and not detract from the performance of others. This will depend partly on the social skills of the individual, but also on the extent to which the person is socialised into the organisational culture.

A further influence of culture on performance is the relationship between culture and technology. Performance will be higher if the culture suits the technology. Research has shown that where the culture is informal and creative, and supports risk taking and conflict, performance will be higher if the technology is non-routine. Routine technology works best when the culture is formally structured and risk-averse, avoids conflict and has a more task-oriented leadership.

6.3   Culture and recruitment/advancement of individuals

Recruitment is one of the most immediate points of contact between the internal culture of an organisation and the outside world. If the recruitment process is carried out thoughtfully and systematically, it is possible to exert a strong influence on the 'incoming culture'. This in turn can be a powerful influence on those already working in the organisation.

Recruitment can have a significant cultural impact at all levels in the organisation. If the management is trying to foster a particular culture generally, it is clearly sensible to ensure that this message is communicated to those contemplating joining the company. Candidates looking to work in a paternalistic environment, for example, are unlikely to be comfortable or successful in a company that is moving towards a culture of independence or entrepreneurship.

Some organisations, such as Marks & Spencer, present a clear culture to job applicants. This culture enables applicants to sense whether they would 'fit in' and advance up the promotion ladder.

7   INFLUENCE ON STRATEGY

7.1   Matching objectives

Peters and Waterman's arguments are very persuasive and supported by much evidence, but can we conclude that a strong culture is always desirable? The first point that needs to be made is that the content of the culture must match the objectives and the environment of the organisation. A strong innovative culture, for example, will only work well if the company wishes to innovate and is operating in a dynamic environment. Strong cultures will always be more difficult to change than weak ones. A strong culture might be based on values that are not compatible with organisational effectiveness; for example, certain loyalties may restrict the process of change. Problems clearly can arise in a merger or acquisition situation where two conflicting organisational cultures are brought together.

Though a strong culture may be a liability, we should not forget the potential benefits. A strong culture increases commitment to the organisation and the consistency of behaviour of its members.

Having a clear mission and agreed values about the means of pursuing it removes ambiguities and can replace the need for more formal controls. An appropriate culture, as Peters and Waterman suggest, can be a crucial factor in determining levels of performance, both for the organisation and for the individual.

7.2   Culture and developing strategy

There are many factors that influence the expectations that people are likely to have of an organisation, as shown in the diagram below:

Influences on strategy

The significance of these factors in the strategic development must be analysed carefully. There are three main questions, which must be addressed:

(a)   Which factors inside and outside the organisation have most influence on people's expectations?

(b)   To what extent do current strategies reflect the influence of any one factor or combination of factors?

(c)   How far would these factors help or hinder the pursuit of new strategies?

7.3   The growth and maintenance of organisational culture

The origins of the culture of an organisation are logically sought in the influence, style and goals of the founders of the organisation. Founders begin with an original idea, unconstrained by previous ways of doing things and therefore are able to impose their vision of how and why things should be done. They play a major role in establishing custom and traditions. The influence of founders and the early members of the organisation often lasts well beyond their life span.

There are many examples of founders of organisations such as Henry Ford at the Ford Motor Company and David Packard at Hewlett Packard who have had profound and lasting effects on their organisation's culture. If we take the example of Thomas Watson at IBM we can see that, though he died in 1956, his influence is still felt in the research and development policies, the mode of dress of employees and the compensation policies adopted by the company today.

We can distinguish three main sources of the maintenance of culture:

(a)   **Top management** - because of their power and influence, top managers have a considerable influence in either sustaining or modifying organisational culture. Other employees will observe their behaviour and they will establish norms of behaviour that will filter throughout the organisation.

(b)   **Selection** - the selection/rejection decision can be taken on the basis that a potential recruit will or will not help in maintaining the existing culture.

(c)   **Socialisation** - organisational socialisation is the process of indoctrination into the culture of the organisation. Frequently this is done by some form of induction training but in many organisations there are also informal practices which serve a similar function. Typically the new employee is told 'how things are done around here' both in the training situation and as words of advice from superior and colleagues.

Culture is often transmitted through the medium of stories, myths, rituals, material symbols and the special language (eg, acronyms and jargon) that are unique to the particular organisation.

7.4   Organisational climate

When applied to organisations, climate relates to the prevailing atmosphere surrounding the organisation, to the level of morale and to the strength of feelings or belonging, care and goodwill among members.

- **Morale** is another general concept that is difficult to measure objectively. It can be considered in terms of the mental attitudes people have towards their tasks and responsibilities. The key ingredients of morale, according to Patrick and Manning, include:

(a)   **A sense of importance in their job** - with challenging and reasonably demanding assignments and a sense of accomplishment based on competent performance.

(b)   **Teamwork among staff** - with a sense of group pride and self-esteem. There should be a high level of human interactions, good relations with co-workers, team effort and the support of other staff, including supervisors and top management.

(c)   **Management concern about staff welfare** - staff should receive fair treatment and just rewards. There should be a clear statement of management with efforts to resolve genuine goal incongruence and a clear attempt to create a feeling of mutual respect and trust with staff.

(d)   **Economic rewards that are fair and individualised** - if fringe benefits are added to pay, management should attempt to meet individual needs and preferences. There should be opportunities for job advancement including promotion and cross-job postings.

- **Commitment** to the organisation is among the factors that contribute to a healthy organisational climate.

    Definition   Organisational commitment is an individual's psychological bond to the organisation, including a sense of job involvement, loyalty and a belief in the values of the organisation.

    It can be describes as 'giving all of yourself while at work'. This means: using time constructively; attention to detail; making that extra effort; accepting change; co-operating with others; self-development; pride in abilities; seeking improvements; and giving loyal support.

- **A sense of belonging** to the organisation builds upon the loyalty essential to successful industrial relations. It is created by managers through ensuring that the staff are informed, involved and sharing in success.

A healthy climate will not, by itself, guarantee improved organisational effectiveness. However, an organisation is most unlikely to attain optimum operational performance unless the climate evokes a spirit of support and co-operation and is conducive to motivating members to work willingly and effectively.

7.5 The management of culture

Organisational cultures will exist, be they weak or strong, planned or unplanned. Sub-cultures and/or counter-cultures are frequently present. The culture of any organisation will be the product of complex human interaction over time. All of these factors make culture something that is difficult to manage or formulate. In essence, you cannot start with a clean sheet in any organisation at any stage.

However, the implications of studies such as those of Peters and Waterman are that there is a clear need to manage organisational culture. It is so intrinsically tied to organisational performance that it would be foolish to ignore it. Culture develops in the light of a particular set of circumstances, at a certain time and in the light of certain conditions. Times and circumstances change and an old culture may well impede rather than help an organisation cope with change. In such cases management would need to intervene to modify the culture by altering those factors which sustain the present culture.

The argument is that if culture can be learned, it can also be unlearned and replaced by a new, more appropriate culture. Thus, management might seek to change culture by appointing people who are sympathetic to the new culture, introduce new training and socialisation devices and change the stories, myths, rituals, language and material symbols that are part of the traditional culture.

8 ETHICS

8.1 Introduction

The *Oxford English Dictionary* defines ethics as:

Definition the 'science of morals, moral principles, philosophy or code'.

Donaldson in *Key issues in Business Ethics*, describes business ethics as 'the systematic study of moral matters pertaining to business, industry or related activities, institutions or practices and beliefs.

There are three contrasting ethical standpoints:

(i) deontological views - where people believe that ethical behaviour requires ethically based actions regardless of consequences;

(ii) teleological values - where people believe that the moral value of outcomes is more important than the process by which they are achieved - the ends justify the means.

(iii) ethical or moral relativism - applies to people who believe that an act is right if it is approved by the social group to which a person belongs and wrong if it is not. Otherwise, moral beliefs should be regarded as the private concern of each individual.

The political, social and ethical environments that the organisation operates in have different components:

- the political environment consists of laws, regulations and government agencies;

- the social environment consists of the customs, attitudes, beliefs and education of different groups in society; and

- the ethical environment consists of a set of well-established rules of personal and organisational behaviour.

8.2   Ethics at three levels

Ethical issues regarding business and public-sector organisations exist at three levels:

(i)   At the **macro level,** there are issues about the role of business in the national and international organisation of society. These are largely concerned with the relative virtues of different political/social systems, such as free enterprise, centrally planned economies, etc. There are also important issues of international relationships and the role of business on an international scale.

(ii)   At the **corporate level,** the issue is often referred to as corporate social responsibility and is focused on the ethical issues facing individual corporate entities (private and public sector) when formulating and implementing strategies.

(iii)   At the **individual level,** the issue concerns the behaviour and actions of individuals within organisations.

8.3   The scope of ethics

Business ethics are concerned with truth and justice and have a variety or aspects including:

- the expectations of society;
- fair competition;
- advertising;
- public relations;
- social responsibilities;
- consumer autonomy; and
- corporate behaviour in the home country, as well as abroad.

The two factors, which have the strongest bearing on ethical standards in management, are public disclosure and publicity, and the increasing concern of a public that is better informed.

These two factors are further compounded by government regulations and education to increase the standard of professionalism among business managers, particularly as there is an element of change, and it is not always for the better. Here the student can consider some of the frauds that have taken place within the City of London, and perhaps the way the advertising industry has deteriorated in recent years, not by telling lies, but by deliberately slating the competition.

8.4   Varying standards of ethics

The problem is compounded by the fact that in a world of multinationals, where competition is now international, the standards of ethics vary from nation to nation. Some countries have higher standards than those of the West, whilst others have standards that are very much lower. The payment of contributions to political parties is an interesting example. In England, it is allowed and it must be declared in the published accounts, but other than in the rare cases such as where the future of the organisation is threatened, it is not tax deductible. This practice is not permitted in the US. However, in several countries of the world, payments to government officials and other persons of influence to ensure the expedition or favourable handling of a business transaction are not regarded as unethical bribes, but rather as payment for services rendered. Indeed, in many cases such payments to ensure the landing of a particular contract are considered a desirable and acceptable way of doing business. There have been instances where foreign nationals have even threatened to close operations down if payments are not met.

This is a very difficult problem and a contentious and emotive area. In addition, standards vary from profession to profession. The student will be familiar with the crisis of ethics that frequently faces the medical profession, and the high ethical standards expected of the members. The famous Hedley Byrne case has enforced high standards of professional care upon the accounting profession and on any profession that gives advice, which people reasonably expect to be accurate. Furthermore, higher standards are expected higher up the social and corporate echelon. What might be considered acceptable among the lower echelons is considered totally unacceptable amongst those who are in the public eye. This may be the root cause of the problem. As democracy spreads, and there are more equal opportunities, the accepted standard of ethics has to be imposed upon people. It could be that they were originally and traditionally outside the scope of such standards of behaviour, and perhaps had a different understanding of what was acceptable. This may suggest that the law needs more frequent review or updating.

8.5   Approaches to business ethics

Lynne Paine argues that, within the organisations that she studied, there were two approaches to the management of ethics - a compliance-based approach and an integrity-based approach.

A **compliance-based approach** is designed to ensure that the organisation acts with regard for and compliance with the relevant law. Any violations are prevented, detected and punished.

An **integrity-based approach** emphasises managerial responsibility for ethical behaviour, as well as a concern for the law. Ethics is an issue of organisational culture and systems. The task of ethics management is to:

- create an environment that supports ethically sound behaviour;
- define and give life to an organisation's values; and
- instil a sense of shared accountability amongst members of the organisation.

8.6   Ethics and the individual

Charles Handy cites the problem where an organisation's standards of ethics may differ from the individual's own standards. For example, what is the responsibility of an individual who believes that the strategy of his or her organisation is unethical? Should the individual report the organisation; or should they leave the employment of the company on the grounds of a mismatch of values? This has often been called 'whistle blowing'.

Indications are that there are practices, which may give a lie to the individual's personal identity. Evidence would suggest that this seems to be most prevalent among the middle order of managers, who aspire to reach the higher echelons. It appears that it is necessary to be more of a company man at those levels than higher up, where it is more possible to be individual.

It is argued that ethics are easier to enforce if the organisation takes precedence over all the employees including the directors, and a system is enforced, whereby ethical standards are adequately monitored. The social audit fashion in the mid-1970s may well have begun to move along this road, although much of its activities were sadly misdirected.

8.7   Expectations of stakeholders

Earlier in the text, we looked at the stakeholder model. The organisational stakeholders are those individuals or groups who have an interest in and/or are affected by the goals, operations or activities of the organisation or the behaviour of its members. They include employees, owners, customers and suppliers.

One of the criticisms of the stakeholder model is that it fails to explain how the management of an enterprise is able to treat each stakeholder in an equitable manner. It is difficult to imagine how they are to prioritise or choose between stakeholders, when critical decisions have to be taken that will result in a benefit to one at the expense of another. For example, who should suffer if a loss occurs during a period of economic recession? Should it be the employees through a factory closure or the shareholders through a cancelled dividend?

Unfortunately a possible clash of values may arise between corporate responsibilities on the one hand and an individual's principles on the other. The organisation should distinguish between corporate social responsibility issues, which should refer to the policies and activities of the organisation, and the decision and actions of individual managers, which should fall within the domain of business ethics.

8.8   Ethics in the real world

The problem lies in applying ethical standards to everyday life in a hard-nosed, fiercely competitive world. J Weber in his treatises on corporate ethics, suggests that there are three ways of succeeding:

(a)   company policy or a code of ethics;
(b)   a formally appointed ethics committee;
(c)   the teaching of ethics in management development programmes.

Of these three suggestions, the code of ethics is the most common, but several large US corporations have gone the full way along the road to introducing ethics into their management development programmes. Perhaps the lack of true recognition of ethical requirements in Europe and especially in the UK stems from the fact that management development programmes are so poorly developed. UK management perhaps does not see the ethical responsibility to develop the staff in whom they have invested.

9   THE ROLE OF GOVERNMENT AND PROFESSIONAL BODIES

9.1   The Government

By formalising certain areas of social responsibilities into legal requirements, successive governments have recognised the importance of organisational ethical behaviour. The legislation covers a wide area of responsibilities including employment protection, equal opportunities, Companies Acts, consumer law, product liability and safeguarding the environment.

Managers must respect and obey the law, even if it is not in their best interests, but they may not co-operate voluntarily with actions requested by the government. Examples include:

*   restraint from trading with certain overseas countries;

*   the acceptance of controls over imports or exports;

*   actions designed to combat inflation eg, limits on the level of wage settlements;

*   assistance in the control of potential social problems eg, displays of health warnings, advertisements and the sale of tobacco.

9.2   Code of ethics

A code is a statement of policies, principles or rules that guide behaviour. Codes of ethics do not only apply to organisations but should guide the behaviour of people in everyday life. Most of us operate with a more or less well defined set of ethical values, principles or rules of thumb that guide decision making. They are seldom spelled out explicitly in a list but if you had to make a list, it would probably include:

*   obey the law
*   be fair
*   avoid harming others
*   prevent harm to others
*   respect the right of others
*   help those in need
*   do not lie or cheat

Codes of ethical conduct have existed for many years in a number of professions and organisations. Their purpose is to guide managers and members of professional institutes in their behaviour as they perform their tasks. Carefully drawn up codes can also reassure customers, suppliers and even competitors of the integrity of the organisation. Because of recent governmental and business scandals, there has been increased public interest in the existence and use of such ethical codes.

The Report on Professional Services, published by the Monopolies Commission (1970), concluded that:
'a number of the restrictive practices carried out by professional groups, on the basis of community welfare, looked rather like arrangements for making life easier for practitioners at the expense of the client'.
This conclusion obviously caused considerable concern both to the public and the professional institutes.

Codes of ethics are usually general statements that are abstract, and are prescriptions for what a person's values should be, rather than descriptions of what they actually are. They are typically statements of principle with which few would disagree. CIMA has issued a set of ethical guidelines, which set out the fundamental principles of ethical conduct. Also, the British Institute of Management publishes a code of conduct, which gives guidance on the ethical and professional standards required of BIM members.

9.3   The British Institute of Management's ethical guide

A Code of Conduct, and supporting Guides to Professional Management, sets out the standards of conduct required of BIM members. Aspects covered by the Code are:

(i)   regard for and compliance with the relevant law;

(ii)   acting with integrity, honesty, loyalty and fairness - not misusing their authority or office for personal or other gains;

(iii)   respect for the customs and practices of any country in which they work.

The supporting guides lay down a number of professional ethics, and the pursuit of the objective of good management, concerning:

* the individual manager
* others within the organisation
* the organisation
* others external to but in direct relationship with the organisation
* the wider community
* the Institute of Management

9.4   The CIMA Ethical Guidelines

The CIMA ethical guidelines state that members have a duty to observe the highest standard of conduct and integrity. They set standards of conduct for professional accountants and state the fundamental principles that should be observed by professional accountants in order to achieve common objectives. These Guidelines also assume that, unless a limitation is specifically stated, the objectives and fundamental principles are equally valid for all members, whether they be in industry, commerce, the public sector, public practice or education.

The guidelines recognise that the objectives of the accountancy profession are to work to the highest standards of professionalism, to attain the highest level performance and generally to meet the public interest requirement. The objectives require four basic needs to be met:

(i)   In the whole of society there is a need for credibility in information and information systems.

(ii)   There is a need for individuals who can be clearly identified by employers, clients and other interested parties as professional persons in the accountancy field.

(iii)   There is a need for assurance that all services obtained from a professional accountant are carried out to the highest standards of performance.

(iv)   Users of the services of professional accountants should be able to feel confident that there exists a framework of professional ethics which governs the provision of these services.

In order to achieve the objectives of the accountancy profession, professional accountants have to observe a number of prerequisites or fundamental principles.

The fundamental principles

(a)   **Integrity** - a professional accountant should be straightforward and honest in performing professional services.

(b)   **Objectivity** - a professional accountant should be fair and should not allow prejudice or bias or the influence of others to override objectivity.

(c)   **Professional competence and due care**

(d)   **Confidentiality** - a professional accountant should respect the confidentiality of information acquired during the course of performing professional services. He or she should not use or disclose any such information without proper and specific authority or unless there is a legal or professional right or duty to disclose.

(e)   **Professional behaviour** - a professional accountant should act in a manner consistent with the good reputation of the profession and refrain from any conduct which might bring discredit to the Institute.

(f)   **Technical standards** - a professional accountant should carry out professional services in accordance with relevant technical and professional standards.

9.5   Ethics committees

Some companies have a voluntary code of conduct. However, simply stating a code of conduct (or ethics) is not enough. The organisation should appoint an ethics committee, consisting of internal and external directors, to institutionalise ethical behaviour. The duties of the committee must be to:

- hold regular meetings to discuss ethical issues;
- deal with 'grey' areas;
- communicate the code to all members of the organisation;
- check for possible violations of the code;
- enforce the code;
- reward compliance and punish violations;
- review and update the code.

An ethics committee decides and rules on misconduct and it may seek advice from specialists in business ethics. This could be an ethics ombudsman, who acts as the corporate conscience.

Although the enforcement of ethical codes may not be easy, the mere existence of such codes can increase ethical behaviour by clarifying expectations. When integrated into the day-to-day operations of an organisation, such codes can help prevent damaging ethical lapses, while tapping into powerful human impulses for moral thought and action. Thus, an ethical framework becomes no longer a burdensome constraint within which the organisation must operate, but the governing ethos.

The Financial Reporting Council, the Stock Exchange and various chartered bodies of the accountancy profession set up a committee, chaired by Sir Adrian Cadbury, to report on *The*

Financial Aspects of Corporate Governance. The main recommendations of the Cadbury Report address issues of investors' rights and management accountability. This includes the role of executive and non-executive directors in both monitoring management's performance and representing shareholders' interests.

9.6   Problems with ethical codes

There are two problems associated with the use of ethical codes.

Firstly, their generality, which makes the translation of abstract concepts into guides for action difficult. Often individual managers have to make their own interpretation of the codes, which can result in different managers acting differently. Other managers may decide that the codes are too vague to be helpful, and disregard them.

Secondly, senior management may not actively support them. This can result in management feeling pressured to compromise ethical standards whilst achieving organisational goals.

To make ethical codes effective, management must enforce them. Unethical managers must be held responsible for their actions. This means withdrawing privileges and benefits and applying sanctions. Although the enforcement of ethical codes may not be easy, the mere existence of such codes can increase ethical behaviour by clarifying what the expected conduct is.

10   SELF TEST QUESTIONS

10.1   What is organisational culture? (1.2)

10.2   Briefly explain the three determinants of culture. (2.1)

10.3   Describe three characteristics that influence an organisation's culture. (3.1)

10.4   What type of culture is often found in construction, advertising and entertainment organisations? (4.2)

10.5   Describe Handy's four classifications of culture. (4.3)

10.6   How can culture influence strategy? (7.2)

10.7   Define ethics. (8.1)

10.8   Explain the expectations placed on a manager by the British Institute of Management's ethical guide. (9.3)

11   EXAMINATION TYPE QUESTION

11.1   Excellent companies

What, according to Peters and Waterman, are the characteristics of the culture of the 'excellent' organisation? Comment on the possible drawbacks of a strong organisational culture.

(20 marks)

12   ANSWER TO EXAMINATION TYPE QUESTION

12.1   Excellent companies

Peters and Waterman identified the following core values that were associated with 'excellent' organisations:

(a)   **A bias for action:** the excellent companies get on with it. They are analytical in their decision making but this does not paralyse them as it does with some companies.

(b)   **Close to the customer:** they get to know their customers and provide them with quality, reliability and service.

(c)   **Autonomy and entrepreneurship:** leaders and innovators are fostered and given scope.

(d)   **Productivity through people:** they really believe that the basis for quality and productivity is the employee. They do not just pay lip service to the notion 'people are our most important asset'. They do something about it by encouraging commitment and getting everyone involved.

(e)   **Hands-on, value driven:** the people who run the organisation get close to those who work for them and ensure that the organisation's values are understood and acted upon.

(f)   **Stick to the knitting:** the successful organisations stay reasonably close to the businesses they know.

(g)   **Simple form, lean staff:** the organisation structure is simple and corporate staff are kept to the minimum.

(h)   **Simultaneous loose-tight properties:** they are both centralised and decentralised. They push decisions and autonomy as far down the organisation as they can get, into individual units and profit centres. But, as Peters and Waterman state, 'they are fanatic centralists around the few core values they hold dear'.

Though Peters and Waterman stress the positive benefits of having a strong organisational culture there are also potential drawbacks:

(a)   Strong cultures are difficult to change.

(b)   Strong cultures may stress inappropriate values.

(c)   Where two strong cultures come into contact eg, in a merger, then conflicts can arise.

(d)   A strong culture may not be attuned to the environment eg, a strong innovative culture is only appropriate in a dynamic, shifting environment.

Despite these problems it is still possible to agree with Alan Sugar, Chairman of Amstrad, who said in 1987 'It is essential to retain a strong corporate culture and philosophy, otherwise the business can drift and become confused and lost in direction'.

There has been an increasing awareness that companies must understand and relate to the outside world. It is futile to ignore changes in the environment that can disqualify the best intentional strategies. It is foolish to pursue policies for profit improvement that will alienate a large proportion of customers, particularly if they will seek out your competitions or provide a growth market for substitute products. The need to relate to the environment has been recognised for many years. Such authors as Barnard, Simon and Chandler, independently, in the 1950s and 1960s drew attention to environmental effects upon a company's organisation and objectives. One leading book states 'to understand the behaviour of an organisation, you must understand the context of that behaviour ... it has been said that all organisations engage in activities which have as their logical conclusion adjustment to the environment.'

Peters and Waterman point out that many of these books are excellent in relating environmental influences upon the company but give inadequate emphasis to the importance of the customer as an environmental factor.

It is important to remember during our discussion of the topics in this session that boundary management involves all areas where the company and its management touch the outside world. Clearly, the customer is an important, continuous contact and it is a group that dictates the wellbeing of the organisation.

5 TRENDS IN BUSINESS MANAGEMENT AND STRUCTURE

INTRODUCTION & LEARNING OUTCOMES

Syllabus area 11(i)
- The different models of organisational management available to achieve goal congruence while maintaining individual motivation (eg, the creation of Strategic Business Units and the encouragement of entrepreneurial behaviour).

- Trends in business management and structure as evidenced in the business press and other mass media (eg, demerger, strategic alliances, virtual organisations, service centres).

The structural design of business organisations is a difficult task for many chief executives. The complexity of the issues involved means that it is not always done effectively. Many previously successful companies have failed through not re-organising their structure in order to remain competitive.

In this chapter we look in more detail at the types of structure that may be found in practice. We begin by looking at the idea that strategy and structure are shaped by the type of environment in which the organisation operates (simple or complex, stable or unstable); and in this context we look at the work of Burns and Stalker on organic and mechanistic organisations.

There is a two-way pattern of influences between the strategy or strategies adopted by an organisation and the structure of the organisation.

- Given a particular strategy, part of the task of implementation is to ensure an appropriate organisational structure for its achievement.

- In choosing strategies, an organisation must take account of limits imposed by its structure, and must also seek to take advantage of particular features in its structural make-up.

Of course, the structure of an organisation is not fixed unalterably for ever, and so we move on to look at the trends in the general management and structure of organisations.

When you have studied this chapter, you should be able to:

- Discuss ways in which the conflict between centralised control and individual creativity can be managed.

- Explain trends in the general management and structure of organisations.

- Evaluate the management of an organisation and recommend improvements.

1 THE MANAGERIAL FUNCTION OF ORGANISING

1.1 Introduction

Management involves the co-ordination of human and material resources towards objectives accomplishment. The four basic elements of management are:

- toward objectives;
- through people;
- via techniques; and
- in an organisation.

Typical definitions suggest that management is a process of planning, organising and controlling activities. Drucker identifies five basic operations that a manager performs:

- **Sets objectives** - by determining the objectives and describing what needs to be done to achieve them.

- **Organises** - by analysing the activities, decisions and relations required, classifying and dividing the work, creating organisation structure and selecting staff.

- **Motivates and communicates** - by creating a team out of staff responsible for various jobs.

- **Measures** - by establishing targets and measurements of performance that focus on the individual and on the organisation as a whole.

- **Develops people** - by directing, encouraging and training.

1.2   The purpose of organising

Whether in business, government, an orchestra or a football team, people who want to co-operate will work together most effectively if they know the parts they are to play in any team operation and the way their role relates to others. Designing and maintaining these systems and structures is based on co-ordination.

We think of organising as:

- the identification and classification of required activities;

- the grouping of activities necessary to attain objectives;

- the assignment of each grouping to a manager or supervisor with the necessary authority (delegation); and

- the provision for co-ordination horizontally - on the same or similar level within the organisation - and vertically - head office, division and department - in the organisation structure.

The organisational structure should be designed:

- to clarify who is to do what tasks;

- to outline who is responsible for what results;

- to remove obstacles to performance caused by confusion and uncertainty of assignment;

- to furnish decision-making and communication networks reflecting and supporting the organisation's objectives.

1.3   Organisational structure and influences

The organisational structure has been described as the links made between a number of people brought together in order to work together as a body to further an aim. The structure must reflect objectives and plans, because activities derive from them. As this is the area where the decisions of the organisation are made, it must also reflect the authority available to the management of the organisation. Whilst each organisation is different and requires a different structure, its decisions are influenced by the environment. For instance, in a manufacturing industry the organisational structure is based on the capacity of its plant, its sales outlets, its costs and access to raw materials. A service industry on the other hand would base its organisation on the product or products to be serviced, the quantity and area involved and the cost of maintaining staff.

The structure of an organisation is therefore concerned with the grouping of the activities carried on so that it can meet its objectives in the best possible way. It achieves this by assigning certain activities to various parts of the organisation and by providing for the necessary authority and co-ordination. However, the groupings and activities and the authority relationships of the structure must take into account people's limitations and customs. It must ensure that there is no duplication of effort since, apart from the additional costs involved, it could result in the organisation not being competitive within the market place. It might not be able to sell its goods or services as cheaply as someone else.

The actual format of the structure adopted will depend on the influences on and circumstances of a particular organisation. In this sense, a workable organisation structure can never be static. No single type of organisation structure works best in all kinds of situations.

2   ENVIRONMENTAL CONSIDERATIONS

2.1   Types of business environment

Unless business planners are able to identify the actual and potential forces of change on their businesses, they will have no means of knowing what steps to take to minimise the danger or to cash in on the opportunities which the changes present. It is incumbent on strategic planners to take the steps necessary to collect, analyse and interpret relevant information on the key factors, or segments. It may be a case of closing the stable door after the horse has bolted if historic information only is produced, that is, after the changes have taken, or are taking, place. Information must be made available which shows the magnitude and rates of change of significant events and activities.

There are four types of business environment - simple, complex, stable and unstable.

(i)   **Simple environment** - some organisations are fortunate to operate in business environments in which they only have to cope with relatively few uncertainties or change agents. It could be said that these organisations are in simple environments. These types of organisations exist both in commercial and non-profit making organisations.

(ii)   **Complex environment** - the more complex an organisation's environment is, in other words the more variables there are that can change, the more uncertainty it faces. Complexity usually relates to the diversity of the environmental segments, and the extent to which they are interrelated. For example, because of their size and the diversity of their product-market involvement, the Hanson Group of companies operates in a very complex business environment.

Organisations operating in a complex environment should try and reduce the environmental complexity, perhaps by structuring the management tasks round specialist operating areas. This would probably involve segmenting the environment into discrete sectors on a basis that reflects the significance of the different environmental influences on the organisation.

Example

The concept of the *Strategic Business Unit (SBU)* was devised by *General Electric (GE)* of America. In the 1960s GE found that despite substantial growth in sales, its profits were not increasing proportionately. GE's top management came to realise that one of the major causes of the inadequate profits was the complexity and number of its product-markets and the lack of balance between them. Accordingly, therefore, in 1971, it restructured its 170 or so departments into just fifty Strategic Business Units. Other large companies were later to imitate GE by applying the same concept. (We shall examine the role of SBUs later.)

(iii)   **Stable environment** - an organisation operating in a stable environment faces no change of significance or relatively little change in the variables that give rise to uncertainty. The organisation is thus able to place confidence in its forecasts and assumptions. The business managers will be guided by their experience of the business environment in which they operate. They will be influenced by past events and the impact they had on organisational performance. The forecasting methods will mainly be **statistical** by nature, based on projecting from past trends. A manufacturer of standardised products such as aluminium cans is an example of an organisation operating in such an environment. There is, however, still a danger of unanticipated or unpredicted change, which should not be ignored.

Burns and Stalker called these stable type of organisations 'mechanistic systems'. Environmental stability is often reflected in an organisation's design ie, stable environments tend to have stable organisation structure, such as bureaucratic structures. A bureaucratic structure, is likely to work well in this environment, because the organisation is handling information that is largely predictable, therefore systems can be developed and implemented to process the information. For example the Inland Revenue is structured to deal with annual tax returns, the format of which is standardised. As long as matters are largely recurrent and familiar, this kind of structure can be very successful.

(iv)   **Unstable environments** - the degree to which the environment is unstable relates to the rate and frequency of change of the factors that give rise to uncertainty. An organisation that operates in an extremely unstable or dynamic environment is faced by rapid, and probably novel change, and thus plans its future facing a very uncertain business situation.

The business planners operating in this type of environment will need to consider the novelty of future events and not be influenced solely by past events and results. They will need to be very sensitive to change, and forecasting will be based on a mix of statistical and intuitive techniques. There is a danger that the organisational structure and culture will be unable to cope with the change required. A dynamic environment is far more risky than a stable environment.

For example technology may evolve quickly, with frequent product or service changes resulting from changes in customer needs. Burns and Stalker have described successful organisations that function in unstable environments as 'organic systems'. Organic organisations have the following characteristics:

- emphasis on lateral and horizontal flows of communications;

- organisational influence is largely based on knowledge rather than one's position in the structure;

- employees see the 'big picture' in respect of their approach to problem solving and goal setting;

- job definitions are relatively flexible.

Communications are largely horizontal rather than up and down. This type of structure could be described as fluid, with employees working together in groups for a given task.

We can see from this that different types of environment can be classified into two major groups: (a) by speed and nature of change (stable or unstable), and (b) by convolution (simple or complex). Four strategic scenarios can therefore be identified, as illustrated in the diagram below.

Nature of change *Convolutions*	**Stable**	**Unstable**
Simple	Simple stable	Simple unstable
Complex	Complex stable	Complex unstable

These four scenarios represent extremes; a continuum of other situations range between them.

2.2   Organic versus mechanistic organisations

We have already referred to the work of Burns and Stalker, who carried out research during the 1950s on twenty companies in the electronics industry. The study looked at how companies adapted themselves to deal with changing market and technical conditions, having originally been organised on the basis of a relatively stable environment. The researchers were particularly interested in how management systems might change in response to the demands of a rapidly changing environment. The results indicated the need for a different structure when the technology of the market was changing. Two 'ideal types' of management systems were identified: mechanistic systems and organic systems.

- **Mechanistic systems** - this type of organisation was adapted to relatively stable conditions. The problems and tasks of management are broken down into specialisms within which each individual carries out assigned, predefined tasks. A clear hierarchy of control exists, and the responsibility for knowledge and co-ordination is with senior management. Vertical communication is emphasised. This system is similar to a bureaucratic type of organisation. The culture of this type of organisation is role based. Mechanistic organisations cope with new problems of change, innovation and uncertainty by referring the situation to the appropriate specialist or, failing that, to a superior. In many situations, the superior may have to refer the matter higher up the hierarchy. A significant number of decisions relating to this type of circumstance are made by the Chief Executive, and it soon becomes apparent that many decisions can only be made by going to the top. Alternatively, committees or a liaison officer may be appointed to deal with these problems.

- **Organic systems** - organisations that face an unstable environment where new problems continually arise, which cannot be broken down and distributed among the existing specialist roles tend to be organistic. This type of organisation continually adjusts and redefines individual tasks and the contribution required, rather than emphasising specialist knowledge. Interactions and communication (information and advice rather than giving and receiving instructions) may occur at any level as required. Burns and Stalker believe this type of system provides for a high degree of commitment to the aims of the organisation as a whole. Organisation charts detailing exact responsibilities etc are not found in this type of organisation; the culture that exists tends to be task based.

2.3   Relative position of the two systems

Burns and Stalker saw these two systems as polar positions between which intermediate forms could exist. They also acknowledged that organisations could move from one system to the other as external conditions change, and some organisations could operate with both systems at the same time.

Burns and Stalker made the point that there was not one favoured system but rather what was important was to achieve the most appropriate system for a given set of circumstances.

One of the major criticisms made against the mechanistic versus organistic approach is that it assumes that change can best be effected by organic types of structure, when this is not always the case.

3   STRUCTURE

3.1   Choice of organisation structure

Among the factors to be considered when deciding on the organisation structure appropriate to a particular company, are:

(a)   **Size** - Clearly a business controlled by one entrepreneur has quite a different structure from a multi-million pound, multi-national giant.

(b)   **Chosen strategy** - A company pursuing a growth strategy will probably need a different organisation structure from one pursuing a non-growth, low risk strategy. It must be able to move quickly, so the organisation structure must allow quick decisions. This means that chains of command should not be too long.

The organisation needs a department specifically concerned with promoting change. The research and development manager will have a high status in the company. The organisation must be forward-looking - it cannot afford to dwell on yesterday's mistakes.

(c)   **Management style** - An ideal organisation structure cannot be imposed on an organisation regardless of management style. For instance, a programme of decentralisation, however desirable in other circumstances, will be doomed to failure if the chief executive is an autocrat who is reluctant to relinquish control to any appreciable degree.

(d)   **Potential synergy** - The greater the potential synergy, the greater the desirability of integrating a new operation or a new acquisition with the existing operations - for if integration is not achieved in some degree, the potential synergy cannot be realised. On the other hand, weak synergy might suggest a holding company/subsidiary company relationship.

(e)   **Extent of diversification** - With very diverse operations there might even be negative synergy if top management try to interfere in areas they do not understand. This points to decentralisation.

(f)   **Extent of geographical separation** - The greater the geographical distance from the centre, the greater the necessity for decentralised control.

Choice of the best structure is not easy as each has advantages and disadvantages. Whatever type of structure is adopted, it is essential that it promotes communication at and between all levels of management. This means that chains of command should not be too long and that the structure defines clearly the areas of responsibility and authority of different managers. In general, the higher up the organisation tree a decision is taken, the longer term its effects will be, the more departments it concerns, and the greater the number of uncertain factors which affect the decision.

3.2   Structure follows strategy?

Chandler, in *Strategy and Structure*, traced the growth and development of a sample of large US corporations from 1909 to 1959 and found that diversification required new administrative systems to ensure the efficient use of resources in the light of changes imposed by new product/market strategies. His research showed that the multi-divisional structure had evolved as an adaptive response to this need and that this created a type of managerial environment that placed a premium on economic performance and the skills of generalists.

The diversified corporations that Chandler was charting were about to become multinational corporations. As markets opened up, the evolution of a product-market strategy would impose changes on the organisation, leading to a transition from a functional to a multi-divisional structure, based on product-market relationships. This is how Chandler's idea that 'structure follows strategy' came about. He also argued that managers who are close to the operational base and its markets, deal with the day-to-day operations of a large organisation's various divisions more efficiently. Long-term strategy, on the other hand, he saw as best undertaken by those who can stand back and take an overview of the whole organisation.

Scott, following Chandler, developed a model of growth and development that viewed the corporation as moving through several stages as its product-market complexity increased. He saw firms as developing from one-person enterprises to functionally organised (sales, production and research) single business organisations. As the firm began to diversify and to develop multiple product lines, it would then adopt a multidivisional structure.

Subsequent studies by Channon, Galbraith and Nathanson confirm the general claim by Chandler that it is impossible for senior managers at the corporate centre to be sufficiently familiar with the different products and markets served by the different divisions of the corporation, and to make informed decisions. Divisionalisation enables each division to concentrate on the problems and opportunities of its particular business environment. The products/markets in which the organisation operates may be so different that it would be impractical to bring the tasks together in a single body. It is more sensible to split the organisation according to the different products/markets or operations and then to ensure the needs of each division are met by tailoring the operations within the division to the particular business needs.

Most writers seem to agree that organisation structure logically follows after strategy has been decided. However, there are some, including Mintzberg, who cast some doubt on this claim. They argue that, whilst the strategic activities need co-ordinating, the existing structure of the organisation is likely to provide a major barrier to change, as the vested interests of existing personnel are tied up in it. Their view is that the structure limits the strategic options and information flow and shapes strategic thinking. To the extent that such a situation prevailed it could then be argued that 'strategy follows structure'. This is because the existing structure:

- forms part of the internal appraisal;

- might need to be changed - and this takes time;

- directs and filters information from inside and outside the organisation (markets and personnel);

- shapes the deployment of value activities and the management of the linkages between them;

- represents the enterprise's existing priorities - as a result of planned or emergent strategies.

3.3   Consequences of structural deficiencies

According to Child, the following deficiencies may arise out of weak structure.

(a)   Motivation and morale may be depressed, because of

- apparent inconsistency
- little responsibility
- lack of clarity as to what is expected
- competing pressures
- overloading due to inadequate support systems.

(b)   Decision-making may be delayed and faulty, because

- information may be delayed in the hierarchy
- decision-making is too segmented
- decision-makers are overloaded – no delegation
- past decisions are not evaluated.

(c)   Conflict and lack of co-ordination, arising from

- conflicting goals that have not been structured into a single set
- no liaison - people working at cross-purposes
- operators not involved in planning.

(d)   No response to change, because

- there is no established specialist in research and development (R&D) or market research (MR)

- R&D and MR do not talk to each other

- R&D and MR are not mainstream activities.

(e)   High administrative costs, associated with

- 'too many bosses, too few workers'
- excess of procedure and paperwork
- some or all of the other organisational problems being present.

3.4   Strategic choice

Structure is affected by various *contingencies*.

(a)   *Technology* at the operating level

(b)   *Environment* at the strategic level

(c)   *Size* relating to complexity

(d)   *Personnel employed*

These contingencies may or may not be interrelated, and may vary from department to department.

However, as stressed by Child, there is a choice of structure available to management in order that they can pursue the chosen objectives for their individual firms, and such a choice does not rest on technical considerations alone. It can be affected by the politics of the situation and by the style of management preferred. In effect, the general system's law of equifinality applies and there can be many routes to the same goal.

3.5   Limited effect of structure

The effect of structure is limited - it is a means to achieve objectives and cannot be successful if the organisation:

(a)   adopts the *wrong strategy;*
(b)   does not possess the requisite *skills;*
(c)   falls foul of *over-politicisation;*
(d)   possesses inherently *bad morale*.

Moreover, structure by itself cannot resolve *conflict*, although it might bring such conflict out into the open.

4   IDENTIFYING THE LINKS BETWEEN STRATEGY AND STRUCTURE

4.1   Introduction

The organisation of resources - manpower, finance, equipment etc - is crucial to the effectiveness of strategy.   Careful resource planning needs to be carried out, which will include asking questions such as:

(a)   What are the key tasks that have to be completed?
(b)   What control systems exist?
(c)   What changes should be made to resources?

As a result of this planning, it is becoming increasingly common for organisations to change their structure in order to meet more closely the strategic requirements. For example, they may move from a centralised to a decentralised structure, if the organisation is following a strategic initiative based on profit centres.   Or, as we have discussed, is the organisation operating in a complex dynamic environment, which requires it to be very adaptive? If this is the case, the structure must reflect this requirement.

Recent management thinking has started to recognise that strategy making is not necessarily a top-down process, and therefore top-down mechanistic structures may not be appropriate.   Careful consideration has to be given as to how the strategic planning process works in practice, and how the organisation's structure can best complement it.

Organisational structure will be discussed in a later chapter, but in this section we will be looking at the relevance of organisation structures to the strategic planning process. There are two points of view.

One view is that the organisational structure is on a par with the analysis of the environment. Both should be analysed at an early stage in the strategic planning process. In particular, the objectives set for a strategic plan are established after taking into account the 'environment' within the organisation. For example, the social/cultural background of the local employees will influence the structure of an organisation located in a South American country. These influences may be dramatically different from the factors bearing on a North American organisation.

Another view is that the strategic plan is developed from an analysis of the environment. An organisational structure is then developed to implement the strategic plan. For example, top management may have particular views on an appropriate leadership style. In one organisation, the view of good leadership may be 'task based'. This view is derived from the scientific management theories of Taylor. The primary concern would be achieving high levels of efficiency with people in the organisation just factors of production.

As is often the case, the truth is somewhere in the middle. Ideally the structure should reflect the plan and not vice versa, but to attempt to change existing structures without care can lead to tremendous difficulties. A pragmatic approach will often be best.

The examination syllabus follows the view that the strategic plan is developed from an analysis of the environment. An organisational structure is then developed to implement the strategic plan.

4.2   Organisational objectives

We have seen how the high level general mission and goal statements 'cascade' through the organisation, progressively becoming more specific at each level as they filter downwards. This delegation of objectives requires an appropriate management planning and control structure. The way in which responsibility and authority are distributed within the organisational structure is an important part of the culture. For example, a company that is structured and managed as a series of separate and competitive units is likely to have a cohesive culture at the level of these sub-units. This makes collaborative ventures between units difficult.

Reward systems are also important indicators of the type of behaviour that is encouraged within the organisation and can be a barrier to the success of some strategies. For example, a company that has individually based bonus schemes, related to volume of output, will find it difficult to promote strategies requiring teamwork and an emphasis on quality, rather than volume.

4.3   Employees and their organisational objectives

The effectiveness of an organisation is determined by how well the objectives of that organisation are being achieved. Organisations are established to accomplish purposes, which cannot be accomplished by individual action. It would be simple to assume that organisational objectives and individual participant objectives are complementary. The classical theorists believed that employees were compensated through monetary and other inducements for their participation in organisational objectives. But this fails to take into account that people have many needs and aspirations that are not easily met in purely economic terms. Many practices that are developed to increase organisational effectiveness may create human dissatisfactions.

There are a number of possible relationships between organisation objectives and the individual objectives of those working for it; the spectrum covers five categories:

(a)   totally opposing;
(b)   partially opposing;
(c)   neutral;
(d)   compatible;
(e)   identical.

If the objectives of an individual are diametrically opposed to those of the organisation then conflict will result as long as the person remains with that organisation.   If the individual's objectives are only partially opposed to those of the organisation, the best outcome for the organisation is that the individual does not actively hamper achievement of the overall organisational objective.   Where a neutral situation exists the individual does not take an active role in the organisation but goes his own way, if allowed to, whilst the organisation pursues its own goals.   Where compatibility is achieved then most personal and organisational goals can be achieved without harming either party. This is called *goal congruence* whereby the organisation works in such a way as to encourage behaviour that blends in with top management goals.   Occasionally, it is possible that the aims of the individual are identical with those of the organisation for which he/she works and there should be a complete absence of conflict.

The requirements are not too difficult to meet as far as organisational objectives are concerned but obvious problems of definition exist when the objectives of individuals are being considered.   Most people have needs, abilities, skills, aspirations and preferences but their objectives may vary in changing circumstances.   Often people's behaviour is difficult to reconcile with their declared objectives and the correct way to motivate them is difficult to find.

Whenever both the organisation and the individual perceive a positive gain in their relationship with each other, the relationship is likely to be successful.   Personal objectives are all-important to the formation and maintenance of organisation.   An understanding of individual needs and objectives enhances effective organisational management.

4.4   Goal congruence at the strategic level

In an ideal world, all managers would make decisions in line with the goals and objectives of all the relevant stakeholders. These would have to be weighted by some appropriate factors, reflecting the influence of the stakeholders and the strength and degree of importance attached by them to the objective under consideration.   In the imperfect reality of strategic business decisions, where the personal goals of the managers happen to concur with the stakeholder objectives (there is goal congruence), they are much more likely to be motivated to implement the strategy wholeheartedly. However, this is not always the case.

For example, the shareholders of an organisation may wish the managers to adopt a high-risk growth strategy to gain big financial returns, relative to their quite small initial investment. If the strategy fails, they are able to offset their losses against gains made elsewhere in their investment portfolio. They can diversify to reduce their risk. The cost of failure to the managers might well be a loss of job. They cannot diversify their employment portfolio to reduce their risk. The potential return to the manager from the complete success of a high-risk strategy may be much smaller than that available to the investor. It may therefore be insufficient to motivate them to take the risk involved in such a high-growth, focused strategy.

4.5   Goal congruence at the individual level

In successful organisations, company objectives will be compatible with the objectives of the individual. However, it will be appreciated that complex interactions take place between individuals, groups and organisations each affecting the other to a greater or lesser extent.   Likert outlines the properties and performance characteristics of the ideal, highly effective group and, with regard to individual goals and organisational objectives, he theorises the following.

- Objectives of the entire organisation and of its competent parts must be in satisfactory harmony with the relevant needs and desires of the great majority, if not all, of the members of the organisation and of the persons served by it.

- Goals and assignments of each member of the organisation must be established in such a way that he or she is highly motivated to achieve them.

- Methods and procedures used by the organisation and its sub-units to achieve the agreed-upon objectives must be developed and adopted in such a way that the members are highly motivated to use these methods to their maximum potential. To achieve this, the reward system of the organisation - salaries, wages, bonuses, dividends, interest payments - must yield them equitable compensation for their efforts and contribution.

5   ENTREPRENEURIAL ORGANISATIONS

5.1   Role of entrepreneurship in business growth and development

According to Buchanan and Huczynski, an entrepreneur is more than one who founds businesses, he is:

'someone who introduces new technical and organisational solutions to old problems, an innovator who introduces new products processes, new organisational arrangements. ...A person with the entrepreneurial spirit has what is called 'executive drive', a need to do a good job and a need for recognition.'

They claim there is a link between the entrepreneurial spirit and self actualising man's need for achievement - in fact they are singling out the opportunistic entrepreneurs who seek out and thrive on uncertainty, believing that such actions can lead to large rewards.

The motivations of small businessmen vary tremendously although Golby and Johns feel that:

'The need for independence sums up a wide range of highly personal gratification provided by working for oneself and not for anybody else - psychological satisfactions which appear to be much more powerful motivators than money or the possibility of large financial gains.'

Anita Roddick, founder of the Body Shop chain, echoes this ambivalence to growth:

'I believe people are confusing entrepreneurship with opportunism. They measure success by the profit and loss account. In reality, entrepreneurship consists of three things:

- first, the idea one wants to get across
- second, the person promoting it
- third, the money that's necessary to make it happen.

The third is the least important of all: the first is what matters - the integrity of the idea. You must have to believe in what you're doing so strongly that it becomes a reality.'

Smith attempts to explain this paradox by claiming that owner managers can be arranged along a continuum whose polar positions are occupied by what he terms the 'craftsman entrepreneur' and the 'opportunistic entrepreneur'. The latter is far more orientated towards and capable of growth than the former, and it is therefore the opportunists whom Governments and the large companies find appealing, and who are the subject of the remainder of this section.

5.2   Characteristics of opportunistic entrepreneurs

According to Deeks, the owner manager and the professional manager possess different characteristic skills as follows:

Small firms entrepreneur

- adaptive
- diagnostic
- exploitation of change; opportunities
- tactical facility
- pragmatic use of techniques as aid to problem solving
- social skill applied on a social basis
- consequence mitigating decision making

Large firm manager

- predictive
- prognostic
- control of charge
- strategic facility
- co-ordination and control specialists
- manipulative skills applied largely on an interpersonal basis
- event shaping decision making

Entrepreneurship can be encouraged within the economy and since 1979 lower tax rates have boosted investment in smaller business as has the Enterprise Investment Scheme (and its predecessor the Business Expansion Scheme), and deregulation of financial markets. However, the main source of finance remains the joint stock banks and the press carried many complaints from small businesses in 1992 and 1993, when it was widely believed that banks were unhelpful in aiding businesses emerging from a recession.

5.3   Entrepreneurship within large organisations

Organisations can only achieve their goals and objectives through the co-ordinated efforts of their members. The nature and extent of employees' expectations vary widely, as do the ability and willingness of the organisation to meet them. Organisations have expectations and requirements that may be in conflict with an individual's expectations. One of the main contradictions of organisational life is the maintenance of individuality and self-responsibility alongside the creation of co-operation and conformity. Employees are expected to work with others and obey but at the same time to show evidence of creativity and independence.

At times, special organisational arrangements need to be made for fostering and using entrepreneurs. Gifford Pinchot makes the distinction between the intrapreneur and the entrepreneur. Specifically, an intrapreneur is a person who focuses on innovation and creativity and who transforms a dream or an idea into a profitable venture by operating within the organisational environment. In contrast, the entrepreneur is a person who does the same, but outside the organisational setting. We will just use the term 'entrepreneur' to mean a person working within or outside the organisation.

It is a managerial responsibility to create an environment for effective and efficient achievement of group goals. Managers must promote opportunities for innovation and take reasonable risks, even if this means tolerating some failures. Because entrepreneurs need some degree of freedom to pursue their ideas, sufficient authority must be delegated. Unfortunately, innovative people often have ideas that are contrary to conventional wisdom and they are their contributions are not always appreciated.

The distinguishing features of the entrepreneurial system are:

(a)   Work rules and regulations established by oneself to insure goal accomplishment
(b)   Rewards accrue consequent to effective task accomplishment
(c)   Responsibility for daily workloads belongs to the individual
(d)   Job results evaluated by the individual
(e)   Competence judged by the individual
(f)   Long hours accepted to gain personal rewards and achievement
(g)   Day to day work decisions determined by personal job goals
(h)   Job changes made by the individual without permission from anyone
(i)   Personal drive is the most valued characteristic of workers
(j)   Risk taking considered necessary for personal achievement
(k)   Pay based on successful task completion
(l)   Daily work judgements determined largely by personal goals
(m)   Personal drive directed to the achievement of personal goals
(n)   Punishments directly related to failure to achieve personal goals
(o)   Advancement based on goal accomplishment

Many large organisations have sought to introduce the approach and benefits of entrepreneurial behaviour, outlined above, beneath the umbrella of a large company. This approach has been termed 'intrapreneurship'.

There is obviously a link between the creative and the entrepreneurial organisation and much depends on the structure adopted to encourage innovation and creativity. Burgelman feels that this structure should be based on the strategic importance of new business to the organisation and how related that business is to the organisation's current activities. This premise leads to nine organisational designs for **intrapreneurship**.

Operational relatedness   **Strategic importance**

	Very important	*Uncertain*	*Not important*
Unrelated	Special business unit	Independent business unit	Complete spin off
Partly related	New products department	New venture division	Contracting
Strongly related	Direct integration	Micro new ventures department	Nurturing and contracting

There are many problems in managing the interface between a bureaucratic and an entrepreneurial system and Thompson, investigating 21 venture efforts that did not become profitable, came to the following conclusions:

'Ventures teams do not easily fit into going concerns and frequently fail, for multiple reasons, including:

(a)   increased costs, uncertainty, or under-financing
(b)   failure to win acceptance within the firm
(c)   insufficient operating freedom for the venture team
(d)   internal power struggles
(e)   a short-term management perspective
(f)   technical rather than commercially orientated venture managers
(g)   lack of financial or organisational resources for commercial success
(h)   the established division's neglect or resistance to them.'

Conclusion   Intrapreneurship offers many advantages of rejuvenation to a large company. However, the 'big company culture' is itself the major obstacle to successful intrapreneurship.

6   STRATEGIC BUSINESS UNITS (SBUs)

6.1   Central strategic planning and strategic business units (SBUs)

In large organisations the traditional central strategic planning system can become unmanageable if there are many products and markets involved. With so many activities, it becomes extremely difficult for strategic planners to conceptualise the total and plan, co-ordinate and integrate the range of diversity into coherent strategies. Quite simply the company is victimised by its cumbersome size. The danger is that strategies can be added willy-nilly without firm direction or meshing. What is required in this situation is the creation of numerous swift-moving self-managed business units, close and responsive to the market.

More recently, organisations have been using an organisational device generally referred to as a Strategic Business Unit (SBU). These are distinct little businesses set up as units in a larger company, to ensure that a certain product or service is promoted and handled, as though it were an independent business. An SBU preserves the attention and energies of a manager and staff, whose job is to guide and promote that product or product line. At the same time, each SBU has its own distinct set of competitors, and its own strategic plan. It might also have its own mission. It is an organisational technique for preserving the entrepreneurial attention and drive and is characteristic of the small company. However, it is an excellent means of promoting entrepreneurial behaviour, which is likely to be lacking in the larger organisation.

6.2   The strengths of SBUs

Tom Peters writing in his recent book, *'Thriving On Chaos'*, about the need for companies to accept the necessity for management revolution asserts:

'Take all the evidence together, and a clear picture of the successful firm in the 1990s and beyond emerges. It will be:

- flatter (have fewer layers of organisation structure);

- populated by more autonomous units (have fewer central-staff second-guessers, more local authority to introduce and price products);

- oriented toward differentiation, producing high value-added goods and services, creating niche markets;

- quality-conscious;

- service-conscious;

- much faster at innovation; and

- a user of highly trained, flexible people as the principal means of adding value.'

In short the principal benefits of an effective SBU decision-making structure are that it will:

(a)   define the company according to the markets it serves - one SBU per market. (In the same way that a small company always does.);

(b)   enable a complex and dynamic environment to be divided into relatively small, more manageable segments;

(c)   serve as a means of meshing the corporate perspective (macro) with local priorities (micro), thus achieving meaningful vertical management teamwork;

(d)   be a fast, responsive, flat, semi-autonomous decision unit able to be fast-paced if needs be;

(e)   provide the capability for the development of strong expertise and experience, business intelligence and decision making ability within narrow areas of business activity;

(f)   exercise the potential of managers of ability at a level lower than the main board of directors;

(g)   develop general management ability, versatility and flexibility;

(h)   reduce corporate management overload;

(i)   give entity and status to the separate units, and thus promote a competitive spirit, creativity, participation and motivation of all levels of staff and managers in general;

(j)   sharpen responsibility and accountability and generally improve financial control.

6.3   Problems associated with SBU structures

An organisation comprising SBUs has built-in structural inefficiencies; it is less efficient in terms of coping with inter-dependence, integration and co-ordination. It is the primary role of corporate management to be aware of these in-built problems and take steps to resolve them by achieving a sensible balance of resources, the integration of separate strategies and careful monitoring. Other problems include the:

(a)   mushrooming of service costs because of duplication;
(b)   need for specific types of management information by each separate SBU;
(c)   build-up of bureaucracy;
(d)   inefficiencies arising from possible parochialism; and
(e)   reluctance of central management to relinquish control over day-to-day activities.

It is a general view of commentators that the benefits of SBUs outweigh the potential problems.

7   TRENDS IN BUSINESS MANAGEMENT AND STRUCTURE

7.1   Expansion of activities

There are many different types of organisational structures that have been used over the years with varying degrees of success. This demonstrates that there is no 'right' or 'wrong' way for an organisation to be structured. Success has far more to do with how well the chosen organisational structure is implemented, and subsequently managed. However, it is also clear that certain types of structure are more appropriate for particular types of business and at different stages of development.

Complex organisations have expanded their activities and boundaries. Goal elaboration has caused organisations to increase their scope, and new technologies have caused them to encompass additional activities. Organisations frequently respond to environmental uncertainties by expanding their domain and bringing within internal control those forces creating the uncertainty.

The development of the corporate form allowed the business to expand its activities beyond that permitted by the resources of the individual owner. In the early part of the 20th century, the movements towards vertical and horizontal integration were an example of boundary expansion by organisations. More recently, the development of large-scale conglomerates, with activities over a wide industrial area, has been a primary example of boundary expansion.

The managerial system of these conglomerates needs to be substantially more flexible and dynamic than for the more simplified one-product or one-service organisation.

7.2 Growth by acquisition

Growth can happen either organically - the business develops new products, increases market share etc - or through acquisition. Acquisitions - takeovers - of other businesses do create management problems in assimilating the products, customers, suppliers, systems and personnel of other organisations. However, this option has advantages as well.

- Growth by acquisition can usually be achieved much more rapidly than a similar level of organic growth.

- Although acquisitions can be expensive, it is usually possible to pay in 'paper' - ie in shares or other securities of the acquiring company - rather than in hard cash. This is not the case with organic growth which usually only occurs as a result of heavy expenditure on development, marketing etc.

- Acquiring a new business usually involves acquiring a base of technical expertise, know-how and goodwill that can benefit the acquiring company in its existing operations as well.

7.3 Demerger

Divestment or demerger is the process of disposing of part of an organisation's activities, and usually the assets and personnel that relate to it. One motive for doing so might be simply an opportunistic attempt to make a swift profit. Another reason might be a strategic decision to focus management effort on core activities while disposing of areas that distract from them. According to Investors Chronicle, at least 20 of the UK's top 300 companies are breaking themselves up or are under pressure from their shareholders to do so. The message is - 'to release value in a company, the best thing to do is to focus on core business, flog off peripheral assets and, if necessary, split yourself into several parts.' It suggests six options for a failing company under pressure to boost its flagging share price:

(i)   split in half;
(ii)   focus;
(iii)   spin off hidden jewels;
(iv)   sell assets;
(v)   break up; or
(vi)   introduce new faces.

In recent years, there have been a number of high-profile demergers of this type (often referred to as 'unbundling'). What was a single entity becomes two or more entities, often with the same owners (shareholders), but typically with separate management teams.

This latter point is well illustrated in the particular type of divestment known as a management buyout. This term describes the case where a strategic business unit (SBU) is sold off, not to another company, but to the existing management team, who become owners as well as managers in the newly formed entity. This procedure has many advantages.

- The people most likely to make a success of the business - and hence to agree a high price for purchasing it - are the managers who are already intimately familiar with its products, markets, strengths, weaknesses etc.

- The investment return demanded by the new owner managers may be less than is required by the head office of a mammoth organisation in which the SBU is just a very small part.

- Managers can put in some of their own capital, but may very likely also attract investment from venture capital providers.

There are several factors, which may lead management to consider a policy of demerger and a number of benefits that might result from this policy.

Each company should ensure that all parts of the organisation are regularly measured in terms of performance compared with objectives and, if weaknesses are identified, management should assess the possible impact of demerger. If poor performance is identified and the situation is not expected to improve to what management considers an acceptable level, there will be a very strong case for demerger.

Other factors influencing management's decision may be:

(i)   the identification of excess capacity, particularly in mature industries;

(ii)   the financial burden of higher interest rates linked to higher levels of inflation;

(iii)   a change of emphasis from growth to profitability; and

(iv)   increased awareness of the risks of conglomerate diversification and a consequent change of attitude towards the policy.

Benefits of demerger

(a)   Providing the company with additional cash resources. These could be used for (i) reinvestment in successful areas of the organisation, (ii) identifying and undertaking potentially successful projects which would be of more benefit to the firm, or (iii) increasing dividends to shareholders.

(b)   Eliminating an unsuccessful area of the business. This could strengthen the company's and management's position in the event of a possible hostile take-over bid.

7.4   Global organisations and multinationals

There are several global products (such as Coca-Cola and Marlboro cigarettes) and some global markets (financial), but no global companies. To be truly global, a company should not really have a home base that is significantly more important to it than any other.

Some multinationals have altered their mission statements to incorporate global aspirations because they find it necessary to develop global strategies to compete effectively. A global strategy can be contrasted with a multi-domestic or multinational strategy, in which separate strategies are developed for different countries and are implemented autonomously. A global strategy is conceived and implemented in a worldwide setting. Some of the components and assembly involved might be located throughout the world in a search for cost advantages. The management may make plant location decisions solely to bypass trade barriers and gain access to markets.

Multinationals take various forms in that they might be focused on a relatively narrow range of products or services, but sell them in a wide range of countries. They can be vertically integrated, and manufacture in one country and sell in another or vertically integrated in several different regions of the world. Oil companies extract oil from a limited number of countries, refine it in other countries and distribute and market the finished product all over the world.

Alternatively, the multinational can be a conglomerate that uses its geographic spread of operations as a way of reducing overall risk or as a way of achieving economies of scale in each area of its operations.

7.5   Strategic alliances

As we noted with SBUs, some organisations are trying to retain some of the innovation and flexibility that is characteristic of small companies. They are balancing between bureaucracy and entrepreneurship by forming strategic alliances (closer working relationships) with other organisations.

Strategic alliances also play an important role in global strategies, where the organisation lacks a key success factor for some market. This may be distribution, a brand name, a selling organisation, the technology, R&D or manufacturing capability. To remedy this deficiency internally would often require excessive time and money.

A strategic alliance is a long-term collaboration bringing together the strengths of two or more organisations to achieve strategic goals. For example, IBM formed links with Ricoh for distribution of low-end computers. This allowed them to move into the Japanese market quickly, inexpensively and with a relatively high prospect for success. It can also help result in improved access to information and technology.

Some organisations are using strategic alliances to extend their reach without increasing their size. Others are motivated by the benefits associated with a global strategy. A strategic alliance can take many forms, from a loose informal agreement to a formal joint venture. They include partnerships, joint ventures and contracting out services to outside suppliers.

7.6   The relationship enterprise

In a study entitled, *The Global Corporation - obsolete so soon,* Cyrus Friedheim predicts that current economic and political developments will mean that today's global firms will be superseded by the 'relationship enterprise', a network of strategic alliances among big firms, spanning different industries and countries, but held together by common goals which encourage them to act almost as a single firm. He reckons that these relationship enterprises will be corporate juggernauts by early next century, and larger than all but the world's six biggest economies.

He has a vision where, early in the 21st century, Boeing, British Airways, SNECMA (a French aero engine maker) Siemans and TNT (an Australian parcel delivery firm) might together win a contract to build ten new airports in China. As part of this, British Airways and TNT would receive preferential routes and landing slots, the Chinese government would buy all state aircraft from Boeing-SNECMA and Siemans would provide all the air traffic control systems for all ten airports.

Friedheim believes the conventional model of the global organisation is flawed because most of the organisations are still perceived as having a home base, with the big decisions kept firmly at home. This home country bias, in conjunction with other external constraints hinders an organisation's efforts to become truly global. For instance, when capital is limited, firms tend to protect their home market at the expense of developing untapped overseas markets. There is also the problem of nationalism - nobody likes foreigners controlling their industries. To the extent that global organisations have a home country, means that governments will perceive this and place them at a political disadvantage. A relationship enterprise is one way to side-step these constraints. A multinational alliance of independently owned firms can draw on ample funds, can dodge antitrust barriers, and with home bases in all the main markets they have the political advantage of being a local firm almost anywhere.

7.7   Virtual organisations

Definition   A virtual enterprise (or organisation) is an association constructed from both administratively and geographically distributed business units or organisations.

For an international company operating worldwide, the creation and transformation of knowledge is paramount. In this environment, the trend in organisation structure is the 'virtual organisation'. It happens where there is cross-border alliance and a network of organisations designed to: share technology or facilities; agree on common standards; or exploit a particular market opportunity. Such an enterprise is, by definition, flexible, dynamic and responsive.

Its aim is to provide an organisational solution to problems posed by the uncertainties arising from increasingly intense global competition. Along with increasing reliance on information technology (IT), the idea of the virtual organisation emphasises:

- the decentralisation of control;
- the creation of more flexible patterns of working;
- a greater empowerment of the workforce;
- the displacement of hierarchy by teamworking;
- the development of a greater sense of collective responsibility; and
- the creation of more collaborative relationships among co-workers.

The key element in supporting the transformation is IT. This is mainly through the systems that facilitate co-ordination and communication, decision-making and the sharing of knowledge, skills and resources.

7.8   Service centres

Service centres are a way of sharing services within an organisation. By taking certain processes that are managed individually by different business units and instead managing them centrally is becoming the new way forward. The organisations of the future are going to embody this approach because it combines the best of the original centralised approach, in terms of expertise and economy, with the best of the decentralised model of organisational structure.

Management thinking in the 1990s has been strongly influenced by the concept of core competencies, where companies focus on what they know how to do well, and outsource activities in which they do not have a particular capability. Setting up a service centre is a way, if not to outsource, then at least to liberate business unit management from the burden of managing non-core activities.

The main aim of a service centre is to increase efficiency and effectiveness. As pan-European and even global competition becomes a reality and, as more and more low cost countries participate in the world economy, it becomes crucial to achieve cost efficiencies in those areas where no other competitive advantage can be achieved. A good example of this would be internal financial support functions. In this case, to achieve minimal human intervention, it requires maximum automation. Since this requires substantial technological investment, it is only economically feasible when a critical mass of transactions is brought together and processes are standardised.

As the European economies integrate and country borders lose their relevance, companies evolve from a multinational (presence within multiple countries) to a transnational operating model (operations across multiple countries). This is often driven by the need to organise customer service support and procurement on a European basis. The trend towards the transnational model means an increase in service centres.

In the current decade, the 'network organisation' will emerge as the next phase in the evolution of organisations. The essence of this type of structure is to let business partners perform those processes with a higher return on investment and for which they have a comparative advantage.

8   SELF TEST QUESTIONS

8.1   What are the five basic operations that a manager performs? (1.1)

8.2   Describe four types of business environment. (2.1)

8.3   What type of system provides for a high degree of commitment to the aims of the organisation? (2.2)

8.4   Explain the consequences of structural deficiencies. (3.3)

8.5   Why is the effect of structure limited? (3.5)

8.6   What are the possible relationships between organisation objectives and the individual objectives of those working for it? (4.3)

8.7   In terms of individual goals and organisational objectives, what are the characteristics of the ideal, highly effective group? (4.5)

8.8   According to Deeks, the owner manager and the professional manager possess different characteristics. Give two examples of each. (5.3)

7.9   What is an SBU? (6.1)

7.10   Explain what is meant by 'demerger' . (6.3)

7.11   Briefly describe a strategic alliance. (7.5)

8   EXAMINATION TYPE QUESTION

8.1   Organic organisation

You are required to describe **five** features of an 'organic' organisation, explaining how these affect the operations of the organisation.   **(20 marks)**

9   ANSWER TO EXAMINATION TYPE QUESTION

9.1   Organic organisation

Answer Plan

(a)   Define 'organic', contrast to 'mechanistic', quote Burns and Stalker
(b)   Five features:
   • management style
   • control
   • communications
   • change
   • structure

Burns and Stalker in their book 'Management of Innovation' studied the relationship between management practices and characteristics of the external environments, in particular, ability to innovate. They defined two main management systems:

• mechanistic where formal communications and hierarchy existed;

• organic where the looser structure was more suitable for coping with unstable conditions and unpredictable problems.

Burns and Stalker discussed five main features that identified an 'organic' organisation.

1   The management style tended to be strongly participative wherein a manager would adopt a role of being a guide and counsellor rather than an issuer of instructions. The manager would talk through problems with staff members, eliciting their involvement by encouraging them to contribute their knowledge, ideas and experience. In such discussions the manager would be a provider of advice and information and seek to achieve a consensus decision. This open approach would encourage staff to understand the difficulties facing the organisation and to adopt the solution as their own. In this way, staff members feel protected when volunteering their ideas and able to exercise initiative when faced with rapidly changing circumstances. Management encourage staff to think of

themselves as tackling a task rather than fulfilling a company duty. This builds a greater sense of action and encourages initiative. Under such an approach, staff feel valued as individuals and their contribution increases. Harvey Jones comments that he never ceased to be surprised in ICI at the performance that young managers could achieve if they were given freedom and encouragement.

2   Inherent in any organic system is the presence of a control system, which is based on results to be achieved rather than the means of getting there. Whereas a mechanistic organisation would exercise tight control through detailed rules and procedures, an organic system relies on motivation to achieve an agreed result. An individual working in isolation cannot achieve many organisational tasks; the motivated efforts of a team of people is necessary. The organic approach encourages this by allowing freedom of action to members of a team to determine their own methods and pursue their own ideas to achieve results. Typically, a management by objectives system evolves whereby a manager will be closely involved in determining the parameters of the task, the obstacles that need to be overcome and the result expected. Once that stage is achieved, the manager will maintain a watching brief and may only become involved in detail if the team members encounter a problem that is beyond their scope.

Control therefore is results based and is effected by means of a network of control rather than being formally exercised by an individual operating through a hierarchy.

3   One feature of an organic system, strongly emphasised by Burns and Stalker, was the nature of the communication system.

In a mechanistic system, communication will flow in a vertical direction, as staff report strictly to their boss within their own function. The nature of such communications tends to be commands and decisions issued downwards and a statement of results achieved passing upwards.   Such communication tends to be formalised between different status levels in the same function. Such a communication system would prevent a task centered control system and open style management. Therefore, an organic structure will ensure that staff at all levels feel involved in the issues and are kept informed of aspects that affect their operations.   This cannot be restricted to vertical communication flows, since team tasks will require substantial horizontal communication.   In addition, a formalised communication system cannot keep pace with rapid changes in environmental factors; it is important to develop a strong information communication system.   The organic structure will achieve this by encouraging lateral communication links, whereby a member of staff could freely contact members of other departments, even where there is a difference in status.

4   An organic structure recognises that adapting to change will require flexibility in assigning work, whereas a mechanistic organisation would have clearly defined roles. This is discouraged in an organic structure where there is continual redefinition of tasks as a result of interaction between individuals.

Fluid definitions of roles and tasks will enable individuals to respond to changes with minimum control. This is important where an organisation faces intense competition or rapid technological changes.   In such circumstances, assessment and re-adjustment to the new order are clearly important.   Tom Peters in his book 'Thriving on Chaos' points out that rapid changes in environmental factors (eg, social demands, economic changes, customer patterns, etc) will intensify and require management to adopt ever more fluid approaches.

Individuals will see their contribution as being part of a team achieving a result, rather than fulfilling an individual role. This will mean redefinition of individual's tasks and a willingness to adopt to new demands.

5   An organic organisation will develop a management structure that enables lateral communication and rapid adjustment to change.

The specialist knowledge of individuals will be recognised as contributing to achievement of team tasks and ultimately, organisation objectives. To bring together the line management and staff advisory functions, an organic organisation will develop a network structure. Here control, authority and communication will operate through networks, not through a strict, formal hierarchy. For example, control will be vested jointly in line managers and technical staff, requiring both parties to co-ordinate to achieve the final goal. A matrix organisation structure is likely to develop as joint ownership of tasks and objectives is defined.

Note: This is a straightforward question if you are familiar with the work of Burns and Stalker. The two main pitfalls to avoid are:

1   merging one aspect with another (eg, management style with structure) so that the identity of each of the five aspects is lost;

2   contrasting organic and mechanistic systems to any great extent. This is not asked for in the question.

6 ORGANISATIONAL MANAGEMENT AND STRUCTURE

INTRODUCTION & LEARNING OUTCOMES

Syllabus area 11(ii)   The different structures which might be adopted by a business organisation and how the various components of those structures interrelate (ie, entrepreneurial, functional, divisional, matrix, network and complex).

There is a two-way pattern of influences between the strategy (or strategies) adopted by an organisation and the structure of the organisation.

- Given a particular strategy, part of the task of implementation is to ensure an appropriate organisational structure for its achievement.

- In choosing strategies, an organisation must take account of limits imposed by its structure, and must also seek to take advantage of particular features in its structural make-up.

We begin this chapter by examining the pattern of influences in more detail. Of course, the structure of an organisation is not fixed unalterably for ever, and so we move on to look at the choice of an optimum structure and the methods of changing the structure if it appears appropriate to do so.

It soon becomes apparent that no one structure is ideally adapted to all of the different types of organisation that may exist and our next step is to revisit 'contingency theory' - the idea that the ideal structure will vary, depending on the circumstances of particular organisations. This leads to a discussion on the problems of comparing organisations.

When you have studied this chapter, you should be able to:

- Explain the relative merits of a range of different organisation structures.

- Recommend and evaluate changes to the structure of organisations.

1   ORGANISATION STRUCTURE AND DESIGN

1.1   The links between strategy and structure

The organising process consists of the following six steps (although the first two are part of the planning process):

(i)   establishing organisational objectives and deciding on the strategy;

(ii)   devising supporting objectives, policies and plans;

(iii)   identifying and classifying the activities needed to accomplish the plans;

(iv)   grouping these activities to suit the human and material resources available;

(v)   delegating the authority to perform the activities to the head of each group; and

(vi)   linking the groups together horizontally and vertically, through authority relationships and information flows.

1.2   The development of structure

Specialisation is the basis on which all structure is founded. For the efficient running of an undertaking which has grown too big for control by a single individual, key activities must be grouped. Roles, tasks and lines of authority and responsibility must be established, and relationships and lines of communication must be specified.

An important feature of any organisation is the number of people who report to any single individual; a point recognised by early writers and elevated to the status of a principle. Attempts by managers to resolve this problem have produced various forms of organisation. The limitation on the number of subordinates that can be directly managed would restrict the size of the organisation if they did not group activities and people into departments.

1.3   Fundamentals of structuring

Lawrence and Lorsch claim that the process of structuring consists of two basic processes, which they term differentiation and integration:

(a)   **Differentiation**

 'The state of segmentation of the organisation into sub-systems, each of which tends to develop particular attributes in relation to the requirements posed by its relevant external environment.'

Differentiation consists of vertical differentiation - establishing a hierarchy; and horizontal differentiation - setting up various departments. Differentiation must occur to achieve economies of scale, including:

- technical economies (machine utilisation and labour specialisation);
- managerial economies;
- financial and marketing economies; and
- risk spreading economies.

(b)   **Integration**

 'The process of achieving unity of effort among the various subsystems in the accomplishment of the organisational tasks.'

Integration consists of both co-ordination and control. Integration is essential for utility of direction - towards the common goal.

1.4   Influences on and dimensions of organisational structure

As we have already noted in an earlier chapter, clearly stated and agreed objectives will provide a basis for the division of work, the grouping of duties into sub-units and a suitable pattern of organisation to achieve those objectives. It will also facilitate systems of communication between different parts of the organisation and determine the extent of decentralisation and delegation. The nature of the organisation and its strategy will indicate the most appropriate organisational levels for different functions and activities and the formal relationship between them.

Certain variables determine the dimensions of organisational structure. They include:

- the grouping of activities - sections, departments, divisions and larger units;
- the responsibility of employees - allocation of tasks, job specialisation and job definition;
- the power, status and hierarchical relationships (authority system);

- the span of control;

- formal organisational relationships - the planned and formalised policies, procedures and controls that guide the activities and relationships of the people in the organisation (administrative system); and

- information technology (IT).

The recent impact of IT will have significant impact on the structure, management and functioning of the organisation because of the effect it has on patterns of work, the formation and structure of groups, the nature of supervision and managerial roles. Computer-based information and decision support systems influence choices in design of production and/or service activities, and may influence the centralisation/decentralisation of decision-making and control systems.

New technology has resulted in fewer management levels because it allows employees at clerical/operator level to not only check their own work, but to take on a wider range of functions.

There are other factors, which could potentially influence the structure of an organisation. They include:

- the size of the organisation;

- the nature of the activity undertaken;

- the inherent complexity of its departments, sections and groups both within themselves and in their relationships with each other;

- the age of the organisation - the length of time it has been in existence;

- the seasonal flow of business during the year;

- the objectives and goals of this organisation;

- the geographical location of the organisation and its various units;

- the degree of centralisation in the organisation;

- the numbers and ratios of differing types of staff eg, administrative and production or technical;

- the degree of automation or mechanisation.

1.5   Organisation charts

Definition   Organisation charts are diagrammatic illustrations of organisation structures. Their purpose is to show:

(a)   **Directions of responsibility** - the chart indicates the direct relationship between a group and its immediate superior and subordinates.

(b)   **Relationships** - charts can show the relationship between the various units, showing the line, functional and staff units.

The following statements can be made by way of explanation of a chart:

(a)   It indicates the lines of authority and accountability.

(b)   There is no significance in some functions, products or areas appearing on the same lateral line. For example, the Northern Region manager might not be of equal status to the International and European manager.

(c)   The chart does not go below middle management level. Thus, there is no illustration of the positions of operatives, assistants, clerical workers, etc. Each functional, product or area could have its own organisation chart.

(d)   The chart does not indicate the full responsibilities. Thus the facilities provided by the management information systems manager, would be available to all departments.

(e)   The chart does not show that in practice several line managers would co-operate and would be in relationship with each other. For example, any production project would involve consultation between at least the production, purchasing, marketing and accounting heads.

(f)   The chart does not indicate channels of communication. Flows would be established, but it is not possible to incorporate them into a chart of this sort (particularly lateral flows).

1.6   Individual authority relationships

Within the organisation, people must be organised so that they know what to do and whom to ask for advice. Generally, you find in most organisations there are four types of individual authority relationships:

(a)   line;
(b)   functional;
(c)   staff; or
(d)   lateral.

With a **line relationship,** authority flows down through the structure. There is a direct relationship between superior and subordinate, with each subordinate responsible to only one person. For example, authority flows from the MD to managers, section leaders, supervisors and so on. Line relationships are associated with functional or departmental division of work and organisational control.

Functional relationships are those between people in specialist or advisory positions, and line managers and their subordinates. The specialist is available to all departments but has no direct authority over staff using the service. For example, the relationship that exists when a specialist such as the IT manager contributes a service to line managers.

Staff relationships occur when senior members of staff appoint assistants. They do the work assigned to them by their manager, but have no authority to do any type of work other than in the name of that manager. They can only exercise representative authority.

Lateral relationships exist between people in different departments or sections - mainly on the same level. They are based on contact and consultation and are necessary to maintain co-ordination.

2.   THE BASIC STRUCTURAL FORMS

2.1   The entrepreneurial structure

This structure is built round an owner-manager who takes all the key decisions. All power and authority resides in one person. This type of business is often started by an individual, who has a great deal of expertise in one of the functional areas eg, manufacturing or selling.

The entrepreneurial structure

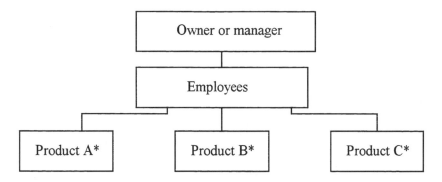

*(Although, throughout, the term 'product' is used to describe the output of a business, this section could apply equally well to companies that produce only 'services'.)

This type of business produces a single product, or a related group of products, and the owner, or manager, is responsible for strategic and operational management. Thus, it is a discrete, self-contained and largely self-controlled business unit. It is equivalent to a strategic business unit (SBU) in a divisionalised organisation. It has the benefits of quick decision-making and short lines of communication. However, it is very dependent on the capabilities of the owner/manager.

2.2   Functional structure

The functional structure shown overleaf is perhaps the most obvious and the most common structure for organising work. It is present in most organisations at some level.   The basic characteristics of:

- **selling** - finding customers, clients, patients, students or members who will agree to accept the goods or services at a price or for a cost;

- **production** - creating utility or adding utility to a good or service; and

- **finance** - raising and collecting, safeguarding and spending the funds of the organisation;

are widely accepted and each has a necessary specialisation. These activities may be co-ordinated through rules, planning systems, the organisation hierarchy and sometimes specialist liaison departments or joint committees. Each functional director then reports to the managing director.

There is often a variation in terminology eg, oil companies are sometimes divided into exploration, production, refining, marketing and finance departments. Hospitals have no selling departments and churches have no production department but this does not mean that these activities are not undertaken - they are either unspecialised or of minor importance and combined with other activities.

The hierarchical structure shown below involves sub-division into specialised departments. There are levels of authority, responsibility and accountability within each department, and with the board of directors. Co-ordination may be achieved through:

- rules and procedures;

- various aspects of planning eg, goals and budgets;

- the organisational hierarchy;

- personal contacts; and sometimes liaison departments eg, there could be a liaison department between production, R&D and marketing to handle design or change problems.

The functional structure

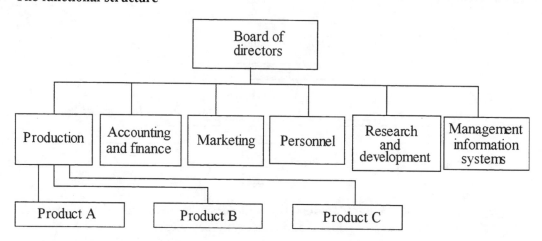

The justification for this type of structure is that by concentrating similar resources in one area of the business, the greatest possible level of economies of scale can be realised. They are felt to be of value when large-scale investments are needed in certain areas, which can only be justified on a group-wide basis. The areas of product and process research and development, IT and many aspects of finance and accounting are good examples where the potential benefits from economies of scale can be significant.

There are two problems with this structure. Firstly, where the organisation is trading with a wide range of products, in a diverse group of markets, there might be a lack of market focus. Secondly, as specialists are given executive authority for their activities throughout the undertaking, there is conflict with the principle of unity of command.

2.3   Product orientated structures

As the number of products produced by an organisation increases, functional design at all levels of the organisation may not be appropriate. In a multi-product organisation, such as Heinz (the food processing company), a product orientation is used as a modification of the functional structure. Usually each major product or product line is managed by a senior manager who in turn reports to the chief executive or board member. This structure establishes each product, or group of products, as an integrated unit within the framework of the company. The main functions of production, sales, people and finance are apportioned to the products, so each product group could have its own specialist of accounting personnel, technical, etc. Such an organisation allows considerable delegation by top management and clear profit accountability by division heads.

The advantages of product divisionalisation are as follows.

*   The focus of attention is on product performance and profitability. By placing the responsibility for product profitability at the division level, they are able to react and make decisions quickly on a day-to-day basis.

*   It encourages growth and diversity of products, for example, by adding additional flavours, sizes, etc. to capture other segments of the market. This, in turn, promotes the use of specialised equipment, skills and facilities.

*   The role of general manager is encouraged with less concentration upon specialisation. This promotes the wider view of a company's operations – 'the helicopter ability' highly prized by John Harvey-Jones and others.

The disadvantages of product divisionalisation are as follows.

*   It is difficult to maintain centralisation of services such as accounting services and R & D economically. There have been instances of product managers having heavy central expenses, over which they have no control.

- As with most divisionalisation approaches, there is a need for central co-ordination to ensure that an overall view is taken at company level, not just at product level. Michael Parker has defined this approach as a 'horizontal strategy'.

- Success is dependent on the ability of the people in charge of a product. Such positions are general management, not specialist, and as already mentioned, there is a shortage of skilled general managers in the UK and also in the USA.

The operating divisions of General Motors detailed below are organised along product lines.

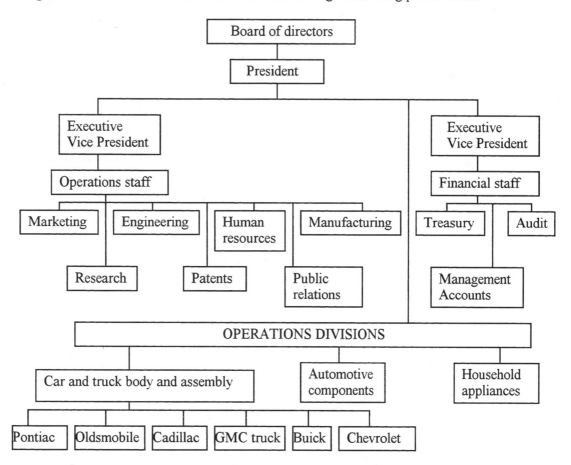

Product divisionalisation is generally preferred over, say, geographic divisionalisation when the product is relatively complex and requires high cost capital equipment, skilled operators and significant administrative costs. This is the situation in the car industry, farm machinery manufacture and electronics industry.

Each product manager is accountable for the division's performance. Usually the product manager has control over most of the major functions that are involved with the product's production and sale. Their responsibilities would include for example:

(a) liaising with production management regarding processing/production schedules;
(b) discussing pricing levels, sales and marketing budgets with the accounts function;
(c) working with R & D on new products and product changes.

2.4   Grouping by geographical location

With geographic divisionalisation, the enterprise is organised by regions or countries. The major international accountancy firms tend to follow this structure. A possible road transport company structure is outlined below:

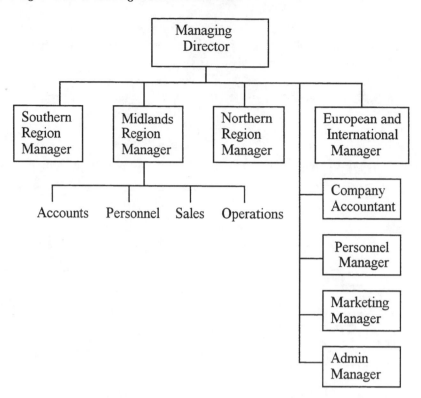

Carried to completion, the geographic division becomes a relatively complete administrative unit in itself. The geographic unit can be organised by function or product. The effect of the geographic division at company level is to draw a territorial boundary around these basic components.

(a)   Geographic divisionalisation is a favoured method amongst companies that have wide geographical areas - where it is important that activities in any area should be grouped and assigned to a manager. Even in international companies, not all functions will be split geographically - for example, finance, management development and training will usually be based at head office.

Geographic divisionalisation is adopted when customer needs, or product characteristics, can best be satisfied on a local basis. In addition, when the product itself is not so complex or capital insensitive as to make the establishment of regional operations too costly or impractical. This would typically happen when the tastes and demands of customers vary greatly between geographical areas and are satisfied by local bases. Consider the differing needs of an estate agency chain, which must be geographically based and that of an insurance agency, which is less clear cut.

(b)   There are important advantages offered by geographical divisionalisation.

(i)   Based in local markets, the organisation can identify and respond quickly to local opportunities.

(ii)   Profitability for each region can be clearly assigned, and delegation is encouraged.

(iii)   Identity with the local community can often provide opportunities not available to a periodic visiting salesperson.

(iv)   It provides goods training ground for general managers.

(v)   It allows companies to take advantage of economies of local operations. For example, a company may be able to expand production in a low-cost area and feed the finished product to other geographical areas. Consider, for example, the current pattern of clothing and electrical goods manufactured in the Far East being shipped to other geographical areas.

(c)   The drawbacks tend to be general and rarely outweigh the advantages where an international company wishes to satisfy customer needs on a local level.

   (i)   There is a requirement for general management abilities.

   (ii)   Despite the great improvements in communications in the last decade, there is still a problem for top management controlling an international company divided between various geographical areas.

   (iii)   The maintenance of central services is difficult, and the pressure to base services such as personnel, purchasing and management locally can increase feelings of independence. Strong central planning is often necessary to ensure overall group performance. Hanson Trust has been very successful in this respect, despite a strong geographical split between UK and USA.

2.5   Divisional structure

This method of grouping is essentially a mixture of functional and geographical or product grouping. Product or geographical grouping is then established within each group. Responsibility is allocated by function, with some functions, for example personnel and finance, existing only at head office. Each division is now responsible for its own functions in relation to a related group of products.

Effectively, each division is a separate business (SBU) operating as a profit centre, having an allocation of capital and being entirely responsible for all stages within its scope of activities. Centralisation would remain to the extent that the activities and scope of the divisions would be subject to the overall strategy and policy of the company.

The divisional structure

Strategic planning in this environment becomes a complex hierarchical process.

(a)   Corporate strategic planning takes place at central board level. This is concerned with guiding the divisions so that the competitive advantages of a diversity of business accrue to the company, and encouraging each division to plan to take maximum advantage of its individual position.

(b)   Divisional planning is concerned with developing a portfolio of products.

(c)   Operational planning is at the functional level within divisions.

Breaking the business down into appropriately defined operating divisions eg, SBUs, is the best way of focusing managerial attention on specific markets and products. The divisional managers are made directly responsible for their unit's operations in a specified market with a specified range of products or services. This should ensure that a clearly defined competitive strategy is developed and implemented in each of the divisions. If this is done, a series of appropriately different, sustainable competitive advantages can be developed.

Such a level of managerial market focus is difficult to achieve in a purely functionally organised group, but the completely divisionalised structure cannot achieve the same economies of scale, particularly if each unit is effectively a stand-alone, self-sufficient business. Not surprisingly, mixed organisational structures have been developed which try to obtain the benefits of both the traditional formats.

2.6   Complex or hybrid structures

There are numerous variations and combinations of different types of organisation structure. In fact, it is unusual for an organisation to have just one organisation form. Most organisations are hybrids or combinations of structures. The reasons for such variations are due to the practical needs of the organisation. Management usually implements structural designs that best meet their needs for efficiency and effectiveness. As time passes, organisations often alter their structure to reflect changes in their goals, strategy and the environment.

2.7   Matrix structures

A limitation of organisation charts is that they tend to appear rigid, and may ignore many vital aspects of the essential relations that exist within an organisation. A matrix structure (shown below) was an attempt to overcome this shortcoming by combining functional and product or project grouping.

The grid/matrix approach came into being because the US Government decided it did not wish to deal with a number of specialised executives when negotiating defence contracts and insisted that contractors appointed project managers. The concept has now been extended to whole organisations (Lockheed Aircraft, British Airways) as well as to major divisions as in ICI and in schools of polytechnics/universities, etc eg:

Course Responsibility (Product)	*BA Business Studies*	*BA European Business*	*MBA*
Subject Responsibility(Function)	Mr R White	Miss J Brown	Mrs T Black
Accounts Miss V Red	Fred	Susan	Simon
Economics Mr A Green	Ian	Frank	Jill
Sociology Mr G Blue	Mary	Tony	Alan

In this approach the course leaders (project/product co-ordinators), responsible for course management, would share their authority with the subject leaders (functional heads), responsible for academic development and research.

The matrix structure may be appropriate where there are at least two significant criteria for success. For example, a multinational company produces three sets of product ranges - Product A, Product B and Product C, and sells the product in three geographical areas - Europe, USA and South America. The management of each product range is equally important, as is the responsiveness to the needs of the different geographical areas. The product managers and area managers have equal weight. Thus the manager of the US area must liaise with the managers of Product A, B and C but does not have authority over them or vice versa.

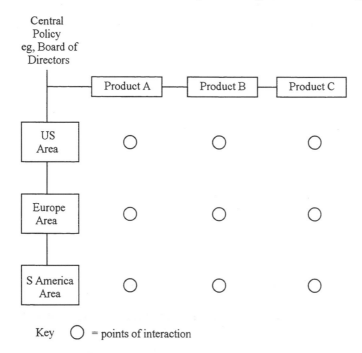

Key ◯ = points of interaction

The advantages of matrix structures include:

- emphasis on the completion of products or projects;

- enforced communication between the heads of the functions and the heads of the projects, products, geographical areas etc;

- the operation of individual accountability.

The problems associated with matrix management are:

- possible role ambiguity in team members, finding that they are seeking to satisfy two bosses;

- the difficulty in balancing authority, responsibility and power between the functional and project heads.

3   MINTZBERG' S THEORY

3.1   Mintzberg's principles of organisational design

When managers are thinking about designing the structure of organisations, they will be swayed by the prevailing orthodoxy. For many years bureaucratic principles were central to management thinking (Taylor and later the Classical School). Today, a major influence on management thinking is the approach of Henry Mintzberg. He advances the view that:

(i)   All labour in an organisation has to be divided into distinct tasks.
(ii)   Co-ordination is needed between the people carrying out the different tasks.

Mintzberg argues that the organisation structure exists to co-ordinate the activities of different individuals and work processes. The nature of co-ordination changes with the increasing size of an organisation. In small organisations, mutual adjustment is sufficient but as organisations increase in size increased reliance is placed upon standardisation as a means of co-ordination.

Co-ordination is achieved in one or more of the following ways.

- **Standardised work processes** - exists where the work is specified, and everybody works in the same way. It is usually the work of the technocrats to design and develop these systems of work.

- **Standardised outputs** - through such things as product or service specifications. Whilst the results are standardised, the means are not.

- **Standardised skills and knowledge** - even though each job is performed independently. This is an important co-ordinating mechanism in professional activities and specifies the kind of training needed to perform the work.

- **Direct supervision** - exists throughout the hierarchy where individuals issue instructions and monitor performance. One person has a specific co-ordinating role.

- **Mutual adjustment** - co-ordination results from internal communication and through informal contact between the people performing their organisational roles. This exists in simple structures where people work closely together. It also applies to some complex tasks eg, in a research project if the outcome is uncertain, colleagues will adjust their activities in the light of new findings.

- **Standardisation of norms** - exists where co-workers share the same beliefs.

The relative complexity of the work affects the method chosen, as shown in the following diagram.

Complexity of work   **Type of co-ordination**

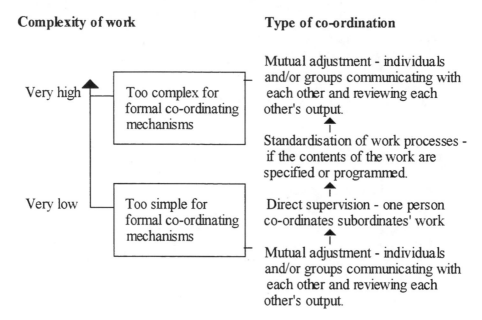

3.2   Building blocks

Mintzberg has suggested that organisational structure is more complex than just differentiating between hierarchical types. His ideas consist of building blocks and co-ordinating mechanisms, which make up the detailed configuration of the organisation. The importance and relative size of these blocks will vary with organisations.

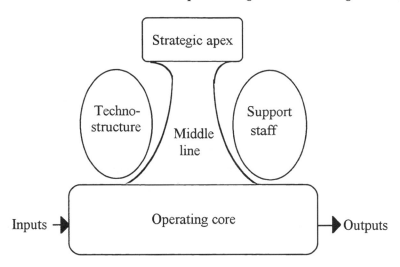

Mintzberg's five groups are:

• **The operating core** - this is made up of the organisational members who are directly involved in the production of goods and services.

• **The technostructure** - refers to staff who provide a technical input without being directly engaged in core activities. The members of this group standardise the work, though its members do not actually supervise detailed production. These include the accountants, computer specialists and engineers.

• **The strategic apex** - refers to the higher levels of management within the organisation. It develops with the expansion of the organisation. Their tasks include strategy formulation and boundary management - imposing general direction in line with the organisation's mission.

• **The middle line** - is the hierarchy of authority between the apex and the operating core. People in this area administer the work done, converting the wishes of the strategic apex into the work of the operating core.

• **Support staff** - provide additional services which, whilst not part of the operating core, provide functions which are essential in the business environment. The support staff includes secretarial, legal, clerical and catering.

There is also an ideology that binds all of this together. It represents the organisational values and beliefs, which provide a common focus for all the other elements.

Whilst Mintzberg suggests the above five parts as an analytical tool, in practice there are several linking mechanisms at work:

(i)   A formally determined hierarchy of decision levels, power and responsibility.

(ii)   A formal flow of information around the organisation.

(iii)   An informal communication network, the 'grapevine'.

(iv)   Formal work constellations whereby sections of the organisation set up and operate formal co-ordinating mechanisms such as working parties and committees.

(v)   A system of ad hoc decision processes whereby the organisation responds in a particular manner when it faces a problem. The aim is to define the problem and find a solution to what may be a unique problem.

3.3   Influence on organisational design

The configuration chosen to support the organisation's strategies depends on the mix of building block and co-ordinating mechanism. Mintzberg discusses six configurations, which broadly cover the combinations already discussed and also the environment, the type of work and the complexity of tasks facing the organisation. These are outlined in the chart below:

	Environment	Internal factors	Key building block	Key co-ordinating mechanism
Simple structure	Simple/ dynamic	Small Young Simple tasks	Strategic apex	Direct supervision
Machine bureaucracy	Simple/ static	Large Old Regulated tasks	Technostructure	Standardisation of work
Professional bureaucracy	Complex/ static	Professional control Simple systems	Operating core	Standardisation of skills
Divisionalised	Simple/static Diverse	Very large Old Divisible tasks	Middle line	Standardisation of outputs
Adhocracy	Complex/ dynamic	Young Complex tasks	Operating core Support staff	Mutual adjustment
Missionary	Simple/ static	Middle-aged Simple systems	Ideology	Standardisation of norms

Simple structure - this corresponds to the entrepreneurial organisation discussed earlier. The strategic apex - possibly consisting of a single owner-manager in a small business - exercises direct control over the operating core, and other functions are pared down to a minimum. There is little or no middle line, and technostructure and support staff are also absent. The fact that co-ordination is achieved by direct supervision means that this structure is flexible, and suited to cope with dynamic environments.

Machine bureaucracy - just as the simple structure is based on predominance of the strategic apex, so the machine bureaucracy arises from the power of the technostructure. The emphasis is on regulation: bureaucratic processes govern all activities within the organisation. This means that speedy reaction to change is impracticable, and this arrangement is best suited to simple, static environments.

Professional bureaucracy - this organisational structure arises from the predominance of the operating core. The name is appropriate, because this type of structure commonly arises in organisations where many members of staff have a high degree of professional qualification (for example the medical staff in a hospital or the analysts and programmers in a software developer). In this type of organisation the emphasis is on maintaining and improving the skills of the professional staff within the operating core. This often implies resistance to interference by 'outside' technical staff. This means that work is decentralised (with each professional acting largely on his own initiative), and the consequence is that reaction to rapidly changing environments is difficult.

Divisionalised form - this is characterised by a powerful middle line, as illustrated in the diagram below.

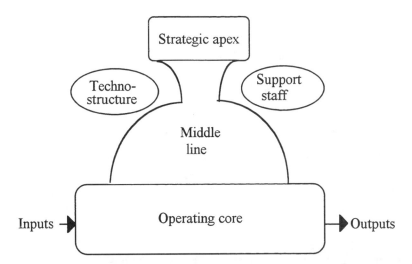

This is of course a common form of business organisation, in which a large class of middle managers each takes charge of a more or less autonomous division. Depending on the extent of their autonomy, managers will be able to restrict interference from the strategic apex to a minimum.

The 'adhocracy' - refers to a complex and disorderly structure in which procedures and processes are not formalised and core activities are carried out by project teams, which form and then unform in a fluid way. It is suited to a complex and dynamic environment. It is not suitable for standardised work.

Missionary organisations - are organisations formed on a basis of a common set of beliefs and values shared by all workers in the organisation. Firm belief in such norms implies an unwillingness to compromise or change, and this means that such organisations are only likely to prosper in simple, static environments.

3.4   Communication

> **Definition**   Communication is the transfer of information and may be defined as: an exchange of facts, ideas, opinions or emotions by two or more persons.

The ability to communicate well is seen as critical to effective management. Indeed it is not surprising that Mintzberg (1973) found that top managers spend over 75 per cent of their time in communication activities. Successful communication within groups and organisations is absolutely vital because it is the ultimate means by which behaviour is modified, change is effected, knowledge is acquired, production and goals are achieved.

In organisations, formal communication channels are normally established as part of the organisation's structure. In a hierarchical structure communication channels may be:

- **Vertical** - chains designed to allow effective communication between managers and subordinates. There is downward communication providing a basis for giving specific job instructions, policy decisions, guidance and resolution of queries Upward communication provides management with feedback from employees on results achieved and problems encountered. It creates a channel from which management can gauge organisational climate and deal with problem areas, such as grievances or low productivity, before they become major issues.

- **Horizontal or lateral** - this refers to communication between people or groups at the same level in the organisation. Co-ordination between departments relies on this form of contact eg, line and staff positions rely heavily on advice passing laterally.

- **Diagonal** - interdepartmental communication by staff of different ranks with no clear line of authority linking them.

4   CENTRALISATION AND DECENTRALISATION

4.1   Tendencies towards centralisation and decentralisation

Centralisation can be defined as the practice of minimal delegation of authority outside senior management.   Conversely, decentralisation is the tendency to disperse decision-making authority in an organised structure.

A centralised structure can be characterised by the retention of the decision-making processes by the senior management.   Authority is *not* delegated. There could be no absolute centralisation of authority in one person because that implies no subordinate managers, and therefore no structured organisation.

A decentralised structure can be characterised by the dispersal of certain decision-making processes throughout the organisation.   Authority and responsibility are delegated. Some decentralisation exists in all organisations because, if managers delegated all their authority, their status as managers would cease, their position would be eliminated and there would be no organisation.

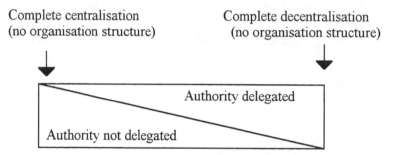

The choice of organisation will depend to a certain extent on the preferences of the organisation's top management, but equally important is the size of the organisation and the scale of its activities. Thus the small business structure is likely to be centralised, and the divisional structure is likely to be decentralised.

Although an organisation might be physically decentralised, it could still be subject to a centralised decision making structure.   In a truly decentralised organisation, the authority to commit men, money and materials is widely diffused throughout each level of the organisation.
Some functions within organisations are easier to decentralise than others eg, production, marketing and sales functions lend themselves to decentralisation, whereas planning, research and development are better administered by a centralised approach.

4.2   Advantages of centralisation

Those who support a high degree of centralisation claim advantages such as:

(a)   co-ordinated decisions and better management control, therefore less sub-optimising;

(b)   conformity with overall objectives;

(c)   standardisation eg, variety reduction and rationalisation;

(d)   balance, between functions, divisions, etc - increased flexibility in use of resources;

(e)   economies of scale - general management, finance, purchasing, production, etc;

(f)   top managers become better decision makers, because:

- they have proven ability;
- they are more experienced;

(g)   speedier central decisions may be made in a crisis - delegation can be time-consuming.

4.3   Disadvantages of centralisation

(a)   Those of lower rank experience reduced job satisfaction.

(b)   Frequently, senior management do not possess sufficient knowledge of all organisational activities. Therefore, their ability to make decisions is narrowed and delegation becomes essential.

(c)   Centralisation places stress and responsibility onto senior management.

(d)   Subordinates experience restricted opportunity for career development toward senior management positions.

(e)   Decisions often take considerable time. This restricts the flexibility of the organisation, as well as using valuable time.

(f)   Slower decision-making impairs effective communication. Such communication problems may affect industrial relations.

4.4   Control and empowerment

Effective performance of organisational tasks depends crucially on employing the right people and giving them the training and opportunities for development that they need. However, this is not sufficient in itself. Another vital ingredient is motivation: staff must feel committed to giving their best efforts, rather than just muddling along with the minimum effort they hope will be considered acceptable.

There are various themes that contribute to employee motivation, including the financial and non-financial rewards earned by staff and the style of management and leadership that they may experience. These themes are taken up in a later chapter. However, in the present context it is relevant to dwell on the difference between hierarchical control based on line authority, and devolved control based on empowered work teams.

The concept of empowerment offers a modern perspective on the improvement of employee performance. Empowerment is seen by many researchers as a key prerequisite for gaining competitive advantage. One definition is as follows: 'by empowerment one means that process by which individuals are informed of the strategic role and purpose of the organisation; come to understand their own role within it; and are given the opportunity to actualise their own role for the good of the organisation'.

This ideal contrasts markedly with traditional ideas of 'top-down management', in which authority passes down through a chain of command from managing director to the lowliest operative. The traditional model inhibits decision making at lower levels in the chain, because each employee must gain approval from his superior. The older system is better suited to stable environments than to the current era of rapid change in business processes, methods and challenges.

More recent developments, of which the concept of empowerment is just one, emphasise the value of rapid response to changing conditions. This is achieved by empowering employees at all levels to take decisions on aspects of work that relate to themselves, cutting out the red tape of hierarchical command structures. This has been an important theme in developments such as quality circles, just in time production and continuous improvement programmes.

Empowerment occupies a key position in the process of transforming ideals into best practice. The reason is that the transformation process can only take place if strategic decisions are communicated to all levels within an organisation.

Traditional ideas of tightly defined functional boundaries inhibit collaboration between departments. To ensure that the organisation derives the maximum value from the resources it uses - and especially its human resources - it is necessary to break down the barriers between functions. On this model, work processes are carried out by multi-functional teams actuated by a common concern for strategic goals known to all members of the teams.

This eliminates the situation in which countless decisions - even decisions of significant importance - are made by staff with little or no idea of the strategic pressures, which should inform them. Instead, members of all divisions should have a clear view of overall strategic aims. Inter-divisional communication must enhance mutual efforts to achieve organisational goals. Senior management must give the process the backing it needs. Public commitment to the value of empowerment is essential.

5   CONTINGENCY THEORY - PROBLEMS OF COMPARING ORGANISATIONS

5.1   Introduction

As mentioned earlier, contingency theory recognises that every organisation is unique, existing in a unique environment. This approach is both analytical and situational, with the purpose of developing a practical approach to a given situation.

As far as organisation design is concerned, numerous formats exist, and according to contingency theory, the choice of structure is dependent upon the organisation's needs. This means the authority and power structure will vary and will influence the way management tasks are performed. This interaction is shown diagrammatically below.

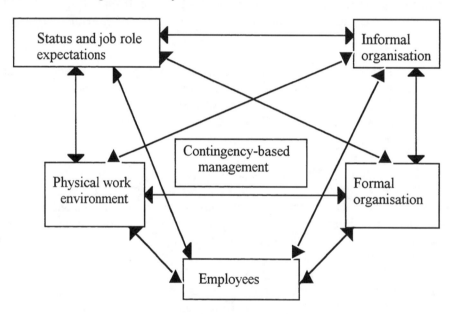

Contingency based approach

This diagram highlights how difficult it is to compare different organisations that follow this approach.

5.2   Considerations of contingency environment, diversity, size, technology and personnel

There is a view that the organisation structure most conducive to high performance can only be formulated by management weighing up the implications for structure of the contingencies they have to face. Contingent factors, such as the type of environment or the size of the organisation, have some direct influence on how successful the organisation is. Secondly it is assumed that the internal structures that determine the way tasks are carried out, that take account of the expectations and needs of employees, the complexity of the operation etc will themselves promote a higher level of effectiveness than a structure ill-suited to the organisation's contingencies. Organisational structure is seen to modify the effects of contingencies upon performance.

The variables identified below are seen as being key when deciding on the most appropriate organisational structure. Each variable is not considered in isolation but reviewed both individually and together.

Environment - according to contingency theory, different approaches to organisational design are conducive to high performance, depending on whether or not the environment is variable and complex in nature or stable and simple.

Diversity - the more diverse the organisation is, in terms of products, markets and locations, the more likely that the structure will be the most appropriate in decentralised divisions. However, geographical speed and organisation size must also be considered.

Size of organisation - the larger the organisation, the more likely it is to have formalised structures allowing for delegation. Specialisation will also be a feature, as will the tendency to be bureaucratic in respect of control structures.

Technology - Joan Woodward's studies suggest that when organisation structures fit their technologies, they achieve a high level of performance.

Human resource policies - the behavioural approach to management suggests that the more jobs are enriched, employees motivated and job satisfaction provided, the more likely it is that employees will perform effectively. Therefore, organisational structures should be developed with these considerations in mind.

5.3 Issues of comparison

Whilst organisations can be compared in respect of performance, the organisations' structures may be quite different. The complexity of the basis of comparison needs to be understood. In order to develop this understanding, studies carried out by Lorsch and Morse are reviewed.

Lorsch and Morse compared two manufacturing plants; one was a high performer, the other low, with two research laboratories, one of which was also a high performer and the other low.

The organisation structures and processes of the high-performing manufacturer, which operated in a relatively certain environment, were:

(a)   high formality;
(b)   short time-horizon;
(c)   highly directive management.

The employees were found to have:

(a)   low tolerance for ambiguity;
(b)   dependency on authority relationships.

The high-performing research laboratory, which operates in a relatively uncertain environment had:

(a)   high tolerance for ambiguity;
(b)   independence of authority.

Yet, both organisations were effective because they were appropriately organised with appropriate employees for their environments and activities. The less effective organisation did not show most of the distinctive characteristics of structure and process to the same degree. The less effective organisation, it appeared, could obtain the appropriate people but did not organise them in the appropriate way. In other cases, failure could be due to having inappropriate people even though they were appropriately organised.

5.4   Limitations of the contingency approach

Child has identified a number of limitations in respect of this approach.

(a)   There is a lack of conclusive evidence to show that matching organisation designs to prevailing contingencies contributes significantly to performance.

(b)   For environmental, strategic and structural relationships, (where the contingency approach is most developed) studies indicate that strategic policies on diversification and growth may make a far more significant contribution to financial performance than the degree to which structural forms have moved in line with strategies.

(c)   There is the possibility that some organisations may be less dependent upon their environments and in a secure position in respect of achieving their goals, therefore a contingency approach is not necessary.

(d)   Multiple contingencies may all be present at the same time. However, only a limited number of contingencies have been focused on eg, size, environment etc, and the extent to which they may be in conflict or harmony and the effect this has on structure has not really been researched.

(e)   Different parts of the organisation may be faced with different types of environment eg, accounting - stable, sales - unstable. Some organisations will have structural variations that take account of variety. However, the contingency approach does not detail the problems this can cause, such as integration of activities and communication breakdowns. Integration mechanisms can be costly in time and resource.

Child believes that contingency theorists have not in the main recognised the organisational design difficulties which may result from the presence of multiple variables. These difficulties occur because of the structural differences, which result when attempts are made at matching the structure of different functions/divisions to the dominant variables, which they face.

6   SELF TEST QUESTIONS

6.1   What are the two basic processes of structuring? (1.3)

6.2   Briefly explain the purpose of organisation charts. (1.5)

6.3   What are the basic characteristics of functional structuring? (2.2)

6.4   Outline the advantages of product divisionalisation. (2.3)

6.5   How do matrix structures overcome the rigidity prevalent in organisation charts? (2.7)

6.6   Draw a diagram showing Mintzberg's five building blocks. (3.2)

6.7   Describe two communication channels in a hierarchical structure. (3.4).

6.8   Differentiate between centralisation and decentralisation. (4.1)

7   EXAMINATION TYPE QUESTION

7.1   Centralisation

Many companies operate through a number of 'divisions'. A division is a form of enterprise structure that has to some degree been 'decentralised'.

Explain the concept of centralisation, and analyse some of the advantages and disadvantages of organisational centralisation and decentralisation.   **(20 marks)**

8   ANSWER TO EXAMINATION TYPE QUESTION

8.1   Centralisation

Answer Plan

Definition; decentralisation; advantages/disadvantages of centralisation; advantages/disadvantages of decentralisation.

Centralisation can be defined as the practice of minimal delegation of authority outside senior management. Conversely, decentralisation can be described as the filtration of authority throughout the organisation.

A centralised structure can be characterised by the retention of the decision-making processes by the senior management. Authority is *not* delegated.

A decentralised structure can be characterised by the dispersal of certain decision-making processes throughout the organisation. Authority and responsibility are delegated.

Whether a centralised or a decentralised structure is preferred depends very much upon the nature of the organisation and its operational market.

Although an organisation might be physically decentralised, it could still be subject to a centralised decision making structure. In a truly decentralised organisation the authority to commit men, money and materials is widely diffused throughout each level of the organisation.

Some functions within organisations are easier to decentralise than others eg, production, marketing and sales functions lend themselves to decentralisation, whereas planning, research and development are better administered by a centralised approach.

Advantages of centralisation include:

(a)   **Unity of control**. There is less chance of any major errors of judgement being committed if control remains centralised.

(b)   **Strategic conformity**. Organisational structures and objectives are known and this leads to the standardisation and formalisation of strategic decision making.

(c)   **Uniformity of policies and standards**. The same quality of product or service is guaranteed.

(d)   **Common culture**. The culture of the organisation would most probably be closely identifiable with the original founder and this culture would permeate throughout the organisation. This commonality of culture might be seen in a very positive way in terms of capability, quality and service.

Disadvantages of centralisation include:

(a)   **Planning process.** There may not be any real understanding by management of the problem of implementing corporate plans.

(b)   **Decision making overload**. Senior management might become swamped with information and the demand for decision making might become such that the decision response time becomes too long for the decision to be effective.

(c)   **Response to change** is almost always slower within centralised structures. This is largely due to the fact that the decision making processes become mechanised and the mechanised process becomes inflexible.

(d)   **Stifles initiative** because people within the organisation are not encouraged or rewarded for using their own initiative.   This may lead to demotivation of staff and/or a high staff turnover.

(e)   **Errors of judgement**. Often decisions are made based on the written information available. Errors of judgement can be made by not knowing the practicalities of a subject.

Advantages of decentralisation include:

(a)   **Prevention of overload**.   Senior managers have more time to concentrate on strategic matters rather than having to make operational decisions.

(b)   **Speed of decision making**. Operational decisions can be made much faster by the relevant line managers.

(c)   **Response to change**. This is faster because the line managers would be aware of the local conditions and factors which affect their unit.

(d)   **Higher awareness of cost and profits**. Decentralisation allows senior managers to view the various cost centres and subsequently evaluate the areas of high cost or high profitability.

(e)   **Motivation** is greater because junior managers are encouraged to use initiative and also to take responsibility for their decisions.

Disadvantages of decentralisation include:

(a)   **Loss of control**. This could result in errors of judgement by junior management.

(b)   **Sub-optimisation** might occur, where each unit is working towards its own objectives without regard to the overall objectives of the organisation.

(c)   **Inconsistency of quality** of either product or service. This may result in dissatisfied customers.

(d)   **Higher calibre staff** are needed to manage the decentralised units. This will inevitably result in higher grades of salary.

As mentioned earlier, the style and type of organisation and its product are all factors, which need to be considered when discussing the merits or otherwise of centralisation and decentralisation.

7 FUNCTIONS IN AN ORGANISATION

INTRODUCTION & LEARNING OUTCOMES

Syllabus area 11(ii) The general operation of the main functional areas of business (ie, operations, marketing, human resource management, finance, research and development, information systems management).

The information required by managers in the various functional areas of a business organisation and the role of the Chartered Management Accountant in identifying and satisfying those information needs.

Business organisations vary in the goods/services they produce and sell, and the way that they are structured. However, it is probably true to say that they all share certain key functions, which must be carried out for them to survive.

In an earlier chapter, we have discussed strategic planning - a very important function, and in later chapters we will be looking, in more detail, at aspects of marketing and human resource management. In this chapter we will be looking briefly at the characteristics and operation of each of the main functions (Marketing, purchasing/procurement, production, research and development (R & D), human resource management (personnel), finance and accounting and management information systems (MIS)), as well as the relationship between them.

Following your study of this chapter, an understanding of the main functions will have formed - not only regarding the nature of the functions in isolation, but also the relations between them. Any organisation is as dependent upon its inter-relationships as it is upon the internal skill within each function.

When you have studied this chapter, you should be able to:

* Explain the relationships necessary between the functional areas in order for an organisation to achieve its objectives.
* Analyse a range of organisations, identifying their component parts, the relationships between those parts and any problems with those relationships.
* Explain the general characteristics and operation of the main functional areas of an organisation.
* Explain the relationship between the work of the Chartered Management Accountant and the functional areas of an organisation.
* Analyse the information needs of managers in each of the main functional areas of an organisation.

1 ORGANISATIONAL ORIENTATIONS

1.1 Managerial orientations

Many companies have passed through the various orientations described below whilst others have chosen to stay with a particular orientation because this suits their current circumstances. The various orientations can be grouped as follows.

(a) **Production orientation** - concentrates on production and the product. Management believes that the product will sell itself provided it can be supplied at low prices and/or with high quality standards.

Such an orientation, adopted by IBM in the early 1990s, meant that it lost touch with its customer needs and persevered with mainframe computers.

(b)   **Sales orientation** - here the organisation is geared to achieving maximum sales and volume is pursued. The claim is that goods are sold not bought and these organisations focus on selling techniques rather than the needs of the consumer.

Aggressive selling can be successfully employed today providing the company is not too worried about repeat business. It is adopted by some insurance and home improvement companies, as well as by those anxious for quick profits on products with short life cycles.

(c)   **Marketing orientation** - 'introduced' by Levitt, aims to create a satisfied customer by establishing what consumer needs and wants are and adjusting production accordingly. Moreover, marketing is not considered to be the preserve of functional specialists but the concern of all employees - being close to the customer is one of the cultural values identified by Peters and Waterman as being held by 'excellent' companies. Although the consumer is regarded as the most influential stakeholder, the importance of generating profits is not ignored.

(d)   **Societal marketing** - the work of Ralph Nader and such organisations as Friends of the Earth has led to legislation relating to the social costs of various activities. Matters covered include pollution, the quality of life and the conservation of irreplaceable resources. Some companies are concerned with long-run consumer and public welfare and have positioned the company and its products in this area. An example would be Body Shop.

1.2   Operative and information sub-systems

As was seen earlier, Handy views organisations as being composed of four main classes of organisational subsystems.   Adaptive systems are linked to strategic decisions and general management and are concerned with fitting the organisation into its environment, shaping its future, dealing with divergencies and deciding its policies. Operative systems control the resources (eg, money, equipment and buildings) that are converted into goods/services to meet stakeholders' satisfaction. Maintenance systems work to keep the organisation healthy and information systems form the decision base of the organisation.

As with all systems thinking, it must be remembered that if the organisation is to survive in the long term, output values must overall be equal to or greater than input values.

There is considerable interrelation between the various operational and informational sub-systems and it is dangerous to think of the four major functional areas - operations management, marketing, personnel and accounting - as distinct areas of activity. Indeed, there are many variations amongst organisations as to how the functional processes are grouped.

1.3   The planning and control of functional processes

The relationship between the various functional processes can be clearly seen when the various stages of tactical planning are investigated.

The elements of tactical planning are:

(a)   **Organisation planning** - when assessing the company's performance and its strengths and weaknesses it is possible that structural weaknesses may be highlighted and any shortcomings should be remedied before proceeding further.

(b)   **Operations planning** - this can be divided into:

- **Short-term profit plan** - strategic planning has a long-term focus and it is important to draw up a short-term profit plan covering a period of, say, four months and compare this with the longer-term plan.   Allowances may have to be made for seasonal fluctuations and for trends indicated by recent results.

- **Marketing plan** - the strategic plan should already have dealt with broad marketing questions such as:

    - What business should the company be in?
    - What segment of that business?
    - When and how should it enter the market?
    - When and how should it grow?

    The more detailed marketing plan will incorporate marketing research and the management of the marketing mix - branding, product mix, pricing, advertising, sales promotion, public relations, packaging and distribution - discussed in a later chapter.

- **Operations plan** - broad operational policies will be included in the strategic plan and the operations plan will cover such activities as plant location and layout, product/service design, warehousing and materials handling.

- **Resources development plan** - the resources of men, materials, machines and money (the four Ms) have to be planned efficiently if the company is to meet its overall profitability target.   The co-ordination of these activities is facilitated by the preparation of detailed short-term plans.

    The manpower plan will endeavour to match the company's needs with its present resources and take effective steps to remedy any imbalance.

- **Product/market development plan** - using the marketing mix to control the buyer's responses and develop the products/services as they pass through the stages of the life cycle - discussed in a later chapter.

2   MARKETING

2.1   Marketing orientations

Marketing is not simply concerned with selling goods and services, it is a means of trying to ensure beforehand that the goods produced or the services offered conform to what potential customers want and will buy. The marketing orientation is closely linked to the notion of the marketing concept strongly advocated by Levitt in the 1960s and expressed as: 'Selling focuses on the needs of the producer, marketing on the needs of the consumer.' It is a consumer and goal-oriented, integrated philosophy for a firm, institution or person.

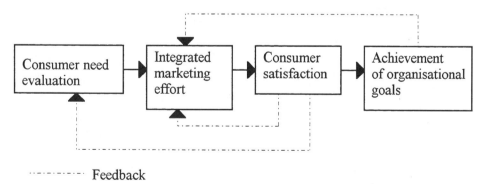

Perhaps it was best summed up by Charles Revlon: 'In the factory we make cosmetics and in the drugstore we sell hope.'

If marketing managers intend to create, build and maintain a market, they must try to persuade customers rather than allow them sovereignty in the market. Philip Kotler in *Marketing Management* suggests that marketing management is demand management concerned with regulating the level, timing and character of demand for one or more products of an organisation.

2.2   The marketing function

Marketing involves products, services, organisations, people, places and ideas. The marketing process is not complete until consumers and customers exchange their money, their promise to pay, or their support for the offering of the enterprise, institution, person, place or idea. Marketing was defined by the Chartered Institute of Marketing as:

(Definition)   'Management process responsible for identifying, anticipating and satisfying customer requirements profitably.'

It is the efficient use of corporate resources to match existing or future demand. This is by the manipulation of all the required means of production, distribution and promotion to make certain that the products or services are in the right place at the right time, and are offered at the right price to meet demand.

The structure may be functional with responsibility assigned on the basis of buying, selling, promotion, distribution and other tasks. It may be product-oriented with product managers for each product or service category and brand managers for each individual brand, in addition to functional categories. Or it may be market-oriented, with managers assigned around geographic markets and customer types, in addition to functional categories.

The marketing function can encompass the following areas of responsibility:

(a)   *Research and strategy* – An important part of the marketing function is the collection of data for market research, collation and analysis of such data and provision of the necessary information to determine strategy for the development of suitable marketing plans.

(b)   *Advertising and press office* – The marketing department is concerned with promoting the company's products and ensuring that data is collected for evaluation of the success or failure of marketing strategy.

(c)   *Sales and distribution* – The marketing function deals with the channels of distribution for the company's products. It is necessary to collect data about the following:

    (i)   processing orders and enquiries from customers;
    (ii)   sales per outlet – retail, credit direct, via agents, etc;
    (iii)   distribution network activity and costs;
    (iv)   sales per product group;
    (v)   budgetary comparisons;
    (vi)   identifying customer demand.

2.3   The implications of the marketing concept

If an organisation has a marketing orientation, the management accepts that the key task is to determine the needs, wants and values of a target market. Then, adapt the organisation to delivering the desired satisfaction more effectively and efficiently than its competitors. As the consumer's needs change, so too must the goods or services that are produced.

This means the application of the marketing concept to management decisions should begin at the strategic planning stage and continue through product development and testing to its eventual sale to the customer.

3   PRODUCTION AND OPERATIONS MANAGEMENT

3.1   The production function

Production is the central activity, the core of the manufacturing business. The production management team are responsible for planning and controlling the range of processes involved in converting the raw materials or components into the finished goods that are required to meet the needs of the organisation's current and potential customers.

As can be seen in the diagram below, it covers the production of both goods and services and is the central part of the conversion process.   However, production management is normally associated with the manufacture of goods and operations management is the term used nowadays to cover all aspects of this functional area.   The points discussed in the remainder of this section deal specifically with manufacturing situations, but most can be easily extended to cover service operations.

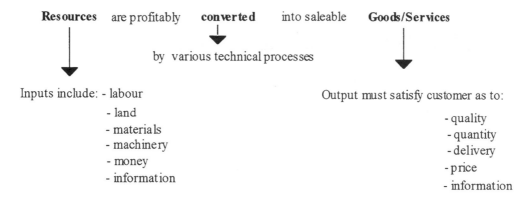

The prime objective is to ensure that resources are utilised in the most effective way to meet customers' product quality and delivery requirements at an acceptable cost.   The interface between marketing and production is critical and this can be very problematic, as the two departments' objectives are often irreconcilable.

The initial concern of the production manager is to acquire the inputs to the production system eg, plant facilities, raw materials and labour.

Once the inputs are assembled, the stage that requires most of the attention - the creation of value - takes place. This section covers the following areas:

Production control - generally provides the administrative framework for productive tasks.   It also generally controls the documentation for recording eg, the authorisation of factory work; the assembly of raw materials for issue to production; and monitoring the work progress through the various productive processes.

Factory operations - the manufacturing system that is concerned with:

* productive activities (the performance of the various manufacturing shops);

* service departments (the provision of maintenance, energy, etc to the manufacturing shops); and

* store-keeping functions (the custody and recording of raw material and finished goods stocks).

The final stage of the production process is the completion of outputs - the finished product and/or service.

3.2   Production planning and control

Having received an indication of what is required from the marketing department, production planning and control must determine how and when the products should be manufactured. The objective is to produce plans and controls which will satisfy marketing demands as to quality (quality control), quantity (stock control) and delivery (progress control), as well as utilise resources available (materials control) in an economical manner (cost control).

The production planning and control department is directly responsible for progress planning and control, the objectives of which are to minimise excessive work in progress, idle time and broken delivery promises.

A typical production process includes the following planning and control elements.

- The customer's needs are translated into instructions for production.

- Production schedules and targets are planned.

- The availability of equipment is planned and arranged.

- The labour requirements are planned and availability arranged.

- The supply of materials and components is planned and arranged.

- Orders progress.

- As actual production progresses, stock purchasing and production records are kept.

- The production activities are monitored against the plans and where necessary corrective action is taken.

In this outline, there is an underlying continuous cycle: plan, produce, monitor against targets and, with feedback, update the plan and the targets. The production schedules are timetables. These are complex and essential. When prepared in advance they map out the details, priorities and prerequisites of the work. They also identify bottlenecks and slack time so that the total time from start to finish is optimised. The schedule provides a target date of completion and progress can be monitored.

The availability of machines, including their loading and capacity, needs have to be carefully planned - material costs and the idle time of machines need to be minimised. Labour costs should also be minimised. This does not necessarily mean paying the lowest wages, but having the lowest labour costs, which follow from motivated, trained and skilled workers producing quality output at high levels of productivity. In planning, production, manning and skill levels need to be considered and decisions taken on training needs, pay and incentives.

The effectiveness of this operation is constrained by the following.

(a)   Conflicting objectives within the organisation eg,

Maximise use of capacity	v	Maintain reserve capacity
Maintain constant output level	v	Be flexible
Minimise finished stock levels	v	Minimise delivery time

(b)   Reliability of sales forecasts and other information.

(c)   Efficiency of production departments.

(d)   Availability of raw materials, which depends on the reliability of suppliers as to quality and delivery, and on the existence of suitable storage space within the organisation.

Production planning and control can pursue two alternative strategies. The first is to maximise the use of capacity, the second is to operate a 'just in time' system of customer flexibility.

American organisations have favoured capacity utilisation, advocating batching items together for long production runs and maintaining stocks of raw material and inter-process goods to smooth out any production disruptions. This creates an element of inflexibility and late changes to customers' orders or special design aspects are unwelcome and may be penalised by excess pricing or extra delay.

Japanese organisations have developed close links with their main suppliers and operate a production system where there is no stock holding. The raw materials required for the current production batch are delivered when production starts and the finished product is despatched to customers, since there is no manufacturing to stock. This means that changes in customer requirements can be easily accommodated, thereby improving customer satisfaction.

3.3   Warehousing and materials handling

Warehousing is an important component of both production and marketing, and can involve extensive capital expenditure on equipment as well as stock holding.

Stocks are held to make production and delivery possible (even though demand fluctuates) and to facilitate economic ordering. Stock control is important as storage costs can be substantial and may easily account for more than 25 per cent of the value of the stocks. There is often a tendency to carry too large a stock of certain items 'just in case' and Pareto's law is applicable in such situations – 80 per cent of the turnover is derived from products accounting for 20 per cent of the stocks.

A tight system of control is therefore required, but if too rigorous this can cause marketing and production problems and alienate these departments from those imposing the control limits - normally the accounting department.

To save money, manufacturers are increasingly relying on suppliers to assist them with their stockholding. Blunden refers to a 'just in time' system, operated by Toyota, as follows:

'Under the Kanban system, component suppliers and the final car assembler (Toyota) integrate their production lines so that there is virtually a continuous flow from primary manufacture to final assembly, crossing formally independent organisational boundaries, with only very low stocks being maintained at each stage.'

3.4   The relationship between the functional areas

A proposal for a new product is assessed in the market place by marketing research. If the proposal seems at first to be viable by the criteria of the organisation, then the next stage, probably in the research and development unit of the firm, is to take the proposal to the prototype stage. The prototypes are tested and if they are satisfactory then the next stage of making pre-production models goes ahead. The aim at this stage is to simulate the production process and its product. Conclusions are reached about production and product issues such as the extent to which the customer's needs are met and the cost of producing to that need. Issues can also be tested at this stage, such as future manufacturing capacity. At the same time, the pre-production products will be tested, possibly including testing by customers. If the feedback from the potential consumer is good and production appears to be economically and organisationally viable, then the main production run can be planned for.

4 **PURCHASING/PROCUREMENT**

4.1 **Cost of inputs**

The cost of raw materials is a major element in the management of production. Purchasing costs may be incurred directly by the production unit and by other units that aid production. In the past, many organisations did not appreciate the importance of the purchasing function in the success of the firm. The role of the purchasing manager had a relatively low organisational status and little management training. This low status is unjustified. The buyer's role not only has internal links with numerous departments and sections but also is a significant link between the organisation and its environment. The purchasing department's primary responsibility is to secure sufficient and suitable raw materials, components and the other goods and services needed to ensure that production is fully supplied in a cost-effective manner. The production department requires the supply of raw materials and so on to be available at exactly the right time in the right quantities and quality.

There is increasing recognition in the manufacturing industry that costs must be minimised. Inventory must be kept low through a very efficient supply of raw materials and components. In some cases this supply involves several deliveries a day. This allows an uninterrupted flow of production without holding expensive buffer stocks.

4.2 **Purchasing function responsibilities**

Typically a purchasing department will set up and maintain effective communications and relationships within the organisation as well as develop good, mutually beneficial relationships with current and potential external suppliers. The range of responsibilities includes:

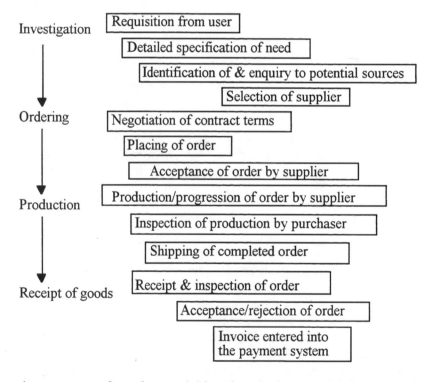

As we can see from these activities, there is the potential for purchasing to play an important role in the company's strategy. Close attention to purchasing is an important characteristic of successful organisations. A central part of this strategy is to develop a mutually beneficial relationship with suppliers.

The active management of this relationship brings benefits in terms of the price, quality and product development of goods/services bought. An example of this strategy is the purchasing practice of Marks and Spencer plc, a British retailer whose policy is not to manufacture themselves but to have an unusually close relationship with suppliers. This results in the company having many of the benefits of their own manufacture. They benefit from the specialist expertise of the supplier, but without the risk and the demands on their limited management resources and capital, which would be needed if they also manufactured the goods they sell.

Although the procedures for purchasing vary widely from one company to another, depending on the size of the company, the variety and nature of the purchases and sources from which they are obtained, certain basic processes are usually common to any procedure. There is no standard procedure. The right procedure for a particular function will be the one which best suits the specific needs of that company in that situation. A purchase of a very expensive piece of plant for the factory, ie, a capital investment, would involve a different set of managers in the decision, than the placing of a routine topping up of 'nuts and bolts' stock order. The first would involve a new contract, the second 'order' would probably be referenced to an existing contract. The first would probably require the authority of the board, the second would be within the day-to-day authority of the buyers.

5   RESEARCH AND DEVELOPMENT

5.1   Introduction

Research and development (R & D) can be defined as 'the organisation of innovation at the level of the firm'. R & D aims to satisfy a market need by developing new products and by improved methods of production. It must also find applications for scientific and technical developments.

The R & D function should have a major innovative role in all organisations. The pressures to introduce new ways of doing things may be 'demand pulled', that is the innovation filling a market need, or it may be 'technology pushed', the innovation coming from the application of discoveries. In many organisations, there is a group of people, not necessarily R & D, whose responsibilities include the creation of new business ideas and techniques.

One of the major tasks of those responsible for the financial management of R & D is to ensure the best choice is made. To do so they must have information about the needs of, and technological capabilities available to, the company. These have to be matched as far as is possible and systems and procedures have to be established which cover the different aspects of the management problem, eg, evaluation, selection, planning and monitoring.

5.2   Types of research and development

Typical R & D activities can be grouped into several types:

- **Pure research** - concerned with advancing the state of knowledge in a particular field without having an immediate commercial application in sight. Most firms are reluctant to engage in pure research. While a discovery may be important and have commercial spin-offs it may be difficult to patent the findings and expensive to develop commercial applications.

- **Basic research** - directed at the advance of knowledge but in an applied field. In undertaking this there is an expectation that some of the findings will lead to product and process innovations with commercial importance.

- **Industrial research** - aims to develop profitable applications of pure and basic research.

- **Development** - seeks to progress from the research findings to the stage of producing a prototype, which has profit-making potential.

- **Design** - the process focused on satisfying customer needs by producing a product with an optimum marketing mix. The design includes elements such as effective operation, product safety, attractive and functional appearance as well as value for money.

In fact the R & D department may work in several of these areas at the same time and will liaise closely with the production and marketing teams. The product design and styling may well be an essential element of all three. The design of cars, for instance, should be such that it makes producing a quality product a straightforward process. Competitive pressures and technical developments in the 1990s have produced leading car designs that have successfully combined sophisticated design complexity with reliability. Now all car manufacturers who hope to be successful in world markets for mass-produced cars must give resources on a huge scale to R & D to match the advanced and successful competition. What makes the competition even more severe is that manufacturers, particularly the Japanese, have in recent years halved the time it takes to develop a new product from initial concept to production. On the marketing side, many consumer products, not the least cars, are sold not only on objective performance criteria but also on the aesthetic and environmental impact of the design. All this makes the R & D functions success ever more important.

5.3   The stimulus for research and development

This comes from two main areas:

- **Consumers** - either directly by feedback through distributors or by market research results;

- **Products** - need to produce new products or variations of existing products to maintain customer appeal or to conform to a more stringent quality standard or to embrace the new findings of a general advance in technology.

In addition to these main stimuli, other pressures can lead to research and development. For example:

(a)   the need to change a dangerous product process or replace a dangerous ingredient of the product, for example, blue asbestos;

(b)   attempts to turn by-products into saleable products;

(c)   interesting results from research in an unrelated field;

(d)   response to public pressure, for example, there is a strong lobby against artificial additives. Change may be vital to maintain product-attractiveness.

It is often difficult to evaluate the return on investment in R & D effort. Clearly, some of the work will lead into blind alleys and cannot yield any profit. Nonetheless, it is a valuable exercise to attempt to calculate the costs and benefits of R & D, otherwise the board cannot judge any case for increasing the level of R & D expenditure.

5.4   Design and estimating

Research and development activities are involved with strategic issues such as the development needs of existing markets, new markets and the corporate rate of growth (both in terms of profit and turnover).

In its relationship with production, research and development ultimately involves design, which has been defined as:

[Definition]   'all the activities relating to the development of a product or service, from inception, through all the developmental stages to the final model. The design activity therefore is an integrating activity that lumps together all sectors of the organisation concerned with product development, manufacture, sales and finance.'

There are therefore many aspects, which include those relating to:

(a)   **Operations** - the designer must have a working knowledge of the process he or she is involved with.

(b)   **Function** - products must be capable of carrying out the tasks required of them and ergonomics (the study of the man-machine interface) and reliability are important considerations in this connection.

(c)   **Aesthetics** - although products should please the eye to attract customers, the appeal of the product may not be solely visual. Other senses are also often involved and sometimes characteristics such as smell, taste or texture may predominate.

For standardised goods the fixing of prices is normally carried out by the marketing department but for contracting organisations manufacturing 'one offs' or for those repairing or servicing equipment **estimating** is somewhat different and according to Appleby:

'Full co-operation between departments is needed ie, financial, production engineering, drawing office, marketing. The final estimate involves considering material content and expected prices, labour hours and rates, overhead costs and profit margins. The use of marginal costing for estimating is advocated by many accountants and this may be appropriate in certain circumstances.'

6   PERSONNEL MANAGEMENT AND HUMAN RESOURCE MANAGEMENT (HRM)

6.1   Introduction

The main theme running through this book is the great significance of the achievement of objectives. Success is achieved by the co-ordinated and controlled use of the resources that are available and can be optimally employed given the technological, social and economic environments of the organisation.

The company uses financial and human resources within its overall strategy - including its human resource strategy. The management of employees in organisations has been developing and changing particularly in the 1980s and 1990s. There have been economic and industrial changes which have had a significant impact on the way organisations view the employment of people.

For a number of years the dominant culture in organisations, especially large ones, was the role of culture. Organisational structure was seen as a hierarchy of positions or 'offices'. Staff filled vacancies, and were then expected to carry out the duties defined for the position. The management of employees was split. The line managers were responsible for the employees' performance in the job, and the personnel managers had a 'staff' or advisory job and looked after many of the administrative aspects of employment, such as keeping the personnel records. Additionally, senior personnel management was responsible for the management of industrial relations and manpower planning. This structure and outlook is still common in British industry, as is the personnel management philosophy that goes with it.

6.2   Employees as the key resource

More recently, a 'human resource management approach' has gained support. Employees are seen as the key resource of the organisation. Their productivity is the key to the organisation's profitability. The attitudes and behaviour of the employees are therefore of great concern to management. The way employees actually behave at work is affected by a number of factors: the work structures, the prevailing organisational culture and the personnel systems and practices. While some may view these as distinct elements in the management of human resources, the increasingly prevalent view is that they should be integrated with each other and with the other organisational strategies.

6.3   The personnel function

Typically the personnel function has responsibility for:

*   personnel policy and strategy formulation and implementation;

*   the staffing of the organisation and advising all managers on employee matters.

The personnel department will have employees working at several levels:

• senior personnel staff involved in policy making and strategic decisions; in these activities they will necessarily be liaising with senior general management, the corporate planners;

• middle managers who will have an advisory and guidance role and also be directly managing the provision of personnel services; they will also be responsible for the implementation of the personnel aspects of corporate planning and strategy, for example, planning staff numbers;

• more junior staff who will provide the various personnel services, especially those required in staffing the organisation, such as recruiting and training staff.

Because they are part of a specialist function, all the personnel managers will be able to concentrate on personnel matters - unlike all other managers who, while personnel matters are an important part of their duties, will have to spend most of their energies on other things.

The relationship between personnel managers and other managers has to be handled carefully. Managerial styles and the organisational culture can affect the way advice on personnel issues is sought, given and received. For instance, given the degree of employment protection afforded to individual employees by legislation, it is in the interest of the firm that industrial relations, both at the collective and individual levels, are handled by experts.

6.4   The nature and importance of personnel services and HRM

In the following paragraphs we will look at the nature, importance and key features of the main personnel services.

(a)   **Organisational structure and manning levels** - in the UK, most organisations, and almost every large one, are structured on bureaucratic lines. Emphasis is on chains of responsibility and authority up and down the organisation. There is a strong commitment to the principle that the tasks the business needs to perform are structured into the work of defined jobs or offices.

For each office a formal job description is documented defining the job category, the tasks to be done and other features. Similarly for each job a personnel specification is drawn up defining the attributes of the ideal person for the job. The jobs as defined make up the organisation's establishment. This establishment gives the details of the 'offices' of the whole company. It includes the numbers of jobs in the organisation, and at each grade, with a defined pay category attached. A major task of the personnel department is to regularly review jobs, numbers of people and the establishment in general so that the numbers and types of employees best match production needs.

(b)   **Redundancy, redeployment, recruitment and selection** - a major asset of organisations not shown in the conventional balance sheet is the carefully recruited labour force. To make the best use of the human resource, there should be regular reviews of staff levels. Human resources plans are updated and decisions taken about recruitment, selection and redundancy. Many organisations feel they have a social responsibility to employees and they are reluctant to make any employees compulsorily redundant. Recruitment is important in that it brings fresh people into the company, and even at times of recession the organisation will want to have an appropriate age profile for its staff.

(c)   **Remuneration issues and procedures** - depending on the nature of the business, labour costs may be the major cost of providing output. Wage costs account for around 60 per cent of the expenses of banks in the UK. The control of such costs is an important element of profit making. Most management nowadays do believe that wages are the primary element of employee motivation and therefore performance-related pay is becoming increasingly widespread.

(d)   **Staff appraisal procedures** - an important tool for motivating and controlling the employee is the formal managerial appraisal of employee performance. As the HRM philosophy becomes increasingly accepted, it is becoming part of the 'common sense' of society that all employees should be subject to performance appraisal and that it is 'irrational' to think otherwise. Staff appraisal requires the careful administration of suitable appraisal techniques and feedback to employees.

(e)   **Employment records** - there is clearly a need for basic information about employees. This data is needed for day-to-day operations and can also be used for the effective planning of staff numbers and the development and training of individuals.

(f)   **Employee communications and relations** - communications with the workforce are an increasingly important aspect - not just as part of a motivation strategy but as part of developing a company culture. This culture is designed to elicit a high degree of commitment from the employee. The employee will identify personal individual interests closely with the interests of the organisation. This involves two-way communication and efficient formal networks through meetings and the circulation of written material. This is of central importance to the HRM approach.

(g)   **Disciplinary and dismissal procedures** - there are several aspects to disciplinary and dismissal procedures. At the legal level the company must ensure that it conforms to the required procedures for the dismissal of employees. There is a requirement in most companies that these are seen to be fair and implemented with justice and uniformity. The company wants to have control procedures, which attempt the improvement of unsatisfactory performance and where necessary make sure unsatisfactory performance is eliminated.

(h)   **Staff training and management development** - the organisation's operations are dynamic - they are always having to respond to change. The relationship with every employee can be seen as part of a cycle. Employees are hired, trained, they may progress in the organisation and, sooner or later, they leave voluntarily or not. In addition to that cycle there are many other changes in a business, some arising from internal pressures, some a response to the external environment.

Central to all these changes is the need for the organisation always to have the optimum number of trained employees. Training is usually expensive and often there is a substantial delay between the identification of the training need and the completion of training.

(i)   **Health and safety procedures and training** - virtually every organisation recognises that not only is it required by UK law that the working environment should be a safe and healthy place to work in, but also that it is part of their social responsibility to employees and all who come into contact with the organisation. This requires that the organisational culture as well as its procedures, practices and training should have a commitment to health and safety.

7   THE KEY ELEMENTS OF THE FINANCE AND ACCOUNTING FUNCTIONS

7.1   Range of activities

If we consider the range of activities of the financial function we can classify them into those that involve financial and management accounting (controller functions) and those that involve the management of finance (treasury functions). Controller functions are principally reporting and interpreting, planning for control, evaluating and consulting, tax administration and economic appraisal. Treasury functions are principally provision of capital, investor relations, short-term financing and investing, banking and custody, credits and collections and longer-term investments.

The design of organisational structure needs to take these functional needs into account. In the UK, a large organisation will typically have an accounting function with a wide area of responsibility and within that role, sections will look after limited areas. For example, an 'internal audit' section focuses on the way the control objectives are being reached. The way the accounting function is arranged will reflect managerial style and cultural preferences. Even the way the function has evolved in the organisation can be an important factor in the divisions of accounting responsibility.

Accounting and other departments in many hierarchically structured organisations specify certain activities as their basic mission, such as the production and sale of goods. These jobs are divided into sub-units and draw a distinction between sub-units or line departments, which are directly responsible for basic activities such as production. They operate with 'line authority' in that they exert their authority directly over subordinates. Staff departments have as their principal task the support or servicing of the line departments. Thus, these staff departments are indirectly related to the basic activities of the organisation. They have the authority to advise but not command. They may advise downward, laterally or even upward.

The accounting department has such a staff function. It has the responsibility for providing other managers with a specialised service including advice and help in budgeting, analysing variances, pricing and the making of decisions. The accounting department does not exercise direct and full authority over the line departments, but has some delegated authority from top management to prescribe accounting and reporting methods.

7.2   Financial accounting

[Definition]   Financial accounting may be defined as 'the analysis, classification and recording of financial transactions, and the analysis of how such transactions affect the performance and financial position of a business.'

The survival of any organisation requires that it fulfils at least two needs. In the longer term if it is not to be subsidised it must at least break even. The second need is for the company to settle its liabilities when they become due. The first need focuses on profitability and the second on cash flow.

Almost every decision taken by management has a financial or accounting aspect. Accounting is a major information system and should provide information for three broad purposes.

* External reporting to investors, bankers, the government for taxation purposes and other interested outside parties;

* Internal reporting to managers for use in making non-routine decisions such as investment, product pricing, formulating overall policies and drawing up plans for the short and long term;

* Internal reporting to managers for use in the controlling and planning of routine operations.

The main function of financial accounting is stewardship. Although reports were traditionally only addressed to the shareholders, there is now an obligation to report to many of those who have a stake in the business. Reports must comply with the requirements of the Companies Act and the regulations, such as Financial Reporting Standards, issued by the accountancy profession. Financial accountants are also normally involved in the issue of share prospectuses, the completion of various government statistics and the compilation of tax returns. Other functions of financial managers include:

* Forecasting availability of, and requirement for cash.
* Planning an appropriate capital structure.
* Obtaining cash from outside the business.
* Investments in fixed and current assets.
* Debtor and creditor management.
* Investing surplus funds.

7.3   Management accounting

Management accounting does not concentrate on recording past events or on presentation of externally published financial statements. The role of management accounting is to support the managers of the organisation in their financial decision-making process and being part of that management team.

> **Definition**   Management accounting is defined by CIMA as: 'the application of professional knowledge and skill in the preparation and presentation of accounting information, in such a way as to assist management in the formulation of policies and in the planning and control of the operations of the undertaking.'

Management accounting integrates the information from all activities of the business and enables management to view operations as a whole.   There are a number of activities associated with management accounting. They include:

(a)   Budgeting and budgetary control.

(b)   Cost accounting - this involves the analysis and allocation of costs.

(c)   Investment appraisal - this involves analysis of whether funds should be committed to projects or not.

(d)   Management of cash flows - this involves techniques such as cash budgeting.

7.4   Internal relationships - link between the functions

As mentioned earlier, the financial and management functions of accounting are linked. For example, if an organisation decides to expand by investing in new machinery and targeting new markets (a decision based on management accounting techniques) it will need to present accounting information to potential investors (financial reporting) to persuade them to provide the necessary funds for expansion (financial management).

In providing such information there is a two way process. The accountancy function needs to communicate with the other functional areas in order to build up an overall company budget as well as budgets by function/division. It needs to know about sales (marketing), labour costs (personnel), production and stocks (production), materials requirements (purchasing) etc. It then communicates back to the other functions what has actually happened ie, information flows back the other way for control purposes.

The accountancy function also brings together information from the various other functions for decision-making eg, whether to invest in new plant and machinery for a new product. Information on expected sales, selling prices and advertising/promotion costs would be required from marketing. Production costs, labour requirements, equipment costs etc would be required from production. Material costs would be required from purchasing. The information can then be integrated and evaluated.

7.5   Using and measuring data

The accounting system is the formal method of gathering and communicating data. This data is to be used to aid the decisions taken to achieve the overall goals of the whole business. The means the accounting data can be classified and reclassified in many ways. One approach is to classify information into three types, each serving as different means, often at various management levels and each answering three basic questions:

- problem solving questions - which decision will lead to the best outcome?
- score-card questions - how is performance?
- attention-directing questions - which areas or activities have problems deserving attention?

The data used in the three areas is not exclusive. It can be used in answering questions in more than one area. For example, data from a performance report can also be used to indicate areas where action is needed. Problem-solving data helps managers when taking long-term and special decisions. Score-keeping and problem-solving data helps managers in the planning and controlling of routine operations.

The score-keeping data is of particular interest to parties outside the organisation who want to know how it has performed in the past. The three basic questions require the gathering of data, and its processing and interpretation, so that informed decisions can be taken. Above all, the accounting systems are means to ends. The ends are better decisions.

The flows of information within an organisation are complex, especially in large firms. Accounting data is systematically gleaned from predetermined sources and reported via the formal channels. The information may be measured and then used for accounting purposes. Sales and production data, for instance, can be quantified in units or as total value.

All types of information, both quantified and non-quantified, can serve important functions in the overall control of the business. An important and basic integrative function is served by accounting information. This is routinely generated and sent out through the formal accounting system. Often the accounting system is the only source of quantitative information that combines the results of all the different parts of the organisation. The accounting information system is of central importance because it represents the only way of assessing the results of the organisation in terms of a single dimension. The primary purpose in the design of accounting tasks is to provide control. The scorecard function is secondary (though often at least a legal necessity).

Accounting information is therefore an important control tool, though it in no way reflects all the activities in the company and only provides information in the one dimension. There is a danger in the use of accounting information in that it can be presented as the only important aspect of the organisation being the only quantitative measure of the activities of a wide variety of disparate units. This tendency has often been reinforced by the dominant position of profit as the principal objective of those in power. Some financial commentators allege that there is an over-emphasis on short-term profit in British firms at the cost of larger profits in the long term.

7.6   The role of accounting information in management control

A significant function of senior management is control of both overall strategy and actual performance. Accounting information is crucial in the effective discharge of both tasks. Traditional management accounting information as a control device must contribute to the overall control system. The primary financial control system of many organisations is budgetary control.

Information is data that has been put into a form which is meaningful to the recipient and which is of real or perceived value for the intended purpose. For the management accountant this purpose is likely to be planning control and other decision making. There is a need for the efficient gathering of enough relevant data and for the data to be processed. From the system's viewpoint, information has some valuable attributes. Rapid feedback of information helps to reduce uncertainty. This is the main reason for wanting information. The more decisions are taken with adequate information, the more likely it is that the decision taken will prove to have been the best possible decision.

Information is usually incremental - it adds to, updates and perhaps corrects information that was already available. It may confirm existing information but information, which has 'surprise' elements is often the most valuable in decision making. This parallels the concept of management by exception, where managerial attention should be concentrated on divergence from the expected.

7.7   Presentation of management accounting information

A number of investigations into the role of accounting information in managerial decisions have shown that much of the information is ignored. To minimise this lack of response, several factors should be considered:

- the economic reality of the information should be clearly presented in a way that demonstrates economic consequences more easily than traditional management accounting statements may do;

- the information should have relevance for the person and purpose for which it is intended. Information for control and performance purposes should generally be limited to those areas for which the manager is responsible;

- it needs to be timely when it comes to the attention of a manager;

- it should be sufficiently detailed and accurate.

7.8   Accounting information as a control technique

Accounting information has a central role to play. Control techniques have different time horizons and organisational levels.   At the short-term operational level, accounting information about performance is judged by comparison with the detailed budget. Budgetary control compares actual reported results with the planned or budgeted results, and reports and investigates any variances. This discipline helps to accomplish plans within agreed spending limits. Budgets therefore have a dual role, as both plans and controls. For budgetary control to succeed a number of conditions need to be met, including the genuine and full involvement of line managers and also a clear definition and understanding of goals and the overall corporate plan.

7.9   Accounting information and strategic planning

In making long-term strategic plans, the financial aspects help to focus on the organisation's environment, the determination of its objectives, the choice of strategies and eventually the tactics used. The accounting information system is required to provide the information for the decisions involved in developing the corporate plan. This will include forecast financial statistics (turnover, capital employed, return on capital and so on), forecast operating statements and balance sheets. It will also include forecast cash flow statements, capital expenditures and treasury operations.

8   INFORMATION SYSTEMS MANAGEMENT

8.1   Introduction - the nature of information

The majority of the functional areas discussed in this section are dealt with in depth in other modules of the CIMA course and it is only proposed here to give a brief resume of the activities in which they are involved and their interrelationships.

All are dependent on information systems for their effective operation. The design of such systems has already been considered alongside the structure with which they are linked. Some basic definitions concerning the nature of information have been formulated by O'Brien:

Definition	**Data** is	'any fact, observation, assumption or occurrence - raw material which is processed into information.'
	Information is	'data that has been transformed into a meaningful and useful form for specific individuals.'
	Information systems	'collect and process data and disseminate information within an organisation.'

A typical business exchanges information with other businesses, suppliers and customers, central and local government, shareholders, financial institutions and trade unions/employers associations.

Some of the most important information for a business is that relating to the market for its goods or services. For example:

- Information on sales levels, profits, suppliers and potential competitors is needed to see if any additional competitive advantage is possible;

- Information on financial circumstances and availability of additional funds is needed to monitor current profitability and plan future expansion.

- Information on profits is needed because shareholders monitor their investment and government requires them for tax and statistical purposes.

For information to be exchanged efficiently it must be organised to meet these needs. A sole trader may collect, record and process all the information needed for their business without any assistance. A large manufacturing company may set up departments to collect, record and process different types of information.

8.2   The value of information

For information to have value, it must lead to a decision to take action that results in reducing costs, eliminating losses, increasing sales, better use of resources, prevention of fraud or providing management with information about the consequences of alternative courses of action. Because the value of the information lies in the action taken as a result of receiving it, asking the following questions would give an assessment of its value:

- What information is provided?
- What is it used for?
- Who uses it?
- How often is it used?
- What is achieved by using it?
- Is it used as often as it is provided?
- What other relevant information is available which could be used instead?

The value of information must also relate to the frequency of its provision, and to the level in the management hierarchy where it is sent and used. Operational management needs more regular control information, perhaps daily or weekly, whereas middle and senior management (tactical and strategic) might need information less frequently - monthly, quarterly or yearly.

8.3   Components of the organisation's information system

A management information system is a system using formalised procedures to provide managers at all levels with appropriate information from all relevant sources (internal and external to the business) for the purposes of planning and controlling the activities for which they are responsible. It should be clear that no single type of system would be capable of this, so in a large organisation there will commonly be a range of components or subsystems that together form the management information system.

There are three broad categories of data processing, which generate information:

- **transactions processing** (routine handling of data for day-to-day operations);

- **management information systems** (provide information to facilitate decision-making and control); and

- **management support systems** (provide support to management in specific circumstances).

Within most management information systems and support systems there are four system types:

(i)   **database systems** which process and store information which becomes the organisation's memory;

(ii) **direct control systems** which monitor and report on activities such as output levels, sales ledger and credit accounts in arrears;

(iii) **enquiry systems** based on databases which provide specific information such as the performance of a department or an employee; and

(iv) **support systems** that provide computer-based methods and procedures for conducting analyses, forecasts and simulations.

8.4 The scope of MIS

To give you an idea of the scope of MIS some typical reports produced in a medium sized manufacturing company might include the following.

(a) **Production and material control**

- Forward loading plans for production cycles
- Machine capacity forecast
- Departmental operating statements
- Stock and work progress reports
- Wastage report
- Labour utilisation report

(b) **Marketing including distribution**

- Market surveys
- Order reports by product and geographical area
- Discount trends
- Transport and warehouse cost statements
- Salesman performance
- Product service and support costs

(c) **Personnel**

- Numbers employed by category
- Overtime hours
- Sickness, absence, lateness
- Training requirements
- Career development plans
- Recruitment policy
- Job descriptions

(d) **Financial and management accounting**

- Annual financial statements
- Monthly profit statements
- Budgets and forecasts
- Sales and contribution analyses
- Cash, management and working capital evaluation
- Capital project appraisal
- Standard cost and variance analysis reports
- Returns to Government departments eg, VAT

9   SELF TEST QUESTIONS

9.1   Distinguish between a sales orientation and a marketing orientation. (1.1)

9.2   Differentiate between organisation planning and operations planning. (1.3)

9.3   Define marketing. (2.2)

9.4   Draw a diagram showing how resources are converted into goods and services in the production process. (3.1)

9.5   Describe two constraints that may affect the effectiveness of the production operation. (3.2)

9.6   Outline the typical R & D activities of an organisation. (5.2)

9.7   What are the main personnel services? (6.4)

9.8   Describe the three broad purposes that financial information is used for. (7.2)

9.9   What are the three broad categories of data processing that generate information? (8.3)

10   EXAMINATION TYPE QUESTION

10.1   Planning and operating decisions

The production process is one by which goods and services are brought into existence. Write a brief account of the planning and operating decisions that the production manager is likely to encounter in a fairly small manufacturing business.   **(20 marks)**

11   ANSWER TO EXAMINATION TYPE QUESTION

11.1   Planning and operating decisions

The basic features of management decision-making are the same, no matter whether a manager specialises in selling, purchasing, production or any other operating function. Similarly, the decisions of a production manager in a car manufacturing business are the same as the decisions of a production manager in a toy car or different type of manufacturing enterprise.

If we assume that the production manager is fairly senior in the management hierarchy and because it is a fairly small organisation, it could be presumed that the production manager would be involved in strategic decision-making, budgeting and weekly or daily production planning and control.

The strategic planning decisions that the manager might be involved with include:

• **Capital expenditure plans** - the production manager will make recommendations about expenditure on production fixed assets. Such decisions would include re-siting the production plant, introducing new production technology or replacing old worn out plant.

• **Planning new products** - product research, design and development might be a specific responsibility of an 'engineering' manager, but there would need to be consultations over operational considerations involving new product development and manufacture. Similarly, the production manager would be involved in decisions to develop existing products, promotion methods and the timing and duration of advertising or promotional campaigns.

• **Quality of products** - this is a key factor in the marketing mix. When a strategic decision is taken about the target market position for the organisation's product, the choice of balance between quality and price will have to be made. The production manager will be involved in this decision to advise on the quality of output that can be achieved with given production resources.

- **Rationalising production** - decisions to shut down a plant or to rationalise production so as to achieve lower costs or greater efficiency are either strategic or budgeting decisions. During economic recessions, survival might depend on the success of management pruning their production capacity and at the same time increasing productivity.

The production manager will also make decisions regarding the production budget. This will be a plan of how many of each product should be made, what resources will be required to make them and how much they will cost.

The resource utilisation budget will maintain the planned requirement for materials, labour and machine time. To determine these requirements, a decision must be made about standard rates of efficiency for material usage, labour productivity and machine operations. The production manager might also be involved in decisions on levels of raw materials inventories and the optimal size of batches, if batch production methods are used.

Standard rates of pay and methods of working might be reviewed periodically and improvements agreed by the production manager in consultation with the work force and the trade union representative.

Where limiting factors exist, for example where some production resources place a constraint on what the business can make and sell, the production manager might need to decide whether to pay extra to overcome the problem, perhaps by sub-contacting some of the work.

Within the framework of the budget, the production manager will make daily and weekly operating decisions. These will include production scheduling ie, deciding on output quotas, the allocation of different jobs to different groups and assigning priorities to jobs. Operating decisions consist of putting plans into effect and control decisions, which might involve some strategic control - monitoring the success or failure of the organisation in achieving its strategic plans. However, most control decisions will be at the tactical or operational level.

Budgetary control involves a comparison of actual results against the budget plan and the highlighting of excessive variances, which might indicate that control action is necessary. Control might then involve decisions about improving efficiency and labour productivity, controlling expenditure levels, postponing spending, reducing idle time, improving capacity utilisation of the plant or quality control. Similar comparisons of actual results against production schedules might be carried out daily or weekly, involving control decisions by the production manager.

8 THE ORGANISATION AND ACTIVITIES OF THE MARKETING FUNCTION

INTRODUCTION & LEARNING OUTCOMES

Syllabus area 11(ii)
- The organisation and activities of the marketing function (ie, marketing research, market segmentation and marketing strategy formulation).

- The concept of the marketing mix and the major tools therein (ie, branding, product mix, pricing, advertising, sales promotion, public relations, packaging and distribution).

In this chapter, we consider the key management function of marketing in more depth and examine the elements in the marketing mix to consider how they might be used to achieve the company's marketing goals.

Jerome McCarthy in his book 'Basic Marketing: A Management Approach' popularised a four factor classification of the 'marketing mix' concept which he called the Four P's - product, price, promotion and place (or distribution). A marketing mix is a company's attempt to find a workable, preferably optimum, combination of controllable marketing factors. There is no such thing as a typical marketing mix because each company prescribes its own unique formula.

When you have studied this chapter, you should be able to do the following:

- Explain the workings of the marketing function of an organisation and the major tools and techniques used by marketing specialists.

---

1 MARKETING ACTIVITY

1.1 Introduction

Marketing is not just relevant to business organisations involved in manufacturing for a profit. It can be applied to those businesses involved in supplying a service such as accountancy firms or travel agents, or to charitable organisations such as housing associations and public and private sector organisations eg, the Health Education Council.

This shows the broadening of the marketing concept to other situations where an exchange takes place and allows us to accept Kotler's revised definition of marketing:

Definition 'Marketing is human activity directed at satisfying needs and wants through exchange processes.'

The exchange can therefore be money for goods, taxes for health services, the fee for advice given, or a charity donation for the feel good factor that you get from contributing.

Although we use the term 'product' throughout this section, the concepts can and are easily applicable to services, ideas, people and so on.

Marketing is the one function of management that is more concerned with what goes on externally than internally. We can think of the organisation as an open system, in that the various activities and people are linked together and are structured to achieve the objectives of the organisation. Marketing activities are conducted mainly across the boundaries of the system.

There are three basic elements in the 'marketing situation'.

(i)   *The company* - which has resources and objectives. The firm's marketing research needs will first be determined by the elements of the marketing environment which are critical to success.

(ii) *The market itself* and the search for marketing opportunities - which may really be a number of sub-markets segmented by various factors. Identifying these factors clearly is important, because each one may have distinct needs and wants. Satisfaction of these represents business opportunities.

(iii) *The marketing process* - which links market needs and company resources. It involves:

- identifying the need - focuses on the unsatisfied and potential wants and any constraints that exist and might limit the satisfaction of those wants. This is the province of market research (more detail later).

- developing the product and service that meets the need - product and service planning. The areas of new product development, product management, product mix, branding, packaging and deletion of old products are all included.

- creating awareness of the benefits offered - planning for effective marketing.

- selling (ie, converting desire to decision) - incorporates advertising, sales promotion, sales force management, publicity, warranties, public relations, displays and communication with the consumers.

1.2   Customer or consumer

Although the terms are used interchangeably, companies should distinguish between the customer and the consumer, so that they can produce goods and services that will sell successfully.

| Definition | **Consumer**: The ultimate consumer of a product, the ultimate user of a product or service; the person who derives the satisfaction of the benefit offered. |

| Definition | **Customer**: A person or organisation actually making the purchase decision, not necessarily the consumer or user. |

For example, a supermarket chain (customer of the manufacturer) purchases a manufacturer's products for selling on to consumers. In a similar way, a housewife (customer of the supermarket) buys a good which is consumed by her family (consumers of the manufacturer).

1.3   The basic functions of marketing

The basic functions of marketing that must be performed by one party or another, and a brief description of them, are outlined below.

- **Customer analysis** - analysing the characteristics and needs.

- **Buying** - procurement, analysis and selection of sellers, terms of purchase and procedure for buying.

- **Selling** - advertising, sales promotion, sales force management, publicity and public relations, customer relations and interaction with consumers, dealer relations, warranties and displays.

- **Product and/or service planning** - new product development, product management, branding, packaging and removal of old products.

- **Social responsibility** - obligation to offer safe, useful and ethical products and services.

- **Price planning** - profitability, level and range of prices, terms and credit availability, cash flow, sales and reductions, budgeting and flexibility.

- **Distribution** - warehousing, wholesaling, retailing and retail site locations, physical distribution and method of transportation, stock management, service levels, allocation and vendor management.

- **Marketing research** - data and information collection and analysis as a basis for future decisions and planning.

- **Opportunity analysis** - appraisal of risks and benefits associated with the decision-making.

The responsibility for these functions can be shifted and shared among manufacturers, wholesalers, retailers, marketing specialists and consumers, but they cannot be eliminated in most situations.

2   MARKET SEGMENTATION

2.1   Explanation

It is important here to define and explain market segmentation. Kotler provides a definition:

Definition   'Market segmentation is the subdividing of a market into distinct subsets of customers, where any subset may conceivably be selected as a market target to be reached with a distinct marketing mix.'

Market segmentation allows companies to treat similar customers in similar ways, whilst distinguishing between dissimilar customer groups. Each customer group has slightly different needs, which can be satisfied by offering each group, or segment, a slightly different marketing strategy. For example, the market for package holidays can be split up into a variety of different sub-markets - the family market, the elderly market, the young singles market, the activity holiday market, the budget holiday market etc. It would be virtually impossible to provide one single holiday package that would satisfy all people in the above markets. Because the people in the different sectors will have different needs and wants, a holiday company has a choice in terms of its marketing approach. It can go for:

(a)   *Niche or target marketing* - (sometimes referred to as concentrated marketing) specialising in one or two of the identified markets only, where a company knows it can compete successfully. It acquires a great deal of expertise in its market segment, which must be large enough to sustain profitability. For example, Saga holidays offer a variety of holidays for the older market niche only. Ramblers concentrate on walking holidays.

(b)   *Differentiated marketing* - offers a variety of products to suit all of the needs. Companies like Thompson Holidays offer a variety of holiday types to appeal to most markets. These holidays may be at different prices, in different resorts, at different times of the year and advertised in different brochures.

(c)   *Mass or undifferentiated marketing* - is the opposite of differentiated marketing, in that it treats all customers and potential customers as identical. In the holiday sector, if a company offers just one type of holiday hoping that it would appeal to the majority of people, it would be competing against all of its rivals, who have become specialists in their own areas.

2.2   Methods of market segmentation

There are different bases used to segment a market. The traditional method was segmentation on demographic grounds. This is still the starting point for many segmentation exercises, though further investigation often finds that demographic influences are not the prime determining factors of purchase.

- **Demographic segmentation** - market research studies are frequently broken down by age, income, social class, sex, geographical area, occupation, family unit, etc. This can be highly relevant with some products. For example, certain brands of breakfast cereals have regular sales, only in families where there are children aged under eight, whereas other brands (eg, Bran Flakes and Shredded Wheat) sell almost entirely to adults. In other areas, demographic influences appear to have no effect - for instance, own label products are believed to sell equally to high and low incomes, to families and single people, and across age groups.

  Socio-economic class is closely correlated with press readership and viewing habits, and media planners use this fact to advertise in the most effective way to communicate with their target audience.

- **Geographic segmentation** - markets are frequently split into regions for sales and distribution purposes. Many consumer goods manufacturers break down sales by television advertising regions.

- **Value segmentation** - is present in most markets. Value can be defined as the customer's view of the balance between satisfaction from the product and its price. Thus, many products have a premium-priced, high quality segment, a mid-priced segment and a low-price segment eg, shoes. In such a market, fashion and quality differences can outweigh price variations. In other markets, eg, petrol and cigarettes, small differences in price can outweigh the small differences in satisfaction perceived by the purchaser.

- **Psychological** - consumers can be divided into groups sharing common psychological characteristics. One group may be described as security-oriented, another as ego-centred and so on. These categories are useful in the creation of advertising messages.

- **Life style segmentation** - a recent trend is to combine psychological and socio-demographic characteristics to give a more complete profile of customer groups. This kind of segmentation uses individuals to represent groups, which form a significant proportion of the consumer market. It defines these individuals in terms of sex, age, income, job, product preferences, social attitudes, and political views.

- **Purchasing characteristics** - customers may be segmented by the volume they buy (heavy user, medium user, light user, non user), by the outlet type they use, or by the pack size bought. These variables, and many others, are useful in planning production and distribution and in developing promotion policy. A food manufacturer will approach supermarket chains very differently to the small independent retailer probably offering better prices, delivery terms, use different sales techniques and deliver direct to the supermarket chain. They might also supply own label product to the large chain but they are unlikely to be able to offer the same terms to the corner shop.

- **Benefit** - customers have different expectations of a product. Some people buy detergents for whiteness, and are catered for by Daz or Persil. Others want economy, for which Surf may fit the bill. Some customers may demand stain removal; one of the biological products is appropriate. An understanding of customers' benefits sought enables the manufacturer to create a range of products each aimed precisely at a particular benefit.

- **Family life cycle segmentation** - a form of demographic segmentation, as shown below, dividing customers by their position in the family life cycle.

Life cycle stage	Characteristics	Examples of products purchased
Bachelor	Financially well-off. Fashion opinion leaders. Recreation oriented.	Cars, holidays, basic furniture, kitchen equipment.
Newly married couple	Still financially well-off. Very high purchase rate, especially of durables.	Cars, furniture, houses, holidays refrigerators.
Full nest (i)	Liquid assets low. Home purchasing at peak. Little money saving.	Washers, TVs, baby foods, toys, medicines.
Full nest (ii)	Better off. Some wives work. Some children work part time. Less influenced by advertising.	Larger size grocery packs, foods, cleaning materials, bicycles.
Full nest (iii)	Better off still.	New furniture, luxury appliances. Recreational goods.
Empty nest (i)	Satisfied with financial position. Home ownership at peak.	Travel, luxuries, home improvements.
Empty nest (ii)	Drastic cut in income. Stay at home.	Medicines, health aids.

The benefits of segmentation to the company adopting this policy is that it enables them to get close to their intended customer and really find out what that customer wants (and is willing to pay for). This should make the customer happier with the product offered and hence lead to repeat sales and endorsements.

2.3   Activity

Give reasons why demographic segmentation, by itself, is not a successful basis for car manufacturers targeting their customers.

2.4   Solution

Reasons include the following:

(a)   A car manufacturer may use buyers' age in developing its target market and then discover that the target should be the psychologically young and not the chronologically young. (The Ford Motor Company used buyers' age in targeting its Mustang car in America, designing it to appeal to young people who wanted an inexpensive sporty car. Ford found to its surprise that the car was being purchased by all age groups.)

(b)   Income is another variable that can be deceptive. One would imagine that working class families would buy Ford Escorts and the managerial class would buy BMWs. However, many Escorts are bought by middle-income people (often as the family's second car) and expensive cars are often bought by working class families (plumbers, carpenters etc).

(c)   Personal priorities also upset the demographic balance. Middle-income people often feel the need to spend more on clothes, furniture and housing which they could not afford if they purchased a more expensive car.

(d)   The upgrading urge for people trying to relate to a higher social order often leads them to buy expensive cars.

(e)   Some parents although 'well off' pay large fees for the private education of their children and must either make do with a small car, or perhaps no car at all.

3   MARKETING RESEARCH

3.1   Introduction

Organisations exist in a constantly changing environment. To be able to respond to these changes, they must collect information on which to base decisions. Decisions based on inadequate information are no more than hopeful guesses. Marketing research has seen major growth in recent years in the United Kingdom for three reasons.

- The environment in which organisations operate is changing fast.

- Technological changes coupled with economies of scale have meant that the risk of substantial loss is much greater, so the producer has to be even more certain that the product will meet market needs.

- The boundaries of markets are expanding, so the cost of failure is becoming much larger.

Marketing research is the systematic and objective search for, and analysis of, information relevant to the identification and solution of any problem in the field of marketing.

It is not just obtaining information, but *involves:*

- framing questions whose answers will provide data to help solve problems;
- asking questions to those best qualified to answer them;
- recording answers correctly;
- interpreting answers; and
- translating interpretations and making recommendations for marketing action.

It consists of:

(a)   *market research* (analysis of the market size, trends, market shares, etc);

(b)   *distribution research* (analysis of present channels of distribution, warehouse and other storage locations, discount policy, transport needs, etc);

(c)   *economic research* (analysis of trends including social and forecasting);

(d)   *evaluation of product(s)* (customer requirements analysis, product life cycles, quality measurements, reliability); and

(e)   *communication analysis* (of the media usage, suggested media combinations eg TV and newspaper advertising, etc).

3.2   Marketing and market research

Marketing research does not itself produce answers but it can produce information that helps decision-makers to arrive at better answers. Marketing research systems need to be designed to meet the information needs of the decision-makers in planning for the future and controlling and adjusting to the present. There is a difference between market research, which focuses on the size and nature of markets, and marketing research, which is wider to include all the aspects of the company's marketing effort. The firm's marketing research needs will first be determined by which elements of the marketing environment are critical to success. Marketing research can be divided into two broad categories: desk research (internal research) and field research (external research).

3.3   Desk research

Desk research - sometimes called secondary research - is concerned with the collection of information from secondary sources. It does not derive information first-hand but obtains existing data by studying published and other available sources of information. Thorough desk research at the beginning of a survey can often eliminate the need for extensive field work, or limit it to checking the main features of the study.

This information may have been collected by somebody else, perhaps for a different purpose. Although the research data is unlikely to be exactly what the current researcher wants and may not be totally up to date, it has the advantage that it is available and at relatively low cost.

Government sources provide a wide range of secondary data by publishing statistics and survey results.   UK government surveys are reliable and available at comparatively modest cost. Commercial organisations, such as the Economist Intelligence Unit and Mintel provide surveys and reports on markets, industries and countries.

There are three main types of information that are collected by desk research:

(i)   **Economic intelligence** - is concerned with such factors as gross national product (GNP), investment, expenditure, population, employment, productivity and trade. It provides an organisation with a picture of past and future trends in the environment, and with an indication of the organisation's position in the economy as a whole.

(ii)   **Market intelligence** - is information about a company's present or possible future markets. Such information will be both commercial and technical, for example: the product range offered by existing or potential competitors; the level of sales of competitors' products and the best overseas markets for a company.

        Specialist libraries provide much of this type of information. The Patents Office Library keeps back numbers of nearly all of the British, and many foreign, technical journals. The Department of Trade and Industry Expert Intelligence Service has extensive information in its library in the City and the libraries of other ministries contain much valuable information and are very willing to help.

(iii)   **Internal company data** - is perhaps the most neglected source of marketing information. Companies tend to record their sales information for accountancy purposes or for the management of the sales force. It is rarely collected in a form that can be readily used by marketing management. The preliminary stages of a marketing study often involve analysing a company's sales. Sales can be analysed by: product type, type of outlet, salesmen, contribution to overheads, total volume and geographical distribution.

3.4   Field research

When desk research is unsuitable, either because of content or being out of date, then relatively expensive field research - sometimes called primary research - has to be considered. There are four main types of primary data collection:

•   **Survey research** - a survey can be taken to achieve one or more aims. For instance, it could be used to judge reaction to a new product or to determine public perception of a brand name. A survey involves careful design of a questionnaire and the use of statistical sampling. The actual survey may be carried out by telephone, mail or structured interview.

•   **Observation** - this involves no interaction with the subject but the recorder watches, listens to and records behaviour. One example is monitoring competitor prices. Another is counting the patterns of the flow of pedestrians through a shopping area.

- **Experimentation** - a range of techniques are used in experimentation. Customer preferences may be determined by 'blind' testing. At a higher level, different marketing strategies may be test marketed.

- **Qualitative techniques** - a relatively expensive method, but one which may yield more valid results, is to conduct unstructured individual or group interviews. The lack of structure may make analysis difficult but the results may be more valid in that they are not the result of the prompting of the structured interview.

Each of these has advantages and disadvantages. The researcher needs to take these into account when designing the programme. A pilot study may be undertaken before embarking on the full-scale study.

3.5   Methods of market research

Market research falls into two chief types: motivational research and measurement research.

(a)   **Motivational research** - the objective is to unearth factors that may be important to the product concerned. It does not discover how important they are, nor does it give particulars of the extent to which the factors exist. Some of the more common techniques in motivational research are:

- *Depth interviewing* - undertaken at length by a trained person who is able to appreciate conscious and unconscious associations and motivations and their significance.

- *Group interviewing* - where between six and ten persons are asked to consider the relevant subject (object) under trained supervision.

- *Word association testing* - on being given a word by the interviewer, the first word that comes into the mind of the person being tested is noted.

- *Triad testing* - where people are asked which out of three given items is least like the remaining two, and why. If the three are brands of a given type of product (or three similar types) replies may show a great deal about attitudes.

In these and other techniques, the basic idea is always to find out what people in general (and the potential customer in particular) believe is relevant to the product.

(b)   **Measurement research** - where the importance of the factors is measured. This type of research uses samples, which should be representative of the population, or some known subsection of it. By finding out how often some features occur in the sample, it can give a reasonable expectation that the same proportions will occur in the whole population. Sample surveys are used to find out how many people buy the product(s), what quantity each type of buyer purchases, and where and when the product is bought.

It is also possible (less accurately) to assess the importance of some reasons in buying or not buying. The main types of measurement are:

- Random sampling
- Quota surveying
- Panelling
- Surveying by post - the mail shot method
- Observation

4   THE MARKETING MIX

4.1   The four Ps

We have suggested that successful businesses are those with a strong marketing orientation to their business culture. The way they think and the choices they make are all directed towards the satisfaction of customer need. The company is affected by external environmental factors beyond its control and must monitor and respond to these changes. In doing so there are a number of variables it can control to influence buyers' decisions. Collectively these controllable variables are called the marketing mix.

The marketing mix is concerned with how to influence consumer demand and is primarily the responsibility of the marketing department. It has been defined by Kotler as:

Definition   'the set of controllable variables that the firm can use to influence the buyers' responses'.

The variables are commonly grouped into four classes that Jerome McCarthy refers to as 'the four Ps' - product, price, promotion and place (or distribution):

Product	**Price**	**Promotion**	**Place**
Brand name	Level	Sales promotion	Distribution channels
Packaging	Discounts	Personal selling	Distribution coverage
Features	Allowances	Publicity	Outlet locations
Options	Payment terms	Advertising	Sales territories
Quality	Delivery options		Inventory levels
Warranty			Inventory locations
Service			
Style appeal			

4.2   Product

By 'product' we mean everything that is used by the organisation to provide consumer satisfaction. A product can be a physical commodity, a service, a group of either of these, or a product-service combination.

It is important to bear in mind exactly what a product is to the consumer. It is really a package of satisfaction. The consumer's image of the product is frequently more significant than the physical description of the product itself. It is what it means to the consumer, not what it means to the seller, that is the key to product policy.

When the outputs of factories are virtually identical, and within a given price range, the conversion of an indifferent (even apathetic) potential customer into a buyer needs effort. Irrespective of whether the product is a toy, a pair of shoes, a lipstick or management consultancy, the existence of competition often means that the successful seller offers more than the actual product itself. The product must be surrounded by value satisfactions, which differentiate that product from others.

The elements of the product mix that the marketer can control include quality, styling, design, packaging, reliability, durability and available sizes. Trade-offs are involved between the various elements of product mix. The build quality of the car may be at a high production cost. The durability of a vehicle may be a trade-off with increased weight, reduced economy and performance. In the 1990s, the potential customers are often wealthier and more discriminating about features such as design and technical specification.

The product mix needs to take into account changes in cultural values and society. Fashions change. Legal requirements change. Environmental pressures may require the repackaging and reformulation of the product. The changing age structure of many countries - with increasing proportions of older people - may shift the emphasis from fashion to durability and utility as the cultural norm.

4.3   Price

Price can be determined on several bases – generally the marketer is interested in 'what the market will bear' which is obviously affected by available substitutes, demand/supply balance, nature of competition, etc. There are two main pricing strategies:

(c)   marketing skimming, when a premium price is charged because your product has a technological advantage or brand loyalty which outweighs a price difference;

(d)   market penetration, a deliberately low price to dominate the market and block competition entry, eg, the Bic biro approach.

Price is a crucial element in the marketing mix. An organisation may decide to reduce its price as a key strategy in its marketing mix. However, if it spends its marketing budget in this area there will be less available for the other three Ps. So the skill of marketing initially lies in knowing what proportion of spend (spread amongst the four Ps) will yield maximum profitable sales.

Setting prices is a difficult part of the marketing mix. While the external environment imposes market constraints on the freedom of the marketer to fully exploit the price element of the marketing mix, the degree of imperfection in most markets gives some discretion. The company generally will have three basic goals in its pricing policy:

•   Establish a presence in the market, typically a low price on entry to penetrate the market, to be increased when established.

•   Achieve and maintain market share against competitors.

•   Earn optimum profits.

These three objectives can often be incompatible. Maintaining market share may require lower prices, or improved products whose cost cannot be reflected adequately in the price. Most products have a lifecycle from launch to eventual decline. The relative emphasis given to each of these three elements changes during the lifecycle. For instance, a newly launched model of a car may be relatively highly priced, because of the degree of improvement over the model replaced. As the novelty wears off, discounts may be introduced to stimulate flagging sales. As the car becomes dated, additional features may be added. Finally, to clear stocks before the launch of the next replacement, deep discounting may be used.

In times of high inflation, price-cutting is less favoured as a marketing tool because customers have lost their perception of a 'benchmark' price, ie, the regular fair price. In this environment, a '5p off' coupon promotion has a greater effect upon sales than a straight price cut.

4.4   Promotion

The promotion mix consists of four elements:

(a)   **Advertising:** paid communications in the media which are designed to influence potential customers favourably regarding a company's products or services. Advertising is sometimes called above-the-line promotion.

(b)   **Sales promotion:** non-media promotional activity aimed at increasing sales. Sales promotion includes a variety of techniques such as give-aways, competitions, coupons and exhibitions. It is sometimes called below-the-line promotion.

(c)   **Public relations:** the creation of positive attitudes regarding products, services, or companies by various means, including unpaid media coverage and involvement with community activities.

(d)   **Personal selling:** the techniques by which a sales force makes contact with potential customers.

Each company has a different promotion-mix setting; even companies in the same product area can successfully adopt widely differing promotion policies.

Advertising can be defined as:

Definition   'any paid form of non-personal promotion by an identifiable sponsor'.

It uses the principal communication media. Sales promotions are the short-term incentives to boost the actual sales of the product. Typically, such incentives are selective and temporary. This element of promotion has been growing rapidly. In the UK, sales promotions involve more spending than advertising. A public relations exercise is the deliberate and planned effort to establish and maintain mutual understanding between the organisation and its public. The term 'public' includes several distinct sectors: the financial community, the media and government, for instance. Finally comes personal selling, on a one-to-one basis with a view to a sale. This is usually more important where the product to be promoted is relatively expensive, complicated and perhaps of a capital nature.

Generally, however, advertising is less important to those selling in the industrial market than to manufacturers of fast-moving consumer goods. In industrial marketing, personal selling is often the most widely used of the above four elements. Sales promotion and public relations are useful in both consumer and industrial marketing: budgets for the former can be as large as the advertising budget for some consumer products.

Companies choose strategies to convince the target market of the benefits of buying their products or services. The starting point is for the company to decide what the purpose of the promotion is. The purpose could be long term, to build up the brand name or it could be short term to boost sales. Advertising is good at achieving longer-term aims while sales promotions can achieve short-term targets such as clearing the remaining stocks of a soon-to-be-replaced model.

Secondly, the organisation should try to show how its product is different from others. If there is a range of similar products on the market, the establishing of a unique selling point (USP) can be an essential element in the marketing mix. There are a wide range of long-term and short-term promotional initiatives, for example money-off coupons, tokens to collect and free samples.

4.5   Place

The final group of factors in the marketing mix is 'place'. While the word 'place' is chosen rather than 'distribution', partly to suit the mnemonic of four P's (product, price, promotion and place), it does have the benefit of emphasising that decisions have to be taken about how to get the goods from producer to purchaser, about the design of the channels of distribution, and about the logistics of the physical distribution management. The process of distribution may involve one or more intermediaries, though in some cases manufacturers may not need intermediaries or may perform this function themselves. The customer will want the goods to be available locally, in the right quantity and form. There may also be a need for sales support staff, and customers may require a local after-sales service. The design of a channel of distribution will be influenced by the type of product, the abilities of the intermediaries and the expectations of the consumer.

5   MAJOR TOOLS OF THE MARKETING MIX

5.1   Branding

The selection of corporate symbols, such as the firm's name (brand), logo and trade characters is a significant element in the establishment of an overall company image. A brand is a name, symbol, term, mark or design that enables customers to identify and distinguish the products of one supplier from those offered by competitors. The supplier has to decide which products to brand, the quality level aspired to and the targeted position in the market place.

A label is an integral element of a product, showing the brand name, its composition and size, recommended user and constraints, promotional offers and details of the manufacturer or distributor.

However, a **brand** is not merely a product with a **label**, but something much more. Just as a person is known by the company he or she keeps, so a brand acquires a reputation related to the type of person who buys it, the ways in which it is used, how it is promoted and its competitive strengths.

Nevertheless, a good product may fail due to unimaginative and inadequate promotion or an unsatisfactory public image. Brand image strategy has to decide on the approach it intends to adopt, by addressing the following questions:

(a)   How shall we present our brand image?

(b)   What are the dominant recognisable strengths of the brand?

(c)   What market position are we aiming for relative to competing brands, (ie, are we aiming for the luxury or middle bracket)?

(d)   Should we concentrate on one market segment or offer a range of brands to cater for a wider market?

In the creation of a brand strategy, an organisation needs to be aware of the effect the brand name can have on the product or service. Some fortunate companies have had their name adopted for the product, regardless of the manufacturer eg, Hoover instead of vacuum cleaner and Sellotape instead of sticky tape. Market research in the UK has shown that most people believe that an organisation with a good reputation would not sell poor quality products. This is a competitive advantage for those companies when it comes to promoting new products.

5.2   Product life cycle

The product life cycle is the concept that attempts to describe a product's sales, profits, customers, competitors and marketing emphasis from its inception until its removal from the market. Ideally, a company will possess a balanced range of products in its portfolio passing through different stages in their respective life-cycles. The six stages are outlined below:

(i)   **Product development**. This is when there are only outgoings since money is invested in design costs and the production of prototypes. After this comes the product launch.

(ii)   **Market introduction**. There is not yet a proven demand for it, sales are low and develop slowly. The cash flow is still negative as a rule.

(iii)   **Market growth**. Demand begins to accelerate and the total market size begins to expand quickly. This could be called 'take-off stage'. Unit production costs fall (due to increased volume of output) and so the product begins to generate profits.

(iv)   **Market maturity**. Demand levels off and increases usually only at replacement rate and new family-formation rate. Profits are still satisfactory, yet at the end of this stage further growth is inhibited by competitive products.

(v)   **Saturation**. More products are available than the market can absorb. Competition is intensified and prices fall.

(vi)   **Decline**. Here few companies can cope with competition and chronic overcapacity occurs widely. This may be when mergers are proposed. Production of the product is concentrated into fewer and fewer hands. Prices and profit margins are depressed.

Our illustration is typical, and therefore acceptable to an examiner.

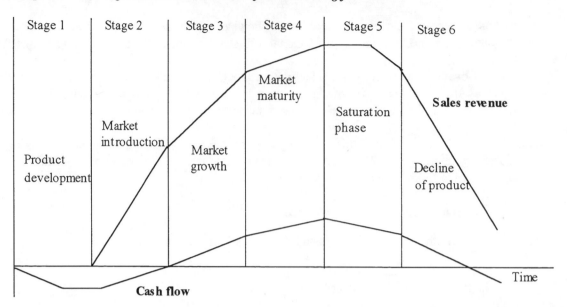

The product life cycle varies according to the type of product, for example, a high fashion product may have a life cycle of several months, whereas a stable product may have many years, eg, Brasso launched in 1927. It can be distorted by:

- finding new uses for old products,
- finding new markets and new user groups,
- changes in the exchange rate (typical of the early 90s),
- the introduction of legislation, enforcing product change, or
- creating a new brand image for an existing product.

It must be appreciated that the curve of the life cycle is a general one and only the experience of the marketing manager can possibly identify the stages of a given product's life cycle

5.3   Boston consulting group (BCG) matrix

The BCG matrix shows the summarised performance of either individual products or a portfolio of products.

The axes of the grid are market share and market growth, allowing four performance descriptions:

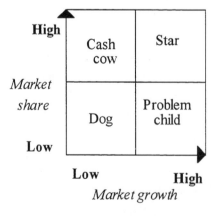

The axes are not calibrated, and therefore **relative** in nature. For instance, a market leader is likely to have a **high** market share. Similarly, market growth is a relative measure. Growth of 8 per cent may be seen as high in one industry and low in another.

Given the high degree of subjectivity, the four subdivisions are described below:

(i)   **Star** - a high market share product in a high growth industry. It generates substantial profits, but requires large amounts of resources to finance continued growth. Techniques to maintain or increase the market share include price reductions, product modifications, and/or greater distribution. As industry growth slows, stars become cash cows.

(ii)   **Dog** - a low market share in a low growth industry is likely to dent the corporate bottom line. A dog usually has cost disadvantages and few growth opportunities. An organisation with such a product can attempt to appeal to a specialised market, delete the product or harvest profits by cutting back support services to a minimum.

(iii) **Problem child** - otherwise known as 'double or quit'. It is a low market share product, but the future potential is considerable (as indicated by the high market growth). This category is sometimes referred to as the 'question mark', because the future of the product is frequently uncertain. It needs substantial cash to maintain or increase its market share in the face of strong competition. The company must decide whether to market more intensively or get out of this market. The questions are whether this product can compete successfully with adequate support and what that support will cost.

(iv)   **Cash cow** - a high market share product in a low growth industry; the product, at least in the short term, is a 'breadwinner'. It generates more cash than is required to maintain its market share. Profits support the growth of other company products. The firm's strategy is oriented towards maintaining the product's strong position in the market. However, because the market growth is low, the product may typically be in the last stages of the product life cycle. This at least means that potential competitors will be unlikely to enter the market.

The primary assumption of the BCG matrix is that the higher the organisation's market share, the lower its costs and the higher its profitability. This is the result of economies of scale (firms can mechanise and automate production and distribution), the experience curve (as projects and operations are repeated, time requirements are reduced) and improved bargaining power.

The grid is most useful when showing a portfolio of products. In the diagrams below, products are represented by circles, the area of which is proportional to product revenue. On some versions arrows are attached to the circles, showing expected future product movements, eg, from problem child to star as shown in Figure B.

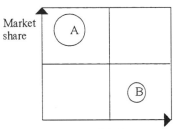

Figure A: Market growth

A cash cow may finance a problem child

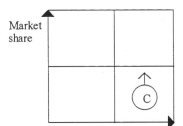

Figure B: Market growth

Expected movement from problem child to a star

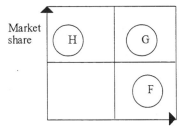

Figure C: Market growth

A balanced portfolio

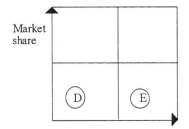

Figure D: Market growth

Funds are probably haemorrhaging from product D, and product E requires investment. Clearly this portfolio may present cash flow problems.

The logic of the portfolio is that cash cows are the financiers of the other segments. Ideally, some problem children are selected to become stars. This will require demands for capital, which will be provided by the cash cows. As a star matures and the market growth slows down, so the star becomes a cash cow for future products. Problem children not selected should be managed to generate cash until they become dogs. Dogs should be harvested or divested from the portfolio.

5.4   Product mix

> **Definition**   The product mix is the composite of products offered for sale by a firm or business unit (American Marketing Association).

This definition could be amended to allow for services, since such organisations as banks and insurance companies face similar mix decisions to those of manufacturers.

After determining the type of products it will offer, an organisation needs to outline the variety and assortment of those products. A product item is a specific model, brand or size of a product that the organisation sells eg, a Penguin classic paperback, a single packet of polo mints, an economy flight ticket etc. Generally, an organisation sells many product items.

A product line is a group of products that are closely related. This may be because they satisfy a class of need, are used together, are sold to the same customer groups, are marketed through the same type of outlets or fall within given price ranges. For example, Campbell sells many types of soup, Macmillan publishes a number of text books on marketing and the airlines provide different services eg, economy, business and first class.

The product mix consists of all the different product lines an organisation offers. For example, Gillette has a product mix, which includes razors, shaving cream, deodorants, shampoos and appliances.

Philip Kotler, in *Marketing Management, Analysis, Planning & Control*, considers the product mix in terms of its width, depth and consistency.

Width refers to the number of different product lines it has - a wide mix enables a firm to diversify its products, appeal to different consumer needs and encourage one-stop shopping. It also requires substantial resource investment and expertise in the different categories of product or service.

Depth refers to the number of product items within each product line - a deep mix can satisfy the needs of several consumer segments for the same product, maximise shelf space, preclude competitors and sustain dealer support. It also means higher costs for stock holding, product alterations and order processing.

Consistency is based on the relationship among product lines in terms of their sharing a common end-use, distribution outlets, consumer group and price range. A consistent mix is easier to handle because it allows the organisation to use marketing and production expertise, create a strong image and generate solid channel relations. However, excessive consistency can leave the organisation vulnerable to environmental threats eg, resource shortages.

The decision as to the mix of products will tend to reflect the nature of the market, the resources of the company and the underlying philosophy of the company's management. The Heinz product mix is both wide and deep, with many different lines (considerably more than 57) and many product items in several of the lines (for example, the varieties of canned soup). Generally, as business organisations become older and larger, they increase the width and depth of their product mix and reduce its consistency.

5.5   Advertising

It is the function of promotion to bring people to the point at which they actually purchase a product or service. Some potential customers might be completely unaware of a product, others could be vaguely interested in it, whilst the remainder may want to own it. There are several complex models which illustrate the stages through which people pass on their way to a decision, but one of the simplest and easiest to remember is the AIDA model:

A - awareness
I   - interest
D - desire
A - action

The customer must be made aware of the product or service, should become interested in it, then desire it and finally act by purchasing.

The following table, taken from *Marketing Theory & Application* (Wentz & Eyrich, Harcourt Brace) relates that model to the task and effect of marketing:

Buyer stage	Promotional task	Advertising effect
Awareness	Establish buyer awareness	Inform potential customers about the product or service.
Interest	Create buyer interest	Stimulate interest in the product
Desire	Create desire	Induce favourable attitude, especially in relation to competing products.
Action	Sell the product	Induce purchase by stressing the immediate desirability of the product.

It is not enough to say that advertising is expected to increase sales. The objective of a campaign must be more precisely stated, eg:

Introduce new products - advertising is the most effective way to acquaint a market with a new or revised product. Some authorities distinguish between informative and competitive advertising. The former type is definitely informative, and is useful in accelerating sales on launch so that profitability is achieved as soon after launch as possible.

Improve the competitive position - the company may decide to increase sales by inducing potential customers to switch brands. It may do this by claiming a product feature or benefit, which is unique. Alternatively, it can claim its product is more efficient than the competition, eg, *'this toothpaste leads to 30 per cent fewer fillings'* or *'this soap powder washes whitest of all.'*

Sell in to dealers - if a product is being heavily advertised, dealers and retailers will be more likely to buy it. The effect can be enhanced both by advertising to the trade and by salespeople briefed to refer to the main promotion.

Develop the company's image - many large companies use institutional advertising to reassure the public about the company's intentions, and to create an image of progressiveness, reliability, or good service. Whilst not directly aimed at selling a product, this type of advertising could have a pronounced long-term effect on sales.

Build or maintain brand loyalty - for a company with a strong brand and a high market share, a major objective is to keep brand loyalty high, ie, to prevent brand-switching. One of the best examples of this type of advertising was the Coca-Cola campaign with its catch-phrase *'it's the real thing'.* Companies in this position sometimes emphasise the tradition and quality of their product.

Bring salespeople and customers together - one of the effects of most advertising is an increase in the morale of sales personnel. Some advertising, however, is specifically designed to put potential customers in touch with salespeople. A good example is the use of return-coupons in industrial advertisements.

There are many other potential objectives in advertising, but the above are among the most important. The objective of a campaign is crucial in determining the message.

5.6   Sales promotion

To refer again to the AIDA model, sales or below-the-line promotion is primarily at the action end. It is intended to stimulate the actual purchase, rather than to be informative or interesting. Sales promotion can be aimed at the ultimate customer, to encourage pull, or at the trade, to push goods into dealerships or the retail system.

The objectives of sales promotion should be considered in more detail, however, because there is a wide range of techniques, which are useful in different marketing situations. Some of the more important objectives and techniques are:

- **'Sell in' to the trade** - appropriate techniques would be dealer discounts (or '11 for the price of 10' offers), trade competitions, or incentive offers to company salespeople.

- **Gain new users** - a company could distribute free samples of the product, offer a trial use, or use a banded pack, in which a sample of a new product is attached to the pack of one of the existing lines.

- **Counteract competition** - price discounting is common. Other possibilities are to offer twin packs at an advantageous price, or to run a consumer competition.

- **Gain repeat purchase** - can be encouraged by coupons on the pack that can be traded in at the next purchase. Other possibilities are to have a series of give-aways in the packs, send-away offers which require several labels or coupons, or a competition which requires proof of purchase of several items.

- **Improve display/shelf position** - shelf display may be improved by the use of free gifts attached to the pack, by container premiums (in which the container is attractive in its own right), by consumer competitions or by competitions in which retailers are given prizes for the best window display.

- **Clear old stock** prior to the launch of a new product.

- **Add excitement** to a well-established product that may be suffering from consumer familiarity.

There are some types of below-the-line activity not listed above. For example, discount cards are issued to encourage loyalty to retail outlets. One of the most important below-the-line activities in industrial marketing is attendance at exhibitions. This is intended to gain new users, but afterwards it is difficult to determine whether a sale resulted from an exhibition or another source.

Examples of types of customer promotion incentives include:

(a)   **Home, magazine or newspaper couponing,** where a coupon with monetary value, redeemable against a specified brand, is either distributed to homes or cut from a magazine or newspaper.

(b)   **Reduced price packs** with a price reduction marked on package by producer. Value of typical price reduction varies between 3 per cent and 12 per cent of retail price.

(c)   **Bonus (or free) packs** where the customer is given an extra product at no additional cost (eg, four for the price of three).

(d)   **Buy 'X' number and get one free** where the consumer sends in packets or labels and will receive a coupon inviting him/her to a free pack or product. (There are a number of variants of this scheme).

(e)   **Free merchandise packs** where the customer gets a gift that is attached to brand package.

(f)   **Re-usable container packs** where the product has a special container with an intrinsic value. The container may be free or involve the consumer paying extra for it.

(g)   **Home sampling** where a free sample is distributed by hand or mail to individual homes.

(h)   **Contests** eg, card and stamp game, rub-off cards, skill competition, sweepstake or draw contest.

5.7   Public relations

The Institute of Public Relations has defined PR practice as being:

[Definition]   'the deliberate, planned and sustained effort to establish and maintain mutual understanding between an organisation and its public'.

The 'public' can include company employees, customers, suppliers, investment managers, financial institutions, shareholders, a particular geographical area and the general public.

At the core of almost all PR exercises is the company's desire to develop and express its corporate identity. Its aim is to spread knowledge and educate people, in order to achieve understanding, according to the prescribed objectives. For example, BP had a campaign showing beauty spots that have oil pipelines laid underground. Lever Brothers can claim the first recorded public relations exercise in the UK; in 1890, they issued the first in-house journal.

There is a wide choice of media facing an organisation that wants to enhance its public relations image. It can choose from newspapers (local/national, daily/weekly), radio, specialist magazines (wide range covering all interests and occupations from accountancy to zoology), house journals, sponsorship and television. TV is the most persuasive medium and reaches the widest audience, so is naturally the most expensive.

Steps in a public relations approach:

(a)   Understand your present situation - analyse your clients and your image.

(b)   Define the objectives - reasons for doing PR and what are you aiming to achieve (eg, dealer activities with customers to inform them of a range of services)?

(c)   Specify the audience - who are you trying to reach?

(d)   Message - what are you trying to tell them?

(e)   Select the media and techniques - how can you get the message over and ensure that it is received and understood?

(f)   Budget - how much do you spend?

(g)   Evaluate the results - did it work? How can you improve it for next time?

It is difficult to evaluate the effectiveness of advertising particularly on a value-for-money basis. This difficulty is even greater with public relations where the benefit can be vague and long term.

5.8   Packaging

Packaging is part of the overall physical distribution function. The design of a satisfactory package is a specialist consideration. Contents and its package may be totally inseparable, and certain products (fluids for instance, as in aftershave or disinfectant) cannot be marketed at all if they are not packaged.

Well-designed packaging can create convenience value for the consumer, whilst at the same time acting as a promotional medium for the supplier. Various factors contribute to the validity of packaging as a marketing tool:

(a)   *Self-service* - the package has to perform the sales task; it must give enough information to allow comparison, but be sufficiently attractive to its intended market to establish the desire to buy. More consumers are now asking for nutritional information to be included on packaging and this must be presented in a clear and attractive way.

(b)   *Consumer affluence* - people are willing to pay more for convenience and appearance and will be attracted by the prestige of better packages. Nowhere is this more true than in the cosmetics and perfumery market. Note the increase in food products, designed to be brought from the shelf and then cooked directly in the microwave.

(c)   *Company and brand image* - well-designed, consistent packaging affords instant recognition of the company and its brand to the consumer. The consumer becomes conditioned to look for certain colours or motifs on the packaging: Kodak film in its yellow box is an example.

(d)   *Innovation opportunities* - the first companies to put beer in ring pull cans attracted many customers, the appeal being 'if it looks new, interesting and clever, let's try it'.

What is also important is the requirement of the reseller (retailer). A 'good' consumer package is one that has display impact. This is what moves goods from the stores shelves. Packages, to the retailer, should be appropriately sized, convenient for stacking, easily price-marked and tough enough to handle normally (not only by shop staff, but by potential buyers) and protect the product, keeping it fresh and in good condition. Thus, a great many decisions have to be made on package design. The aspects include size, shape, materials, colour, the text that appears on the package, the text for any enclosed leaflet and the brand mark.

After a package has been designed, it should be tested to make sure that it answers all the particular requirements of the product and of the company, the dealer and the customer:

(a)   *a physical test* to make sure it can meet the conditions of delivery, display and use;

(b)   *visual tests* to ensure that the package text can be read and that it delivers the desired message; to ensure also that the whole design is effective and the colours and motif are in harmony;

(c)   *dealer tests* to determine whether dealers find the package attractive and easy to handle;

(d)   *consumer tests* to determine whether the package is attractive to the final consumer.

Of course, this makes attractive, well-designed packages costly to produce. The cost is part of the overall cost which, with the required profit, is the price the customer will be asked to pay. Consideration of this will determine company policy on packaging.

5.9   Distribution channels

Distribution is concerned with gap closing. The gap is because:

• production is centralised but customers are widely dispersed;
• production is in bulk but consumers purchase singly;

- production needs to be continuous but purchases may be seasonal; and
- consumers are unaware of the location of supplies.

It covers the effective use of distribution networks and the selection of distribution chains. Whether to use a wholesaler will be determined by many factors, but the decision will usually be made by a procedure known as risk analysis. The wholesaler, by specialising, can hold stock at a lower cost than the manufacturer, and so reduce the risk involved in holding those stocks. Other factors include the degree of after-sales service required and the expertise of retailers.

In the consumer market there is a range of distribution channels. Examples are the traditional high street shops, and more recently out-of-town shopping precincts or malls. So-called 'direct selling' involves a producer selling directly to the consumer. While this may appear to cut out the cost of the middle man, the producer is undertaking that role.

In retail book sales by mail order, companies have the advantages of postal or courier delivery countrywide, but also the additional cost of packing and postage. Mail order is an attractive channel of distribution to those who are unable to visit a bookshop. Direct sales by publishers are not widely promoted by publishers in Britain.

6   MARKETING STRATEGY FORMULATION

6.1   Goals and objectives

A marketing strategy is designed to guide management towards getting products or services to the customers and encouraging them to buy. Marketing strategies are closely related to product strategies. They must be inter-related and mutually supportive.

To arrive at a coherent set of goals and an overall strategy, there are certain important questions, which the company may ask itself. These are:

(a)   What business are we in? Some well-known restaurants, for example, consider they are not in the food selling business, but that they exist to provide a good evening out for their customers, selling foods as an incidental.

(b)   What broad markets does the company wish to serve? Can the company serve them? Our restaurant could aim to serve the lunch market, the afternoon coffee trade or the evening meals market. It could also try to cover all three markets, although this would be difficult.

(c)   What specific market segments does the company wish to concentrate on? Assuming the restaurant decides to go for the business lunch market, it must then decide which segments it wishes to aim its service at. Examples include office workers wanting a quick snack, managers wanting to entertain customers at lunchtime in a more formal setting and shoppers wanting a rest and a sandwich and so on.

(d)   What proportion of total effort should be concentrated upon each market segment (and associated plans and services)? In other words, how many eggs and what baskets?

(e)   What are the basic customer needs of each market segment? For our restaurant, this will have a bearing on the menu, seating arrangements, staffing, pricing and times of opening.

(f)   What size markets is the company now in, or will be in? What is the likely growth pattern?

(g)   At what market standing does the company aim? (A big fish in a small sea, or vice versa?)

(h)   What are the company's strengths and weaknesses?

As a result of asking these questions and analysing the market it will be possible to plan and determine a marketing strategy.

6.2   Market analysis

Market analysis also helps identify the appropriate marketing strategy. This analysis will include the following:

(a)   Appraisal and understanding of the present situation. This would include an analysis for each product showing its stage in the product life cycle, strength of competition, market segmentation, anticipated threats and opportunities, customer profile.

(b)   Definition of objectives of profit, turnover, product image, market share and market position by segment.

(c)   Evaluation of the marketing strategies available to meet these objectives. Such strategies as pricing policy, distribution policy, product differentiation, advertising plans, sales promotions, etc.

(d)   Definition of control methods to check progress against objectives and provide early warning, thereby enabling the marketing strategies to be adjusted.

There are two purposes of the analysis. The first is to identify gaps in the market where consumer needs are not being satisfied. The second is to look for opportunities that the organisation can benefit from, in terms of sales or development of new products or services.

6.3   Marketing audit

Part of the marketing research is concerned with the way an organisation responds to the demands of the market place. The best way to evaluate its marketing effort is to carry out a marketing audit, which examines the organisation's marketing objectives, marketing activities and marketing environment with the aim of assessing its present effectiveness and recommending future action. A comprehensive audit would cover the following aspects of the organisation's marketing system.

The marketing environment will provide information on economic and demographic trends, technological change, legal developments, social change, markets, customers, competitors (relevant market shares, product developments and promotional plans) and suppliers.

The marketing strategy consists of corporate objectives, marketing objectives, the marketing plan, marketing resources and the strengths and weaknesses of the organisation.

The marketing plans and control incorporate sales forecasting, product development, control procedures and market research.

The marketing mix includes product evaluation (price acceptability, suitability for customer requirements, quality and reliability), advertising and sales promotion, sales force, pricing policies and distribution activities (analysis of current channels of distribution, discount policies, warehousing and transportation).

Profitability and cost effectiveness includes the profitability of products, markets and marketing costs.

6.4   Strategies and approaches

An organisation often has to select a strategy from among two or more alternatives. For example, a company that has the objective of achieving a market share of 45 per cent may accomplish this in several ways. It can improve the product or service image through extensive advertising, add salespeople, introduce a new model, lower prices or sell through more/different outlets. Each alternative strategy has different ramifications for the marketing managers. A price strategy may be very flexible, because the price can be raised or lowered more frequently than product modifications can be introduced. However, a strategy based on price is the easiest to copy and may lead to a price war.

Attempting to gain market dominance by being first to launch a new product is known as an offensive strategy. This strategy can be successful and result in the market being captured by the first entrant eg, VAX produced a combination floor cleaner for domestic use. This strategy is the high risk strategy and careful market analysis is important in order to reduce the risk of launching a product that is not currently wanted.

The defensive strategy involves a more cautious approach to the market, often allowing a competitor to test the demand and build up a consumer response before launching their own product. The approach is to ensure that the company adopts a strategy, which makes use of developments. The exploitation of developments may make use of product innovations of competitors, seeking to improve on them or at least differentiate from the original merchandise.

There are many examples of approaches that might be used to halt a product's declining profitability. They include cost reduction and price modification, conversion of non-users or winning competitors' customers, entering new market segments, increasing the frequency of use or developing new and more varied uses, re-launching the product or many types of improvements and modifications to features, style, communication mix and distribution.

7   SELF TEST QUESTIONS

7.1   What are the three basic elements in the 'marketing situation'? (1.1)

7.2   Explain market segmentation. (2.1)

7.3   Marketing research consists of a number of activities; describe three of them. (3.1)

7.4   Outline the three main types of information that are collected by desk research. (3.3)

7.5   What are the four Ps? (4.1)

7.6   Describe the main pricing strategies. (4.3)

7.7   Draw an illustration of a product life cycle. (5.2)

7.8   What is the difference between a star and a problem child? (5.3)

7.9   Explain the meaning of the letters of the AIDA model. (5.5)

7.10   What are the factors that contribute to the validity of packaging as a marketing tool? (5.8)

7.11   What does a marketing audit examine? (6.3)

8   EXAMINATION TYPE QUESTION

8.1   Marketing mix decisions

You are required to:

(a)   describe the role of advertising as an element in the marketing communications mix for companies manufacturing and marketing:

     (i)   chocolate confectionery, and
     (ii)   fork-lift trucks;   **(10 marks)**

(b)   describe how 'below-the-line' promotional activity differs from advertising as such, and explain what major factor must be considered when planning an advertising campaign;
                                                                     (8 marks)

(c)   explain why manufacturers use brand names and discuss the advantages and disadvantages to both the manufacturer and retailer, of the production and sale of goods under the retailers 'own brand'.   **(7 marks)**

(Total: 25 marks)

9   ANSWER TO EXAMINATION TYPE QUESTION

9.1   Marketing mix decisions

(a)   For both types of product, advertising is one of four main elements of the **promotion mix.** The other three are personal selling, sales promotion and public relations. We shall accept, to depict the way in which promotion works, the model AIDA:

A   =   awareness
I   =   interest
D   =   desire
A   =   action

Advertising can be effective in making people aware of products, in generating interest in them, in encouraging desire for them, and in stimulating the actual purchase. Sales promotion is effective mainly at the action end. Sales forces are more successful if advertising has been used to promote awareness and interest, and public relations is concerned with improving attitudes to the product and to customers.

(i)   A manufacturer of chocolate confectionery may well spend as much as, say, 6-7 per cent of the sales price of the product on the advertising budget. Much of this may be spent on TV and daily press advertising. The message would be designed to promote brand preference. The message would be simple and clear, and might exploit psychological characteristics such as the need for 'belongingness' or friendship. If the product were already well-known, the advertisement would be expected either to improve customer preference ('desire') for the brand or to stimulate interest in it in some other way.

(i)   A fork lift truck manufacturer would probably spend a lower proportion of the goods' price on advertising, with trade magazines and perhaps up-market newspapers selected as the media. In industrial advertising, it is common to find advertisements designed more explicitly as an aid to the sales force (for example, the use of a return coupon). The message would be more complex, to persuade economically-conscious managers about claimed product advantages. The promotion mix in industrial marketing is more sales-force oriented than in consumer marketing, and sales promotion also is less important.

(b)   Whereas 'advertising' refers to promotional messages transmitted through the media (TV, radio, press, posters, cinema), below-the-line' promotion refers to the use of non-media methods, such as competitions, free gifts, retail displays, etc.

The major factors to be considered in planning an advertising campaign are the advertising budget, the message to be communicated, the media to be used, and the location and timing of the advertisement.

The budget size should be considered in relation to the resources available, the effect on company profitability, and the estimated advertising expenditures of competitors. Advertising expenditure is often fixed by companies as a proportion of the sales for each line, but his criterion, and the others mentioned, may be overridden in order to achieve a particular objective.

Message design involves the creation side of advertising – what is said, what images appear on the TV screen, the layout and pictorial features of press advertisement. Creative factors must be appropriate to the market segments at which they are aimed, catering for the tastes and needs of that segment.

Media selection depends upon the viewing, reading or listening habits of the potential customer. Cost-effectiveness is the major criterion, and the ratio used is cost per thousand of the target audience. The decision as to which media are actually used generally rests with the advertising agency; there is no 'either-or' choice, since many products use several media in integrated campaigns.

Location and timing (in TV and radio advertisement placing), and frequency of placement must be decided.   The placement of the advertisement should be next to items or programmes of particular interest to the target audience, and the size or duration of the advertisement must be decided in relation to the budget, the required response, and the complexity of the message.

(c)   Branding is a means of identifying a product or group of products. It provides a means of distinguishing the product clearly from competitive items and frequently, in the mind of the consumer, symbolises the particular qualities which apply to the branded manufacturer. It tells the customer roughly what to expect of the product, and is of great value in promotion of the company's goods.

The manufacturer making goods for a retailer's 'own branding' would clearly lose the benefit of those points mentioned above.   He would have no control over the pricing and distribution of his product; in fact, the retailer gains by assuming direction of these variables.

For the manufacturer, selling to large retail outlets may be a relatively economical form of trading.   An annual contract, for example, does not require frequent visits from his sales team. The predictability afforded by a guaranteed, large, sale means that production can be more closely and efficiently planned.   Distribution, in large planned batches rather than small, highly varying quantities, will be cheaper, and promotional expenditure will be greatly reduced.   The manufacturer relies on the 'pull' generated by the retail outlet for his sales; indeed, the retailer may advertise extensively.

The manufacturer may well continue to make the product using his own, manufacturer's brand label.   However, the retailer will often take a significant proportion of the manufacturer's turnover.   The retailer may thus expect to exercise considerable influence on his supplier, especially in terms of quality and of regular supply.   He will receive 'own-branded' goods relatively cheaply, and will sell them at a lower price than the manufacturer's brand, thereby attracting more people to his stores.

Some customers, of course, will still prefer the original manufacturer's branded product, but the stores can cater for this by stocking a quantity of the manufacturer's brand. This 'double stocking' is one of the disadvantages to a retailer, but is nevertheless widely practiced.

One of the main disadvantages for both parties is the question of a heavy reliance on a single source or customer. In the event of extreme business problems (such as bankruptcy) or drastic policy changes by either partner, the other may experience a severe drop in the profitability of the product concerned.

9 HUMAN RESOURCE PLANNING

INTRODUCTION & LEARNING OUTCOMES

Syllabus area 11(iii)

- The relationship of the human resource plan to other types of business plan.

- The determinants and content of a human resource plan (i.e. organisational growth rate, skills, training, development, strategy, technologies, natural wastage).

- The problems which may be encountered in the implementation of a human resource plan, and the ways in which such problems can be avoided or solved.

- The human issues relating to recruitment, dismissal, retirement and redundancy, and how to manage them.

It has become fashionable to speak of the human assets of the organisation, rather than staff, personnel or manpower. It is also useful because it reminds us that although people only appear as costs in the formal accounts, they are assets in the sense that they are, or should be, a productive resource. Like other resources, they need maintenance and proper utilisation, have a finite life, and have an output greater than their cost.

Human resource planning is a strategy to maintain and improve the ability of the organisation to achieve corporate objectives, through the development of strategies designed to enhance the contribution of manpower at all times in the foreseeable future.

Expanding this idea, we see that human resource planning deals with human activity directed towards a specific economic aim, and so provides the organisation with the right number of employees who have the skills to achieve the organisation's objectives.

When you have studied this chapter you should be able to:

- Explain the process of human resource planning and its relationship to other types of business plan.

- Produce and explain a human resource plan for an organisation.

- Analyse the issues involved in managing the dismissal, retirement and redundancy of individual staff.

---

1 THE CONCEPT OF HUMAN RESOURCE MANAGEMENT

1.1 Overview

The effectiveness of an organisation's operations and functions depends very largely on the staff it employs - everything comes back to people. All managers are concerned that the personnel in their own department are successful. To ensure this, they recognise the importance of a planned and systematic approach to recruitment and selection of staff. If the people appointed do not have the right ability, temperament and willingness, all the theories on motivation, empowerment and commitment are not going to be of any use.

Human resource management (HRM) is described by Michael Armstrong as:

Definition 'a strategic approach to acquiring, developing, managing and motivating an organisation's key resource.'

This involves looking at the development of human resources, gaining employees' commitment to the values and goals of the organisation and aiding in the development of human resources to add value to products or services.

There are two important elements to the definition - 'key resource' and 'strategic'. As Armstrong mentions, the people in most organisations are the key resource. For the vast majority of organisations, it is the people who make things, take decisions and sell the goods or services. People costs represent the greatest capital outlay.

The strategic element refers to the observation that, in order to make an effective contribution, human resource management must complement and advance the organisation's strategic business objectives. It should have clear and consistent policies and encourage all employees to be committed to the organisation's goals. It must be flexible and responsive to internal and external change and work within the framework of constraints and opportunities whilst still contributing to the overall corporate aims.

Most cynics will say it is only a new name or modern approach for personnel management with an involvement in the strategic planning process. We will contrast the modern approaches, emphasising the need for empowerment or passing authority down the line as far as is sensible, with the traditional approaches.

1.2   Traditional and modern view

The traditional view of 'personnel management' includes activities which are described by Michael Porter as 'maintenance' functions. They include record maintenance, manpower planning, recruitment and selection, placement and termination, training and career development, grievance and discipline procedures, welfare, terms of employment, negotiations on wages and other matters and procedures for avoiding disputes. These are necessary tasks, but have left the personnel function without a genuine insight into how its actions affect the organisation's achievement of its objectives.

The traditional role offered scope for specialisation, leading to the personnel function being staffed by people who have spent their entire careers in the personnel field. They may have started by specialising in job analysis and have ended up as company personnel manager or personnel director, but only in rare instances with a seat on the board.

The HRM approach believes firmly in what is known as 'empowerment'. This means passing authority as far down the line as practicable and sensible for the enterprise. The role of HRM is seen as:

- suggesting a strategic approach to the personnel function;

- serving the interests of management;

- dealing with gaining employees' commitment to the values and goals laid down by the strategic management;

- aiding in the development of the human resources which helps the organisation add value to their products or services.

It can be defined as the process of achieving outstanding organisational performance through empowering people to achieve and give of their best. As such, it is directed at building a sustainable competitive advantage and is a strategic activity. Because of this approach it is not the exclusive province of the specialist in the human resource area. It is an activity which should actively involve not only line managers, but also all those responsible for the strategic direction of the organisation.

1.3   Differences between manpower planning and human resource planning

Manpower planning has been defined by the IPM Edinburgh group as:

> **Definition**   'a strategy for the acquisition, utilisation, improvement and preservation of the human resources of the enterprise.'

It is through manpower planning that a company can determine its recruitment and selection needs, and can assist in the planning of its training needs. Its purpose is to reduce uncertainty in the environment and assist in shaping a company's human resource policies.

The stages of manpower planning consist of a series of sequential steps as follows:

(i)   an estimate of the organisation's future manpower needs in terms of numbers and skill composition;

(ii)   an analysis of labour flows into, within, and out of, the organisation, and the ability of relevant labour markets to supply existing or future demands;

(iii)   the identification of gaps between supply and demand and the development of policies and plans to close these.

In the diagram of manpower planning below, we show the basic flow of people through the organisation:

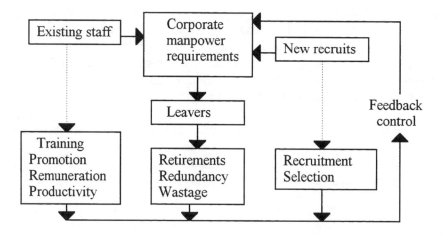

Human resource planning encompasses what used to be called manpower planning, but in recent years it has been recognised that there is more to people planning than quantitative estimates of the demand and supply of personnel. Nevertheless, manpower planning still provides a good starting point for the development of a human resource plan.

Human resource planning entails:

•   the use of qualitative techniques for estimating future manpower requirements, such as scenario setting;

•   a more explicit link with corporate and business strategy;

•   a willingness to develop people so that they have the skills to meet the future needs of the business; and

•   an interest in improving the performance of all employees in the organisation by using appropriate motivation techniques.

The relationship between human resource planning and the organisation's corporate and business strategy is outlined in the following diagram:

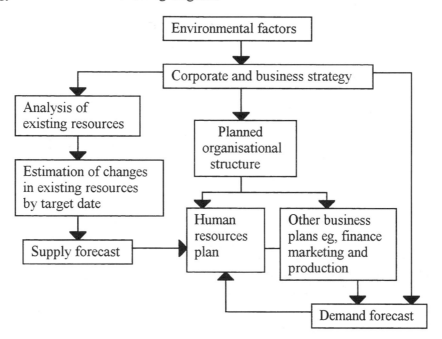

The human resource plan must take account of the following:

- The organisation's basic strategy, accompanied by the detailed objectives and tactics that make that strategy a reality, will define the human resource needs. For example, a strategy based on internal growth means that additional people will have to be hired.

- Changes in the external environment. For example, in a growth economy an organisation may want to expand but there may be fewer job candidates because unemployment is low.

- The external and internal environments will define the limits within which the human resource plan must operate. Internal organisation will establish the most effective structure ie, the degree of decentralisation, autonomy and relationships between different functions to enhance communication, decision-making and responsiveness to change.

- Once these limits have been established, the future human resources required are compared with the existing human resources situation to determine what recruitment, training and development programmes are necessary.

| Conclusion | The strategic approach to HRM involves the integration of human resources considerations into the organisation's overall strategic planning process.

2   HUMAN RESOURCE STRATEGY

2.1   Introduction

New themes in planning are concerned with the improvement of competitive performance. We are in the middle of an industrial revolution based on a wave of new technologies: electronics, computers, robotics and automation, biotechnology, and various new materials. The success of Japanese industry has encompassed all of the above, but another competitive edge is their manpower strategies and their ability to engage, involve and motivate people, thus tapping their energy and ideas. This success has encouraged many western firms to re-examine their approaches to personnel. Multinational companies are now investing as much in human resource programmes on leadership, competitive benchmarks, quality improvement and employee involvement as they are spending on new equipment. We are seeing the emergence of flexible organisational arrangements such as short-term contracts, teleworking, part-time working and the use of consultants and bought-in services.

2.2   Objectives of human resource strategy

Human resource plans and corporate plans cannot exist in isolation, since each will automatically influence the other. Heads of all company functions are involved in the process of considering the changing staffing needs over the period of the corporate plan, starting from the present position. HRMs responsibility is that of drawing the functional requirements together within the framework of company human resource policy, including funding. The basic aim is to assess the quantity and quality of people required at each level within each department of the business and to ensure that these positions are filled on a continuous basis.

Effective human resource planning will, therefore, help to remove the need for redundancies and avoid shortages of labour. Age planning can deal with some of the people problems arising from time to time. An effective human resources strategy must include realistic plans and procedures. The objectives will include the following:

(i)   Identifying, in precise terms, the kinds of talent the organisation needs to achieve its strategic goals in the short, medium and long term.

(ii)   Recruiting an adequate supply of people with the potential to become outstanding performers, allowing for wastage and for the actions of competing organisations.

(iii)   Developing people's potential by training, development and education.

(iv)   Retaining as high a proportion as possible of those recruited in this way whose potential is demonstrated in the early years in employment.

(v)   Ensuring that everything possible is done to prevent poaching of talent by competitors.

(vi)   Recruiting an adequate number of talented people of proven experience and accomplishment, and easing their adjustment to a new corporate culture.

(vii)   Downsizing to reduce staff numbers when necessary.

(viii) Motivating the employees to achieve high levels of performance and to build ties of loyalty to the organisation.

(ix)   Searching for ways of improving performance and productivity.

(x)   Creating an organisational culture in which talent is nurtured.

3   HUMAN RESOURCE PLANS FOR DIFFERENT SCENARIOS

3.1   Introduction

We have already indicated that the main differences between manpower planning and human resource planning is the use of qualitative techniques for estimating future manpower requirements, such as scenario setting, and a more explicit link with corporate and business strategy.

Michael Porter, in *Competitive Advantage*, argues that all firms face uncertainty but one of the problems with forecasting is that many managers underestimate the probability of rapid change or discontinuous change. According to Porter, a scenario is 'an internally consistent view of what the future might turn out to be'.

3.2   Scenario setting

A sign that strategy formulation within an organisation is maturing is the fact that various methods and concepts now exist which have the potential to provide structured, analytical approaches to strategy development. Examples include portfolio models, experience curves, scenario analysis, market structure analysis and technological forecasting.

[Definition] Scenario analysis is a way of creating and using future scenarios to help generate new strategic options and evaluate strategies.

Scenario setting is a technique used where a future scenario is stimulated by strategic questions or environmental opportunities or threats. For example, the strategic question 'will e-commerce affect the way we do business?' could lead to both 'yes' and 'no' scenarios relevant to the human resources plan. The approach attempts to match specific options with a range of possible future situations (or scenarios). It is essentially used as a means of addressing some of the less well structured or uncertain aspects of evaluation. There are many ways to construct a scenario and the following outline is just an example:

(i)   Use the industry scenarios and develop a set of assumptions about the task environment. At 3M, for example, the general manager of each business unit is required annually to describe what his or her industry will look like in 15 years.

(ii)   For each strategic alternative, develop a set of optimistic, pessimistic, and most likely assumptions about the impact of key variables on the organisation's future financial statements.

(iii)   Construct detailed statements for each of the strategic alternatives, using optimistic (O), pessimistic (P). and most likely (ML) proforma statements for each alternative.

3.3   Environmental analysis

To make a valid contribution to the enterprise, human resource planners must look both within and outside the internal environment. The organisation does not exist in a vacuum but is influenced by political, economic, social and technological factors (PEST). By analysing these areas, the planner can consider changes that have taken place or are likely to occur in society at large and build them into scenarios to clarify plans for the future.

Political factors - a change of government could affect the way people are employed. Legislation can be introduced that changes industrial relations procedures. This could result in fewer days lost through industrial action. Governments may introduce incentives to encourage young people to remain in full-time education, or they may fund businesses to encourage training and development for them. Specific areas of the economy may be given special attention, in the form of funding, to encourage growth.

Economic factors - National economies may experience growth or decline and governments may have a special commitment to change cultures through economic interventions. Companies in the South of England looking to relocate and/or recruit new staff might develop scenarios based on the environmental forecasting associated with buying or renting houses in the area. Experts could be asked to assess probabilities directly. Factors considered could be buoyancy of housing market in general, availability and price of existing and planned housing stock in designated area, the local infrastructure, interest rates and availability of mortgage funds.

Social factors - in recent years, customers tastes have changed towards certain products eg, environmentally friendly and genetically modified products. There may be significant changes in the composition of the labour force eg, the average age of workforces may increase because of a fall in the birth rate or more women may be represented in traditionally male sectors because of changes in social attitudes.

Technological factors - new production methods may be developed that reduce the need for operational or supervisory staff. The advent of new technologies may spark a requirement for the acquisition of new skills to maintain the new machines. Old skills and knowledge, which were previously valued, may become superfluous.

4   HUMAN RESOURCE PLANNING

4.1   Determinants and content of a human resource plan

Human resource planning cannot, of course, be considered in isolation. It is related to all other resources strategies and particularly to capital investment. Capital investment often means less manpower. It can, however, lead ultimately to an increased manpower requirement, but with a change in the mix of grades required.

Capital investment brings economies, which lead to lower prices, leading to growth, leading to greater manpower requirement. The mix of grades will tend to change from unskilled to skilled, from production to maintenance, from technical operating to planning, researching, marketing, purchasing and accounting. Such changes must be planned for as far in advance as possible. Re-training schemes must be organised.

If an overall drop is going to be necessary, an attempt should be made not to build up too much only to be cut back later. (The 'hire and fire' attitude is definitely 'out' these days.) If any cuts are necessary, planned use should be made of early retirement schemes, voluntary redundancy etc.

The main aim of human resource planning is to acquire and retain the number and kinds of people needed by the organisation, looking inside the company to develop suitable people, as well as buying in from outside. It should also consider organisational design and job analysis to see if there are better ways of organising the way that people perform at work. This consideration has powerful implications for staff development and for flexibility of workers.

A typical human resources plan should look forward from three to five years in an organisation's lifetime. It is a cyclical process having four main stages.

(i)   Analysing corporate and departmental objectives - to determine the overall shape and size of the organisation required, and the strategies and tactics to be employed in the implementation of operational plans.

(ii)   Demand forecasting - projecting future staffing requirements required to achieve the corporate objectives by the target date.

(iii)   Assessing present human resources and producing a supply forecast, which is an estimation of likely changes in the existing staff resources by the end of the forecasting period ie, target date.

(iv)   Devising policies and plans, in detail, whereby shortages or excesses in labour numbers and skills deficiencies can be overcome.

The human resources planning process should also consider the broader environmental factors. These include:

*   changes in population trends (eg, ageing populations);

*   patterns of employment - more flexible structures of work organisation;

*   competition for labour from other organisations;

*   changes in the educational system;

*   developments in information technology and automation; and

*   government intervention eg, initiatives on employment, training and enterprise programmes and information technology, and employment legislation.

4.2 Stages in a human resource plan

Human resource planning can be described as a strategy for the acquisition, utilisation, improvement and retention of an organisation's human resources. The four main stages are auditing, forecasting, planning and controlling resources.

- The auditing stage involves the analysis of the strategic environment (trends in population growth, education, pensions, employment rights of women and ethnic minorities) in the light of the organisation's strategic objectives. The strategy chosen will have implications on the numbers of employees and the mix of skills required.

- The forecasting stage analyses the demand for and supply of labour in terms of number, type and quality of people the organisation should employ to meet planned requirements and cover expected turnover.

- The planning stage involves policies to recruit, train and develop the labour force indicated in the forecast.

- The controlling stage involves measuring the effective use of the human resources and their contribution towards the achievement of the organisation's objectives.

The stages of human resource planning are outlined in the diagram below:

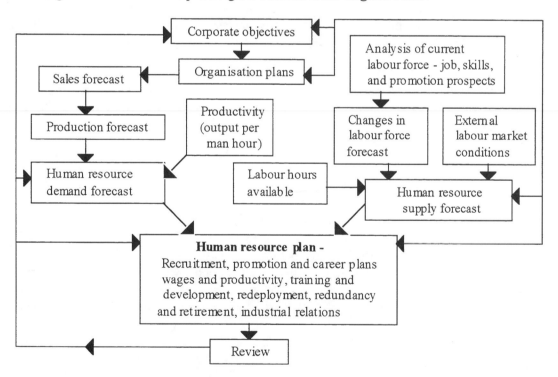

4.3 Analysing corporate and departmental objectives

Human resource strategy is a reconciliation process between what an organisation might do (opportunities) and what it can do (resources). This is an impossible process without consideration of human resource requirements. Similarly, human resource planning needs, as its base data, predictions of future output and some indication of available finance. Within this framework, human resource planning serves two functions.

(a) It fulfils a problem-solving role by identifying human resource requirements, controlling the flow of labour, developing skills and increasing adaptability.

(b) It also has a strategic role in contributing towards the shape of the organisation as required by external and internal changes.

In both cases, human resource planning represents an important flow of information to aid decision making and the formulation of policies.

The management accountant can assist the HR manager in the control stage of the plan. Any control system needs to set objectives, measure performance, note deviations and act to eliminate them. The management accountant will be able to advise the HR manager if any of the environmental factors - economic, technological or market trends - changes in an unpredicted way. This will allow the recruitment, training or redeployment plans to be updated accordingly.

4.4   Demand and supply forecasting

Demand forecasting is closely linked with an organisation's corporate strategy. Any strategic decisions will have a manpower implication, eg, decisions to invest in new equipment, to reorganise, acquire, increase or decrease productivity, to change the method of production, to diversify into new product markets and to market products more effectively. Demand forecasting is, therefore, tied in with changes in the state of the economy, technological innovation, the product market, demand for services, collective agreements and government legislation.

Future demand for employees is generally measured by managerial judgement, ratio-trend analysis or work study.

- **Managerial judgement** - is where managers consider future workloads and decide how many people they need. The process may be 'bottom up', when line managers submit proposals for agreement with top management, or 'top down', with senior management forecasts being verified by the line managers.

- **Ratio-trend analysis** - looks back over several years at trends in the numbers of staff and the numbers of products or services made or sold. It then projects these ratios forward, taking into account the new targets and the effects of new technology and new working practices.

- **Work study** - is suitable for circumstances where work can be easily measured. It looks at output plans and at how long each unit takes to produce, to give the planner required annual hours - taking into account absenteeism, turnover and new technology.

People are a crucial resource, and therefore long-term plans are needed to ensure availability of the right type of skills. The main problem with human resource planning is that with the speed of change in technology, it is difficult to predict not only how many workers will be needed in *n* years time, but also what type of skills they will need. Some jobs, which now form a major part of the work content, may be completely automated within a few years. In addition the rate of growth of the firm's business cannot be accurately predicted. There is thus considerable uncertainty on the demand side.

Supply forecasting begins by assessing present human resources and analysing:

- staff numbers by age, abilities, grade, type, skills and experience etc;
- turnover of staff and rates of absenteeism;
- overtime rates and periods of inactivity;
- staff competencies and potential.

Analysis by age would enable the department to draw a graph to show when the vacancies due to retirement would occur, and would enable the personnel department to draw up better detailed pension plans. In addition, analysis by age would remove 'bottle-necks' or 'age gaps' within the company. It would show where the bulk of people were and if any likely problems could occur in the future, because of a particular age spread (eg, if the bulk is at age 55-58 and retirement proposed to be brought forward to age 60).

Analysis by ability would involve appraisals of the staff in the department. This would require written reports, at six monthly intervals, from the manager for whom each member of staff worked. These reports are read through by both the manager and the person being appraised, and discussed together. They should cover his or her ability in detail. All the skills of each employee must be detailed, not merely the ones he or she uses at present.

One of the problems with supply forecasts is that people cannot be treated like other resources. They are unpredictable and might leave the company. Although there is uncertainty on the supply side, an attempt must be made to assess the numbers, which will be required in each type of work for some years ahead, even though the estimates will be subject to wide error. Demand and supply must then be reconciled, with decisions being taken as to the level of recruitment required, the extent of internal promotion, the amount of internal training needed, etc. This in turn will lead to decisions about the size of the personnel department needed to handle interviews, training, etc.

The management accountant can assist the HR manager in both of the forecasting stages. Because labour must be recruited and trained or shed and made redundant as required at the most appropriate time, the forecast must be based on the predictions gathered from the analysis of all the organisation's forecasts. The management accountant can quantify the objectives for a given period in the future (generally five years) and draw up a list of current and future requirements.

4.5   Changes affecting human resource requirements

In organisations that are large enough to draw up business plans from the overall corporate objectives, it is important that there is a relationship between the various business plans drawn up in different functional areas. This link can be highlighted when we look at the areas of change affecting an organisation's human resource requirements.

(i)   Expansion or contraction of the enterprise - expansion will almost certainly involve the planning of recruitment while contraction may involve decisions concerning redundancy.

(ii)   Changes in the demand for output - certain products or services may be showing increasing demand while others may be declining. This may well involve changes, if not in the numbers employed, then certainly in the skills' composition of the workforce, necessitating retraining. These changes may be of a seasonal nature, as in the hotel industry, and organisations must plan for such fluctuations in demand.

(iii)   Product changes may affect the composition of the labour force. For example, an organisation that has traditionally supplied fitted kitchen furniture to the highest specification may decide to change to factory-produced home assembly kits. Different skills may well be required to manufacture these.

(iv)   Changes in the method of output brought about by changes in technology will undoubtedly affect manpower requirements. Automation in a production department or the introduction of a computer in an accounts or records department will undoubtedly call for different skills if not a reduction in the number of people employed.

(v)   Finally, changes in productivity may occur through techniques to improve efficiency or productivity bargaining. This, too, will affect the quantity and perhaps the skills required of the labour force.

It can be seen that some of these changes will affect most organisations at some time or another. Recently, strong arguments have emerged for the application of human resource planning techniques to cope with such changes. These are:

(i)   In many firms, wage costs are a significant proportion of total costs. Firms, therefore, need a clear indication of likely future wage costs for effective budgeting exercises.

(ii)   The increased importance given to training and career planning, because of technical change and the expectations of the workforce, necessitates some form of human resource planning.

(iii)   Firms are now under much greater pressure to appear socially responsible. Both social expectations and successive legislation have affected traditional policies of 'hire and fire' according to market demands. Human resource planning is a key technique in avoiding over-recruitment or lay-offs and redundancy.

4.6   Policies and plans to plug the gap between supply and demand

A human resource plan provides the trigger for a HRM action programme aimed at reconciling differences between supply and demand. It provides a framework in which action can be taken to help overcome staffing difficulties facing the organisation. HR planning is a continuous process, which seeks to ensure flexible resourcing related to internal and external environmental influences.

Acquiring adequate numbers of staff of the right grades is not the end of human resource planning. HRP involves promotion, recruitment, training and promoting good industrial relations. It also involves a continuous review of working conditions by comparison with other organisations: pay, wage comparisons between different grades, pensions, holiday and sickness pay, physical working conditions, safety aspects, sports and social facilities, other fringe benefits.

Tactical plans to implement these policies include pay and productivity bargaining, conditions of employment, career development, organisation and job specifications, redundancy, recruitment, training and retraining.

•   Shortages or surpluses of labour that emerge in the process of planning may be dealt with in various ways. A deficiency may be met through internal transfers, promotion, training, external recruitment and reducing labour turnover (by reviewing possible causes). A surplus may be dealt with by running down staff levels by natural wastage, restricting recruitment or, as a last resort, redundancies.

•   Recruitment - to recruit the appropriate numbers of employees the supply of labour must be such that workers are available of the right skills, age and health in the area. Labour generally is regarded as relatively immobile. Many organisations will decide where to locate new operations on the basis of knowledge about available labour. The labour that is required could be attracted away from existing employers if higher salaries are offered.

•   Redundancy - selection of labour for redundancy is a very difficult task. The bond of loyalty between organisation and employee may be considerable and threats of redundancies will usually result in a demotivated workforce who fear for the future. The impact on the level of motivation and on company performance has to be taken seriously by management.

•   Training - changes in products and methods of production often require a new skill or understanding on the part of the workforce. The personnel function will often establish a training programme to cope with changes in the work environment and to increase the motivation of employees. In situations where an expansion requires more skilled workers, the training programme may be used to upgrade the skills of existing workers, or to provide the skills for new employees. This is particularly likely to be the case when the local labour supply cannot provide sufficient numbers of the appropriately skilled workers.

•   Management development - the level of education and training available in the existing labour supply is unlikely to provide potential employees with the exact skills, experience, and enterprise required for management within a particular organisation. Managers must therefore be trained to fulfil the role expected of them. The management team must also keep abreast of developments in all areas of business, which may often require training programmes and attendance at various courses. Frequently the emphasis is on self-development.

- Estimates of labour costs - a forecast of the labour requirements will enable organisations to estimate the associated costs. The factors influencing these will not simply be the numbers and grades required, but also the state of the labour market. A labour surplus in an area may lead to the lowering of wage rates, although trade union pressure may not allow this. The market availability of labour with the appropriate skills will reduce the need for, and consequently the costs of training.

4.7   Recruitment, dismissal, retirement and redundancy

The organisation should have a responsible attitude towards employment legislation requirements and codes of practice, union activities and communications with staff.

When general principles are converted into practice, they should take the form of good pay and working conditions and high quality training and development schemes. They should also extend to recruitment, redundancy and retirements policies.

Recruitment of staff is very important. If an organisation recruits individuals who turn out to be unsuitable, they will have to sack them. Dismissals will be inevitable in any large organisation, but careful recruitment methods should manage to keep such demoralising events to a minimum.

Organisations have different ways of providing for staff nearing retirement, apart from pension schemes. One of the problems for retired people is learning what to do with their leisure time. Some companies provide training courses and discussion groups to help them plan their future time constructively.

Dealing with redundancies is a more difficult problem. Even for organisations that show an ethical sense of responsibility towards their employees, there may be occasions when parts of the business have to be closed down, and jobs lost. In such a situation, the organisation should have a meaningful and cost-effective programme to deal with staff identified as surplus to future requirements. This might include redeployment and redundancies, although more creative schemes will also involve early retirement provisions, flexible pension planning and secondments. For employees that are made redundant, there are measures the organisation can take to help them to get a job elsewhere, for example:

- providing funds for training in other skills that employees could use in other industries and organisations;

- counselling individuals to give them suggestions about what they might try to do;

- providing generous redundancy payments that employees could use to either set up in business themselves, or tide them over until they find suitable employment again.

4.8   Problems with human resources planning

People resources are costly and like all other resources of the company have to be carefully planned. Apart from problems of providing the funds to meet 'labour cost', other current problems underline the need for human resource planning. Knowledge, expertise and skill are constantly changing. Rapid social and technical change represents more problems in the environment within which planning takes place.

All types of forecasting are subject to several potential drawbacks. These are:

(i)   Problems may arise due to the uncertainty of the environment. Significant changes can occur which can render earlier predictions virtually useless. For example, cheap imports can seriously affect developments in the British industry. The strength of the pound against foreign currencies adversely affects the tourist industry and hence employment in the hotel, catering and entertainment industries. Unforeseen changes in legislation may have an impact on manning levels in affected sectors and rapid technological developments may seriously affect earlier manpower forecasts.

(ii)   Such forecasts cannot take complete account of factors related to the unpredictability of human behaviour.

(iii)   The data being used by the planners may be incorrect or wrong estimations may be made of unknown data.

The value of human resource planning is that it can assist organisations to foresee changes and identify trends in staffing resources, and to adopt personnel policies that help to avoid major problems.

Effective HR planning can anticipate future difficulties while there is still a choice of action. Coupled with good communications, consultation and participation with staff involved, planning should help alleviate harmful effects to individual members of staff or to the performance of the organisation.

5   SELF TEST QUESTIONS

5.1   Define the modern view of HRM. (1.2)

5.2   How does human resource planning differ from manpower planning? (1.4)

5.3   Briefly describe three objectives of the human resource strategy. (2.2)

5.4   What is 'scenario analysis'? (3.2)

5.5   What are the factors in a PEST analysis? (3.3)

5.6   Why is demand forecasting linked with the organisation's corporate strategy? (4.4)

5.7   When assessing present human resources, how are they analysed? (4.4)

5.8   What are the main problems associated with predicting manpower requirements? (4.5)

6   EXAMINATION TYPE QUESTION

6.1   Human resource planning

(a)   Describe the human resource planning process.   **(10 marks)**

(b)   Why is human resource planning an important feature of the strategic management of organisations that employ significant numbers of accountants and other professionally qualified staff?
                                                                                                        (10 marks)
                                                                                                    (Total: 20 marks)

7   ANSWER TO EXAMINATION TYPE QUESTION

7.1   Human resource planning

(a)   Human resource planning is 'a strategy for the acquisition, utilisation, improvement and retention of an organisation's human resources'. It attempts to predict how many and what types of people will be needed in the future and the extent to which these needs are likely to be met. It should take into account how existing conditions might change, both inside and outside the organisation, and devise appropriate policies to ensure that the demand for staff is met. Its purpose in both the short and the long term is therefore:

- to estimate the (uncertain) demand for each grade and skill of employee;

- to estimate the (uncertain) supply of labour of the appropriate grades and skills;

- where there is a discrepancy between demand and supply to take measures, which will reduce the demand or improve the supply.

In other words, have the right people in the right jobs at the right time.

The process that the organisation might use for human resource planning is shown below:

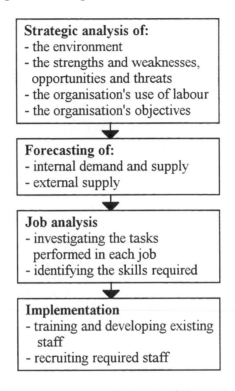

The human resource plan is prepared on the basis of the analysis of labour requirements and the implications for productivity and costs. The plan may consist of various elements, according to the circumstances. For example:

- The recruitment plan - numbers and types of people and when they are required, culminating in the recruitment programme.

- The training plan - numbers of trainees required and/or existing staff needing training, culminating in the training programme.

- The redevelopment plan - programmes for transferring and retraining employees.

- The productivity plan - where and when redundancies are to occur; policies for selection and declaration of redundancies; redevelopment, retraining or relocation of redundant employees; policy on redundancy payments etc.

- The retention plan - actions to reduce avoidable labour wastage.

The plan should include budgets, targets and standards. It should allocate responsibilities for implementation and control - reporting and monitoring achievement against the plan etc.

(b)   One of the most valuable assets owned by an organisation is its staff. They sit at the centre of strategic planning. Whilst strategic planning seeks to minimise the uncertainty of the enterprise's environment (within a given set of constraints on its actions), it is the employees that actually implement the strategy ands take the opportunities offered. They must be motivated and developed and this is of the greatest importance when the people under consideration are professionally qualified. This is for a number of reasons:

(i)   If the organisation seeks excellence, it must realise that high quality of product and service is crucially dependent on a similarly high quality of staff. Excellence and human resource planning are closely related.

(ii)   Developing such staff is generally quite expensive, and there are therefore quite considerable investment implications for the medium to long term. This is emphasised by the relatively long lead-time required in such development. If this is combined further with the high level of uncertainty inherent in attempting to develop individuals to a very high level of expertise and performance, the potential investment in these employees is clear. The uncertainty arises because some will fail to reach the required standard if the standard is very high, and even those that do reach it may take their expertise elsewhere.

(iii)   Since professional skills tend to be at a premium, the development of 'home grown' experts may well be desirable. The influence of competitive employment markets is reduced and it may well be that professional employees, that are developed in-house, will show greater commitment and loyalty to the organisation as a result.

Professional employees are highly important to an organisation because it is through them that vital skills are acquired for such processes as the management of innovation, change and development. If accountants are taken as an example, the management of cash flows from new product lines is crucial to the flow of funds for the continuing development and success of future products. They will also be necessary for the budgeting process and the analysis of variances from the budgeted figures.

10 THE RECRUITMENT, SELECTION AND INDUCTION PROCESS

INTRODUCTION & LEARNING OUTCOMES

Syllabus area 11(iii)
- The process of recruitment and selection of staff using different recruitment channels (ie, advertisement, agencies, consultants, executive search)

- The content and format of job descriptions, candidate specifications and job advertisements

- The techniques that can be used in the selection of the most suitable applicant for a job (ie, interviews, assessment centres, intelligence tests, aptitude tests, psychometric tests)

- The importance of negotiation during the offer and acceptance of a job

  The process of induction and the importance thereof

Organisations succeed largely through the efforts of the individuals working within them. It follows that recruiting and selecting the right individuals is of fundamental importance and a cornerstone of good management. Recruitment is the part of the human resource plan, which is concerned with finding the applicants. This means going out into the labour market, communicating opportunities and information and generating sufficient interest to elicit a response from suitable candidates to come forward for final selection.

Recruitment campaigns are followed by the selection process. Selection is the process of choosing between applicants for the job; a process of eliminating unsuitable applicants. Selection activities are designed to identify those candidates who, on the evidence available, appear to be the most suitable for the vacancy concerned.

The selection process starts with the sifting and sorting of paper details - the application forms and submitted CVs. Once the shortlist is drawn up, the next stage is to determine the best methods of further assessment. The selection interview is probably the most popular of these methods, although other techniques - assessment centres, psychometric testing and ability testing - will all be considered.

The consequences of good selection are often clear, whereas those of poor selection are not always obvious. The cost of advertising, the management time involved in selection and training and the expense of dismissal are easy to calculate but the longer term effects such as lowering of morale, reduced business opportunities and reduced quality of product or service are possibly more serious.

When you have studied this chapter you should be able to:

- Produce a plan for the recruitment, selection and induction of finance department staff
- Produce a plan for the induction of new staff into the finance department of an organisation

---

1 THE IMPORTANCE OF RECRUITMENT AND SELECTION

1.1 Introduction

 Recruitment is the process of selecting a supply of possible candidates for positions within an enterprise.

Selection is the choosing from a number of candidates the one most suitable for a specified position.

1.2   Recruitment and selection policy

Recruitment and selection plays an important part in the organisation's strategy. It is inextricably linked with the organisational goals and objectives and much of the training and development, which follows it. Its position is shown in the diagram below:

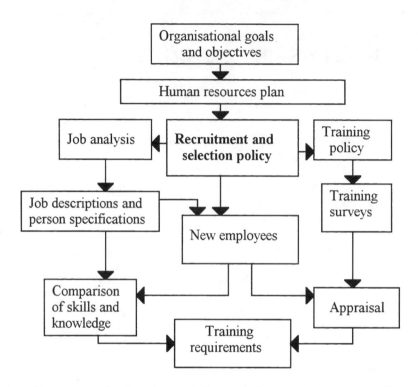

The aim of most organisations is to produce goods or services at a profit, so the people working in these organisations will need to be good at their jobs. There is always the possibility of training someone to do the job efficiently but it is obviously better if people are placed in jobs where their natural abilities and interests are reasonably suited.

Choosing the right candidate for the job, or selecting the right person for promotion, is a critical organisational decision for a number of reasons. Incorrect decisions can lead to frustrated employees and poor performance levels for the organisation. Selection and appraisal procedures can be costly and time-consuming and it is annoying to have to repeat them to recover from previous errors.

1.3   Outline of the recruitment and selection process

Recruitment and selection are part of the same process and some people often refer to both as the recruitment process. This is not entirely accurate; the process of recruitment, as distinct from selection, involves the attraction of a field of suitable candidates for the job.

There is no 'ideal plan' for recruitment and selection - no super model to be followed. All organisations have their own way of doing it, with varying degrees of success. What is important is for an organisation to be aware of what has been useful and successful in the past and try to develop a system that is well designed and properly applied.   When selecting staff, there are two basic questions that need addressing:

(i)   If you do not know what you are looking for, how will you recognise a suitable candidate when you see one?

(ii)   If you do not know what you want your staff to do, how can you judge their ability to do it, train or develop them to do it more effectively or assess their performance?

The process of recruitment involves several stages, shown in the diagram below.

*   The clarification of the exact nature of the position to be filled - is the job really necessary or can it be covered adequately by reorganising or re-allocating to other jobs? If the job is necessary, what does it entail? What are the duties and responsibilities attached to the job?

*   Determining the skills, aptitudes and abilities required for the job - what qualities and attributes are required for a person to perform the job effectively?.

*   Establishing a profile of the ideal candidate.

*   Attracting candidates by advertising or other means - is it necessary to recruit outside the organisation? If so, where are suitable applicants most likely to be found? Which are the best sources of labour and methods of recruitment?

Once this has been achieved, the selection processes begin; these are aimed at selecting the best person for the job from that field of candidates. The processes include collecting information about the candidates and planning the selection process to decide on the most appropriate methods of selection.

The last part of the recruitment and selection process is the induction and follow-up - how to undertake the socialisation process and introduce the new member of staff to the policies, procedures and working practices of the organisation.

A general outline of the recruitment and selection process is shown below:

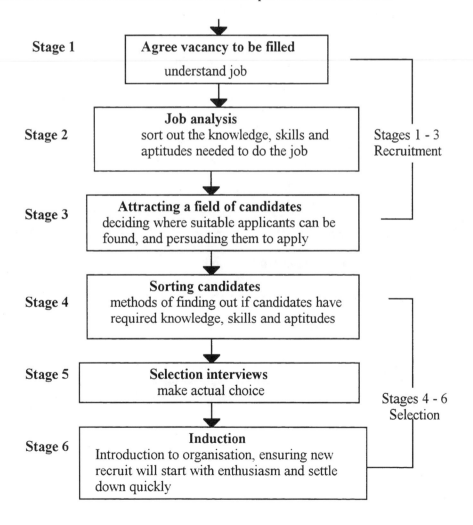

1.4   Assessing the need to recruit

When considering recruitment, there are two questions that managers must address. The first is whether there is really a job, and the second is whether there is someone suitable who is already employed by the organisation. There are many alternatives to recruitment eg,

- promotion of existing staff (upwards or laterally)

- secondment (temporary transfers to another department, office, plant or country) of existing staff, which may or may not become permanent.

- closing the job down, by sharing out duties and responsibilities among existing staff

- rotating jobs among staff, so that the vacant job is covered by different staff, on a systematic basis over several months.

- putting the job out to tender, using external contractors.

1.5   Alternative employment arrangements

The majority of new recruits are still appointed on a full-time, permanent basis. However, because the profile of working people is changing in the UK, organisations are beginning to turn towards other methods of employing staff.

Alternative working arrangements include:

- Homeworking (or teleworking) - technical advances mean that a great deal of work can now be done from home.

- Job-sharing - where two or more employees split a job between them, normally doing the whole job for half the time.

- Flexitime - where core hours must be worked but employees can arrange how they make up sufficient hours over a period of a week or a month.

- Term-time contracts - where employees are contracted to work only during school term time.

There are many more ways of solving staffing problems and organisations are attempting to become more responsive to employee needs. Many organisations are beginning to adopt a 'flexible firm' model, which is characterised by a central core of permanent workers, surrounded and supported by contractors, temporary staff, seasonal workers and part-timers, who are brought in as and when required.

2   JOB ANALYSIS

2.1   Introduction

The job analysis will consider the collection of tasks ie, the job, to be undertaken by the job holder, procedures involved, relationships with other jobs and job holders, responsibilities of the post, the personal qualities, experience and qualifications required of the applicant. According to the British Standards Institution, job analysis is:

[Definition]   'The determination of the **essential** characteristics of a job' (BSI 1979).

It is a vital preliminary to any recruitment activity and involves three main aspects; these are

(a)   An analytical study of a job to determine accurately the work done.
(b)   Achieving an understanding of the work in relation to other tasks in the organisation.
(c)   An identification of the qualities required of the job holder.

Such an exercise is frequently necessary since all too few organisations have a precise picture of the work that people do to achieve organisational objectives. It has often been said that discrepancies occur between what superiors believe is taking place, what job-holders believe is taking place, and what subordinates believe is taking place and all these can differ from what is actually taking place.

2.2   Analysing the job

An initial interview between the person responsible for selection and the head of the relevant department should meet the following objectives and decide:

- whether or not to alter the nature of the job;
- on the key characteristics of the job and the person to fill it;
- a time schedule for selection, based on the urgency of the vacancy;
- how the exercise is to be handled: internally /externally;
- details of the terms and conditions on which the job will be filled.

For routine vacancies, many of these issues will not arise, but it is important to be able to identify the circumstances in which a more detailed analysis is required. These include a senior vacancy, a newly created job, a 'problem' job, subject to high labour turnover or poor performance or a job where the present job holder has undertaken the job for many years. In these cases a full job analysis is required. The elements of job analysis are shown below:

- Job description - the recording, under an appropriate job title, of the tasks and responsibilities involved in a job

- Job evaluation - the process of analysing and assessing jobs to ascertain their relative worth, using the assessments as a basis for a balanced wage structure.

- Job classification - the process by which jobs similar in content, remuneration and status are classified into designated groups.

- Person specification - a specialised job description emphasising personnel requirements, designed to assist in the selection of employees.

2.3   The process of job analysis

The process starts with a detailed study and description of the tasks that make up a job. This is then analysed further under headings such as:

Job requirements: skill; knowledge; physical effort; and mental effort.

Responsibility: for people; materials; and to customers.

Working conditions: physical environment; and hazards

The job analysis forms the basis of a job specification, which is a description of the individual qualifications - age, sex, education and experience required of a person who is to do the job.

It will be seen that the detail and approach to job analysis are dictated by the purpose for which the job is being analysed.

A job analysis can be used for the placement, selection, training and promotion of employees. It can also be used for job evaluation, which allows for the rating of jobs against each other according to comparative skills, responsibilities etc.

2.4   Methods of job analysis

Various methods may be used, all with advantages and disadvantages depending upon the nature of the task to be analysed. The main methods are as follows

(a)   **Observation** - may be carried out by a manager or, in some cases, a job analysis specialist. While this technique is adequate for simple repetitive jobs it is generally poor for more complex work. General observation has been found to be a particularly useful method of identifying the learning difficulties of new recruits.

(b)   **Interviews with the job holder** - this is probably the most popular method of job analysis, and the most acceptable to job-holders themselves who may resent being observed without participating in the exercise. It is based on the notion that no one in the organisation knows more about the job than the actual job-holder. Its accuracy depends upon a full interview, a trained interviewer and a lack of bias on the part of the job-holder. Some job-holders may exaggerate the difficulty of their work or inflate its importance; this can occur especially in a job evaluation exercise where job analysis is being used as a basis for wage negotiation.

(c)   **Interviews with management** - this method is helpful to gain an overall picture of the relationship of the tasks to other jobs in the work process. It is also a useful check on the accuracy of the job-holder's account. It may, however, lack the precision of the previous method since the manager may not be aware of all the intricacies of every job under his supervision.

(d)   **Questionnaires and checklists** - are useful adjuncts to the interview methods and may be designed to enable relatively inexperienced managers to carry out an accurate job analysis.

(e)   **Procedure manuals** - many jobs already have written accounts and such manuals often abound in training departments where they were specially devised to assist in the training process. However, many jobs change frequently and the process of job analysis should be continuous.

2.5   Job description

A job description specifies the tasks, details responsibilities, sets authority limits, distinguishes accountability and outlines the organisational relationships that the job entails. It can be used in job evaluation, which is a process of analysing and assessing jobs to ascertain their relative worth and using the assessments as a basis for a balanced wage structure.

After a full job analysis has been carried out, a job description can be drawn up identifying the precise nature of the job in question. There are various methods of classification but most include all of the following points

(i)   The title of the job and the name of the department in which it is situated.

(ii)   The purpose of the job, identifying its objectives in relationship to overall objectives.

(iii)   The position of the job in the organisation, indicating the relationships with other jobs and the chains of responsibility. For this purpose, many firms refer to existing organisation charts.

(iv)   Wage/salary range

(v)   Principal duties to be performed, with emphasis on key tasks, and limits to the job-holder's authority. Usually under this heading is included an indication of how the job differs from others in the organisation.

(vi)   A further breakdown of principal duties is made identifying specific tasks in terms of what precisely is done and in what manner, and with some explanation, both in terms of quantity and quality.

(vii)   Aspects of the 'job environment' should be considered. Descriptions should be made of how the organisation supports the job, in terms of management and the provision of key services. The working conditions should be considered in terms of both the physical environment and the social environment (is the job part of a group task?). The opportunities offered by the job should be identified; these are especially important in a recruitment exercise. Such opportunities should be those offered by the job, and not those open only to talented individuals and may include such factors as promotion prospects and general career development. The rewards offered by the job should be taken into account, including the wage rate, bonuses, the amount of expected overtime and the related fringe benefits. Finally, some assessment should be made of the temperamental demands placed upon the job-holder such as the uncertain nature of the work and the amount of stress involved.

(viii) No job description is complete without a full identification of the key difficulties likely to be encountered by the job-holder.

2.6   Job evaluation

Definition   'Job evaluation is the comparison of jobs by the use of formal and systematic procedures in order to determine the relative position of one job to another in a wage or salary hierarchy'

Job evaluation is used to determine wage and salary differentials. It is essentially concerned with relationships not absolutes. It provides data for developing basic pay structures but cannot determine what the pay levels should be. It is the job that is evaluated, not the person doing the job. However, job evaluation methods depend, to some extent, on a series of subjective judgements made in the light of concepts such as logic, justice and equity and the progressive refinement of job evaluation techniques is an attempt to minimise the subjective personal element.

Methods of job evaluation are both non-analytical and analytical. Non-analytical methods include job ranking and job classifications.

Job ranking - the simplest method of evaluation is an attempt to determine the relative position of each job in the undertaking in comparison with all other jobs though without indicating the extent of the difference between jobs at different levels. A committee usually undertakes the ranking.

Job classification - is similar to job ranking, except that instead of ranking jobs and then devising grades, the grades are pre-determined and the jobs are then evaluated and allocated to a grade identified by a number or letter. This system is used in the Civil Service with eight grades A-H in ascending order of work complexity.

Analytical methods include points rating and factor comparison.

Points rating - involves several steps:

*   the definition of job factors eg. skill, responsibility, education, working conditions;

*   determination of the number of points to be awarded to each factor eg. skill 100-300 points, responsibility 100-500 points, education 100-400 points;

- breaking down of factors into a number of degrees on which jobs will be compared; thus education may be 4 GCSE levels or equivalent = 50 points, A levels =150 points, HNC = 200 points, second class honours degree = 300 points, higher degree = 400 points;

- ranking of each job on each factor and determining the total number of points;

- multiplying the total number of points by the value allocated to a point or group of points.

Factor comparison - like the points system, this is based on the assumption that jobs can be broken down into factors. Points, however, are not awarded to each factor; instead jobs are compared with each other on the basis of common factors. The steps involved are:

(a)   a number of representative 'key' jobs (15-20) are selected for comparison;

(b)   the representative jobs are ranked according to the factors selected eg. skill, education;

(c)   the portion of the current wage attributable to each factor for each representative job is chosen and the apportionment ranked.

Analytical methods allow a finer distinction to be drawn between jobs and so provide a more acceptable basis for showing whether jobs which have changed in content should also change in pay. Control over the wage structure is thus made easier. The main cause of wage inflation is that workplace bargaining often takes place in a piecemeal fragmented way, giving rise to anomalies and compensatory counterclaims from individual work groups. Job evaluation means the comparison of jobs, not employees, in a systematic analysis to determine their place in a hierarchy. It offers a basis for a structure of pay, which can at least be presented as rational. Job evaluation forces on management the same disciplined approach to personnel problems as is required in other spheres. For the employee, job evaluation means that increased skills and responsibility can be rewarded and recognised.

| Conclusion | Methods of job evaluation are both non-analytical and analytical. Non-analytical methods include job ranking and job classifications. Analytical methods include points rating and factor comparison. |

2.7   Person specification

This is variously referred to as the personnel specification, the job specification and even the man specification. Its aim is to construct a blueprint of the qualities required of the job-holder. It is based firstly on the job description and secondly upon an analysis of successful as well as unsuccessful job-holders. Such a specification is of obvious value in framing recruitment advertisements and as a guide to the selection process. The main problems involved with all types of specification are detail and flexibility. Some writers feel that over-specification is as bad as being too vague, in that too detailed a specification may be aimed at the ideal candidate who just does not exist; it may, therefore, prove to be too limiting in the recruitment and selection exercise. Probably the most appropriate policy is to apply a detailed specification with a certain degree of flexibility. Several classifications have been produced, the most famous of which is undoubtedly the **Seven Point Plan** devised by Alec Rodger in the 1950s. Rodger's classification involves the following factors:

(i)   **Physical make-up** - this can be extremely precise, as in the case of listing minimum height requirements for recruits to the police force, or it can refer to more general attributes such as a pleasant appearance, a clear speaking voice and good health.

(ii)   **Attainments** - relate to both job attainments and educational attainments. It is quite common for organisations to stipulate minimum entry requirements in terms of the number of GCSEs, A-levels or a degree, and in some cases, as with jobs in the Civil Service, the class of degree. People aspiring to the professions, as in the case of accountancy, must have minimum educational qualifications to enable them to tackle the required professional examinations. Many jobs require applicants to possess specific work experiences such as typing speed, experience of working with certain types of computer language or proven ability at operating a certain machine.

(iii)   **General intelligence** - many attempts have been made by psychologists to link measured intelligence levels with the ability to do certain jobs. Many jobs require such abilities as a good memory, verbal and numerical skills and problem-solving.

(iv)   **Special aptitudes** - some jobs carry specialised requirements such as the ability to drive a car or bus, the ability to type, or the ability to speak a foreign language.

(v)   **Interests** - certain interests may be appropriate to certain jobs. Any interest in helping people may be considered a necessary requirement for social work. Candidates for certain teaching posts may be favoured if they express an interest in extra-mural activities such as drama or running a soccer team.

(vi)   **Disposition** - all firms require their employees to be honest and reliable. A friendly disposition is usually essential in jobs which involve a great amount of contact with the general public as in the case of a receptionist. Jobs without close supervision invariably call for employees who are self-reliant and can make decisions.

(vii)   **Circumstances** - may include such factors as availability for working irregular hours or the home address of the candidate. For example, if a firm requires its employees to be on regular call, it may be difficult for someone living in an isolated rural community.

A similar blueprint was devised by Munro-Fraser. He referred to it as the **Five Point Plan**, to include the following considerations:

(i)   Impact on other people - appearance, speech and manner;
(ii)   required qualifications - education, training, and experience;
(iii)   innate abilities - 'brains', comprehension and aptitude for learning;
(iv)   motivation - determination and achievement;
(v)   flexibility and adjustment - emotional stability, ability to get on with others and capacity for stress.

2.8   The purpose of specifications

Whichever classification system is used it must be adapted to the job in question. It may be useful to distinguish between essential and desirable attributes. Plumbley suggests that it is also important to identify contra-indications ie, attributes that would disqualify a candidate. Such contra-indications may include such factors as shyness or, in the case of a Liverpool retailer requiring Saturday shop assistants, disqualifying candidates who expressed a strong support for one of the city's soccer teams. It can clearly be seen that a person specification can be helpful in not only the recruitment process but also as a template by which candidates may be selected. It is important to reiterate an earlier point about the need to be flexible and to draw up the specification in terms that can be recognised and measured - not a list of abstract human qualities. Finally, care must be taken not to transgress one of the laws relating to discrimination, as in the case of a job advertisement seeking 'a female Scottish cook and housekeeper', which was barred both on the grounds of race and sex discrimination.

Conclusion   A person specification is useful in many ways. Initially, it enables the recruiter to get a clearer picture of the sort of person who has the potential to succeed in the vacancy. It can be used when sorting through application forms to help produce a suitable shortlist and it can also be used at the interview stage to provide a firm basis for selection decisions, such as whether to reject or accept a candidate.

2.9   Justification of job analysis

Effective recruitment depends upon accurate job analyses. Precision in identifying the type of person required by an organisation can save time and money and avoid unwanted personnel. For instance, if the exact nature of the job is known, then it facilitates precisely worded advertisements, which assist in attracting a suitable field of candidates. If the advertisement is loosely worded, based upon an insufficient analysis, then totally unsuitable candidates may be attracted to apply, thereby causing an increase in the costs of recruitment. Job analysis is helpful to the recruitment process in another way, since it may establish that the job is no longer necessary or that it can be done elsewhere in the organisation or that it can be shared amongst other employees. Thus, job analysis may eliminate the need for recruitment. However, apart from its value in the recruitment process, job analysis as a technique is useful in many areas of personnel work. The list below gives an indication of its many uses.

(a)   To assist in determining the most appropriate method of selection.

(b)   To help identify the need for training and the most appropriate training method.

(c)   As part of a job evaluation exercise. Job analysis is the first step in establishing differences between jobs so that wage and salary differentials may be determined.

(d)   As an important preliminary to any job redesign exercise, as in work improvement through job enrichment.

(e)   It may be useful in the field of industrial relations by providing information vital to negotiating exercises.

3   ATTRACTING CANDIDATES

3.1   Internal or external recruitment

Once the content and value of each job and the ideal requirements of the job-holder have been determined, recruitment can begin. Management must make a decision as to whether the organisation is seeking to recruit from within or from outside. Each has its own advantages and disadvantages.

Internal recruitment occurs when a vacant position is filled by one of the existing employees. It generally applies to those jobs where there is some kind of career structure, as in the case of management or administrative staff. Most firms invariably recruit supervisors from their own shop floor staff. If a policy of internal recruitment is to be pursued the following points should be noted:

(a)   Recruiting from within by promoting existing employees can act as a source of motivation and may be good for the general morale of the workforce.

(b)   In dealing with existing staff, selection can be made on the basis of known data. The old adage of 'better the devil you know' applies here.

(c)   The internal recruit may be fully conversant with the work involved and will certainly know the people with whom he will be dealing; he may even have been carrying out the duties either as part of his own job or as the understudy to the incumbent.

(d)   It can save considerable time and expense in recruitment and selection.

(e)   If training is required this can be costly, but generally no induction is needed, and the firm may be able to train employees to its own specifications.

External recruitment occurs when an organisation seeks to bring in someone from outside the organisation to fill a vacancy. In general its advantages and disadvantages are opposite to those of internal recruitment, but the following specific points should be noted

(a)   External recruitment may be essential if an organisation is seeking specific skills and expertise that is not available internally. At some stage external recruitment is necessary to restore manning levels, depleted by employee wastage and internal promotion policies.

(b)   It may be necessary to inject new blood into an enterprise. People from outside the firm often bring with them new ideas and different approaches to the job, gleaned from their experience working in other organisations. With internal promotion policies there is a real danger of producing a succession of employees all with the same ideas; indeed, this may be a barrier to progress in the organisation. On the other hand, it should be remembered that newcomers can be equally set in their ways and have difficulties of adjustment to new techniques and approaches.

(c)   Although training costs may be reduced since there is the opportunity to recruit personnel with the required expertise, external recruitment does add to replacement and selection costs, and induction is still necessary.

(d)   Bringing in someone from outside may create dissatisfaction among existing employees.

(e)   In order to attract people to change their jobs a firm may have to pay initially higher wages.

There are no hard and fast rules concerning internal and external recruitment. If internal recruitment is used, then a limited number of methods are available. The most usual is really a form of direct invitation. Assessments are made of employees, and on the basis of these, management decides who will be offered a promotion opportunity. Some firms, however, allow employees to compete for vacancies by advertising internally, either through newsletters or by using notice-boards; normal selection procedures then follow. In some concerns it is obligatory that all promotion opportunities be open to competition, although this does not preclude management inviting certain chosen candidates to apply. Even where external recruitment is the main policy it does not prevent an existing employee from applying. The remainder of this section will focus on the techniques of external recruitment beginning with an assessment of recruitment advertising.

3.2   Recruitment advertising

Before embarking upon an advertising exercise, an organisation must be clear about its objectives in so doing, ie, precisely what to say and how to say it and a choice must be made as to the most appropriate media.

(a)   Defining the objectives - the three objectives of recruitment advertising are:

   •   To produce a compact field of suitable candidates and deter the unsuitable from applying.

   •   To achieve a balance between coverage and cost.

   •   To facilitate future recruitment by presenting an attractive image of the organisation.

(b)   What to say – this is based on a careful job analysis, followed by a selection of those key aspects that provide necessary information to prospective job candidates. Several research studies have been carried out to determine the type of information required and there is a measure of agreement that the most important factors are a succinct description of the work involved, the location, the remuneration, and a brief indication of the type of person required. Plumbley suggests that the information should be factual, relevant and unambiguous. Examples abound in most newspapers of evasive advertising making statements such as the job will be located in the North of England or the salary will be commensurate with the seniority of the position. Such statements do nothing to attract candidates and may actually deter potentially suitable applicants.

(c)   How to say it - generally advertisements should be concise and attractively written. Unfortunately in some organisations the job of writing the advertisement is given to an inexperienced personnel officer or is the product of a committee; both can result in poor advertisements. The following factors may be of importance:

- an attractive eye-catching heading, possibly incorporating a company symbol or logo;

- a job title that will leave the applicant in no doubt as to what the job entails;

- a written style that holds interest; and

- the offer of further information, perhaps inviting applicants to telephone for further information and to discuss their suitability.

All these factors are important considerations before actually placing an advertisement. Some companies employ management consultants for the entire undertaking, although this incurs a consultancy fee as well as the cost of the advertisement. The advantages and disadvantages of various forms of advertising are discussed below.

3.3   Types of advertising

The national press - is probably most suitable for the recruitment of managerial, some professional and senior technical staff. More popular daily papers such as the Daily Mirror may be used where large numbers of skilled or semi-skilled workers are required, and incentives are offered for moving area. The main advantages include the following:

(i)   There is regular publication, so space is usually available for an immediate insertion.

(ii)   The layout is usually attractive.

(iii)   There is a wide circulation and readership, thereby increasing the field of potential candidates.

(iv)   Many British newspapers are sold in other countries, so that overseas coverage is achieved at no extra cost. This may be important in recruiting for jobs requiring the experience of working in another country, as in some marketing posts.

(v)   Certain newspapers such as The Times have a certain status, which may enhance the reputation of the firm.

(vi)   Some newspapers have regular job features. The Guardian, for instance, devotes particular days to certain types of job advertisements; Monday is devoted to media appointments, Tuesday to teaching appointments and so on.

The main disadvantages include the following:

(i)   The fact that approximately 95% of the circulation is wasted.

(ii)   The advertisement has a relatively short life; many people do not keep daily newspapers beyond the day of issue.

(iii)   Since national papers are popular sources of recruitment, competition is fierce. A firm may find that its advertising is surrounded by others of a similar nature, perhaps offering more attractive jobs.

(iv)   The national press is very expensive. A column centimetre can cost anything from £10 – £20 and a large block display can be £1,000 or more; and these rates apply for only one issue.

Local newspapers - are probably most suited for the recruitment of skilled manual, clerical, local authority and lower management positions. The main advantages include the following:

(i)   It is usually much cheaper than the national press (but it still may constitute a considerable expense for some firms).

(ii)   It can reduce recruitment and selection costs by eliminating the costs of resettlement in that readers are usually from the local area.

(iii)   The firm may already be well known so that the length of advertisements may be reduced.

(iv)   The use of local papers has the added advantage of contributing to good public relations and vacancies may attract editorial coverage.

(v)   Most local papers have a longer life than their national counterparts.

The main disadvantages include the following:

(i)   A sufficient number of people with the necessary requirements may not be available in the local area.

(ii)   Circulation is usually limited and issues are often only on a weekly basis.

(iii)   The quality of layout is very variable.

Specialist journals - include the publications of the professional bodies and various trade journals. As such they are most suited for recruitment in the professions and specialist trades. The main advantages include the following:

(i)   The readership is particularly homogeneous; there is already a degree of pre-selection, which may reduce eventual recruitment and selection costs.

(ii)   Many, because of their small circulation, have relatively cheap advertising rates, although this may not be the case for the more popular accounting journals.

(iii)   It may be assumed that likely readers are those who wish to keep up-to-date with developments in their field.

The main disadvantages include the following:

(i)   Closing dates for advertisements usually occur well before publication; this can inhibit speedy recruitment.

(ii)   Because they are so specialised there is considerable competition from other advertisements.

(iii)   Many give little space to job advertisements.

(iv)   Circulation can be slow and haphazard, particularly where it involves subscription readership.

Radio and television - using radio and television is increasing in popularity particularly since the advent of commercial radio. Whilst there is wide exposure, the desired audience may not be listening or watching. In some cases firms using television have been overwhelmed by the response, which creates significant problems of selection. Although television advertising can be more expensive than the national press, the use of television, along with the cinema, may be appropriate for mass-recruiting in situations of severe labour shortage.

Other methods of recruitment include:

•   Nominations by existing employees - can be a selective method of recruitment, since generally only suitable applicants are recommended.

- Casual enquiries - places the onus on job candidates and as such is unpredictable and offers the firm no control over the process. Some firms see it as an indication of motivation on the part of the job-seeker and some facilitate enquiry by posting notices of vacancies outside the premises.

- Government employment services - the unemployed register presents firms with a reservoir of potential employees categorised according to skill and pre-selected according to suitability. The separation of the benefit and employment functions by the creation of Job Centres also provides details of vacancies to people already holding a job.

- Employment agencies - tend to specialise in separate market sectors such as clerical and secretarial, accounting or computing. Some provide such an efficient service that they are the most cost-effective way of obtaining good candidates. Many of these agencies undertake initial screening of potential candidates, so that the recruitment officer sees only the most suitable applicants.

- Advertising agencies - assist a firm by taking over responsibility for its recruitment advertising and gain substantial income not only from the fee charged but the discounts they receive from the press and journals.

- Management consultants - as with employment agencies there has been a considerable increase in the numbers of consultants specialising in recruitment and selection. Such firms specialise in the recruitment of senior management and senior technical staff. There is often an overlap with the role of advertising agencies and candidate registers. In the latter case some consultants offer firms an executive search service which entails the pre-selection of a group of likely candidates.

- Recruiting direct from schools and colleges - is often a cheap method of obtaining trainees and sometimes involves pre-selection by the schools and colleges themselves.

3.4 Activity

What might happen if the organisation failed to keep internal applications for vacancies a secret from the applicant's line manager?

3.5 Activity solution

It could result in the line manager blocking attempts by their staff to move into another job, especially if it is a post outside their department. Alternatively, and worse, such employees may be 'blacklisted' by their line manager, who may see their request to move jobs as a personal slight against them.

4 THE PURPOSE AND EFFECTIVENESS OF THE JOB APPLICATION FORM

4.1 Purpose of the application form

A common procedure is to invite inquirers to complete a standard application form accompanied by a short hand-written letter of application. The application form usually seeks information about the applicant on several fronts, namely:

(i)   personal details of address, age, family background, nationality;
(ii)   education and experience history;
(iii)   present employment terms and experience;
(iv)   social and leisure interests.

The application form should be regarded by the applicant as an opportunity to qualify for the interview. It usually includes a general section enabling the applicant to express career ambitions, personal preferences, and perhaps even aspects of motivation, ambition and character, in his or her own words.

The application form has advantages over the personal CV in that it allows for standard comparisons between applicants and it includes all areas of interest to the company. As well as obtaining all the essential information about the applicant, the purposes of the application form are:

- To eliminate totally unsuitable candidates; a standardised form speeds the sorting and short-listing of applicants and can be most useful where the ratio of applicants to vacancies is high. At a basic level it is a test of literacy and the ability to understand simple instructions.

- To act as a useful preliminary to selection interviews. Basic information can be gained which would otherwise take up valuable interview time. Some interviewers use the form as the framework for the interview itself; it can be a particularly useful guide for inexperienced interviewers. Some organisations have extended the role played by the application form compared to the interview by asking for much more detailed information, sometimes asking candidates to answer questions relating to their motivation towards applying.

- It forms the nucleus of the personal record of individual employees. A well designed application form contains all the relevant data relating to address, age, qualifications, previous experience and so on. This should be updated at regular intervals.

4.2   Effectiveness of the application form

The design of the form is crucial. So often we find forms with not enough space to enter the appropriate information. Attempts have been made to link the characteristics of applicants as described on the application form with the characteristics of successful job holders. The method used is to take a large sample of current employees and categorise them into good, average and bad workers, or whichever classification is most suitable. The next step is to look for a correlation between the personal characteristics of workers and their work records to use as a basis of selection. For example, if all good workers were twenty-three years of age or older on application, married and with at least two years' experience in a similar job, then this may be a blueprint for successful selection. Extra weight can be given to this information at the application form stage.

5   APPLICANT REFERENCES

5.1   Introduction

Generally the personnel department issue a standard letter requesting a reference because this is relatively easy, but it places a considerable workload on the referee. Using the telephone as a means of gaining a reference, although more time-consuming, often leads to better and more accurate information on the applicant.

The type and number of references taken up varies with different organisations. Many companies suggest going back five years or two previous jobs. Applicants' present employers are contacted only after a decision has been made to make an offer of employment.

5.2   The purpose of references

References are used by most employees as a key part of their selection process, but mainly to verify facts about the candidate rather than as an aid to decision making. The reference check is usually the last stage in the selection process and referees should be contacted only after the applicant has given permission. Good referees are almost certain to know more about the applicant than the selector and it would be foolish not to seek their advice or to treat the reference check as a mere formality.

As well as the applicant's suitability for employment, the reference may provide information on strengths and weaknesses, training needs and potential for future development.

5.3   The problems with references

Unfortunately, references are notoriously poor predictors of future performance. Some referees take the task seriously but many do not, and because most of them are well known to the applicant, they hesitate to say anything critical.

Where people are dissatisfied or frustrated in their present jobs, they could come out badly in a reference. Star students can turn out to be less than star employees, and sacked employees could turn out to be real winners in a different organisation. Employers wishing to rid themselves of an unsatisfactory employee could write a glowing reference, or one that leaves a lot unsaid. Some references are too ambiguous to be useful eg, 'Any manager would be lucky to get Miss Jones to do the accounts'. The skilful reference reader learns to look for what is conspicuous by omission, although there is a risk that the writer merely forgot.

The poor predictive validity of the reference may be due to the blandness of the request. To overcome this, employers should ask direct and meaningful questions. One question that might be included is whether the employer would re-employ the candidate and, if not, why not.

5.4   Activity

Why might an employer give a poor reference to a member of staff?

5.5   Activity solution

A poor reference may be submitted on a worker an employer does not wish to lose.

Conclusion   Recruitment, as distinct from selection, involves the attraction of a field of suitable candidates for the job. Only when this is done does the selection process begin, the aim being to select the best person for the job from that field of candidates.

6   SELECTION

6.1   Selection process

Selection is the process, at the end of which a decision is made as to whether an individual is offered and takes up employment with an organisation. Not only is the firm selecting the individual but, invariably the individual is making decisions as to the suitability of the job offered, the terms of employment and the firm.

Methods of selection include the shortlisting of applicants, collecting information about the applicants and the design and preparation of the selection process.

The diagram below outlines the process:

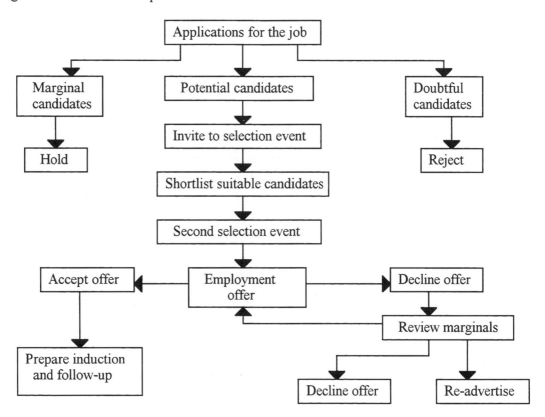

6.2 Screening and shortlisting

Before selection can take place the number of applicants must be reduced to manageable proportions. The employer must decide the criteria that are essential and desirable to do the job effectively. Candidates should be screened according to these conditions and placed in one of three categories eg, potential, doubtful and marginal. The doubtfuls should be sent a standard letter briefly, but tactfully, dismissing them. The marginals will be kept on hold and informed of the situation and the potentials, assuming there are enough, will be invited for a selection event.

In general, selection events should be tailor-made for a particular organisation and job. The thoroughness of the procedure will depend on a number of factors

- The consequences of faulty selection; obviously an organisation will take more care in selecting its Financial Director than it will in selecting its car-park attendant.

- The time and finance available; these are both constraints on the process. A firm may have neither the time nor the money to invest in lengthy, complicated selection methods.

- The company policy, which may lay down certain rules for the composition of selection panels or the use of certain tests. Some companies have policies of over-hiring certain types of trainees, to ensure that the most able graduate is available for all positions. This will often offset losses through labour turnover.

- The selection process becomes more important the longer the length of the training period, since this represents a considerable investment on the part of the organisation.

The selection event can include the application form, interviews, tests, references, medical examinations, group selection methods, situational tests and/or assessment centres.

We have already discussed the application form and references.

6.3   The interview

The interview is a third stage in the selection process. It is defined as:

[Definition]   a formal discussion where an employer assesses an applicant for a job.

The purpose of the interview must be clear. It has three main aims:

• Finding the best person for the job.

• Making sure that the candidate understands what the job is and what the career prospects are.

• Making the candidate feel that they have been given fair treatment in the interview.

Other objectives to be achieved at the interview include:

• To confirm and expand on the information about candidates given in the application form, in other documents or on the telephone.

• To assess candidates' personality and motivation.

• To obtain further details on certain matters.

• To ensure applicants have a reasonable knowledge of the job and the organisation and to provide them with more information if required.

• To evaluate the suitability of the candidates for the job.

• To encourage the most suitable candidate to take the job.

• To agree terms of employment

6.4   Interview process

An interview process can be:

A face to face interview - carried out once by a single representative, usually of the employing organisation. It is considered the best situation for establishing rapport and is certainly cost effective in terms of people employed. While it does have the advantage of placing candidates at ease, enabling the interviewer to gain a true picture of the applicant, the selection decision relies heavily on the judgement of one individual.

A problem-solving interview - this is a face to face interview where the candidate is set a hypothetical problem. For example, a problem may be posed to a prospective industrial relations trainee concerning the action he or she would take following a fight between a foreman and a shop steward where both participants told a different version of the incident and a work stoppage had ensued. The drawback with such interviews is that the quality of the answers is very difficult to assess and compare to those given by other candidates.

A stress interview - this is another face to face interview, where the candidate is put under deliberate stress usually by an aggressive interviewer, who attempts to disparage the candidate's answers at every opportunity. This method of interviewing proved successful during the war for selecting undercover agents and was in vogue a few years ago for selecting managers, based on the theory that their ability to handle stressful situations was the best test of their ability. Research evidence concerning stress interviews suggests they are of dubious value and can actually cause harm by alienating favourable candidates.

A succession of interviews - by different interviewers (eg, operating manager and personnel officer). Common practice in leading companies is to conduct several face to face interviews, rather than a single panel interview. Obviously this type of exercise is more costly and can be more wearing on the candidate, but it may enable a more balanced judgement to be made.

A group interview - where candidates are brought together and observed by assessors, who give the group a problem to discuss or a situation to sort out. It is a sort of committee exercise. This method can identify personal reactions such as tact, dominance and persuasiveness.

A panel of people - candidates are interviewed before a panel of two or more people, in some cases as many as six or seven. For some senior posts in some local authorities in Britain, panels of twenty or more can be found. The usual panel size is between two and six interviewers, depending upon the nature of the job and the customs of the employing organisation. Panel interviews have the advantage of sharing judgements and most panels have the authority to reach immediate decisions. Their main drawback is the question of control: with so many people, irrelevancies can be introduced and a particular line of questioning can soon be destroyed. The success of a panel interview often depends upon careful planning and effective chairmanship. While they can be impressive in terms of ritual, panel interviews can be particularly unnerving for some candidates.

Conclusion   The main aim of the selection interview process is to find the best person for the job and encourage him or her to accept the position with terms that are agreeable to both parties. Finding the best person means: confirming, expanding or obtaining further information than already given on the application form; assessing the knowledge, personality and motivation of the candidate and addressing any questions they may have. All candidates should feel that they have been treated fairly.

6.5   Selection testing

Definition   A test is a standardised type of examination given to an individual.

Selection testing includes medical examinations, attainment testing, psychological tests and observation of the candidate in group situations. The tests used usually take the form of pencil and paper tests, and it is argued that such testing helps:

(a)   to assess the ability and quality of existing employees;
(b)   to assess the potential of shortlisted future employees;
(c)   to reduce the cost of recruitment by cutting down the time spent on subjective interviewing;
(d)   to eliminate or at least reduce the risk of making costly mistakes;
(e)   to minimise staff turnover, which is also costly.

The main problem with any form of selection test is ensuring that it is relevant to the type of appointment. A brief description of the main types of testing follows.

Intelligence tests - such as general IQ tests. These involve the setting of some kind of task or problem, which is designed to gauge levels of reasoning, understanding, memory and speed of thought. The need for such tests is not considered necessary where existence of a formal education path can be shown.

Aptitude tests - aim to measure some inborn potentiality of a certain kind, rather than acquired skill or knowledge. They are basically used to obtain information about such skills as mechanical ability, clerical and numerical ability and manual dexterity.

Competence tests - sometimes called attainment tests, measure the depth of knowledge or grasp of skills which have been learned in the past. For example, a car mechanic could be asked to tune a car engine using a machine that he claims to be experienced in using.

Personality tests - usually take the form of personality inventories. These are lists of multiple choice questions where the aim is to reveal 'what a person really is' or how a person would react in certain situations. The importance of personality in employment is that what people are determines what they do. A typical personality test asks people to report on their likes, dislikes, attitudes and what they would do in certain situations. A typical personality test is the Bernreuter Personality Inventory, consisting of a large number of 'yes', 'no' and 'undecided' questions. By comparing the answers with a stencil, it is possible to categorise the subject's personality as emotionally unstable, extroverted, self-sufficient, dominant or submissive.

Medical examinations - eliminate candidates with health problems that might affect their attendance at work or endanger the health or safety of colleagues, and protect prospective staff from being employed in work for which they are physically unsuitable. These are mandatory for some jobs, notably for airline pilots, bus drivers and hospital workers. Apart from a general check on fitness they can assist in the placement of employees, especially when dealing with disabled candidates. In some firms a medical examination is required as part of that firm's agreement with an insurance company.

Group selection methods - the classic format for such methods is where a group of leaderless candidates are presented with a simulated work problem. Such tests are much used by the British Army as part of their officer selection programme and are also used by several large organisations in the selection of graduate trainees. Such exercises are tests not only of problem solving and intellectual skills but of social skills as well, indicating how a candidate is able to get on with and influence others.

Situational tests - are developed to meet the criticism of most other types of test, where answers are either right or wrong. Those in favour of situational tests argue that most work situations are probabilistic and the most useful tests are those of problem-solving and creative thinking in a work simulated setting. The classic format for such tests is in group selection.

6.6   Assessment centres

These are centres where groups of around six to ten candidates are brought together for one to three days of intensive assessment. They are presented, individually and as a group, with a variety of exercises, tests of ability, personality assessments, interviews, work samples, team problem solving and written tasks. As well as being multi-method, other characteristics of assessment centres are that they use several assessors and they assess several dimensions of performance required in the higher level positions.

Traditionally, the main purpose of assessment centres has been to contribute to management decisions about people, usually the assessment of management skills and potential as a basis for promotion decisions. Assessment centres are better at predicting future performance than judgements made by unskilled managers, and it is the combination of techniques that contributes to their apparent superiority over other approaches.

6.7   The criteria for effective selection

The selection decision is a very important one. It should be as objective as possible by using the job analysis, a clear interview plan containing meaningful comments, a fair grading scheme and by acknowledging the following criteria.

Discrimination - whichever method of selection is used, the manager must be able to discriminate between candidates to make a selection decision. For example, if ten candidates are given a written test as part of the selection procedure and all score 100%, then the test has failed to discriminate between candidates. This criterion is particularly important in the design of tests; in some cases questions must be eliminated which prove to be too difficult or too easy for all candidates.

Reliability - this is a question of the dependability of the method of selection.

Regardless of the method and approach chosen, good selection will ultimately rest on the firm understanding of the requirements of the job and job holder and a sensible use of techniques, which will objectively measure the extent to which the candidates possess those qualities and skills.

6.8   Making the offer of employment

Once an eligible candidate has been found, an offer can be made, in writing or by telephone, subject to satisfactory references.

The organisation should be prepared for its offer to be rejected at this stage. An applicant may have received and accepted another offer, may have disliked his first view of the organisation, may have changed his mind or may have just been testing the water in applying in the first place. A small number of applicants will be kept in reserve to cover this eventuality.

An effective offer of employment must not contain anything that cannot be delivered and should contain the following elements:

- must be a written document - a written statement is a legally binding document, which should help to seal the offer. A telephone call to break the good news to the successful candidate is fine, but should not go into too much detail about the offer in conversation.

- must contain sufficient detail - must contain the job title and location with details of pay, benefits, hours of work, holiday as well as the terms and conditions of employment, including notice period, sickness payment schemes, pension scheme details, disciplinary and grievance procedures and an outline of the probationary period where one is in force.

- should offer an opportunity to make further contact before a final commitment is made - a clear but informal opportunity for further discussion, which may lead to negotiation on terms and conditions of employment.

6.9   Negotiation

After the offer of employment is made, it may be necessary to reach a mutually agreeable compromise over some aspects of the employment contract. This could mean negotiating over pay, hours of work, holiday arrangements or the type of car on offer.

Negotiating is an activity that seeks to reach agreement between two or more starting positions, enabling parties with opposing interests to bargain. This bargaining leads to a situation of compromise and agreement. Regardless of the nature of the dispute, the same principles will apply and the aim will be to reach a solution that is acceptable to both parties.

7   INDUCTION

7.1   Purpose

Induction involves the introduction of a new member of staff to other members and to the environment of the organisation, its culture, policies and practices. It is an opportunity to affirm corporate values and objectives while the employee is still likely to be comparatively receptive and before he or she has been subjected to dissenting views. It is also an opportunity to provide the employee with an organisational context for his or her own duties and responsibilities. Induction covers the rules and regulations, methods of operation and personal training and development needs. Effective induction is an extension of the recruitment and selection procedure, starting with the selection process and covering the first few months at work.

A new entrant's first impressions can be very important in shaping his or her attitude to the company and colleagues. A warm welcome, introductions to other members of the organisation and a well-planned induction programme will reassure the new member. Reassurance will aid motivation and attitude to work performance.

7.2   The induction programme and follow-up

Induction courses are arranged for new recruits to an organisation to enable them to familiarise themselves with the firm and to adjust to the requirements of the organisation. The first stage might involve a tour of the offices and factory, talks or films on the history and products or services of the organisation, and an explanation of the policy relating to holidays, sickness, trade union membership, flexitime, etc. On the first day, the paperwork will need to be sorted eg, P45, banking details, confirmation of educational qualifications etc. Induction is a matter of telling and showing, to build familiarisation swiftly, enabling new entrants to maximise their contribution to the company in the minimum time.

Someone joining an accounts department would then require an introduction to the structure of the departmental organisation and his or her role in it. Here, the idea is to familiarise the new recruit with colleagues. Arrangements should be made at this stage for someone to go to lunch and/or tea with the new person, mainly because it can be very lonely on your first day sitting on your own in the canteen. If at all possible the new employee's manager and head of department should be available over the first few days to give a clear indication of their commitment to ensuring that things work out well. Details of the methods of working would also be given (much of this may be embodied in an office manual) and instruction given by a supervisor on the requirements of the post for which the recruit was engaged.

For staff who are seeking membership of one of the accountancy bodies the selection of the most appropriate qualification and methods of study will have to be determined in discussions between the student, the accountant and the training officer (this may have been agreed at the selection interview).   In addition a training programme must be initiated so that the correct practical experience is obtained to satisfy the requirements of the accountancy body.

Within the accountancy profession there is much emphasis on post-qualifying education (PQE) and details of courses provided by all the accountancy bodies, and other organisations, should be readily available.   Staff should be encouraged to attend to keep their knowledge up to date and, in some instances, staff may be directed to attend, eg, to update skills and knowledge.

Staff at all levels should be encouraged to develop their knowledge and abilities to as far as they are capable (and wish).   In accounts departments, there are many opportunities to specialise and this should be encouraged, provided it is compatible with the policies and requirements within the organisation, and there are understudies for all areas of knowledge.

After about two months on the job, it is good practice to arrange a meeting where the new employee can discuss areas of concern and find out how they are getting on. The meeting may be timed to coincide with the end of the probationary period or with the presentation of the formal statement of terms and conditions of employment.

This follow-up should be designed to explore issues of satisfaction, expectation and motivation. Attention should be given to the quality of training received and the nature of interpersonal relationships within the workgroup. The outcome should be a positive one but, when it is negative, action must be taken to investigate areas of dissent to help that employee and to make sure it does not happen in the future.

8   SELF TEST QUESTIONS

8.1   Define selection (1.1)

8.2   Draw an overview of the recruitment and selection process (1.3)

8.3   Briefly describe three alternatives to recruitment (1.4)

8.4   List the elements of job analysis (2.2)

8.5   What methods are available for job analysis? (2.4)

8.6   What is job evaluation used for? (2.6)

8.7   Outline 4 factors that feature in Alec Rodger's 7 point plan (2.7)

8.8   Describe the types of recruitment advertising an organisation might run (3.3)

8.9   What advantages does the application form have over the personal CV? (4.1)

8.10   Describe one of the problems with references (5.3)

8.11   What type of interview processes are there? (6.4)

8.12   Briefly describe 3 selection tests (6.5)

8.13   At what stage of the induction programme would management organise the follow-up? (7.2)

9   EXAMINATION TYPE QUESTION

9.1   Engineering company

You work for a large engineering company, which is under severe pressure to significantly reduce costs and improve performance. Your Chief Accountant is retiring after a lifetime's service with the firm. In recent years he has lost interest and his department has performed badly - producing poor quality information behind schedule. Although there are some able people in the department everyone has become demoralised and demotivated. Sickness and absenteeism is high. There is confusion over areas of responsibility within the section, systems are out-dated and you sense that there is a lot of duplication.

Against this background describe the recruitment and selection process the company would go through to fill this vacancy, describing the options that are available to you and the reasons for your choices.

10   ANSWER TO EXAMINATION TYPE QUESTION

10.1   Engineering company

The first step will be to decide whether to keep the job in its current form or, particularly in view of the difficult financial climate, whether to combine the duties with another job or reallocate the duties. The Managing Director would need to be involved in this decision.

There is a clear requirement to analyse the post carefully because it is a senior vacancy, where there have been specific problems of performance where the job-holder has done the job for a long time and where there is confusion over areas of responsibility. Therefore, it will be essential to draw up a proper job description, clarifying the key responsibilities of the role. It will then be necessary to determine the person specification - the type of person sought to fill the job. Clearly a qualified, high-calibre accountant is required. But there are other requirements. The section has been poorly managed and uses out-dated systems. The person will need strong management skills and experience, perhaps with a qualification or experience. Part of the company's strategic plan may be to invest in a new system and, if so, the person appointed would need to demonstrate a knowledge of the latest systems. He/she will have a successful track record to date, will be dynamic with strong leadership, inter-personal and social skills.

Because of the problems of the firm as a whole and the section in particular, a strong candidate is clearly required. It is likely therefore that the job will need to be evaluated to ensure that candidates of sufficiently high-calibre are attracted. For example it will be necessary to determine a salary and benefits package which is competitive in the market place, will be attractive to the right candidate but which does not completely distort the pay differentials within the firm.

Once the decisions have been taken about the job description, the person specification and the value of the job, the recruitment and selection can take place. First there is a need to decide whether there are any suitable internal candidates. There are some bright young staff in the department with the potential for development but it is unlikely that any of them will have the experience or all-round breadth of skills required for the job. However it might be a good idea to give them a chance to apply - it is good for morale and there might be a surprise!

It is unlikely that there will be anyone on file who has written 'out of the blue' but it would be worth checking. There will be a need for the company to decide whether to advertise the post themselves or use recruitment consultants or head-hunters although head-hunters and agencies are expensive and times are hard!

It is therefore probably best to advertise. It will probably be more beneficial to advertise nationally to attract a sufficient breadth of applicant - because there is a requirement for a broad range of skills at a senior management level. A combination of the national press (Sunday Times) and trade magazine (Accountancy Age) would be advisable. The company should arrange for an attractive advert to be designed - making sure details of the broad-range and level of skills required as well as what the job can offer the candidate in terms of career growth and development are identified. Details of the job and salary and benefits range will also be included. Applicants who reply to job advertisements are usually asked to fill in a job application form, or to send a letter giving details about themselves and their previous job experience (their CV) and explaining why they think they are suitable for the job.

The application form or CV should be used to find out whether the applicant is obviously unsuitable for the job or whether they may be of the right calibre and worth inviting to an interview. It is likely that the Finance Director with the help of the personnel manager will select an initial list of people to interview. It may be decided, because the job is important and inter-personal and social skills are required, to subject the final short-list candidates to psychometric testing.

Interviewing is a crucial part of the selection process because it gives the company a chance to assess the applicant directly and it also gives the applicant a chance to learn more about the organisation. Because of the importance of the post a short-list of the two to three best candidates from the first interviews may be drawn up and then seen at a final interview with the Managing Director and the Finance Director.

With the personnel manager, the Finance Director should ensure that the interviews are properly organised and structured with key questions being prepared and detailed notes being taken and the action at the end of each interview agreed.

Finally, once the preferred choice is agreed upon and references are sought and acceptable, the job offer is made.

11 HUMAN BEHAVIOUR AND MOTIVATION

INTRODUCTION & LEARNING OUTCOMES

Syllabus area 11(iii)
- The design of reward systems

- A range of models of human behaviour and motivation and their application in a business context (eg, Taylor, Schein, McGregor, Maslow, Herzberg, Handy)

One of the most important aspects of human resource management is making sure that the people within the organisation are motivated to perform their jobs effectively and efficiently. This motivation should accord with the objectives and culture of the organisation.

Motivated people are those who have made a conscious decision to devote considerable effort to achieving something that they value, although this will differ from one individual to another. Effective management will recognise this fact and will be aware of the techniques available to keep the employee interested and keen to achieve. Managers should carefully assess their reward structures and through careful planning, and clearly defining duties and responsibilities, the effort-performance-reward-satisfaction system can be integrated into an entire system of managing.

When you have studied this chapter you should be able to do the following:

- Evaluate the tools, which can be used to influence the behaviour of staff within a business, particularly within the finance department

---

1 MOTIVATION

1.1 Psychological factors affecting work performance

An organisation has goals that can only be achieved by the efforts of its employees. Individuals also have their own goals in life, and these are likely to be different from those of the organisation. After recruitment, the employee might be subjected to a number of techniques designed to enhance performance. A major consideration for management is the problem of getting the employees to work in such a way that the organisation achieves its goals; in other words, employees must be motivated.

We can attribute four major psychological factors to each individual - personality aspects, perception, ability and motivation, each having major implications for management of people, and affecting performance and attitudes in work:

(i) **Personality aspects** - the personality of the individual has an important influence on how they behave and how well they perform at work. Indeed many organisations use personality tests as part of their recruitment procedure in order to get the right fit between the person and the job. But what is personality? The term is often misused when we speak of someone having lots of personality or not much personality.

> **Definition** We can define personality as the individual's characteristics and behaviours, which are organised in such a way as to reflect the unique adjustment the individual makes to his or her environment.

(ii)   **Perception** has been defined as 'the active psychological process in which stimuli are selected and organised into meaningful patterns'. In understanding organisational behaviour, these processes are of key significance. No matter how hard a manager tries to send a clear message, the message is still subject to distortion as the receiver will select parts of the message, interpret it in the light of experience and organise the information in a form that makes sense to him. Our perceptions then form the basis for our actions. If a person's perception of what is expected of him in his or her job is correct then the result can be effective performance. If, on the other hand, the perception is distorted and gives an unreal picture of reality then the result will be inappropriate behaviour and ineffective performance.

(iii)   **Abilities** - a person's ability is obviously a vital influence on his or her behaviour and performance at work. No matter how well motivated or enthusiastic the individual, if the ability is missing, the performance will be less than adequate. In discussing ability we can distinguish between two elements which determine levels of competence, namely aptitude and learning. Aptitude refers to a person's innate capacity to perform some particular task effectively eg, a person may be tone deaf and lack any musical aptitude whilst, on the other hand, the same person may have a high level of athletic aptitude. Learning can be an important category because ability does not simply depend on innate factors. It is also determined by the chances that the individual has, to acquire abilities through learning. In organisations, these opportunities are provided on a formal basis through training, and on a less formal basis through work experience.

People differ not only in their ability to complete a task but also in their 'will to do' or motivation.

(iv)   **Motivation** is concerned both with why people choose to do one thing rather than another and also with the amount of effort or intensity of action that people put into their activities.

Definition   Motivation can be defined as the will to do, the urge to achieve goals, the drive to excel.

The motivation of a person depends on the strength of his needs. Motivation is concerned with why people do (or refrain from doing) things. Needs are motives for action and can be classed as wants, drives or impulses within the individual. These needs can be conscious or sub-conscious and direct a person to achieve certain goals.

There are five major motivators - values, beliefs, attitudes, needs and goals - as outlined below.

Definition   Motivators are forces that induce individuals to perform, forces that influence human behaviour.

1.2   Values

The values a person holds can influence motivation in two particular ways. First they affect the types of activities the person will find appealing and secondly, values influence a person's motivation towards specific outcomes such as money, power and prestige.

People with different values tend to end up in different jobs; for example, the values held by people in social work professions differ from those held by people in the armed forces. Even within organisations, patterns of values held by different groups can vary considerably eg, between levels (senior management as compared with shop floor workers) and between functions (production versus research and development).

On a more specific level, the way in which people value particular organisational rewards has a major effect on their motivation. If people value monetary rewards highly and find themselves in a situation where effective performance leads to greater income, they are likely to be highly motivated. On the other hand if, in the same situation, a person values friendship above income this person might be poorly motivated. Understanding an individual's values is a crucial element in determining a motivation approach.

1.3   Beliefs

There are two ways in which beliefs are particularly important to motivation. Employees must believe that what the organisation requires of them is possible to achieve. If they believe work demands to be impossible they are going to be poorly motivated. Also employees need to believe that by performing well they will personally benefit from their efforts. Again poor motivation is the outcome if a person believes that effective performance will not bring personal rewards.

Beliefs may be correct or incorrect. In terms of the impact on motivation this does not matter. A person who mistakenly believes he or she is not capable of doing the job will be as poorly motivated as the person who is correct in his or her belief. The problem of incorrect beliefs is that they often lead to irrelevant or inappropriate behaviour. Managers must make sure that people hold realistic beliefs, both about their own capacities and the likely consequences of effective performance.

1.4   Attitudes

Definition   Attitudes refer to persistent feelings and behaviour tendencies directed towards specific persons, groups, ideas or objects.

They are important to our understanding of motivation because of the links that exist between them and behaviour. A person with a negative attitude to another department in the organisation may be unlikely to behave in a friendly or co-operative way with members of that department. A person with a positive attitude toward the company will be more likely to come to work regularly and stay with the company even if offered a job in another organisation.

However, it should be remembered that people sometimes act in ways that are inconsistent with their attitude, ie, the person says one thing and does another. We should not be too surprised by this because, while the concept of attitudes is valuable, a full understanding of why people actually behave the way they do requires us to take into account the many additional factors that influence individual motivation and behaviour.

1.5   Needs

People can be thought of as having a variety of different needs that influence their motivation. As we shall see later a number of theories, notably Maslow's, have identified needs as the key feature of all human motivation. Needs are seen as varying from basic needs such as food and shelter to more complex needs such as the needs for friendship, self-esteem and self-realisation. Motivation is said to relate to need in that a person with a particular need will be motivated to engage in behaviour that will lead to the gratification or satisfaction of that need. The implication for organisations is that to motivate employees it is necessary to set up situations in which people are able to satisfy their most important needs by engaging in behaviour most desired by the organisation for effective performance.

There is no generally agreed, comprehensive list of human needs. It is very easy to become confused in distinguishing what a person wants and what a person needs. The very simplicity of need theories of motivation, which makes them initially attractive, may also be their greatest weakness. Motivation is a complex process with needs being only one component of that process.

1.6   Goals

Goals influence motivation in two ways. First, a goal provides a target to aim at, something to aspire to. This means the existence of a goal generates motivation in a person to work towards the achievement of the goal. Second, goals provide a standard of performance. A person is doing well if they have achieved a goal or are on the way to achieving it. On the other hand failure to achieve a goal or at least to make some progress toward it is evidence of unsatisfactory performance.

Research has investigated the importance of goals in motivation and concludes that for goals to be significant motivators they must be specific, sufficiently difficult to be challenging and they must be accepted by the person as their own particular goals and not as something imposed from outside.

2   MOTIVATION MODELS

2.1   Introduction

There has been much research undertaken in an attempt to understand what motivates individual employees at work and how managers can improve motivation.

The motivational strategy that is decided upon will depend on the beliefs held, and the culture that prevails, in an organisation and by its managers. There are radically different views held within different organisations about people's nature, the influence of work and what motivates them to work harder and more effectively. There are two radically different views, the traditional and the human relations, which represent the nature of the employee.

2.2   The traditional view

This view stems from the work of FW Taylor and the school of scientific management. Taylor believed that there was a right (meaning best) way to perform any task and that it was management's job to determine the right way. At its extreme, the traditional view holds that:

- people dislike work
- people will only work for money;
- employees are not capable of controlling their work or directing themselves;
- employees should be closely supervised and tightly controlled so that they meet standards;
- simple, repetitive tasks will produce the best results;
- extra effort must lead to greater reward.

Workers gain from this approach because the right way is easier and pay is enhanced as a result of increased productivity.

Although this ideology was first developed in the 1920s, it still has echoes in many organisations today.

2.3   The human relations view

This view draws heavily on Elton Mayo's conclusions from the Hawthorne experiments. The Hawthorne studies were originally carried out by Western Electric in Chicago to test different methods of lighting and work organisation. Mayo and his co-workers developed the theory that the strongest motivating force behind most employees' behaviour at work was the preservation and nurturing of social relationships with their colleagues. The human relations' views are as follows:

- people want to be made to feel valued and important;

- people want recognition for their work;

- people want to be controlled sensibly;

- managers must discuss the plans they make for their subordinates and take any objections on board;

- managers must encourage self-regulation on routine tasks.

This view leads to an approach towards employees that encourages contribution and self-direction, advocating full participation on matters of significance to improve the quality of decision-making and the nature of supervision.

2.4   Theory X and Theory Y managers

In his book *The Human Side of Enterprise*, published in 1960, McGregor referred to the managers who hold these juxtaposed views (traditional and human relations) and presented two opposite sets of assumptions implicit in most approaches to supervision. He called these two sets of assumptions **Theory X** and **Theory Y**, which are the opposite extremes. Within these two extremes there are a number of possible combinations of the two. Theory X assumptions are

(a)   The average human being has an inherent dislike of work and will avoid if it he can.

(b)   Because of this human characteristic of disliking work, most people must be coerced, controlled, directed and/or threatened with punishment to get them to expend adequate effort towards the achievement of organisational objectives.

(c)   The average human being prefers to be directed, wishes to avoid responsibility, has relatively little ambition, and wants security above all.

This is the traditional approach greatly influenced by the results of specialisation, standardisation and mass production techniques. Jobs have been sub-divided to such an extent that initiative and discretion have been reduced; conformity, obedience and dependence have been demanded from the members of the organisation. This appears to be the approach of the scientific managers and classical theorists and the supporters of Weber's type of bureaucracy. The theory may provide an explanation of some behaviour patterns in industry, but McGregor regards it as an extreme and unacceptable set of assumptions about human beings. Unfortunately, it can often be a self-fulfilling prophecy, since people tend to behave in the way expected of them.

McGregor derived a new set of assumptions, which he called Theory Y

(a)   Expenditure of physical and mental effort in work is as natural as play or rest. The average human being does not inherently dislike work that can be a source of satisfaction.

(b)   External control and the threat of punishment are not the only means of bringing about effort towards organisational objectives. People can exercise self-direction and self-control to achieve objectives to which they are committed.

(c)   Commitment to objectives is a result of the rewards associated with their achievement. The most significant of those rewards is satisfaction of the self-actualisation needs.

(d)   The average human being learns, under proper conditions, not only to accept, but to seek, responsibility. Avoidance of responsibility, emphasis on security and low ambition is the result of experience and are not inherent in man's nature.

(e)   Capacity to exercise a relatively high degree of imagination, ingenuity and creativity in the solution of organisational problems is widely, not narrowly, distributed in the population.

(f)   Under conditions of modern industrial life, the intellectual potential of the average human being is only partially utilised.

The dichotomy between different managerial ideologies is obviously a simplification. McGregor felt that Theory Y assumptions provided a better explanation of human nature and indicated that the need for a different managerial strategy in dealing with people if they were to be correctly motivated.

Professor Lupton, Deputy Director of the Manchester Business School, sounds a note of caution regarding McGregor's work; managers should approach all prescriptions, whatever their origins, sceptically and critically. He believes there is insufficient evidence to support the view that the adoption of Theory Y is, in itself, followed by an improvement in the indicators of organisational performance. Much more research needs to be carried out on this, and other, prescriptions.

Other criticisms of the theory include

(a)   Not all people want self-direction, individual freedom and autonomy; many could not cope with such freedom.

(b)   It over-emphasises the workplace as the primary source of the satisfaction of needs. With the accent on a shorter working week and greater leisure time, it is more important to seek off-the-job satisfaction.

(c)   Theory X is not necessarily the cause of the conflict between the individual and the organisation; the universal conflict may be inherent in all organisations, not just in modern industry. If this is the case, then Theory X may not be the cause and Theory Y, therefore, not the cure.

2.5   Schein's model of motivation

In 1965 Professor Edgar Schein published a classification of the assumptions about what motivates people, based on management's assumptions about people. Like McGregor's Theory X and Theory Y, Schein's classification is essentially a set of assumptions about behaviour. Schein identifies four sets of assumptions as follows:

Rational-economic man - this view states that the pursuit of self-interest and the maximisation of gain are the prime motivators of people. It lays stress on man's rational calculation of self-interest, especially in relation to economic needs. According to Schein this set of assumptions places human beings into two categories: (a) the trustworthy, more broadly motivated, moral elite who must organise and manage the mass, and (b) the untrustworthy, money-motivated, calculative mass. In practice the rational-economic approach was an important assumption in the minds of Frederick Taylor, the Scientific Managers and the entrepreneurs of mass-produced technology.

Social man - this view sees people as predominantly motivated by social needs and finding their identity through relationships with others. Acceptance of this view by managers concentrates on people's needs rather than task needs. Studies have shown that productivity and morale can be improved by fostering social relationships in order to improve co-operation and teamwork.

Self-actualising man - this concept is based on Maslow's theory of human needs which sees not social needs but self-fulfilment needs as being the prime driving force behind individuals. 'Self-actualising man' needs challenge, responsibility and a sense of pride in his work. The managerial strategy, which operates under this set of assumptions, provides challenging, demanding work aiming for greater autonomy at work. Studies have shown that this model of motivation appears to be strong amongst professional and skilled grades of staff. However, it is less clear whether it applies as strongly to lower graded employees.

Complex man - as you would imagine, this view sees people as being more complex and variable than the previous ones. The requirement for management is an ability to diagnose the various motives, which may be at work with their staff. A consequence of this is that managers need to be able to adapt and vary their own behaviour in accordance with the motivational needs of particular individuals and teams.

Schein himself sees motivation in terms of a 'psychological contract' based on the expectations that the employee and employer have of each other, and the extent to which these are mutually fulfilled. Ultimately, the relationship between an individual and the organisation is an interactive one.

3   MOTIVATION THEORIES

3.1   The needs, expectancy and goal theories

The subsequent theories can be categorised as follows:

(a)   **Content theories (needs)** offer ways to profile or analyse individuals to identify their needs. Often criticised as being static and descriptive they appear to be linked more to job satisfaction than to work effort. Maslow, Herzberg and McGregor take a universalistic approach whereas McClelland and Argyle list forces and drives that will vary in relation to different individuals.

(b)   **Process theories (expectancy and goal)** offer a more dynamic approach and try to understand the thought or cognitive processes that take place within the minds of people and which influence their behaviour. Adams' equity theory and various expectancy and goal theories adopt such an approach and complement rather than compete with content theories.

   Motivation can be either positive or negative. Positive motivation, sometimes called anxiety-reducing motivation or the carrot approach, offers something valuable to the individual such as pay, praise or permanent employment for acceptable performance. Negative motivation, often called the stick approach, uses or threatens punishment by dismissal, suspension or the imposition of a fine if performance is unacceptable.

   Douglas McGregor, in his book, *The Human Side of Enterprise*, believed that 'Mature, self-disciplined persons do not require external discipline from others, or the stick. But it seems certain that our world is still populated by many persons who must depend upon others for their discipline'

4   CONTENT THEORIES

4.1   Principles

Content theories are sometimes known as 'need' theories and focus on the needs served by work. The motivation of a person depends on the strength of their needs. The basic needs model is shown as:

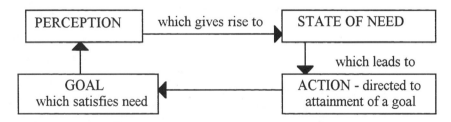

The above simplified model depicts motivation as prompting a person to take action to satisfy a state of needs or desires by achieving a perceived goal. Motivation can be viewed as **tension reducing.**

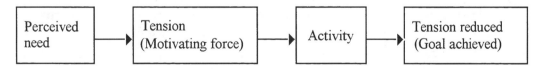

If efforts to motivate employees are to be successful management must either

(a)   **Create** needs within an individual; or

(b)   **Offer means** of satisfying an individual's existing needs.

Needs vary between individuals and within individuals according to the situation, the time of day and the stage reached in their life cycle.

4.2   Maslow's hierarchy of needs

Apart from the biological determinants of behaviour, activated by deprivation, we all have emotional or psychological needs. In the mid-1950s, Abraham Maslow outlined five innate needs - the first two being the primary needs:

(i)   *Basic or physiological needs* - the things needed to stay alive eg, food, shelter and clothing. Such needs require satisfaction before other needs manifest themselves, and such needs can be satisfied by money.

(ii)   *Safety or security needs* - people want protection against unemployment, the consequences of sickness and retirement as well as being safeguarded against unfair treatment. These needs can be satisfied by the rules of employment, eg, pension schemes, sick fund, employment legislation etc.

(iii)   *Social needs* - the vast majority of people want to be part of a group and it is only through group activity that this need can be satisfied. The way that work is organised eg, by enabling people to feel part of a group, is fundamental to satisfaction of this need.

(iv)   *Ego needs* - these needs may be expressed as wanting the esteem of other people and to think well of oneself. While status and promotion can offer short-term satisfaction, to build up the job itself and to give people a greater say in organising their work (participation) is to give satisfaction of a more permanent nature.

(v)   *Self-fulfilment needs* - this is quite simply the need to achieve something worthwhile in life - the fulfilment of personal potential. It is a need that is satisfied only by continuing success.

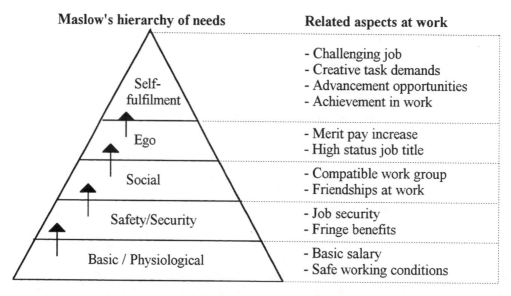

The peak of each level must be passed before the next level can begin to assume a dominant role. Needs do not have to be completely satisfied before higher needs emerge: as Simon puts it 'they only need to be satisfied'. In other words, a sufficient level of satisfaction is acceptable as opposed to the maximum or optimum level.

The significance of Maslow's hierarchy of needs is that it underlines the relative importance of money. Status has no satisfaction for the man desperate for food and shelter. Equally it demonstrates that money alone is not enough, and indeed as basic and safety needs become satisfied people are likely to concentrate their attentions on social and ego needs. For management to fail to offer the satisfaction of properly structured group activity and allow people a greater say is to drive them to seek similar satisfactions in unofficial groups, the objectives of which are frequently counter-productive. Perhaps the supreme example is the motor industry where, in spite of high rates of pay, the boss-subordinate relationship has not been good. In short, you cannot buy the whole man with pay alone.

Activation and motivation of workpeople thus depends not only on money but also on the whole employment package embracing such other aspects as:

(a)   pension, sick fund, canteen arrangements;
(b)   nature of the work done;
(c)   interest and challenge in the work;
(d)   scope in the job for self-expression and self-determination;
(e)   style of management used.

Maslow shows that a satisfied need is not a major motivating force - it is the immediate level of unsatisfied needs that is the prime motivator. In the words of Maslow: 'When the need is fairly well satisfied, the next higher need emerges, in turn to dominate the conscious life and to serve as the centre of organisation of behaviour since gratified needs are not active motivators.' So a satisfied need is not a motivator.

It is often overlooked in textbooks that Maslow devised his hierarchy of needs as a social analysis of the whole person, not just in the context of behaviour at work. This can be important in that need levels can be satisfied outside of work. For example, a person's basic and security needs may be satisfied through work but they may seek satisfaction of social and ego needs from social activities.

Maslow also stated that the various levels of the hierarchy can overlap and an individual may be seeking satisfaction at two levels at once. Indeed, an individual can have differing strengths of needs at the different levels at the same time. Even so, there is a discernible trend to progress from basic to self-fulfilment in stages.

4.3   Herzberg's theory of motivation

Herzberg developed his 'two-factor' theory of motivation from research into the job attitudes of two hundred accountants and engineers, who were asked to recall when they had experienced satisfactory and unsatisfactory feelings about their jobs. The replies led Herzberg to conclude that there are two important factors in work situations, satisfiers (or motivators) and dissatisfiers (or hygiene factors). The term 'hygiene' was derived from the concept of drains - they act to prevent ill health, but do not in themselves produce good health.

Motivators include achievement, recognition, challenging work, responsibility and advancement.

Herzberg pointed out that these factors were related to the **content** of work. Satisfaction of the motivating forces will encourage an individual to grow and develop in a mature way, often raising overall ability and performance. Herzberg encouraged managers to study the job itself (ie. the tasks done, the nature of the work and responsibility), and provide opportunities to satisfy the motivating factors. Such extrinsic factors attract people to the job and persuade them to remain – the 'Golden Handcuffs' of many organisations.

The hygiene factors, or dissatisfiers, relate to the **context** or environment of work rather than to job content. The most important hygiene factors include company policy and administration, supervision - the technical aspects, salary, relationships with others and working conditions.

Optimisation of these factors will remove job dissatisfaction, but will not create positive job satisfaction; they do not in themselves produce any growth in worker output, but can prevent losses in worker performance due to work restriction. That is to say, if these hygiene factors are satisfied then they will not be the cause of any dissatisfaction; but the fact they are satisfied will not lead to any improvement in worker output.

Other authors have used the term 'maintenance' as a substitute for 'hygiene', thus illustrating the need to maintain standards in these factors if dissatisfaction is to be avoided. Since 'maintenance' and 'hygiene' are interchangeable terms, it is important to note that either could be used in an examination question.

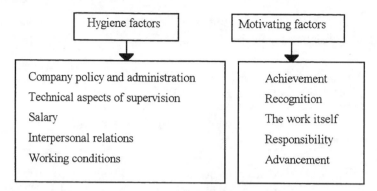

It is interesting to consider the lists of hygiene and motivation factors against Maslow's hierarchy of needs. We will see a general fit between hygiene factors and Maslow's lower level of needs and similarly a close match between motivating factors and Maslow's higher levels of needs.

As distinctly separate factors are associated with job satisfaction and job dissatisfaction, Herzberg concluded that the two feelings are not the opposite of one another, but that they are concerned with two different ranges of man's needs. Hygiene factors are purely preventive: if the organisation provides them it will prevent the workers from being dissatisfied with their job, but they will not motivate positively. To help them to do creative, satisfying, responsible work the organisation must provide motivators.

4.4   D McClelland

Herzberg defined achievement as a factor with the ability to satisfy. McClelland researched individual needs and found that the need for achievement is a distinct and powerful source of motivation. However, this does not exist equally among all people. Individual differences have been acknowledged in his work. He emphasised three fundamental needs in particular as motivators, the need for achievement (n-Ach), affiliation (n-Aff) and power (n-Pow).

Achievement - most of the research carried out concentrated on this particular need. McClelland describes n-Ach as 'behaviour towards competition with a standard of excellence'. This need is to attain something related to a specific set of standards. There are very real individual differences in the extent to which people have this need. Some people are highly competitive and continually set challenging standards for themselves, while others are simply not interested. The majority lie somewhere in between. High n-Ach people have the following characteristics:

•   they seek out situations where they can exercise a high level of control and responsibility for the outcome;

•   they seek out quite difficult tasks; and

•   they seek out feedback on how they are doing.

Affiliation - is a need to develop interpersonal relationships on a friendly basis. Some people want this at all costs and most enjoy working in an environment in which friendly co-operation is possible.

Power - this is the need to influence others and lead them into behaving in a way in which they would not normally behave.

Writing in the early 1950s, McClelland showed that managers have a high level need for achievement, a relatively high need for power, but a low need for affiliation. The general idea is that the entrepreneurs have a high need for achievement, and relatively high need for power; chief executives of larger organisations tend to have a high need for power, but because they have reached their sought-after level they are less in need of achievement.

4.5   M Argyle

This writer produced another listing of 'drives' that affect motivation. The idea here, however, is that they are on a provisional basis, because individuals may be unaffected by some of them and would in any case be affected differently by each one.

(a)   **Biological drives** - affect social behaviour, eg hunger and thirst.

(b)   **Dependency** - assistance, guidance and counselling obtained from those in power. New situations at work can give rise to dependency upon people who have the relevant facts.

(c)   **Affiliation need** - the need here is to socialise, which can be carried to the extreme and allow work to be neglected as a secondary activity.

(d)   **Dominance** - this drive is to achieve influence and to control other people's actions. People with this drive attend meetings and do most of the talking.

(e)   **Sex** - on a social level this drive is generally directed to people of the opposite sex, eg colleagues at work.

(f)   **Aggression** -this is the need to cause harm to others. It is usually on a verbal basis (including rumours).

(g)   **Self-esteem** - this drive varies between individuals.

(h)   **Additional drives** -include needs for achievement and money. Persons who rank highly in this area tend to be those most concerned with the work that is being done. Others may have an affiliation drive, which makes them much more concerned with 'getting on' with other people.

4.6   Adams' equity theory

Adams argues that inequities exist whenever people feel that the rewards obtained for their efforts are unequal to those received by others. Inequities can be negative or positive.

When people sense inequities in their work they will be aroused to remove the discomfort and restore a state of felt equity to the situation by

(a)   Changing work inputs.
(b)   Changing rewards received.
(c)   Leaving the situation.
(d)   Changing the comparison points.
(e)   Psychologically distorting the comparisons.

People who feel overpaid (feel positive inequity) have been found to increase the quantity or quality of their work, whilst those who are underpaid (feel negative inequity) do the opposite.

Feelings of inequity are determined solely by the individual's interpretation of the situation. The fact that a manager feels that the annual pay review is fair is immaterial.

4.7   Activity

List the hierarchy of needs and hygiene/motivation factors. What parallels can you draw between the two approaches?

4.8   Activity solution

Hierarchy of needs	Motivating factors	Hygiene factors
Self fulfilment needs Esteem needs Social needs Safety needs Basic needs	Opportunity for advancement Acknowledgement Increased responsibility Work challenge	Sports/social facilities Working conditions Pension Pay

There is a clear relationship between Herzberg's 'Hygiene Factor' and the lower levels of Maslow's 'Hierarchy of Needs'. Likewise there is a close correlation between the motivating factors and Maslow's higher needs.

5   PROCESS (EXPECTANCY) THEORIES

5.1   The V H Vroom Model

Vroom believes that people will be motivated to do things to reach a goal if they believe in the worth of that goal and if they can see that what they do will help them in achieving it.

Vroom's theory is that people's motivation toward doing anything is the product of the anticipated worth that an individual places on a goal and the chances he or she sees of achieving that goal. Vroom's theory may be stated as

Force   =   valence x expectancy

Where   force   =   the strength of a person's motivation;

valence   =   the strength of an individual's preference for an outcome; and

expectancy   =   the probability that a particular action will lead to a desired outcome.

When a person is indifferent about achieving a certain goal, a valence of zero occurs. Likewise, a person would have no motivation to achieve a goal if the expectancy were zero. The force exerted to do something will depend on both valence and expectancy. For example, a manager might be willing to work hard to achieve company goals for a promotion or pay valence.

Vroom's theory recognises the importance of various individual needs and motivations, and avoids some of the simplistic features of the Maslow and Herzberg approaches.

5.2   The Porter and Lawler Model

Porter and Lawler derived a more complete model of motivation. They have applied this model primarily to managers. It is summarised in the following diagram.

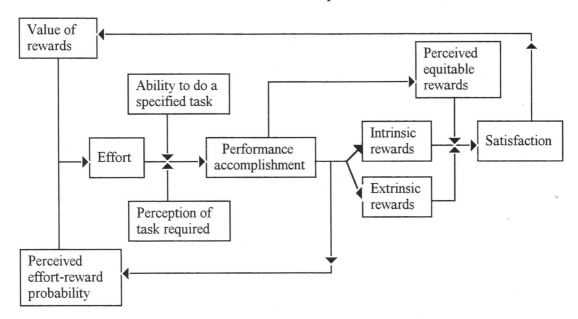

This model indicates that the amount of effort exerted depends on the value of a reward, plus the amount of energy a person believes is required and the probability of receiving the reward. The record of actual performance also influences the perceived effort and probability of getting a reward.

Actual performance in a job is determined principally by effort expended. But it is also greatly influenced by an individual's ability to do the job and by his or her perception of what the required task is. Performance is seen as leading to intrinsic rewards (such as a sense of accomplishment) and extrinsic rewards (such as working conditions and status). These rewards lead to satisfaction. What the individual distinguishes as a fair reward for effort will affect the satisfaction derived. Likewise, the actual value of rewards will be influenced by satisfaction.

To the practising manager, this model means that motivation is not a simple cause and effect matter. It shows that managers should carefully assess their reward structures and that through careful planning, and clearly defining duties and responsibilities, the effort-performance-reward-satisfaction system can be integrated into an entire system of managing.

5.3   Handy's motivational calculus

Handy is a member of the **contingency school** of management. His idea is that how a person is motivated at a given time will depend upon a number of factors influencing that person at that time.

Note that this is quite different from the approaches of the other writers we have been looking at. Maslow, Herzberg and McGregor all adopt a theory applying to everybody. McClelland and Argyle list forces and drives which will differ in relation to different individuals.

The idea put forward here is that each person has a specific 'motivation calculus' in respect of every decision taken - and this can be on a conscious or a subconscious basis. This assesses three factors:

Needs - these may be defined in accordance with the ideas of Maslow or any other researchers, and they are the person's needs at that time.

Desired results - these are what a person is expected to accomplish in the work.

Expenditure (E) factors - these relate to the expenditure of effort, energy, excitement in attaining the desired results.

As a result of this assessment we have a 'motivation decision'. This is the strength of the motivation to achieve the desired results. It will have to be dependent upon:

- the strength of the needs of the individual;
- the expectancy that the expenditure will achieve the desired results; and
- the expectancy that these desired results will assist in the satisfaction of the needs.

Given that the expectancy (either for expenditure or results) is high, then the motivation to undertake the work will also be high.

What we discover in this approach is that there is no theory of motivation that can be absolutely correct. The earlier researchers appear to have been right in that we can identify motivational forces, but the problem here is that different individuals will react to different forces motivating them in accordance with:

- the kind of person he or she is;

- the way the motivational needs relate to the job being done; and

- the individual's own idea of the probability of his or her personal efforts being able to accomplish the standards set by management.

Charles Handy therefore suggests that:

- each individual must know exactly what is expected;

- he/she should participate in the setting of targets in accordance with personal objectives; and

- feedback, on a regular basis, is necessary to inform individuals of their performance in relation to the targets.

Handy's motivational calculus has gained acceptance as being the most meaningful and practical approach to date. It is one that practising managers can directly apply in their own situations and it provides a model to analyse how people's behaviour changes over time.

5.4   Reinforcement theories

Skinner developed an approach called positive reinforcement or behaviour modification. It states that individuals can be motivated by proper design of their work environment and praise for their performance and that punishment for poor performance produces negative results. It emphasises the removal of obstructions to performance, careful planning and organising, control through feedback, and the expansion of communication.

Skinner and his followers analyse the work situation to determine what causes workers to act the way they do, and then they initiate changes to eliminate troublesome areas and obstructions to performance. Specific goals are set with workers' participation and assistance, prompt and regular feedback of results is made available, and performance improvements are rewarded with recognition and praise. Even when performance does not equal goals, ways are found to help people and praise them for the good things they do. Positive reinforcement theory has not gained universal acceptance.

6   THE DIFFERENCE BETWEEN CONTENT AND PROCESS THEORIES

6.1   Content theory

Content theory focuses on the question of what arouses, sustains and regulates good directed behaviour, that is what particular things motivate people. There is the assumption that everyone responds in much the same way to motivating pressures and that there is, therefore, one best way to motivate everybody. The best known work in this area is that of Maslow's needs hierarchy, McClelland's achievement motivation and Herzberg's two factor theory.

6.2   Process theory

Process theories change the emphasis from needs as in content theory to the goals and processes by which workers are motivated. They attempt to explain and describe how people start, sustain and direct behaviour aimed at the satisfaction of needs or the elimination or reduction of inner tension.

Equity theory provides a very useful elaboration of the process theory of motivation. It focuses on individuals' feelings of how fairly they are treated when compared with how others are treated. The theory has two main aspects. First it considers that individuals evaluate their social relationships in just the same way as they weigh up economic transactions such as buying or selling a house or car, or any other exchange process, ie, they set what they contribute against what they are likely to gain. Second, it argues that in evaluating any form of transaction, social or any other, individuals always compare their situation with that of others.

6.3   Relevance of content and process theories

If we consider the relevance and applicability of content and process theories, especially the expectancy theory, to management in the 2000s there are several features to support their use. Together they claim to give a comprehensive view of the motivational process. They take account of the ways the individual judges their situation and the link to effective performance. They imply that job satisfaction (intrinsic) follows from rather than precedes effective job performance. Expectancy theory has led to the redesign of work giving emphasis to intrinsic job satisfaction (to a degree the motivating factors of Herzberg's hygiene-motivation theory). Further, in a world of increased emphasis on cost-efficiency, minimum manning levels and employee flexibility, they provide a fruitful direction for managers to take.

> **Conclusion**   Theories of motivation stress different factors contributing to job satisfaction. Content theories, such as those of Maslow and Herzberg, stress the satisfaction of needs. Process theories, such as those of Vroom, emphasise the importance of rewards.

7   THE IMPORTANCE OF THE REWARD SYSTEM

7.1   Reward systems

Management action is usually designed so that employees are highly motivated. By this it is usually implied that the staff meet the performance standards. Achievement of high performance may be through offering positive rewards. Equally, achievement may be through the employees having the perception that if they do not perform up to standard then something unpleasant may result. It may be reduced pay, less chance of promotion, or in the current world employment climate, reduced job security or no job at all. Either way, it is important to identify opportunities for development and advancement and conduct regular performance reviews so that performance can be monitored.

7.2   Psychological contracts

Psychological contracts exist between individuals and the organisations to which they belong, be they work or social, and normally take the form of implied and unstated expectations. According to Handy, the individual has a set of results that he expects from the organisation, results that will satisfy certain of his needs and in return for which he will expend some of his energies and talents. Similarly, the organisation has its set of expectations of the individual and its list of payments and outcomes that it will give to him.

An individual belonging to more than one organisation will have more than one psychological contract. Only if each contract is perceived identically by all parties to it will conflict be avoided.

Psychological contracts can be classified as follows.

(a)   **Coercive contracts** are those which are not freely entered into, and where a small group exercise control by rule and punishment. Although the usual form is found in prisons and other custodial institutions, coercive contracts exist also in schools and factories.

(b)   **Calculative contracts** are those where control is retained by management and is expressed in terms of their ability to give to the individual 'desired things' such as money, promotion and social opportunities. Most employees of industrial organisations 'enter into' such a contract.

(c)   **Co-operative contracts** are those where the individual tends to identify with the goals of the organisation and strive for their attainment. In return the individual receives just rewards, a voice in the selection of goals and a choice of the means to achieve such goals. Most enlightened organisations are moving towards such contracts but it must be emphasised that if they are to be effective then the workers must also want them. If such a contract is imposed on the workforce it becomes a coercive contract.

In all cases the employees must know the results of their increased efforts and the management must understand the individual's needs.

7.3   Money as a motivator

Money in the form of pay is a powerful motivator and can be viewed as all-embracing, as a basis for comparison or as a reinforcement. The multiple meanings of pay can be related to the motivational theories examined as follows

(a)   **Maslow** - pay is unique in that it can satisfy all types of need. This will be directly in the case of lower level needs, and otherwise indirectly, for example the prestige of being on a high salary level can be a source of ego-fulfilment.

(b)   **McClelland** - high-need achievers view pay as performance feedback and as a measure of goal accomplishment. Group bonuses are attractive to high-need achievers. Those seeking power could view pay as a means of buying prestige or as a way of controlling other people.

(c)   **Herzberg** - pay is normally viewed as a hygiene factor but it can be a motivator when it occurs as a merit increase that gives special recognition for a job well done.

(d)   **Equity theory** - pay is an object of social comparison and is a major reason for felt inequity.

(e)   **Expectancy theory** - pay is only one of many work rewards that may be valued by individuals at work. When instrumentality and expectancy are high, pay can be a source of motivation.

Money is a complicated motivator that is associated with several levels of needs, not just the basic level. Economists, accountants and many managers tend to regard money as a prime motivator but behavioural scientists tend to place it low on the scale. Probably, neither view is correct because, as an all-embracing approach, it depends on the individual.

7.4   Payment by results

The most direct use of money as a motivator is payment by results schemes whereby an employee's pay is directly linked to his results. All such schemes are dependent upon the belief that people will work harder to obtain more money. Whyte carried out extensive research on incentive pay schemes for production workers. He concluded that 'money is not an almighty' motivation and estimated that only 10% of production workers would ignore group pressure from workmates and produce as much as possible in response to an incentive scheme.

7.5   Power and status

In discussing money as a motivator it is necessary to recognise its effects at two levels.

(a)   Money in absolute terms, as an exact amount, is important because of its purchasing power. It is what money can buy, not money itself, that gives it value. Saul Gellerman *(Motivation and Productivity)* sees the main significance of money in its power as a symbol. Because money can be exchanged for satisfaction of needs, money can symbolise almost any need an individual wants it to represent. The next increase in salary could mean affording a better car, or an extra holiday.

(b)   Money is also important as an indication of status. Increasing differentials between jobs creates feelings of a senior status in the person enjoying the higher salary. Money is a means of keeping score.

8   WAYS IN WHICH MANAGEMENT CAN MOTIVATE STAFF

8.1   Role of management

Everyone has a range of performance within which they carry out their work. The range varies from an upper limit dictated by ability, both intellectual and physical, and zero performance, which is the lower limit. Within that range is the level of acceptability, below which is disciplinary time. Management's responsibility for the performance of staff can be summarised into three main functions:

*   Motivating staff to perform at the upper limit of performance;

*   Coaching staff so they develop their ability and increase their potential for high quality work;

*   Clarifying and enforcing the level of acceptability so that poor performers are given the opportunity to discuss and evaluate their performance.

It is important to understand these as three separate functions. Motivation can only improve performance so far; then it becomes a matter of developing new or additional skills. An athletics coach cannot make an Olympic sprinter out of an overweight novice purely by motivation. He or she will have to teach sprinting techniques and use training programmes to develop particular muscles and improve lung function.

Motivation is a process that arouses, sustains and regulates behaviour toward a specific goal or end. Obviously this process is of interest to everyone. To the supervisor or manager, whose job it is to get others to perform tasks, it is vitally important. He or she has to become involved with the motivation of the employees so that the performance requirements of the organisation can be met and the employees' needs and expectations satisfied. It means knowing something about motivation theory and understanding how it can help him or her carry out his or her duties and responsibilities effectively.

8.2   Increasing motivation

There are many ways that managers can increase the motivation of their employees. As we have previously discussed, pay and incentive schemes are frequently regarded as powerful motivators.

There are other methods, which are non-financial motivators that have been suggested by various writers. These include participation in decision-making and quality of work life.

We have already noted the content theories of Herzberg etc. which point to the job itself as a source of motivation. The job content can be interesting and challenging. It can meet needs for advancement, social standing, professional recognition, self-esteem etc. This can sometimes compensate for lower earnings and cause people to hold back from pursuing a higher paid position, because the job content is seen to be less interesting. The methods used include job enrichment, job enlargement and job rotation.

8.3   Participation

The use of participation is frequently quoted as a means of stimulating motivation. There is no doubt that people are motivated by being involved in the actions and decisions that affect them. Participation is also a recognition of the value of staff, since it provides a sense of accomplishment and 'being needed'. A manager seeking to raise performance by increasing motivation could involve staff in the planning and inspection aspects of the work encouraging staff to participate in the design of the work planning schedules. Staff would be motivated to achieve the targets that they had helped establish.

The use of participation is not an automatic recipe for increased motivation. Hopwood writes that it is 'naive to think that participative approaches are always more effective than authoritarian styles'. It depends upon the individual people and circumstances involved. There are certain guidelines that must prevail if participation is to be effective in raising motivation.

(i)   The matters for participation must be meaningful and relevant. If staff believe that the items are trivial or outside of their scope then there will be an adverse reaction that will damage existing levels of motivation.

(ii)   The participation must be seen as part of a continuing approach not just a 'one-off' exercise.

(iii)   Staff must be fed the results of their involvement as quickly and fully as possible. Herzberg said 'a manager cannot motivate staff in a vacuum'. Feedback is essential if motivation is to grow.

(iv)   The participation must be genuine. It should be defined for staff in the first stage whether their participation is limited to consultation 'where staff's ideas are sought but management makes the decision' or whether there is a sharing of authority in that staff are involved in the final decision.

(v)   People must have the ability, equipment and will to be involved. For example, you cannot motivate someone to do a job for which they have not been trained. Also, if staff feel dissatisfied in work because of deficiencies in the maintenance/hygiene factors, then participation will fall on deaf ears.

8.4   Quality of work life

An interesting approach to motivation is the recent development of 'quality of work life programmes'. Introduced as a concept by Davis and Cherns (1975), one of the main advocates in the UK has been Eric Trist. There are many case studies published in such companies as General Motors, Proctor and Gamble etc. Basically the approach is a very wide-ranging application of the principles of job enrichment.

The intention is to improve all aspects of work life, especially job design, work environment, leadership attitudes, work planning and industrial relations. It is an all-embracing systems approach, which usually starts with a joint management and staff group looking at the dignity, interest and productivity of jobs.

8.5   Job design

Herzberg defines three avenues that management can follow in attempting to improve staff satisfaction and motivation.

(i)   **Job enrichment** - a deliberate, planned process to improve the responsibility and challenge of a job.   Typical examples include delegation or problem solving for example, adding query-solving to a clerk's routine duties or staff signing own letters instead of passing them through for manager's signature.

Job enrichment, in this sense of improving responsibility and challenge, has been called 'vertical job enlargement' by Argyris and other authors.   Although Herzberg's term 'job enrichment' is the more descriptive and commonly accepted, it is important to note the alternative term which will be mentioned in many textbooks and could occur in an examination question.

(ii)   **Job enlargement** - widening the range of jobs, and so developing a job away from narrow specialisation.   There is no element of enrichment.   Argyris, Seashore etc. term this as 'horizontal job enlargement'.   Herzberg contends that there is little motivation value in this approach.

(iii)   **Job rotation** - the planned rotating of staff between jobs to alleviate monotony and provide a fresh job challenge.   The documented example quotes a warehouse gang of four workers, where the worst job was tying the necks of the sacks at the base of the hopper after filling; the best job was seen as being the fork lift truck driver.   Job rotation would ensure equal time being spent by each individual on all jobs.   Herzberg suggests that this will help to relieve monotony and improve job satisfaction but is unlikely to create positive motivation.

8.6   Types of feedback

The feedback that we get comes in different forms:

(i)   Intrinsic feedback comes from within our bodies - the muscles and skin eg, the reaction to touching a hot surface is the pulling away of the hands.

(ii)   Extrinsic feedback comes from the environment eg, the visual and aural information needed to drive a car.

(iii)   Concurrent feedback comes during an act and can be used to control it while doing it.

(iv)   Delayed feedback comes after the task is completed and can be used to affect future performance.

Staff must be fed the results of their involvement as quickly and fully as possible. Herzberg said 'a manager cannot motivate staff in a vacuum'.   Feedback is essential if motivation is to grow. The feedback should be clear and frequent. Intrinsic feedback is inadequate in learning job skills and the trainer has to provide the relevant extrinsic feedback. Concurrent feedback is better than delayed feedback when developing job knowledge, skills and performance. Recognition, praise and encouragement create feelings of confidence, competence, development and progress that enhance the motivation to learn.

9   JOB SATISFACTION

9.1   Sources of job satisfaction

> Definition   Job satisfaction refers to the way in which people feel about their work.

Job satisfaction is seen as being high when people report strong positive feelings about their work and, conversely, low when they report strong negative feelings in the form of complaints about real or imaginary problems.

Job satisfaction is the outcome of a wide range of variables. Writing in 1976, Locke identified three main approaches - factors external to the work content, human relations and the 'work itself' school.

(a)   The first approach sought to explain job satisfaction in terms of factors such as working conditions and payment systems, ie, factors external to the work content such as:

Pay - wages do form an important factor in determining job satisfaction. Research has consistently shown positive correlation between rates of pay and satisfaction with the job. This seems to hold true for manual workers, white-collar workers and managers. Pay is seen as important in job satisfaction not only because of the material benefits it provides but also because of its symbolic importance as a measure of achievement and recognition.

Working conditions - again there does appear to be a positive correlation between working conditions and satisfaction at work. Factors such as temperature, humidity, ventilation, noise, hours of work, cleanliness and adequate tools and equipment have their effect on job satisfaction. The reasons for this are straightforward. Good working conditions lead to greater physical comfort, they enable the job to be done more effectively and safely and, finally, good conditions such as a shorter working week or flexitime will facilitate the pursuit of off-the-job activities like hobbies or pastimes.

There is a risk, however, in over-stressing the importance of working conditions. Whilst people respond to the extremes of good and bad working conditions, in many situations where the working conditions may be described as 'average' then there is little relevance.

(b)   The human relations' approach expressed the importance of the work group and leadership style on determining levels of job satisfaction.

The work group - by providing its members with the opportunity for social interaction, the work group can be a source of job satisfaction. People who are socially isolated at work tend to dislike their job whilst those who are members of a cohesive group with similar attitudes and values find the group a strong source of satisfaction.

There is some research, which suggests that though group membership is a source of satisfaction, it may have been overestimated by the Human Relations' school. In particular the work of Dubin suggests that individuals gain much of their social satisfaction outside the work situation.

Leadership - there are two major aspects of leadership that have been identified as sources of job satisfaction. Firstly the leader who has a supportive relationship with their subordinates and takes a personal interest in them is seen to contribute positively to job satisfaction. Secondly the leader who encourages involvement and participation in the group similarly enhances job satisfaction. Likert's research in this field was instrumental. However, though it can be said that there is a positive relationship between employee-centred leadership and job satisfaction, the relationship is not always consistent or strong.

(c)   The 'work itself' school emphasised that job satisfaction could only be provided by allowing individuals to exercise choice, responsibility and challenge in work. Thus, it is the type of work and the way in which the work is organised that influences job satisfaction levels.

Control over methods and pacing of work - it is argued that where the individual has little control over the methods and pace of work job satisfaction will be low. Where there is more control exercised by the worker job satisfaction will be higher and positive feelings about the job will increase.

Variety of tasks - high levels of specialisation with the attendant monotony and repetitiveness leads to a decrease in job satisfaction. Where a job offers more variety and less specialisation job satisfaction is likely to be higher.

Use of full range of skills and abilities - job satisfaction is found to be higher in those jobs, which make a full use of an individual's skills and abilities. Using valued abilities and skills provides employees with a self-pride, a sense of competence and self-confidence.

Promotion and recognition - where an employee feels they have failed to gain recognition for their achievements and have been unjustly overlooked for promotion this does appear to have a major effect on producing a low level of job satisfaction. Promotion and recognition obtained will heighten job satisfaction meeting, as it does, a desire for higher earnings, the desire for social status, the desire for psychological growth and, in as much as the promotion is earned, the desire for justice.

Following the publication of *The Motivation to Work* by Herzberg, Mausner and Snyderman in 1959 much attention and support has been given to the 'work itself' approach. It has also been the subject of a certain amount of criticism, particularly because of its lack of emphasis on pay.

9.2   Theories of job satisfaction

Within these three main approaches we can briefly examine some of the major theories which seek to explain the nature and causes of job satisfaction.

(a)   **Subtractive theory**

Put forward by Vroom this theory suggests that job satisfaction is a function of the difference between what an individual expects from a job and what they get from a job. In other words, a person enters a job with a certain perception of what the job entails, the benefits and the drawbacks and then, as a result of experience in the job, this perception is shown to be more or less realistic. A person will obtain job satisfaction if experience is aligned to their initial perception or expectation about the job while job dissatisfaction will be the outcome if the job in some way falls below the expectations.

(b)   **Instrumentality theory**

This theory states that job satisfaction is determined by the extent to which the job provides a means of achieving certain valued outcomes. These outcomes may be job related, eg the development of skill, promotion, prestige, or they may be separate from the job, eg a high standard of living, good holidays, plenty of spare time. If the job is seen as providing a means of achieving these objectives job satisfaction will be high, otherwise it will be low.

(c)   **Social influence theory**

In contrast with the preceding two theories this theory suggests that when people enter jobs they have no clear perception or expectations of what it will be like. Rather people are influenced by others in the same or similar jobs as to whether a job is particularly satisfying or dissatisfying. Thus it is argued that job satisfaction is a learned phenomenon acquired through social influence and affected by comparison with others.

(d)   **Herzberg's two factor theory**

This theory suggests job satisfaction is dependent on two distinct sets of factors - the hygiene factors, which are related to dissatisfaction and the motivators which are related to job satisfaction.   Thus motivators such as recognition, autonomy, responsibility and the work itself can only affect satisfaction and not dissatisfaction. Hygiene factors such as pay, working conditions, relationships with supervisors are simply potential sources of dissatisfaction and could not provide a source of positive job satisfaction. Hygiene factors are often termed 'maintenance factors'.

(e)   **Maslow's need hierarchy**

The implication of Maslow's theory is that job satisfaction will occur when an individual's job helps satisfy the needs, which correspond to their position on the need hierarchy. Thus a person seeking to satisfy esteem needs would report job satisfaction in so far as the job permitted the satisfaction of these needs.

Conclusion   The benefits to the organisation from having workers with a high level of job satisfaction include: high staff loyalty and low staff turnover; better timekeeping and attendance; good general morale; and pleasant working relationships with a high level of trust.

9.3   Implications for management

(a)   Although intuitively it might appear that high job satisfaction would be linked with high levels of performance this has been shown not to be the case. Major surveys by Seashore have shown that performance levels of people with low or medium job satisfaction can be equal or superior to those with high job satisfaction.
Why is this the case? The main explanation is that satisfaction and performance are often unrelated.

Although motivation has a direct link with effort and performance, the same is not true of job satisfaction. A person can be high on motivation but low in job satisfaction and vice versa, or clearly high or low on both. The main benefit of high job satisfaction is not direct work performance but rather, the absence of dissatisfaction, which could cause absenteeism, turnover, poor health etc.

Complex behaviour such as that involved in the performance of a job is clearly influenced by a wide range of factors and many of these factors do not relate to job satisfaction. That is not to say that job satisfaction is unimportant to performance since for example:

(b)   A dissatisfied employee is more likely to leave their jobs permanently or to be absent from work more often.

Labour turnover has significant disruptive effects in the organisation, interfering with normal operations, causing morale problems with those who remain and increasing costs in selecting and training replacements. Studies constantly show labour turnover to be highest amongst groups with the lowest levels of job satisfaction. However it must be noted that labour turnover is related to other factors too, notably the state of the labour market.

(c)   Similarly, high levels of absenteeism and low levels of job satisfaction are directly related. Studies have shown that by increasing levels of job satisfaction management can do much to improve the pattern of absenteeism in their organisation.

(d)   A lack of job satisfaction has been linked to many physical ailments. It has been seen as related to symptoms such as fatigue, headaches, high blood pressure, and heart attacks. Some writers have gone as far as to say that the best overall predictor for longevity is job satisfaction.

Similarly, with mental health job dissatisfaction is seen as being very harmful. For example the University of Michigan's Institute for Social Research carried out research studies showing that worry, tension and inter personal relationships were affected.

Whilst physical and mental health have other contributory factors it is still true to say that job dissatisfaction has major negative consequences for the mental and physical well-being of the employee.

Conclusion There is no direct link between improved job satisfaction and increased effort and performance at work.

A high performer is just as likely to be dissatisfied with the organisation as a low performer. However, there is a link between increased dissatisfaction and increased levels of absenteeism, turnover and ill health.

9.4   The assessment of job satisfaction

Since job satisfaction can have such an important influence on behaviour at work it is necessary for management to have on hand appropriate ways of measuring and monitoring levels of satisfaction in their own organisations.

Two basic approaches are used:

(a)   Indirect measures; ie, the use of indicators such as labour turnover, absenteeism, conflict or productivity.

(b)   The job satisfaction survey; the use of appropriately constructed questionnaires which seek to elicit responses which indicate levels of job satisfaction, often conducted for a specific purpose.

9.5   Activity

Compare and contrast 'motivation' and 'job satisfaction'

9.6   Activity solution

Motivation is the will to do. A motivated worker feels challenged by the work and aims to produce more/achieve higher workmanship.

Typified by:	Results in:
- outspoken criticism of other sections' shortcomings - sense of urgency in 'norm of activity'; - need for feedback of results.	- higher output; - better quality; - less waste produce; - suggestions for improvement.

Job satisfaction exists when an individual or group has a favourable attitude towards the organisation.

Typified by:	Results in:
- high level of employee trust; - identification with organisation's aims; - pride in corporate image.	- lower staff turnover; - less absence, better time-keeping; - good general morale; - pleasant working relationships.

Job satisfaction does not result in increased productivity or better work standards.
A dissatisfied worker who becomes 'satisfied', does not necessarily increase his/her output.
A high performer is just as likely to be dissatisfied with the organisation as a poor performer.

10   SELF TEST QUESTIONS

10.1   Define motivation (1.1)

10.2   Does Theory X relate to the traditional or the human relations' view of employees? (2.4)

10.3   What does the needs model depict? (4.1)

10.3   Draw Maslow's hierarchy of human needs 4.2)

10.4   List Herzberg's most important hygiene factors (4.3)

10.5   What is meant by 'valence' and 'expectancy' in the work of Vroom? (5.1)

10.6   Distinguish between content theories and process theories of motivation. (6.1, 6.2)

10.7   What is meant by a 'psychological contract'? (7.1)

10.8   Explain the process of job enrichment (8.5)

10.9   How does Herzberg's theory view money as a motivator? (7.3)

10.10   List some non-financial motivators (8.2)

11   EXAMINATION TYPE QUESTION

11.1   Norman's motivation

Norman is a recently qualified management accountant. He chose this profession because he understood that high salaries could be earned by successful accountants in senior positions.

After training in various departments of a large firm he was offered a position in the consultancy division in a department concerned with advising companies in the London area on management accounting systems. The department is growing, partly because its expertise in management accounting systems is widely known. The department is therefore well provided with technical support and other resources. He enjoyed the analytical work involved and received high merit ratings in each of his two annual reviews. These resulted in substantial pay increases.

Norman is married, has a two-year old son and another baby due shortly. He loves playing with his son, and is a keen member of a choir, which practises twice a week. He has purchased a house with a mortgage that is just within his financial means, and he enjoys making do-it-yourself improvements to the house.

A large organisation, which has over 100 establishments throughout the country, has asked Norman's employers to advise them on the management accountancy systems in each of these establishments.   Each of the establishments differs in its structure, due to varying local environments. Because Norman's performance has been so good, it has been suggested that he should take charge of a small new department, which will be specially set up for this business.

You are required, on the basis of any relevant motivation theory (such as Vroom's Expectancy Theory or Porter and Lawler's), to analyse Norman's personal motivation and how it may be affected by the suggested change of job.   **(20 marks)**

12   ANSWER TO EXAMINATION TYPE QUESTION

12.1   Norman's motivation

Victor Vroom's expectancy theory is expressed as $V \times E = M$ ie, Valence (strength of a person's preference or desire for a particular outcome) x Expectancy (the belief that achieving a certain outcome will lead to satisfaction of their needs). The culmination of these two factors dictates the strength of motivation that is applied by an individual.

Therefore, a strong desire coupled with a strong belief will lead to high motivation levels. However, if desire or belief are low then motivation levels will fall. A person must believe that the rewards are attractive to them and that they are able to achieve the performance necessary to gain those rewards.

Norman's present job is concerned with advising companies in the London area. This would enable Norman to return home on most or all evenings. His social needs are family based with young children, home improvements and twice-weekly choir practice. Such interests are not highly demanding in financial terms, however, they do make extensive demands on time and the ability to regularly fulfil social dates. Although Norman would welcome extra money to assist with the mortgage on his new house, he may be unwilling to lose family time and social interests in exchange.

From the work angle, Norman gains motivation through:

-       enjoyment of the job;

-       high merit ratings;

-       substantial salary increases;

-       a work pattern that enables him to meet his family and social needs.

The rewards that Norman may seek could include higher salary, promotion bringing greater responsibility and challenge.

These rewards are being met by his present employment and needs for promotion and higher salary could be met in the near future, given the substantial pay increases earned in the last two annual reviews.

The new employment offer would put Norman in charge of a small specialist department advising over 100 establishments throughout the country. This would offer promotion, increased job responsibility and presumably enhanced salary. These are factors that would weigh heavy in the valence aspect of Vroom's formula. The belief could exist that taking the new position would unable Norman to enjoy these factors (expectancy). If these were all the factors involved then Norman would be motivated to accept the new job.

However, the new job will require extensive travelling and probably, absences from home. This will disrupt Norman's family life and his social pattern. If his needs for recognition, promotion and higher salary outweigh family and social factors then the valence will be strong enough to motivate Norman to accept the new job. However, if the job terms show only marginal improvement over his present position, then he is unlikely to be motivated to accept the new position. Ultimately, the strength of valency and expectancy will determine Norman's motivation to accept the new position. It will also be influenced by Norman's expectation of the rewards developing in the immediate future through his present occupation.

Note: many management authors believe that Vroom's expectancy theory is accurate but difficult to apply in practice. Such authors point to the difficulty of measuring valence which overlaps social and business needs. We can recognise this difficulty in constructing this answer.

Lawler and Porter's model is more complete and is based on Vroom's work. It states that the amount of effort depends on the value of a reward, plus the demand for energy that a person believes is required and the probability of receiving the reward.

Probably the most practical theory of motivation to apply would be Handy's motivational calculus. It would be good practice to base an answer for Norman's situation on the motivational calculus approach.

12 TRAINING AND DEVELOPMENT

INTRODUCTION & LEARNING OUTCOMES

Syllabus area 11 (iii)
- The distinction between development and training and the tools available to develop and train staff (ie, education, training methods, management development programmes, promotion, succession and career planning, job redesign)

- The stages in the planning and conduct of a training course, the features and benefits of the various tools and visual aids used and the importance of feedback during and after a training course

Training, management development and appraisal systems play significant roles in providing motivation and job satisfaction for all levels of employment.

Training begins with a clear definition of the organisation's training needs. Different types of training can be identified to meet the differing needs and staff involved.

Management development is the finding, tracking and developing of people for positions of responsibility in the organisation. It is based on providing training and experience to enable an individual to assume progressively more challenging and senior positions.

Before specific training and development programs are chosen, three kinds of needs must be considered. The needs of the organisation include such items as the objectives of the enterprise, the availability of staff and the turnover rates. Needs related to the operations and the job itself can be determined from the job descriptions and the performance standards. Data about the individual training needs can be gathered from the performance appraisals, interviews with the job-holder and surveys. Because there are so many types of training an organisation can use, it is important to identify the needs carefully and match them with the right programme.

Human resource planning also requires a method of plotting succession and career progression so that the organisation can ascertain at what rate employees progress, and whether factors such as age-spread will lead to promotion blockages or the over-promotion of inexperienced employees.

When you have studied this chapter you should be able to:

- Explain the process of succession and career planning

- Produce a training and development plan for the staff of a finance department and analyse the major problems associated with the design and implementation of such a plan

- Explain the importance of human resource development planning

- Produce and explain a plan for the delivery of a training course on a finance-related topic

---

1 THE IMPORTANCE OF TRAINING AND DEVELOPMENT

1.1 Introduction

Human resource development is the process by which the knowledge, skills and attitudes of the employees are enhanced to the benefit of the organisation, the individual, the teamwork and the community.

Any development activity would be integrated with the strategic objectives and the organisational culture and would also be subject to the environmental constraints or social responsibilities.

A measurement of how the human resource development function is given a high profile within the strategic objectives of the organisation can be seen in times of recession. A car manufacturer in Detroit USA, during the recent recession, reluctantly laid off a large proportion of its skilled workforce, leaving the remaining employees anxious and demoralised and the community angry about the increase in unemployment. A Japanese manufacturer, in the same industry and suffering the same economic downturn, instead of laying off staff that they had invested in and would need when the upturn came, used the time available to train the car workers in maintaining the manufacturing equipment. This strategy meant that, not only did they retain their staff and keep the morale of the workforce high, but when the recession lifted, the Japanese plant could benefit from reduced maintenance costs and machine down-time and a co-operative workforce.

The culture within the organisation is also an important factor in the development of employees. Introducing an elaborate programme of self-managed learning into an organisation where there has previously been no formal training policy would require a revolutionary change that needed some powerful persuasion by management.

Personal objectives exist, and individual decisions to join, stay with, or leave the organisation will relate to these. The same constraint applies to decisions concerning the extent of co-operation with particular management strategies, and whether to accept transfer to other work and so on.

The environmental constraints and social responsibility factors must also be taken into account. Government policy on training and development, as well as grants available from different sources would be built into the organisation's strategy; the human resources manager would be aware of the strategic benefits and competitive advantages, which might accrue to the organisation.

Legal aspects arise, together with social and ethical considerations, which determine the manner in which manpower may be utilised, the controls imposed, replacement, rates of pay, and also standards used in selection for recruitment and promotion.

External influences affect the demand for manpower (eg market conditions, government policy) and its supply (eg education policy, competing employment opportunities).

1.2 Development and training

Human resource development (HRD) may be seen as a process of building and enhancing the skills, knowledge and attitudes of employees. Apart from the benefits accruing to the individual worker - greater versatility, extra skills etc - many advantages accrue to the organisation. Employees become more flexible, the productivity and quality of work should improve, job satisfaction might increase - with consequent reduction in absenteeism and staff turnover rates - and the organisation need not fear the consequences of new technology.

A common confusion that exists is the distinction between training, development and education. In practice the distinction is often blurred but for the sake of clarifying the following discussion, we shall use the definitions given below:

> **[Definition]** Education is considered to be instruction in knowledge and skills to enable people to be prepared for various roles in society. Its focus is mainly broadly based for the needs of the individual and to a lesser extent, the needs of society.

> **[Definition]** Training is a planned process to modify attitude, knowledge, skill or behaviour through learning experiences to achieve effective performance in an activity or range of activities. Its focus is much more narrowly based than education or development, and is job-oriented or task-oriented. Its purpose is to develop the abilities of the individual and to meet the current and future human resource needs of the organisation.

Definition   Development is concerned more with changes in attitudes, behaviour and potential than with immediate skill. It relates more to career development than job development. It is a learning activity concentrating on the future needs of the organisation. Development programmes usually include elements of planned study and experience, and are frequently supported by coaching or counselling.

The definition of training stresses the relationship between training and human resource planning.

The definition of development, on the other hand, suggests a fulfilment of innate potential and ability through continuous involvement rather than just timely interventions to satisfy gaps in knowledge and ability.

1.3   Training and development policies

As with recruitment and selection, training and development is inextricably linked with the organisational goals and objectives. Organisations formulate training and development policies in order to:

(a)   define the relationship between the organisation's objectives and the current and future human resource needs;

(b)   provide a framework for facilitating development, and training;

(c)   provide information for employees. For example, to stress the performance standards expected and to inform employees of opportunities for training and development;

(d)   enhance public relations. For example, to help attract high calibre recruits, reassure clients and the public about the quality of products or services.

An organisation policy will be influenced by variables such as:

* size, traditions and culture;
* products or services;
* economic and social objectives;
* obligations to provide professional updating training eg, nurses;
* senior management's views on the value of training;
* the labour market;
* resources that can be allocated to training;
* training needs of the organisation;
* expectations of employees.

1.4   Commitment to training and development

Evidence shows that 93% of the top performing organisations in the UK train their workforce, but what is more significant, 81% of the poor performers did nothing. Similar organisations in Germany, when compared in every way with their competitors in the UK, are 63% more productive. From these and other statistics, management has to accept, or at least consider, that spending on people is as essential to success as is spending on equipment, buildings, maintenance, transport etc.

Training must, however, relate to the needs of the organisation. Training for the sake of it, as a prestigious 'me too' panacea is a costly waste of time and money. It is this situation that has fostered the attitude that training is a low priority, low status function that can be readily cut from the budget when times are hard. What should be considered is the trade-off from investing in training. On the commercial side, the availability of a trained workforce could mean savings on quotes for much needed orders.

2   THE BENEFITS OF EFFECTIVE TRAINING AND DEVELOPMENT

2.1   Training in the organisation

It is important that any organisation should adopt a systematic approach to training. The increasing pace of technological change is perhaps the single biggest impetus for training programmes. In the first half of this century, workers acquired their skills through apprenticeships and college courses that equipped them with knowledge and skills sufficient for their working lives. Today, however, few people can expect to do the same work in the same way for more than a few years and the number of jobs for untrained workers has declined.

A systematic approach to training will involve:

(a)   Defining training needs.

(b)   Deciding what training is required to satisfy these needs.

(c)   Using experienced trainers to plan and implement training.

(d)   Following up and evaluating training to ensure that it is effective.

This approach can be illustrated diagrammatically:

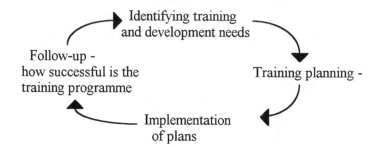

2.2   Benefits to the organisation

The benefits to the organisation of effective training and development are:

*   Provision of trained manpower;
*   Improvement of existing skills;
*   Increased employee knowledge;
*   Improved job performance;
*   Improved customer service;
*   Greater staff commitment;
*   Increased value of the organisation's human assets; and
*   The personal development of employees.

2.3   Benefits to the individual

The benefits to the individual of effective training and development are:

(a)   increased motivation;
(b)   individual goals equating with those of the organisation;
(c)   needs and aims to develop abilities and talents satisfied;
(d)   newly acquired skills for future use.

Conclusion   The purpose of training in the work situation is to develop the abilities of the individual and to satisfy the current and future manpower needs of the organisation.

3   ANALYSING TRAINING AND DEVELOPMENT NEEDS

3.1   Job training analysis

The training needs will be indicated by a job training analysis. This can be defined as:

Definition   the process of identifying the purpose of the job and its component parts, and specifying what must be learnt in order for there to be effective performance.

A job analysis will reveal the 'training gap' which is the difference between the knowledge and skill required for the effective performance of a specific job and the knowledge and skill already possessed by the employee.

3.2   Identifying training needs

Training must have a purpose and that purpose can only be defined if the training needs of the organisation and the groups and individuals in it have been identified and analysed. Training needs can be broadly defined as the gap between the knowledge and skill requirements and the knowledge and skill already possessed by employees.

Some of this training requirement will relate to the longer term, for example where a company has a strategy to enter a particular overseas market or move into a new industry. The knowledge and skill gap will be defined for the future needs of the organisation and expressed for each of the future time periods. It will then be detailed in the human resources plan and used to define training and development needs as well as the recruitment and promotion of staff.

There are a number of means which are used to assess training needs. These range from a very broad analysis of organisational goals and corporate strategy to the details of individuals' performance appraisal.

(a)   **Organisational analysis** - an analysis of the features of an organisation and a diagnosis of its problems may well indicate that training is necessary. Such an analysis may involve consideration of the following factors:

- The overall performance of the organisation or any part of it in terms of output, sales, profit, costs and so on. For example, if materials wastage is high for a batch of new recruits, it might show a need for improvement in the training programme they have been through.

- The policies of an organisation may involve training as a means of achieving future goals. Forecasts of technical change and plans for expansion have implications for training with the requirements to train for new skills or increase the supply of traditional skills. Similarly changes in personnel policies eg, a new promotion policy or a career development plan, will create new training needs.

- There are various indicators of organisational health, which may well suggest that training is necessary. Such indicators might include labour turnover, absenteeism or the level of grievances. For example, several studies have shown that inadequate training often leads to workers failing to achieve production targets, which affects their chances of gaining financial incentives. Many such employees experience frustration, which manifests itself in grievances and labour turnover.

- Governmental influences, and legislation in particular, have caused and still do cause organisations to reconsider their position concerning the provision of training.

(b)   **Performance appraisal** - individual training needs can be established by feedback on individual assessments. As we shall see later, a major objective of appraisal schemes is to make both superior and subordinate aware of the need to train and/or re-train employees.

(c)   **Job analysis** - this is an important part of assessing training needs, in that a detailed job analysis will indicate those areas of a job where training is necessary. By defining the duties, responsibilities, tasks, knowledge and skill, which make up a job, and specifying the training accordingly, relevance must result. There are a variety of approaches to job analysis which involve greater or lesser degrees of detail but the basic procedure is similar for all and covers the following stages:

- A broad analysis of the requirements of the job and any special problems surrounding it as seen by the job-holder, the superior and, possibly, colleagues.

- An analysis of the particular skills needed to do the job.

- A detailed study of the responsibilities, duties and tasks carried out. This forms the basis of the job description.

- An analysis of the knowledge and skills required by the job-holder. This forms the basis of the job specification.

- A description of the training requirements for the job ie, the training specification.

(d)   **Other approaches** - include information gained from records of employee performance, feedback from customers or simply from observation of employees. Other methods available include surveys of staff with questionnaires or interviews of superiors and subordinates and customer surveys covering their satisfaction and dissatisfaction.

3.3   Training objectives

Once training needs have been established it is then possible for the organisation to set its training objectives. Such objectives should include the following considerations:

(a)   **Prerequisite experience and abilities.** Many training programmes are based on the trainees having some prior experience and aptitude. This is where training overlaps with selection.

(b)   **Educational objectives.** Often general in nature eg, language training.

(c)   **Behavioural objectives,** ie, specifically related to changing management and staff attitudes

(d)   **Criteria for assessment**

It should be remembered that the setting of objectives is often constrained by both resources available and the demands for work output. For example, a firm may well identify a training need in several of its staff but be able to take little action because of the lack of training facilities or finance or both. Training objectives have to be set alongside other organisational objectives to ensure they are realistic and attainable.

3.4   The role of the trainer

The trainer has four prime responsibilities:

(i)   Planning and organising training activities - this will involve establishing physical training facilities and equipment and also identifying human training resources (ie, lecturers, course leaders, instructors); there may be a need to train the trainers.

(ii)   Determining and managing training activities - this involves establishing curricula or syllabi, establishing a manual or computer record system.

(iii)   Directing training activities - the monitoring of standards and activities.

(iv)   Consulting and advising - both on training matters and on technical matters.

Frequently the trainer is a member of the personnel department, though in a large organisation there may be a separate training department.

4   METHODS USED IN DEVELOPING INDIVIDUALS IN THE WORKPLACE

4.1   Training and development methods

Training and development methods vary tremendously depending on the person, the job, the resources, the organisation and the economic environment. We can divide them into on-the-job and off-the-job training methods, structured or unstructured, participatory or self development, sitting in front of a computer screen or 'sitting with Nellie'. The methods that we will be looking at include training courses (both external and in-house), on-the-job training, mentoring, coaching; computerised interactive learning, planned experiences and self-managed learning.

When developing managers we tend to use methods that are highly participative eg, case studies, syndicates and the T group system. The first confronts the trainee manager with a potential real life problem, the second encourages participative management; the third, and more controversial, method forces the individual to see himself as others see him and thereby encourages him to develop his management potential. The unstructured nature of T groups has brought criticism in recent years.

Business games, either in the sophisticated format of the computer based profit seeking programme or as the simple leadership games centred around packs of playing cards, are also effective tools of management development. The list of games available is endless; all involve high participation levels

4.2   Internal training and development methods for the individual

The types of training and development that can take place at work include:

- *The apprenticeship* - This requires the trainee to learn and apply skills in the work situation over a period of time, often years. Learning-while-you-work is normally supplemented by courses of related education in a company school or a college of further education.

- *Induction courses* - These are arranged for new recruits to an organisation to enable them to familiarise themselves with the firm and to adjust to the requirements of the organisation.

- *Job instructions* - This is a systematic approach to training for a particular job, normally used by supervisors when training those who report to them. It can be a cost-effective way of satisfying training needs and can also be linked to a competence-based qualification such as NVQ, which is supervised by the trainee's immediate superior. This type of training develops trainee-supervisor links. However, the trainer might have bad habits that would, inevitably, be passed on to the trainee. Another problem for all on-the-job training will be the normal distractions and pressures of the workplace.

- *Internal training centres* are sometimes used to provide customised training programmes eg, where there would be a risk if the trainee made a mistake. Some hairdressers have special evenings where trainees are allowed to test their skills on clients who agree to be 'guinea pigs' and only pay a nominal amount.

- *Job rotation* - The training idea of moving an employee from one job to another is that it broadens experience and encourages the employee to be aware of the total activity.

- *Films and closed circuit television (CCT)* - Films are useful as explanatory devices for, say, describing company situations, how the different functions of an organisation relate to one another, or for presenting an overview of production. They are of little use in the teaching of craft, technical and social skills. CCT is used increasingly in management training to illustrate how managers behave and to show how such behaviour can be modified to enable beneficial changes in their interpersonal and problem solving skills.

• *Computer based training (CBT) and computer assisted learning (CAL)* - Some training packages and skills training can be designed for use on computers. User-friendly systems enable trainees to work at their own pace, working on set programmes. A few computer-based training packages adhere strictly to the principle of programmed learning where you are not allowed to progress until you have answered a question correctly or performed a task. ·

• *Programmed learning* - consists of the presentation of instructional material in small units followed immediately by a list of questions the trainee must answer correctly before progressing to more difficult work. The advantages are that trainees can move at their own pace, become actively involved in the learning process and can do their training independently without the need for an instructor.

• *Coaching* - is a specialised form of communication. It is useful when there is a need to extend the depth and range of an employee's knowledge very quickly for reasons which may range from the introduction of new techniques to the need to train for a particular job, perhaps on the unexpected retirement of the present job holder. Coaching is a considerable drain on managerial time and is also subject to work pressures. Support has to be given from the planning stage and will continue during the learning process, with the value of constructive criticism being particularly relevant

• *Mentoring* is used by organisations to show junior employees how things are done. The mentor is expected to guide the new recruit through a development programme and 'socialise' them into the culture of the enterprise. It is a route for bringing on 'high flyers' by allowing them to make mistakes under supervision.

• *Delegation by supervisor* can increase the scope of a trainee's job and provide greater motivation but, without supervision, the employee may make mistakes or may fail to achieve the task.

• *Secondments* are temporary transfers to another department or division to gain a deeper understanding, or learn more about certain aspects within an organisation. For example, a sales manager in an international corporation might work in one of the company's European offices to learn more about the customer requirements and to learn a foreign language.

• *Work shadowing* is a method where one employee shadows another, often in a more senior position, to experience what it is like working at that level.

4.3   Internal training and development methods for groups

Group training encourages participants to learn from each other through discussing issues, pooling experiences and critically examining opposite viewpoints. Instructors guide discussions rather than impart knowledge directly. They monitor trainees' understanding of what is going on, ask questions to clarify points and sometimes, but not always, prevent certain members from dominating the group. Some of the most popular methods follow:

(a)   *The lecture method* - This is regarded as an economical way of giving a large amount of information to many people. Some people prefer listening to reading and good lecturers can help learning and assist understanding. Lectures are of little value if the aim of training is to change attitudes, or develop job or interpersonal skills.

(b)   *Discussion methods* - Discussion and participation are known ways of securing interest and commitment. Discussion methods in this respect are useful ways of shaping attitudes, encouraging motivation and securing understanding. Discussion methods can also underline the nature and the difficulties of group problem solving.

(c)   *Case study method* - In this approach to training, learning occurs through participation in the definition, analysis and solution of the problem or problems. It demonstrates the nature of group problem solving activity and usually underlines the view that there is no one best solution to a complex business problem. Casework creates interest and enthusiasm among members but, when they lack knowledge and experience, the exercise can fail.

(d)   *Role playing* - This method requires trainees to project themselves into a simulated situation that is intended to represent some relevant reality, say, a confrontation between management and a trade union. The merit of role-playing is that it influences attitudes, develops interpersonal skills and heightens sensitivity to the views and feelings of others. However, it requires careful organising and giving tactful feedback is not easy unless the exercise is filmed in such a way that instant playback is possible.

(e)   *Business games* - Games simulate realistic situations, mergers, take-overs, etc in which groups compete with one another and where the effects of the decision taken by one group may affect others. The benefits are said to include development of an appreciation of the complex character of decision taking; understanding of risk and the nature of teamwork. Although business games and case studies can be devised to correspond to real life situations, the classroom environment means that participants might not take them seriously.

(f)   *T-group exercises* (the T stands for training) leave the group to their own devices. The trainer simply tells them to look after themselves and remains as an observer. The group itself has to decide what to do and, understandably, the members feel helpless at first and then they pool their experiences and help each other. They eventually form a cohesive group, appoint a leader and resolve any conflicts within the group. The advantages claimed for T-group exercises are that members recognise the need to learn from experience and from each other. They also observe how others react to offers of help. Since the group begins in a leaderless state and ends by appointing a leader, it de-mystifies the process of leader selection. They exercise interpersonal communication skills and learn to understand group dynamics.

Conclusion   In an exam question you might be asked to identify some training and development methods to suit a particular scenario. Because there are so many, you will need to be able to compare and contrast their relative advantages and disadvantages so that you can identify the ones that the examiner is looking for.

4.4   Self managed learning

Self managed learning is a form of development where the employee takes the initiative in learning new skills, knowledge and attitudes with the support of the organisation. Personal development programmes are highly personalised and tailored to individual needs, involving a mix of different training interventions and a variety of goals to achieve. Support from the organisation may take the form of payment of fees, allowing time off work to attend classes or by setting up a learning resources centre in-house.

4.5   Outdoor management training

An interesting recent development has been the use of outdoor training which assumes the existence of direct parallels between the personal qualities necessary for management and those cultivated through participation in outdoor pursuits such as canoeing, sailing or rock climbing. The essential demands of these activities - planning, organising, team building, dealing with uncertainty, direction and control - are supposedly the same as those needed for management. In either situation, individuals must be able to identify relevant and feasible objectives and initiate and organise activities aimed at their achievement. Such duties require capacities for leadership, communications, co-ordination and the motivation of subordinate staff. Creativity, and the ability to efficiently implement measures needed to solve immediate problems, are highly valued skills.

4.6   Activity

What does your own personal development programme look like?

4.7   Activity solution

Your immediate ambition is to achieve your accounting qualification. You may be undertaking this entirely on a distance learning basis or you may be attending college on a day release or full time basis. You may be receiving support from your organisation for this in terms of money and time. Or you may be entirely self-financing. This qualification may just be one element in a complex and highly structured development programme which might also include secondments, rotation, in-house training or mentoring or it may stand alone as the only example of career development your organisation has planned for you.

4.8   Training effectively

There are some points about the presentation of the methods of training outlined above, that you need to consider.

With a lecture, it is estimated that only 20% of what is said will be retained and the audience may unconsciously retain parts that resonate with them, but have no significance. They may only just recall the broad gist of the presentation.

A presentation is more effective when:

- the information is prepared thoroughly in advance;
- the plan is to get only a handful of key points across;
- there is a structure to it eg, preview, content then summary;
- the different elements of the presentation are linked;
- the delivery is paced, allowing time for reflection;
- a variety of good quality visual aids are used;
- jargon is avoided and technical information is simplified;
- the audience is given material to take away.

4.9   Plan for the delivery of a training course on a finance related topic

Suppose the company that you work for has identified a need to train some line managers who will be taking responsibility for profit centres. The skills they will need to develop will be to plan and control the activities that generate revenue in their department. Also, because these line managers are key change agents in the company, there will be a greater emphasis on the course manager to make them feel comfortable with the new structure and be able to 'sell' it to their subordinates as being of benefit to everyone concerned. The course details are:

'Profit centre management - Strategies, Techniques and Tools'.
A two day course, divided into four sessions
Course hours 9.30am - 4.30pm with an hour lunch break and refreshment breaks mid morning and afternoon.

The benefits of the course:

- This course transforms financial and accounting language and concepts into basic business tools that line managers can use successfully every day. Course participants will return to their jobs ready to apply the fundamentals of profit centre management to improve profits, sell new ideas, implement realistic budgets and analyse and monitor performance. The course will help you to influence and persuade your colleagues and provide leadership in your organisation.

The first step for the course manager is to analyse the gap between the knowledge and skill requirements in detail, decide on the requirements of the training programme and draw up the training objectives. These must be tangible, observable targets that can be achieved by the end of the course. For example, at the end of this course, you will be able to:

- apply the financial concepts and policies behind the management decision process;
- construct a set of budget forecasts;
- reduce complications inherent in the budgeting process;
- communicate effectively with financial personnel;
- interpret and understand financial statements;
- obtain useful management accounting reports;
- draw up a set of action plans to correct adverse performance;
- convince others to buy into decisions; and
- use knowledge and competence to influence others.

Once the learning areas and targets are established, the appropriate methods of training can then be put into effect. As this is likely to be a small group, they should be more involved (active) in the training process. Lecturing would be totally ineffective in this instance; it will probably be a mixture of presentations, discussions, case studies and individual action planning. The course content, outlined below, is divided into four sessions, covering the two days. The first day will be mainly presentations and discussions and the second day will incorporate workshops for case studies and individual action planning

Session 1	Session 2
Introduction and overview - profit centres Background to the new profit centre structure What it means to your company Explanation with examples of profit centred organisations Key features - benefits and problems associated with profit centres Responsibilities for line manager - extent of new learning required Line manager's role in the implementation Timetable for implementation Explanation of ongoing help and counselling after implementation	Using influence effectively Coping with changeover to the new structure Explaining the process to others Understanding the difficult person's point of view How to effect change successfully How to deal with resistance

Session 3	Session 4
Developing budgets Determining revenue Preparing budgets Establishing standard costs Pricing policy implications	Budgets and control Tracking variances Constructing action plans to respond to variances Determining what information is available to you Extracting management reports Profit centre and cost centre reporting

Through case studies, discussion groups and learn-by-doing exercises, participants will:

- draft and analyse financial statements
- set up budget
- solve problems in the budget process
- report on the status of a project

The training process should be monitored against expected results to see how effective it is, and alternative training programmes should have been considered so that they can be implemented if necessary.

5   EVALUATION

5.1   Evaluating the training and development programme

Wherever the training takes place a good training and development initiative must measure itself against its original objectives to ensure that learning has taken place. This is the important process of evaluation.

> **Definition**   The evaluation of training has been defined by Hamblin as 'any attempt to obtain information (feedback) on the effects of a training programme and to assess the value of the training in the light of that information'.

Evaluation leads to control, which means deciding whether the training was worthwhile and what improvements are necessary to make it better. Evaluation is not always easy because it is hard both to set measurable objectives and to obtain the information or results to see if objectives have been met. Hamblin suggests that there are five levels at which evaluation can take place:

- **Reactions** - of the trainees to the training, their feelings about how enjoyable and useful it has been etc.

- **Learning** - what new skills and knowledge have been acquired or what changes in attitude have taken place as a result of the training.

- **Job behaviour** - at this level evaluation tries to measure the extent to which trainees have applied their training on the job.

- **Organisation** - training may be assessed in terms of the ways in which changes in job behaviour affect the functioning of the organisation in which the trainees are employed in terms of measures such as output, productivity, quality etc.

- **Ultimate value** - this is a measure of the training in terms of how the organisation as a whole has benefited from the training in terms of greater profitability, survival or growth.

5.2   Evaluation process

The very least the trainer can do is ask the trainees whether they found the programme useful and enjoyable. For many organisations this is where the process begins and ends, but the process should be much more investigative.

The trainer or manager should establish whether the trainees have learned anything and whether the learning can be applied back at the workplace. To do this the trainer can collect data, which can be used to see whether the learning has taken place, and learning objectives have been met. This can be achieved with:

- attainment tests;
- rating scales;
- questionnaires;
- interviews; and
- observation.

Whatever evaluation method is used it should be done before, during and after the event.

- Before the event - evaluation will clarify the existing skills, knowledge and attitudes to help the trainer plan the event and provide a yardstick to measure them by.

- During the event will determine the rate of learning, allowing the trainer to pace the learning to suit the trainee and offer remedial help where needed.

- After the event can be immediately after the training or over a long time.

5.3 Evaluation problems

Unfortunately, some training programmes are difficult to evaluate because the changes in behaviour noticed could have been caused by something other than the training course.

The benefits of long-term management courses may also be difficult to measure because of the time involved in some courses eg, several years for an MBA.

If training is to be effective, it is important that the criteria used in the classroom or course situation resemble the working environment. There could be a situation where a course participant, away from the work place, is rated excellent by his or her peers, when measured against the group's criteria. But, on returning to the workplace and attempting to transfer the new values and behaviour to the job, he might meet resistance and outright hostility from the superior and co-workers. This shows that manager development may be improved using a situational approach where the objectives and methods match the characteristics of the organisation.

6 THE PROCESS OF LEARNING

6.1 Learning in the workplace

For a training and development intervention to be considered effective, learning must take place. This might be the acquisition of knowledge, a new skill or modified behaviour. Learning is the result of experience. People use the knowledge of the results of past behaviour to change, modify and improve their behaviour in future. Learning cannot take place without appropriate feedback. The experience may be planned, as in studying this book, or it may be accidental eg, learning from one's mistakes. However, learning cannot be seen; it can only be inferred by observing changes in behaviour. Learning frequently occurs when an individual has to deal with a situation new to them. It is about developing new skills, competencies and attitudes to meet new situations.

The basic process is simple. All learning begins when we ask ourselves a question. This may be a simple question of a factual nature eg, when we ask how much of product X we sold last year, or a question about process such as how to arrange for financial results to be available three days earlier each month. It could be a question about purpose eg 'what is the main aim of this organisation?' Whatever the source of the question, the situation will demand an answer. Then the answer needs to be tested out in practice. If it works then something has been learned. If it does not then the process starts again with the question.

The ability of employees to learn is more important to organisations that are preoccupied with controlled performance; needing to know what the staff must do, how they are to do it and how well they are expected to perform. In these organisations the induction of new recruits, job training, reward systems and performance evaluation have all been influenced by learning theories.

6.2 Learning theories

There are four theories of learning; the first two are 'behavioural theories' concentrating on observable behaviour, and the others are 'cognitive theories', focusing on what goes on internally to create learning. Behaviourists and cognitive psychologists agree that experience influences behaviour, but disagree over how this happens.

(i)   Reinforcement theory - Burrhus Skinner states that we learn by being conditioned to understand that a particular stimulus evokes a particular response which leads to a desired outcome. We are continually looking for ways to achieve more positive reinforcement, in terms of rewards, and avoid negative reinforcement ie, punishment, so we learn to adjust our behaviour according to which pattern produces the best results for us.

(ii)   Information theory - looks at the way that learners seek out feedback from all parts of their environment. This information is received by the learner and used to control performance and modify behaviour in an automatic way like a thermostat in a central heating system.

(iii)   Cognitive or problem-solving approaches to learning argue that behaviourism is unnecessarily restricting; that it excludes those aspects that make people interesting and different. Reinforcement is always knowledge about the results of past behaviour, it is feedback on how successful our behaviour has been. That knowledge is information, which can be used to modify or maintain previous behaviour. The information has to be perceived, interpreted, given meaning and used in decision-making about the future behaviour.

(iv)   Experiential learning theory - Kolb, Rubin and McIntyre see learning as a continuous cyclical process with four stages:

- Experience; either planned or accidental.

- Reflective observation; which is looking back at the experience and introspectively reviewing the general issues raised.

- Abstract conceptualisation; seen as generalising from reflection and developing hypotheses based on experience and knowledge.

- Active experimentation; which is consciously trying out hypotheses in other situations.

6.3   Learning organisations

Learning organisations encourage questions and explicitly recognise mistakes as part of the learning process. They encourage testing and experimentation. Because they want to find new answers, they recognise that failed answers are as important as successful ones.

Pedler, Burgoyne and Boydell are the main proponents in the UK of the 'Learning Company'. It can be defined as:

(Definition)   'An organisation that facilitates the learning of all its members and continuously transforms itself.

The aim is to design an organisation which is capable of adapting, changing, developing and transforming itself in response to the needs, wishes and aspirations of people, inside and outside. These organisations will be able to achieve their objectives without predatory takeovers, mergers or divestments. They will be able to avoid the large scale restructuring that is now commonplace in industry. Actions that are carried out therefore have two purposes. The first is to resolve the immediate problem and the second is to learn from the process.

Pedler, Burgoyne and Boydell believe that the current state of an organisation is due to three forces - the idea behind it, the phase of its development and the era it is in. Although these three perspectives are in principle independent, in practice they may be linked. When an organisation is going through a development phase that integrates its activities, employees and ideas, this is when the organisation starts to take a 'learning approach' to change.

Self-development and action-learning is also one of the foundations of the learning organisation; as the organisation learns from the actions that it carries out so does the individual.

6.4   Role of management

The role of management in a learning organisation is to encourage continuous learning and acquisition of new knowledge and skills and to transform these into actual behaviour, products and processes within the organisation. To enable learning to take place within the organisation, management should adopt the following approach:

- The process of strategy formulation should be designed with learning in mind, and should incorporate experimentation and feedback.

- All members of the organisation should be encouraged, and given the opportunity, to contribute to policy making as part of the learning process.

- Information should be seen as a resource to be exploited by all members of the organisation, not as a 'power tool' reserved for a chosen few.

- Accounting systems should be designed in such a way that members of the organisation can learn how the cash resource is used.

- Employees should be encouraged to see internal users of their outputs as 'customers'.

- Employees should be encouraged to see the diversity of rewards they enjoy (not just cash), and there should be openness about why some people are paid more than others.

- The structures of the organisation - everything from office layout to managerial hierarchy - should be regarded as temporary arrangements which can be altered in response to changing conditions.

- Employees who have contacts outside the organisation - salesmen, customer service staff, purchasing staff etc - should impart the knowledge they determine from such contacts to improve the organisation's knowledge base.

- Management must foster a climate in which workers understand that part of their task is to improve their own knowledge, and to share knowledge with other members of the organisation.

- A priority for management should be the provision of opportunities for structured learning - courses, seminars, etc.

6.5   The individual's motivation to learn

The conditions necessary for effective learning must start with the individual's motivation to learn in the first place. The advantages should be clear - money, opportunity, valued skills or whatever. Vroom's expectancy theory states that the strength of an individual's motivation to do something will depend on the extent to which the results of the effort contribute towards the desired outcomes. Charles Handy suggested that for any individual decision, there is a conscious or unconscious 'motivation calculus' which is an assessment of three factors:

- the individual's own set of needs;

- the desired results - what the individual is expected to do in his job;

- 'E' factors. Handy suggests that as well as effort, there is energy, excitement in achieving desired results, enthusiasm, emotion, and expenditure (of time, money etc).

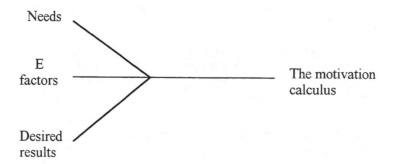

The motivation decision will depend on the individual's judgement about the strength of his or her needs, the expectancy that expending 'E' will lead to a desired result and how far the result will be 'instrumental' in satisfying his or her needs.

If the motivation to learn is good, the next step is to set clear objectives and standards, so that each task has some meaning. Each stage of learning should present a challenge, without overloading the trainee or making him or her lose confidence. Specific objectives and performance standards for each will help the trainee in the planning and control process that leads to learning, providing targets against which performance will constantly be measured.

Active participation is more telling than passive reception (because of its effect on motivation, concentration and recollection). If a high degree of participation is impossible, practice and repetition can be used to reinforce receptivity, but participation has the effect of encouraging 'ownership' of the process of learning and changing - committing the individual to it as his or her own goal, not just an imposed process.

6.6   Feedback

It is hard for us to behave or learn at all without appropriate feedback. Consider the student who consistently fails exams but is never told why. The plans that we choose to follow depend on our needs, motives, values and beliefs about ourselves and our environment. The conduct of these plans depends on our ability to draw on our knowledge and skills and on learning from the successes and failures of previous plans. Feedback is therefore vital to learning. Information on how things went in the past is used to control future actions. Feedback, rewards and punishments and knowledge of results have a motivating effect on our behaviour.

7   DEVELOPMENT OF BUSINESS PROFESSIONALS

7.1   Management development

[Definition]   Armstrong defines management development as 'a systematic process which aims to ensure that the organisation has the effective managers it requires to meet its present and future needs'.

According to Torrington and Hall it can be distinguished from management training in four ways:

(a)   Management development is a broader concept and is more concerned with developing the whole person rather than emphasising the learning of narrowly defined skills.

(b)   Management development emphasises the contribution of formal and informal work experiences.

(c)   The concept of management development places a greater responsibility on managers to develop themselves than is placed on most employees to train themselves.

(d)   Although in training generally there always needs to be a concern with the future, this is especially emphasised in management development. Managers are developed as much for the jobs they will be doing as for the jobs that they are doing. Management development is a vital aspect in career management, and from the organisation's point of view both are methods of satisfying human resource needs while allowing individuals to achieve their career goals (Torrington and Hall 1987).

You may wonder what the difference is between developing managers and developing staff. The answer is that there is little or no difference apart from the hype surrounding management development because most organisations invest heavily on development of managers. However, there is a good reason for this: it is because managers are the key decision-makers and carry the responsibility for the success or failure of the enterprise. If development is to be effective it must make those managers into better managers from the point of view of the company employing them. It must also take into account the future managers and what their potential is likely to be. Thus, to establish a management development programme the following steps should be taken:

- Assess the strengths, weaknesses and training needs of existing managers and future managers.

- Chart the planned growth of the organisation over the next five or ten years.

- Match the potential strengths to future posts.

- Develop potential strengths to meet future posts.

7.2   Management development programmes

They may take many forms. The main schemes are:

(a)   Student sponsorship - the method by which the armed services recruit and train graduates and a method favoured by many large concerns. The undergraduate attends university sponsored by his or her future employer with an undertaking to join them on qualification. For the undergraduate the advantages include a salary whilst training and the prospect of a definite job, whilst the employer benefits by the early training and recruitment of staff, of potentially high ability.

(b)   Professional and technical qualifications - such as membership of CIMA. Schemes like this mean that the employee is given an opportunity to develop his or her skills and the employer is assured of well-trained, often externally examined and highly motivated staff.

(c)   General management development - the UK is well behind the USA in its use of business degrees and the existence of business schools. The realisation that management is a skill to be learned and that there is much research to be done is gradually gaining ground in the UK. There are now courses of one and two years' duration at the various business schools intended to attract the already professionally qualified manager who now wishes to add business skills to his abilities in order to enhance his promotion prospects.

(d)   Internally organised management development - good management training can be obtained in the sophisticated multinational companies simply by being seconded to a variety of departments to learn how to run them and their area of work. More and more, however, entry to such schemes is becoming dependent upon a business-related degree or qualification, rather than merely upon the possession of any degree.

7.3   Training and development plan for staff of finance department

Training is a process that begins with the identification of training needs in relation to the organisational objectives. A job analysis will reveal the 'training gap', which is the difference between the knowledge and skill required for the effective performance of a specific job and the knowledge and skill already possessed by the employee.

The process moves on to the identification of appropriate target groups for training and the design of suitable training experiences. The steps are outlined below:

(i)   A decision on the scale and type of training system needed, and whether it can best be provided by the organisation's own staff or by external consultants;

(ii)   The allocation of responsibilities for training within the firm, including a co-ordinator for any external training;

(iii)   Planning specific training courses and ensuring that they are properly timed to allow normal operations to continue; and

(iv)   Reviewing the system on a regular basis to ensure that it is still satisfying the organisation's training needs.

This process is more complex than the description might suggest and the figure below gives a more complete account of what is involved.

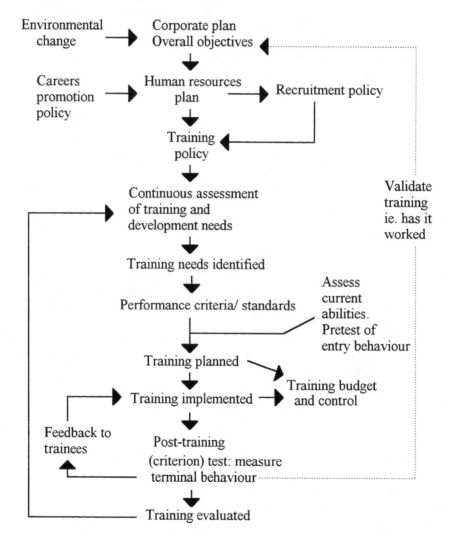

A company's greatest asset is its people and it is important to ensure that every person is adequately trained for the job they have to do and that they can, in due course, develop and take on responsibilities. Training should ideally meet both the needs of the job and the individual.

Most finance departments will have staff at different levels and of mixed ability. Not all of them will need training or developing. For staff who are seeking membership of one of the accountancy bodies the selection of the most appropriate qualification and methods of study will have to be determined by discussions between the student, the accountant and the training officer (this may have been agreed at the selection interview). In addition a training programme must be initiated so that the correct practical experience is obtained to satisfy the requirements of the accountancy body.

Within the accountancy profession there is much emphasis on post-qualifying education (PQE) and details of courses provided by all the accountancy bodies and other organisations should be readily available. Staff should be encouraged to attend to keep their knowledge up to date and, in some instances, staff may be directed to attend, eg. to acquire knowledge of a new accounting standard, tax changes, computing course, etc

Staff at all levels should be encouraged to develop their knowledge and abilities to as far as they are capable (and wish). In accounts departments there are many opportunities to specialise and this should be encouraged, in so far as it is compatible with the policies and requirements within the organisation and the need to ensure that there are understudies for all areas of knowledge. Some may wish to concentrate on computers, others on management control systems and yet others on taxation. So long as the knowledge gained is appropriate and there is adequate cover while members of staff attend courses, there should be worthwhile benefits to the organisation from any investment made in training.

There is a range of training types available to the finance department depending on the purpose for which it is required. The types of training may be classified as follows:

(i)   Induction training - this is the means whereby a new employee is introduced to the organisation in as effective a way as possible.

(ii)   Operative training - this could be a learning while doing type of training, providing a logical breakdown of jobs so that instruction can be given in the different elements. For example, staff may be taught how to use the different parts of an accounting package, such as Sage or Pegasus. The skills are thereby learned faster with security incorporated at each stage.

(iii)   Technical training - Courses may be of the 'sandwich' type ie. periods at college alternating with practical experience at work eg, AAT.

(iv)   Professional training - depending on the size of the company, it will probably assist employees aiming for professional qualifications through the provision of study leave and payment of fees. Professional update courses may also have to be organised where changes have taken place, which require specific training eg. budget affecting corporation tax.

(v)   Office training - There is much more systematic training for office workers, eg. clerks, computer operators, than there used to be. It has been recognised that 'picking up' the job from colleagues is not the best method for such training.

(vi)   Management training - There is a strong body of opinion that believes that management cannot be taught; it can only be experienced. Although management training is in some respects a natural process, the techniques, after formal education, include on the job training, group learning sessions, conferences and counselling.

Training may also relate to special activities such as safety training or to particular groups such as employees requiring preparation for retirement courses.

The training and development process should be monitored against expected results to see how effective it is, and alternative training programmes should have been considered so that they can be implemented if necessary. Evaluation leads to control which means deciding whether the training was worthwhile and what improvements are necessary to make it better. Evaluation is not always easy or immediate because it is hard both to set measurable objectives and to obtain the information or results to see if objectives have been met.

7.4   Problems associated with the design and implementation of the plan

As with any plan, because there is a certain amount of forecasting involved, there are bound to be problems somewhere in the process.

The analysis of the organisation's training needs is based on a comparison of the skills possessed by its employees with those needed for its smooth operation. There are two variables that could go wrong here - the skills needed for operation could change if environmental changes wreaked havoc with the organisation's sales or technology or level of competition. The other variable is the employees involved. They can move to another company, have an accident, retire early or be dismissed.

Once the decision is made on the scale and type of training system to be used, there can be problems associated with the staff or external consultants chosen to deliver the programmes. On-going evaluation may point to problems with training delivery or funds may not be available to continue with programmes already started.

The person responsible for co-ordinating any external training may leave suddenly and not have any immediate successor.

There are many other problem areas that you could probably identify, faced with a scenario question in an exam. Every organisation has to cope with a different external and internal environment. They change constantly and corporate plans, as well as human resource plans, must be flexible enough to cope with these changes.

8   CAREER AND SUCCESSION PLANNING

8.1   What is career management?

Career management was once the chosen way of ensuring that the organisation had the right people in the right places at the right times. It meant understanding the direction and objectives of the organisation, grooming and developing the appropriate staff, managing individual career expectations and matching them with the current and future needs outlined in the human resources plan. It also involved succession planning to ensure a stock of skilled and trained people to fill anticipated vacancies.

This type of planning still exists and succession planning and career management are still a part of many organisation's human resource plan. However, the current situation in some industries is a little different. They are seizing the opportunity, offered by delayering and restructuring, to influence the way individuals think about their career. Businesses like banks used to have a grading system that encouraged an expectation of promotion and life-long employment. This is now unrealistic and creates false career aspirations. Because of the removal of levels of management and changes to jobs through technological advances, these types of organisation have people who are at a plateau and are unlikely to move any further in the company.

From our understanding of motivation theory, we know that, among other things, people seem to place a high value on responsibility, opportunities for achievement, advancement and clear links between performance and reward. Many of us will want a greater say in how we organise our work and there are a number of ways in which jobs can be redesigned to improve the satisfaction and productivity of those who do them.

8.2   Development and career planning

If the organisation does not address the problem of career development it will have to rely on filling vacancies by **ad hoc** methods either from internal or external sources. The risks are great that the correct human resources will not be available or that current managerial resources will be wasted, with consequent effects on commitment and morale. The questions raised by this area are:

(a)   What basic job and professional training needs to be provided to prepare new and existing staff to fulfil their roles satisfactorily?

(b)   Should we concentrate on in-service training or external courses?

(c)   How can induction procedures be improved?

(d)   What special programmes need to be developed to deal with re-training and updating?

(e)   How can internal procedures be improved to aid the movement of staff to jobs where they can exercise greater responsibilities?

(f)   What new succession plans need to be drawn up for key management and supervisory roles?

(g)   How well is training linked to career development?

Human resource planning also requires a method of plotting career progression so that the organisation can ascertain the rate of the employees' progress, and whether factors such as age-spread will lead to promotion blockages or the over-promotion of inexperienced employees. Managing careers is a difficult part of human resource planning. Expectations of employees seem to change and higher levels of education may add to the difficulty. A key decision is whether careers are expected to fall within specialist areas, such as the professions, or in departments, or whether a broader base is required.

8.3   Objectives

Many organisations have elaborate schemes for planning the career progression of all, or most, of their managerial staff. This is generally done with the objectives of:

(a)   providing each individual with as far as possible a satisfactory career; and

(b)   ensuring that the organisation makes the best use of its managerial resources.

Charles Handy argues that career planning in many organisations is not a development process, so much as a weeding-out process. Because career development is a series of hurdles - appointments and levels of authority - only the strong survive to the end. The need to provide a large number of hurdles, or promotion possibilities also leads to clutter in the organisation, with many more levels of authority than often necessary.

Most managers are not only interested in their current job but are concerned about where this job is going to lead to in the future. The objective of many managers is to ensure that they 'grow' during their career. This objective can obviously benefit the organisation as well as the individual. It is the personnel department's responsibility that the career-growth cycle is achieved.

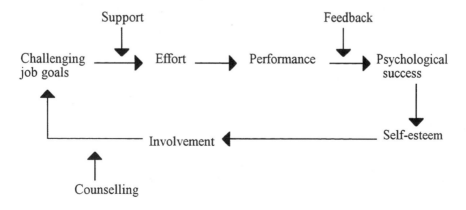

The growth is triggered by a job that provides challenging, stretching goals. The clearer and more challenging the goals, the more effort the person will exert, and the more likely it is that good performance will result. If the person does a good job and receives positive feedback, he or she will feel successful (psychological success). These feelings will increase a person's feelings of confidence and self-esteem. This should lead to the person becoming more involved in work, which in turn leads to the setting of future stretching goals.

8.4   Succession planning

Succession planning should be an ongoing process so that the personnel department is continuously working with heads of departments so that the staff requirements are anticipated and met within the dynamic framework of the corporate plan.

Consideration of the process might be assisted by starting from the present position. An assessment of current staff resources should be available, analysed by departments, the types of jobs at each level (job description) and the number and quality of staff in those jobs (staff appraisal).

A forecast of the staffing requirements, by grades and skills, should then be assessed and agreed within the corporate plan (both the short and long-term needs) to highlight any surplus staff as well as shortages.

In the case of a mismatch between job specification and existing employees, every opportunity should be made to provide retraining or to undertake staff development. Again, the personnel appraisal records should indicate staff who have been willing or who are keen to widen or change their skills.

Where there are shortages, recruitment programmes should be agreed. Vacancies should be identified and using the job description and job specification, recruitment and selection of appropriate staff should be carried out. The plan may require that training should then be provided for new recruits, as they will be unlikely to have the specific job knowledge required. In such cases, recruitment would be geared to the selection of people with the necessary ability and aptitude.

Succession planning is a difficult task. Whilst the process must seek to achieve the organisation's goals and objectives, it must also take into account the aspiration of individuals in trying to achieve a realistic fit between the person and the job.

8.5   Management succession

One of the most important aspects of human resource planning is ensuring the management succession. It is, of course, both possible and desirable to bring in top managers from outside the company, thereby adding a breadth of experience to the top management team, but it is still necessary to have people at the top who have come from within the business. They bring specialist knowledge of different aspects of the firm itself and provide an inspiration for more junior managers who can aspire to the same position. It is thus essential that people with management potential are identified early in their careers.

Good training schemes must be provided for such people, to integrate with planned career patterns, including a number of development moves, to widen experience. However, care must be taken that grooming the chosen few does not take precedence over everyone else's career: if certain people are known to have been singled out, resentment will be caused and the company may miss out on spotting late developers. This points to the need for a thorough appraisal system throughout the organisation. Everyone should be made to feel that his actual and potential contribution is of value.

Management succession planning will probably entail compiling:

(a)   for each post, a list of perhaps three potential successors; and

(b)   for each person (at least from a certain level upwards) a list of possible development moves.

These lists then form the basis for long-term plans and development moves, and in addition supply a contingency plan to provide a successor for any post which becomes suddenly and unexpectedly vacant (eg, through death).

9   SELF TEST QUESTIONS

9.1   What does the definition of development suggest? (1.2)

9.2   Draw a diagram showing what the systematic approach to training will involve (2.1)

9.3   Outline the benefits to the individual of effective training and development (2.3)

9.4   What will a job analysis reveal? (3.1)

9.5   The trainer has four prime responsibilities - briefly describe them (3.4)

9.6   What are discussion methods used for? (4.3)

9.7   How can you make a presentation more effective? (4.8)

9.8   List the potential sources of information that can provide data for the evaluation of training (5.2)

9.9   What are the objectives of career progression? (8.3)

10   EXAMINATION TYPE QUESTION

10.1   Installing a training system

(a)   Describe the steps that should be taken to set up a training system in an organisation.

(10 marks)

(b)   Identify five ways in which such a system would benefit the accounting function.

(10 marks)
(Total 20 marks)

11   ANSWER TO EXAMINATION TYPE QUESTION

11.1   Installing a training system

(a)   All organisations, whatever their size and level of complexity, will need some form of training if staff resources are to be used properly. Even smaller firms who tend to recruit staff ready trained will need to train existing staff to cope with new systems and to teach new staff the finer details of their working practices. The main difference between the different types of organisation is likely to be the degree of formality involved in the training system.

The steps that should be taken to set up a training system will depend on its formality, but would normally include:

(i)   An analysis of the organisation's training needs, based on a comparison of the skills possessed by its employees with those needed for its smooth operation;

(ii)   A decision on the scale and type of training system needed, and whether it can best be provided by the organisation's own staff or by external consultants;

(iii)   The allocation of responsibilities for training within the firm, including a co-ordinator for any external training;

(iv)   Planning specific training courses and ensuring that they are properly timed to allow normal operations to continue; and

(v)   Reviewing the system on a regular basis to ensure that it is still satisfying the organisation's training needs.

(b)   The most likely benefits of a training system for the accounting function of an organisation are:

(i)   More efficient use of staff resources as staff understand their duties more clearly, so that, for example, difficult accounting entries will be dealt with more intelligently;

(ii)   Greater flexibility of operation as more staff acquire more skills, allowing for replacement of those concerned with maintaining one set of records by those working on others if workload or absences demand it;

(iii)   Greater ease in introducing new techniques as a training system will exist to help with the changeover, particularly useful if the accounting records are being computerised;

(iv)   Greater capability for dealing with staff turnover as the training programme automatically provides for career succession; and

(v)   General improvements in efficiency and staff morale.

13 APPRAISAL

INTRODUCTION & LEARNING OUTCOMES

Syllabus area 11 (iii)   • The importance of appraisals, their conduct and the problems often associated with them

   • The relationship between performance appraisal and the reward system

A competence is an observable skill or ability to complete a particular task. It also includes the ability to transfer skills and knowledge to a new situation. The general purpose of any assessment or appraisal is to improve the efficiency of the organisation by ensuring that the individual employees are performing to the best of their ability and developing their potential for improvement.

Of all the activities in human resources management (HRM), appraisal is the least popular among those who are involved. Managers do not seem to like doing it and employees see no point in it. However, it is an accepted part of management orthodoxy that there should be some means by which performance can be measured.

Appraisal acts as an information processing system providing vital data for rational, objective and efficient decision-making regarding improving performance, identifying training needs, managing careers and setting levels of reward.

When you have studied this chapter you should be able to:

• evaluate a typical appraisal process

---

1 THE IMPORTANCE OF APPRAISALS

1.1 The process of competence assessment

[Definition]   Competencies are the critical skills, knowledge and attitude that a job holder must have to perform effectively

Competencies are expressed in visible, behavioural terms and reflect the skills, knowledge and attitude (the main components of any job) which must be demonstrated to an agreed standard and must contribute to the overall aims of the organisation. As a general definition, a competent individual can perform a work role in a wide range of settings over an extended period of time.

Some competence-based systems are development-led - they focus on the development of competence and are linked to training and development programmes to develop people to a level of performance expected at work. Other systems are achievement-led - they focus on assessment of competent performance - what people do at work and how well they do it.

This is an important distinction when considering competence-based systems as the system may include many components, each linking to a different aspect of human resource activity within an organisation.

1.2   Process

For any competence based system the process is the same:

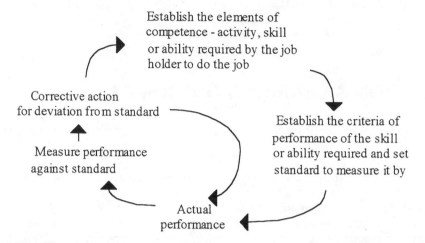

Conclusion   Although it is not a work-based activity, think of the process of passing a driving test. It is an observable skill, which is measured against set standards. In the case of failure a list which outlines the failed areas is given to the learner driver and is used to form the basis of any corrective action needed before re-applying for the test.

1.3   Performance appraisal and HRM

An early HRM model, developed by Fombrun *et al*, shows four key constituent components - selection, appraisal, development and rewards, as outlined below:

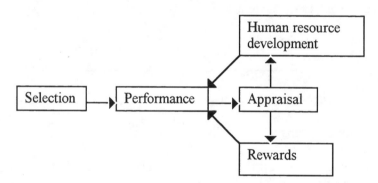

As the diagram shows, the information relative to the behaviour and performance of an individual can lead to activities in the human resources department. Performance appraisal data can be used as predictors in the planning, recruitment and selection processes and can determine employee rewards.

1.4   The appraisal scheme and the organisational structure

The organisation's appraisal scheme is inextricably linked to its control structure. It clarifies specific jobs, it assesses competencies, it uses feedback and reward to improve performance, it links performance to organisational goals and it aims to make the behaviour of employees predictable and, hence, controllable

The overall purpose of appraisal must be to create a more effective organisation where employees know, not only what is expected of them, but also the reason for doing the job the way they do it, and how good/bad they are at their work. The other side of this is that management is fully aware of what the staff are supposed to be doing and how they are actually doing it. This can be achieved if performance criteria are established jointly, appropriate on-the job behaviour is mutually understood and the review is a continual process focussed on growth and development.

Assessment is the process used for obtaining information about an individual employee's past and current work behaviour and performance. This allows appraisal, which may be defined as:

[Definition]   The regular and systematic review of performance and the assessment of potential with the aim of producing action programmes to develop both work and individuals.

Performance appraisal is a procedure where the managers or supervisors in an organisation discuss the work of their subordinates. They see each person individually and consider the progress they have been making in their job, their strengths and weaknesses and their future needs as regards training and development and the employee's potential for promotion.

1.5   Appraisal as a management tool

In a sense all individuals are constantly appraised but a systematic appraisal involves more than a casual assessment of individual performance.   Systematic performance appraisal is a vital management tool for the following reasons:

(i)   It enables a picture to be drawn up of the human 'stock' of an organisation - its strengths and weaknesses, enabling more effective human resource planning.

(ii)   By identifying weaknesses in an individual's performance it may identify training needs and once training has taken place, performance appraisal enables some evaluation of training effectiveness.

(iii)   It allows managers and subordinates to plan personnel and job objectives in the light of performance.

(iv)   In some circumstances it may be used to assess the level of reward payable for an individual's efforts, eg, in merit payment systems.

(v)   By encouraging two-way communication it permits an evaluation of a subordinate's strengths and weaknesses and the reasons for them.   Thus, for example, if a subordinate's failure to perform is due to some failure in the work system corrective action can be taken quickly.

(vi)   It is the ideal situation for assessing potential.   At the organisational level this permits career and succession planning.   At the individual level it permits superior and subordinate to assess the most effective development plans for the subordinate.

It is, however, important if the appraisal is to fulfil the last point that it is regular and systematic, based on objective criteria and permits a two-way flow of communication in a reasonably trusting atmosphere.   No subordinate is likely to admit to weaknesses or training needs in a climate of distrust.

1.6   Categorising training needs

Training needs may be identified from the appraisal process, in which actual performance is compared with pre-defined objectives. Shortcomings or 'gaps' in performance are then used as indicators of the training required to achieve improvements. At the same time, training based upon the appraisal process can be used to develop and build individual personal capacity and competence and to develop and build group/departmental capacity and competence.

The process of appraisal may also be used to review and develop departmental role objectives and job descriptions, from which further training needs' analysis can be undertaken. Actual training needs may be categorised on the basis of:

(i)   competencies associated with work quality eg, accuracy and consistency, exercise of judgement and discretion, communication skills and cost consciousness.

(ii)   competencies associated with work quantity eg, personal planning and time management, capacity to meet deadlines or work under pressure and capacity to cope with upward variations in work volume.

(iii)   supervisory and managerial skills and competencies eg, planning and organising, communication and interpersonal skills, directing, guiding and motivating, leadership and delegation, co-ordination and control, developing teamwork and developing and retaining staff.

1.7   The benefits of appraisal

(i)   Effective appraisal is grounded in the belief that feedback on past performance influences future performance, and that the process of isolating and rewarding good performance is likely to repeat it.

(ii)   Agreement on challenging but achievable targets for performance motivates employees by clarifying goals and setting the value of incentives offered.

(iii)   Effective appraisal can allow employees to solve any workplace problems and apply creative thinking to their jobs.

2   THE CONDUCT OF APPRAISALS

2.1   The appraisal process

The process of performance appraisal usually entails:

- clarifying a person's job;
- identifying criteria for assessment;
- assessing competence
- interviewing the job holder;
- identifying and agreeing future goals and targets;
- agreeing action points eg, training needs;
- giving regular feedback.

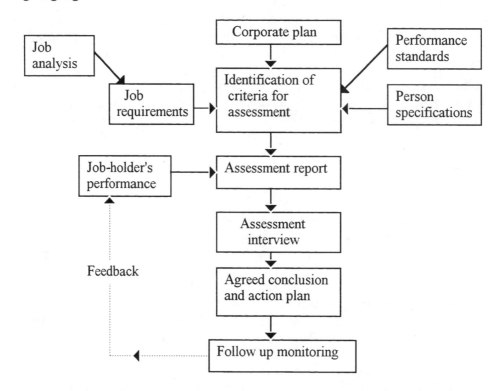

Appraisal can be highly motivating if it builds on expectations of appropriate effort leading to desired performance, and includes positive reinforcement with rewards that are equitable in the eyes of all parties concerned.

2.2   Who appraises?

In any organisation there are a number of alternative individuals or groups who might be involved in the appraisal of others. In this section we shall briefly examine the alternatives.

Appraisal by the immediate superior - this is the most common arrangement. The advantage of this is that the immediate superior usually has the most detailed knowledge of the tasks and duties carried out by the subordinate and the most intimate awareness of how well they have been carried out. The formal appraisal session should also be seen as part of the continuous appraisal and feedback process that goes on all the time between a superior and subordinate.

Appraisal by superior's superior - he or she may be involved in the appraisal process in two ways. First, they may be required to countersign the appraisal of the immediate superior in order to legitimise it and show that it has been carried out fairly. Secondly, the superior's superior may directly carry out the appraisal. This is felt to offer a fairer appraisal in many situations, reducing the chances of 'victimisation' and ensuring that common standards are applied.

Appraisal by the personnel department - frequently it may be responsible for the administration and organisation of the appraisal system but this does not normally mean that it actually carries out appraisals. However, it can happen in situations where there is no logical immediate supervisor to do the job, as, for example, in a matrix organisation.

Self-appraisal - how people rate themselves is of crucial importance to the realisation of many of the objectives of an appraisal system. If a person feels the present system is unfair and that criticisms of performance are ungrounded then the individual is not going to be concerned about self-improvement and development. Self-appraisal as the sole form of appraisal is very rare but an element of self-appraisal is quite common. This may consist of getting individuals to prepare for the appraisal meeting by filling out a self-appraisal form or perhaps to complete one section of the superior's assessment form. This differs from full self-appraisal in that it is always the superior who has the final say.

Appraisal by peers - it can be argued that a person's peers will have the most comprehensive view of their performance, and hence will be able to make the most acceptable and valid appraisal. However, managers do not often accept this method.

Appraisal by subordinates - though not widely used certain benefits may be claimed for this approach. In particular, subordinates are likely to be very closely aware of the performance of their boss. As part of a more comprehensive appraisal method an appraisal by subordinates can play a useful role.

Assessment centres - are used to appraise the potential of employees as supervisors or managers. They use tests, group exercises and interviews to assess this potential.

The openness of the appraisal process is one of the most crucial issues in performance appraisal and it concerns the extent of participation by the job-holder in the assessment of his/her own performance. However, what is meant by participation in appraisal? In many cases it is used only to denote that the employee has been allowed to see the appraisal. In only a minority of cases does the employee actually participate in assessing their performance as an integral part of the appraisal system.

2.3   General principles of appraisal

The following list represents the generally agreed set of criteria, which should be fulfilled for an appraisal scheme to be effective:

- It should be systematic in that all relevant personnel should be appraised using the same criteria.

- It should be objective. Critical remarks that are factual may be acceptable but citing personality defects or subjective judgements is not.

- It should be based on factors that are relevant to the performance on the job and not consider those factors, which may relate more to the personal prejudices of a particular assessor.

- It should be carried out on a regular basis so that the assessment of any individual is based on current information.

- Wherever possible it should be mutual and there should be a large amount of agreement between superior and subordinate about the subordinate's performance. This is seen as essential for motivation purposes if the subordinate is to improve performance.

- It should be constructive, helping the improvement of performance. Destructive appraisals will lead to resentment and a worsening of superior/subordinate relations.

- Before an appraisal scheme is established there should be an agreement between management and the trade unions involved concerning the need for appraisal, the uses that will be made of it and the method of operation.

- There should be adequate training given to those responsible for carrying out the appraisal.

- The standards should be consistently applied in all functions at all levels.

Conclusion   Appraisals should be fair, consistent and disciplined in approach, relying more on objective than subjective input and aiming to help the person being appraised consider future planning.

3   APPRAISAL PROCESS METHODS

3.1   Types

There are a few types of staff appraisal processes in use, these include the **review and comparison** method, **management by objectives** and the **task-centred** method.

Review and comparison - This consists of the individual being assessed and analysed in terms of objectives, tasks, workflows and results achieved. These are then compared with previously agreed statements of required results and performance levels.

Management by objectives - This is a system whereby managers agree certain objectives with their subordinates and then review the results achieved. It is a common-sense approach to staff appraisal based on the idea that if subordinates know their objectives they are more likely to reach them. Motivation will also be higher as they have more control over the setting of objectives and targets and also the methods by which those objectives and targets can be met.

The **task-centred method** - This relates to what the subordinate is doing and how he does it. It avoids the more formal approach to staff appraisal and adopts a continual assessment approach. After the completion of each task an assessment is carried out and performance monitored.

Whichever type of appraisal method is used the criteria must be clearly stated, understood and agreed by the subordinate. Subordinates must also be clear about the objectives and results required.

The objectives set, and statement of results required, must also relate to the job description, personnel specification and salary grading. The appraisal criteria may include the following.

(a)   Volume of work produced eg, within time period, evidence of work planning, personal time management and effectiveness of work under pressure.

(b)   Knowledge of work eg, gained through experience, gained through training courses and gained prior to employment.

(c)   Quality of work eg, level of analytical ability, level of technical knowledge, accuracy, judgement exercised and cost effectiveness.

(d)   Supervisory or management skills eg, communication skills, motivation skills, training and development skills and delegation skills.

(e)   Personal qualities eg, decision-making capabilities, flexibility, adaptability, assertiveness, team involvement, personal motivation and commitment to the organisational goals.

3.2   Techniques of assessment

(a)   **Employee ranking** - employees are ranked on the basis of their overall performance. This method is particularly prone to bias and its feedback value is practically nil. It does, however, have the advantage that it is simple to use.

(b)   **Rating scales** - under this method the individual's performance is usually broken down into several characteristics or areas of performance, such as

    (i)   quantity of acceptable work;
    (ii)   quality of the work;
    (iii)   understanding of the work;
    (iv)   initiative; and
    (v)   application.

The individual's performance in each of these areas is then rated. The rating scales used for this exercise vary. The simplest methods used are those where a score (eg out of 10) or a grade (eg A, B, C, D and E) is awarded. A commonly used method is the *Graphic Rating Scale*. In this method each characteristic is represented by a scale, which indicates the degree to which the individual possesses the characteristics. It is called 'graphic' because the scale visually graphs performance from one extreme to the other. The advantage of this method is that the person rating often finds it easier to relate to descriptions of performance rather than allocating a score or a grade.

The main problem associated with rating scales is the 'clustering' of results around the 'average' or 'satisfactory' level with little use made of the extreme levels. This negates the whole purpose of an appraisal scheme. To overcome this, some specialists replace terms like 'poor', 'satisfactory' or a numbering system with a series of statements. Each statement is tested for best match with the job-holder's performance.

Despite their popularity there are problems with the use of rating scales. They provide little information to the individual as to how to improve his/her performance. There is no identification of training needs so it is difficult to design training programmes on the results of rating scales. Frequently rating scales will induce resistance on the part of superiors doing the rating because they are required to assess on factors where they do not feel they have adequate information. For the person being assessed, rating scales can readily provoke resistance, defensiveness and hostility. Telling someone that they lack initiative or that their personality is unsatisfactory can strike at the heart of their self-identity and self-esteem.

(c)   **Checklists** - with this method the rater is provided with a list of statements relating to job performance. The rater must choose the most (and sometimes the least) appropriate statements for each individual.

(d)   **Critical incident method** - this is based on the assumption that performance is best assessed by focussing on critical incidents. An incident is considered critical when an employee has done, or failed to do, something that results in unusual success or unusual failure in some part of the job. Such a method involves spotting critical incidents and then recording them on a record sheet for each employee. While the method is useful in highlighting strengths and weaknesses in important areas, it relies upon critical incidents being identified by a superior. It can also be extremely time-consuming.

(e)   **Free reporting** - this method usually involves the completion of a report on each employee. It has the advantage of giving complete freedom in the assessment process. However, it does make comparisons difficult to draw between employees, and to a certain degree depends upon the standard of literacy of the assessor.

(f)   **Results oriented methods** - advocates of methods such as Management by Objectives claim their superiority in assessing performance. The method involves setting individual targets and identifying the actions necessary to achieve them. At the end of a period of time (usually six months), results are reviewed. Studies carried out at the General Electric Company in 1966 revealed that where targets had been jointly agreed between superior and subordinate, there was a distinct improvement in performance. Certain advantages are claimed for this method of appraisal; it is assumed that it strengthens superior and subordinate relationships and unlike other methods of appraisal has an achievement (and therefore motivation) factor. However, some writers feel that such a method leads to an over-reliance on results at the neglect of individual counselling. Another major criticism is that results may not reflect performance but may be the product of external factors outside the control of any individual.

3.3   Bias associated with rating scales

Bias can occur when using rating scales for a number of reasons:

Halo effect - this refers to the tendency of people to be rated similarly on all of the dimensions or characteristics being assessed. Thus if quality of work is rated as fair, then there will be a likelihood that all other factors in the assessment will be rated as fair. The term halo is used because all of the ratings fall within a narrow range or within a halo.

Recency bias - though appraisal should normally relate to a person's performance over the whole period since the last appraisal it is found that, in fact, assessors tend to be most strongly influenced by their most recent observations. Thus what is supposed to be an annual review is actually based on performance only in recent weeks.

Bias through the contrast effect - this can happen when appraising a number of subordinates within a short space of time. A manager's appraisal of an individual can be affected by the evaluation of the preceding subordinate. For example, a poor performance by one individual can make the next person to be appraised look excellent in comparison even though the performance is really only average.

Attribution errors - since we are appraising a person, good and bad performance will be explained in personal terms. Success or failure will be attributed to factors in the individual rather than any situational factors that have had major effects on performance.

3.4   Reducing rating errors

Though it is difficult to eliminate all sources of error it is possible to minimise them by applying the following general guidelines:

(a)   Superiors should be encouraged to observe performance regularly and keep records of their observations.

(b)   Rating scales should be constructed so that each dimension on the scale is designed to measure a **single**, **important** work activity or skill.

(c)   Appraisers should not be required to appraise a large number of subordinates at any one time.

(d)   Those rating should be made aware of the common sources of error and helped to avoid them.

(e)   There should be training in the effective use of performance appraisal techniques and in the conduct of an appraisal interview.

3.5   Behaviourally anchored rating scales (BARS)

These differ from the common rating scale in two major respects. First, rather than rate personality, BARS evaluate employees in terms of the extent to which they exhibit **effective behaviour** relevant to the specific demands of their jobs. Secondly, each item to be assessed is 'anchored' with specific examples of behaviour that correspond to good performance, average performance, poor performance and so on.

A simplified example is given below which relates to performance in communicating and co-operating with others in a production control environment.

Rating	Behaviour
Excellent	Reports, oral and written, are clear and well organised; speaks and writes clearly and precisely; all departments are continually informed; foresees conflict and handles with initiative.
Good	Conveys necessary information to other departments; does not check for misunderstandings, but willingly tries to correct errors.
Unacceptable	Does not co-operate with or inform other departments; refuses to improve on reports or to handle misunderstandings.

To arrive at the behavioural examples for all jobs in an organisation is a complex task, which involves the collection of much data and the discussion and participation both of management and of those who are to be appraised.

(a)   **Advantages of BARS**

- Rating errors can be reduced because the choices are clear and relevant.

- Performance appraisal can become more reliable, meaningful and valid for both the appraiser and the appraisee because of their participation in establishing the scheme.

- The degree of conflict and defensiveness is reduced because people are being assessed in terms of specific job behaviour and not their personalities.

- The feedback that is generated can clearly identify deficiencies and identify needs for training and development activities.

(b)   **Disadvantages of BARS**

- Decision-making, inventiveness and resolution of problems are difficult to incorporate.

- The time, effort and expense involved is considerable and the investment may only be worthwhile if there are a large number of people doing the same or similar jobs.

- Since BARS are concerned with **observable** behaviours then jobs with a high mental content such as a research scientist or a creative writer do not lend themselves to evaluation using BARS.

- There is an inevitable level of generalisation involved, so that BARS cannot hope to cover all examples of employee performance at all levels.

- Overall it is felt that BARS are superior to graphic rating scales and they are increasingly popular.

3.6   The appraisal interview

The interview is a common feature of many appraisal schemes and is normally used in conjunction with one of the rating methods discussed above. It is the vehicle for giving feedback to the employee where they can find out about their strengths and weaknesses and discuss what steps to take to improve future performance. As such it is a crucial part of the appraisal process. However, the fact that an interview takes place does not inevitably lead to desirable outcomes. It requires skill and insight on behalf of the appraiser to ensure that feedback is positive and the motivational effects are beneficial to the individual and the organisation.

The effectiveness of the interview will depend very much on the skill of the superior conducting the interview. It is important to listen to the subordinate and be prepared to change an evaluation in the light of new evidence. The emphasis should be on the future rather than the past, stressing opportunities rather than trying to apportion blame. There is a better chance of progress in an appraisal interview if the discussion centres on specific job behaviour or results rather than on general issues of personality or attitude. The focus should be on an employee's strengths so that they know those behaviours which they should maintain and develop as well as where there are weaknesses to be remedied.

A properly conducted appraisal interview can have a major effect on an individual's self-appraisal and it is this self-appraisal which will be the main determinant in the continuation of excellent performance and the willingness to improve and develop in those areas where necessary.

However, problems can readily arise. The person being assessed will experience a conflict between presenting themselves in the best possible light to get the best evaluation and being frank and open about weaknesses to gain help and coaching to deal with difficulties. Appraisal interviews can readily lead to defensive reactions to critical statements. People feel threatened and self-esteem is seen as being under attack. This is common where pay discussions and appraisal are merged.

4   EFFECTIVE STAFF APPRAISAL

4.1   The criteria of effectiveness

A key issue in performance appraisal is determining what constitute valid criteria or measures of effective performance. The problem is made more difficult because almost all jobs have many dimensions so that performance appraisal must employ multiple criteria or measures of effectiveness in order to accurately reflect the actual job performance of the employee.

Although it is impossible to identify any universal measures of performance that are applicable to all jobs, it is possible to specify a number of characteristics that a criterion of job performance should possess if it is to be useful for performance appraisal:

(a)   A good criterion should be capable of being measured reliably. The concept of reliability of measurement has two components. Firstly, stability, which means that measures taken at different times should yield the same results. The second is consistency, which means that if different people use the criterion, or a different form of measurement is used, the results should still be more or less the same.

(b)   A good criterion should be capable of differentiating among individuals according to their performance. If everyone is rated the same the exercise rapidly becomes pointless.

(c)   A good criterion should be capable of being influenced by the job-holder. If a person is to improve performance after appraisal then it must be about matters over which the individual has discretionary control.

(d)   A good criterion should be acceptable to those individuals whose performance is being assessed. It is important that people feel that their performance is being measured against criteria that are fair and accurate.

A key issue that has to do with the criteria of effectiveness is the question of whether they should focus on the activities (tasks) of the job-holder or the results (objectives) achieved. For example, a salesman might be assessed in terms of activities eg, number of cold calls or speed of dealing with complaints or in terms of results eg, total sales volume or number of new customers. Measures of results pay no attention to how results were achieved.

There are advantages and disadvantages of using either results or activities as criteria. Appraisal based on results has the advantage of encouraging and rewarding the results desired by the organisation. However, it has the disadvantage that it might encourage people to break rules or go against company policy to get the desired results. It may lead to frustration if the failure to achieve results is due to factors beyond the control of the individual. Assessment in terms of results also has the shortcoming that it does not generate information about how the person is doing the job and hence has limited value in suggesting ways of improving performance.

A major advantage of appraising in terms of activities is that it helps in generating information that can help in the training and development of poor performers. However, it may only encourage people to concentrate on their activities at the expense of results achieved. This can result in excessive bureaucratic emphasis on the means and procedures employed rather than on the accomplishments and results. There are then problems in incorporating the successful non-conformist into the appraisal system.

An effective appraisal system needs to have a balance of both measures of results and measures of activities.

4.2   The negative effects of appraisal

There have been studies on the effects of appraisal, which show some negative effects eg:

*   criticism had a negative effect on goal achievement;

*   subordinates generally reacted defensively to criticism during appraisal interviews;

*   inferior performance resulted from defensive reactions to criticism;

*   repeated criticism had the worst effect on subsequent performance of individuals who had little self confidence.

4.3   Barriers to effective appraisal

Too often appraisal is seen as a personal criticism session, and therefore staff become very suspicious and uncooperative as it may announce financial disadvantage or lost promotion opportunity. The superior might show bias towards certain employees or may be reluctant to 'play God' with the subordinate's future.

Any appraisal scheme is doomed to failure and will cause frustration among the staff if:

*   the top management does not give the appraisal system continuous support;

- the appraisal procedures are not made clear to everybody;

- the scheme does not get full support at all management levels. As wide a range of staff as possible should be involved in the formulation of the scheme;

- potential appraisers are not given experience of interviewing before they are involved in appraisals. Too often a manager has not been trained in this field and his valuations simply reflect his own temperament;

- interviews designed to improve performance are often trying to weigh up at the same time salary and promotion issues;

- fear, ignorance, lack of involvement and the suspicion of unfairness can create open hostility. A scheme should be seen to be fair, with an appeals procedure for those who consider themselves unfairly treated;

- the facts are not recorded;

- uncontrollable factors are introduced; and

- it is not felt to be taken seriously.

4.4   Problems with appraisal systems

Despite the growing popularity of performance appraisal schemes in many organisations, several problems have been revealed and various criticisms have been made of appraisal as a technique. The main problems and criticisms are as follows:

(a)   Many organisations seek too many objectives with their appraisal schemes. To try to use them to assess potential, to motivate employees, to review salaries, to control training etc is asking too much of such schemes.

(b)   Many appraisal schemes generate a mass of paperwork, which is wasteful of management time and costly to administer.

(c)   Some studies have revealed a lack of commitment to such schemes by top management which means that the schemes are not properly implemented. This often means a lack of follow up to appraisal so that adequate provision for increased training or new levels of pay has not been made.

(d)   Assessments made in appraisals are very prone to errors of judgement because of subjectivity, prejudice, inappropriate criteria, pressures of time etc.

(e)   Frequently there is little attention given to the training of people to carry out appraisals.

(f)   In some organisations appraisal becomes little more than an annual ritual with little concern for its consequences and even less concern for critically reviewing the process itself.

(g)   The criticism of 'recency' is often made. Superiors may appraise subordinates only in terms of recollections of events immediately preceding the appraisal.

(h)   Employee resistance to appraisal is not uncommon. This is particularly noticeable when a scheme has been introduced without full consultation with all the interested parties.

Conclusion   Despite these criticisms, appraisal is becoming more widespread and is seen as an important part of staff relationships.

5   RELATIONSHIP BETWEEN APPRAISAL AND THE REWARD SYSTEM

5.1   Types of reward

Reward refers to all forms of financial returns and tangible services and benefits employees receive as part of an employment relationship. The three main objectives of reward management are:

- to attract and retain suitable employees;
- to maintain or improve levels of employee performance; and
- to comply with employment legislation and regulations.

The types of reward used in an organisation will result from decisions made concerning the nature of the effort in relation to the reward.

5.2   Pay and performance

Relating pay to performance comes from the theories of motivation. The 'need' theories emphasise what motivates people, rather than how people are motivated. Maslow argued that higher order needs become progressively more important as lower order needs are satisfied. Herzberg found that pay becomes significant as a source of satisfaction when it is seen as a form of recognition or reward.

An incentive scheme ties pay directly to performance. It can be tied to the performance of an individual or a team of employees. The scheme includes the following performance-related pay:

- piecework - or payment by results - is a system where rewards are related to the pace of work or effort. The faster the employee works, the higher the output and the greater the reward;

- bonus schemes; and

- commission - this a reward paid on the performance of an individual, typically to salaried staff in sales functions, where the commission earned is a proportion of total sales.

Conclusion   Appraisals should be fair, consistent and disciplined in approach, relying more on objective than subjective input and aiming to help the appraisee consider future planning. As an examination area the subject of appraisal should not be viewed in isolation because it can also be used in answers to questions on motivation, reorganisation and payment schemes.

5.3   Activity

If an appraisal session does not include a discussion on salary, then what is its relevance?

5.4   Activity solution

Current practice suggests that involving pay matters in appraisal sessions inhibits discussion on other aspects. The appraisee is reluctant to be open in case it affects the salary award and will react defensively to criticism

Without pay discussions, the appraisal session can fulfil its key purpose of staff counselling and development. This would involve such matters as:

(a)   Feedback on performance and problems encountered;
(b)   Career development;
(c)   Identifying job interests and likely development areas;

(d)   Define performance targets;

(e)   Review promotability;

(f)   Enable individuals to appreciate where their jobs fit in the overall company scheme.

6   SELF TEST QUESTIONS

6.1   What can performance appraisal data be used for? (1.3)

6.2   Give three examples where performance appraisal is a vital management tool (1.5)

6.3   Identify the stages in the performance appraisal process (2.1)

6.4   What is the main problem associated with rating scales? (3.2)

6.5   What does the acronym BARS stand for? (3.5)

6.6   Outline a problem associated with appraisal interviews. (3.6)

7   EXAMINATION TYPE QUESTION

7.1   Appraisal systems

You have been asked to write a report on performance appraisal systems and in it you have been asked to describe the following:

Required:

(a)   The purpose of an appraisal system.   **(5 marks)**

(b)   The objectives of appraisals from the viewpoint of:

        (i)   The individual   **(5 marks)**
        (ii)   The organisation   **(5 marks)**

(c)   The barriers to effective appraisal   **(10 marks)**
                                                                         (Total: 25 marks)

8   ANSWER TO EXAMINATION TYPE QUESTION

8.1   Appraisal systems

Report on Performance Appraisal Systems

For the attention of Accounts Manager

June 20X9

1.   **Terms of reference**

        This report was requested to provide the following information:

        (a)   The purpose of an appraisal system.
        (b)   The objectives of appraisals from the viewpoint of:
                (i)   The individual
                (ii)   The organisation
        (c)   The barriers to effective appraisal

2.   **The purpose of an appraisal system**

The general purpose of any assessment or appraisal is to improve the efficiency of the organisation by ensuring that the individual employees are performing to the best of their ability and developing their potential for improvement. It enables a picture to be drawn up of the human 'stock' of an organisation - its strengths and weaknesses, enabling more effective personnel planning.

Staff appraisal is a procedure where the managers or supervisors in an organisation discuss the work of their subordinates. They see each person individually and consider the progress they have been making in their job, their strengths and weaknesses and their future needs as regards training and development and the employee's potential for promotion.

The purpose therefore is:

*   to assess the level of reward payable for an individual's efforts by measuring the extent to which the individual may be awarded a salary or pay increase compared with his or her peers.

*   to review the individual's performance, identify training needs and plan follow-up training and development. By encouraging two-way communication, it permits an evaluation of a subordinate's strengths and weaknesses and the reasons for them. Thus, for example, if a subordinate's failure to perform is due to some failure in the work system, corrective action can be taken quickly. This will help the individual to do his or her job better and assist the organisation to achieve its objectives.

*   to review the individual's potential by attempting to predict the type and level of work that the individual is likely to be capable of in the future. At the organisational level, this permits career and succession planning. At the individual level, it permits superior and subordinate to assess the most effective development plans for the subordinate.

3.   **The objectives of appraisals from the viewpoint of the individual**

An appraisal is a process where the progress, performance, results and sometimes personality of an employee are reviewed and assessed by his or her immediate superior. The objectives of an appraisal from the individual's point of view include the following:

*   it compares the individual's performance against a set and established standard;

*   it identifies work of particular merit done during the review period;

*   it provides a basis for remuneration

*   it establishes what the individual has to do, regarding the objectives of the organisation;

*   it determines the future employment of the individual eg, to remain in the same job, be transferred, promoted or retired early.

*   it determines whether the individual is in a job where proper use is being made of his or her skills and talents;

*   it establishes key results which the individual needs to achieve in work within a set period of time

*   it identifies training and development needs

4.   **The objectives of appraisals from the viewpoint of the organisation**

An appraisal system is used by the organisation to review and change, to inform and monitor and to examine and evaluate employees. The objectives from the organisation's point of view include the following:

- it monitors human resource selection processes against results;

- it identifies candidates for promotion, early retirement etc;

- it helps to identify and provide a record of any special difficulties/hazards surrounding the job, perhaps not previously realised;

- it identifies areas for improvement;

- it provides a basis for human resource planning;

- it helps formulate the training plan;

- it improves communication between managers and the managed where the organisation adopts the joint problem solving approach in their appraisal system

5.   **The barriers to effective appraisal**

There have been studies on the effects of performance appraisal that show some negative effects eg:

- criticism had a negative effect on goal achievement;

- subordinates generally reacted defensively to criticism during appraisal interviews;

- inferior performance resulted from defensive reactions to criticism;

- repeated criticism had the worst effect on subsequent performance of individuals who had little self confidence.

Too often appraisal is taken as a personal criticism session, and therefore staff become very suspicious and uncooperative as it may announce financial disadvantage or lost promotion opportunity. The superior might show bias towards certain employees or may be reluctant to 'play God' with the subordinate's future. Since its very basis is face to face meetings, it is subject to particular barriers, and may be seen as:

- confrontational because of a lack of agreement on performance, badly explained or subjective feedback performance based on recent events or disagreement on longer term activities;

- judgmental - where appraisal is seen as a one sided process based entirely on the manager's perspective;

- an informal, loosely constructed and badly managed conversation without purpose;

- a bureaucratic system based on forms, devised solely to satisfy the organisation's personnel department, which make no attempt to identify individual and organisation performance and improvement;

- unfinished business and not part of a continuing process of performance management;

- an annual event which sets targets that quickly become out of date.

14 AUTHORITY, RESPONSIBILITY, POWER AND DELEGATION

CONTEXT & LEARNING OUTCOMES

Syllabus area 11(iv) • The concepts of power, authority, responsibility and delegation and their application to organisational relationships

One of Fayol's principles of management is authority and responsibility. He proposed that the holder of an office should have enough authority to carry out all the responsibilities assigned to him. The organisational chart shows the formal relationships which exist between positions, indicating positional authority, where those people occupying positions at upper levels in the hierarchy have more power and exercise more control than those at the lower levels. Responsibility relationships can be traced by following those same lines upwards.

Authority and responsibility go together but neither can be effective without the art of delegation. You would not expect the managing director to produce a detailed business plan himself, for he or she would probably not be aware of the detail. It is usual for this work to be allocated to, say, the finance director who in turn would delegate the work to perhaps the head of the management accounts section who may again delegate the detailed work to the group responsible. You would find that certain individuals within the organisation would spend most of their time during a particular part of the financial year assembling the information. They have been delegated to do this work and consequently have become experts at preparing it.

When you have studied this chapter you should be able to:

- Explain the concepts of authority, power, responsibility and delegation
- Analyse the relationships between managers and subordinates

1 AUTHORITY AND RESPONSIBILITY

1.1 Introduction

The way that an organisation functions will not just be determined by the design of the structure, but how power, authority and delegation operate to ensure that decisions are made and tasks are completed. The organisation structures will determine where the power lies for example centralised structures maintain the power base at the corporate centre. However, power, authority and the nature of delegation are complex considerations for an organisation and cannot be viewed purely from a structural perspective.

1.2 Definitions

Fayol defined authority as:

Definition 'the right to give orders and the power to exact obedience'.

He differentiated between official authority which 'derives from office' and personal authority which is 'compounded of intelligence, experience, moral worth, ability to lead and past services'.

McGivering, while Reader in Organisational Behaviour at Bradford University, defined the terms power, authority, delegation and responsibility in the following ways:

(a) Power is the ability to exert a positive influence over objects, persons or situations.

(b) Authority is the right to exercise power.

(c)   Delegation is the act by which a person or group of persons possessing authority transfers part of that authority to a subordinate person or group.

(d)   Responsibility. The term is also used to mean a duty or activity assigned to a given position or (in the plural) the aggregate of such duties.

(e)   Accountability refers to the fact that each person, who is given authority must recognise that the position above them, will evaluate the quality of their performance.

It will be recalled that the classical approach to organisation placed great emphasis upon the need to define clearly a manager's responsibilities and the fact that these should be committed to written schedules to show how they were connected with authority and duties.

In stressing this inter-relationship McGivering states:

'It is axiomatic in organisational processes that responsibility should be equal to authority, for power without corresponding responsibility is likely to lead to behaviour uncontrolled by the organisation and hence to unintended and probably undesirable consequences. Although it is possible to delegate both duties and the necessary authority, it is not possible to delegate responsibility. That is to say, the superior is always responsible for the actions of his subordinates and cannot escape this responsibility by delegation.'

Not every theorist or practitioner would agree with this statement but perhaps the words of ex-President Truman, 'the buck stops here', express the majority opinion.

1.3   Nature of authority

Authority can be defined as the right that an individual has to require certain actions of others ie, it is the right to use power. It is necessary to distinguish between authority and power. Authority in an organisation is the right in a position to exercise discretion in making decisions affecting others. As such, it is one type of power. Power is a broader concept, which can be defined as the ability to influence the actions of others. So, it is quite possible to have authority without power (eg, a weak and ineffective supervisor) or power without authority (eg, a trade union shop steward). Authority can arise from any of three main sources:

(a)   *formal* - where the organisation bestows the authority upon the individual by means of his job title and the reporting relationships specified;

(b)   *technical* - where the authority arises due to personal skills or special knowledge or training. Here the authority exists only within the scope of that special knowledge or skill;

(c)   *personal, informal* - this authority is not recognised in any organisation chart. It exists because, without regard to the position he holds, the person is accepted as being particularly respected, or an elder citizen or is simply popular and recognised by his colleagues as being efficient.

Administrative organisation creates superior/subordinate relationships and it is vital that these are properly defined and clearly understood. The right to use power should be sufficient to enable the proper discharge of duties assigned and the person should be held accountable for the proper use of power.

Organisations differ in the extent to which authority is relied upon as a means of achieving control or motivation. In the authoritarian or classical approach, great emphasis is placed upon formal relationships where communication upwards to the superior is discouraged; orders are given and obeyed, sometimes without question. Initiative and personal involvement with the allocated tasks are minimised. Current thinking favours a relationship in which the exercise of authority between a superior and his subordinate is replaced by personal influence through *good leadership*.

1.4   Responsibility

The *Oxford English Dictionary* defines responsible as 'liable to be called to account, answerable'. The definition goes further by describing the responsible individual as one who is 'morally accountable for actions, capable of rational conduct, of good credit or position or repute, respectable, and apparently trustworthy'. From this, therefore, responsibility is 'in charge of something for which one is accountable'.

Responsibility can also be defined as 'the obligation to use delegated powers', and the late Douglas McGregor in his book *The Professional Manager* points out that there is often a reluctance on the part of managers to use powers delegated to them. He believed that this is due to the authority of a manager being circumscribed in many ways. He or she cannot discipline or dismiss a subordinate without following an elaborate set of formal procedures. Even then, there is a risk that a strike will occur or that the action will be overruled either by a superior or by an arbitrator.

The union contract is seen as only one of many restraints on managerial authority; others include budgeting for capital and revenue expenditure, cost control, personnel policies and legal restrictions on his freedom of action. In addition, managers know that they will be judged by their ability to get on with people, which often means playing a cautious political game, rather than utilising the power the position seems to carry.

Many would assert that a manager has but one responsibility - to contribute to the economic performance of the enterprise. But there is now a strongly held view that management has major social responsibilities in addition to purely economic ones. Such responsibilities include those to employees, the local community, the government, education and charities.

On the one hand, the manager is respected and admired and he enjoys high status, but on the other he or she is feared and under constant suspicion of manipulating people (employees, customers, shareholders and the government) for personal power or economic gain.

The chief executive is unlikely to have responsibilities for the direct operation of anything, as his time will be spent on matters of company policy, planning, assessing company performance and analysing the causes of inadequate performance. At a lower level, managers must demonstrate their competence as operating managers, dealing successfully with day to day problems; less of their time will be available for looking into an uncertain future.

1.5   Authority and accountability

As we have already noted, authority is the right or power to make decisions or give instructions or orders. Accountability is the obligation to give an account of the stewardship of the authority given, to a superior. Such superiors in turn are accountable to their superiors. This reporting, or accounting chain is what Fayol refers to as the scalar chain. Some contemporary writers refer to it as the job task pyramid.

Authority and accountability go hand in hand. A fair system means that every manager or supervisor should be answerable for his or her actions. Just because a manager delegates a job to someone else, it does not mean the manager ceases to be accountable for the job being carried out. A manager is still accountable directly to higher or other authority for authority delegated and for tasks assigned to their direct reports.

In some organisations, certain employees are reluctant to be responsible and to account to someone is undoubtedly the cause of much organisational ineffectiveness and friction.

Many employee relations issues have been caused by the refusal of one or both sides to accept full responsibility for performing their assignments.

1.6   Balance of authority, power, responsibility and accountability

Authority, power, responsibility and accountability for every position and employee in the organisation must be balanced if a stable equilibrium is to be achieved and maintained.

The principal problem that exists in organisations is that employees at all levels may try to maximise their own authority and power. At the same time they may try to minimise their own responsibility and accountability. Similarly, managers may attempt to maximise the responsibility and accountability of their staff, while minimising the amount of authority and power delegated to their subordinates.

The result, in organisations where individuals are often seeking what they perceive to be their personal best interest is to produce instability, in terms of the authority-power-responsibility-accountability relationship. It is one of management's tasks to ensure employees accept the balance between these four factors.

The organisation structure provides management with the tool to make these factors balance. A manager may structure authority, power, responsibility and accountability in the organisation through the process of delegating, assigning tasks and exacting accountability.

2   POWER

2.1   Types of power

The essence of power is that the persons exercising power are enabled to assume that power by their followers. So, although a person may not have any formal authority, he or she is able to assume power over others through the willingness of those to act as followers. Conversely, a manager may have formal authority but having lost the respect of his/her staff is unable to exercise power or influence over them. There are a number of different types of power, some personal and some positional:

(a)   **Reward power** - a person has power over another because he or she can mediate rewards such as promotions, recommendations or answers to questions.

(b)   **Coercive power** - this enables a person to mediate punishments for others: for example, to dismiss, suspend, reprimand them, or make them carry out unpleasant tasks.

Reward power and coercive power are similar but limited in application because they do not extend beyond the limits of the reward or punishment, which can be mediated. Such power is often diminished by a failure to exercise it.

(c)   **Referent power** - is based upon the identification with the person who has the resources, or the desire to be like that person. It could be regarded as 'imitative' power, which is often seen in the way children imitate their parents. It is not necessarily connected to the reward power or coercive power that parents may have over their children.

Psychologists believe that referent power is perhaps the most extensive since it can be exercised when the holder is not present or has no intention of exercising his influence.

(d)   **Expert power** - is based upon one person perceiving that the other person has expert knowledge of a given subject and is a recognised authority in a given situation; such knowledge may be theoretical but is more likely to be practical in its application.

(e)   **Legitimate power** - is based on agreement and commonly held values which allow one person to have power over another person: for example, an older person, or one who has longer service or is seen to be charismatic.

Psychologists believe that power is effective only when it is held in balance; as soon as power is used it gets out of balance because the person against whom it is used automatically resorts to some activity to try to correct the imbalance. This can occur through the coalition of weaker members as a defensive measure against authority or by a search for alternative relationships.

Power can therefore arise from personal characteristics, unrecognised by the organisation, but operating through the consent of followers.

2.2   Legitimacy

Weber's contribution to the study of the organisation was his interpretation of legitimacy. He identified two media by which commands are obeyed:

(i)   *power*, the ability to force people to obey, regardless of their resistance;

(ii)   *authority*, where orders are voluntarily obeyed by those receiving them, and subordinates accept the ideas and directives from above because they are legitimate.

Weber went on to stress the way authority was legitimised.   He identified three types of administrative apparatus or organisation - charismatic, traditional and rational-legal.

(i)   *Charismatic leadership* - Here the individual has some special quality of personality. Classic entrepreneurs such as Sir Francis Drake, Lord Nuffield and Henry Ford, and even religious leaders such as John Wesley, all had this charisma.   Structure and commands depend upon such inspiration. However, unless the leader has created an organisation that can survive without his physical presence, an inbuilt instability exists. When the leader leaves or is lost, there is jockeying for position, leading to schism and eventually giving way to a more traditional or legalistic organisation.

(ii)   *Traditional* - This authority is based upon custom and practice. Status is largely inherited - eg, father to son, with a distinctly patriarchal attitude towards officials and subordinates. Alternatively there is a feudal form, where loyalty to the leader is traditional but officials have a measure of independence of action. Although rooted deep in history, both types of traditional leadership still exist today.

(iii)   *The rational-legal* - This is Weber's classic bureaucracy. It is rational because its means are expressly designed to achieve certain goals with maximum efficiency. It is legal because authority is exercised by means of a system of rules and procedures through the office that the individual occupies. Weber's characterisation is the most technically efficient form of organisation possible, identified with precision, speed, knowledge, continuity, discretion, unity, strict subordination and minimisation of friction and material and personal costs.

2.3   Activity

Name two modern charismatic leaders - one international and one national.

2.4   Activity solution

There are many to choose from but examples might include Nelson Mandela and Richard Branson.

2.5   Status

There are many definitions of status.

(a)   A position in a social system.
(b)   Evaluation of a position, person or group on a scale of relative esteem.
(c)   Worth of an individual is estimated by a group or class of persons.

Status, like power, is conferred by others though it may be inferred from a person's behaviour; it is not a thing that a person possesses on his own.

Status may derive from:

(a)   position in an organisation;

(b)   knowledge and education;

(c)   wealth, or lack of it;

(d)   membership of an exclusive club or institute;

(e)   conditions of employment;

(f)   birth eg, hereditary titles;

(g)   association with other persons eg, wives tend to be accorded the status of their husband (particularly in the armed forces);

(h)   social background.

As far as business is concerned, status is an important part of the reward system designed to motivate people; the reward system generally coincides with the status system.   Where such correlation is absent there is likely to be dissatisfaction shown by those whose rewards are not commensurate with their status.   Status symbols, though often frowned upon if carried to excess, (perhaps as in the Civil Service) serve a useful purpose since their absence can create uncertainty and give rise to status ambiguity.   The more casual the attitude to status the more conflict is to be expected; most people place some emphasis upon it and few can ignore it altogether.

2.6   Negative power

If power is used contrary to accepted practice or outside the accepted boundaries, the power is seen as disruptive and illegitimate.   This can be called a negative use of power.   This type of power has the capacity to stop things happening, to delay them, to distort or disrupt.   An example is employees who give information to their managers on the basis that they only let them see what they want them to see.   Negative power does not operate all of the time, but often at times of low morale, irritation, stress or frustration at the failure of other influence attempts.

The use of negative power breeds lack of trust by superior for the subordinate.   The superior will then start checking procedures and using alternative information channels to thwart the use of negative power.   This may be seen by the subordinate as a diminution of his job and further provocation to activate his negative power.

3   DELEGATION

3.1   Reasons for delegating

Responsibility, authority and delegation are three inter-related terms. Responsibility cannot exist without authority and vice versa. By delegating authority to a particular individual, responsibility is usually automatically delegated.   We have already looked briefly at delegation and defined it as giving 'someone else the freedom and authority to do a job for which you are accountable'.

Delegation is an important aspect of organisation and effective management. Without delegation formal organisations could not exist.   Without delegation the chief executive would be responsible for everything and would be the only person with the authority to do anything; consequently nothing much would ever get done. Because management is the act of getting things done (accomplishing objectives) through the work of other people, it is obvious that management could not succeed without delegation. Of course, management could delegate completely the tasks, and the associated authority for planning, co-ordinating, controlling, organising and monitoring; to do so would be to abdicate the management role. Of necessity, however, the manager has to give some of the work to subordinates.

The main reasons for delegating authority are:

(i)   *Training* - Training by doing is acknowledged to be a very effective method. By delegating more and more and further and further down the line, and by insisting on full briefing and consultation between managers and subordinates, training becomes not a special process to be done at rare intervals, but a general day-to-day activity.

(ii)   *Management succession* - Gives others a chance of acclimatisation. They not only need to get to know the routine but also to accustom themselves to the advantages and disadvantages of advancement.

(iii)   *Performance evaluation* - The virtue of gradually getting used to exercising authority is that a subordinate can be tested under actual conditions, before being permanently promoted. By regularly ensuring a free flow of delegation, there will be continuous trying and testing of persons, accepted as a matter of routine.

(iv)   *Relief of stress* - Not just in the self-interest of managers is delegation valuable; it relieves pressure on them but its other advantages weigh heavier.

(v)   *Job satisfaction* - The most valuable advantage of delegation is job satisfaction for subordinates. By ensuring that the mix of delegation is appropriate, some of the interesting jobs will be delegated and not only the tedium. By increasing employees' enjoyment in their jobs, employers can encourage better work.

3.2   Activity

Can you list some more reasons for delegating authority?

3.3   Activity solution

More reasons for delegation include:

(i)   Managers can be relieved of less important or less immediate responsibilities;

(ii)   It enables decisions to be taken nearer to the point of impact and without the delays caused by reference upwards;

(iii)   It gives organisations a chance to meet changing conditions more flexibly;

(iv)   Makes subordinate's job more interesting;

(v)   Allows career development;

(vi)   Brings together skills and ideas;

(vii)   Team aspect is motivational;

(viii)   Allows performance appraisal.

3.4   Process of delegation

Delegation embraces both authority and responsibility. Authority can be delegated readily, but many problems of delegation stem from failure to provide the necessary information and resources in order to achieve expected results, or from failure to delegate sufficient authority for subordinates to fulfil their responsibilities. Delegation is a process where a manager or supervisor:

- determines the results expected;
- allocates duties to subordinates;
- grants them authority to enable those duties to be carried out;
- holds them responsible for the completion of the work and achievement of results.

To delegate effectively managers must:

(a)   Define the limits of authority delegated to their subordinates.

(b)   Satisfy themselves that the subordinate is competent to exercise that authority.

(c)   Discipline themselves to permit the subordinate the full use of that authority without constant checks and interference.

Rosemary Stewart in her book *Managers and their Jobs* stated that there are three questions that a manager should ask about any of his activities.

(a)   Should it be done at all?

(b)   If so, when should it be done?

(c)   Should it be delegated?

Most frequently in her opinion, based on specified research, the manager will find some of his work ought to have been delegated. One of the conclusions at the end of her book is that few managers will have sufficient time unless they know how to delegate. They should have taught their subordinates what they can do without reference to the manager, what things they should tell the managers for information, when the subordinates should consult managers and at what times managers are available for discussion.

There are immense differences between the processes of delegation employed in different organisations; you can find one firm where delegation flows freely and informally and another where it is only reluctantly employed. However, there is one feature that is common to almost all variants and that is its direction. It is almost always downwards.

At one extreme we could have what could be called 'off-hand' delegation, or casually emptying one's 'in basket' into the basket of a subordinate. As a contrast we have thorough delegation that involves the senior in carefully briefing the junior. Although the careless style was quoted as an extreme example, it is not as rare as it should be.

3.5   The manner of delegation

There is no 'correct procedure' for delegation, and even if there were you would not become a good delegator by learning it. 'It is not what you do, it is the way that you do it.' Let us take as examples different manners of delegation.

(i)   *By abdication* - At one extreme, it is not uncommon to leave everything to a junior, which is a very crude and usually ineffective method.

(ii)   *According to custom and practice* - In some organisations it is customary to have work done by the age-old system whereby precedent rules. This method scarcely sounds progressive but it is common enough in the bureaucracies both of the Civil Service and major companies.

(iii)   *By explanation* - This more progressive way involves the manager in 'briefing' his subordinate along the lines of how the task should be done, without explaining too much because that could verge on actually doing the job. This is one of those cases when explanation is wanted - not too little and not too much - a fine balance that requires the art of management.

(iv)   *By consultation* - Prior consultation was once quite novel in manager/union relations and also between managers and subordinates, but nowadays prior consultation is considered to be important and very effective. Another thing that has been realised by some, though not admitted by all, is that the middle grades of worker are immensely powerful; by contributing or withholding their co-operation they make the success of their seniors by no means automatic.

Conclusion   Delegation is one of the main functions of effective management. In essence, delegation is the process whereby a manager assigns part of his authority to a subordinate to fulfil those duties.

3.6   Chain of delegation

Delegation is associated with the organisation structure, authority and responsibility. At the top of a typical organisation chart is generally the managing director but we must realise that in most situations, he or she cannot take all the decisions and do all the work. However, subordinates cannot do the work without the necessary authority and power. The chain of delegation in an organisation begins with the shareholders and ends with the operatives who are responsible for the performance of various tasks. This chain is illustrated below with the arrows down showing the delegation and the arrows up showing accountability.

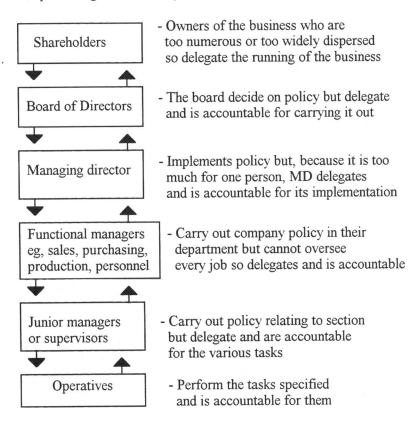

3.7   Problems with delegation

Many managers are reluctant to delegate, preferring to deal with routine matters themselves in addition to the more major aspects of their duties. There are several reasons for this:

- seniors often believe that their subordinates are not able or experienced enough to perform the tasks;
- some managers believe that doing routine tasks enables them to keep in touch with what is happening in the other areas of their department;
- where a manager feels insecure he or she will invariably be reluctant to pass any authority to a subordinate.

Other problems with delegation include:

- failure to delegate sufficient authority;
- need for higher managerial skill;
- loss of direct control;
- danger of a less satisfactory outcome/lower productivity;
- fear of losing one's job to a good subordinate;
- boss is secure and comfortable in his old job;
- subordinate may become impatient for monetary recognition;
- doubt over what to delegate and what to keep;
- failure to monitor and counsel.

Conclusion   Remember - Authority is the right to use power and delegation is the act by which a person transfers part of their authority to a subordinate person.

4   METHODS OF INFLUENCE

4.1   Ways to influence

Influence can be defined as:

Definition   Any changes in behaviour of a person or group due to anticipation of the response of others

Behaviour changes can be caused either by ideas, or by some other inanimate factor eg, a change in the weather may influence someone to abandon a picnic. However, influence systems typically refer to situations where behavioural changes take place as a result of relationships among people.

You will often see the term influence used in conjunction with power and authority, with influence covering those ways of influencing behaviour that cannot be termed wither power or authority. A range of ways to influence behaviour is outlined below:

- **Emulation** - although it requires no direct contact between individuals, it is a powerful influence on behaviour. People often pick out certain behaviour patterns and strive to equal or surpass them. In organisations, participants are aware of the behavioural patterns of co-workers and various executives. Certain individuals become 'models' with their behaviour patterns being adopted by others, hoping to attain similar success

- **Suggestion** - is an explicit attempt to influence behaviour by presenting an idea or advocating a particular course of action. Typically this mode is used when several alternative behaviour patterns for individuals or groups are acceptable and the person influencing is merely suggesting a preferred pattern. If this tolerance for different behaviour were not present, the influencer would use some other mode such as persuasion or even coercion.

  Persuasion - implies urging and the use of some inducement in order to evoke the desired response. It involves more pressure than a mere suggestion but falls short of the type of force implied by the term coercion.

  Coercion - involves forcible constraint, which may include physical pressure (arm-twisting). In organisations, salaries and / or promotions can be used to constrain or influence behaviour. In many cases the threat of dismissal is also a powerful influencer.

4.2   Relation to power sources

The types of power described earlier allow individuals various ways to exercise the power. Influence can be divided into two types; the overt and the unseen. Handy has related these two types of influence to sources of power.

Power source	Physical	Resource	Position	Expert	Personal
Overt methods of influence	Force	Exchange	Exchange rules and procedures		Persuasion
Unseen methods of influence				Ecology	Magnetism

- **Force** - individual instances of force can be found in business or government organisations but they are rare, are usually related to a particular individual, and tend to be short-lived. Economic force, such as a long dole queue and poor profits, is close to Etzioni's coercion. Whatever the source of the force, the long-term results are universally acknowledged to be undesirable. Coerced labour will eventually revolt, will not work as efficiently as required, and will always look for conflict with management. It is certainly not the situation whereby trust can develop.

- **Exchange, bargaining, cajoling or even bribery** - can follow from any power source depending on what is offered, but resource and position powers are the most frequent bases. If the exchange is going to work, then A has to offer something that B wants, and the payment has to be worth the effort or expenditure. Frequently, the recipients' expectations, such as union wage demands are totally unrealistic and doomed to disappointment. Ideally, both parties should trust one another, and receive profit from it. For example, management may offer employees a pay rise in exchange for more flexible working practices. Once the reward has been agreed and paid, the exchange is complete, and the continuance of the behaviour needs to be enforced by the threat of withdrawal of the reward.

- **Rules and procedures** - perhaps the most dominant form of influence in our society is exerted through rules and procedures. If an organisation is going to use rules and procedures to influence they must ensure there is the perceived right to institute the rules and procedures (McGivering) and the means and will to enforce them ie, the appropriate power base. Rules can be used in a positive way to protect liberty and approve actions.

  Without these the influence attempt will fail. Rules and negotiations, therefore, derive largely from position power, backed by resource power. Experts can also exert influence through rules and procedures.

  It has been argued that one way to increase your power in an organisation is to circumscribe your opponent with rules and regulations whilst retaining the maximum degree of uncertainty relating to your own position. This is essentially how the French protect their own organisations from competition outside France (eg, English meat imports) and even outside the community (consumer goods from Japan).

- **Persuasion** - this method relies on logic, the power of argument and the evidence of the facts. It is the preferred method of influence of most people and is usually the method of first resource. In practice, it nearly always gets contaminated by one of the other methods. For example a manager who genuinely attempts to reason with a member of staff may not be seen as persuading but really a subtle form of enforcement of rules and procedures. Persuasion frequently has more power if the argument is presented in a charismatic manner, or the source of backup information is highly credible.

- **Ecology and physical environment** - embraces the relationship between the organisation and the individual. All behaviour takes place in an environment, and therefore the influence it has on individuals needs to be taken account of. For example dangerous surroundings increase tension and lower productivity. To adjust the environment in order to remove constraints or facilitate some aspects of behaviour is indirect influence.

- **Magnetism** - this can arise from charisma, but Handy prefers to note the impact of trust or respect, and the conviction that a leader has ability, high principles, or demonstrates loyalty to us. Empathy is also another aspect of magnetism, the sharing of convictions or views. Usually, magnetism stems from particular sources of power, usually personal or expert, and as such it is only as effective as its sources. To increase it, we must work on those sources, to maintain it we must be careful to nourish those sources, for some of them, such as trust, are very fragile indeed.

5   SELF TEST QUESTIONS

5.1   Distinguish between reward power, coercive power, referent power, expert power and legitimate power. (1.2)

5.2   Briefly describe the three main sources of authority. (1.3)

5.3   Outline the five different types of power. (2.1)

5.4   Identify Weber's three types of legitimate authority (2.2)

5.5   What are the main reasons for delegating authority? (3.1)

5.6   List the process of delegation. (3.4)

5.7   Which direction does the authority and hence the delegation generally flow on an organisation chart? (3.6)

5.8   Describe the ways that behaviour can be influenced. (4.1)

6   EXAMINATION TYPE QUESTION

6.1   Delegated authority

'The reasons for delegation are mainly practical, but there are a few that are idealistic'

(a)   What advantages, both practical and idealistic, may be gained from the delegation process in an organisation? Are there any potential disadvantages?   **(13 marks)**

(b)   What is needed in practice to ensure that delegated authority is matched with responsibility?
(12 marks)
(Total: 25 marks)

7   ANSWER TO EXAMINATION TYPE QUESTION

7.1   Delegated authority

(a)   Delegation is the process whereby a manager or supervisor transfers part of his or her legitimate authority to a subordinate. Along with authority goes responsibility but whilst authority can be delegated, responsibility remains with the delegator; eg, while a Board of Directors may delegate authority to the managers, the directors are still responsible directly to the shareholders.

In all but the smallest of organisations some degree of delegation is necessary, as there are physical and mental limitations to the work that can be undertaken by any manager. This in turn allows subordinates to gain experience and demonstrate how they can perform. From these points the following practical advantages can be derived:

(i)   The workload of the manager is reduced leaving him more time to concentrate on strategic duties.

(ii)   Subordinates can gain good experience for future management.

(iii)   Delegation can lead to decentralisation which can allow divisional or branch managers to react quicker to local changes than managers at Head Office.

(iv)   Allowing subordinates to perform work of a higher grade can aid their development.

(v)   Management can see how subordinates tackle work of a higher grade, and how they cope with extra authority.

(vi)   Effective deployment of resources fulfils value for money criteria.

Idealistic advantages could be seen as those that suggest delegation aids motivation in subordinates, and allows for an individual to grow in his work. Where job satisfaction is gained by an employee, the employer is able to have the benefit of much better work performance - which might thus also be regarded as a practical advantage.

Whilst there are many advantages to be gained from delegation, care must be taken to ensure that the process is carried out carefully, otherwise there may be potential disadvantages:

(i)   If there is not the right mix of duties passed down, a subordinate may only have the tedious tasks and quickly lose interest and motivation.

(ii)   The superior must recognise that he is still accountable for the performance of the subordinate - he must not abdicate his responsibility.

(iii)   With decentralisation, local managers may develop their own procedures which may act against the objectives of the organisation.

On the whole, delegation of duties should be employed wherever possible and appropriate as the advantages will outweigh the disadvantages. With careful management control, the disadvantages can be minimised and optimum performance obtained.

(b)   It is very easy to say, as a matter of theory that authority must be matched by responsibility in an organisation. Both are usually thought of as being determined 'from above', but in practise this matching process is hard to achieve.

In the first place, it is necessary, in determining authority and responsibility to know accurately what each member of the organisation should do (and what he in fact does). Thus an accurate formal organisation chart is of great assistance.

This may well need to be augmented by means of an informal organisation chart as well, since people very rarely operate in the way in which they are officially expected to. Once the organisation chart has been prepared, job descriptions can be established. These will first state the responsibilities and then organise the necessary authority to match those responsibilities. Of course, once again there is likely to be a difference between the formal and the informal pattern. Thus a forceful personality can very easily make up for a lack of formal delegated authority.

The process of delegating authority will vary very considerably from one organisation to another. It is essentially a question of power, and how power is exercised. It is of little use for a manager to have the authority to hire employees if he lacks the power to advertise for applicants, or to determine the rates of pay. But even if he has both of these, it will avail him little unless there are willing applicants. His authority cannot usually exceed that of his superiors, the significant exceptions being where he has specific technical knowledge, or unusual personal qualities.

For authority to be exercised responsibly, it is necessary for policies to be established for the exercise of the authority. These have to be set out clearly for the guidance of the subordinates involved, and control must be established by some suitable mechanism (based on a flow of appropriate information). A manager can only hold his subordinates responsible provided that he has made it clear what is expected, knows what has been achieved, and has some means of taking corrective action where necessary.

15 LEADERSHIP AND MANAGEMENT STYLES

INTRODUCTION & LEARNING OUTCOMES

Syllabus area 11(iv)
- The characteristics of leaders and managers

- Management style theories (eg, Likert, Tannenbaum and Schmidt, Blake and Mouton)

- The advantages and disadvantages of different styles of management

- Contingency approaches to management style (eg, Adair, Fiedler)

There are many ways of looking at leadership, and many interpretations of its meaning. Essentially it is a relationship through which one person influences the behaviour or actions of other people. Leadership is related to motivation, communication and delegation, as well as the activities of groups.

This chapter describes and comments on a number of the theoretical and practical aspects of leadership. A review of the main leadership theories is followed by a discussion on the alternative management or leadership styles available to a person in a management or supervisory position.

When you have studied this chapter you should be able to:

- Analyse situations where problems have been caused by the adoption of an ineffective or inappropriate management style and recommend remedial action

1 LEADERSHIP

1.1 Definition

Influence systems provide the broad setting within which leadership occurs. People often have their own views of leadership. Some see it as a special attribute possessed by relatively few whilst others see it as a set of skills which most people can acquire through appropriate training.

 Buchanan and Huczynski define a leader as 'someone who exercises influence over other people'. Leadership is seen as 'a social process in which one individual influences the behaviour of others without the use or threat of violence'.

Leadership can be viewed from three standpoints:

- an attribute of a position eg, the managing director;
- a characteristic of a person - a natural leader;
- a category of behaviour.

From the position of leadership at work, the latter standpoint is most applicable and can be considered as something one person does to influence the behaviour of others. Defining the role of leadership we could say:

Leadership is a dynamic process in a group (or team), where one individual influences the others to contribute voluntarily to the achievement of group tasks in a given situation. The role of the leader is to direct the group towards their goals. In an informal group these roles will have been agreed by the group itself, whereas in a formal group the goals will generally be set by senior managers outside the group.

1.2   Formal and informal leaders

Leadership can be formal ie, having the delegated power and authority that Weber wrote about. Informal leaders can initiate action but do not have the same authority.

The formal leader is the appointed leader, who holds a particular rank or position. The leader may have been elected to the position or selected by some process in a typical bureaucratic organisation.

The informal leader is the natural leader, chosen or selected by the group to which he or she belongs. Leadership is both a function and a status grouping. Directors, managers and supervisors would be included in the status grouping and their identification has been important in studying the phenomenon of leadership in the past.

1.3   Leadership - the job

Leadership is all about moving people and things on, getting them from 'a' to 'b'. It involves improving performance, changing the way things are done, making a new product or whatever, and if the designated leader cannot communicate the why, how and when of moving from 'a' to 'b' then he or she will neither behave like a leader, nor succeed in the task.

As a function, leadership involves facilitating the achievement of group goals and has been defined in many ways from 'that which leaders do' to long, complex paragraphs including many elements. Fiedler, in one of his definitions, writes that a leader is 'the individual in the group given the task of directing and co-ordinating task-relevant group activities or who, in the absence of a designated leader, carries the primary responsibility for performing these functions in the group'.

From the definitions given (and there are lots more) you may still wonder what leadership is. Are leaders born or made? Can anyone be a leader, or only the favoured few? Is there a particular trick to it, or a particular style, something that, if we could learn it, would transform our lives? Are there models we should imitate, great men we can learn from? Do you have to be popular to be an effective leader? Can you be both well-liked and productive? The search for answers to questions like these has prompted a large number of studies and, unfortunately, none of these has produced a definitive solution to the leadership puzzle.

Theories of leadership can be classified as follows:

- Trait based
- Activity based
- Contingency based
- Style based; and
- Continuum based.

We will be discussing each of these theories separately, even though there is a considerable overlap between them eg, style being shown on a continuum and activity based theories being classed as a contingency theory by some writers.

2   TRAIT THEORIES OF LEADERSHIP

2.1   Leadership qualities

Early studies of leadership were based on the assumption that leaders were born and not made. Trait theories sustain the belief that the best way to study leadership is to analyse the personalities of successful leaders. They try to seek out the common personality characteristics (or traits) so that they have a basis on which to recognise actual and potential leaders by knowing their traits and comparing them with the traits of known leaders.

This approach has much in common with the 'great man' theory of history, which states that the great events of history are set in motion by great men. Thus, those who display leadership in one situation would probably be the leader in any other situation. They are leaders because of some unique and inherent set of traits that set them apart from normal people. Lists of leadership qualities were compiled that included:

- physical traits, such as drive, energy, appearance and height;
- personality traits, such as adaptability, enthusiasm and self-confidence; and
- social traits, such as co-operation, tact, courtesy and administrative ability.

2.2   Types of traits

A major problem with the trait approach is the question of exactly which traits are important. Despite research there is no agreed set of traits which enable us to predict the successful leader. This lack of agreement can be seen in the following two lists of traits put forward by different authorities.

List 1 - contains the 15 traits, cited by Rosemary Stewart, in an American study.

Judgement	Initiative	Integrity
Foresight	Energy	Drive
Human relations skill	Decisiveness	Dependability
Emotional stability	Fairness	Ambition
Dedication	Objectivity	Co-operation

List 2 - in contrast the psychologist Ghiselli suggests that the following six traits characterise effective leadership:

- Supervisory ability
- Occupational achievement
- Intelligence
- Self-actualisation need
- Self-assurance need
- Decisiveness

These lists show only one characteristic in common ie, decisiveness.

2.3   Situational approach

Another version of the trait theory is the situational approach. The theory here is that leaders are products of particular situations eg, Hitler in Germany of the 1930s, Churchill in England of the early 1940s and Mao in China after 1946. A given set of factors exist in certain situations eg, economic depression, weak government, high unemployment and a disenchantment with traditional politics. The theory suggests that a leader emerges, who recognises the problems and has characteristics or traits that fit the needs of the situation.

Studies in America have found that the implication for managers in successful leadership can partly depend on them correctly interpreting and responding to the values, feelings and personalities of the group they lead, as well as the economic environment.

The trait approach refers to what a leader is. Another approach to understanding leadership success concentrates on what a leader does.

3   ACTIVITY BASED THEORIES

3.1   Leadership as an activity

Behavioural theories have emphasised the functions of the leader (ie, what does the leader do) and the style of the leader. Leadership is seen as an active process, a process of goal attainment involving complex relations between leader and follower with actions performed both by and for the leader.

If we regard leadership as an activity, practising leadership means doing things. For example, a leader will issue orders, persuade and motivate people and get tasks done.

Urwick approved of definitions that described leaders as people to whom others would go for advice and get it, and whose influence guided others. He argued that leadership was demonstrated by example. The activities he described were characteristic of a managing director eg, representing the company to the outside world, initiating innovation, administering the undertaking and imposing order.

3.2   Action centred leadership

Professor Adair's action-centred leadership model is where task, group and individual needs are interconnected in the context of total leadership. The basic idea behind his theory is that the leader in any group or team has to strive constantly to achieve three major goals while at the same time maintaining a position as an effective leader. The first goal is the consideration of the task needs. These are the objectives to aim for using the efforts of everyone in the group. The second goal is a similar consideration of the group needs, concentrating on team building, developing interdependence and keeping the members of the group well informed. The third goal is to consider individual needs and motivating, developing and supporting individuals. Successful leadership is achieved by all three goals being reached.

The diagram below shows the overlap of the task, group and individual needs, and indicates some measure of interrelation between these factors.

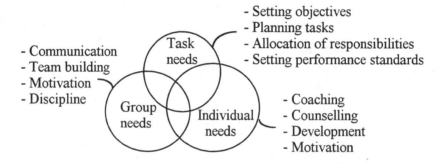

Adair's model of leadership is more a question of appropriate behaviour than of personality or of being in the right place at the right time. His model stresses that effective leadership lies in what the leader does to meet the needs of task, group and individuals. This takes the model nearer the contingency approaches of modern theorists, whose concern is with a variety of factors - task, people and situation - all having a bearing on leadership and leadership styles.

4   CONTINGENCY BASED THEORIES

4.1   Fiedler's contingency theory

Most simply put, contingency theory sees effective leadership as being dependent on a number of variable or contingent factors. There is no one right way to lead that will fit all situations; rather it is necessary to lead in a manner that is appropriate to a particular situation.

Fiedler's contingency theory of leadership has been particularly influential and offers a systematic way of analysing situations and then prescribing the most effective leadership response to that situation. First of all Fiedler developed a new way of assessing leadership style based on the measurement of the leader's LPC (least preferred co-worker) score. This score is obtained by asking the leader to think of the person with whom they can work least well, their least preferred co-worker. Then they are required to rate that person on sixteen dimensions, each with a positive and negative aspect.

Examples of these dimensions are given below.

Positive					Negative

Pleasant					Unpleasant

Cheerful					Gloomy

Helpful					Frustrating

The leaders who rate their least preferred co-worker negatively get lower LPC scores and are said to be task orientated. Those who get high scores and see positive value, even in those they find it difficult to get on with are said to be relationship oriented. These measures provide a new and original method of assessing a person's leadership orientation.

Fiedler goes on to show that there is no direct correlation between a leader's LPC score and his effectiveness as a leader. People with very different LPC scores can be equally successful and people with identical scores are seen to succeed or fail as leaders independent of whether they are task or relationship orientated. He argues that effective leadership is also dependent on a further set of variables namely:

(a)   The extent to which the task in hand is structured.
(b)   The leader's position power.
(c)   The nature of the existing relationships between the leader and the group.

Since these factors are likely to vary from group to group there is no one way of leading; rather the approach to leading must be modified in the light of task structure, position power and whether existing relationships are good or bad. From his analysis Fiedler is able to identify three typical situations which require a very different response from a leader.

Situation 1 - is where:

• The task is highly structured.
• The leader's position power is high.
• Subordinates feel the relationships with the leader are good.

Under these conditions the task-oriented leader (low LPC) will get good results. Operating under these favourable conditions the low LPC leader will detect that events are potentially under control, set targets, monitor performance and get excellent results.

The relationship-oriented leader (high LPC) does not perform well under these circumstances. This type of leader seeks to get work done by maintaining good inter-personal relations but here these relations are already good. The relationship orientation is irrelevant here and the group may well under-achieve under such leadership.

Situation 2 - is where:

• The task is unstructured.
• The leader's position power is low.
• Subordinates feel that their relationships with the leader are moderately good.

Relationship-oriented leaders get the best results under these conditions. Maintenance of good relations is important here both to the ability of the leader to exert influence over subordinates and to the accomplishment of the task. The task oriented leader will not succeed in these circumstances because any deterioration in relationships will be ignored and, since the task lacks structure and position power is low, leadership/subordinate relations will be the key factor in producing good results.

Situation 3 - is where:

- The task is unstructured.
- The leader's position power is low.
- Subordinates feel that their relationships with the leader are poor.

Fiedler says that task-oriented leaders are most effective under these conditions. A relationship-oriented leader is unwilling to exert pressure on subordinates, avoids confrontations that might upset or anger them, gets involved in attempts to repair damaged relations and ignores the task. On the other hand, the task-oriented leader will be impatient, attempt to structure the situation, ignore resistance from subordinates, reduce ambiguity and uncertainty surrounding the work and thus achieve a good performance.

From an analysis of these three situations it does appear that leadership depends on the particular requirements of a situation and there is no single style suitable for all occasions. For Fiedler, the effective leader is the person who can successfully identify the important features of the context (the contingent factors) and then adopt the style relevant to that context.

4.2   The importance of contingency theory

Contingency theory demonstrates that there is no ideal personality, nor one best style for a leader. The theory also provides a basis for developing people as leaders. By making people aware of the factors affecting the choice of leadership style and providing a basis for increased self-awareness the theory gives a useful starting point for leadership training.

Contingency approaches to leadership have been the object of some criticism. Notably, Schein has pointed out:

(a)   The key variables of task structure, power and relationships are difficult to measure in practice and may depend more on intuition than on measurement.

(b)   The framework does not take into account the needs of subordinates.

(c)   The theory ignores the need for the leader to have technical competence relevant to the task.

The major difficulty for any leader seeking to apply contingency theory is to actually modify his/her behaviour as the situation changes.

5   STYLE THEORIES

5.1   Behavioural theories and the question of management style

Style is a difficult factor to measure or define. The style of a manager is essentially how he or she operates, but it is a function of many factors. The early approaches sought to identify one style that was 'best'.

Since the 1950s several theories about leadership and management style have been put forward. Most have been expressed in terms of authoritarian versus democratic styles, or people-oriented versus task-oriented styles. The two extremes can be described as follows:

(a)   **Task centred leadership** - where the main concern of the leader is getting the job done, achieving objectives and seeing the group as simply a means to an end.

(b)   **Group centred leadership** - where the prime interest of the leader is to maintain the group, stressing factors such as mutual trust, friendship, support, respect and warmth of relationships.

Huneryager and Heckman identified four different styles of leadership:

Dictatorial style - where the leader forces subordinates to work by threatening punishment and penalties.

Autocratic style - where decision-making is centralised in the hands of the leader, who does not encourage participation by subordinates. Many of the most successful businesses have been led to success by autocrats who are paternalistic leaders, offering consideration and respect to the workforce, but retaining full rights in decision-making. This is typified by the Quaker companies in the early years of this century (eg, Cadbury, Rowntree, Reckitt and Colman).   Such a style is frequently found today in professional firms. Often they find it hard to delegate, to bring on successors, to stand down at the right moment, to switch off and go home, and to appreciate the views of others.

Democratic style - where decision-making is decentralised, and shared by subordinates in participative group action. It is important not to allow a preference for democratic social systems to blind managers into favouring democratic management styles in all situations. Businesses can stand (and often need) firmer, more single-minded management than nation states would generally find healthy. Those who lead using the democratic approach suffer from being unable to move as quickly as competitor businesses led by autocrats and from people in the ranks not being clear as to exactly which direction they should be pulling in.

Laisser-faire style - where subordinates are given little or no direction at all, and are allowed to establish their own objectives and make all their own decisions.

As we shall see from various studies (outlined below) a considerate style of leadership is frequently found to be the most effective and leads to greater job satisfaction, though task centred styles are often associated with high employee performance and, on occasions, with employee satisfaction as well.

5.2   Theory X and Theory Y

We have already discussed Douglas McGregor's authoritarian - democratic approach to management style. His Theory X manager - the authoritarian - is tough and supports tight controls with punishment/reward systems. The contrasting style is that of the Theory Y manager - the democrat - who is benevolent, participative and a believer of self-controls.

5.3   Ohio State University Studies

These studies were carried out by Edwin Fleishman and his colleagues in the late 1940s and are a classic and very influential attempt to make sense of the complexity and diversity of leadership behaviours.   They developed a questionnaire (which they called the Leadership Behaviour Description Questionnaire or LBDQ) which asked people to analyse and comment on the behaviour of their superiors in their organisation.   From their results it was easy to identify the two major dimensions of leadership:

(i)   **Initiating structure** - the concern with organising the work to be done, the definition of roles and the ways of getting jobs done.

(ii)   **Consideration** - the concern with the social organisation of the group, maintaining good relations and giving opportunities for group involvement and participation.
This distinction, more commonly referred to today as the difference between a job-centred approach and an employee-centred approach, has been very influential.

The studies state clearly that the approaches are not mutually exclusive and that the most effective leaders that they studied were those who combined both approaches. This finding was developed by Robert Blake and Jane Mouton in their concept of the managerial grid.

Inconsiderate leaders who stress task achievement tend to have subordinates who complain a lot, show a higher labour turnover and have relatively unproductive work groups. Most subordinates prefer considerate leaders and dislike those who are simply task oriented.

5.4 Likert's four management systems

Likert's book *New Patterns Of Management* distinguished between four key styles or 'systems' of leadership.

System 1 - Exploitative autocratic - which relies on fear and threats. Communication is downward and superiors and subordinates are psychologically far apart, with the decision-making process concentrated at the top of the organisation. However undesirable this may ostensibly appear, there are certain organisations, such as the Church, civil service and armed forces, where there must be little room for questioning commands, for doctrinal, procedural or strategic reasons.

System 2 - Benevolent authoritative - there is a limited element of reward, but communication is restricted. Policy is made at the top but there is some restricted delegation within rigidly defined procedures. Management tends to hear only what it wishes to hear. The student should be able to envisage the resultant style of leadership: an arrogant personality at the top, possibly fanatically committed to an ideal and determined to see it through to the ultimate conclusion desired, whatever the consequences. Criticism or dissent, even other viewpoints, are not tolerated and frequently are suppressed. The result is a leadership hierarchy supported by yes-men.

System 3 - Participative - the leader has some incomplete confidence in subordinates, listens to them but controls decision making, motivates by reward and a level of involvement and will use the ideas and suggestions of subordinates constructively. Communication is both up and down, but upward communication remains rather limited. Scope is given for some local input

System 4 - Democratic - management gives economic rewards, rather than mere 'pats on the head', utilises full group-participation, and involves teams in goal setting, improving work methods and communication flows up and down. There is a close psychological relationship between superiors and subordinates. Decision-making is permitted at all levels and is integrated into the formal structure with reference to the organisation chart. Each group overlaps and is linked to the rest of the organisation by link pins that are members of more than one group. A cost accountant is such a person. He is a member of the finance function, but because he attends the weekly cost review meetings, he is closely involved with the management of the production function. Such management, advocated Likert, produces high productivity, greater involvement of individuals and better labour-management relations.

Likert recognised that each style is relevant in some situations; for example, in a crisis, a system 1 approach is usually required. Alternatively when introducing a new system of work, system 4 would be most effective. His research shows that effective managers are those who adopt either a System 3 or a System 4 leadership style. Both are seen as being based on trust and paying attention to the needs of both the organisation and employees.

While accepting that technically competent, tough job-centred management can achieve high productivity, especially if reinforced by rigid control methods, Likert suggested that such environments generate a latent rebellious attitude in subordinates, with high utilisation costs in waste and scrap, higher levels of conflict, stoppages and grievances etc. This type of management, he suggested, only works well in certain environments. Even so, irrespective of the environment, there will come a point at which the system will break down, and conflict will then escalate out of control.

5.5 Adair's five essential leadership characteristics

More recently, other writers have developed some basic ideas, either in parallel with, or directly following from Likert's research. John Adair (*Training for Leadership*, Gower, 1968) identified five essential leadership characteristics, the use and mix of which are largely determined by the demands of local situations:

(a)   intelligence;
(b)   scholarship;
(c)   dependability in exercising responsibilities;
(d)   activity and social participation;
(e)   socio-economic status.

Adair also emphasised the importance of the situation. He recognised that the situation dictates the type of leader required at a given time, and relates closely to authority of position, personality or knowledge. Product type, size of firm, position and performance of the company will also influence leadership types and requirements.

5.6   The studies of Kurt Lewin and Ronald White

Although their studies have sometimes been criticised as rather artificial (eg, studies of children in laboratory conditions) they have none the less been very influential. One famous experiment illustrates their approach. It involved groups of children making paper mache masks. The groups were exposed to three different styles of leadership ie, democratic, authoritarian and laissez-faire.

The responses of the children were monitored and the results both in terms of task performance and general behaviour were carefully studied. The conclusion reached can be summarised as follows:

Work quality and quantity - output was highest under authoritarian leadership but quality was at its best under the democratic style. *Laissez-faire* leadership produced the lowest levels of quality.

Motivation - the children were best motivated under democratic leadership. Work continued under democratic leadership even after the leader had left the group. Whenever the authoritarian leader left the room it was a signal for work to cease. Interest in the task was at its highest in the democratic group.

Efficiency - the *laissez-faire* style was shown to be clearly inefficient. However, in terms of technical efficiency there was little to choose between the democratic and authoritarian styles.

Member satisfaction - the members of the group expressed a strong preference for the democratic style. Hostility to the leader was frequently expressed in the authoritarian group. Democratic group members were more friendly and 'group-minded' than members of the authoritarian group. Submissive and dependent behaviour was a characteristic of much behaviour under authoritarian leadership.

In general, the study provides support for a democratic style of management though it should be noted that studies, such as this, might not transfer easily to the surroundings of the complex modern organisation.

5.7   Criticisms of the behavioural approach

The behavioural approach to leadership has provided useful insights into the nature and processes of leadership. It has usefully stressed the values of democratic, participative styles and, in identifying styles, it has helped in the perception of leadership as a range of choices open to the manager rather than one limited and universal set of behaviours.

However, the behavioural approach is also subject to certain criticisms. Despite a level of agreement between different researchers there are also confusions and some contradictions. The various definitions of style illustrate this problem. What are the exact differences and similarities between, say, a democratic style, a participative style and a paternalistic style?

The theories perhaps underplay the importance of task achievement. Groups are formed to perform tasks and achieve goals and a concentration on group relationships may be to the detriment of performance.

Perhaps the most important criticism of the style approach is that it does not consider all the variables that contribute to the operation of effective leadership. By concentrating on style there is a neglect of other factors, which impinge on the issue such as the needs and expectations of the followers, the nature and objectives of the organisation and the general social and cultural environment in which the leader operates.

It is the consideration of this wider set of variables that has led to the development of the contingency approach to leadership style of Blake and Mouton.

5.8   Blake and Mouton's managerial grid

Blake and Mouton started from the assumption that a manager's job is to foster attitudes and behaviour which promote efficient performance, to stimulate and use creativity, to generate enthusiasm for experimentation and innovation, and to learn from interaction with others. They argued that managerial competence can be taught and learned. Their managerial grid, shown below, provides a framework for understanding and applying effective management and sets guidelines for an approach to management which has been successfully applied in many countries, and in a variety of functions and organisations.

The grid derived its origin from the precept that management is concerned with production and people. Developing this concept a little further, concern for production is not confined simply to the Taylor ideal of effective factory performance. Production may mean the number of good research ideas generated or accounts processed, the volume of sales, quality of service and possibly warranty claims, as well as top policy decision-making and the number of successful decisions. Likewise, concern for people embraces friendships and relationships, task commitment, self-respect, equity and integrity. The grid suggests that any combination of concern for production and concern for people may be present within an organisation.

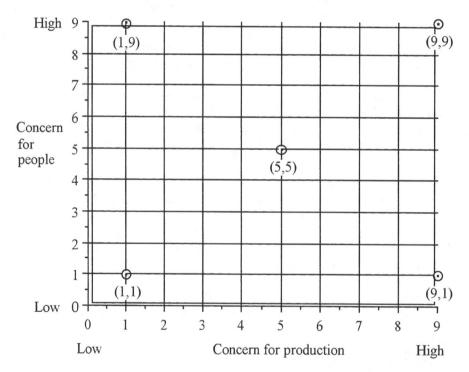

A high concern for production will score 9 and a high concern for people will also score 9, the two co-ordinates on the grid indicating the proportion of each concern present. The five styles outlined on the grid are explained below:

(a)   The **task-orientated** style (9.1) is in the best Taylor tradition. Men are treated as a commodity, like machines. The manager will be responsible for planning, directing, and controlling the work of his subordinates. However, while this style can achieve high production, there are noticeable deficiencies. It is a Theory X approach, and in certain environments creative energy may be channelled into trying to beat the system. Subordinates can become indifferent and apathetic, or even rebellious.

(b)   The **country club** style (1.9) emphasises people. People are encouraged and supported, and any inadequacies are overlooked, on the basis that people are doing their best, and coercion may not improve things substantially. The 'country club', as Blake calls it, has certain drawbacks. This style often pervades in inefficient, quasi-monopolist, time-serving organisations. Many disputes, such as within the railways, the health service, local government, the newspaper publishing industry and the coal industry, have arisen largely from this style of management having taken the easy option in the previous year.

(c)   The **impoverished** style (1.1) is almost impossible to imagine. Certainly no commercial organisation could survive with such impoverished management, and it is doubtful if any non profit-making organisation could either. This style may exist on the micro-scale, however, eg, the supervisor who abdicates responsibility and leaves others to work as they see fit. A failure, for whatever reason, is always blamed down the line. Contact is frequently minimised, and commitment to problems raised is almost non-existent. Typically, the 1.1 supervisor or manager is a frustrated individual, passed over for promotion, shunted sideways, or has been in a routine job for years, possibly because of a lack of personal maturity.

(d)   The **middle road** (5.5) is a happy medium. This viewpoint pushes for productivity and considers people, but does not go 'over the top' either way. It is a style of 'give and take', neither too lenient nor too coercive, arising probably from a feeling that any improvement is idealistic and unachievable.

(e)   The **team** style (9.9) may be idealistic; it advocates a high degree of concern for production which generates wealth and for people who in turn generate production. This style endeavours to discover the best and most effective solutions, aiming at the highest attainable level of production to which all involved contribute and in which everyone finds his own sense of accomplishment.

The implication is that managers should aim for the 9,9 combination, a goal-centred team approach that seeks to gain optimum results through participation, involvement, commitment and conflict-solving where everyone can contribute. According to Blake and Mouton, individuals can adapt their style to become more effective personally, and, working in a team, can build the synergy needed to raise output above the level that could be achieved individually.

Critics of the grid complain that, being two-dimensional, it inevitably over-simplifies a highly complex and fluid relationship between manager and staff. However, the simplicity of Blake and Mouton's original conception has probably been the main reason for its success.

5.9   Activity

Blake and Mouton define 9.9, team centred results based leadership as the theoretical ultimate. Identify some situations where 9.9 may not be the best approach but 1.9 or 9.1 may provide a better basis.

5.10   Activity solution

A manager may find that a 9,1 approach is better in situations of crisis where survival is at stake. Also, when a timetable has gone wrong and urgent action must be taken. Many managers also find that in handling dismissals or issuing final warnings it is better to reduce the people aspect and concentrate only on the achievement of the task.

There are fewer instances where a manager can move from 9,9 or 9,1 towards a people based 1.9 with reduced attention to results. Staff welfare issues, and some public relations exercises could occur as examples.

6   CONTINUUM OF LEADERSHIP BEHAVIOUR

6.1   Tannenbaum and Schmidt

Some of the leadership theories present two basic choices - a task centred leader on the one hand and an employee-centred one on the other. Likert's theory offers four choices and the managerial grid offers five. The adaptation of leadership styles to varying contingencies, was initially defined by Tannenbaum and Schmidt in 1958 with their ideas of a leadership continuum, which is represented in the diagram below:

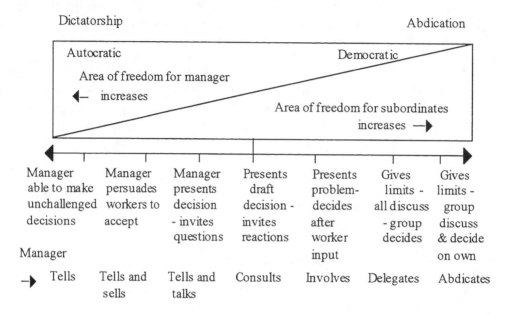

The continuum suggests a range of styles between authorisation and democratic without any suggestion that any one style is right or wrong. Tannenbaum and Schmidt's continuum recognises that the appropriate style depends upon:

(a)   the leader (personality, values, natural style etc);

(b)   the subordinates (their knowledge, experience, attitude etc);

(c)   the situation (such forces as the organisation's culture, time pressures, levels of authority and responsibility etc).

Reappraising their theory in 1973, Tannenbaum and Schmidt added the influence of the environment on management style, for example, ecology pressures, education changes, union power base etc.

6.2   John Adair

The continuum has been further developed by John Adair. On the question of the appropriateness of style, Adair goes further to suggest that style may need to vary in different working situations, within the same group. Groups that may work in crisis situations, where the split second correct decision of one man is required, and there is no room for debate or discussion, such as fire-fighting crews, or the military, obviously need the boss-centred approach. However, the same groups, when in training, can profit from exploring the possibility of finding more appropriate positions along the continuum. In the commercial world, a rescue strategy might require a highly boss-centred approach, if only to ensure that the process is done correctly and expeditiously. However, where there is a growing market and a less volatile competitive situation, there is scope to move along the spectrum.

Adair concludes that the intelligent selection of style requires:

(a)   personal qualities of character which in turn must be supported by appropriateness to the general situation and an adequate level of knowledge and experience;

(b)   an ability to guide the group towards its appropriate goal;

(c)   the capacity to maintain and build the unity of the team; and

(d)   balancing the right mix of input from the team.

6.3   Ashridge Management College

A further development of the continuum was published by the Ashridge Management College in 1966. Basically, they suggest four distinct management styles:

(a)   *Tells* - the autocratic dictator. The manager makes decisions, issues orders and expects obedience. Communication is downward with no feedback until after the event.

(b)   *Sells* - the persuader. The manager makes the decisions and tries to persuade staff that it represents their best interests.

(c)   *Consults* - partial involvement. The manager retains the decision-making authority but seeks to elicit other opinions before reaching his decision. Ashridge points out that this must be an honest approach not an attempt to hoodwink staff where the manager has no intention of changing a predetermined decision.

(d)   *Joins* - the democrat. Here the leader joins with the staff and operates from within the team, seeking to reach a consensus decision. It is clearly most effective where all members within the group have knowledge and experience to contribute so that an evenly-balanced informed discussion can lead to the best decision.

The findings from the study are that employees prefer to receive the 'consults' and 'joins' styles, but most managers were scored as being 'tells' and 'sells'. This was further reflected in the fact that staff satisfaction in work tended to be higher with staff who saw their boss as 'consults' and 'joint'.

A further important conclusion was the need for consistency in leadership style. The least favourable attitudes were found in staff who professed themselves unable to see a consistent style in their boss.

7   MANAGEMENT STYLES

7.1   A spectrum of style

Although style is seen to vary along a continuum from autocratic to democratic, the most effective style must be appropriate to the situation. For example, a production environment will have a demand for a different style of management to that of say the sales office, or again a service industry, or even an accountants' office. Equally, over the years, the working environment has changed. A hundred years ago, when FW Taylor was developing his scientific management, the working environment treated men as machines, and while Taylor was paternalistic in his attitude, an autocratic environment was the order of the day. Now, things have changed irreversibly. Even factory operatives are better educated, more widely read, and better informed about their rights than ever our grandparents were. As a result, there is almost an expectation from the work force to be consulted about the way they are expected to work.

7.2   Style in practice

In an examination situation, you could be confronted with a scenario, and asked to suggest an appropriate style of management to deal with the problem. It will not be sufficient to merely regurgitate Likert, or describe 'Blake's Grid'. Rather, you will be expected to use your own experience, and your wider reading and knowledge to answer the question. Some examples are now quoted to help you relate academic knowledge to the practical situation.

Rover

The rescue of any company is a traumatic exercise, requiring very specialist styles. From the previous experience, when it was British Leyland, the following factors were significant:

(a)   A situation that demanded a very tough, capable type of manager with a good track record. Sir Michael Edwardes was head hunted from Chloride. The current situation at Rover requires a similar type of manager.

(b)   A team that was small and could be objective. All too often management climbs down because of its own vested interest. Management that has independent wealth is neither frightened of being fired nor afraid to use resignation as a powerful weapon if their solutions are not adopted.

(c)   Subordinate management who were prepared to manage in a working environment of very powerful unions, and take unpopular decisions.

(d)   The problems related to a large organisation that was geographically dispersed throughout the UK and sold its products through a network of dealers.

(e)   The products were out of date, there was no money to replace them, and competition was eating into the market place both within the UK and overseas.

(f)   There were political constraints particularly with the numbers employed and the dependency of the component industry.

Similar problems apply at Rover, and at other car manufacturers, mainly because of the strong pound and a depressed market for new cars. There is an oversupply of certain cars and the company will probably need to shed jobs and increase productivity if it is to stay in business. Unfortunately, this time the Government cannot step in to sort the management problem out, but a strong manager should be appointed to make some unpleasant decisions. He or she will be an autocratic type to persuade staff that it represents their best interests.

British Petroleum (BP)

BP was traditionally a cradle to the grave organisation. In 1990, BP began a fundamental change of its culture, strategy and organisation, downsizing and de-layering to position itself to face future challenges. The company now focuses on its core activities, with the non-core being outsourced or bought in.

For the employees remaining with BP, the changes have been dramatic. Individuals have learned to adjust to new ways of working and the leaders have been pivotal in the change process. Before the changes, the manager's roles were clearly defined. There were rules and procedures and many personnel procedures. Authority was clearly delineated and controlled. In an organisation where all recruits were qualified, managers were selected on technical or professional excellence.

In the new cost-conscious organisation, strong technical and professional skills are not sufficient. The leader's role has changed, become more complex and is critical to BPs success. Leaders have to recognise and learn new skills to build empowered teams and deliver the new agenda. While maintaining performance and rebuilding moral, they need to encourage creativity and risk taking and develop skills for the future whilst delivering the current year's targets. The ability to understand and influence people and develop and maintain strong personal networks is critical.

8   **SELF TEST QUESTIONS**

8.1   What are the three standpoints that leadership can be viewed from (1.1)

8.2   List three theories of leadership. (1.3)

8.3   Give two examples of a personality trait. (2.1)

8.4   What are the three major goals in Adair's action-centred leadership? (3.2)

8.5   Describe one of the criticisms of contingency theory. (4.2)

8.6   Outline the two extreme leadership styles. (5.1)

8.7   Briefly describe Likert's four management systems. (5.4)

8.8   What do the axes on the managerial grid represent? (5.8)

8.9   According to Tannenbaum and Schmidt, what does the style depend on? (6.1)

9   **EXAMINATION TYPE QUESTION**

9.1   **Blake and Mouton's managerial grid**

Six supervisors from accountancy departments are on a management development course. A, one of them, has reported his proposals about a case, which they have been studying. The other five have rated A by placing crosses on Blake and Mouton's managerial grid. The results are as shown.

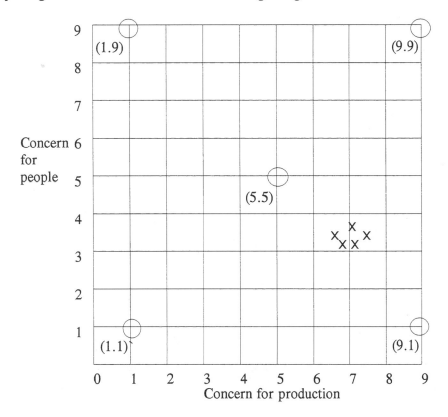

(a)   Explain what the consultant in charge of the exercise should tell the group about the significance of the result.   **(6 marks)**

(b)   Make **seven** suggestions how A could improve his management style.   **(14 marks)**
                                                                                 (Total: 20 marks)

10 ANSWER TO EXAMINATION TYPE QUESTION

10.1 Blake and Mouton's managerial grid

(a) The positions of the ratings on the managerial grid show a remarkable degree of unanimity on the part of the other participants. They are close enough to the central co-ordinates (5,5) to identify A as an example of Blake and Mouton's 'middle of the road' type of manager, and the exact position (around 7,3) shows more concern for production and less for people. Blake and Mouton believe that the compromise position of 5,5 results in inadequate attention being given to output and the needs of the employees. Given the close agreement of all the ratings the imbalance that this shows is probably significant enough to justify concern.

(b) A's management style needs to show more concern for people if it is to improve and move towards Blake and Mouton's ideal of 9,9, where concern for both people and production reach a maximum. Possible ways of achieving this include the following means of improving his communications with his subordinates:

(i) showing greater confidence in them in the way he allocates and supervises work;

(ii) being prepared to accept their suggestions for improvements in work practices;

(iii) restructuring his decision making so as to involve them in it as fully as possible;

(iv) attempting to empathise more with their work problems and helping them to find solutions;

(v) being prepared to help them discover answers to problems rather than simply delivering a managerial decree;

(vi) providing them with proper feedback to motivate improvements in performance; and showing a general interest in their current work and future career prospects.

16 GROUP DEVELOPMENT, BEHAVIOUR AND ROLES

INTRODUCTION & LEARNING OUTCOMES

Syllabus area 11(iv) • Theories of group development, behaviour and roles (e.g. Tuckman, Belbin)

Leadership is a dynamic process in a group (or team), where one individual influences the others to contribute voluntarily to the achievement of group tasks in a given situation. The role of the leader is to direct the group towards their goals. In an informal group these roles will have been agreed by the group itself, whereas in a formal group the goals will generally be set by senior managers outside the group.

The work of an organisation is generally achieved by the collective efforts of individuals working together, often in small teams or groups. This adds a new dimension to the psychological factors investigated previously, and it is the purpose of this chapter to look at the new dimension.

We begin by isolating a number of general features relating to group working, including the balance between formal and informal relationships, the establishment of group norms and the morale within a group. From these we move on to an area which has been widely researched: the question of identifying stages in the development of groups. The work of Tuckman is important here. We then look at approaches to maximising group effectiveness. This is obviously an important topic for managers, and links in closely with our earlier coverage of motivation theory.

When you have studied this chapter you should be able to:

- Explain the formation of groups and the way in which groups and their members behave
- Identify the different roles adopted by members of a group, and explain the relevance of this to the management of the group

1 GENERAL FEATURES OF GROUPS

1.1 Introduction

A group is basically a collection of individuals, who share a sense of common identity and contribute to some common aim under the direction of a leader. A group is more than a collection of people; four individuals added together does not constitute a group. A crowd of people getting off a train is not a group. Groups only exist when there are inter-relationships.

In the work place, most tasks are undertaken by groups and teams, rather than by individuals. Group associations range from spontaneous, informal social gatherings, to work on a mass production assembly line to membership of the armed forces. Most of man's knowledge and values comes from group experience. Man's objectives, and his way of achieving them, are largely determined by groups. His behaviour in groups is necessary to an understanding about behaviour in organisations. It is difficult to imagine how man could manage without groups since it is only through them that he can achieve his goals.

Because we use the terms groups, teams and committees interchangeably, it will be helpful to clarify the difference between the three.

A **group** can be an informal collection of people, related perhaps to skill, training, or department on a permanent or temporary basis. They will tend to have a leader, a standard of social behaviour, a reason to exist and a clear sense of identity.

A **team** is a formal group. It has a leader (or captain) and a distinctive culture, geared towards a final result, be it product, service or sporting victory. A good team is highly task-oriented, working towards a common goal, against a common enemy and obliterating individual objectives and most status and style differences.

A **committee** is again a formal group usually with a chairman and a secretary, and it formalises its meeting with an agenda and minutes. There is usually a fairly rigid procedure about speaking, proposing meetings, voting rights, construction of the agenda and communication. Unlike a team, which is usually formed within one discipline, a committee will have the advantage of being inter-disciplinary, in that it could embrace accounts, sales, personnel and operations, but also at different levels.

Any of the above three classifications could be permanent (ie. regular meetings at set times, declared purpose, usually recognised by the organisation); or temporary (ie. set up to resolve a particular problem, meet a defined target).

1.2   Group characteristics

Groups have certain characteristics, which distinguish them from a random collection of people.

- A clear sense of **identity** exists - members of the group feel a sense of belonging (as an individual does within a family group). There are established boundaries to the group so we can define those who are accepted as members and those who are not. There is a sense of sharing that adds to the identity; it may be a common use of property, a common bond of knowledge or a common activity. This identification is perceived by the group members themselves, and this feeling marks the distinction between a random collection of people and a group.

- There is usually a **purpose or aim,** which helps to forge the group. For instance, a village threatened by a new road may form a Residents' Action Committee. The group will form and develop in response to the external threat.

- The third main distinguishing characteristic is the existence of **group norms**. These norms may include output, productivity, attitudes towards the company, manner of dress, non-acceptance of authority etc. Obedience to the norms of the group is usually an implied requirement of membership. The norms of a group bind the members together, distinguish it from other groups and provide an entry barrier to outsiders.

There must be **communication** within the group, often informal and personality based. A group cannot form in the absence of communication. This communication is often a necessary part of the adoption of roles within the group. Typical roles could be leader, cynic or group conformist.

1.3   Classification of groups

Groups can be classified in several ways:

(a)   **Formal and informal groups**

Groups can vary from the formal (an appointed work group, a project team, a board of directors) to the informal (corridor meetings, lunch groups, ad hoc groups).

Formal groups are usually appointed for a specific purpose by the management of an organisation and, as such have a formal structure and are concerned with the co-ordination of work activities. The people appointed will become involved with the task for which they are selected and will often form teams which deal with certain aspects of the work. Leaders may be selected within the group, and may be given some form of official recognition. Formal groups are often permanent groups, eg standing committees (such as a finance committee), a board of directors etc. Formal groups are often cross-functional, eg with representatives from marketing and purchasing, and may be cross hierarchical, ie with the boss and a subordinate in the group. It is also possible to find temporary formal groups which have been appointed to carry out a specific project only (eg, computerisation of the stores department).

Informal groups on the other hand are based more on personal relationships and agreement of group members, rather than on defined role relationships. Informal groupings are found in most organisations and may take the form of people who get together informally to exchange information (eg, social committees), or groups of people who meet outside the workplace (eg darts teams etc). This sort of loose grouping usually has a floating membership and the leaders usually emerge as a result of personal power. The aims of informal groups are usually related to personal and group satisfaction. Informal work groups will almost always arise if the opportunity exists, and very often can work against organisational pressures. Informal groups can become very powerful and in extreme cases undermine the formal objectives of the organisation. It has been suggested that managers who fear this sort of influence might design the work so as to eliminate interaction, or rotate the members of the group to prevent any stable group structure emerging.

It was probably not until the Hawthorne Investigations in the late 1920s that it was realised that informal relationships are established within the formal structure as laid down by the organisation chart.

There is a strong tendency for employees to form small groups with their own status systems, patterns of behaviour, beliefs and objectives different from and often opposed to the requirements and objectives of the formal organisation. These social groups and their associated behaviour have been called the informal organisation to distinguish it from the formal organisation that officially exists. Stryker claims that:

'The informal organisation that pervades every company is so complex that it probably could never be completely charted. But it is this hidden operating structure that gets the work done. Indeed, it is the biggest intangible asset - and usually the touchiest open secret - of any management.'

Informal groups therefore often have the following characteristics:

- they are not recognised by the organisation;
- membership is on a personal basis;
- there is no formality of roles or procedures;
- the group may have goals directly opposing those of the organisation.

(b)   **Cohesive and loosely formed groups**

Groups can be cohesive or loosely formed. A cohesive group is one whose sense of identity is sharply defined and it operates as a tight unit. There is no ambiguity about whether a particular person is a member of that group or not. Likewise, outsiders are in no doubt that in attacking one individual member they can expect a total group response. This cohesiveness can be valuable for management as the whole team responds as a unit, though of course their cohesive strength could be used against the company if the group feels threatened.

The factors that dictate the degree of cohesiveness are several.

- The size is significant (generally it is difficult to be cohesive when members exceed ten).
- A clear common goal will encourage cohesiveness and identity.
- Some mutual characteristic will enhance cohesiveness eg, geographical area, specific skill or background factor.
- Time span - cohesiveness develops over time and is not instantly available.

(c)   **Effective and ineffective groups**

Whether a group is seen as effective or ineffective can be measured by company standards imposed from outside. Examples include:

- meeting output, quality and timetable targets;
- or posing problems for management;
- acquiescent to change.

On the other hand, self-imposed targets, evolved within the groups could measure effectiveness. Such as:

- frustrating management initiatives;
- protecting weak members of the group;
- being recognised as the best performing group.

The approaches to creating an effective group are discussed in more detail later in this chapter.

1.4   Goal congruence

In successful organisations, company objectives will be compatible with the objectives of the individual. If the objectives of an individual are diametrically opposed to those of the organisation then conflict will result as long as the person remains with that organisation.

It must also be borne in mind that groups have objectives too; this is likely to give rise to conflicts and pressures affecting members of groups. According to Likert, in such situations:

'To minimise these conflicts and tensions, the individual seeks to influence the values and goals of each of the different groups to which he belongs and which are important to him so as to minimise the inconsistencies and conflicts in values and goals. In striving for this reconciliation, he is likely to press for acceptance of those values most important to him.'

It will be appreciated that complex interactions take place between individuals, groups and organisations each affecting the other to a greater or lesser extent.   Likert gives the following properties and performance characteristics of the ideal, highly effective group:

(a)   Members are skilled in all the various leadership and membership roles and functions required for interaction between leaders and members and between members and the other members.

(b)   The group has been in existence long enough to develop a well-established relaxed working relationship among its members.

(c)   Members of the group are attracted to it and are loyal to its members, including its leader.

(d)   Members have a high degree of confidence and trust in each other.

(e)   Values and goals of the group are a satisfactory integration and expression of the relevant values and needs of its members. They have helped shape these values and are satisfied with them.

(f)   In so far as members of the group are performing linking functions they endeavour to have the values and goals of the groups which they link in harmony, one with the other.

(g)   The more important a value seems to the group the greater the likelihood that the individual member will accept it.

(h)   Members of the group are highly motivated to abide by the major values and to achieve the important goals of the group.

(i)   All of the interaction, problem-solving, decision-making activities of the group occur in a supportive atmosphere.

(j)   The superior of each work group exerts a major influence in establishing the tone and atmosphere of that work group by his leadership principles and practices.

With regard to individual goals and organisational objectives, he theorises that:

'Objectives of the entire organisation and of its competent parts must be in satisfactory harmony with the relevant needs and desires of the great majority, if not all, the members of the organisation and of the persons served by it'. We shall see later, in discussing the topic of conflict, that there are other views.

'Goals and assignments of each member of the organisation must be established in such a way that he is highly motivated to achieve them.

Methods and procedures used by the organisation and its sub-units to achieve the agreed-upon objectives must be developed and adopted in such a way that the members are highly motivated to use these methods to their maximum potential.

Members of the organisation and the persons related to it must feel that the reward system of the organisation - salaries, wages, bonuses, dividends, interest payments - yields them equitable compensation for their efforts and contribution.'

1.5   Detrimental effects of groups

Having mentioned some of the favourable effects of groups, it must be mentioned that a group can have detrimental effects:

(a)   It may restrict, inhibit or even smother individuals.

(b)   Pressure to conform in ideas and behaviour may produce the negative results of:

   (i)   workers producing more work than an unreasonably low group norm may be punished by being fined, suspended or ostracised; and

   (ii)   personal distress of individuals attempting to solve conflict.

(c)   Unfair treatment of, and prejudice against, non members of the group.

(d)   Distortion of attitudes, judgements and perceptions by members wishing to belong to the best groups - group competition can be counter-productive.

(e)   Resistance to change imposed by management can be very destructive (as instanced in the factory visited by Gouldner where attempts were made to substitute an authoritarian approach for one which had been previously a pattern of indulgence). Unofficial strikes are also a good example of detrimental effects.

1.6   Group norms

[Definition]   A norm may be defined as: 'A standard of specific behaviour expected of and by the members of a social group'

In speaking about his work at the Hawthorne works of the Western Electric Company in Chicago, Mayo found that the company's payment by results scheme was being blocked by work groups setting their own norms of output and behaviour. The pressure from work colleagues within the group was a more potent force than the financial incentive offered for extra output. Elton Mayo stated that 'the itemised changes experimentally imposed could not be used to explain the major change - continually rising production'.

The eventual explanation put forward was that the girls experienced a tremendous increase in work satisfaction because they had greater freedom in their working environment.   As a result of removing the girls from a normal work situation and by intensifying their interaction and co-operation, informal practices, values, norms and social relationships had been built up giving the group high cohesion. The norms of output were those that the girls felt the researchers desired ie, they responded to the attention not the individual improvements in working surroundings.

Instances in which group norms are **less** than those expected by management are common as a defensive measure if the introduction of new machinery or new practices is seen as a threat to the group through redundancy. Even Taylor recognised **systematic soldiering**, which restricted output as a defence mechanism by the workers. He believed that scientific management could overcome such an obstacle to efficiency.

1.7   Types of industrial groups

Following research on a large number of work groups in a variety of different industries in America, four general work group types were identified:

(a)   **Apathetic groups** - usually made up of low paid, unskilled workers who were not likely to challenge the decisions of management or unions. Grievances and pressure tactics were rare, leadership was not clearly defined nor accepted and there was evidence of suppressed discontent, internal disunity and friction.

(b)   **Erratic groups** - found where jobs are similar and worker controlled; a large worker interaction occurs and the group were easily moved to adverse and inconsistent behaviour. There was highly centralised leadership and quick conversion to good relationships with management.

(c)   **Strategic groups** - hold better jobs than the two previous groups. They possess high self-interest and engage in activity in the union; skills are identified with the ability of the worker to make decisions on the performance of his work. There is a high degree of internal unity, evident from sustained union participation and relatively good production records in the long run.

(d)   **Conservative groups** - usually found at the higher end of promotional and status ladders, they are self-assured and successful with restrained pressure for highly specific objectives.

Clearly, different group types require different managerial approaches if they are to be used productively in a business organisation.

1.8   Morale

Morale is greatly affected by group behaviour and changing a group's existing structure can often destroy morale, if imposed.

Definition   McGivering defines morale as: 'The extent to which the members of a group identify with the aims and activities of the group.'

He suggests that this is the current usage, which has replaced the earlier view that morale applied to the emotional state of individual persons divorced from a group context. There are bound to be occasions when some individuals may not identify completely with the aims and activities of the group and the state of morale may be indicated by:

(a)   Degree of interest and involvement in group activities.

(b)   Level of absenteeism and labour turnover (though there may well be other variables involved).

However, opinions vary:

(a)   Mary Parker Follett believed that one of the benefits of participation is increased motivation and higher morale.

(b)   Urwick was convinced that a logical structure is better for efficiency and morale than one allowed to develop around personalities.

(c)   Brech believes that the morale of an organisation is largely a reflection of the outlook of its chief executive.

(d)   Initially, Mayo thought that the improvement in morale of workers in a spinning mill in Philadelphia was due to the frequency and duration of rest pauses that had been introduced; he later came to the conclusion that a stable social relationship in the work situation was the really important element.

(e)   Elliott Jacques, in the Glacier investigations, also discovered the importance of allowing group members to take part in setting departmental policy. Furthermore, recent evidence supports the view that an inability to exert a positive influence over its situation is likely to lead to low morale in the group.

(f)   Extensive research has failed to establish any direct correlation between high morale and high productivity although in the long run there is likely to be some measure of positive correlation.

2   THE DEVELOPMENT OF GROUPS

2.1   Reasons for the formation of groups

People come together in groups for a number of reasons which fall under two broad headings: 'personal' or 'situational'. Under the heading of 'personal' we could include such reasons as achieving personal goals, developing common interests (eg, a cricket team), achieving satisfaction of personal needs, or seeking protection from outside threats. In the case of situational groupings however the reasons for coming together are a bit more precise - the need to perform a specific task, to pass information amongst themselves, or because people are in the same geographic location. In the case of situational groups we may also find that the reasons for the grouping will also persist, as in the case of a research group who have a specific task to carry out.

Charles Handy (*Understanding Organisations*) suggests a number of reasons why groups are formed:

*   *for the distribution of work* - to bring together a set of skills, talents and responsibilities, and to allocate them to particular duties.

*   *for the management and control of work* - to allow work to be organised and controlled by appropriate individuals with responsibilities for a certain range of work.

*   *for problem solving and decision making* - to bring together a set of skills, talents and responsibilities so that the solution to any problem will have all available capacities applied to it.

*   *for information processing* - to pass on decisions or information to those who need to know.

*   *for information and idea collection* - to gather ideas, information or suggestions.

- *for testing and ratifying decisions* - to test the validity of a decision taken outside the group or to ratify such a decision.

- *for co-ordination and liaison* - to co-ordinate problems and tasks between functions and divisions.

- *for increased commitments and involvement* - to allow and encourage individuals to get involved in the plans and activities of the organisation.

- *for negotiation or conflict resolution* - to resolve a dispute or argument between levels, divisions or functions.

- *for inquest or inquiry into the past.*

Because a group is not a random crowd, it has certain characteristics.

- It has a *sense of identity*. Whether the group is formal or informal, its presence is recognised by its members who will recognise who does and who does not belong to the group. In general, people will want to belong to a grouping of some sort because they will have something in common with other members.

- There is *loyalty to the group norms*. This generally shows itself in abiding by group behaviour, and excluding from the group those who do not conform. Conformity may be found in such things as taking oaths of loyalty, or simply by abiding by group norms.

- It has *purpose and leadership*. Most groups have a specific purpose or objective, and will appoint leaders to help them achieve these goals. The factors determining who shall be leader may include age, seniority, or status. This hierarchy will be necessary to ensure that the group achieves its purpose.

2.2   Stages in the development of groups

Groups evolve over time in prescribed stages. Tuckman has defined four main stages of formation.

(a)   **Forming:** in this first stage members meet and try to find out about each other. They learn the purpose of the group. At this stage, there is no clear structure or behaviour pattern.

(b)   **Storming:** this stage sees manoeuvrings for roles, competition for leadership and questioning.

(c)   **Norming:** this is a settling period when standards and roles are accepted. Trust and morale should now increase.

(d)   **Performing:** at this stage group performance should achieve expected standards and the group identity be established.

In real life, these stages may blur and may occur rapidly or slowly. The manager will endeavour to bring the group through its first three stages quickly to reach expected performance.

3   CREATING AN EFFECTIVE WORK GROUP

3.1   Belbin

According to Belbin the success of a group, in terms of morale, behaviour and performance, can depend significantly upon the balance of individual skills and personality types within the group. He has designed a series of questionnaires whereby people can be identified as belonging to a particular group type. He suggests that there are eight main character types that a well balanced group would contain. (He has subsequently added a ninth).
These eight types are:

- **the leader or chairman** - co-ordinating (not imposing) and operating through others;

- **the shaper** - committed to the task, may be aggressive and challenging, will also always promote activity;

- **the plant** - thoughtful and thought-provoking;

- **the monitor-evaluator** - analytically criticises others' ideas, brings group down to earth;

- **the resource-investigator** - not a new ideas person but tends to pick up others' ideas and adds to them; is usually a social type of person who often acts as a bridge to the outside world;

- **the company worker** - turns general ideas into specifics; practical and efficient, tends to be an administrator handling the scheduling aspects;

- **the team worker** - concerned with the relationships within the group, is supportive and tends to defuse potential conflict situations;

- **the finisher** - unpopular, but a necessary individual; he is the progress chaser ensuring that timetables are met.

Different team roles indicate different types of behaviour, which are not necessarily linked to job and task skills. For instance, a person might be naturally imaginative - a 'good ideas' person. Another might be good at checking details to make sure everything has been covered. Yet another might be the person to make sure decisions are implemented and the task carried through to completion. Even though these team roles are not associated with particular job and task skills, they are considered crucial to task and goal achievement in that their presence or absence is said to influence significantly the work and achievements of teams. Consequently, most team role exponents maintain that, for a team to be high performing, it should be 'balanced'; that is, there should exist amongst the typical behaviours of members, the full range of team roles.

The description of Belbin's eight roles does not mean that a team cannot be effective with fewer than eight members. Members can adopt two or more roles if necessary. However, the absence of one of these functions can mean a reduction in effectiveness of the team. With no shaper, the team can get bogged down, with no finisher, important details can be missed, with no monitor-evaluator the team can be swayed by the very bright, articulate and possibly impractical shaper and so on.

3.2   Contingency approach to group effectiveness

Handy takes a contingency approach to determine what makes a group successful, in which, he proposes, three categories need to be considered:

- **The givens** - the group; the task; the environment;
- **The intervening factors** - motivation of group; processes and procedures; leadership style;
- **The outcomes** - the productivity of the group and the satisfaction of the group members.

Handy stated that in the short term group leaders cannot vary the 'givens' but they must understand each aspect since it presents a constraint within which they must operate. Within the givens, the characteristics of the group include the size of the group, member characters, group norms, individual members' objectives and roles, and stage of development of the group.

On the other hand 'intervenings' are within the influence of the team leader and should be operated to maximise the 'outcomes'. It should be noted that two outcomes are specified as reflecting effectiveness. Firstly, productivity relating to the group task and secondly, member satisfaction in being a part of the group exercise.

Conclusion   Handy's contingency approach should be carefully examined since it provides an analytical method for improving group effectiveness.

3.3   Pressures on group members

Pressures within a group need not be obvious, but may be implied, so that something as simple as being 'out of line' with the rest of the group may act as a pressure to get into line. Because groups develop their own identity, a member of a group is expected to conform to that identity. Therefore individual members of the group have a number of choices:

- complying with the group simply as a matter of convenience;
- accepting the group's ideas;
- rejecting the group's ideas.

Handy *(Understanding Organisations)* suggests that there is strong pressure on the individual when:

- an issue is vague, not clear cut;
- a person works in close proximity to other group members;
- a person lacks support for his view or behaviour.

It is also suggested that people will differ in the degree to which they conform:

- more intelligent people are less prepared to conform;
- people who conform to group pressures lack self-confidence;
- people who conform tend to be more anxious.

If there is any change in a person's expected behaviour we may find definite stages in the group's control process:

- *initial tolerance* - where the group may note the weakness and ask for an explanation;

- *attempts to correct* - group members have noted the shift from group behaviour and deliberately try to correct it;

- *verbal aggression* - if the shift from expected behaviour continues, then the group may become abusive with the implied threat of aggression;

- *physical aggression* - in the main this is likely to be used by groups at the lower levels (not by senior management);

- *rejection* - this is the last stage in the group's control process, and once a member has been rejected the group will rebalance its role.

Finally in this section it is worthwhile to reflect on the potential for actual conflict both within a group and between different groups. This issue is taken up in a later chapter.

4   SELF TEST QUESTIONS

4.1   What characteristics do groups have? (1.2)

4.2   How can groups be classified? (1.3)

4.3   What is meant by 'goal congruence'? (1.4)

4.4   List some of the reasons why groups form (Handy). (2.1)

4.5   List the four stages of group development (Tuckman). (2.2)

4.6   What type of personality does the 'plant' have? (3.1)

4.7   What does Handy mean by 'givens' and 'intervenings'? (3.2)

5   EXAMINATION TYPE QUESTION

5.1   Groups

You are required to

(a)   distinguish between 'formal' and 'informal' groups;   **(5 marks)**

(b)   list, with examples, **five** conditions which will encourage highly cohesive groups.**(15 marks)**
                                                                                               (Total: 20 marks)

6   ANSWER TO EXAMINATION TYPE QUESTION

6.1   Groups

(a)   **Formal groups**

The functional organisation of Henri Fayol places people into formal groups, which may be further sub-divided by sections or departments. As a result, such formal groups will consist of people working on the same project or product, similar skills but matched to different clients, salesmen who serve a similar locality or territory, a shift team or, as in the Trist and Bamforth experience, gangs working on a specific coal face.

Such groups can vary enormously. Project groups may be together just for the duration of the project. Similar situations exist for audit teams, who will go out on an audit and may be disbanded at its completion. A warship crew will be together for the completion of a commission, perhaps two or three years. Formal groups will vary in the degree of cohesion and size, but all will have a common purpose and a set of rules which governs their relationships.

Informal groups

Within the framework of formal groups, and transcending their boundaries, a network of informal groups will develop. Such groups will provide their membership with important benefits such as companionship, emotional support, assistance and even a form of protection. Such groups are likely to be highly cohesive.

(b)   **Common enemy/goal**

Members of a group who feel either threatened or well motivated will form a highly cohesive group. Where there is scope for strong union development trade union members will unite to form a common front. The NUM was a strongly cohesive union, and some of the public sector unions are exhibiting similar cohesion. Bowman cites the high cohesion of a well motivated entrepreneurial management team; what Peters and Austin might call a 'skunk works' will also be very cohesive.

Size

Small size will always encourage group cohesion. In the naval situation the crew of a small vessel, such as a mine-sweeper (about 45) will have the greater opportunity to interact - from the captain to the lowest rating. There will be strong ship loyalty. However, above a destroyer (about 300) there will be less scope for such interaction, and in the large ships the cohesion will be in levels of rank and messes.

Duration

A ship will usually commission for about two to three years. Once the crew has worked up (storming) and are running the ship well, a high degree of cohesion will develop. If, however, the group is together for a short time, then there is little opportunity for the cohesion to develop. Passengers on a cruise are a group, but they do not form a very cohesive one, since they are likely to be together for a relatively short time.

Homogeneity

Where there is a common interest, belief, education, age and gender will all help in the development of mutual understanding and cohesion. Where there is a good training scheme that tends to retain the people, there will be an informal group made up of the various cohorts of trainees.

Communication

If groups can communicate effectively, cohesion will develop. The secret of success among the trade unions arises from effective communication, even where it is of disinformation.

Cohesion may not always lead to the desired objective or result. The operatives in the famous Elton Mayo experiments formed a very cohesive elitist informal group. Mayo did not get the results he expected because the operatives formed a group who would do anything for the professor. Whatever the variation, they still worked very hard. By contrast, groups who are alienated will combine together to work negatively against the desired objectives.

But cohesion is not always a bad thing, nor is it confined to informal groups. The second part has been deliberately worded to emphasise the positive aspects of cohesion in formal groups.

17 DISCIPLINARY PROCEDURES

INTRODUCTION & LEARNING OUTCOMES

Syllabus area 11(iv)   •   Disciplinary procedures and their operation, including the form and process of formal disciplinary action and dismissal

An important part of any employee relations policy to be followed by management is to provide a clear statement of what behaviour is expected of an employee and the procedures to be followed in controlling behaviour. Inevitably there are times when an employee's conduct is of sufficiently poor standard to warrant disciplinary action.

If an employee can show that he or she was dismissed without just cause or excuse, they may bring a claim before the Industrial Tribunal under the Employment Protection (Consolidation) At 1978, and may qualify for compensation or other remedies.

The problems attached to dismissing incompetent employees include the unpleasantness of the task, combined with the fear of being taken to an industrial tribunal. To avoid some of the difficulties the personnel department should design written procedures for discipline and dismissal.

When you have studied this chapter you should be able to:

•   Explain the problems of maintaining discipline and evaluate the tools available to help a manager achieve it

---

1   DISCIPLINARY MATTERS

1.1   Discipline

An important part of any employee relations policy to be followed by management is to provide a clear statement of what behaviour is expected of an employee and the procedures to be followed in controlling behaviour. As one of Henri Fayol's principles, discipline was seen as:

Definition   'respect for agreements directed at achieving obedience, application, energy and respect. Discipline should be maintained by a fair disciplinary system with penalties judiciously applied by worthy superiors.'

Henri Fayol saw that for the smooth running of a business, discipline and precise and exact obedience at all levels was a necessity. He also thought that discipline was what leaders make of it.

Discipline is best obtained by:

•   good superiors at all levels;
•   agreements as clear and as fair as possible; and
•   sanctions (penalties) judiciously applied.

Where breaches occur, we should look at both the offending worker and at the leadership. In the last resort, penalties must be exacted from the offenders.

1.2   Effective discipline

A basis for effective discipline is good motivation and sound, clearly given instructions. It is essential for good communications to be used so that employees know what they are required to do. Ideally, discipline should be based on co-operation and a high morale, which will ensure rules and conditions are obeyed willingly.

Discipline can be obtained by rewards although it is usually by punishment where accepted norms of behaviour are not upheld. Some methods of disciplining are by reprimand, downgrading, suspension, refusing a wage increase, transfer or dismissal. By virtue of his or her position, a superior has the right to command and enforce obedience, if necessary. It also gives the right to punish, because of the harm that might be done to the group's purpose.

Disciplinary action should contribute towards improved behaviour, but certain matters must be noted.

- Behaviour expected must be communicated to those concerned. This is best done in the period of induction.

- Discipline should be exercised fairly, with no favouritism or excessive penalties. This should be done as soon after the breach as possible.

- Management should not break rules itself. A good example is essential.

- The quality of discipline can vary with the type of leadership and the understanding of the common purpose.

1.3   Discipline and punishment

It is important that students make a sharp distinction between 'discipline' and 'punishment'. They are quite different. Discipline may be defined as:

[Definition]   either a code of acceptable conduct or a system of rules establishing behaviour patterns.

Punishment means disciplinary action, which occurs as the result of some form of breakdown in the code of conduct (or the breaking of the code as a deliberate action). The idea behind discipline itself is to avoid reaching this point of breakdown.

Although discipline has the connotation of punishment, it should be seen as a more positive part of the function of management. As well as giving a means of control, correct imposition of discipline should provide an ordered, safe environment in which there is equity of treatment, team spirit is encouraged and initiative can be developed to the full.

Note: two types of generally accepted discipline can arise. Either:

- behavioural codes which are 'accepted'; or
- legally enforced regulations or rules, which are 'imposed'.

The two types provoke different reactions. If an 'accepted' code of behaviour (eg, a group 'norm') is not adhered to, then colleagues are likely to regard the code-breaker as an 'outsider' and inflict penalties upon him or her (eg, pressure to withdraw from that part of the organisation concerned). On the other hand, where a law is broken (eg, a minor traffic offence) then colleagues may actually sympathise. It is also possible for both types of reaction to occur for the same event.

As far as the organisation's own 'legal' rules are concerned, these are established to satisfy the requirements of the environment concerned, and these fall into four basic categories:

(a)   organisational image;

(b)   basic standards making for the organisation's and the personnel's well being;

(c)   prevention of loss of any kind, ineffectiveness and inefficiency;

(d)   behavioural codes which allow personnel of all grades to work in a satisfactory manner and to interact reasonably.

1.4   Disciplinary problems within the workplace

Problems within the organisation include:

- Excessive lateness in arriving at work, which delays any tasks done on a team basis or in the provision of a service for a client.

- Poor work performance, due to lack of care with shoddy work or a large number of rejects.

- Violation of safety rules, with potential danger either to the employee or his/her colleagues.

- Insubordinate attitude, which may affect the motivation of a group and which may create unnecessary stress or tension in the workplace.

- Failure to wear correct clothing, for reasons of hygiene with potential damage to output.

- Failure to wear appropriate standard of dress, which may affect the public image of the organisation.

- Abuse of 'time off' provisions which may affect the management attitude for all employees.

- Absence for no good reason, or without warning, with consequent adverse effect on work planning within the organisation.

- General non-compliance with the rules, regulations and procedures, negotiated for the well-being and safety of all employees.

1.5   Disciplinary problems outside the workplace

Whilst all employees might quite correctly resent any disciplinary procedures being involved within the organisation for behaviour outside the workplace, there may still be problems which could be seen as legitimate concerns for the supervisor:

- involvement with competition or undertaking private work to the detriment of the employer;
- personal abuse by alcohol or drugs which adversely affect performance at work;
- law-breaking activities which might reflect adversely on the employer.

2   EFFECTIVE ORGANISATIONAL PROCEDURES

2.1   Procedural agreements

These are agreements made between employers and employee representatives eg, staff associations and trade unions, defining the steps to be taken for the settlement of a specific issue without resort to any industrial action. Procedures are both treaties of peace and devices for the avoidance of war. Procedural agreements may relate to:

- grievances;
- discipline;
- disputes;
- promotion;
- redundancy.

2.2   Grievance policy

The procedures agreed should flow from a published statement of grievance policy agreed with the workforce. The Employment Protection Act requires the statement of terms and conditions of employment to which full time employees are entitled to name a person to whom grievances can be addressed. Grievance policies should: be simple; fair; provide for rapid settlement with prescribed time for each stage; and provide for settlement as near as possible to the point of grievance.

2.3   Dealing with disciplinary matters

If disciplinary action is to be administered fairly and consistently, the concept of progressive application might be considered appropriate for less serious misconduct:

(i)   informal chat with employee to clear up a relatively minor breach of discipline;

(ii)   formal oral warning with the supervisor stressing the possibility of more serious action if the misconduct is continued;

(iii)   formal written warning which becomes part of the employee's record;

(iv)   disciplinary action, such as suspension or layoff, to reinforce formal written warning;

(v)   dismissal is the final drastic action, which should only be applied if all other previous action fails.

Because of the serious implications of disciplinary action, there should be clear guidelines as to the level of management, which might be permitted to carry out suspensions, demotions or dismissals. However, all management, including supervisors, have an important role to play. Thus, it is vital that there should be clearly stated procedures in writing, communicated to all concerned and administered fairly and consistently within an environment that allows both sides to state their cases properly.

An organisation should institute a model disciplinary procedure, which aims to correct unsatisfactory behaviour rather than to punish it. Good practice should be based on the Advisory, Conciliation and Arbitration Service (ACAS) guidelines (or similar) which would normally only stipulate immediate dismissal or suspension followed by dismissal for gross misconduct.

2.4   Criteria for grievance and disciplinary procedures

ACAS suggest that procedures should be agreed with staff or union representatives and need to satisfy the following criteria:

	Disciplinary procedure	Grievance procedure
1. In writing	X	X
2. Timings of each stage laid down	X	X
3. Third party presence allowed	X	X
4. Managers trained in procedure	X	X
5. Definition of punishment for a given offence	X	N/A
6. Definition exists for each offence eg, what is lateness?	X	N/A
7. Appeals procedure	X	N/A
8. How long does offence stay on record?	X	N/A
9. Which manager is responsible for action?	X	X
10. Nature of grievance specified in advance?	N/A	X

Clearly, careful investigation should accompany any disciplinary procedure. Employees should be provided with detailed information on any punishments to be imposed and they should have a basic right to appeal - for which there should be a standard procedure.

3   THE ROLE OF MANAGEMENT IN RESPECT OF DISCIPLINARY MATTERS

3.1   Correction or reprimand

There is a difference between the two disciplinary matters which the manager or supervisor must clarify before dealing with. To deserve a reprimand (and possibly incur a penalty) the employee must be blameworthy. If he or she has done something wrong, but was not to blame eg, mistake due to poor training or unforeseeable circumstances, a correction should be the outcome. When employees feel that criticism is unjustified they may be uncooperative, argue their side fiercely or nurse a grudge, depending on their temperament.

3.2   Disciplinary situations

Imposing disciplinary action tends to cause resentment and such action is usually hated by both supervisors and their subordinates and, for that reason, are often avoided. Failure to act can only lead to increasing problems with a steady erosion of the control of the manager or supervisor within the department.

The challenge for the superior is to apply the action so it causes the least resentment. The rules should be easy to follow:

- The disciplinary action should take place straight after the offence is noticed or brought to the supervisor's attention.

- All employees must know what is expected of them and what a breach in their behaviour will lead to.

- The disciplinary action must be consistent. Inconsistency lowers the morale of other employees and diminishes the respect they have for the supervisor.

- Make the disciplinary action as impersonal as possible by removing the personality element from it. Bear no grudges afterwards.

- Try to keep the disciplinary action private to avoid the spread of conflict and the humiliation (or martyrdom) of the employee concerned.

4   THE DISCIPLINARY PROCESS

4.1   The procedure

A disciplinary procedure should:

(i)   be in writing;

(ii)   specify to whom it applies;

(iii)   provide for matters to be dealt with quickly;

(iv)   indicate the disciplinary action which may be taken;

(v)   specify the levels of management which have the authority to take the various forms of disciplinary action;

(vi)   provide for individuals to be informed of the complaints against them and to be given an opportunity to start their case before decisions are reached;

(vii)   give individuals the right to be accompanied by a trade union or by a fellow employee of their choice;

(viii) ensure that, except for gross misconduct, no employees are dismissed for a first breach of discipline;

(ix)   ensure that disciplinary action is not taken until the case has been fully investigated;

(x)   ensure that individuals are given an explanation for any penalty imposed;

(xi)   provide a right of appeal and specify the procedure to be followed.

4.2   Types of warning

The following types of warning might be appropriate in a disciplinary action:

Type	Issued by	Notes
Informal verbal	Immediate supervisor	No record would be kept of these
Formal verbal	Supervisor or manager	The warning will be formal in the sense that there is normally a formal interview or hearing, where the employee may be represented by a union official or colleague. A record will be kept of the warning but this is not confirmed in writing to the employee
Formal written	A senior manager	There is an interview and the outcome of the warning is confirmed in writing to the employee.
Final written	A senior manager or possibly the personnel manager	

4.3   Pre-interview

Before the interview, carry out a full investigation of the circumstances surrounding the employee's actions and collect the evidence required to substantiate the company's complaint against the employee.

The employee involved should also be notified and, if necessary, interviewed in order to ascertain his or her version of events.

Also, notify the individual's colleague or union representative who will be attending the interview.

4.4   Disciplinary interview

These are very formal affairs where the manager controls the proceedings and can plan in advance how he or she will deal with the guilty party and future consequences. This type of interview seeks to establish the facts and, assuming the complaint is valid, confirms to the offending employee that he/she has broken a company rule and warns the employee that a penalty is or will be enforced, either now or possibly in the event of further misconduct. The seriousness of the offence, such as gross misconduct, is identified, and at this stage the consequences of further offences must be discussed. It is hoped by this means to prevent further misconduct and so ensure the future efficiency and appropriate conduct of the employee.

Quite often, the employee can bring a friend as a witness to the details of the interview.

4.5   The features of an appeals procedure

ACAS outlines the right of the employee to appeal against supervisory discipline. It should not be the case that a supervisor will tell their subordinate that they can appeal to higher management and then bear a grudge if they do.

It is an obligation on the management of an organisation to provide an appeals procedure. At this appeal the disciplinary penalty given by the supervisor may be upheld, set aside or reduced. It is the senior manager's right to query the supervisor's verdict as this ensures justice for the employee.

5   DISMISSAL

5.1   Introduction

Dismissal is usually seen as the last step, the ultimate sanction in any disciplinary procedure. However, dismissals occur most frequently in the form of redundancy. Statistics published by the Department of Employment list the major reasons for dismissal as redundancy, sickness, unsuitability and misconduct in that order. Legislation in Britain during the 1970s, notably the *Industrial Relations Act 1971*, the *Trades Unions and Labour Relations Act 1974* and the *Employment Protection Acts 1975* and now the *Employment Protection (Consolidation) Act 1978* makes it a difficult and costly business to dismiss employees. There are now provisions for employees to challenge the employer's decision. However, in recent statistics published by the Department of Employment, it was revealed that only a proportion of cases of unfair dismissal actually reach Industrial Tribunals. Most are dealt with by some form of conciliation and arbitration.

5.2   Fair dismissal

There is a general presumption that all dismissals, with or without notice, are unfair unless the employer can prove otherwise. The employer is under a statutory obligation to show that a dismissal is fair. In this case a dismissal is fair if it is related to

(i)   **A lack of capability or qualifications** - this involves cases where the employee lacks the qualifications, skill, aptitude or health to do the job properly. However, in all cases the employee must be given the opportunity to improve the position or in the case of health be considered for alternative employment.

(ii)   **Misconduct** - this includes the refusal to obey lawful and reasonable instructions, absenteeism, insubordination over a period of time and some criminal actions. In the last case, the criminal action should relate directly to the job; it can only be grounds for dismissal if the result of the criminal action will affect the work in some way or other.

(iii) **A statutory bar** this occurs when employees cannot pursue their normal duties without breaking the law. The most common occurrence of this is the case of drivers who have been banned.

(iv)   **Some other substantial reason** - this is a separate reason and will include good work-related reasons for dismissal (eg a need for the business to change and the employees refusing to adapt to the change required).

In cases of dispute, if the organisation has a proper system of warnings and reprimands, it might be seen as evidence of fairness.

5.3   Dismissing incompetent staff

To avoid the unpleasantness associated with firing employees who do not reach the required standards, despite all efforts, the organisation should draw up some well-designed procedures for dismissal. These might include:

- Standards of performance and conduct, that are clearly defined and communicated to all employees.

- A system to warn employees where a gap is perceived between the standard and their performance.

- A defined period for improvement that is reasonable, with clear improvement targets and help and advice where necessary.

- Disciplinary procedures and ultimate consequences of continued failure made clear to the employee.

5.4   Unfair dismissal

In all cases of unfair dismissal there are two stages of proof. Firstly, the circumstances which represent fair grounds for dismissal must be established, and secondly, the tribunal must decide whether dismissal is fair in the circumstances of the case in question.

For dismissal to be automatically unfair, it must be for one of the following reasons:

(a)   Trade union membership or non-membership; or

(b)   Pregnancy; or

(c)   Sex or race discrimination; or

(d)   Revelation of a non-relevant spent conviction.

5.5   Provisions for unfair dismissal

If an employee can show that he or she was dismissed without just cause or excuse, they may bring a claim before the Industrial Tribunal under the Employment Protection (Consolidation) Act 1978, and may qualify for compensation or other remedies. The tribunal will normally refer the case to ACAS (Advisory Conciliation and Arbitration Service) in the hope of gaining an amicable settlement. Some form of conciliation and arbitration settles most cases. The possible solutions or remedies for unfair dismissal are set out below.

(a)   **Withdrawal of notice** - by the employer. This is the preferred remedy as stated in the *Employment Protection Act*.

(b)   **Reinstatement (order of Industrial Tribunal)** - this treats the employee as though he had never been dismissed. The employee is taken back to his old job with no loss of earnings and privileges.

(c)   **Re-engagement (order of Industrial Tribunal)** - in this case, the employee is offered a different job in the organisation and loses continuity of service. Both reinstatement and re-engagement were provisions introduced by the *Employment Protection Act*.

(d)   **Compensation (order of Industrial Tribunal)** - if an employer refuses to re-employ, then the employee receives:

- compensation made up of a penalty award of 13-26 weeks' pay (more in the case of discrimination);

- a payment equivalent to the redundancy entitlement; and

- an award to compensate for loss of earnings, pension rights and so on.

Some form of compensation may also be appropriate in cases of reinstatement and re-engagement.

5.6   Instant dismissal

It is worth noting that in spite of the legal protection against unfair dismissal an employer still retains the right to dismiss an employee instantly, without notice or money in lieu of notice. However, it is a severe action and justified only in the most exceptional circumstances. Furthermore, whether the employer is justified in an instant dismissal is always to be judged according to the facts of each case.

6   SELF TEST QUESTIONS

6.1   How is discipline best obtained? (1.1)

6.2   Outline some methods of disciplining. (1.2)

6.3   Distinguish between 'discipline' and 'punishment' (1.3)

6.4   Outline the types of disciplinary action that can be taken for less serious misconduct (2.3)

6.5   Why must disciplinary action be consistent? (3.2)

6.6   Why would the supervisor try to keep the disciplinary action private? (3.2)

6.7   What type of record is kept of an informal verbal warning? (4.2)

6.8   At appeal, can a senior manager set aside a penalty given by a supervisor to a subordinate? (4.5)

6.9   Briefly describe two cases where dismissal would be deemed to be fair. (5.2)

7   EXAMINATION TYPE QUESTION

7.1   Discipline v motivation

'One has only to think of the way in which the application of discipline at work can discourage interest and commitment, reduce effort and lower morale to appreciate that the discipline of staff in an organisation is likely to have a bearing on the level of work motivation and vice versa.'

(a)   Distinguish between 'discipline' and 'motivation'.   **(10 marks)**

(b)   What is self-discipline and how important is it for effective discipline in the workplace?
                                                                                          (5 marks)

(c)   Explain the inter-relationship between discipline and motivation proposed in the quotation.
                                                                                         (10 marks)
                                                                                   (Total: 25 marks)

8   ANSWER TO EXAMINATION TYPE QUESTION

8.1   Discipline v motivation

(a)   Discipline and motivation are both means by which the management of an organisation seek to ensure that employees make the effort necessary to achieve the objectives of the organisation.

Discipline means the establishment and maintenance of rules of orderly behaviour in an organisation, and the creation of sensible rules which promote the efficient working of an organisation. The term 'discipline' implies that some of the necessary rules are going to be unpopular to some extent with employees, and thus that disciplinary rules need to be enforceable by some sanction or other.

Motivation inspires employees to work hard independently of disciplinary rules. A highly motivated employee may need few disciplinary rules because the high level of motivation itself ensures that the orderly behaviour which discipline seeks to impose is automatically adopted by the employee. Motivation is generally achieved by satisfying the needs of the employees - perhaps by offering financial incentives, relating income directly or indirectly to output, but often equally importantly, by providing opportunities for self-realisation and fulfilment and the enjoyment of high status and esteem.

(b)   Self-discipline is the ability to impose orderly behaviour patterns upon oneself without the need for externally imposed rules. It is important in the workplace because if employees have it, or can be motivated to develop it, the need for detailed rules and regulations imposed by management is greatly reduced. A self-disciplined workforce is also likely to need less supervision and it implies that they are likely to approach their work with intelligence, realising that it is in their own interest to maximise productivity, provided, of course, that the package of remuneration and other benefits available reinforces this view.

(c)   The quotation suggests that the imposition of strict discipline may operate as a demotivator, and its implication is that a highly motivated workforce is likely to need less discipline. These concepts are probably valid, but it remains necessary for management to ensure that some discipline is there, since even highly motivated staff may take advantage of the absence of disciplinary rules. They may even be spurred on by their high motivation to disregard disciplinary rules, which have been introduced for safety reasons.

As pointed out in (a) above, both discipline and motivation exist in an organisation to promote the prosperity of the organisation by encouraging (or forcing) the staff to work. The trick for management to achieve is to balance the two. The optimum situation is a highly motivated workforce accepting the need for minimum disciplinary rules as necessary controls providing the background to their own self-discipline, but such a situation is not always easy to achieve. If the workforce is disaffected and lacks motivation the response of management is likely to be to impose strict discipline, perhaps with harsh penalties for infringements of the rules.

The management style of the organisation is also something that will affect the relationship and relative importance of the two factors. Even within the same organisation, departments may vary greatly in the extent to which discipline is relied upon and detailed rules enforced. Managers will seek to improve motivation and one way to do so may be to let the employees see that high motivation and self-discipline displayed by them is 'rewarded' by a slackening of disciplinary rules imposed by management.

18 LEGAL ISSUES AFFECTING HUMAN RESOURCE MANAGEMENT

INTRODUCTION & LEARNING OUTCOMES

Syllabus area 11(iv)   The nature and effect of legal issues affecting work and employment, including the application of appropriate employment law (ie, law relating to health, safety, discrimination, fair treatment, childcare, contracts of employment and working time)

In this chapter we look at legislation on recruitment and employment. Because of the concern to avoid exploitation and discrimination, a legal framework surrounds the whole area of human resource management that organisations must work within.

Employment law deals almost exclusively with civil law, where a plaintiff takes action against a person who committed a wrongful act. This means that the outcome of any case, if successful, will result in an award for damages or compensation, as opposed to imprisonment under criminal law.

We examine the roles and responsibilities assigned to employers and employees under the Health and Safety at Work Act 1974, as well as those allocated to safety representatives appointed by trade unions. The current legislation is designed to ensure reasonable safety in all places of employment.

When the organisation is devising its health and safety policy, it should apply good practices to every area that is affected. The policy should cover provisions for health and safety made in job descriptions, design of work systems, patterns of work, training and development, accident prevention and counselling.

Discrimination may operate in all kinds of areas including sex, sexuality and marital status, race and colour, religion, politics, disability and conviction of a criminal offence. Forward-looking organisations will have a positive attitude to equal opportunities and operate non-discriminating procedures to all aspects of human resource management, including recruitment and selection programmes, advertisements, access to training and promotion, disciplinary procedures, redundancy and dismissal.

When you have studied this chapter you should be able to:

- Explain how the legal environment influences the relationships between the organisation and its employees, and between the employees of an organisation

- Explain the responsibilities of the organisation, its managers and staff in relation to health and safety and advise how a manager can promote the health and safety of subordinates

- Explain the various ways in which fair treatment of employees can be achieved, and the role of government in ensuring this

1 A LEGAL FRAMEWORK

1.1 Background

Because of concern by successive governments to avoid exploitation and discrimination, human resource management is perhaps more subject to legislation than any other aspect of corporate management.

When we consider employment law, we are dealing almost exclusively with civil law, where a plaintiff takes action against a person who committed a wrongful act. This means that the outcome of any successful case will normally be an award of compensation and/or damages, as opposed to prosecution and possible imprisonment under criminal law. Employers can be imprisoned under certain specific conditions eg, where negligence is proved under the health and safety legislation, but there are very few cases.

In the UK, Acts of Parliament mainly determine the conduct of employment relations. Codes of practice are also important; these are recommended procedures that describe good practice in such areas as recruitment, discipline, equal opportunities and redundancy, even though there are laws surrounding these areas. Bodies such as ACAS (Advisory, Conciliation and Arbitration Service), the EOC (Equal Opportunities Commission) and the CRE (Commission for Racial Equality) are among the main providers of such recommendations.

1.2   Institutions controlling employment relations

There are three main British institutions that control the conduct of employment relations through law - Industrial Tribunals, ACAS and EATs (Employment Appeals Tribunals).

Industrial Tribunals are relatively informal courts, which hear and pass judgement on claims made under employment law. Applicants and respondents (employees and employers) may be legally represented or may represent themselves.

ACAS was formed with a specific remit to promote the improvement of industrial relations and encourage the development and reform, where necessary, of collective bargaining mechanisms. Advice is generally one-off enquiries, surveys and some projects. Conciliation is the settling of individual or collective disputes and arbitration is the judgement when conciliation and negotiation are exhausted.

Employment Appeals Tribunals act as appeals courts for industrial tribunal decisions, which have been challenged, either by the employee or the employer. Their role is to reconsider the industrial tribunal decisions and pass judgements that will satisfy the aggrieved party and prevent the dispute from going higher up in the legal hierarchy.

2   CONTRACT OF EMPLOYMENT

2.1   Introduction

It is important to differentiate the contract of employment (sometimes referred to as a 'contract of service') from other contracts under which one person agrees to perform work for another. Many statutory rights are conferred only on persons employed under contracts of employment.

When a person is newly employed, a contract of employment has to be exchanged. This is of considerable significance in the determination of the legal rights and obligations of both parties. In some parts of the world, this individual contract is not so significant since the obligations, rights and remedies of the parties involved in it are determined by collective agreement. However, in the UK these collective agreements themselves create legalities if and when they are specifically incorporated into the contract.

2.2   Sources of the contract

The contract of employment normally derives from several different sources - some express, some implied. Examples of these sources are:

(a)   an agreement between the parties;

(b)   an agreement between unions and employers which the parties agree to operate;

(c)   a term being implied from common law;

(d)   the custom of a trade;

(e)   a statutory provision which requires the parties to the contract to observe a certain term (for example, the Employment Protection (Consolidation) Act 1978 provides for employees who are laid off to get guarantee payments).

2.3   Terms of the contract

Note that there are two kinds of terms to a contract of employment, express and implied.

Implied terms - the contract does not have to be in writing. There are implied terms and conditions, which are established by custom or general usage in the industry or in the organisation. What is *implied* is that the employer should pay the agreed wages/salaries, and adopt reasonably safe procedures in the workplace. But, as a rule, the employer is not *obliged* to provide work. Also, on the part of the employee, he or she must co-operate with the employer, use skill and care in obeying lawful instructions, and give a faithful service.

Express terms - the present trend is for contracts of employment to be in writing, as a result of the provisions of the Contracts of Employment Act 1963, which are now contained in the Employment Protection (Consolidation) Act 1978.

Under the Trade Union Reform and Employment Rights Act 1993, an employer must give employees covered by the Act, within thirteen weeks of the beginning of the period of employment, a written statement which:

(a)   Identifies the parties.

(b)   Gives the date when the period of continuous employment began, and where employment with a previous employer counts as part of the employee's period of continuous employment, the date when the previous employment began. If the contract is for a fixed term the statement has to give the date of expiry.

(c)   Gives particulars of the following terms of employment:

   (i)   the scale or rate of pay and payment intervals;
   (ii)   hours of work;
   (iii)   holidays, holiday pay and entitlement to accrued holiday pay;
   (iv)   sick pay/leave provisions;
   (v)   pensions and pension schemes;
   (vi)   notice required for termination by employer and employee;
   (vii)   job title (not job description).

There are, in addition, certain statutory conditions laid down in respect of particular industries (eg for road haulage, hotel and catering, etc) and these cannot be in any way limited by any employer-employee agreement. Additionally, the written statement must have a note stating what disciplinary rules are applicable, to whom the employee can appeal against a disciplinary decision or to whom the grievance can be taken. Any appeals procedure must also be stated.

Furthermore, there are *working rules,* which have been established by employers and unions, and these are normally issued in booklet form and set out agreements reached on issues such as public holidays, night work shifts, payments for certain conditions (eg for dirty work), bonuses and tea breaks; etc.

This does mean that employers are, overall, restricted as to the conditions of service statements by industrial agreement - the union usually supporting the idea that both employer and employee must abide by these.

Organisational regulations also exist, especially in very large firms, and these are usually set out in pamphlets or booklets, which are available to employees. The broad rules are usually indicated to the new recruit upon engagement. The topics these cover will include

(a)   the suggestions system;

(b)   punctuality;

(c)   special leave of absence for, say, local councillors who are employees, or for Territorial Army members;

(d)   complaints procedure;

(e)   medical examinations; and

(f)   parking.

Finally, there are, always, informal rules and regulations, which have arisen as conventional, acceptable standards of behaviour in the organisation. These have a very wide range, from the unofficial inferences drawn concerning some official (formal) rules which have arisen over the years, to understood ways of going about things. The recruit has to learn of these from colleagues, usually by experience.

The important point to grasp is that, wherever possible, the employee should be given a statement of the conditions and the regulations of service in writing. This should be completely understood by the employee and he or she should be able to ask for any clarification - which should be offered willingly. Only in this way can there be a clear understanding and the avoidance of conflict in these issues.

2.4   The employer's duties

Imposed upon the parties to a contract of employment are various implied obligations. Though based on common law, these obligations have been considerably elaborated upon by statute.

(i)   **Duty to pay wages** - the payment of wages is sometimes described as the employer's primary duty - in that a failure to pay on the part of the employer will be regarded as breach of a fundamental term of the contract, entitling the employee to leave immediately. Deductions from wages and method of payment of wages are governed by the Payment of Wages Act 1960.

(ii)   **Provision of an itemised pay statement** - by the Employment Protection (Consolidation) Act 1978 every employee is entitled to an itemised pay statement containing the following details:

  (i)   gross pay;

  (ii)   variable and fixed deductions and their purposes;

  (iii)   net pay;

  (iv)   where different parts of net wages are paid in different ways, the amount and method of payment of each part.

(iii)   **Payment during sickness** - where a contract of employment is silent regarding wages during the employee's absence through sickness, the employer remains liable to continue paying wages so long as the contract is not ended by giving proper notice.

(iv)   **Equal pay for equal work** - The *Sex Discrimination Act 1975* requires employers to pay men and women equally.

(v)   **Duty to indemnify** - it is implied in every contract of employment (unless the contrary is expressly stated) that the employee who incurs expense on his employer's behalf is entitled to be indemnified.   The expense or payment must have been made in the course of the employee's duties.

(vi)   **Duty to provide work** - it is sometimes said that an employer is under a duty not just to pay wages but also to provide work. The accepted view is that an employer will not be failing in his contractual duties by not providing work, provided he continues paying wages except:

   (i)   in the case of a piece-worker who requires to be given work to earn wages;

   (ii)   in the case of public performers who require the opportunity of work to maintain and enhance their reputation;

   (iii)   where failure to provide work extends over such a length of time as to indicate a deliberate intention not to carry out the contract.

   Also an employer who agrees to employ an employee for '40 hours per week' is required to pay the employee for 40 hours whether work is available or not. The employer has no right unilaterally to reduce the working week.

(vii)   **Duty to provide for the employee's safety** - it is the duty of every employer at common law to take reasonable care for the safety of his employees, and failure to do so will render the employer liable in damages to an injured employee or his dependants. Statutes lay down other duties regarding the health and safety of employees and others (non-employees), eg. Factories Act 1961, Health & Safety at Work Act 1974. Some of these statutes or regulations made under them create specific duties for particular types of work.

2.5   The employee's duties

There is an underlying duty of faithful service implied into every contract of service. Often, of course, contracts of employment will contain express provisions regarding the employee's duties and these may provide additional or supplementary obligations.

(a)   **Duty of care** - there is implied into every contract of employment a duty that the employee performs his contract with proper care.

(b)   **Duty of co-operation** - even where the employer promulgates a rulebook containing instructions for the execution of the work, the employee is under an obligation not to construe the rules in a way designed to defeat the efficiency of the employer's business.

(c)   **Duty of obedience** - in the absence of express provisions an employee is required to carry out all reasonable and lawful orders of the employer. Some orders clearly do not require obedience eg, falsify sales records on employer's instructions; drive an unroadworthy vehicle, which may lead to his prosecution under the Road Traffic Acts.

(d)   **Loyal service** - this duty may be expressed, in general, as follows:

   •   To use all reasonable steps to advance his employer's business within the sphere of his employment.

   •   Not to do anything which might injure the employer's business.

2.6   Termination of employment - by notice

At common law the contract of employment may be terminated by either party for any reason or for no reason upon giving notice of a reasonable length, unless the contract is one for a fixed term or unless it specifically restricts the reason for which it may be terminated. Proper notice may be either:

(a)   what the contract provides;

(b)   what is reasonable if there is no contractual term regarding notice;

(c)   what is provided by the Employment Protection (Consolidation) Act 1978.   A contractual term providing for notice shorter than is specified in the 1978 Act is void and therefore unenforceable.

The Employment Protection (Consolidation) Act 1978 lays down minimum periods of notice for both employer and employee. A contract of employment may not permit either side to give less than the minimum period of notice. However, either party may waive his or her right to notice, or take a payment in lieu. The Act does not affect the right to terminate a contract without notice in the event of gross misconduct.

2.7   Summary termination

As we have already discussed in the section on dismissal, at common law either party may lawfully terminate the contract summarily eg, sacked without giving any notice, if the other party has committed a serious breach of the contract. The general principle justifying summary dismissal is that the employee's conduct prevents further satisfactory continuance of the employer-employee relationship eg, misconduct including disobedience, insolence and rudeness, committing a criminal act such as stealing or causing injury through practical jokes.

3   HEALTH AND SAFETY

3.1   The reasons for health, safety and security requirements

Every year in the United Kingdom there are thousands of accidents in the office, which result in injury. The latest estimates amount to around 50,000 office accidents each year, 5,000 of them being serious. Health and safety at work should be a concern for ourselves and our colleagues, and if we are managers or employers we also have a responsibility for the health and safety of our employees. Typical hazards in an office might include desks/chairs too near to doors, trailing wires, cables and leads, unlit or poorly lit corridors and stairs, top-heavy filing cabinets, unmarked plate glass doors and wet floors. There are of course potentially many others; this list is not intended to be comprehensive.

The consideration, design and implementation of the working environmental factors will be governed by appropriate legal regulations. Although there are many statutes which affect the relationship between an organisation and its employees, the main Acts of Parliament which are relevant to the office environment are outlined below.

3.2   The Health and Safety at Work Act 1974

The Act was designed to have far-reaching consequences upon employers' premises and methods of work. The Act of 1974 can be seen to apply in four general areas, in addition to the detailed new legislation. These four general areas are:

(a)   Employee's responsibilities present under common law are restated, namely:

(i)   to take reasonable care of himself and others;
(ii)   to allow the employer to carry out his duties and responsibilities;
(iii)   not to deliberately or recklessly alter or operate any machinery or equipment.

(b)   The replacement of many of the provisions of the 1963 Offices, Shops and Railway Premises Act. This earlier Act listed environmental first aid and fire prevention provisions, many of which are now superseded by the general codes of practice recognised by the Health and Safety at Work Act. Some detailed rules which are specified include:

(i)   an allocated allowance of floor area per person;
(ii)   temperature to be 16°C within one hour of work commencement time;
(iii)   sanitation, washing facilities and fresh drinking water must be provided;

(iv)   first aid facilities and named employees available, who are trained in first aid.

(c)   Fire Precautions Act 1971 provisions were re-emphasised in 1974. In particular:

(i)   presence of effective fire alarm system, fire lighting equipment and fire drills - these must be known to employees;

(ii)   regulations regarding fire exits.

(d)   General aspects for the employer involve:

(i)   Provision of a safe working environment with minimum risk to health. The extent of this liability is being tested with cases of employees suing their employers for health problems arising many years later, as in the case of the asbestos workers and the recent case of passive smoking-induced cancers. This general provision covers such areas as heating, ventilation, lighting, noise, pollution, sanitation and washing.

(ii)   To ensure the proper and safe operation, handling, storage and movement of all goods and materials (including dangerous substances). There is also a requirement to provide protective clothing free of charge.

(iii)   Reporting certain injuries, diseases and dangerous occurrences to the enforcing authority. New regulations - the Reporting of Injuries, Diseases and Dangerous Occurrences Regulations (RIDDOR) – unify all previous reporting arrangements.

(iv)   To supply information, training and supervision regarding training matters.

(v)   To provide and publish a safety policy.

(vi)   To appoint safety representatives to check on safety matters.

(vii)   To provide and maintain safe machinery.

(viii)   To provide first aid facilities and trained personnel.

(ix)   To extend the safety provisions to cover members of the public, as well as employees, so that they will not be at risk on company premises. An example would be the requirement for visitors to wear a 'hard hat' when visiting a construction site.

The *Health and Safety at Work Act 1974* is an umbrella statute under which regulations are being made to strengthen and gradually replace the provisions under the earlier statutes such as the *Factories Act 1961*. Enforcement of safety regulations is now made under the *1974 Act* by Health and Safety Inspectors.

3.3   Employers' obligations under the Act

Except where fewer than five people are employed there is a duty on employers to prepare and, as appropriate, revise written policy statements relating to the health and welfare of employees. These statements and their revisions must:

(a)   be brought to the notice of all employees;

(b)   give details of the organisation and arrangements that are in operation for the implementation of the policy;

(c)   be incorporated into appropriate procedures and rules.

Policy statements should, before issue, be approved by the recognised trade unions.

3.4 Safety representatives

The Act introduced Safety Representatives to achieve maximum employee involvement in safety matters. This part of the Act was amended by the *Employment Protection Act* in that the safety representative must come from a recognised trade union. Certain functions of the safety representative have been identified; these are

(i) to investigate potential hazards
(ii) to investigate complaints
(iii) to make representations to the employer
(iv) to carry out inspections
(v) to represent the employees
(vi) to receive information from inspectors.

A safety representative must be permitted to take time off with pay for the purposes of performing these functions.

3.5 Enforcement of the Act

The enforcement comes within the control of the Health and Safety Commission and Executive, which were set up to administer the provisions of the Act.

(i) An *improvement notice* is served on a person who is contravening a requirement of the Act by an inspector. The person is required to remedy the contravention within a specified period.

(ii) A *prohibition notice* is served where, in the opinion of the inspector, an activity gives rise to risk of serious personal injury.

4 APPLYING GOOD PRACTICE

4.1 Health and safety policy

M Armstrong in his book *A Handbook of Personnel Management Policy* made an idealised statement of health and safety policy. Its provisions are

(a) The safety of employees and the public is of paramount importance.

(b) Safety will take precedence over expediency.

(c) Every effort will be made to involve all managers, supervisors and employees in developing and implementing procedures.

(d) Legislation is to be complied with in the spirit as well as to the letter of the law.

Within this idealised framework, some or all of the following courses of action may be appropriate

(a) *Job descriptions*, which stress the health and safety aspect of the job.

(b) *The design of work systems* to reduce health and safety hazards; using engineering design to build in safety controls.

(c) *Creating patterns of work* to reduce accidents directly, eg the introduction of rest pauses, or indirectly, eg by reducing stress by introducing flexitime, job enrichment and so on.

(d) *The training of employees*, identifying what employees must know concerning health and safety and then devising the most appropriate method of instruction. The actual training is comparatively simple; the real difficulty is in ensuring that workers comply with the safety regulations once they have been trained. Follow up campaigns using posters, films, discussion groups and the like have been shown to have a limited effect only and need to be repeated at regular intervals. However, safety training may be handicapped by unfavourable images of the safe worker. Recent research by Piriani and Reynolds concluded that the safe worker was perceived by management as being slow and overcautious and by his workmates as being unsociable.

(e)   *Formal procedures* are set up by most organisations. They range from employing a safety officer and a medical officer, to establishing disciplinary procedures to deal with rule-breaking.

(f)   *Accident prevention* by carrying out an analysis of accidents.

(g)   *Participative management* in an attempt to involve the workforce in the question of health and safety. We have already seen that involvement has been institutionalised in the Health and Safety at Work Act by the introduction of safety representatives. In some industries, such as mining, there is an obvious commitment on the part of employees toward a shared objective of safe working. In other firms, involving the workforce in safety matters is a problem that no amount of committees or publicity has yet solved. The problem may lie in an attitude generated by management who may see safety work as having a low status.

(h)   *Employee counselling* has met with some success, particularly in reducing stress, an area of a great deal of current concern and research.

4.2   The welfare function today

The *Shops Offices and Railway Premises Act* laid down a law as to the minimum amount of space for an individual worker to occupy. It also addressed such basic issues as washing and toilet facilities and working temperatures. All of this is now expected and accepted by employees and employers and today's welfare issues concern such things as the handling of hazardous substances. Social issues are also now regarded as a welfare concern; these include things such as smoking within the working environment.

Due to this increase in complexity, the modern role of welfare in organisations is less easy to define. In its widest context, welfare, as the concern for people as individuals, can be seen in most personnel management policies, in selection interviewing, counselling, appraisal schemes and so on. In a narrow context, welfare can be viewed as a set of provisions that have a great deal of overlap with fringe benefits. For example, because of the increased attention to equal opportunities and also the need to recruit more women returnees to the workforce, many organisations are improving their child care arrangements. These provisions have been identified by Thomason as canteen and recreational facilities, information services such as legal aid, the provision of houses, nurseries, transport and the like, further education provision and medical services.

Thomason feels that such provisions may enable people to work better within the normal functioning of the enterprise and may have an effect on such factors as recruitment, loyalty and length of service. The evidence, however, is far from conclusive. A study carried out in the United States in 1970 by Metzger found that most employees preferred higher wages to welfare provisions, which they had to accept irrespective of whether they suited individual needs.

5   EQUAL OPPORTUNITIES AND DISCRIMINATION

5.1   Legislation

There are five main statutes, which relate to equal opportunities and discrimination:

(a)   The *Equal Pay Act 1970*;

(b)   The *Sex Discrimination Act 1975*;

(c)   The *Disabled Persons (Employment) Acts, 1944 and 1958*;

(d)   The *Race Relations Act 1976*; and

(e)   The *Rehabilitation of Offenders Act 1974.*

5.2   The Equal Pay Act 1970

The Act is intended to prevent discrimination between men and women with regards to the terms and conditions of employment. It makes it clear that the provisions apply equally to men and women (ie, a man can also claim if he has a less favourable term than a woman has). The Act did not come into force until 1975 to give employers time to bring their terms and conditions into line with the legislation. The Act covers all conditions and terms of employment and not just pay. It aims to ensure that where men and women are employed in like work or work of an equivalent nature, they will receive the same terms and conditions of employment.

5.3   The Sex Discrimination Act 1975

This Act renders it unlawful to make any form of discrimination in employment affairs because of marital status or sex. This applies especially to the selection process as it offers protection to both sexes against unfair treatment on appointment. Note that there are two kinds of discrimination, direct and indirect (see also below):

(a)   **Direct discrimination** - occurs when someone is treated less favourably than someone of the opposite sex - perhaps by being banned from applying for a job because of being a woman. This type is not difficult to discover.

(b)   **Indirect discrimination** - in this case, an employer may relate a condition to an applicant for a job which does not actually seem relevant to it, but which suggests that only one sex would be acceptable. An example of this may be advertising so that only men are encouraged to apply.

5.4   The Disabled Persons (Employment) Acts, 1944 and 1958

The power to enforce the provisions of these Acts is not extensive and co-operation has been developed between employers and the government, with special official advisers being available for consultation.

The Acts introduce a *quota system* obliging employers to employ a percentage (standing now at 3%) of people handicapped by disablement. It is an offence to employ additional non-disabled persons if the quota has not been reached.

5.5   The Race Relations Act 1976

This makes it unlawful to discriminate on grounds of race, colour, nationality, and ethnic or national origin.

Direct and indirect discrimination are included. There is also a *code of practice* to eliminate racial discrimination and to establish equal opportunity in employment, published by the Commission for Racial Equality. As a result of this code, employers are able to adopt anti-discriminatory policies - ensuring that management is aware of the legal position.

5.6   Rehabilitation of Offenders Act 1974

Although this Act declares that former convictions are not relevant and do not have to be stated at interviews for jobs, many exceptions are given and no remedy is forthcoming where someone is discriminated against during selection.

6   PROMOTION OF NON DISCRIMINATION

6.1   Equal opportunities

'Equal opportunities' is a generic term describing the belief that there should be an equal chance for all workers to apply and be selected for jobs, to be trained and promoted in employment and to have that employment terminated fairly. Employers should only discriminate according to ability, experience and potential. All employment decisions should be based solely on a person's ability to do the job in question, no consideration should be taken of a person's sex, age, racial origin, disability or marital status.

6.2   Developing good practice

A number of employers label themselves as *equal opportunity employers*, establishing their own particular kind of equal opportunity policy. However, while some protection is afforded by employment legislation, the majority of everyday cases must rely on good practice to prevail.

Developing and applying good working practice should cover all of the aspects of human resource management including the following:

(a)   recruitment;
(b)   terms and conditions of employment;
(c)   promotion, transfer and training;
(d)   benefits, facilities and services; and
(e)   dismissal.

The main areas where good practice can be demonstrated are:

•   *Job analysis* - person specifications must not be more favourable to men or women.

•   *Advertisements and documentation* - advertisements must not discriminate on sex or marital status grounds. This means that job titles must be sexless eg. 'salesman' becomes 'sales person'.

•   *Employee interviewing and selection* - questions must not be asked at interviews, which discriminate by implication eg, asking a woman whether or not she intends to have children.

•   *Redundancy* - if a redundancy situation becomes inevitable management must:

        (a)   indicate the reasons for the situation, and what steps they have taken to avoid it;

        (b)   indicate the numbers and categories of people likely to be affected;

        (c)   indicate the timetable in accordance with the legislation;

        (d)   identify a manager to be responsible for the implementation and to have executive responsibility on behalf of the company.

(This will be important, since redundancy is always news, and there will be all kinds of people who will be asking questions about what is going on.)

7   MATERNITY RIGHTS

7.1   Statutory rights

The provisions that apply to pregnant women, under the Employment Protection (Consolidation) Act 1978 give those who qualify the following statutory rights:

(i)   Maternity pay for up to six weeks of confinement.

(ii)   Entitlement to return to work, based on the duration of employment and other factors. This is the right to return to the job done for her employer at the time when she stopped work due to pregnancy. The right normally has to be exercised within 29 weeks of the birth. The employee is entitled to return to work without any alteration in the capacity in which she had been employed, the place employed, the seniority, pension and similar rights. Only if the job previously done has become redundant is the employer permitted to offer 'alternative employment'.

The Employment Act 1980 provides two cases where the right to return to work may be excluded:

(a)   where there are five or fewer employees and it is not reasonably practicable to reinstate or offer a suitable alternative;

(b)   if reinstatement would mean a redundancy and the employer does offer a suitable alternative.

The onus is on the employer to show that the exclusion of the right is justified.

(iii)   Should an employer dismiss a woman because she is pregnant, the woman is considered, prima facie to have been unfairly dismissed. However, this provision does not apply if the woman was incapable of performing her normal work (due to her pregnancy; or, if her continued employment would be contravening other legislation).

Note: Paid time off must be given for ante-natal care (under the *Employment Act 1980*).

8   SELF TEST QUESTIONS

8.1   What does EOC stand for? (1.1).

8.2   Why was ACAS formed? (1.2).

8.3   Explain 'express terms' in a contract. (2.3).

8.4   Briefly describe one of the duties of an employer. (2.4).

8.5   What fire precautions are outlined in the Health and Safety at Work Act 1974? (3.2).

8.6   List some of the functions of the safety representative. (3.4).

8.7   In what area has employee counselling met with some success? (4.1)

8.8   Briefly outline the main provisions of The Equal Pay Act 1970 (5.2)

8.9   Employers can discriminate in some areas - what are they? (6.1)

9   EXAMINATION TYPE QUESTION

9.1   Legal framework

You are the newly appointed Chief Accountant of the subsidiary of a publicly quoted company. You have just had a meeting with John Harrison, the senior Management Accountant, about a problem in his department. Your notes from that meeting are set out below.

Notes

Eileen Skinner joined the Accounts Department four years ago from Watt and Armitage, a local firm of accountants. She had already passed the final examinations of the Association of Accounting

Technicians and came with excellent references. Her performance until recently has been good. She has scored well in every annual review, never getting an overall performance rating of less than 7 out of 10, and has been viewed as a strong candidate for promotion to a higher grade.

In recent weeks the quality of her work has deteriorated and she has taken to arriving late and leaving early. She has also begun to take days off, sometimes without offering a proper explanation. Her immediate superior has tolerated the situation because of Eileen's past record. However, other members of staff are beginning to complain that Eileen is not pulling her weight and, as one colleague put it, 'if she can get away with it, why can't we?'

John doesn't want Eileen Skinner to be dismissed but he can see no other way out if morale in the department is to be maintained. The parent company has a policy of being a 'good' employer and of meeting its legal obligations in full. Prepare a Memorandum for John Harrison setting out your proposals for dealing with the problem.

Required

(i)   Set out the legal framework covering the situation   **(15 marks)**

(ii)   What procedure would you follow if Eileen is to be disciplined or dismissed?   **(10 marks)**

(Total: 25 marks)

10   ANSWER TO EXAMINATION TYPE QUESTION

10.1   Legal framework

MEMORANDUM

To: John Harrison
From: Chief Accountant
Date: 15th April 20X0

Subject: Eileen Skinner

(i)   **Legal framework**

There are a number of points to raise on the legal situation.

From the notes it is not clear whether Eileen is employed by the company ie, has a contract of employment or is self employed and has a contract for services. Assuming she is an employee, working full time under a degree of supervision for a salary, Eileen has a contract of employment.

The Employment Protection (Consolidation) Act 1978 requires that all employees receive a statement of their terms and conditions of employment. As well as details of pay, this statement should outline the normal working hours, holiday entitlement, sickness procedures and periods of notice to be given by both the employee and employer. Where disciplinary and grievance procedures exist, these should be detailed in the statement. As a new recruit Eileen should have been informed of the following:

- disciplinary procedures, including the number of warnings, oral or written, which will be given before suspension or dismissal;

- grievance procedures, outlining who is responsible for dealing with complaints about any aspect of employment which the employee is not satisfied with;

- what constitutes a disciplinary offence;

- how many stages there are to the disciplinary procedure;

- what the rights of appeal and representation are.

A contract of employment places duties on both employer and employee. The employer's duties include provision of remuneration and work, holidays, sick pay and maternity provision. The employee's duties under the contract include fidelity, skill and care and obedience in carrying out lawful and reasonable instructions.

A contract of employment can end either by mutual agreement, by giving notice, by passage of time in the case of a fixed term contract, by dismissal or by redundancy.

Dismissal will be unfair if:

(i)   it relates to trade union membership or activities;

(ii)   the employer fails to prove the reason for dismissal relates to:

- the capability of the employee to perform the work;
- the conduct of the employee;
- redundancy;
- the employee contravening a restriction imposed by law by continuing employment;

(iii)   a female employee is dismissed because of pregnancy.

Acts of gross misconduct include the refusal to obey lawful and reasonable instructions, absenteeism, insolence and rudeness, committing a criminal act such as stealing or causing injury through practical jokes.

Other legal issues to take into consideration are:

(a)   The *Equal Pay Act 1970*;

(b)   The *Sex Discrimination Act 1975*, making it unlawful to discriminate, either directly or indirectly, because of sex or marital status;

(c)   The *Disabled Persons (Employment) Acts, 1944 and 1958*;

(d)   The *Race Relations Act 1976*, making it unlawful to discriminate because of race, colour, nationality or ethnic origin.

(ii)   **Recommendations**

Eileen seems to have problems, which she is not sharing with either her colleagues or her superiors. She has not committed any gross misconduct, which would justify immediate dismissal and her behaviour is only recently changed.

The company's disciplinary code follows the guidelines laid down by ACAS and I suggest that we initiate this procedure. The steps, which should be agreed with Eileen and formally written down are as follows:

(a)   Investigate and record the frequency of Eileen's late arrivals, early departures and days off work. Have an informal talk with Eileen to establish the cause of her recent change in behaviour. There may be problems at home or she may be unwell. She may be experiencing some difficulties in the office, such as sexual harassment or discrimination, which is making her behaviour different. Explain the feelings of the rest of the department and express your concern about the situation, using the results from the investigation.

Eileen may have decided that she would like to work fewer hours or in a different department and the company may be able to help her, if this is the problem.

If the poor conduct continues the disciplinary procedure will continue.

(b)   An oral warning given to Eileen reminding her that her conduct is not acceptable. The quality of work and conduct we expect should be brought to her attention.

(c)   A written warning, outlining the consequences of her continuing misconduct.

(d)   A second written warning.

(e)   Dismissal or other disciplinary action (which will be agreed with the personnel department after her oral warning).

19 CONFLICT IN ORGANISATIONS

INTRODUCTION & LEARNING OUTCOMES

Syllabus area 11(iv) • The sources of conflict in organisations and the ways in which conflict can be managed to ensure working relationships are productive and effective.

Conflict is an important aspect in the understanding of organisational behaviour. It is accepted that not all conflict is harmful and that perhaps a certain level of conflict is inevitable and desirable. The task for managers is not just to resolve or suppress all conflict but to manage it so as to reduce its harmful effects and benefit from its good effects.

When you have studied this chapter you should be able to:

• Analyse the causes of inter-group and interpersonal conflict in an organisation and recommend ways in which such conflict might be managed

1 THE CAUSES OF CONFLICT WITHIN AN ORGANISATION

1.1 The nature of conflict

Conflict can be caused by behaviour intended to obstruct the achievement of the goals of another person.

Definition Conflict is any personal divergence of interests between groups or individuals

Conflict occurs when organisational units are interdependent, share resources, and perceive their goals as incompatible. It can be identified on three levels:

(a) **Perception** - realisation that conflict exists because goals of the two parties are incompatible and the opportunity for interference is present.

(b) **Feelings** - conflict may cause feelings such as anger or mistrust between the groups.

(c) **Behaviour** - conflict results in behaviour, which is a reaction to the first two levels.

A certain amount of conflict in an organisation is not only inevitable it is often beneficial, for conflict is both a cause and an effect of change.

We can distinguish between 'organised' and 'unorganised' conflict. The feelings of 'organised' conflict are often expressed through recognised procedures, eg, grievance and disputes procedures between company and union. 'Unorganised' conflict tends to be personal and ad hoc, expressing itself through poor morale, grumbling, lack of trust, absenteeism, lack of discipline etc.

Mary Parker Follett distinguished between two types of conflict - constructive and destructive.

Constructive conflict is beneficial to the organisation because it can:

(a) challenge accepted, 'old-fashioned' ideas;

(b) stimulate the development of a climate of change and innovation;

(c)   define responsibility and authority limits more closely;

(d)   provide an opportunity for anxieties or personality challenges to be brought out into the open;

(e)   provide a fresh approach, often widening the range of options available for dealing with a problem.

The essence of constructive conflict is that it is not personality-based and therefore does not create a legacy of 'bad will'.

Destructive conflict, on the other hand, is usually damaging to personal working relationships. It therefore is detrimental to both the organisation and the individuals involved. Such conflict can cause alienation between individuals, between groups and between the individual group and the company.

The essence of destructive conflict is that it is often personality-influenced and creates ' bad will'. This will encourage negative, 'dog in the manger' attitudes and block achievement of company goals.

1.2   Signs of conflict

Conflict may manifest itself in many different ways:

- official or unofficial strikes;
- restriction or reduction of output, or activity which jeopardises income;
- demarcation disputes;
- lock-outs;
- absenteeism;
- sabotage;
- high labour turnover;
- poor time-keeping;
- refusal to obey instructions;
- working to rule;
- unwillingness to accept more efficient methods of production;
- racial prejudice;
- unhealthy rivalry between groups and between individuals;
- refusal to work with colleagues, or the ostracism of individuals; and
- closed-shop restrictions.

1.3   Causes of conflict

The causes of conflict are often difficult to determine accurately, as individuals may themselves be unsure of their motivation and behaviour. Some authorities suggest the following:

(a)   misunderstandings;
(b)   insensitive and non-supportive relationships;
(c)   failure to communicate openly and honestly; and
(d)   a climate of distrust, unreasonable pressure, or competition.

Charles Handy in *Understanding Organisations* explains that the causes of conflict can be many and various but they all start from two fundamental issues - differences over territory and/or objectives and ideologies.

Differences in objectives and ideologies leading to conflict can be caused by:

(a)   the overlapping of formal objectives;

(b)   the overlapping of role definitions, eg, possible conflict for an accountant between professional codes and organisation needs;

(c)   the contractual relationship is unclear, where parties may view their priorities differently;

(d)   the existence of concealed objectives.

Differences over territory can cause conflict in the following circumstances:

(a)   where there is violation of territory, ie, infringing another department's responsibilities;

(b)   overcrowding where there are too many people for the amount of work or responsibility;

(c)   territorial jealousy - the drive to obtain and enjoy the role and privileges of others; for example, to become a member of a particular committee or control a particular routine.

The conflicts that arise from these causes will often cause individuals to distort the communication process. To win the conflict, an individual might be selective in the information that he is willing to release, or narrowly interpret rules and regulations to enhance their own influence.

1.4   Organisational politics

One type of conflict can be described as 'organisational politics'. This has been described as 'the process whereby differentiated but interdependent individuals or interest groups exercise whatever power they can amass to influence the goals, criteria or processes used in organisational decision making to advance their own interests'. (Miles, R H)

The existence of this kind of behaviour is familiar to everyone. Clearly it tends to upset the rational model, according to which organisational goals are passed down through the hierarchy and form the basis for the actions of all members of the organisation.

The 'individual interests' referred to in the definition above may include:

*   acquisition of individual power
*   'empire building'
*   career advancement
*   favourable allocation of organisational resources.

The techniques for achieving these objectives may include:

*   enhancement of individual position power and expert power;
*   exploiting the informal organisation by forging networks and alliances with other managers
*   developing links with 'external' sources of power, such as shareholders.

From the organisational perspective, the aim in dealing with this kind of political behaviour must be to channel it in such a way that it supports, rather than conflicts with, overall objectives.

2   CONFLICT BETWEEN WORK GROUPS

2.1   Inter group conflict

We have considered what makes groups tick but now let us look at some aspects of group conflict. When groups come into contact with other groups, politics and conflicts can arise, such as problems of control, power struggles, empire building and other well-known features. Such conflicts will never be eliminated but there are some ideas of how to manage them. Another feature is that they are not always negative eg, differences between the internal auditors and the payroll department may highlight the need for improved internal control procedures. Another example is where the sales manager has continual problems with the production manager over out-of-stock items, which may lead to improved forecasting techniques being introduced.

A few conflicts that are typical in most organisations include:

(a)   *'It's the system'* - where individuals feel powerless against a particular group or the organisation as a whole; one person may become isolated and can cause considerable difficulties, for example, holding up decisions. Equally, the 'voice in the wilderness' may occasionally be right.

(b)   *Interpersonal conflicts* - such as those that arise between two powerful managers. For example, the marketing director who wants to go for sales and product growth, and the finance director who says: 'We can't afford the expansion' because of lack of capital. This can often turn into a power struggle and such struggles have been known to destroy companies.

(c)   *Fundamental differences on the solution* - people will have different ideas about a particular problem; a typical example is an old conflict on centralisation v decentralisation. Again, is it a real conflict, bearing in mind that often there is no one right answer?

2.2   Traditional and modern views of inter-group conflict

Early writers in the field of organisational conflict saw it as a process, which was essentially harmful to the organisation. It was seen as the result of poor management or the product of trouble-makers. The negative consequences were always stressed and conflict was seen as an avoidable feature of organisational life. This view of conflict as a destructive and harmful phenomenon can be contrasted with a more modern perspective, which emphasises the constructive and beneficial outcomes of conflict. Robbins summarises this modern view, stating that a contemporary approach to conflict:

(a)   Recognises the absolute necessity of conflict.

(b)   Explicitly encourages opposition.

(c)   Defines conflict management to include stimulation as well as resolution methods.

(d)   Considers the management of conflict as a major responsibility of all administrators.

| Conclusion | Conflict can be constructive (generating new ideas) or destructive (destroying morale and motivation). |

It is now generally believed that conflict is both valuable and necessary. Without it there would be few new challenges, there would be no stimulation to think through new ideas, organisations would become stagnant and apathetic.

However, it is also true to say that conflict needs to be carefully managed to avoid the harmful effects.

2.3   Sources of inter-group conflict

Dessler classifies four major sources of conflict:

(a)   *Interdependence and shared resources* - conflict is most likely to occur where groups are dependent on each other to achieve their goals and use shared resources in pursuit of these goals. An example of this might be a dispute between a production department and a research and development department where both claim priority over access to a particular piece of equipment.

(b)   *Differences in goals, values and perceptions* - groups are distinctive social units and will have special interests, particular views of what is important and what is not and will tend to see the world in a way, which supports the maintenance and success of the group.

(c)   *Authority imbalance* - where a group's authority is inconsistent with its responsibilities or prestige conflict is likely to occur. If it has too little then it will aggressively seek more; if it has too much it will be the target of others who feel the need to enhance their own authority or prestige.

(d)   *Ambiguity* - conflict is a familiar event where a group's responsibilities are unclear or ambiguous. Power vacuums arise and inter-group conflicts ensue as each department or group seeks to fill the vacuum.

2.4   Types of inter-group conflict

(a)   *Institutionalised conflict* - eg, that between Trade Unions and management.

(b)   *Hierarchy based conflict* - those based on inequalities of power built into the organisational hierarchy.

(c)   *Functional conflicts* - interdepartmental conflicts of a lateral (rather than hierarchical) nature where departments conflict over goals and resources eg, a conflict between production and sales.

(d)   *Line/staff conflicts* - professional staff employed in a staff capacity often regard line management as being unimaginative, dull and inflexible whilst line management sees the staff group as abstract, impractical, over-educated, inexperienced and too young.

(e)   *Formal/informal conflict* - the existence of two sorts of groups, one determined by the formal structure and rules of the organisation and the one resulting from social interaction can often result in conflict. Custom and practice may well be at variance with formal procedures and the two can easily come into conflict.

(f)   *Status conflict* - where groups compete for status and prestige conflict often follows.

(g)   *Political conflicts* - these can take many forms and political processes, such as the formation of cliques and conspiracies, are commonplace features of organisational life.

2.5   The dynamics of inter-group conflict

When groups come into conflict the patterns of the group behaviour change, relationships between groups change, new strategic moves are adopted and at the final stage of the conflict the parties have to adjust to winning or losing. Changes within the group experiencing conflict include:

(a)   Loyalty to the group becomes more important.

(b)   There is an increased concern for task accomplishment ie, more pressure for the group to perform at its best.

(c)   Leadership in the group becomes more autocratic.

(d)   The organisation and structure of the group become more rigid.

(e)   Group cohesiveness increases.

2.6   Changes in relations between groups experiencing conflict

(a)   Perceptions about one's own group and the other group are distorted. Out-group members are often stereotyped whilst, in one's own group, it is common only to perceive the strengths and deny any weaknesses.

(b)   Interaction and communication between groups decrease. Groups become more isolated, overlooking shared interests and exaggerating differences.

(c)   There is a move from a problem-solving orientation to other groups to a win/lose orientation. Ignoring long-term consequences of the conflict, groups become obsessed with winning in the particular situation.

(d)   There is increased hostility to the rival group. People become part of the 'enemy' rather than colleagues.

2.7   Strategies groups use to gain power

(a)   **Contracting** - this refers to the negotiation of a *quid pro quo* agreement between two groups. Each side makes some concessions to the other. This is often found in union/management bargaining.

(b)   **Co-opting** - this takes place when a group gives some of its leadership position to members of other groups and thus blunts any criticism of its activities by the out-group.

(c)   **Forming coalitions** - two or more groups can combine to increase their power over groups not in the coalition.

(d)   **Influencing decision criteria** - this is sometimes referred to as 'moving the goal posts' and involves trying to win by changing the criteria by which success and failure are judged.

(e)   **Controlling information** - by selectively giving or denying information a group can strengthen its position.

(f)   **Forcing and pressure tactics** - this consists of the use or threat of direct action eg, the use of a strike or work to rule.

2.8   Consequences of winning or losing on the group

(a)   **The effects of success** - the winning group has a stronger belief in the negative stereotype of the losing group. Winning reinforces the group's positive self-image. The group becomes more concerned with the satisfaction and needs of individual members. The work atmosphere becomes more casual and complacent as group cohesiveness and co-operation increases. At least in the short run concern with task accomplishment decreases and there is little interest in change.

(b)   **The effects of failure** - the losing group tries to explain away its failure as a matter of luck or unfair tactics by the winners rather than admitting that the other group was better or more deserving. There tends to be a decline in the quality of inter-personal relations within the group with people blaming one another for the loss. There is more tension in the group, less cohesiveness, less co-operation and less concern for the needs of individual members. These are mainly short-term reactions and groups can and do learn from their failures and can reorganise to be more effective in the future.

3   MANAGING CONFLICT

3.1   Introduction

Any divergence of interests between groups or individuals or lack of adjustment between an individual and his job or the circumstances of his job can be termed conflict. Current management thinking suggests that when conflict arises it is advantageous to express it openly so that conflicting points of view can be discussed before the decision is taken, in order that some level of commitment may be sponsored. Consequently, continuing open communications between management and staff and frequent consultations tend to minimise the damage caused by destructive conflict.

There are obviously a variety of different ways to handle conflicts and you have probably heard some of the following said in your own organisation:

(a)   'Try to avoid things going too far; provide friendly counsel; avoid trouble at all costs.'

(b)   'Keep personalities out of this; let's concentrate on the facts.'

(c)   'Let's get this out in the open; come to the point; don't drive the conflict underground.'

One writer has suggested that at least three essential conditions are required to avoid conflict:

(a)   a friendly atmosphere with clear common goals which are recognised and accepted by other group members;

(b)   a clear idea of the various tasks to be accomplished; and

(c)   a reasonably steady environment such as the market in which a firm operates.

3.2   Possible approaches for dealing with conflict

Five possible approaches for dealing with conflict are:

(a)   *Authority* - order them to stop fighting, although people are less and less willing to accept 'orders from above'.

(b)   *Political* - these include modifications of claims, compromises, promises in the future, finding satisfactory solutions for all concerned, recognising that there is no clear-cut winner or loser.

(c)   *Overall or corporate objectives* - attempting to establish an overriding aim or goal which unites all groups to a common purpose; sometimes a crisis will help such matters.

(d)   *Confrontation* - this is one way of resolving issues - however, most managers will tend to avoid this, but if a problem is not resolved it will tend to get worse; at least the confrontation means that the opposing sides meet and discuss the problem rather than suppress it.

(e)   *Right of appeal to an external or higher authority* - this is often a useful device in matters where a conflict cannot be resolved or one party feels aggrieved at a decision.

3.3   The Handy way

Handy suggests that in tackling conflict a manager should seek to turn the conflict into a possible argument or engender fruitful competition.   Only if this is not possible should the conflict be controlled. Handy nominates two types of strategy for tackling conflict.

The first set of strategies he terms 'control by ecology', because they create the environment for constructive relationships. Such strategies include:

(a)   agreement and knowledge of common objectives;
(b)   providing meaningful information to the participants;
(c)   building communication and trust between the individuals/groups;
(d)   ensuring that individuals' roles do not counteract the organisation goals;
(e)   developing suitable co-ordination mechanisms for the departments involved.

Since it is not always possible to arrange the ecology as desired, management may need to control and regulate the conflict. Unlike the long-term ecology strategies, which involve developing a better system for the future, the control strategies are short-term. The problem with such short-term solutions is that the causes of the conflict are not resolved and can arise again in the future. There is also the danger of short-sightedness in concentrating on the short-term, urgent solutions whilst ignoring the more important long-term issues.

Such short-term regulation strategies include:

(a)   the use of an arbitration authority;

(b)   the development of detailed rules of conduct;

(c)   creating a position to manage the area of conflict, eg a budget liaison officer;

(d)   using confrontation or inter-group meetings to analyse the conflict openly;

(e)   separating the conflicting parties;

(f)   ignoring the conflict problem in the belief that it is a temporary situation that will 'blow over'.

3.4   Coping with conflict

The generally accepted techniques of coping with conflict are:

(a)   Co-operative, problem-solving relationships between antagonising parties.

(b)   Search for superior goals (those which are compelling for both parties and cannot be ignored, but which cannot be achieved by the efforts or resources of one party alone).

(c)   The third party, or peacemaker, role.

(d)   Improvement of interpersonal skills, for instance, to give to parties to a conflict the interpersonal skills necessary to resolve the conflict themselves. Rogers, a clinical psychologist, suggested that in a dispute between management and labour, if labour was able to state management's point of view accurately in a way that management could accept and management could state labour's case in a way that labour agreed was accurate, then it would be possible to guarantee that some reasonable solution could be reached.

3.5   Pluralist approach to conflict

In contrast to the human relations' approach, the underlying assumptions of the pluralist approach to conflict are:

(a)   Conflict is often desirable, but it should be managed in such a way as to prevent it getting out of hand.

(b)   Conflict is the sign of a healthy organisation.

(c)   Conflict is inevitable and results from:

   (i)   a struggle to achieve the needs of (for example) food, power, status and responsibility; and
   (ii)   innate instincts in man of aggression and competitiveness.

(d)   Genetic and physiological determinations of aggressive behaviour are more important than the environmental influence.

(e)   Man is driven by the instincts of selfishness, competitiveness and aggression.

The views of this school of thought are supported by Follett and Tannenbaum. Experimental studies of creativity and innovation suggest that groups are more productive when a dissenter is present than when dissenters are absent, although, given the opportunity, the dissenter is the first person the group gets rid of. The weaknesses of this approach are:

(a)   conflict of interest can be dysfunctional;

(b)   dissension among union members can reduce the effectiveness of the union; and

(c)   differences can be magnified out of all proportion; and, for example, in collective bargaining, the resolution of even moderate differences may be difficult to achieve.

Whereas the human relations' supporters try to obviate conflict, the pluralists try to make constructive use of it by exploiting conflict to effect changes and enhance organisational performance. According to Follett, there are three methods of dealing with conflict:

(a)   *Domination.* A strong management can win against a weak union, or a strong union can completely destroy a company; this type of behaviour only results in grievances being perpetuated.

(b)   *Compromise.* In a compromise situation, both sides give ground in the interests of a short-term solution to the dispute; it is often not a real solution to the underlying problems.

(c)   *Integration.* This is Follett's suggestion as the best approach; from the conflict of ideas and attitudes, the opposing forces move towards common objectives. She believed that this would happen if there was frank and open discussion of the real problems. This led to her view of power with, rather than over people, and of joint responsibility and multiple leadership.

Townsend despised compromise. Rather, he advocated, there must be domination. One side must win, and the winning side must appreciate the consequence of victory, total accountability.

More recent research suggests that the pluralist approach to conflict management is most effective when:

(a)   neither party dominates the other;

(b)   both parties see some advantage in their continued association, even though their relationship may change as a result of the conflict;

(c)   neither party is able, or wishes, to annihilate the other; and

(d)   cross loyalties or affiliations exist which prevent complete separation of conflicting parties into distinct camps.

The human relations' approach to conflict has had some success in several conflict situations, but it ignores many of the basic causes of conflict, for instance competition over scarce resources. Conflict is inevitable and even desirable, so long as it does not produce prejudice and hostile relationships, which broaden and prolong the conflict.

The conflict resolution techniques suggested by the human relations theory may be morally superior, but are they realistic in today's industrial climate?

Research was carried out in 1964 into the characteristics required for success in business; most executives replied that these were aggressiveness, self-confidence, assertiveness and dominance. The pluralists point to the free enterprise system and to the two-party political system as indicators of the success of their approach to conflict with inbuilt checks and balances. Whenever one of the opposing parties in any system finds itself opposed to another there is no reason why it should not attempt to destroy the other and it can be expected to do so. As soon as there are divisions of loyalty, neither party can destroy the other without jeopardising some of the interests of its own members.

3.6   Managing inter-group conflict - Robbins

There are many approaches to the management of conflict and the suitability of any approach is to be judged only in terms of its relevance in a particular situation. There is no universal right way, rather it depends on the goals and requirements of management in a specific setting. In some situations it is correct to compromise, in others nothing less than complete victory is required. Robbins provides the following classification of possible ways of solving conflict:

(a)   *Problem solving* - the groups are brought together to find a solution to the particular problem.

(b)   *Super-ordinate goal* - finding a common goal for conflicting groups that will override their differences.

(c)   *Expansion of resources* - ending conflict over resources by giving extra resources to all.

(d)   *Avoidance* - withdrawing from the conflict or concealing the incompatibility.

(e)   *Smoothing* - playing down the differences and stressing common interests.

(f)   *Compromise* - getting a solution without there being a definite winner or loser.

(g)   *Authoritative command* - judgement over the conflict is made by someone in authority.

(h)   *Altering the human variable* - changing attitudes, beliefs and perceptions about the conflict.

(i)   *Altering the structural variable* - merging departments, reorganising work relationships etc.

It is apparent from Robbins' analysis that it is possible to manage inter-group conflict and avoid the dysfunctional aspects, which damage organisational effectiveness. It is important to note that certain management techniques have been shown to be more effective than others have. In particular, confrontational techniques which involve recognising the reality of conflict have been shown to be more effective than those which avoid or try to simply smooth over the problem.

3.7   Blake and Mouton's theories of conflict management

Blake and Mouton believe there are five basic theories associated with managing conflict. These theories represent various styles of management, which they believe managers may change over time.

The diagram below illustrates these five theories.

High 9	**1,9**								**9,9**
	Disagreements are smoothed over, or					Valid problem solving takes place			
8	ignored so that surface harmony is					with varying points of views.			
	maintained in a state of peaceful co-existence					Objectivity evaluated against facts;			
7						emotions, reservations, and doubts			
						are worked through.			

High

9 | 1,9 — Disagreements are smoothed over, or ignored so that surface harmony is maintained in a state of peaceful co-existence | 9,9 — Valid problem solving takes place with varying points of views. Objectivity evaluated against facts; emotions, reservations, and doubts are worked through.

Concern for people

6   5.5 — Compromise, bargaining and middle-ground positions are accepted so that no one wins - nor does anyone lose. Accommodation and adjustment lead to 'workable' rather than best solutions.

Low 1   1,1 — Neutrality is maintained at all costs. Withdrawal behind walls relieves the necessity of dealing with situations that would arouse conflict.

9,1 — Conflict is supressed through authority obedience approach. Power struggles are decided by the most senior shared manager or third party arbitrator

1   2   3   4   5   6   7   8   9
Low   Concern for production of results   High

Blake and Mouton believe that on the whole people do conform to the expectations of others, this readiness to conform reduces conflict and is what permits regularity, order and predictability. To adhere to common norms provides a basis for organised effort. From conformity can come a sense of identification and belonging. Alternatively, failure to conform may stir conflict with one's colleagues and associates so that the nonconformist is rejected.

3.8   The best approach

Thomas points out that research suggests that collaboration is the best way to settle conflict. Derr disagrees and argues that each of the above conflict management strategies is most appropriate under certain circumstances.

Collaboration - this is a useful way to resolve conflict when the following conditions exist.

(a)   There is at least a moderate amount of required interdependence among the parties to the conflict.

(b)   A felt power equality exists between the two parties - equality is necessary for the openness required to solve the problem.

(c)   The mutual advantage of collaboration must be seen by both sides.

(d)   There must be organisational support for the collaborative process.

Competition - this operates on a different set of assumptions than collaboration. Derr suggests the following reasons why competition may be likely.

(a)   Autonomy seeking - for those who want to keep their true commitment to an organisation to a minimum and yet become important.

(b)   Avoiding vulnerability.

(c)   Obtaining flexibility - informal groups may use their power to resist a change in working methods.

(d)   Solving ideological disputes.

Compromise - this can be a bridge between collaborative approaches and power-play.

| Conclusion | To be successful in avoiding or resolving conflict, managers must understand the nature of the conflict issue, the behaviour and norms of the group and their own balance of leadership style. |

4   STRESS

4.1   Introduction

Conflicts at work are an undeniable cause of stress. Cooper in his book, *Papering over the Cracks*, has indicated the high incidence of stress throughout organisations, irrespective of job and seniority and has suggested that 'every job has its own stress fingerprint'. Stress is individually defined; one person's stress can be another's excitement and energiser. Everyone has a range of comfort where they can feel steady and safe. Stress occurs when the individual feels they are working outside this comfort zone. It can be argued that most people need some form of stress to bring out their best performance, but if the stress is of the wrong form, or too much, it becomes damaging. Research also shows that personality plays a part in the stress process. Individuals who have a personality that is classified as 'type A' are more likely to suffer from heart disease under severe stress than individuals with a 'type B' personality. One of the major tasks of management in organisations is to control the level of stress.

4.2   Symptoms of stress

Stress shortens time-horizons, polarises issues, exaggerates the importance of the present, makes difficulties into crises and inhibits creativity. Headaches, muscular tension, fatigue and hypertension have all been cited as effects of stress. Usually people under stress exhibit the following symptoms:

(a)   Tension - expressed by for example, excessive preoccupation with trivia.

(b)   Low morale - often expressed as low confidence in the organisation.

(c)   Communication difficulties - employees may become withdrawn, absenteeism is an extreme form.

According to McKenna, in *Business Psychology and Organisational Behaviour*, any situation that is seen as burdensome, threatening, ambiguous or boring is likely to induce stress. There tends to be the feeling that this situation should not exist, but because of it the person feels disappointed or annoyed and eventually is prone to anxiety, depression, anger, hostility, inadequacy and low frustration tolerance.

4.3   Causes of stress

The main causes of stress at work are:

(i)   Intrinsic to the job - here again there is a range of factors that may cause or contribute to stress.

●   Work overload or work underload.

●   Fatigue - perhaps partly caused by a long and difficult 'commute' to work, as well as long hours on the job itself.

●   Coping with change, eg in dealing with more automated ways of carrying out the work.

●   Poor working conditions (inadequate lighting, insufficient physical space etc).

(ii)   The individual's role in the organisation - factors that can cause stress include the following:

- Unclear reporting lines - an individual may feel torn between the requirements to two superiors, unsure of which one is his 'boss'.

- Role ambiguity, especially where the individual suffers from insufficient information about his organisational objectives.

- Lack of career prospects, particularly at later stages of an individual's career, where a 'plateau' may be reached. This may often be combined with a feeling of being threatened by younger employees striving for promotion.

(iii)   Features of the individual's working relationships - the importance of good relationships within work groups has been emphasised in an earlier chapter. In addition, an employee's relationships with his direct superiors and subordinates can affect the level of stress he experiences. For example, a reluctance or inability to delegate to subordinates can lead to work overload, as well as causing anxiety about work performance.

(iv)   Organisational structure and climate and the extent of rules and regulations - the main variables are the stability of the organisation and the style of management.

- If the stability of the organisation is disrupted - perhaps because of a threatened takeover, or a danger of insolvency - then individual security can also be upset, and this is a primary cause of stress.

- If the style of management is autocratic, middle and lower managers may struggle to cope with targets laid down arbitrarily from above, and this too can lead to overwork and stress.

(v)   Home-work interface - features of the individual's life outside work, particularly the growth of dual career families. Individuals under stress in their private lives may carry their problems over into the organisational setting. The possibilities are obviously numerous; financial difficulties, friction within the family as a result of long working hours and/or shift working etc.

4.4   Implications for organisations

Stress is largely inherent in the managerial role. The factors that cause managerial stress cannot all be avoided or eliminated. But the stress that they cause can be managed or mitigated. Some of the ways organisations can achieve this are detailed below.

(a)   Create stability zones - this is a place or time for rebuilding energy reserves. This means that organisations need to ensure that employees take their holidays and do not work every weekend.

(b)   Specialisation, simplification and blocking - managers have to deal with vast amounts of information and data, which needs to be analysed, and the results form the basis of decisions. By ensuring that the information received by managers is specific specialist information, which is presented in a simple format, thereby blocking non-essential details, this can relax time pressures, and workload.

(c)   Use of catalysts - most often non-executive directors, consultants, or working parties perform this function, allowing management 'to see things differently'. Catalysts can be valuable in restoring perspective.

(d)   Compartmentalisation - this approach focuses on organising work by a time-dimension rather than by topic. Most meetings are topic-centred eg, marketing review; few are time-centred. As a result the agendas of most meetings cover a variety of time-horizons.

The organisation of work is usually haphazard; meetings are scheduled on first come first seen basis. Some organisations make an attempt to compartmentalise by having:

(i)   Monday morning - where are we at - meetings, to plan the immediate workload.

(ii)   Long-term planning meetings held regularly away from the office.

(iii)   Providing time management courses.

(iv)   Computerised project planning support systems.

5   SELF TEST QUESTIONS

5.1   Distinguish between 'organised' and 'unorganised' conflict. (1.1)

5.2   What are the signs of conflict? (1.2)

5.3   Explain the difference between the traditional and modern views of inter-group conflict (2.2)

5.4   Describe two types of inter-group conflict (2.4)

5.5   Briefly describe the changes within a group experiencing conflict (2.5)

5.6   What are the effects of failure on a group? (2.8)

5.7   Outline two possible approaches for dealing with conflict. (3.2)

5.8   Explain 'smoothing' as a way of solving conflict. (2.6)

5.9   Draw a grid outlining Blake and Mouton's theory of managing conflict. (3.7)

6   EXAMINATION TYPE QUESTION

6.1   Conflict

What are the symptoms of conflict in an organisation? How can a manager convert conflict into constructive competition?   **(20 marks)**

7   ANSWER TO EXAMINATION TYPE QUESTION

7.1   Conflict

Conflict can be described as a failure to reach common agreement. It can also be an indicator of poor relationships within the organisation. The existence of it is often reflected in the struggle for power.

The reason for the human resources function addressing industrial relations matters is because of the tendency for conflict to occur, in most organisations, in some shape or form. Industrial relations personnel have the specific responsibility for 'managing conflict' to ensure that, with effective negotiation, conflict can be resolved and utilised as a mechanism for building understanding and common purpose within the enterprise, such that harmony is created.

Conflict becomes a problem for an organisation when disagreements, or differences of opinion, between people are handled badly or allowed to last for too long. When this happens they upset the atmosphere of the working environment such that a disruptive, uncooperative or negative culture begins to develop.

The symptoms of conflict are many and varied but they all have a common factor. It is the expression by employees of dissatisfaction with the current situation in the work environment and a need to express it - in the main overtly. Employees, either as individuals or a working group, may develop entrenched viewpoints and they refuse to budge from their strongly held views. They may develop erratic behaviour patterns, directing their pent up emotions against people or objects (throwing a spanner in the works). This can be evidenced in a range of behaviour from actually damaging industrial equipment to a tendency to display a 'short fuse' eg, losing their temper quickly and being particularly resentful towards management. A more common symptom of conflict is 'negativity', which is the propensity to look at everything that goes wrong in the organisation, or at every initiative management attempt, in a negative manner. A spirit of 'non co-operation' may emerge where there is underlying conflict. Employees may, short of taking industrial action, insist on working to rule ie, only performing the essentials of the requirements of their contracts of employment and refusing to co-operate in any other activities.

There are other, less overt, symptoms of conflict to consider.

•   Employees may fantasise - because they feel helpless to change the day-to-day situation, they switch off from work and daydream to escape the reality of the conflict culture of the organisation. These employees are usually apathetic to both their jobs and to relationships at work. It follows that poor quality work is one of the consequences of such behaviour.

•   Employees may exhibit regressive tendencies - returning to an earlier and less mature personality to cope with the frustrations brought on by the conflict. Some individuals may even start to behave like children.

•   Employees may repress their feelings - anxiety levels will grow to the extent that they may eventually suffer from stress (thought by some behavioural scientists to be the industrial disease of the late 90s). Under such conditions, the people involved will often be sick from work for long periods of time. High sickness rates can be symptomatic of an organisation in conflict.

Charles Handy summarises the symptoms of conflict as follows:

•   poor communications in all directions (vertical, horizontal and lateral);

•   interpersonal friction;

•   inter-group rivalry and jealousy;

•   low morale and frustration;

•   proliferation of rules, norms and myths and

•   widespread use of arbitration, appeals to higher authority and inflexible attitude towards change.

Conflict can be positive, especially where managers use it to develop competitiveness within the organisation. Conflict is an essential part of change and creativity, especially when considered with regard to the management and development of teams. To maximise individual or group potential, management must first eliminate insecurity. Development of a detailed and mutually acceptable grievance procedure will ensure that employees feel that any conflict arising from working conditions or unfair treatment will be dealt with fairly. Once this is developed, the manager will be free to focus on personality conflicts between people and between work groups.

By creating a positive open culture and through development of carefully selected work teams, a manager can use conflict to increase productivity and enhance performance. The members of a well structured group will display loyalty to each other and a high level of work commitment to the group. With planned targets, well briefed and well led teams competing against one another can do much to harness natural conflicts and develop the potential of the organisation as a whole. A manager will need to consider the application of motivational techniques and incentives and performance rewards to maximise the effectiveness of competition. These might include the creation of quality circles, job enrichment and delegation to improve the performance potential of work teams.   Notice boards, in-house newspapers, periodic team appraisals and team prizes would demonstrate to all involved the rewards of team competition.

The benefits of competitions are that they:

- set standards by establishing best performance by comparison;
- motivate individuals to better efforts;
- identify the best performers.

To be useful, competition must be perceived by the participants to be open, rather than closed. Open competition exists where all participants can increase their gains eg, productivity bargaining. Closed competition exists where one party's gain will be another's loss. This is a win-lose, or zero-sum, situation.   One party can only do well at the expense of another in competition for resources and recognition. If competition is perceived to be open, the rules are seen to be fair and the determinants of success are in the competitors' control, competition can be extremely rewarding. The observations of Peters and Waterman, on the motivational effect of comparative performance, supports this view. If these pre-conditions are not met, competition may degenerate into conflict again.

20 ORGANISATIONAL CHANGE

INTRODUCTION & LEARNING OUTCOMES

Syllabus area 11(v)
- The impact on the organisation of external and internal change triggers (eg, environmental factors, mergers and acquisitions, re-organisation and rationalisation)

- The importance of managing critical periods of change (e.g. start-up, rapid expansion, re-organisation, merger, redundancy programmes, close-down) and the ways in which these periods can be managed effectively

In this chapter we will consider the nature of change and its effects upon organisations. Management has been defined as 'the management of change' and certainly, change is ever present and occurring at an ever-increasing rate.

Organisations inevitably change because they are open systems in constant interaction with their environment. Although the impelling force for change can be attributed to internal or external stimuli (or both), the underlying impetus is the exposure of system boundaries that allow new technologies, skills, values and demands to affect the organisation.

We begin by explaining why change is inevitable in organisations, and why it is often met with resistance. This is followed by a brief discussion of the main causes of change and the strategies that organisations use to grow or shrink by acquiring new businesses or divesting themselves of existing businesses.

We then look at a model - Greiner's model - which illustrates the life cycle of an organisation moving through five phases of growth. This is introduced partly to indicate the differences between evolutionary and revolutionary growth, and partly to emphasise the impact on management processes and styles during each of the phases.

When you have studied this chapter you should be able to:

- Evaluate the determinants of change in organisations and the different levels at which change must be managed
- Evaluate how the organisation and its managers might deal with major critical periods in the development of the organisation

---

1 ORGANISATIONAL CHANGE

1.1 Introduction

We have discussed change throughout this book, although we have not dealt with it as a separate topic. Towards the beginning of the book, we suggested that different forms of organisational structure might be required to cope with changing environments. We looked at the possibilities of changing motivation and personality, as well as the changes in behaviour and performance with training and development. We also explored how leaders change their subordinates' behaviour and how the leaders themselves might change their management or leadership style.

Whilst there is no doubt that change affects all our lives, considerable debate is currently taking place as to the desirability of some of the changes and the necessity for their rapid introduction. Tofler argues that change is out of control and that man is suffering from the increased pace of life and its accompanying transient relationships. Others argue that change is being introduced too slowly and that organisations, particularly within the UK, are left behind by their major competitors.

Much depends on the organisation's relation with its environment discussed later. As a consequence of the environment becoming more turbulent and complex, there is a need for organisations to develop more effective adaptive response systems. Change should not be regarded as a panacea for corporate ills but can have some remedial action and may be introduced for its own sake.

1.2   Definition and classification

Change is defined as the 'substitution or succession of one thing in place of another; substitution of other conditions; variety'.

Change can be a gradual evolution or a sudden transformation. This speed of change is often outside the control of the company. The rate of change may be dictated by technology, competition or environmental factors. Some companies constantly operate in fast-changing surroundings, eg. those in the fashion industry.

An important consideration is the cascading effect of change, where a change in one area leads to changes in others. If a company loses an important customer, it does not mean that the company will simply produce less. Instead it is likely that there will be changes in its marketing approach, pricing, advertising, packaging, production and purchasing; there may even be changes in management responsibilities. So we should not consider one change in isolation but instead as one stage in a continuing sequence of changes.

Change can be classified into two categories - planned and unplanned.

Planned change - is deliberate and conscious effort designed to meet forthcoming input changes that can be seen or predicted. For example, changes in the buying patterns or customer requirements, the effects of new legislation or the need to conform to a new industry-wide code of practice. It can also be a planned change to prepare for some improvement in the organisation itself. For example, the upgrading of premises, the introduction of e-commerce or opening new outlets.

Unplanned change - is thrust upon the organisation by environmental events beyond its control. For example, changes in the bank rate, sudden changes in the value of a currency, unexpected scarcity of a raw material or a serious fire.

1.3   The role of management

The role of management is to anticipate the need for change, create an atmosphere of acceptance of change and manage the stages of introduction and implementation. The manager can expect resistance to change since all major changes threaten somebody's security or somebody's status. There are many spectacular examples of companies and industries, which failed to adapt and change. For example, the failure of Volkswagen to introduce a new model to replace the Beetle, caused severe problems to the group for several years and the resistance to change by London Dock workers encouraged the automation of Rotterdam, which is now a thriving, international port while London Docks have closed.

1.4   Forces for change

The forces for change can come from within the organisation or from the external environment. The internal forces that bring about change:

(a)   cascading effect - the continuous reaction to historical changes, as the initial change works its way through the system.

(b)   innovation - the company may develop a new product or a new manufacturing process that alters the economics of the market place;

(c)   individual executives' ambition;

(d)   unforeseen internal events, for example, incapacity of senior executives;

(e)   pursuit of growth - Starbuck has suggested several driving forces that stimulate company growth:

   (i)   companies may seek dominance of a particular market or area;

   (ii)   a company may seek to grow in size in order to achieve 'critical mass', ie that state that enables a company to dictate the terms of its market and/or purchases, thereby generating stability for the future;

   (iii)   growth may enable a company to reap economies of scale. This may be linked to the desire to maximise capacity utilisation;

   (iv)   to seek maximisation of profit;

   (v)   executives may seek the challenge and adventure of new projects. For example, a restless entrepreneur who is successful in one field may lose interest as that field becomes more stable and predictable;

   (vi)   growth may increase the power, job security and earnings of executives. There is therefore an in-built desire amongst the management team to achieve growth.

1.5   Change triggers

Buchanan and Huczyknski claim there are four basic features of organisational change:

Triggers - some kind of disorganising pressure or trigger, arising either within or outside the organisation, initiates change. For example, changes may be triggered by the discovery that one of the company's main suppliers is closing down, or by changes in legislation that affect the ways in which employees have to be treated.

Interdependencies - the various parts of an organisation are interdependent. Change in one aspect of an organisation creates pressure for adjustments in other aspects. The introduction of dealing on the stock exchange over the Internet has created a new type of investor and new methods of working, as well as new technologies, for brokers, which is likely to change the balance of relationships between the traditional and electronic brokers.

Conflict and frustrations - the technical and economic objectives of managers may often conflict with the needs and aspirations of employees and this leads to conflicts which in turn create pressures for and resistance to change. The new technology that management want to introduce may lead to demands for a new training and reward system from the staff who will have to operate it.

Time lags - change rarely takes place smoothly. Instead it happens in an 'untidy' way. Some parts of the organisation change more rapidly than others do. People and groups may need time to 'catch up' with everyone else. The maintenance staff may still be learning new skills months after that new machine has been installed.

Organisational change is triggered by many factors. However, there are three most obvious reasons:

   (i)   Internal changes may be introduced to cope with developments outside the organisation. These can be changes in technology, consumer tastes, competitor activity, raw materials or legislation.

   (ii)   There may be a desire to modify the attitudes, knowledge, skills and relationships within the organisation to improve performance. This may be achieved by making changes to jobs, product design, layout of premises, allocation of responsibility and/or technology.

(iii)   The organisation may anticipate developments and find ways of coping with them in advance. This is known as proactive change.

1.6   Internal and external triggers

Internal triggers for change are those factors that can cause organisational disequilibrium and include:

(a)   questioning authority and intra-organisational conflicts;

(b)   adverse organisational climate;

(c)   poor performance - unstable labour relations, low output and high costs;

(d)   presence of entrepreneurs and other innovators;

(e)   changes in or reordering of organisational goals;

(f)   favourable changes experienced in the past.

The internal triggers may, or may not, be related to external forces operating within the organisation's environment which, according to Martino, revolve around:

(a)   changes in knowledge both technical and social;

(b)   economic opportunities;

(c)   distribution of political power;

(d)   demographic make-up of the population;

(e)   ecological considerations;

(f)   ideological and culture factors.

2   TYPES OF CHANGE

2.1   Changes in the external environment

Changes in the environment can lead to the organisation having to re-think its corporate strategy. The general environment for any organisation includes technological, economic, legal, political, demographic, ecological and cultural factors. These can include changes in the law, changes in social behaviour or in the general economic environment eg, recession. Within this environment, each organisation has a more specific set of factors that are relevant to its decision-making processes. This is its task environment. Competition is also a source of impetus for change because an organisation will adjust its strategy when direct competitors provide new products or services.

Changes in products or markets can lead to problems in managing the resources. Bringing new products or services onto the market requires new designs and new methods of selling and marketing. The process itself has its difficulties, but it is often the cause of other changes.

The factors of change from the external environment will be many and will be different for different companies. However, several trends that are currently under way, that can lead to organisational and management changes are as follows:

(a)   the increasing use of computers, information technology and telecommunications. Now available to even the smallest organisations, the new technologies are affecting work patterns and location of businesses;

(b)   changes in education and training. A growing recognition that training should continue throughout a life-time's employment;

(c)   change in the balance of employment with the shift to knowledge and service workers and away from manufacturing industries;

(d)   greater co-operation between government and industry with jointly funded projects;

(e)   multinational companies will continue to spread internationally and managers in different countries must learn to communicate and adapt to each other;

(f)   changes in global trade patterns developing.

Companies can respond to these sorts of changes in various ways. One way is simply to react to a crisis. This is a weak, inefficient response since it abdicates all initiative and control. A more fruitful approach would be to deliberately plan the change and face up to the need to follow the changes through all affected areas of the company's operations.

2.2   Changes in the internal environment

Changes in structure - these may be related to changes in other sub-systems, but there are many structural adjustments that take place when all other aspects are relatively stable. Different ways of dividing the work and/or new means of co-ordination can be designed to make an existing organisation more effective and efficient. Addressing a lack of defined responsibility for a particular part of the business the organisation may change to a vertical structure. This may have been a change from a horizontal structure that was more suitable for increasing the communication links within the organisation. The creation of new structural forms, such as conglomerates or multinational corporations, usually leads to many other adjustments. If there is a change in the financial structure, due to a takeover or merger, then it may lead to a more general structural change.

Changes in culture - are the most difficult changes to manage. The banks in the UK have been faced with a change in the market caused by competition from other financial organisations, leading to a change in the range of products offered. The associated problem of a change in culture from one of stable conservatism to being customer-focussed and profit-seeking is a huge change that is difficult to manage.

3   RESISTANCE TO CHANGE

3.1   Change, work and self-identity

We have already seen that major changes in the life of the individual such as unemployment, retirement and redundancy pose threats to self-identity. In addition we need to consider the general issue of changes at work on the individual. Rapid and major changes can easily undermine a self-identity, which has been built up over time in reasonably stable conditions. For example, technological innovations can make a person's skills no longer relevant; re-organisation can reduce status and prestige; entering new markets can devalue experience of the traditional markets. The threat to self-identity is one of the main factors leading to resistance to change.

The fears and worries of the individual facing change have been the subject of considerable study. It is possible to classify them in terms of job factors, personal factors and social factors.

Job factors

- Fear of technological unemployment.
- Fear of changes in working conditions.
- Fear of demotion and reduced pay.
- Fear of increased effort and less bonus.

Personal factors

- Resentment of the implied criticism that present methods are inadequate.
- Resentment of the implied criticism that present performance is inadequate.
- Fear that skill and ability are no longer needed.
- Fear of increased boredom and monotony and a decreased sense of personal worth.
- Inconvenience of having to unlearn present methods.
- Inconvenience of having to learn new methods.

- Fear that harder work will be required.
- Fear and uncertainty of the unknown.

Social factors

- Dislike of having to make new social adjustments.
- Dislike of need to break present social ties.
- Fear that the new social situation will bring less satisfaction.
- Dislike of outside interference and control.
- Dislike of those initiating change.
- Resentment over lack of consultation and participation in the change.
- Perception that the change will help the organisation at the expense of the individual, the work group or society.

3.2   Why people may resist change

Schermerhorn identifies the following sources of resistance

Sources of resistance	Suggested responses
• Fear of the unknown	• Information, encouragement, involvement
• Need for security	• Clarification of intentions and methods
• Felt no change needed	• Demonstrate problem or opportunity
• Vested interests threatened	• Enlist key people in change planning
• Contrasting interpretations	• Disseminate valid information, facilitate group sharing
• Poor timing	• Await better time
• Lack of resources	• Provide supporting resources and/or reduced performance expectations.

Such sources of change should be compared with those identified by Schein who differentiated between **economic fears** eg, pay reductions and redundancies and **social fears** eg, impaired status, reduced satisfaction, implied criticism of past performances and break up of working group

Resistance to change can be directed against the change itself, the change strategy or the change agent and should be viewed as a form of negative feedback by those managing the change which could be constructively employed to modify their approach.

4   CHANGES IN STRATEGY

4.1   Patterns of strategy development

Organisational strategy is a function of factors such as environmental opportunity, internal competence and resources, managerial interest and desires and social responsibility. Most planned organisational change is triggered by the need to respond to new challenges or opportunities presented by the external environment, or in anticipation of the need to cope with potential future problems. The strategy adopted by the organisation should improve the ability of the organisation to cope with changes in its environment.

Because we associate strategy with the long-term direction of an organisation, we think of it in terms of major decisions about the future. However, it would be a mistake to think that the strategy is developed through one-off major changes; it is more likely to be developed over a period. Once an organisation has developed a particular strategy then it tends to develop gradually from within that strategy, rather than fundamentally changing direction.

Mintzberg's studies showed that, although 'transformational' or 'revolutionary' change did take place, the more typical changes were incremental or piecemeal. There were periods when strategies remained unchanged and also periods of flux, where the organisation seemed to have no clear directional strategy. The diagram below outlines the different patterns of strategic change.

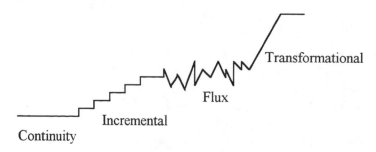

In some respects, organisations should seek to manage strategy to achieve a gradual change. No organisation could function efficiently if it were to undergo frequent major revisions and, realistically, it is unlikely that the environment will change so rapidly that this would be necessary.

Incremental change may be viewed as an adaptive process in a continually changing environment. Arguably, it is beneficial for an organisation to change incrementally, because it will build on the skills, routines and beliefs of those in the organisation. Unfortunately, environmental change may not always be gradual enough for incremental change to keep pace and, if the change lags behind, the organisation may get out of line with the environment and need more fundamental or transformational change at times of crisis. Transformational change may come about either because the organisation is faced with major external events that demand large-scale changes or because the organisation anticipates such changes and therefore initiates action to make major shifts in its own strategy.

4.2   Strategic options

Whenever the organisation can identify differences between where it is and where it wants to be on any dimension, it can engage in a process of planned change or organisational improvement.

There are a number of strategic choices management can make in order that an organisation may achieve its stated objectives - firms pursuing virtually the same ends do not have to employ the same change strategies.

In 1980 Glueck classified the alternatives and identified the following usage frequencies:

* Growth   54.4%
* Stability   9.2%
* Retrenchment (defensive)   7.5%
* Combination of the other three   28.7%

Such strategies can be pursued internally using the company's existing resources and competencies or external means can be employed such as acquisition, merger or collaborating with other organisations.

5   ORGANISATIONAL GROWTH

5.1   Greiner's model of organisational growth

> **Definition**   Organisational growth can be defined as: 'Change in an organisation's size, or any movement towards a given objective.' (Hicks 1987)

The concept of size is problematic and growth can have many characteristics, a number of which are mutually exclusive. In the context of strategic change, growth is normally viewed in terms of output and this is often an attractive option for management. Traditionally literature about organisational growth is written from the stance of an industry leader operating in growth markets. In the case of the public sector it would be a position of expanding budgets. Growth follows the product/market strategies closely, but inevitably the organisation diversifies as growth opportunities dry up.

L E Greiner specifies five aspects of organisational growth.

(a)   Age of the organisation - the older the organisation, the more difficult it is to change.

(b)   Size of the organisation - the larger the organisation, the more complex the change process becomes due to co-ordination and communication issues.

(c)   Stages of evolution - management are stable and only minor change is required. Management are focused on growth.

(d)   Stages of revolution - serious unrest in management due to major turbulence. Management are focused on solving the problems that are hindering growth.

(e)   Growth rate of industry - affects the pace of change, the organisation undertakes.

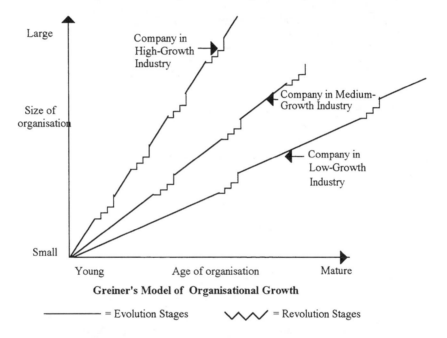

Greiner's Model of Organisational Growth

————— = Evolution Stages   ＶＶＶ = Revolution Stages

The diagram above illustrates the combined effect of these aspects on organisations. Each dimension influences the other over time; when all five elements begin to interact, a more complete and dynamic picture of organisational growth emerges.

Greiner identifies five phases of growth. Each evolutionary period is characterised by the dominant **management style** used to achieve growth, while each revolutionary period is characterised by the dominant **management problem** that must be solved before growth can continue.

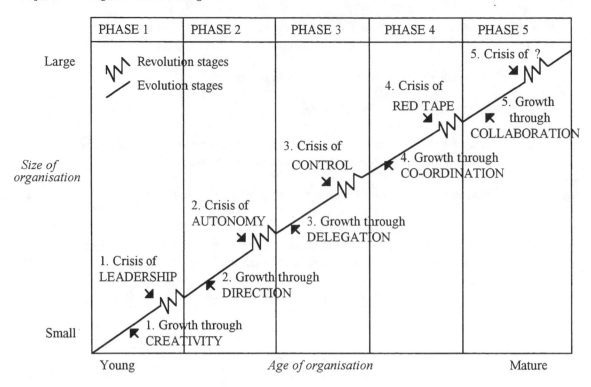

It is important to note that each phase is both an effect of the previous and a cause for the next phase. For example, the evolutionary management style in phase 3 (above) is 'delegation', which grows out of, and becomes the solution to demands for greater 'autonomy' in the preceding phase 2 revolution. The style of delegation used in Phase 3, however, eventually provokes a major revolutionary crisis that is characterised by attempts to regain control over the diversity created through increased delegation.

The principal implication of each phase is that management actions are narrowly prescribed if growth is to occur. For example, a company experiencing an autonomy crisis in Phase 2 cannot return to directive management for a solution - it must adopt a new style of delegation in order to move ahead.

Phase 1	**Creativity** - making and selling, this is the creative stage. Control comes from the feedback gained from customers/clients. As the organisation grows, production becomes more efficient. Management is required to take on additional responsibilities. Unless more sophisticated business techniques can be introduced and maintained, the organisation may stagnate and die.
Phase 2	**Direction** - the organisation becomes 'structural' with a hierarchy of positions and jobs moving to greater specialism. Accounting systems covering for example purchasing are introduced, as one standard of working practices. Growth during this phase is usually evolutionary. This phase of growth exposes weaknesses in the functional structure, which need to be resolved before the organisation can continue to the next phase.
Phase 3	**Delegation** - growth is achieved through delegation. The organisation structure moves to becoming decentralised and geographically based. Profit centres may emerge and formal reporting processes are emphasised. Management focus on expansion of the market.
Phase 4	**Watchdog** - the organisation structure during this phase moves into product groups with line reporting relationships. Control is exercised through planning. Management reward emphasises profit share and stock options, which focus on both short and long term growth. This phase concentrates on the consolidation of the organisation.

Phase 5	**Participation** - growth is encouraged through participation, and mutual goal setting. Management focuses on problem-solving activities which ensure the organisation's survival, but also emphasises innovation to ensure growth and survival. The structure will be team based, with good performance being rewarded through team bonus schemes.

The implications for management of this model are detailed in the table below, which shows the specific management actions that characterise each growth phase. These actions are also the solutions, which ended each preceding revolutionary period.

CATEGORY	PHASE 1	PHASE 2	PHASE 3	PHASE 4	PHASE 5
Management Focus	Make and sell	Efficiency of operations	Expansion of market	Consolidation of organisation	Problem solving and innovation
Organisation structure	Informal	Centralised and functional	Decentralised and geographical	Line-staff and product groups	Matrix of teams
Top management style	Individualistic and entrepreneurial	Directive	Delegates	Watchdog	Participates
Control system	Market results	Standards and cost centres	Reports and profit centres	Plans and investment centres	Mutual goal setting
Management reward emphasis	Ownership	Salary and merit increases	Individual bonus	Profit sharing and stock options	Team basis

5.2 Ansoff's product-market matrix

An alternative approach to this area is that of Igor Ansoff, who attempts to identify the strategies open to an organisation seeking growth. Ansoff's analysis is summarised in a 2-by-2 matrix, with 'market' on one axis and 'product or service' on the other.

	Existing product	New product
Present market	Expansion ie, increase in market penetration	Product development or innovation
New market	Market development (sometimes called 'exploration')	Diversification

To illustrate how this works, consider the following possibilities:

- A business seeks growth while offering its **present** products to its **present** market; this is a strategy of market penetration, ie achieving wider adoption of an existing product by the existing target customers.

- A business seeks growth by offering **new** products to its **present** market; in other words, a strategy of new product development.

- A business seeks growth by offering its **present** products in **new** markets; this is a strategy of market development, ie, finding new customers who may wish to acquire the products already on hand.

- A business seeks growth by offering **new** products in **new** markets; this is a strategy of diversification. In effect, managers conclude that existing products and markets do not offer the most attractive option, and they look for something better.

Market penetration, market development and **product development** are often grouped together as intensive strategies. These are followed by firms that have not fully exploited the opportunities of their current products or market, ie the product has not reached the decline stage of its life cycle and its market is not yet saturated.

Such intensive strategies are normally deemed to be pursued internally but, **horizontal integration** ie, the taking over of competitors, encompasses either market penetration or market development or both.

Diversification strategies are normally appropriate when a company cannot grow into its present industry with its current products (because they are approaching the end of their life cycle), nor within its current markets (because they are becoming saturated).

The choice of growth option depends on many factors including the stage the industry has reached in its growth cycle. Heuss talks of four stages:

(a)   **Development/introduction** - this is a time for vertical integration as there is often a scarcity of suppliers of raw materials, components and machinery and their secrecy and time consideration regarding customers.

(b)   **Growth** - there is a need for liquid resources to finance trade and new plants and so concentration with its vertical disintegration takes place - it becomes more advantageous to buy in many items from specialist firms. Imitators enter the market place attracted by the rapidly increasing sales and high profits that can be earned - horizontal disintegration is rife.

(c)   **Maturity** - often accompanied by an oligopolistic shake out leading to horizontal integration. Input scarcities and sales bottlenecks can lead to vertical integration.

(d)   **Saturation/decline** - lead to diversification.

The parallels between this industrial growth cycle and the product life cycle should not be ignored.

5.3   Market leaders and followers

Johnson and Scholes in 'Exploring Corporate Strategy' identify the different actions undertaken by market leaders and followers.

(a)   **Growth** - the market leaders stay ahead of the field during growth, offering unique products or services or cost advantages. The followers may have entered the market to meet excess demand, developing by imitation. Alternatively acquisition may allow the follower to catch up.

(b)   **Maturity** - this phase can be difficult for any organisation whether it is in the public or private sector. Expectations and strategies need to be reviewed. Each organisation needs to assess how it can compete against its competitors.

In the public services there is a realisation that the service cannot cope with being a monopoly supplier, covering the entire 'market'. Senior management are being forced to define the activities that they can perform, with the emphasis on 'contracting out' services to private contractors, ranging from waste removal to canteen staff.

Johnson and Scholes identify three ways a market leader may choose to consolidate its position during this phase of the life cycle.

(i)   By exploiting their superior cost structure.

(ii)   By raising structural barriers ie, high levels of marketing, geographical expansion, encouraging government policies which would make entry difficult.

(iii)   By making it less attractive for other organisations to challenge the leader's position. An example is the 'price match' strategy the John Lewis partnership.

The followers on the other hand will tend to:

•   Enter price wars.

•   Reduce costs, which will allow expenditure on for example more effective distribution.

•   Adopt a 'niche' market sector.

Geographical spread is a strategy favoured by many organisations. Japanese companies challenging and displacing market leaders in electronics is such an example. The attempts being made by organisations to move into the Eastern European market are another example.

(c)   **Decline** - when demand is reducing, divestment or withdrawal options have to be considered. Sometimes market leaders will close down their own capacity and buy competitors in order to ensure supply is decreased.

Follower organisations tend to concentrate on differentiating themselves.

5.4   Development versus growth

Definition   Organisation development is 'the formation of new combinations of resources, or the formulation of new attainable and visionary objectives'.

Development involves policy decisions that will change objectives, while growth involves technical or administrative improvements, which will allow the organisation to achieve its objectives more effectively. Development is a broader concept, and can happen through innovation and/or acquisition, providing a framework for growth.

Growth occurs during a particular stage of the organisation's development; it is an evolutionary process. Hicks states:

'Growth asks: how does the organisation get more out of what it now has?

Development asks: how does the organisation achieve something different?'

Development usually changes the organisation fundamentally and can be 'revolutionary', which results in resistance to the changes.

Growth and development, while separate and distinct concepts, are also interrelated. Development creates the potential for new growth, and as growth reaches its limit, pressures often occur for development. New innovations or markets will lead to development, which if successful will create the opportunity for growth. This interaction is depicted below:

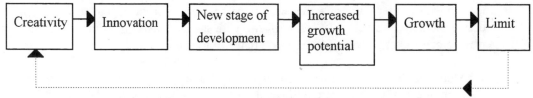

Relationship of creativity, development and growth (Hicks).

5.5   Growth by diversification

We have already seen from our study of Ansoff's product-market growth matrix that diversification is a strategy that entails the deployment of a company's resources into new products and new markets. The company thus becomes involved in activities that are different from those in which it is currently involved. Diversification strategy means the company selectively changes the product lines, customer targets and perhaps its manufacturing and distribution arrangements.

Johnson and Scholes stress that a company engaging in diversification considers: 'All directions of development away from its present products and its present market at the same time'.

Such activities are not new - Steiner talks of the sixteenth century House of Fugger engaged in spices, textiles and banking. However, there is an increasing trend towards diversification - of the top 500 US companies, 6.5% were diversified in 1959, 33% in 1980 and 38% in 1990.

They can be split into those related to the firm's core marketing system (**vertical integration***),* those related to the business of the firm (ie **concentric diversification**) and those unrelated to the firm and beyond the boundaries of its industry (ie **conglomerate diversification**). Diversification strategies can be pursued internally or externally.

Peters and Waterman are against conglomerate diversification. They argue that: 'Organisations that do not branch out (whether by acquisition or internal diversification) but stick very close to their knitting out-perform the others. The most successful of all are those diversified around a single skill - the coating and bonding technology at 3M for example. The second group, in descending order, comprises those companies that branch out into related fields - the leap from electric power generation turbines to jet engines (another turbine) from GE, for example. Least successful, as a general rule, are those companies that diversify into a wide variety of fields. Acquisitions especially, among this group, tend to wither on the vine.' Despite this, major conglomerates like Hanson Trust, BTR, Williams Holdings continue to generate successful business performance.

Because of the extent of the change with diversification, there is clearly more risk involved than in a strategy of product-market expansion (ie, remaining within the existing product-market scope), so we must consider the reasons why companies nevertheless diversify. Ansoff suggests three main reasons:

(i)   Objectives can no longer be met without diversification. This would be identified by the momentum line (status quo) forecast and gap analysis. The reason for the dissatisfaction with the present industry might be either due to poor return caused by product decline, with little opportunity for technological innovation in the same field, or due to lack of flexibility eg, unavoidable dependence on a single customer or a single product line.

(ii)   The company has more cash than it needs for expansion. Whether it prefers to invest this outside the business, or to seek opportunities for diversification, will depend on the relative rates of return obtainable.

(iii) Companies may diversify even if their objectives are being or could be met within their industry, if diversification promises to be more profitable than expansion.

Steiner suggests that it may be for the company to make greater use of an existing distribution system, or to avoid the company depending on only one product line.

More reasons put forward by other writers are:

- For the company to expand horizontally into other industries and use the synergy obtainable to strengthen its existing products.

- For the company to compete at all points with a competitor. If a competitor is obtaining synergy from its product-market mix, which provides it with some form of competitive advantage, the company might be compelled to also diversify to achieve the same advantageous mix.

- To take advantage of downstream opportunities such as by-products, etc.

If a company is unable to reach a decision about the relative merits of expansion and diversification due to lack of quantifiable information, it might continue to search for diversification opportunities, short of actually committing resources. In other words it delays the decision until better information is available, as has already been advocated.

An organisation may diversify by developing its own new product-market area (organically) or by acquiring or merging with a company already operational in the proposed new field. The former implies an active research department initiative. The latter can lead to quicker entry into the new area (time is often of the essence) and to **start-up** economies, but is not without its own difficulties.

5.6   Stability strategies

Although concerned with maintaining the status quo these do not necessarily involve **no action** although such a course is commonly adopted when the company is doing well and there is no envisaged change in the company's values or its environment.

The consequences of growth are not always seen as beneficial. For example, the owner of a small business may be content to continue at the existing level of operations for a number of reasons:

- If the business is already supporting the owner in a reasonable life style there may be no motivation to change.

- Growth will probably require finance and the owner may not relish borrowing.

- Growth may mean that the owner is unable to stay close to all aspects of the business, which could reduce personal enjoyment and satisfaction.

- Growth may lead to sacrifice of overall control.

Another 'no-growth' scenario is where future growth is sacrificed for **present profits** by, for example, reducing expenditure on R & D, maintenance or advertising. This can only be a temporary measure if long-term stagnation is to be avoided. For example, Rolls Royce reduced R & D expenditure by 33% in 1992.

Finally, after a period of rapid growth and even when things are going well, a company may wish to consolidate its position and either temporarily or permanently cease growth activities.

6   MERGERS AND ACQUISITIONS

6.1   Growth by acquisition versus internal growth

Companies may make mergers or acquisitions for a number of reasons:

- as a means of achieving growth;

- to put up more effective barriers to the entry of new firms by acquisition in their own industry;

- in order to diversify;

- to cut costs by economies of scale;

- to obtain skills;

- to obtain liquid resources (the acquiring company can defray the purchase price by the issue of additional equity capital, particularly where the price earnings ratio is high) etc.

A company might wish to be acquired because the owner wants to retire to obtain additional cash or to use the larger company's R & D facilities to assist its expansion or to provide more extensive career opportunities for the owner/directors, etc.

Among factors to be considered when deciding whether to grow internally or make an acquisition are:

- **Timing** - if analysis of the proposed product-market area shows that time is of the essence, acquisition of a company already in the field is indicated, as this can generally be achieved very much more quickly. The exceptions to this would be in the case of the relatively small number of industries where the lead time for product development is of the order of weeks or a few months rather than years, or where start-up synergy is large enough to allow a quick start.

- **Start-up cost** - if the cost of entering a new area will be high it might be better to acquire.

- **Synergy** - if the new area has relatively little synergy with the old, acquisition might be better.

- **Structure of the new industry** - if the competitive structure of the new industry would not admit another member, or if barriers to entry are high, acquisition is the only way. If there are no attractive acquisition opportunities in the area, internal growth is the only way.

- **Relative cost and risk** - acquisition is often more costly than internal development because the owners of the acquired company will have to be paid for the risks they have already taken. On the other hand, if the company decides on internal growth it has to bear such risk itself, so that there is a trade-off between cost and risk.

- **Relative price-earnings ratio** - if the price-earnings ratio is significantly higher in the new industry than the present one, acquisition may not be possible because it would cause too great a dilution in earnings per share to the existing shareholders. On the other hand, if the present company has a high price-earnings ratio it can boost earnings per share by issuing its own equity in settlement of the purchase price.

- **Asset valuation** - if the acquiring company believes that the potential acquisition's assets are under-valued it might acquire in order to undertake an *asset stripping* operation, ie, selling off or using the company's assets rather than operating it as a going concern.

6.2   Activity

List all the possible motives you can think of for a company attempting to acquire the ownership of more, or all, of another company

6.3   Activity solution

Among possible motives are the general, marketing, manufacturing, purchasing and financial benefits. These aims include:

General:
- to obtain joint synergy,
- to buy management talent,
- to buy time while the strategy of the acquiring company develops.

Marketing:
- to preserve the balance of market power;
- to control spheres of influence of potential competitors;
- to break into a new market (perhaps export or beachhead);
- to take advantage of joint marketing synergies (for example by the way of rationalising distribution, advertising, sales organisation and sales costs in general);
- to re-position markets and products;
- to obtain the reputation or prestige of the acquired company;
- to take over 'problem child' products;
- to obtain a critical mass position.

Manufacturing:
- to acquire technical know-how;
- to amalgamate manufacturing facilities to obtain synergies (economies of scale, group technology, shared research, rationalisation of facilities and working capital, and so on);
- to extend manufacturing involvement (for example the provision of field maintenance services).

Purchasing:
- to control spheres of supply influence;
- to safeguard a source of supply for materials;
- to obtain operating cost synergies;
- to share the benefits of the suppliers' profitability.

Financial:
- to acquire property;
- to acquire 'cash cow' organisations;
- to obtain direct access to cash resources;
- to acquire assets surplus to the needs of the combined businesses and dispose of them for cash;
- to obtain a bigger asset backing;
- to improve financial standing (market price and earnings per share);
- for speculative gain purposes.

6.4   Distinction between merger and acquisition

A merger involves two companies, often of similar size, who decide that it would be to their mutual advantage to join forces.

An acquisition involves a company gaining control of another company for its own benefit, possibly against the wishes of the other company (though of course in the case of a public company the shareholders must consent). Usually it is a larger company gaining control of a smaller company.

Mergers and acquisitions are often made to achieve diversification but equally a company might choose to merge with or take over another in its own industry. The same considerations apply. The failure rate for mergers and acquisitions shows that there are considerable risks and the operation should therefore be carefully planned.

6.5   Activity

What behaviour problems are likely to arise from changes imposed by a parent company upon a company it has recently taken over?

6.6   Activity solution

In the event of a takeover or merger, behavioural problems will arise out of fear of change and there will be resistance to it. They will manifest themselves as follows:

(a)   **A conflict of loyalties** - many people who were loyal to the old firm or organisation will find it difficult to adjust to the new arrangement. This will manifest in an inability to integrate, to accept changes in work pattern and new managers. This in turn will lead to poor performance, possibly even outright opposition or even a possible attempt to undermine the new managers' authority.

(b)   **Fear** - this will arise initially from the changes at higher levels. Suspicion of changes will cause doubts and uncertainty. The fear will develop if the merger leads to redundancies. This will especially hit higher levels of management since there will be no requirement for two chief accountants or two marketing directors.

(c)   **Loss of status** - the loss of status can cause serious problems even where jobs and autonomy remain. For example, the chief accountant of the firm which is taken over may remain as divisional controller but report only functionally to a general manager, having another chief accountant senior to him. The job remains unchanged but the person may well grieve over lost status, especially if any privileges are removed. The situation may be further aggravated by the fact that an internal struggle may take place, possibly arising from the downgraded accountant being technically superior to the new function head.

6.7   Reorganisation

Changes in the organisation's structure might involve creating new departments and divisions, greater delegation of authority or more centralisation, changes in the way plans are made, management information is provided and control is exercised.

Although reorganisation is intended to respond to changes in the organisational environment, there may be other compelling reasons. Those related to the enterprise environment include changes in operations caused by acquisition or sale of major properties, changes in product line or marketing methods, business cycles, competitive influences, new production techniques, changes in the number of people employed, government policy or the current state of knowledge or trends in organising.

The need for reorganisation may become apparent with the deficiencies in an existing structure. Some of these arise from organisational weaknesses, excessive spans of management, too many committees, slow decision-making, excessive costs or breakdown in financial control. Personality clashes between managers may be solved by reorganisation and staff-line conflicts may develop to such an extent that only reorganisation will resolve them. Other deficiencies may stem from management inadequacies or a lack of skill or knowledge on the part of a manager. These may have been avoided by moving the authority for decision-making to another position.

Some older companies provide ample evidence of inflexibility. Examples include an organisation pattern that is no longer suited to the times, a district or regional organisation that could be either abolished or enlarged because of improved communications, or a structure that is too highly centralised for an enlarged enterprise requiring decentralisation.

The need for reorganisation is outlined below:

Causes	Examples
Changes in the organisational environment.	Greater competition may create pressure for cost cutting, leading to a reduction in employees.
Diversification into new product/service market areas.	As the organisation becomes more complex, there is a need for better lateral and vertical integration. There is also the problem of when or whether to switch from a functional to a divisional organisation structure.
Growth	As more people are employed there are problems with extended hierarchies and poor communication.
Technology	New developments can lead to fewer staff required in certain skills and shortages of staff in others.
Changes in the capabilities of the staff.	Changes in educational levels and the distribution of occupational skills, as well as the attitude towards work, can have an impact on the structure of the organisation.

7   DEFENSIVE STRATEGIES

7.1   Types of strategy

Firms that are under-performing sometimes adopt defensive strategies. They are consequently unpopular with managers 'in office' as they imply failure of their previous strategies.   Five principal classes have been identified:

(a)   **Operational turnaround** is pursued by companies following Glueck's maxim: 'Slow down and catch your breath: we've got to do better'

It often follows a period of sustained growth or successful strategic turnaround and should not be confused with the latter as it assumes that the firm's basic corporate objectives and strategy are sound and appropriate. Neither should it be confused with the stability strategy of consolidation, which is not appropriate when a firm is under-performing.

Major approaches include:

- **Cost reductions** - cutting staff and improving productivity

- **Increasing/rationalising revenues** - generating more sales and profits without increasing expenditure by more effective advertising, sales promotion etc; increasing prices where possible; focusing on high margin products; better investments of cash and current investment; tighter inventory controls; better collection of debts and stretching of payments to creditors

- **Reduction of assets** - selling land, buildings and equipment no longer needed.

(b)   **Strategic turnaround** is pursued when the company's objectives or corporate strategy is not yielding the desired performance. Normally the board of directors is involved and the top management team is changed - Schendel reported that of the 54 firms he studied, 39 made significant changes to their management teams including the Managing Director during strategic turnarounds.

(c)   **Divestment** involves the selling off or liquidation of a SBU (specific business unit) and is appropriate when that SBU is unable to fit in with the rest of the organisation. Exxon disposed of its office systems division because the managers did not understand it as well as the oil industry. It is also employed to generate a lot of cash from the sale which can be used to reduce debt and buy time eg, Pan American sold off the profitable Intercontinental Hotels chain to prop up its loss making airline.

(d)   **Liquidation** - the selling off or voluntary winding up of an organisation is preferable to a compulsory liquidation. However, it is a difficult policy to adopt as top management does not notice that crises are developing and often makes light of them when they do occur in the hope that they will go away.

(e)   **Captive company**: the reduction of major functional activities and the decision to sell 75% or more of its products/services to a single customer. The company becomes dependent on the stronger firm but in return it achieves some security and can reduce its expenditure.

The choice of defensive strategy depends on the match between the firm's current operating health and its current strategic health. If the former is strong, and the latter weak, a strategic turnaround is called for; if the situation is reversed an operating turnaround is required; whereas weakness in both could lead to liquidation.

7.2   Reasons for and reactions to decline

Organisations may go into decline due to a range of reasons such as:

(a)   declining market;
(b)   over capacity in the market;
(c)   increasing costs and declining profits;
(d)   poor management;
(e)   lack of innovative products/services;
(f)   cash-flow problems.

How organisations react to decline will obviously depend on the reasons that have caused it. In a declining market for example one of the most difficult decisions for organisations in both the public and private sector is whether to reduce capacity either temporarily or permanently. If turnaround cannot be achieved fairly quickly it is likely that exit from the product/market will be necessary.

Also the organisations' reaction will depend on whether it is a market leader or follower. Market leaders will tend to:

(a)   redefine scope;
(b)   divest themselves of peripheral business;
(c)   'encourage' departures from the market.

Market followers on the other hand will attempt to:

(a)   differentiate their products/services;
(b)   identify new opportunities.

Organisations usually face very difficult decisions regarding retrenchment, divestment and withdrawal from products/markets. Sometimes organisations have no option but to sell out to another organisation who may then introduce radical change.

Often in a decline situation redundancies will result and will usually result in a demotivated workforce who fear for the future. The impact on the level of motivation and on company performance has to be taken seriously by management.

7.3   Divestment/rationalisation

This is the process of disposing of part of an organisation's activities, and usually the assets and personnel that relate to it or pulling out of certain product or service market areas. One motive for doing so might be simply an opportunistic attempt to make a swift profit. Another reason might be a strategic decision to focus management effort on core activities while disposing of areas that distract from the core activities or are vulnerable. The most common reason is to rationalise an enterprise as a result of a strategic appraisal. This could mean deciding to concentrate on its core business and sell off fringe activities, or to sell off subsidiaries where performance is poor or where growth prospects are not good.

In recent years there have been a number of high-profile demergers of this type (often referred to as 'unbundling'). What was a single entity becoming two or more entities, often with the same owners (shareholders), but typically with separate management teams.

This latter point is well illustrated in the particular type of divestment known as a management buyout. This term describes the case where a strategic business unit (SBU) is sold off, not to another company, but to the existing management team, who become owners as well as managers in the newly hived-off entity. This procedure has many advantages.

- The people most likely to make a success of the business - and hence to agree a high price for purchasing it - are the managers who are already intimately familiar with its products, markets, strengths, weaknesses etc.

- The investment return demanded by the new owner managers may be less than is required by the head office of a mammoth organisation in which the SBU is just a very small part.

- Managers can put in some of their own capital, but may very likely attract investment also from venture capital providers.

7.4   Redundancy

Redundancy is a complex human and business issue, which demands sensitive handling by management.

For the individual faced with redundancy an initial concern is with financial security with the loss of a secured and predictable income. Psychologically redundancy can be a blow, reducing self-esteem and suggesting a lack of appreciation for past efforts. There will be fears, real or imaginary, of unemployment. Clearly redundancy does serve to increase unemployment and typically takes place in areas or industries, which already have an unemployment problem.

For the organisation facing redundancies there are both commercial and humanitarian considerations. People are often the most valuable assets of the business. It is their skill and ability, energy and creativity that allows the organisation to prosper. To dispose of these assets in such a way as to harm morale in those employees who remain or in an inhuman way, which harms the company's reputation is clearly bad management. To ensure that these humanitarian and commercial considerations are taken into account an organisation needs to develop a redundancy policy, which should cover the following matters:

(a)   **Objectives** - the objectives of a redundancy scheme are to reduce costs and at the same time protect the interests of individuals. How this is to be done should be quantified as precisely as possible.

(b)   **Different redundancy situations** - redundancy may arise because of circumstances forced on the business, eg loss of sales, or because of changes that will benefit the organisation, such as technological advances. The scope for compensation is likely to be much greater in the latter situation than the former.

(c)   **Avoiding redundancy** - all alternatives should be considered before unavoidable redundancies are implemented. It is possible to reduce the amount of compulsory redundancy by schemes such as early retirement, relocation, retraining and voluntary redundancy.

(d)   **Selection for redundancy** - the question of who should be made redundant is a difficult one but some statement about it should be incorporated into a redundancy policy. A common approach is 'last in – first out' though businesses also use other criteria such as skill, competence and attendance record.

(e)   **Consultation** - there are statutory rules governing the requirements for consultation and the time scale and information that must be provided. Even without such legislation common sense would suggest that they are necessary.

(f)   **Notice of redundancy** - again there are statutory requirements concerning the required length of notice.

(g)   **Compensation** - minimum compensation rates are required by law. The amount varies according to a formula, which takes account of age, length of service and earnings. This is a minimum figure and many employers are more generous.

(h)   **Pension rights** - legally pension rights must be preserved for employees aged over twenty-six who have completed at least five years service.

(i)   **Re-engagement** - if circumstances change, employees previously made redundant may be re-engaged. It is necessary to clarify the position with regard to matters such as pensionable service.

(j)   **Redeployment** - because of the traumatic effect of redundancy, many organisations try to assist with redeployment. Such assistance may take a number of forms eg, financial arrangements and assistance with finding a new job.

The human problems of redundancy are increasingly recognised by employers and there have been a variety of managerial initiatives to mitigate the effects. One of the most constructive has been a redundancy counselling service. Sometimes this is administered by the personnel department whilst other organisations use external services.

8   SELF TEST QUESTIONS

8.1   Give two examples of events thrust upon the organisation by environmental events beyond its control. (1.2).

8.2   What are four basic features of organisational change? (1.5).

8.3   What does the general environment for any organisation include? (2.1).

8.4   Outline the main sources of resistance to change. (3.1).

8.5   Describe the strategic choices management can make to achieve its change objectives (4.2).

8.6   Draw a diagram showing Greiner's five phases of growth (5.1).

8.7   Explain the four sectors of Ansoff's product-market matrix. (5.2).

8.8   Briefly describe a 'no-growth' scenario. (5.6).

8.9   Describe three of the five defensive strategies that can be adopted by the organisation. (7.1)

9   EXAMINATION TYPE QUESTION

9.1   Strategic objectives

Until quite recently, many firms pursued a policy of conglomerate diversification. This was usually linked with the strategic objective of growth and often effected by mergers. However, a contrary form of policy has now become popular – that of 'demerger' or 'unbundling'.

Required

(a)   Assess the appropriateness of growth as a strategic objective.   **(6 marks)**
(b)   Explain why a company might follow a policy of conglomerate diversification.   **(13 marks)**
(c)   Explain why a company might follow a policy of demerger.   **(6 marks)**
                                                                                          (Total 25 marks)

10   ANSWER TO EXAMINATION TYPE QUESTION

10.1   Strategic objectives

(a)   The survival of the organisation is usually considered to be the prime objective of any business. It is a commonly held view, however, that if a company is not growing, then it is dying. If the total market is expanding, it is likely that most competitor companies are planning to grow and firms who remain static will be out-performed by other organisations in the industry. Therefore, many companies include a 'growth objective' in their strategic plan, considering this as a more aggressive policy, which will help ensure the firm's survival.

There are a number of additional reasons why growth is seen as an attractive objective. Systems of taxation generally influence the owners of a firm to favour growth. As shareholders must pay tax on dividends they generally prefer the majority of profits to be reinvested, thus resulting in capital gains which will reduce the total liability of the shareholders as individuals. The management of a company will opt for growth as a means of enhancing their personal position. Association with a larger firm will be perceived as desirable and the managers' individual goals will play a part in the formulation of a strategic plan.

There are several definitions of the term *growth*. It may be viewed as an increase in sales or market share, or alternatively in terms of increased profitability and shareholders' returns. Another important factor is that growth should have a specific purpose; that is, as a means of achieving the stated objectives of management and not be seen as an end in itself.

It is normally assumed that the objective of a company will be to maximise shareholders' wealth and growth is one way of achieving this. Another view holds that each company has multiple objectives. One of these may be survival, with growth and profit maximisation seen as a means of achieving this aim.

The concept of growth must be placed within the context of the past performance of the company and the average for the particular industry. The strategy adopted by management will be influenced by an accurate view of the environment, the strategies adopted by competitor companies and the available resources.

(b)   Management can consider several growth strategies as follows.

(i)   *Market penetration* - This is increasing sales of present products in present markets and can be accomplished by inducing current customers to purchase more of the firm's products, attracting non-users or by persuading competitors' customers to purchase from the company.

(ii)   *Market development* - This involves increasing sales in previously untried geographical locations or new market segments.

(iii)   *Product development and diversification* - An important distinction must be drawn between these two strategies as they involve different levels of risk.

Product development entails providing the present market with a new product, whereas diversification involves both new products and new markets. In order to establish which strategy should be developed, it is important to draw up forecasts about present products. If the current market environment is favourable in terms of customers and products, then market penetration or market development and diversification will be suitable strategies to adopt. If, however, the current market environment is not viewed as favourable for growth, management would be advised to adopt a strategy of product development and diversification.

Of the possible strategies, diversification entails most risk as it involves the development of both new products and new markets. Means of minimising the risk should therefore be assessed by firms embarking upon this strategy. One method, defined by McNamee as an organisation acquiring 'totally, or in part, another organisation whose business is not related to the acquiring organisation's business', is that of *conglomerate diversification*.

Although conglomerate diversification can be adopted by a company as a means of achieving rapid growth with relative ease, the nature of the strategy as defined above necessarily means that the acquiring and acquired firms will be operating in different areas. This means that considerable risk is involved. Nevertheless, there are several reasons why management may opt for conglomerate diversification.

(i)   Management may consider profit as the sole objective of the firm.

(ii)   If the acquiring firm has a high level of specialisation, conglomerate diversification may be the only possible strategy for expansion.

(iii)   If the threat of a decline in current markets is forecast, the position of the company may be jeopardised and conglomerate diversification may be seen as a solution.

(c)   There are several factors, which may lead management to consider a policy of demerger and a number of benefits, which might result from this policy.

Each company should ensure that all parts of the organisation are regularly measured in terms of performance compared with objectives and, if weaknesses are identified, management should assess the possible impact of demerger. If poor performance is identified and the situation is not expected to improve to what management consider to be an acceptable level, there will be a very strong case for demerger.

Other factors influencing management's decision may be

(i)   the identification of excess capacity, particularly in mature industries;

(ii)   the financial burden of higher interest rates linked to higher levels of inflation;

(iii)   a change of emphasis from growth to profitability; and

(iv)   increased awareness of the risks of conglomerate diversification and a consequent change of attitude towards the policy.

Benefits of demerger

(i)   Providing the company with additional cash resources. These could be used for (i) reinvestment in successful areas of the organisation, (ii) identifying and undertaking potentially successful projects which would be of more benefit to the firm, or (iii) increasing dividends to shareholders.

(ii)   Eliminating an unsuccessful area of the business. This could strengthen the company's and management's position in the event of a possible hostile take-over bid.

21 IMPLEMENTING CHANGE

INTRODUCTION & LEARNING OUTCOMES

Syllabus area 11(v)
- The stages in the change process

- Approaches to the management of organisational development and major cultural and structural change (e.g. Kanter, Lewin and Peters)

The introduction and management of change are central to success in any management position. The only certain factor is that everything will change in time. Harvey Jones in his reflections on leadership, states 'change is a continuous industrial process' and whilst we can recognise that 'change, or the prospect of change, will frighten everybody,' it is the 'task of leadership ... to make the status quo more dangerous than launching into the unknown'.

In this chapter, we look in detail at a structured approach ('organisational development') to modifying behaviour and culture in response to change, as well as a variety of other approaches.

When you have studied this chapter you should be able to do the following:

- Explain the process of organisational development and the problems associated with it

- Recommend ways in which planned change can be implemented at the organisational and departmental levels

- Identify opportunities to improve the management of change and communicate recommendations to appropriate managers

---

1 THE DYNAMICS OF CHANGE

1.1 Framework for the management of change

The idea of change that is planned assumes that the management can identify gaps between current conditions and desired conditions on the following dimensions:

(i)   How can this organisation be more effective?
(ii)   Can we operate more efficiently?
(iii)   How can we make it a more satisfying place to work?

Whenever the organisation can identify differences between where it currently is and where it would like to be on any of the dimensions, it can pursue planned change or improve the organisation. Systems can be implemented to identify and diagnose particular problems within these general areas eg, poor morale, inefficient computer programs, lack of quality control or inadequate downward communication. Depending on the problem, a suitable change effort can be designed.

If the process of planned change is to become part of the culture of the organisation, provisions must be made for introspection and self criticism on a routine basis. It should also be followed up as a natural part of the managerial style.

1.2 Why change is a challenge to management

The managerial role involves coping with accelerating change in both the external environment and the internal subsystems that affect the managerial process. Accelerating change can lead to increasing complexity, making the job of the manager increasingly difficult. They need a tolerance for ambiguity and an ability to diagnose situations and identify opportunities and problems.

As decision-makers, managers are the ultimate change agents, whether they are centrally involved or merely guiding and co-ordinating activities. Change can stem from adjustments in managerial behaviour eg, leadership style, approach to planning and controlling or degree of participation in decision-making. When the focus is more technical, structural or psychosocial, managers may respond to suggestions from others or actively instigate changes.

There are external or internal consultants that facilitate organisational change. Specialists in economic and marketing research, industrial relations and organisational development are all examples of change agents.

1.3 Targets for organisational change

Harrison claims that there are a number of levels of intervention and that the depth of intervention ought to be as shallow as the problem permits.

- Cognitive and rational problem-solving techniques such as those used in management accounting and operational research are located at the shallow end of the continuum of available strategies.

- Industrial psychology based methods, focusing on the individual and his task relationships are at a somewhat deeper level and include job enrichment and management by objectives (MBO).

- At the deepest level are those instrumental approaches, which attempt to change attitudes and social orientations as well as task-related behaviour. Organisational development is such an approach: see later in this chapter.

Many managers focus their change efforts at a specific level within the organisation such as the level of the:

(a) **Individual** - in the belief that organisational behaviour is determined by the characteristics of its members. The aim is to improve individual skill levels, attitudes and motivation. Techniques employed include education and training and management development

(b) **Organisation structure and systems** - claiming that organisational behaviour is determined by the characteristics of the organisational situation in which people work. The aim is to direct member's behaviour to organisational goals and techniques involving structural and procedural modifications such as divisionalisation, matrices, size, job redesign, reward systems and management by objectives (MBO).

(c) **Organisational climate and interpersonal style** - such managers believe that emotional and social processes, which characterise the relations among members, determine organisational behaviour. Their aims are to create a system with a wide climate of high interpersonal trust and openness and a reduction in the dysfunctional consequences of excessive social conflict and competitiveness. The principal technique is organisation development.

Obviously no one level should be focused on exclusively and a balance of approaches should be the aim.

2   THE CHANGE PROCESS

2.1   Implementation of changes

People do not like change. Comfortable routines have to be altered and there is no guarantee at the outset that the new system will work as well as, let alone better than, the old one. When change is in the air, many members of the organisation can be seen to go about muttering that it was good enough for them, so why should it need to be changed now?

The first lessons in implementing change are thus as follows.

(a)   Change should never be for change's sake.

(b)   Good communication is essential from the outset; do not let rumour take over.

(c)   Create an awareness of the need for change; let the doubting members see the problems of the existing system and encourage them to call for changes themselves.

(d)   Nominate one person or a group of people to the initiating role and be prepared to accept their amendments to the change to be introduced in the light of their experience.

(e)   The change should be regarded as the idea of the whole department or team. If people do not align with the change, they will not support it.

(f)   Be prepared to accept something that is a little less than perfect if it means it will work and have the support of the team (effectiveness = change x likelihood of success).

(g)   Remember that it will be a slow process to introduce complete change; be prepared to accept phasing if it will mean effective change.

(h)   On the other hand do not allow the necessary changes to disappear under a bed of lethargy.

The organisation that can change with changing situations is the organisation that will survive. Management must be innovative and dynamic; it must know how to introduce change without disruption; it must be prepared to be totally flexible in its attitudes.

2.2   Lewin's 3-step model of change

Kurt Lewin developed a programme of planned change and improved performance, involving the management of a three-phase process of behaviour modification. He demonstrated the effectiveness of using group norms and consensus decision-making to change individual and organisational behaviour. His research programs included Weight Watchers and the effect of group discussion and commitment in changing eating habits. The key findings were that behaviour change is more likely to occur and persist when commitment is on a group basis, rather than an individual one.

The process of change, shown in the diagram below, includes unfreezing habits or standard operating procedures, changing to new patterns and refreezing to ensure lasting effects.

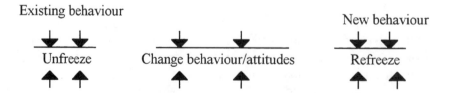

The process of change comprises three stages:

(a)   **Unfreezing** - implies that a change will mean abandoning existing practice before new practices can be successfully adopted. If individuals are to change, their current behaviour patterns must be unfrozen as a way of reducing resistance to change. Unfreezing will lead to doubts and to fear of the unknown. It will create the initial motivation to change by convincing staff of the undesirability of the present situation. This is an opportunity for managers to introduce education and training. However, in some cases an ethical question may arise regarding the legitimacy of deliberately creating discomfort that may initiate change.

(b)   **The change process itself** - mainly concerned with identifying what the new behaviour or norm should be. This stage will often involve new information being communicated and new attitudes, culture and concepts being adopted. If people have been educated, then the change is more likely to be successful.

(c)   **Refreezing or stabilising the change** - Lewin argued that even if the change is successful, the fruits of the success could be short-lived because the group's behaviour may revert to its previous ways. A new stable point of equilibrium must be established. People need to feel happy with the new values and culture and to see evidence of the success of the change. This implies reinforcing the new pattern of work or behaviour by rewards (praise etc) and developing the belief that the changed situation satisfies organisational and personal values.

2.3   The Bullock and Batten model

A few models have been developed from Lewin's three-step model. One of them is the integrated four phase model, developed by Bullock and Batten. The four steps are:

(i)   **Exploration** - this phase considers what changes are to be made and commits resources to the planning phase. The enterprise has to be aware of the need for change and will probably use a consultant to facilitate the process.

(ii)   **Planning** - this phase is concerned with understanding the problem. Research will be undertaken to collect and analyse information. The solution will be chosen and support will be gained for the proposed changes.

(iii)   **Action** - the planned changes will be implemented. This includes arrangements for managing the change, gaining support for the change as it takes place, evaluating the feedback of results and making adjustments where necessary.

(iv)   **Integration** - this phase consolidates the completed change so that it becomes part of the everyday operation of the enterprise. This will involve reinforcement of the new processes through feedback and reward systems. The consultant will move on and, the success will be publicised and staff will be undergoing the training to maintain the changes.

3   ORGANISATION DEVELOPMENT

3.1   Introduction

Organisation development, typically shortened to OD, is a systematic, integrated and planned approach to improving organisational effectiveness. Bennis states:

> **Definition**   'Organisation development is a response to change, a complex educational strategy intended to change the beliefs, attitudes, values and structure of organisations so that they can better adapt to new technologies, markets and challenges, and to the dizzying rate of change itself.'

The essence of an organisation development programme is that it aims to improve enterprise effectiveness in all aspects of the company, ie it considers the company as an entity. It is seen as a continuous, all embracing process that is focused on change.

3.2   Objectives of organisation development

Organisation development is a contingency approach, designed to solve problems that decrease operating efficiency at all levels, using the diagnostic and problem-solving skills of an external consultant in collaboration with the organisation's management. Such problems may include lack of co-operation, excessive decentralisation and poor communication.

The objective of OD, and therefore of the consultant or change agent, are to:

(a)   create an open, problem-solving environment in the organisation;

(b)   supplement the authority of role or status with that of the authority of knowledge and competence;

(c)   locate decision-making and problem-solving responsibilities as close to the sources of information as possible;

(d)   build trust among individuals and groups in the organisation;

(e)   maximise collaboration and make competition constructive;

(f)   develop reward systems which recognise the development of people as much as the achievement of organisational objectives;

(g)   increase acceptance of company objectives by active participation; and

(h)   increase the degree of autonomy for individuals in the organisation.

The techniques may involve sensitivity training, managerial grid training and survey feedback. Some OD practitioners also use process consultation, role analysis, job enrichment, organisational behaviour modification (coaching, counselling and team building), job design, stress management, career and life planning and management by objectives as part of their approach.

The managerial grid of Blake and Mouton is used in OD, but the emphasis is on the team or group rather than the individual. People who work together meet to identify barriers to effective functioning of the group. The team members develop change objectives and action plans to make the group more effective in achieving the organisation's goals.

3.3   OD process

Although various techniques are used, the process often includes the steps outlined below.

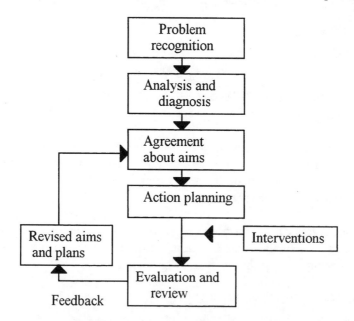

(i)   The preliminary stage is where the discussion of the aims and the implications of the programme takes place. The role of the third party is also sorted at this stage.

(ii)   The analysis and diagnosis stage includes obtaining and analysing data to identify and clarify problems.

(iii)   After analysing the data, management and the third party agree on aims and objectives of the programme.

(iv)   The action planning involves planning the sequence of activities designed to improve the organisation, in the light of the problems diagnosed.

(v)   As with any planning activity, the progress needs evaluating and reviewing.

(vi)   Resulting from the review, new plans may be required.

The interventions in the process may include a change in the organisation structure, a more effective procedure for handling customer complaints and/or the establishment of a team charged with the responsibility of implementing a cost reduction programme.

OD must be considered as a continuous process - planned, systematic and focussed on change. The aim is to make the organisation more effective.

3.4   Diagnosis

The consultant will explore the possibility of embarking on a programme of OD and will investigate the people, products, processes and environment of the client, looking at the systems and sub-systems in use for answers to the following questions:

(a)   Are the learning goals of organisation development appropriate?
(b)   Are the client's set of values such as to be conducive to a system of OD?
(c)   Are the key people involved?
(d)   Are individuals in the client system ready for OD?
(e)   What are the main problems confronting the organisation?

With regard to the last question, OD practitioners claim that goals vary in clarity and kind and that they are always in the process of changing. Bennis stated that when he felt certain that he knew what the problem was, he began to worry. He tried to develop a set of hoped-for outcomes, which were measurable in terms of either productivity or human satisfaction.

Attempts can be made to diagnose the client's key problems under six basic areas:

(a)   integration - congruence of the organisation's goals and the individual's needs is necessary (goal congruence);

(b)   power and authority - distribution of the sources of power and authority must be satisfactory;

(c)   collaboration - conflict needs to be resolved or managed;

(d)   adaptation - changes induced by the environment must be responded to appropriately;

(e)   identity - acceptance of clear organisational goals and commitment to their achievement;

(f)   revitalisation - how should the organisation react to growth and decay?

There may be a need for one or more of the following:

(a)   changing the organisation's culture (from a family concern to a professionally-managed company for instance);

(b)   changing managerial strategy;

(c)   changing the way work is done;

(d)   adapting to changes in the environment;

(e)   changing communications and developing trust between staff and line groups.

3.5   Education of managers

Management of change has become one of the most important parts of managers' jobs, and much more emphasis needs to be placed on the type of education needed to enable managers to cope with change. The qualities that are necessary, either within the company or externally, include:

(a)   interpersonal competence - skill in communication, ability to manage conflict, and self-awareness can be improved by laboratory training activities, grid and sensitivity training;

(b)   training in problem-solving and decision-making;

(c)   goal-setting skills;

(d)   planning skills;

(e)   better understanding of the processes of change;

(f)   skills in systems diagnosis.

It is true that there is not much evidence that education or training will, in itself, influence attitudes; these might be improved in the process of the individual undergoing training, but his ability to apply a changed attitude to real-life situations may be limited. An awareness of problems is, however, a first step to accomplishing desirable changes in attitude.

3.6   Evaluation

The final phase of OD is the evaluation of the effects of a change programme on the organisation as a whole; this is a continuous process which does not stop once the consultant, or change agent, has left the client's premises. This evaluation may take the form of attitude surveys, survey-feedback projects, research projects by behavioural scientists, and internal employee-relations research groups.

A serious problem is the evaluation of an individual's contribution to the organisation. The evaluation of progress is often highly subjective; some, such as Blake and Mouton, use productivity figures, whilst others use a variety of other indicators, for example, satisfaction, communication patterns, morale, etc. Bennis endeavoured to determine whether the organisation was, after his assignment, able to maintain and continue its own organisation development programme. Initially, he saw his role as that of a catalyst, a necessary ingredient in the process of change in the early stages of OD. With guidance, the client should become less and less dependent upon the change agent, and more capable of self-support.

3.7   Role of change agent

An agent of change is needed to act as a catalyst. He or she may be from inside or outside the organisation. The aim is to help the company to solve its own problems and the focus is on organisational, group and interpersonal processes. Members are encouraged to speak more openly about problems and inter-group activities are encouraged.

The role of the third party is important. To be a change agent requires particular qualities and abilities. These include the ability to listen, to establish and maintain comfortable relationships with people and to be aware of personal strengths and weaknesses.

The change agent is frequently a management consultant who, being a senior outside adviser, has several important advantages.

(a)   Confidentiality is assured.

(b)   An objective assessment is obtained, the consultant is unbiased and not party to any previous decisions taken within the company therefore 'has no flag to defend'.

(c)   Many consulting firms have considerable expertise and experience in organisational matters. This experience is often gained in other industries and so the consultant is able to provide examples of good practice elsewhere.

(d)   The assignment can be accomplished more quickly.

(e)   The OD consultant should not be a prescriptive, solution-oriented individual (like the traditional consultant). The role can be described as containing three elements:

      (i)   *collaboration* - working with clients rather than for them;

      (ii)   *research* - assisting clients to collect the information necessary to diagnose their own problems;

      (iii)   *process expertise* - focusing on how decisions are made (the dynamics of group behaviour) rather than on the type of decision.

The main disadvantages of using outside consultants are that the consultant is an outsider and it may be costly.

4   CHANGE MANAGEMENT

4.1   Why people resist change

Resisting change means attempting to preserve the existing state of affairs against pressure to alter it. Some examples of the many reasons why people resist change are as follows:

(a)   changes create an unknown future. This causes fear and resistance. People like to feel secure and have an influence on the events of their lives;

(b)   not knowing the reason for the change. Indeed those affected by the change and expected to make it work may be unclear as to why any change is necessary;

(c)   change could pose a threat of reduction in status and power, loss of security or removal of challenging, interesting work.

4.2   Force field analysis

Force field analysis is very similar to OD. It a general-purpose diagnostic and problem-solving technique, developed by Kurt Lewin. In any situation there are forces that push for change (driving) as well as forces that hinder change (restraining). If the forces offset each other completely, it results in equilibrium and status quo. Change can be brought about by increasing the driving forces or by reducing the restraining forces.

The force field model suggests two ways of dealing with change. The first is by strengthening your own side and the second is by weakening the opposing forces.

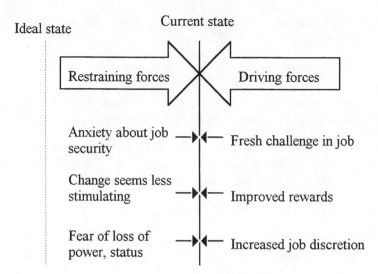

Restraining and driving forces in a change situation

Lewin advocates that managers should recognise that there exists a current state of equilibrium with forces pushing for change on the one hand and equally, forces resisting change aiming to maintain the present situation.

Change can be brought about by either increasing the driving forces or by reducing the restraining forces. The tendency is to increase the pressure of the driving forces. Lewin contends that this is often counter-productive, because it causes increased pressure from the restraining forces. It is better practice to analyse the restraining forces with a view to reducing or eliminating their pressures. This can then move more smoothly to the new state of equilibrium.

Involvement in understanding the need for the change and also in the framing of the changes will achieve this reduction of restraining forces. The change process consist of:

(i)   Identifying the restraining forces and overcoming/removing/getting round them.

(ii)   Carrying out the change.

(iii)   Stabilising the new situation by reinforcing the (now changed) behaviour of individuals and work groups with praise and encouragement.

Using a common individual and organisational problem, that of lack of time, we can illustrate the use of force field analysis. To work on the problem effectively we need to state the situation in terms of current and desired conditions, where we are and where we want to be. The current condition = no time spent on planned change and the desired condition = large blocks of time to critically appraise the organisation.

In order to understand the situation, we have to identify the forces that are keeping us in equilibrium ie, no change from the current condition.

Driving forces

knowledge of theory that says it would be 'better'
ling that it would be 'better'
ss stories about increased productivity from current literature
tories from acquaintances in similar organisations
elling the virtues of a new approach

ases to absorb available time

- current deadlines leave no time to analyse the problem of lack of time
- we seem to be doing satisfactory work, there is no sense of urgency
- reluctance of participants to rock the boat by analysing group processes
- assumption that time is not currently wasted

This list is not exhaustive but it leads to the next step, which is to pick one or more of the forces, starting with restraining forces and generating ideas for increasing them or decreasing them.

After alternatives have been evaluated, action plans can be designed and implemented.

4.3   Leavitt's model of change management

Leavitt argued that approaches to change that succeeded in one organisation were not necessarily successful in another. He suggests that the chosen approach to change in a particular organisation should reflect the underlying beliefs within that organisation.

Whilst change can never be fully planned due to unexpected problems and follow on effects, many organisations are adopting a positive attitude to the need for change. Leavitt recognised four variables, which can be affected by change and claimed that these 'entry points' can become specific targets for managerial efforts to instigate change. The variables are

- (a)   task;
- (b)   structure;
- (c)   technology;
- (d)   people.

Each of these can give rise to different approaches to change.

- (a)   *Task approach* – Seeking improved solutions to tasks will be largely technical, that is, seeking to improve the quality of decisions. The task approach, even where it involves clear changes of methods, is clearly interrelated to the other three approaches.

- (b)   *Structure approach* – This approach covers:

    - (i)   the traditional performance approaches of ensuring proper division of labour, levels of authority and responsibility, defining chain of command, span of control etc.;

    - (ii)   decentralisation - the creation of project centres and localising of decision-making creating a high level of local autonomy;

    - (iii)   communication patterns - the consideration of communication channels and flows; thus for repetitious, predictable work a highly centralised communication structure seems most efficient - whereas for novel, loosely structured tasks, a more open multi-channel communication network seems more appropriate.

- (c)   *Technological approach* - Taylor's Scientific Management is an early example of this approach category which includes method study approaches where an outsider views the work pattern and suggests changes in a technological approach. Updating and replacement of equipment is a natural example of an external approach. The essence is that the approach occurs outside of the work group itself.

- (d)   *People approach* - Group working, attitude training, changes in styles of management are examples of the people approach.

Each change can therefore be approached by one of these main four methods but it must be remembered that there is strong interaction between these categories. For example, a change in *technology* (introduction of a computer) will influence *tasks* (output may be quicker or greater) and a change in structure could mean fewer staff needed. A change in any category is likely to have an effect upon the people approach.

The interdependence of these four variables can be illustrated as follows

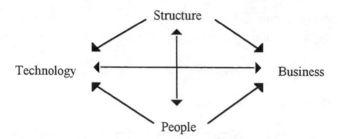

As a result of these interdependencies changes in one variable could lead to unanticipated, and possibly undesirable, changes to other variables. Moreover, it is possible to deliberately change one variable to bring about a desired change in another variable - the increasing adoption of mass production technologies has led to the spread of capitalist structures.

Leavitt points to the fact that, if there is too much rigidity in an organisation, it does not allow creative ideas to be introduced. Some methods used to overcome this are:

*   **diversification** - enterprises with too narrow a product base may buy interests in other industries;

*   **decentralisation** - the parent company has overall control but units are given authority to make major decisions and the unit managers are held accountable to the parent company;

*   **venture groups** - a group is given the resources to develop a new idea, which may have come from a group member.

4.4   Key issues in successful change management

As we have seen, people tend to be resistant to change. Members of the organisation should not perceive new ideas and innovations as threats. The efforts made by management to maintain the balance of the socio-technical system will influence people's attitudes and behaviour, which will affect the level of organisational performance and effectiveness. It is important, therefore, for management to adopt a clearly defined strategy for the initiation of change.

J Kotter and L Schlesinger suggest six specific methods for overcoming resistance to change. They are:

*   participation and involvement;
*   education and communication;
*   facilitation and support
*   power/explicit and implicit coercion;
*   manipulation and co-optation;
*   negotiation and agreement.

Participation - this approach aims to involve employees, usually by allowing some input into decision-making. This could easily result in employees enjoying raised levels of autonomy, by allowing them to design their own jobs, pay structures etc.

Employees are more likely to support changes made and give positive commitment as they 'own' the change. Another advantage of participation is the improved utilisation of employee expertise. Coch and French in their book *'Overcoming Resistance to Change'* suggest involving the people affected as early as possible, as deeply as possible.

The possible disadvantages include:

* The time element - the process can be lengthy due to the number of people involved in the decision making process.

* The loyalty element - there is a need for a strong trusting relationship to exist between management and workforce.

* The resistance element - management may suffer from restricted movement as the amount and direction of change acceptable to employees will have some influence.

Education and communication - usually used as a background factor to reinforce another approach. This strategy relies upon the hopeful belief that communication about the benefits of change to employees will result in their acceptance of the need to exercise the changes necessary. The obvious advantage is that any changes could be initiated easily. However, employees may not agree about the benefits of proposed changes as being in their best interests. Also, the process of education and persuasion can be lengthy to initiate and exercise unless there is a firm mutual trust. Without this they are not likely to succeed.

Facilitation and support - employees may need to be counselled to help them overcome their fears and anxieties about change. Management may find it necessary to develop individual awareness of the need for change.

Power/coercion - this strategy involves the compulsory approach by management to implement change. This method finds its roots from the formal authority that management possesses, together with legislative support. Management can fir, transfer, or demote individuals. They can also stifle their promotion or career prospects. When there is a state of high unemployment, management enjoys greater power and is therefore able to use this strategy with more success. The advantages of this method are that changes can be made with speed and adhering to management's requirements is easy when opposition is weak from the work force. The disadvantages include the lack of commitment of the workforce and determination to reverse policy when times change and also poor support resulting in weak motivation, low morale and performance. Future implications also need to be considered. For example, when employees enjoy a stronger position ie, union representation, they are less likely to co-operate due to their experiences of past management treatment.

Manipulation and co-optation - involves covert attempts to sidestep potential resistance. Management can put forward proposals that deliberately appeal to the specific interest, sensitivities and emotions of key groups involved in the change. The information that is disseminated is selective and distorted to only emphasise the benefits of the change. Co-optation involves giving key people access to the decision-making process.

Negotiation - this particular strategy is often practised in unionised companies. Simply, the process of negotiation is exercised, enabling several parties with opposing interests to bargain. This bargaining leads to a situation of compromise and agreement. Branching from this are two strategies:

* Each party involved seeks to negotiate for itself, at the cost of the other parties involved.
* Each party aims to find an agreement with aspects advantageous to all concerned.

The advantage of negotiation strategy is that it offers the company the opportunity to note possible conflict and allows it to be dealt with in an orderly fashion. This hopefully prevents such problems as industrial action. Also, when an agreement has been made, the outcome can be to encourage commitment, preserve morale and maintain output. The main disadvantage is that this approach may be time consuming, and should opposition be strong enough the management may choose to adopt a power strategy instead.

Where strategic change is sought, it is also suggested that different styles might be more effective in some circumstances, for example:

- Participation and education and communication are likely to be best suited to incremental modes of change or to situations of transformational change in which time horizons are long.

- Coercion and power are likely to be effective only if there is a crisis or need for rapid transformational change, unless change is taking place in an established autocratic culture.

4.5   Activity

Changes in organisations can be seen as threatening. You will possibly know this from your own experience. Think about the possible effects of change and then list the reasons why people might fear or resist organisational change.

4.6   Activity solution

People tend to resist change because they fear one or more from the following list:

(a)   A loss of job security.

(b)   A loss of status.

(c)   The loss of work they enjoy.

(d)   Possibility of having to work for a different manager.

(e)   A break up of working relationships.

(f)   Having to work in a different location (moving home, etc).

(g)   Having to work at a different time (shift work, etc).

(h)   An inability to cope with new duties/responsibilities.

(i)   Inconvenience of the change (training etc).

(j)   The closing of potential promotion (career implications).

(k)   Economic aspects (loss of overtime etc).

4.7   Coch and French

The book *Overcoming Resistance to Change* by Coch and French includes the results of a series of experiments checking management success in introducing change. The authors itemise experiments, which cover the full range of imposed, participative and delegated approaches. In one experiment, the company was introducing new production techniques and working methods. These changes were accompanied by the introduction of a revised bonus payment system.

The workers were divided into two groups.

(a)   *Group A* – Here, management decided the change was necessary and worked out the new bonus scheme and working methods. These decisions were explained to the group of workers and the benefits of the changes fully listed. Management sought to answer any questions that staff may have had and welcomed questions at the briefing meeting.

(b)   *Group B* – With this group, before management decided on any changes, the group discussed the need for new methods. A sub-group of workers was involved in discussing and finalising the new methods: they suggested many improvements. The group, as a whole, was involved in implementing the new methods.

The results in terms of productivity were that, whereas both groups were achieving some 60 units per hour before the introduction of the new methods, afterwards, group A's output fell to 45 units per hour while group B's output increased to 75 units per hour. The differences in introducing the change to the groups also had an effect upon the morale.

In the period of forty days after the change:

(a)   *Group A* - much hostility against management was recorded. There were many complaints, especially about the new bonus rates. 17% of the labour force left the department. There was evidence of a rigid norm of output at the level of 45 units per hour and a norm of non-co-operation with management;

(b)   *Group B* - only one hostile act was recorded and generally the group members were co-operative and permissive. There were no staff leavers and the norms were positive, seeing continuing improvement.

4.8   Activity

All change is a threat since it involves moving into the unknown. How can managers introduce change and minimise staff's anxieties?

4.9   Activity solution

Change introduced through the use of power or manipulation is likely to add to anxiety. Education and communication will rarely succeed on their own in introducing major change. However, they are useful as a support for a negotiation or participation approach. The negotiation approach requires the existence of organised representatives and a formal procedure which is suitable for some items such as change in employment terms but would be inadvisable for other items of changing procedures, organisational changes, decentralisation etc. In these cases, participation offers the best opportunity of allaying staff anxieties by involving them early in the change process and continuing that involvement through to completion. Coch and French summarise the approach as 'involve those affected as early as possible, as deeply as possible'.

5   CREATING THE CONDITIONS FOR CHANGE

5.1   How organisations can create readiness for change

The senior management group has responsibility for establishing the organisation's vision and objectives and for making sure that the whole organisation pursues the same vision. The managers are then responsible for creating the conditions that will promote change and innovation. To manage the change process successfully, the culture of the organisation will need to be permissive and flexible. Bureaucracies are very slow to change because they do not have this culture.

Managers need to encourage individuals to use their initiative and must put the emphasis on teamwork. An autocratic management style is not conducive to change because the manager should act as a facilitator of change rather than just telling people what to do. Ronald Corwin, in his book *Strategies for Organisational Intervention*, argues that an organisation can be changed more easily:

•   if it is invaded by creative and unconventional outsiders with fresh ideas;

•   if those outsiders are exposed to creative, competent and flexible socialisation agents;

•   if it is staffed by young, flexible, supportive and competent boundary personnel;

•   if it is structurally complex and decentralised;

•   if it has outside funds to lessen the cost of innovation;

- if its members have positions that are sufficiently secure and protected from status risks involved in change;

- if it is located in a changing, modern urbanised setting where it is in close co-operation with a coalition of other organisations that can supplement its skills and resources.

5.2   Thriving on chaos

Some companies seek to create a climate of change. Some of the fast-growing companies of recent years (eg. Digital, Amstrad) stress that they changed their corporate method of operation from a static to a constantly changing environment. Peters called this concept 'thriving on chaos'. However a constant changing environment does not necessarily mean chaos, but instead it may just mean that companies can handle the introduction of change.

The advantages of having a climate of change are that:

(a)   innovation of products and methods are actively sought and welcomed;

(b)   people who are used to change tend to accept it without the frustration and rejection that can occur when change is postponed until it results in an imposed revolution;

(c)   staff tend to develop an external viewpoint and are less insular and defensive.

However, there are possible disadvantages in that morale may be damaged and staff may become more involved in time-wasting office politics because of the anxieties of possible organisational changes.

Peters outlines five areas of management that constitutes the essence of proactive performance in a chaotic business world:

(i)   An obsession with responsiveness to customers - via developing customised products or services that create new market niches and adding more value (features, quality, service) to achieve or maintain true differentiation.

(ii)   Constant innovation in all areas of the firm - every activity should be engaged in small starts that will enhance and further differentiate every product and service offering, whether in the development or mature phase of products or services.

(iii)   Involve everyone in everything - the wholesale participation of and gain-sharing with all people connected with the organisation. There are no limits to what the average person can accomplish, if well trained, well supported and well paid for performance.

(iv)   Leadership that loves change (instead of fighting it) and instils and shares an inspiring vision - through listening, assessment of the external situation and obtaining all points of view, develop a succinct vision that is clear and exciting, and at the same time leaves wide latitude for the pursuit of new opportunities.

(v)   Control by means of simple support systems aimed at measuring the 'right stuff' for today's environment - focus on flexibility rather than rigidity and make the process of developing objectives truly 'bottom up'.

5.3   Rosabeth Moss Kanter

Another American management author, Rosabeth Moss Kanter, compares two ways of approaching problems - integrative and segmentalist. Seeing problems integratively is to see them as wholes related to larger wholes and challenging established practices. Segmentalism is concerned with compartmentalising actions, events and problems and keeping each piece isolated from the others.

The integrative approach is associated with an entrepreneurial spirit producing innovation. There is a willingness to move beyond received wisdom, to combine ideas from unconnected sources, to embrace change as an opportunity to test limits. Organisations using this approach reduce rancorous conflict and isolation between units. They create mechanisms for exchange of information and new ideas across organisational boundaries. Innovation flourishes in this team-oriented co-operative environment.

The contrasting style of thought - segmentalism - is anti change and prevents innovation. Organisations adopting this type of approach find it difficult to innovate or handle change.

Echoing Burns and Stalker's mechanistic and organic systems, Kanter also distinguished between conventional segmentalist structures and change-oriented integrative structures.

- Segmentalist structures are appropriate for conditions of stability. They are typified by formal organisation, vertical communication and set rules with precise job descriptions. However, they are unsuitable in conditions of change because they tend to deal with it in a cumbersome way eg, in dealing with unfamiliar problems authority lines are not clear. Matters are referred higher up and the top of the organisation becomes over-burdened by decisions. Jobs and departments are created to deal with the problems caused by change, creating further and greater problems. Committees are set up as a temporary problem-solving device, but the situations that create the problems are not temporary.

- Integrative structures are appropriate for conditions of change. They rely heavily on expert power, team work and lateral, informed communication and, as there is great commitment to the organisation, formal and informal systems become indistinguishable.

5.4   A model for cultural change

Cultures take a long time to develop, and once socialised, people are likely to be very resistant to changes in their culture. Some critics have said that the timescale of managing cultural change makes it an impractical proposition. Employees may well have chosen to work in an organisation because they find it compatible with their own norms and values and any attempts to change culture will lead to aggression, apathy, absenteeism or a high labour turnover.

Robbins suggests the following list of activities that can be undertaken to accomplish cultural change:

(a)   Have top management become positive role models, setting the tone through their behaviour.

(b)   Create new stories, symbols and rituals to replace those currently in vogue.

(c)   Select, promote and support employees who espouse the new values that are sought.

(d)   Redesign socialisation processes to align with new values.

(e)   Change the reward system to encourage the acceptance of a new set of values.

(f)   Replace unwritten norms with formal rules and regulations that are tightly enforced.

(g)   Shake up current sub-cultures through extensive use of job rotation.

(h)   Work to get peer group consensus through utilisation of employee participation and the creation of a climate with a high level of trust.

Andrew Mayo describes a simple model of cultural change illustrated by the diagram below.

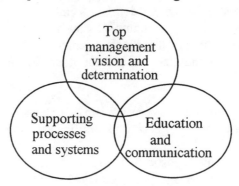

Each circle must be in place or change will not be effective, Mayo argues.

Top management vision and determination - senior management must share and own the end goals so that they visibly drive and articulate the changes needed. Employees tend to follow the lead of senior management.

Education and communication - in order to change the way people think in an organisation, educational programmes are required; first for management and then for all staff. In this way employees are encouraged to think through the implication of the desired culture change for themselves and work out what they must do to help achieve it.

British Airways invested in education programmes in order to achieve cultural change, first through a programme entitled 'putting people first' and then 'managing people first'.

The Chief Executive, Colin Marshall, attended nearly every course to reinforce his beliefs in the cultural message.

Systems and processes - these are the lifeblood of the organisation and will affect every employee. Ensuring that the organisation systems and processes are designed to support the desired culture is essential.

Conclusion   There is no easy method or choice when handling change. Much will depend upon the nature of relationships between the workforce and management, market conditions, the amount of power parties involved possess, as well as the degree of change proposed. The culture of the organisation will have a significant influence upon the approach used.

6   CHANGE AGENTS

6.1   The role of the leader

There must be a leader of the change process who accepts the responsibility. Such a leader must have certain skills and attributes, such as:

- inspiration;
- interpersonal skills;
- ability to resolve a multitude of interdependent problems;
- ability to plan;
- opportunist;
- gift of good timing.

To maximise the advantages and minimise the disadvantage of the change process, the role of the leader should be to:

(i)   Give all staff concerned the maximum possible warning of impending change to give them time to get accustomed to the idea.

(ii)   Explain as far as possible the reasons for change as the provision of both adequate and accurate information scotches rumours before they can be circulated.

(iii)   Involve individuals and/or work groups in the planning and implementing of change as much as possible. Employees will be more likely to become committed to change if they feel they can have some influence on the change and its outcome. It is also a way of gaining valuable suggestions.

(iv)   Keep lines of communication going, monitor progress, giving regular feedback and communicate results.

(v)   Try to introduce changes gradually; phased change stands a better chance of success.

(vi)   Offer and provide appropriate training.

(vii)   Ensure the workforce are aware of the benefits to them of the change eg, increased responsibility, job enrichment.

(viii)   Consider the effects of change on individuals, giving counselling where necessary.

(ix)   Follow up regularly and be supportive.

(x)   Develop a favourable climate for any subsequent changes envisaged.

6.2   Power skills

The change agent in the modern enterprise appears to rely less on technical expertise and more on the social and interpersonal skills of communication, presentation, negotiation, influencing and selling. Kanter identifies seven 'power skills' that change agents require to help them overcome resistance and apathy and enable them to introduce new ideas.

(i)   Able to work independently, without the power and sanction of the management hierarchy behind them.

(ii)   An effective collaborator, able to compete in ways that enhance rather than destroy co-operation.

(iii)   Able to develop high trust relations, with high ethical standards.

(iv)   Possessing self-confidence, tempered with humility.

(v)   Respectful of the process of change as well as the substance.

(vi)   Able to work across business functions and units - multi-faceted and ambidextrous.

(vii)   Willing to stake rewards on results, and gain satisfaction from success.

Kanter speaks of this management style in terms of 'business athletes' and a new entrepreneurial style. The new heroic model is an athlete that can manage the amazing feat of doing more with less, and who can also juggle the need to conserve resources and pursue growth opportunities.
She outlines some techniques that change agents can use to block interference:

Wait them out	They might eventually go away
Wear them down	Keep pushing and arguing, be persistent
Appeal to higher authority	You better agree because he does
Invite them in	Have them join the party
Send emissaries	Get friends in whom they believe to talk to them
Display support	Have 'your' people present and active at key meetings
Reduce the stakes	Alter parts of the proposal that are particularly damaging
Warn them off	Let them know that senior management are on your side
And remember	Only afterwards does an innovation look like the right thing to have done all along.

6.3   Implementing change through power politics

If transformational change is required in an organisation, it is likely that there will be a need for the reconfiguration of power structures. Any manager of change needs to consider how it might be implemented from a political perspective. For example, a critical report by an outside change agency such as market research findings on customer perceptions of service may be 'rubbished' by the board because it threatens their authority and power.

Understanding these systems, there is a need to plan changes within this political context. The political mechanisms include:

(i)   **the control and manipulation of organisational resources.** Acquiring, withdrawing or allocating additional resources, or being identified with important areas of resource or expertise, can be an important tool in overcoming resistance or persuading others to accept change. Being able to manipulate the information opposing the changes can also be important.

(ii)   **association with a powerful group or elite** can help build a power base. This may be useful for the change agent who does not have a strong personal power base to work from. Association with a change agent who is seen as successful or who is respected can also help a manager overcome resistance to change.

(iii)   **handling the subsystem effectively** can achieve acceptance of change throughout the organisation. Building up alliances and a network of contacts and sympathisers may help win over powerful groups.

(iv)   **symbolic devices** that may take different forms. To build power the manager may become involved in committees, which reinforce and preserve the change model. Symbolic activity can be used for consolidating change by positive reinforcement towards those who most accept change. These rewards include new structures, titles and office allocation.

7   SELF TEST QUESTIONS

7.1   Describe the levels in the organisation where managers can focus their change effort (1.3).

7.2   What are the stages in Lewin's 3-step model of change? (2.2).

7.3   Outline the steps in the integrated four-phase model. (2.3)

7.4   Draw a diagram showing the process of organisational development. (3.3)

7.5   Describe the two ways of dealing with change suggested in the force field model. (4.2)

7.6 Explain the four interacting variables identified by Leavitt which give rise to a different approach to change (4.3)

7.7 List the five strategies for managing change (4.4)

7.8 Distinguish between conventional segmentalist structures and change-oriented integrative structures. (5.3)

7.9 Outline the skills and attributes that a leader must have. (6.1)

8 EXAMINATION TYPE QUESTION

8.1 Managing change

You are required to explain **four** strategies for managing change, giving the advantages and disadvantages of **each**. **(20 marks)**

9 ANSWER TO EXAMINATION TYPE QUESTION

9.1 Managing change

(a) **Participation** - this approach seeks to involve employees in the decision making process. There are cases where this has been extended to the designing of own jobs, payment systems etc. The advantage of this method is that it enhances commitment to change, since the employees have developed their own change. In addition, the wider range of input into the change process will bring in an equally wide range of knowledge and experience.

However, there are a number of significant disadvantages. First of all, there must be the culture and climate to permit participation in change. Townsend boasted how change worked in Avis but the type of person working for a car-rental firm is likely to be different, and probably more adaptable, than someone who is in a very highly programmed job with little scope for creativity.

Secondly, the greater number of people in the decision making process can give rise to an extremely protracted decision making process, because no-one is responsible and hence accountable for the decision.

Thirdly, there is a need for a high degree of trust between the management and their subordinates. Again, there may not be the culture and tradition of this, with the result that the invitation to participate will be treated with considerable suspicion.

Fourthly, participation must be honest. Pseudo-participation is always exposed for the sham that it is, and only serves to exacerbate the problem. This can easily happen, since with the wide variety of people being involved, there is a high risk that plans for change degenerate into a talking shop.

(b) **Education** - there is a mistaken view that if people are better educated and trained, then they will be receptive to change. While better education and training may make changes easier, and create an environment where people are prepared to participate in the change process, it will also raise the expectation of the individual. This could mean an increased turnover as people become more marketable, or an exacerbated hostility derived from frustration where enhanced expectations have not been met.

(c) **Communication** - this assumes that if the plans for change are effectively communicated, then people will understand the need for change and accept the changes. This would lay the foundations for change to be implemented fairly easily and painlessly.

Sadly, the communication of the plans for change is subject to misinterpretation and, if the wrong medium is selected, can be manipulated into disinformation by self-seeking interests. In addition, communication can be a two-edged sword. People may learn of the need for change and morale may drop, exacerbating the current situation. Similarly, the more marketable people may move, and this will also create a situation where change is needed, but the best people to implement it have left.

(d)   **Power** - this is where management exerts what is perceived as its 'right to manage' and imposes change unilaterally. Management has the formal authority to do this within the parameters of appropriate legislation, and the de facto situation in relation to the labour market. In periods of high unemployment, management may elect to take this option, knowing that if employees do not like the situation, then they should look very carefully at the alternatives. It is argued that this draconian method is a viable option only in times of high unemployment, but it could be argued that in times of full employment those people who are not prepared to go along with the changes can be eased out less painfully.

Such a strategy has the obvious advantage of being easy and quick to implement, especially if the workforce is in a weak and demoralised position. However, there are two significant potential disadvantages. First, in the short term, there is the obvious problem identified by Etzioni that such a coercive strategy will fail to gain the wholehearted support of the workforce, with the result that the desired levels of motivation, morale and output will not be achieved. Secondly, in the long term the company may be building up further problems for itself. Unions have long memories, and a coerced, demoralised workforce provides a fertile area in which confrontation and antagonism will develop. As a result, when the time becomes ripe for a more co-operative approach, the management is unlikely to find the unions and the employees very helpful, or predisposed to comply with managerial wishes.

(e)   **Manipulation** - this can be very similar to the power strategy. It is ostensibly less coercive. A management team may use the media of pseudo-participation and pseudo-effective communication to persuade the workforce about the need for change. Ideally it will be done through a mass meeting, similar to union meetings outside the factory gate. Agreement comes from position power and an unwillingness to step out of line. The benefits are the same as from the power strategy, as are the considerable disadvantages.

(f)   **Negotiation** - this moves along the spectrum from autocratic styles to a more consultative approach, usually through the media of the unions. The objective is an acceptable compromise solution. Two possibilities exist. First, that one side wins and one loses. Compromises are often unsuccessful, so this approach may be the best way. Secondly, is the possibility to work towards a compromise. This option may not exist or it may be very unpalatable. The obvious example is where rationalisation is required. The unions may resist the closures, but the future of the whole company or even the industry may be at stake. This may mean that the path towards a compromise is really not available. It also means that one party to the negotiations is fighting with a considerable handicap.

The obvious advantage of negotiation is that it recognises potential conflict and seeks a solution without running the risk of creating damaging industrial disputes. It has the further advantage that the resultant agreement will produce a commitment to the changes and maintain the morale of the workforce and the output that management requires. However, it can be a protracted process and if it goes on too long, patience may be lost on both sides. It also depends upon the level of confidence that exists in the union and the negotiating team. If there is a feeling that the unions have sold the employees out, if they could have got a better deal, and if they feel they have been the victims of cynical manipulation, then the whole process will fail.

Note. Any four of the above strategies would be sufficient for a complete answer.

FOULKS LYNCH
4 The Griffin Centre
Staines Road
Feltham
Middlesex, TW14 0HS
United Kingdom

HOTLINES: Telephone: +44 (0) 20 8831 9990
           Fax: +44 (0) 20 8831 9991
           E-mail: info@foulkslynch.com

For information and online ordering, please visit our website at :

www.foulkslynch.com

PRODUCT RANGE

Our publications cover all exam modules for the new CIMA syllabus to be examined from May 2001.

Our CIMA product range consists of:

Textbooks	£17.95 - 18.95	Lynchpins	£9.95
Examination Kits	£9.95 - £10.95	Distance Learning Courses	£85

OTHER PUBLICATIONS FROM FOULKS LYNCH

We publish a wide range of study materials in the accountancy field and specialize in texts for the following professional qualifications :

- **Association of Chartered Certified Accountants (ACCA)**
- **Association of Accounting Technicians (AAT)**
- **Association of International Accountants (AIA)**
- **Certified Accounting Technician (CAT)**

FOR FURTHER INFORMATION ON OUR PUBLICATIONS:

I would like information on publications for: ACCA ☐   AAT ☐
                                      CAT ☐   AIA ☐
                                      CIMA ☐

Please keep me updated on new publications : ☐   By E-mail ☐   By Post ☐

Your name ....   Your email address:...

Your address: ....

....

....

....